Treaties with American Indians

Treaties with American Indians

An Encyclopedia of Rights, Conflicts, and Sovereignty

VOLUME III

Donald L. Fixico

EDITOR

A B C ☰ C L I O

Santa Barbara, California • Denver, Colorado • Oxford, England

Library of Congress Cataloging-in-Publication Data

Treaties with American Indians: an encyclopedia of rights, conflicts, and sovereignty / Donald L. Fixico, editor.
    p. cm.
    Includes bibliographical references and index.
    ISBN 978-1-57607-880-8 (hard copy: alk. paper)—ISBN 978-1-57607-881-5 (ebook)
1. Indians of North America—Legal status, laws, etc.—United States—Encyclopedias.
2. Indians of North America—United States—Treaties—Encyclopedias.   3. Indians
of North America—Government relations.   I. Fixico, Donald Lee, 1951–
    KF8203.6.R74 2008
    342.7308'72—dc22
                            2007027797

12   11   10   09   08   1   2   3   4   5   6   7   8

Senior Production Editor: Vicki Moran
Editorial Assistant: Sara Springer
Production Manager: Don Schmidt
Media Editor: Caroline Price
Media Resources Coordinator: Ellen Brenna Dougherty
Media Resources Manager: Caroline Price
File Manager: Paula Gerard

ABC-CLIO, Inc
130 Cremona Drive, P.O. Box 1911
Santa Barbara, California 93116-1911

This book is also available on the World Wide Web as an ebook. Visit www.abc-clio.com for details.

This book is printed on acid-free paper. ∞

Manufactured in the United States of America

*This important study of Indian
treaties is dedicated to the people of my
tribes, who have suffered, endured, and
now prosper again:*

*To the Shawnee,
To the Sac and Fox,
To the Seminole, and
To the Muscogee Creek*

—Donald L. Fixico

Contents

VOLUME I

Thematic Essays
Regional Essays

VOLUME II

U.S. and Canadian Indian Treaties
Important Treaty Sites
Primary Source Documents

VOLUME III

Historical Chronology
Biographies
Treaty Related Issues

Volume III

Introduction, xiii

Historical Chronology

Biographies

Treaty Related Issues

Introduction

PEACE AND FRIENDSHIP is the most commonly used phrase in the language of Indian treaties. The intent of the United States as a young country was to persuade Indian communities to deal only with the United States. Many things were unsettled following the American Revolution, and the tribes found themselves in the middle of it. In the early years of U.S.-Indian relations, the tribes also had common interest with the British, the French, and the Dutch.

Indian agents and other government officials in the United States negotiated more than four hundred treaties and agreements with American Indians; treaty talks occurred for more than one hundred years. Interestingly, Indian and white leaders met at various sites that often had been the meeting places for previous trading and council meetings. Negotiating in Native languages and English through interpreters was difficult, although some Native people spoke some of the white man's tongue. Beginning in 1778 with the Delaware, when the United States negotiated its first successful treaty with an Indian tribe and ratified it, a historic precedent was set, one that has made Native Americans a unique minority in their own country. For the record, Indian tribes in what is now the United States also made treaties with the British, the French, the Confederate States during the Civil War, and with other Indian tribes.

In Canada, the federal government negotiated seventeen treaties with the First Nations peoples, starting in 1871 and ending in the twentieth century. These consist of thirteen numbered treaties plus the four Robinson and Williams treaties.

The mid-nineteenth century represented the zenith of treaty making; during the next twenty years, the practice sharply declined. A rider attached to a congressional appropriations act in 1871 ended the Indian treaty-making business in the United States, although agreements were negotiated until 1917. The Act of 1871 did not end the recognition of Indian treaties, however; it merely halted the treaty-making process.

U.S.-Indian treaties often included more than one tribe, and some tribes signed many treaties.

There are 374 ratified treaties and 16 agreements. The first treaty was concluded in 1778; the last one, during the late nineteenth century. The shortest treaty is with the Kickapoo in 1820. The treaty is 16 lines long, with 8 Kickapoo leaders and 6 American officials who signed, involving $2,000 to be paid for Kickapoo removal. The longest treaty is the Treaty with the New York Indians of 1838 at Buffalo Creek in New York; that treaty is 15 pages long. The Potawatomi signed the most treaties of any tribe, a total of 26. The biggest gathering was the council held at Medicine Lodge, Kansas, during October 1867, at which 500 soldiers met with more than 15,000 Plains Indians gathered from the Cheyenne, Arapaho, Apache, Kiowa, and Comanche. The largest number of treaties were signed in 1825 and 1836, 20 each year; 19 treaties were signed in 1855, 18 in 1865, and 17 in 1832.

In regard to categories, 229 treaties involve ceded lands; 205 are about payments and annuities; 202 include the phrase *peace and friendship;* 115 are about boundaries; 99 address reservations; 70 include civilization and agriculture; 59 are about roads and free passages; 52 address the sovereignty or the authority of the United States or tribes; 49 include allotment and guaranteed lands; 47 contain gifts, goods, or presents; 38 contain provisions on education; 34 contain provisions on hunting, fishing, and gathering rights; 28 authorize forts and military posts; 25 include trade; 12 address railroads; several include agents for the tribes; and a few treaties deal with one or more of the following: stolen horses, returning prisoners, slavery, returning criminals, intruders, scalping, alcohol, missions, and mail routes.

Treaties between Indian tribes and the United States are binding agreements. For Native peoples, each step of the negotiation was important, not just the resulting words on a piece of paper. Indian agents, military officials, and officials of the Indian Office met with Native leaders to begin negotiations, which usually began with a council held at a previously agreed-upon site. To Native people, the chosen site was important, and the talk itself was just as significant as the resulting treaty or agreement. The site itself, such as the one near Medicine Lodge in southwestern Kansas and Prairie du Chien in western Wisconsin, set the tone of the council. Medicine Lodge has made a lasting impression and is re-enacted every five years.

The first meeting, or council, between Indian and white leaders likely made or broke the tone of the talks. The council was a fundamental concept among the Indian nations, and tribal protocols varied from tribe to tribe. Unsure of how to approach the various tribes, federal officials depended upon local whites, guides, and traders to introduce them to the tribes in their areas. Familiar with the ways of the Indian tribe, these individuals advised officials how to approach Native leaders.

In learning the protocol for dealing with tribes, federal officials experienced difficulty in meeting with more than one tribe at the same time. They made the mistake of trying to get enemy tribes to meet at the same council. Even tribes who met only sometimes, such as the Plains Indians, who gathered annually during the summer to hold the Sun Dance, had a mutual understanding of the importance of the arrival at camp, as exemplified by the Medicine Lodge Council in 1867. Dressed in their finest ceremonial garb, a tribe also sometimes wanted to be the last to arrive so that other tribal groups would acknowledge that an important group had arrived.

Protocol is involved in any type of summit, council, or important discussion involving conflicting interests, especially if there are deep differences between cultures. In the general situation of treaty talks, white officials learned a lot about the importance of kinship relations in forming an agreement, especially if it resulted in an alliance between the two sides. Early treaties—those concluded before the mid-nineteenth century—were often peace treaties, for the United States wanted tribes to acknowledge their relationship with the new nation and abrogate relations with the British and the French. Bringing about peace following a battle or other conflict created balance between two opposites, and this tranquil state of existence fostered mutual respect between the two parties and a need for ceremonial acknowledgement. Thus, smoking the pipe was germane to solidifying the new relationship of nonconflict.

The language barrier between the two sides caused great skills in diplomacy to be exercised. During the height of contact between Indians and whites in the seventeenth and eighteenth centuries, more than 250 indigenous languages were spoken. The role of interpreters, both Indian and white, became crucial to treaty negotiations. The varying protocols among tribes for holding councils compelled American officials to learn about tribal leaders before talks of a serious nature began. Cultural differences added to language barriers as problems arose, often intensifying the clashing views of Indians and whites over land. One perceived land and what it meant economically, and the other understood the earth philosophically and celebrated it with ceremonies. The same commodity became homeland for both sides, and ensuing treaties named who owned the land. A new culture of treaty making emerged from the older Indian way of holding council and talking.

Gift giving played a crucial role in the early contact and negotiations between Indian and white leaders. Federal officials typically brought gifts of inexpensive items such as mirrors, metalwork, and beads to get the Indians into a peaceful frame of mind that would lead to the discussion of bigger issues, such as land cessions. As mentioned, at least forty-seven treaties contained provisions for giving gifts and presents. Officials understood the importance of generosity and sharing among Native peoples and used this against them, hence the "Great White Father" in Washington held a position of respect and generosity.

The cultural difference between Indians and whites proved to be enormous. In addition to the language barriers, both sides operated from different mind-sets; each held different ideas about what was important for the negotiations and what the negotiations meant. Native leaders and federal officials had a challenging situation to overcome before they could begin successful discussions. It is said that, on one occasion Osceola, the noted leader of the Seminole in Florida, disagreeing with tribal leaders who signed the Treaty of Fort Gibson in 1833, stabbed his knife through the two pieces of paper on the table. This was his angry response to all treaties, letting others know that his mind was set on going to war. It is likely that this did happen since there is a hole in the original treaty kept in a vault at the National Archives in Washington.

"Touching the pen" became a common occurrence during Indian treaty making. Native leaders were unable to write their names because they did not know the English language, and therefore white officials asked Native leaders to "make their

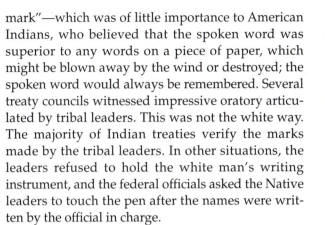

mark"—which was of little importance to American Indians, who believed that the spoken word was superior to any words on a piece of paper, which might be blown away by the wind or destroyed; the spoken word would always be remembered. Several treaty councils witnessed impressive oratory articulated by tribal leaders. This was not the white way. The majority of Indian treaties verify the marks made by the tribal leaders. In other situations, the leaders refused to hold the white man's writing instrument, and the federal officials asked the Native leaders to touch the pen after the names were written by the official in charge.

The most important concern for Native peoples in treaty negotiations was their sovereignty. Sovereignty is an important issue of concern resulting from the U.S.-Indian and Canada-First Nations agreements. The signing of a treaty creates binding responsibilities between both sides and includes the respectful recognition of each for the other. Theoretically, the relationship between the two sides is one of a sovereign forming an agreement with another sovereign—that is, government-to-government in a lateral relationship of similar status. The status is one of international law and based on each party to the treaty having faith in the agreement and recognizing each other as being sovereign.

Trust is a meaningful legal responsibility between two nations and their people, and treaties established this reciprocal relationship. Both sides of a treaty agreement must abide by the provisions and must continue to fulfill the responsibilities outlined in the document. That trust responsibility continues into this century, in the hands of the assistant secretary of the Department of the Interior, who supervises the Bureau of Indian Affairs for all tribes in the United States.

Treaties were a systematic procedure for dealing with Indian tribes. By examining the history of these agreements, some assessment can be made about them in stages or phases. For example, treaty negotiations, talks, or councils were the first step in this system of agreements. During these important gatherings, significant Indian individuals were recognized and acknowledged so the representatives of the United States would know who they were dealing with. In some cases, such as the Prairie du Chien meeting, "making chiefs" occurred; this happened more than once when government officials persuaded certain individuals to sign for their tribes as leaders. The federal government operated on the political philosophy that a head of state represented

a nation, thus an Indian nation must have one significant leader or chief. This was not the case with many tribes, such as the Muscogee Creek, the Ojibwa, and others, who had leaders for each town or village and settlements scattered over a vast region of the country.

Discussion of the treaty's provisions was another critical phase of Indian treaty making. Both sides met with an agenda of needs, according to their thinking, and they lobbied to obtain agreement from the other side. Some acute Native leaders saw that education was an important part of the future of their people and wanted educational assistance in the form of teachers. Common provisions included goods and annuities over a number of years and perhaps blacksmiths. Most of all, large sums of money were paid to the tribes for their lands.

The next phase consisted of the results of treaties—some of which caused important changes, such as the exchange of enormous tracts of land for perpetual gifts, or changes in fishing or hunting rights on ceded lands. The treaties led to a new era in Indian-white relations and actually marked the decline of the strength of Indian nations. This decline became evident as tribes such as the Potawatomi, Delaware, Chippewa, and others signed several treaties with the United States. After 1800, the federal government almost always had the leverage in treaty talks.

Strategies of treaty-making involve several motives, all of which resulted in the decline of the Indian nations. These strategies involved introducing the idea of one nation, one leader; setting boundaries; manipulating leadership; making chiefs; courting treaty signers; and giving gifts to influence tribes and their leaders. Such actions almost always were directed toward Indian men, not toward women (although, in many tribes, women held the authority to select their leaders).

Peace was the main objective in the early U.S. treaties until about 1850. The federal government found it much easier to make peace with the Indian nations than to fight them, which proved costly, especially as great effort was needed just to find them. The United States signed 374 treaties but fought more than 1,600 wars, battles, and skirmishes against Indian tribes. The Navajo Treaty of 1849 and the Fort Laramie Treaty of 1851 were negotiated with peaceful objectives in mind rather than more land cessions. The Fort Laramie agreement involved multiple groups of the Northern Plains, Sioux, Gros Ventre, Mandan, Arikara, Assinaboine, Blackfeet, Crow,

Cheyenne, and Arapaho. Boundaries were set to keep them apart, with additional provisions for roads and military posts included as part of the treaty.

The establishment of boundaries for tribes was another goal for government officials as they treated with Indian leaders. Many tribes hunted over vast territories; government officials were able to contain tribes within certain areas, and they reminded leaders of the boundaries established in the agreements. Officials introduced Native peoples to the idea of land ownership and individual ownership. In 1858, the Sisseton and Wahpeton Sioux signed a treaty in Washington, D.C., agreeing to new reservation boundaries. This led to the surveying of the tribal land for division into individual eighty-acre allotments. In this way, tribal lands were reduced in size.

At times, the United States undermined and manipulated leadership to get the lands it wanted. The importance of kinship played a vital role in treaty making between Indians and the United States. Federal officials learned of the importance of kinship and symbolic bonds in tribal communities and used this knowledge to develop a tribal dependence on the "Great White Father" in Washington. When the leaders of tribes refused to negotiate, federal officials sought out other Indians who were more easily persuaded to sign treaty documents.

Land acquisition was the principal reason for treaties and was pursued to such an extreme extent that, by the end of the nineteenth century, American Indians held less than 2 percent of the land that they had once possessed totally. The unleashed white settler became an uncontrollable force to consume Indian lands. Such was the settlers' greed that federal officials were forced to deal with tribes, which resulted in many Indian removal treaties or war. A domino effect occurred as eastern tribes moved onto lands of interior groups, who moved onto lands of western tribes, and so forth.

Expansion of the United States was another goal of government officials. During the Civil War, federal officials negotiated, and the government ratified, eighteen treaties that called for expanding the territory held by the Union. During the three years between March 1862 and March 1865, federal officials concluded treaties with the Kansa, Ottawa, Chippewa, Nez Percé, Shoshone, Ute, Klamath, Modoc, Omaha, Winnebago, and Ponca Nations. These agreements included land cessions and fur-

ther diminished the territories of the tribes. Indian lands were further reduced by the systematic creation of "permanent" reservations.

Control of tribal movements was the final strategy and result of the treaties. With treaties in place and with military power greater than that of the tribes, the United States could enforce control over the weakened Indian nations. Once the leaders were undermined and control exerted over them, Indian superintendents controlled the Indians and conditions on the almost two hundred reservations throughout Indian country.

Land was the central issue of U.S.-Indian treaties. As more settlers arrived from England and other countries, the need for more Indian land placed considerable pressure on the Indian tribes. A domino effect began to occur as eastern seaboard tribes of the Atlantic coast retreated inland, thereby encroaching on the hunting domains and farming areas of tribes nearby to the west. The expansion of white settlement across the Appalachian Mountains caused the newly formed United States to treat with the inland tribes. British agents and traders worked among the Indian nations to gain their allegiance and convince them to reject the proposed talks of federal officials.

At the same time, other European interests in the form of French, Scots, and Irish traders proved successful in obtaining acceptance among tribes. These trading activities made it more difficult for the United States as more Americans pushed into the Ohio Valley and the back country of the Southeast.

The most obvious kind of treaty called for tribes to surrender their lands. In less than thirty years, from 1801 to 1829, federal officials made thirty-one treaties with the Chickasaw, Choctaw, Muscogee Creek, Cherokee, and Florida tribes. These cession treaties extinguished Indian title to all of the area east of the Mississippi River from the Ohio River to the Gulf of Mexico.

Officially, treaties had to be ratified by the U.S. Congress and signed by the president of the United States. Congressional ratification was most active during the 1800s, as federal officials met with Native leaders at an increasing rate. Treaty making fell into a pattern: More and more treaties were negotiated with eastern tribes, who were thus forced to keep moving westward; the Delaware, for example, were forced to remove at least nine times.

Unratified treaties were agreements not confirmed by the U.S. Congress. Naturally, many agree-

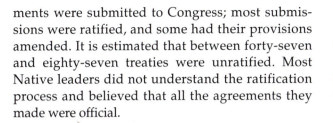

ments were submitted to Congress; most submissions were ratified, and some had their provisions amended. It is estimated that between forty-seven and eighty-seven treaties were unratified. Most Native leaders did not understand the ratification process and believed that all the agreements they made were official.

Organization of the Encyclopedia

This encyclopedia is intended as a comprehensive reference tool for anyone interested in American Indian treaties with the United States. In these three volumes, the larger number of U.S.-Indian treaties, their lengths and complexity, and the complexity of Canada-Indian treaties are described. The volumes are organized in sections. The first volume consists of major essays that explain various perspectives on Indian treaties, and regional treaties. In the second volume, entries are included that describe each treaty; short entries address treaty sites and terms; and there are primary source documents of many treaties. The third volume contains a historical chronology, brief biographies of noted individuals involved in the treaties, and a section on treaty-related issues.

Acknowledgments

This three-volume project has been the work of many people. I have often felt like an academic Sisyphus, facing the enormous task of rolling the big boulder up the mountain. More than three hundred people have helped, supported, and written entries or essays for this encyclopedia. I am grateful for the help of the following individuals, who assisted with this project in the early years at the Center for Indigenous Nations Studies at the University of Kansas: research assistants Viv Ibbett, Melissa Fisher Isaacs, David Querner, and Elyse Towey. I appreciate the support given my work by Chancellor Robert Hemenway, Provost David Shulenburger, former Associate Dean Carl Strikwerda, and former Dean Kim Wilcox at the University of Kansas.

I would like to express appreciation to the following individuals at Arizona State University, who have been helpful in the completion of this project over the last two years: President Michael Crow; Executive Vice President and Provost Elizabeth Capaldi; former Provost Milton Glick; Vice President David Young, Divisional Dean Debra Losse; former Chairperson Noel Stowe of the History Department; and Chairperson Mark von Hagen. I am grateful for the support from the ASU Foundation, which sponsors my Distinguished Professorship of History, and for ASU as a leading university that supports scholarship in American Indian history. I especially want to thank Clara Keyt as a research and editorial assistant. I thank my research assistants during the final phase: Matt Garrett, Cody Marshall, and Kristin Youngbull; they have helped to track down a lot of information as well as doing other chores. With their help, after I moved to Arizona, the boulder was pushed the rest of the way to the top of the mountain in the sun with a smile.

Appreciation is also expressed to all the contributors who wrote entries and the noted scholars who wrote the essays for the encyclopedia. Nor would this project have been possible without the patience, effort, and tremendous understanding of my good friend and editor, Steven Danver. Thank you to Caroline Price for the tremendous illustrations; and to April Wells-Hayes for the thorough copyedit of the manuscript. I wish all editors were like Vicki Moran who guided this project smoothly through all its production stages. I am especially grateful to my wife, Professor April Summitt, whose words of support encouraged me to complete this project. I am also grateful to my son, Keytha Fixico, who has patiently waited for me so that we could go to a movie and do other son-and-dad stuff. Always, I am grateful for the support of my parents, John and Virginia Fixico; and I want to acknowledge my four tribes—the Shawnee, Sac and Fox, Seminole, and Muscogee Creek—to whom this three-volume encyclopedia is dedicated.

Donald L. Fixico
Arizona State University

Treaties with American Indians

Historical Chronology

Articles of Capitulation of Montreal, September 1760

Provisions concerning aboriginal rights were included in the terms of the Capitulation of Montreal which, on September 8, 1760, sealed the surrender of France and brought an end to the Seven Years' War on North American soil. This act, drafted without the input of Native representatives, articulated the foundations of Britain's policy regarding indigenous peoples in the newly conquered territories. France's former allies would in no way be molested for having played a part during the hostilities. More important, their territorial rights and religious freedom would be protected.

During the summer of 1760, the British mounted a vigorous offensive against Montreal, the strategic heart of the French colony since the fall of Quebec the year before. When it became clear that reinforcements were not forthcoming from Europe and that further resistance would prove futile, the governor general of New France, Marquis Pierre de Rigaud de Vaudreuil de Cavagnial, resolved to surrender. On September 8, Jeffrey Amherst, commander-in-chief of the invasion force, signed the Act of Capitulation. This guaranteed that the vanquished regular troops would safely return to France and that the civil and religious liberties of the population that now found itself under de facto British rule would be maintained. Of the fifty-five articles that make up this capitulation, only five allude to American Indians. Three of these in fact pertain to the protection of French soldiers and Canadian colonists (Articles 9, 47, and 51), and the other two are directly concerned with the welfare of the latter's traditional allies. Article 8 specifies that the British would provide medical care to the injured and sick Native warriors. Most significantly, Article 40 stipulates that "[t]he Savage or Indian allies of his most Christian Majesty [the king of France], shall be maintained in the Lands they inhabit; if they choose to remain there; they shall not be disturbed on any pretense whatsoever, for having taken arms, and served his most Christian Majesty," adding that they would also be free to retain their Catholic religion and missionaries.

Jeffrey Amherst fought in the French and Indian War and against Pontiac in 1763. (Library of Congress)

During the final stretch of the Seven Years' War in North America, British officials had made comparable assurances directly to aboriginal representatives. At Oswegatchie (February 13–14, 1760), Fort Lévis (August 18), and Longueuil (September 5), treaties of neutrality were concluded; at Kahnawake (September 15–16) a further round of negotiations transformed the relationship between France's former allies in the St. Lawrence valley and the British from one of amicable neutrality to a formal alliance. The Act of Capitulation, it must be stressed, was in contrast an agreement between two European powers. Its outcome was confirmed by the Treaty of Paris (February 10, 1763), although the subsequent Royal Proclamation (October 7, 1763) largely superseded Article 40 by elaborating in clearer terms the basis of future indigenous policy in British North America.

Even so, the Act of Capitulation was brought to the attention of the Canadian government on several occasions throughout the nineteenth century to bolster the land claims of the Iroquois of St. Regis (Akwesasne) and of the Lac-des-Deux-Montagnes (Kanesatake), as well as those of the Abenakis of Odanak and of the Montagnais of the Lac-Saint-Jean region. More recently, it was famously alluded to in the *R. v. Sioui* decision of the Supreme Court of Canada (1990). At issue was whether or not Article 50, which stipulates that the Act of Capitulation of Montreal extinguished all prior acts of capitulation, rendered obsolete the central piece of evidence in the trial, a disputed treaty between James Murray and the Hurons of Lorette dated September 5, 1760. The court concluded that the article in question applied only to preceding acts signed on behalf of France (such as the Act of Capitulation of Quebec) and that there was no reason to believe that it was intended to extinguish a treaty independently concluded between an aboriginal nation and the British. Article 40, it was reiterated, constituted a legal undertaking by Great Britain not to dispossess the former allies of France of the territories they occupied in 1760.

Jean-François Lozier

See also Canadian Indian Treaties; Royal Proclamation of 1763; Treaty of Montreal–August 7, 1701.

References and Further Reading

Delâge, Denis, and Jean-Pierre Sawaya. 2001. *Les traités des Sept-Feux avec les Britanniques: droits et pièges d'un héritage colonial au Québec.* Sillery, QC: Septentrion.

Doughty, Arthur G., and Adam Shortt, eds. 1918. *Documents Relating to the Constitutional History of Canada, 1759–1791.* 2nd ed. Ottawa: King's Printer.

Vaugeois, Denis. 2002. *The Last French and Indian War: An Inquiry into a Safe-Conduct Issued in 1760 That Acquired the Value of a Treaty in 1990.* Trans. Kathe Roth. Montreal, QC: McGill-Queen's University Press.

Royal Proclamation of 1763

King George III issued the Royal Proclamation of 1763 in response to the British conquest of North America. Most importantly, the proclamation reserved the interior of North America for Natives and banned all white settlement therein. It also defined the boundaries of Britain's newest colonies—Quebec, East Florida, West Florida, and Grenada—and outlined their governance. In Canada, the proclamation is viewed as the Magna Carta of Native rights, and its importance is cited in the Constitution Act of Canada, 1982. In the United States, in 1831 and 1832, the proclamation influenced

William Johnson (1715–1774), British superintendent of Indian affairs in the American colonies, 1755–1774. Johnson concluded the Treaty of Fort Stanwix with the Iroquois, persuading them to relinquish claims to territory along the frontiers of New York, Pennsylvania, and Virginia, clearing the way for European-American immigration in these areas. (National Archives of Canada/C-083497)

American Supreme Court Justice John Marshall's decisions in the *Cherokee v. Georgia* and *Worcester v. Georgia* cases that Indians were "domestic dependent nations." These decisions continue to define the U.S.-Indian relationship. Finally, by denying colonists the interior, the proclamation is one of the causes of the American Revolution.

The Royal Proclamation was intended to be a temporary measure to provide an orderly establishment of British authority while imperial policies were established. Pontiac's War of 1763 confirmed that the Indians would not permit the usurpation of their land by the land-hungry thirteen colonies. The proclamation was not a direct response to Pontiac's War; it had been developed and issued before news of Indian victories reached England. Through the proclamation, Britain hoped to curb American west-ward expansion and ease tensions with the interior tribes by securing, at least temporarily, their lands. This assurance did help end Pontiac's War.

First, the proclamation placed the Indians under the King's protection but at the same time denied them the status of "subject." Second, it affirmed that the Crown held the underlying title to all land east of the Mississippi, whereas the Indians held a right of possession. Third, it reserved for the Indians all land east of the Mississippi, west of the Appalachian height of land, south of the Hudson Bay watershed (Rupert's Land), and north of Florida. According to the proclamation, these lands, known as Indian Country or Indian Territory, could not be surrendered to the British unless all the Natives concerned in those areas had been consulted in a public assembly by a duly appointed representative of the British Crown. This process was designed to curb "great Frauds and Abuses" and slow westward expansion while preventing frontier wars. Nevertheless, the new process was open to abuse, as the protection of Indian property was placed with the Crown and its agents, the same agents and Crown responsible for obtaining land surrenders from the Indians. The Treaty of Fort Stanwix in 1768, which extended the proclamation line to the west, represents one of several adjustments to occur before 1775. Fourth, new settlement west of the proclamation line was banned, and all settlers currently living beyond the pale were "forthwith to remove themselves." Fifth, Native nations governed their lands according to their own laws, but fugitives from British justice were to be pursued and captured on Indian lands if necessary. Sixth, it opened the Indian trade to all British colonists. Licenses were to be provided "without fee or reward" to all applicants, provided they agreed to follow "[r]egulations as We shall think proper to prescribe."

The colonists, particularly Virginians, resented British attempts to limit westward expansion. In practice, settlers ignored the boundary line, or the proclamation line, and began establishing settlements in the interior. Similarly, it was impossible to regulate traders once they crossed the frontier.

To explain imperial policies in late 1763, Sir William Johnston, with proclamation in hand, called for a gathering of Native nations at Niagara. In the summer of 1764, more than two thousand people representing more than forty nations arrived to discuss the Royal Proclamation and peace. This meeting was recorded in wampum and in the Niagara Treaty of 1764. Essentially, the treaty affirmed the Royal Proclamation of 1763 as well as recognized the nation-to-nation relationship between the Indians and the British. Pontiac, one of the key leaders of anti-British sentiment, however, was not present; he signed a separate peace in 1765 warning that the British were not to be trusted despite their promises (Borrows 1997, 155–172).

Although it is generally accepted that the proclamation acknowledged Native claims to the land, broader interpretations in Canada maintain that the document recognized aboriginal sovereignty and rights. Nonetheless, by denying Indians the status as "subject," the proclamation effectively denied Indians rights and sovereignty (Dowd 2002, 177). Regardless of the interpretation applied to the document, the proclamation continues to form the basis for Indian title and land claims in Canada.

Karl S. Hele

See also *Cherokee Nation v. Georgia*, 1831; Constitution Act (Canada), 1982; Pontiac; Treaty Conference with the Six Nations at Fort Stanwix– November 1768; *Worcester v. Georgia*, 1832.

References and Further Reading
Borrows, John. 1997. "Wampum at Niagara: The Royal Proclamation, Canadian Legal History, and Self-Government." In *Aboriginal Treaty Rights in Canada: Essays on Law, Equity, and Respect for Difference*, ed. Michael Asch, 155–172. Vancouver: University of British Columbia Press.
Del Papa, Eugene M. 1975. "The Royal Proclamation of 1763: Its Effect upon Virginia Land Companies." *Virginia Magazine of History and Biography* 83(4): 406–411.
Dickason, Olive Patricia. 2002. *Canada's First Nations: A History of Founding Peoples from Earliest Times.* Toronto: Oxford University Press.
Dowd, Gregory Evans. 2002. *War Under Heaven: Pontiac, the Indian Nations, and the British Empire.* Baltimore: John Hopkins University Press.
Great Britain. Parliament. 1824. "By the King: A Proclamation." In *A Collection of the Acts Passed in the Parliament of Great Britain and of Other Public Acts Relative to Canada*, 26–35. Quebec: P. E. Desbarats.
Nichols, Roger L. 1998. *Indians in the United States and Canada: A Comparative History.* Lincoln: University of Nebraska Press.
Parmenter, Jon William. 1997. "Pontiac's War: Forging New Links in the Anglo-Iroquois Covenant Chain, 1758–1766." *Ethnohistory* 44(4): 617–654.

Albany Conferences of 1754 and 1775

At the Albany Conference of 1754, the commissioners of the British colonies in North America sought an alliance with the Six Nations to fight against the French. With the growing hostility between the colonists and Great Britain in 1775, the American patriots foresaw the importance of securing the support, or at least the neutrality, of the Indian tribes along the colonial frontiers. And so, on July 12, 1775, the Continental Congress created three Departments of Indian Affairs—the Northern, the Middle, and the Southern—and appointed commissioners "with the power to treat with the Indians in their respective departments, to preserve peace and friendship, and to prevent their taking any part in the present commotions" (Journal 1836, 75). On July 13, Congress appointed Volkert P. Douw, Major-General Philip Schuyler, Colonel Turbot Francis, Colonel Oliver Wolcott, and Major Joseph Hawley to the Northern Department, the jurisdiction of which included the Six Nations and the tribes to the north of them.

The following month, the northern commissioners, except for Major Hawley (who could not serve because of ill health), went to Albany, New York, where they met with the sachems and warriors of the Six Nations. There they explained the colonists' grievances, which they attributed to King George III's "evil" and "wicked" ministers, and asked the Six Nations to remain neutral in the war between Great Britain and the Twelve United Colonies: "We are now necessitated to rise, and forced to fight," they told the Indian league. This "is a family quarrel," and "You Indians are not concerned in it." And so, "We desire you to remain at home, and not join either side, but keep the hatchet buried deep." The commissioners also warned against English interference and, after smoking the peace pipe, told the Six Nations to acquaint their allies to the north, "the Seven Tribes on the river St. Lawrence," with what had taken place at Albany (Journal 1836, 89–90, 91).

On August 31, the Six Nations replied to the colonists, announcing that they would not "take any part, but as it is a family affair," they would "sit still and see you fight it out . . . for we bear as much affection for the King of England's subjects on the other side of the water, as we do for you, born upon this island." They also said they would inform the neighboring tribes of what had been transacted at Albany and warned the Americans to keep the war outside Indian territory, to which the Americans agreed, saying that "whatever may happen between us and our enemies, we never will injure or disturb the peace of the Six Nations, but preserve invariable the friendship that is now established, even unto death" (Journal 1836, 94, 99).

After the treaty, the British and the Americans alike refrained from involving the Six Nations in their family quarrel. Hostilities increased in the summer of 1776, forcing both sides to actively pursue an alliance with the Iroquois. Divisions within the Six Nations were clearly visible, as the Mohawk chief, Joseph Brant, convinced four Iroquois nations to take up arms against the Americans. At the council meeting at Irondequoit in July 1777, the Iroquois, except the Oneida and the Tuscarora, joined the British side and officially entered the war at the Battle of Oriskany the following month. The Oneida and Tuscarora sided with the Americans and were spared when Generals John Sullivan and James Clinton marched into Iroquois territory in 1779 and attacked the Mohawk, Onondaga, Cayuga, and Seneca. Internal divisions and General Washington's scorched-earth policy regarding villages and cornfields eventually took their toll on the Iroquois Confederacy. At the Treaty of Fort Stanwix in 1784, where the Iroquois ceded western Pennsylvania, New York, and Kentucky to the United States, their numbers were half of what they had been before the war.

Michael A. Sletcher

See also Brant, Joseph; Indian Country; Indian Territory; Treaty with the Six Nations–October 22, 1784.

References and Further Reading

Graymont, Barbara. 1972. *The Iroquois in the American Revolution.* Syracuse, NY: Syracuse University Press.

"Journal of the Treaty Held at Albany, in August, 1775, with the Six Nations by the Commissioners of the Twelve United Colonies, Met in General Congress at Philadelphia." 1836. *Collections of the Massachusetts Historical Society,* 3rd Series, 5: 75–100.

Snow, Dean R. 1994. *The Iroquois.* Cambridge, MA: Basil Blackwell.

Pre-Confederation Treaties (Canada)

In Canada, the term *pre-confederation treaties* refers to four groupings of treaties. The earliest group consists of the treaties commonly referred to as "peace and friendship treaties." Next is a group of treaties concluded between 1764 and 1836 in Upper Canada, which today forms part of the province of Ontario. The third group of treaties was also concluded with First Nations in Ontario, after the creation of the province of Canada in 1850. Finally, the Vancouver Island treaties were concluded during 1850–1854 between the First Nations on the west coast of Canada and Governor James Douglas on behalf of the Crown.

Many of the peace and friendship treaties were concluded by the British Crown with First Nations whose territory lay on or close to the east coast of Canada, such as the Mi'kmaq, the Maliseet, and the Abenaki. Others were concluded by the British with First Nations in the province of Quebec, such as the Huron, the Mohawk, and the Algonquin. The focus of these treaties was peace, cessation of military hostilities, and alliances. Treaties often included guarantees on the part of the Crown to protect the rights of their First Nations allies, including rights to land and religion.

In its recent decision in *R. v. Marshall* ([1999] 3 S.C.R. 456), the Supreme Court of Canada found that a series of peace and friendship treaties between the Crown and the Mi'kmaq in 1760 included a treaty guarantee of a right to exchange for goods the products of hunting, fishing, and harvesting. The court translated the formulation of rights in 1760 as a modern-day treaty right to earn a "moderate living" from harvesting activities, including hunting and fishing.

Some peace and friendship treaties have received government recognition only in recent years. For instance, a document signed in 1760 by a representative of the British Crown guaranteed the Huron the right to their customs and religion, including the rights to hunt and to conduct activities incidental to hunting in a provincial park. The government took the position that, because the document was a unilateral, written act, it could not constitute a treaty. In its 1990 decision in *R. v. Sioui* ([1990] 1 S.C.R. 1025), the Supreme Court of Canada ruled that the document represented solemn, bilateral undertakings between the Crown and the Huron and included a treaty right to hunt and carry on activities incidental to hunting on Crown lands.

Another peace and friendship treaty that has received government recognition only recently is the Treaty of Swegatchy, concluded in 1760 between William Johnson on behalf of the British Crown and communities of the Mohawk, Abenaki, Huron, and

Algonquin Nations. No written copy of the Treaty of Swegatchy exists. However, in *R. v. Côté*, the Quebec Court of Appeal relied on later references to it by First Nations representatives, as well as numerous references to it in William Johnson's journal, to find that it constituted a valid, existing treaty that is a continued source of rights ([1993] R.J.Q. 1350).

The second group of pre-confederation treaties was negotiated in southern Ontario following the enactment of the Royal Proclamation of 1763, by which the King of Britain proclaimed that Indian lands could only be purchased by the Crown in its name through a public process. There are more than twenty-five of these treaties. Most were concluded with the Chippewa, the Mississauga, and the Ottawa Nations, although other First Nations were also involved.

The purpose of these treaties for the Crown was to secure land for incoming settlers through a treaty process, in conformity with the Royal Proclamation. As with many treaties concluded between the Crown and First Nations during this period, it can be difficult to know the intentions of the First Nations in entering into treaty, for the written instruments are in English and, although interpreters were often used, at issue is the quality of the interpretation as well as the ability of the interpreters to translate concepts culturally alien to the First Nations parties. Moreover, the British records of some of the earlier treaties were inaccurate, incomplete, and sometimes even nonexistent. Thus, new treaties were required, to cover areas regarding which treaties supposedly had already been concluded.

The third group of pre-confederation treaties includes the Robinson Huron and Robinson Superior Treaties of 1850 as well as the Manitoulin Island Treaty of 1862. The Robinson Huron and Robinson Superior Treaties are particularly noteworthy because they became the models for treaties that were concluded after confederation in 1867. These treaties were concluded with the Ojibway, the Chippewa, and the Ottawa Nations. As with the earlier treaties in Ontario, the aim of the Crown in entering into these treaties was to open territory up for settlement. But, as with the earlier treaties, due to language and cultural obstacles it is difficult to ascertain completely the intentions of the First Nations parties.

The Vancouver Island treaties were recognized as valid by Canada only about a hundred years after they were concluded. Until 1965, Canada held the position that the agreements concluded between Governor Douglas on behalf of the Crown, and certain First Nations on Vancouver Island, lacked the requisite formalities to constitute treaties. In 1964, the British Columbia Court of Appeal confirmed an earlier trial judgment in which the agreements were found to constitute valid and subsisting treaties that protected the rights to hunt and fish. The judgment of Justice Thomas Norris of the B.C.C.A. on this issue has been repeated time and again. He concluded that " . . . treaty is not a word of art and in my respectful opinion, it embraces all such engagements made by persons in authority as may be brought within the term 'word of the white man' the sanctity of which was, at the time of British exploration and settlement, the most important means of obtaining the goodwill and co-operation of the Native tribes and ensuring that the colonists would be protected from death and destruction" (*R. v. White and Bob* [1964], 50 D.L.R. [2d] 613 at p. 649).

The judgment of the British Columbia Court of Appeal was approved by the Supreme Court of Canada in 1965 (52 D.L.R. [2d] 481). Since that time, the conclusions of Justice Norris have been cited numerous times by Canada's highest court on the issue of what constitutes a treaty between the Crown and aboriginal peoples.

Anjali Choksi

See also Articles of Capitulation of Montreal, September 1760; Colonial and Early Treaties, 1775–1829; *Connolly v. Woolrich* (Canada), 1867; Constitution Act (Canada), 1867; Robinson Huron Treaty (Second Robinson Treaty)–September 9, 1850; Robinson Superior Treaty (First Robinson Treaty)–September 7, 1850.

References and Further Reading

R. v. Côté [1993] R.J.Q. 1350; affirmed on other grounds [1996] 3 S.C.R. 139.
R. v. Marshall ([1999] 3 S.C.R. 456).
R. v. Sioui ([1990] 1 S.C.R. 1025).
R. v. White and Bob, (1964) 50 D.L.R. (2d) 613 at p. 649.
St. Germain, Jill. 2001. *Indian Treaty-Making Policy in the United States and Canada, 1867–1877*. Lincoln and London: University of Nebraska Press.

Commerce Clause and Native Americans

The commerce clause of the U.S. Constitution empowers Congress to regulate commerce with foreign nations and Native American tribes. It is one of the few pieces of jurisprudence giving the federal government authority over Native Americans.

Laws imposed by Congress to control the Native population have a long history. Many early treaties and laws were controversial because of the limitations they placed on Native American rights. The first laws regarding Indian policy were the Trade and Intercourse Acts. These acts segregated Indians and used federally licensed agents within that population to monitor and regulate trade. Next, the Indian Removal Act of 1830 pushed the Native Americans farther west beyond the Mississippi. Over the years, these laws, along with the commerce clause of the Constitution, have plagued the Native American population.

The commerce clause is the foundation of legislation passed by the U.S. government regarding the Native American population. Congress is invested with the power to collect taxes and duties in a uniform way throughout the United States. Within the Native American territories, which are scattered among various states, the power of the federal government is limited; however, beyond the boundaries of the reservation, Native Americans are subject to the same laws and punishments as everyone else. Regardless, the law states that all actions must be undertaken in good faith, that a violation of this principle authorizes a tribe to file a lawsuit against the state in a federal court. Many Native people believe that the commerce clause constitutes a violation of their civil rights, that they should not be subject to these laws, and that they should be exempt from them because of the boundaries of their reservations.

Laws regarding gaming on Native American reservations are beyond the control of the federal government. Gambling with cards or slot machines in casinos is very common on reservations relative to the rest of the United States. It is difficult to run a legal casino in the United States outside Las Vegas or Atlantic City; but on the reservations, casinos have flourished because federal gaming laws had no jurisdiction prior to the passage of the Indian Gaming Regulatory Act of 1988. The governing powers on the almost three hundred reservations are separate tribal councils, which may or may not be similar to the state or federal government. A major reason for the high degree of gaming activity allowed by tribal councils is the generation of revenue. Gaming allows reservations, with their own forms of government, to be more economically self-sufficient.

Gaming takes place at the discretion of the tribe and under its supervision. The federal government simply allows it under the Indian Gaming and Regulatory Act but has no say in the regulation of Native American casino operations. However, the state government has some power to control Class III gaming, which includes slot machines, blackjack, craps, and chance machines, all of which may be restricted by the state in which the tribe is located. Compacts can be made, but the state exercises a certain level of authority in regard to the gaming activities that take place within the compounds of the reservation. This is relevant to the commerce clause in that the federal government may still levy taxes and regulate trade in and out of the reservation. Yet, the federal government faces many limitations in dealing with the Native American population. Any drastic action undertaken by the federal government could cause controversy over civil rights issues to flare.

The commerce clause allows casinos with all forms of gambling on Native American reservations. Whereas the state determines the types of operations allowable, the federal government may regulate the capital and revenue generated by the Native American tribes. Native American society is included with the rest of the United States because it must pay taxes and duties very much like all American citizens and businesses.

Arthur Holst

See also Bureau of Indian Affairs (BIA); Indian Gaming Regulatory Act, 1988; Indian Removal Act, 1830; Sovereignty; Treaty; Trust Doctrine.

References and Further Reading

Prucha, Francis Paul. 1984. *The Great Father: The United States Government and the American Indian.* Lincoln and London: University of Nebraska Press.

Prucha, Francis Paul. 1994. *American Indian Treaties: The History of a Political Anomaly.* Berkeley: University of California Press.

Wilkins, David E., and K. Tsianina Lomawaima. 2001. *Uneven Ground: American Indian Sovereignty and Federal Law.* Norman: University of Oklahoma Press.

Washington's Address to the Senate, September 17, 1789

On September 17, 1789, George Washington addressed the U.S. Senate on the status of earlier treaties between the United States and the Wyandot,

George Washington (1732–1799) played a crucial role in the founding of the United States. He commanded American forces in the American Revolution against England, helped to ratify the U.S. Constitution, and was elected the new nation's first president in 1789. (Library of Congress)

Delaware, Ottawa, Chippewa, Potawatomi, Sac Nations, and the Six Nations (without the Mohawks), which had been concluded by Arthur St. Clair at Fort Harmar on January 9, 1789. With respect to the second clause of Article II, Section 2, of the newly framed Constitution of the United States, the president had been granted the "Power, by and with the Advice and Consent of the Senate, to make Treaties, provided two thirds of the Senators present concur." The authority of the executive office to make such treaties, as Washington then understood it, included the right to negotiate treaties not only with foreign powers but also with North American Indians, or as he put it in the first sentence of the address, "It doubtless is important that all treaties and compacts formed by the United States with other nations, whether civilized or not, should be made with caution, and executed with fidelity" (Twohig 1989, 51).

But Washington was still uncertain about the Senate's role in the ratification process of these earlier treaties. On May 25, 1789, he had handed several treaties to the Senate regarding their ratification. The Senate responded on September 8, resolving that

"the President of the United States be advised to execute and enjoin an observance of the Treaty concluded at Fort Harmar on the 9th day of January 1789" (De Pauw 1974, 38). Uncertain of the Senate's advice, Washington readdressed the question to them on September 17: "If by my *executing* that treaty," he inquired, "you mean that I should make it (in more particular and immediate manner than it now is) the act of Government, then it follows that I am to ratify it." But, he continued, "[I]f you mean by my *executing it*, that I am to see that it be carried into effect and operation, then I am led to conclude either that you consider it as being perfect and obligatory in its present state and therefore to be executed and observed, Or that you consider it as to derive its completion and obligation from the silent approbation and ratification which my proclamation may be construed to imply" (Twohig, 1989, 52).

Washington thought that the Senate had intended the latter, but he was still unclear about their de facto counsel. What is more, he did not understand why the treaty with the Six Nations was not included in their response on September 8. And so he addressed the Senate on both questions, to which he received the following instructions on September 22: "that the Senate do advise and consent that the President of the United States ratify the Treaty concluded at Fort Harmar on the 9th day of January 1789, between Arthur St. Clair, Governor of the Western Territory on the part of the United States, and the Sachems and Warriors of the Wyandot, Delaware, Ottawa, Chippawa, Pattawatima [Potawatomi] and Sac Nations." Regarding the treaty with the Six Nations (except the Mohawks), the Senate decided that it "may be construed to prejudice the claims of the States of Massachusetts and New York and of the Grantees under the said States respectively" and was therefore "postponed until the next session of the Senate" (De Pauw, 1974, 43).

Washington proceeded to ratify the treaties and established a strong, independent role in foreign relations for the presidency; or, as one historian summed up Washington's future foreign policy: "Thenceforth, Washington initiated foreign policy on his own, seeking no counsel from the Senate at all. Furthermore, ever after, only 'weak' presidents, those who entrusted foreign relations to the secretary of state, worked through the Senate as a matter of course; every 'strong' president like Washington has as little to do with the Senate as possible" (McDonald, 1974, 28).

Michael A. Sletcher

See also Fort Harmar, Ohio; St. Clair, Arthur; Treaty with the Six Nations–January 9, 1789; Treaty with the Wyandot, Etc.–January 9, 1789.

References and Further Reading

De Pauw, Linda Grant, ed. 1974. *Documentary History of the First Federal Congress of the United States of America, March 4, 1789–March 3, 1791,* vol. 2, *Senate Executive Journal and Related Documents.* Baltimore: John Hopkins University Press.

McDonald, Forrest. 1974. *The Presidency of George Washington.* Lawrence: University Press of Kansas.

Twohig, Dorothy, ed. 1989. *The Papers of George Washington,* vol. 3, *Presidential Series.* Charlottesville: University Press of Virginia.

Battle of Fallen Timbers, 1794

The Battle of Fallen Timbers on August 20, 1794, was significant not as a military classic but because it marked the initial collapse of the Indian-British alliance that had stood defiant against U.S. frontier growth in the Great Lakes or Northwest Territory region between 1783 and 1794. The defeat led to the Jay Treaty of November 1794, which allowed British evacuation to Canada, and the Treaty of Greenville on August 3, 1795, which validated U.S. settlement on lands north of the Ohio River. Afterward, Native Americans found themselves squeezed between unreliable British allies in Canada who supplied vital arms and forts, and American frontier expansion in the form of treaties, raids, and wars. Only an offensive war by British-Indian allies could hope to deflect the American population of more than three million people from full settlement of the Northwest Territory. Such hope arose with the great leader Tecumseh and the War of 1812.

Historical causes of the battle began with the British defeat at Yorktown in 1781, followed by the Treaty of Paris in 1783. The treaty ended the American Revolutionary War and ceded the Northwest Territory to the fledgling United States. This expansion led fragmented Native tribes to cede the eastern and southern Ohio River valley to the United States in three separate treaties with the U.S. Confederacy during 1784–1786. Border raids on both sides led to a meeting on the Detroit River in December 1786 and the formation of a confederacy of many tribes. Anishinaabeg, Delaware, Iroquois, Huron, Miami, Mingo, Ottawa, Potawatomi, Shawnee, Wyandot, and the Wabash Confederacy of Wea, Piankashaw,

Kickapoo, and Mascoutin joined the effort. The larger confederacy agreed to seek British alliance from Canada. In July 1787, the U.S. Congress responded with the Northwest Ordinance, which reaffirmed American ownership of the region. Article III of the ordinance claimed that Indians would not be deprived of their lands or rights without consent unless by "just or lawful wars authorized by Congress." Such claims proved hollow when Congress sold Native lands, and U.S. settlers found them occupied! The treaty at Fort Harmar in January 1789 and the Indian Trade and Intercourse Act of 1790 also failed to resolve matters before conflict began.

President George Washington sent a one-thousand-man force, which was repelled, followed by a three-thousand-man force. On November 4, 1791, at camp on the Wabash River, this mixed U.S. force suffered a severe defeat by Indian forces. A one-

General Anthony Wayne's American troops defeat the a force of warriors from several tribes at the Battle of Fallen Timbers in August 1794. (Library of Congress)

thousand-man force of Indian confederation warriors under Little Turtle deployed with surprise in classic crescent moon formation and inflicted more than nine hundred casualties with only twenty-one Indians killed, despite the presence of U.S. cannon and the three-to-one advantage of U.S. forces.

The Indian confederation now held negotiating power, and U.S. envoys assured the Wabash in a treaty on September 27, 1792, that the land was Indian and the U.S. would protect Indian interests. However, the treaty went unratified by Congress and Wabash warriors. Further treaty attempts proved futile, and the border war was renewed with vigor.

The United States then formed the Legion army (5,190 men in 4 groups), trained in frontier warfare by Major General Anthony Wayne. The force departed from Fort Washington (Cincinnati) in the spring of 1794, marching north to push back the Indian confederation to British outposts. On August 20, 1794, the superior legion engaged the 400-man Indian force in a grove of fallen timber and drove it toward the British Fort Miami. However, the British refused to open the gates for their Indian allies; 9 Indian leaders were killed and their force scattered. The loss exposed British reluctance for war with the United States and broke united Indian resistance for a time. The former allies then signed two separate treaties (the Jay and Greenville treaties) allowing U.S. presence in the Northwest Territory at the cost of Native land. By 1800, there were 45,000 American settlers in Ohio, outnumbering Native Americans three to one.

Chris Howell

See also Battle of Horseshoe Bend (Tohopeka), 1814; Battle of the Thames, 1813; Fort Harmar, Ohio; Right of Occupancy/Right of the Soil; St. Clair, Arthur; Vincennes, Indiana; Wabash River, Indiana; Washington's Address to the Senate, September 17, 1789; Wayne, Anthony.

References and Further Reading

McConnell, Michael. 1992. *A Country Between: The Upper Ohio Valley and Its Peoples, 1724–1774.* Lincoln: University of Nebraska Press.

Starkey, Armstrong. 1998. *European and Native American Warfare, 1675–1815.* Norman: University of Oklahoma Press.

Steele, Ian K. 1994. *Warpaths: Invasions of North America.* New York and Oxford: Oxford University Press.

Tebbel, John, and Keith Jennison. 2003. *The American Indian Wars.* Edison, NJ: Castle Books.

Originally published 1960 by Harper and Brothers, New York.

Utley, Robert M., and Wilcomb E. Washburn. 1977. *Indian Wars.* Houghton Mifflin.

Battle of Tippecanoe, 1811

The Battle of Tippecanoe took place between U.S. and Native American forces near Prophetstown in Indiana Territory on November 7, 1811. Increasing tensions between the United States and the Shawnee leaders Tecumseh and Tenskwatawa over the American policy of expansion led Indiana governor William Henry Harrison to march on Prophetstown (near the confluence of the Tippecanoe and Wabash rivers). The inhabitants of that village were followers of Tenskwatawa (Tecumseh's brother, also known as the Shawnee Prophet) and other young warriors who supported Tecumseh's quest to unite the Native American tribes. Tenskwatawa had promised to defer military engagement during the absence of Tecumseh, who had traveled south in an effort to mobilize the southern tribes. However, the presence of a substantial military force near the village provoked an attack before dawn on November 7. Wyandot, Kickapoo, Potawatomi, Winnebago, Ojibwa, Sac, Miami, and Shawnee warriors confronted a well-organized force of regulars and militia commanded by Governor Harrison personally. More than two hours later, the Native Americans retreated and dispersed, allowing Harrison to claim a decisive victory, raze Prophetstown, and shatter the image of the Prophet's invincibility.

Tenskwatawa had established Prophetstown in 1808 following an invitation from Main Poc of the Potawatomi. The influence of the Prophet and his more martial brother increased as they voiced criticism of the 1809 Treaty of Fort Wayne and made the growing village into a center for anti-American activities. During the Fort Wayne meeting, Harrison had gained substantial land concessions from government-friendly chiefs of the Delaware, Miami, Potawatomi, and other tribes. The Shawnee leaders denounced the government chiefs and denied the validity of the treaty, using it to rally the northwestern tribes against American settlement. Tecumseh wanted to unite the tribes in a confederacy strong enough to withstand American expansion, and Tenskwatawa's prophetic religion was to function as a mobilizing force conferring religious sanction upon the budding resistance movement.

William Henry Harrison attacked while the Shawnee leader, Tecumseh, was away recruiting more warriors. The American commander reported the battle as a victory while losing many men and forcing Indians from the area. (Library of Congress)

In an 1810 meeting at Vincennes, Tecumseh demanded the return of lands, openly admitted to his plan to unite the tribes against the Americans, and threatened to kill government-friendly chiefs responsible for land cessions. By the summer of 1811, preparations were made for a major confrontation, and Tecumseh arrived in Vincennes with hundreds of warriors on his way to mobilize the southern tribes. Governor Harrison was greatly alarmed and decided to strike against Prophetstown in the absence of the Shawnee war chief.

Harrison's mixed force of regular army troops and Kentucky and Indiana militia departed from Vincennes on September 26. A stockade, named Fort Harrison, was built near the present site of Terre Haute. On October 29, the American force resumed its northward march, and by November 5 Harrison's army stood about ten miles from Prophetstown. The next day, the governor met with representatives of the Prophet, who suggested a council the next morning and promised peace in the interim.

Notwithstanding these gestures of reconciliation, Harrison's men entered bivouac with their weapons loaded and ready to enter battle formations on a moment's notice. Meanwhile, Tenskwatawa sought the advice of the Master of Life and offered

magic remedies to warriors preparing for a surprise attack, claiming they would be invulnerable. A select group was assigned to kill the governor himself.

The battle commenced just after 4:00 p.m. when a sentry fired on approaching warriors. Some Native Americans had already penetrated the army lines, and a chaotic situation ensued. In the blinding darkness, the U.S. troops were at a disadvantage until the many campfires had been put out. Harrison soon took command and reorganized his confused forces with vigor, despite the enemy bullets that pierced his hat and shot his horse from under him. Major Joseph Daveiss led his dragoons into a brief counterattack, but he and many of his men were killed. The U.S. force, although slightly larger (probably about eight hundred troops to seven hundred warriors), was reduced to holding the lines in defensive action. Finally, at about 6:30, the Native Americans recognized the shortcomings of the Prophet's magic and the futility of the attack. When they retreated, the battle had already claimed several hundred casualties, including approximately fifty dead on either side. The next morning, U.S. troops destroyed the abandoned Prophetstown.

The dispersed warriors continued to raid frontier settlements, but they no longer believed in the magic of Tenskwatawa. The Battle of Tippecanoe and the destruction of Prophetstown did not end Tecumseh's quest to unite the tribes, but it undermined its spiritual foundation and discredited the once powerful Prophet.

Knut Oyangen

See also Harrison, William Henry; Tecumseh.
References and Further Reading
Edmunds, R. David. 1983. *The Shawnee Prophet.* Lincoln: University of Nebraska Press.
Reid, Richard J. 1983. *The Battle of Tippecanoe.* Published by author.

Battle of the Thames, 1813

The Battle of the Thames on October 15, 1813, in British Canada ended British-Indian alliances in North America. Tecumseh, the great Shawnee leader of the pan-Indian confederacy east of the Mississippi River, died in the battle. The American victory led to the Treaty of Ghent in 1814 and massive deportation of Indians to west of the Mississippi River.

From the American Revolution, which ended in the Treaty of Paris in 1783, to the War of 1812, which ended with the Treaty of Ghent in 1814, American

Shawnee leader, Tecumseh, was shot at the Battle of the Thames on October 5, 1813. The battle was a victory for General William Henry Harrison in the War of 1812. (Library of Congress)

Indians east of the Mississippi River lost power to a fast-growing United States. The Iroquois League in New York, the Northwest Territory confederacy of 1795, Tecumseh's Indian confederacy, and the Cherokee Nation in the Southeast lost their lands.

Native people turned to spiritual prophets such as the Iroquois Handsome Lake and the Shawnee Tenskwatawa in modern Indiana. Tenskwatawa prophesied a new pan-Indian religion and drew adherents to Tippecanoe village after correctly predicting a June 16, 1806, eclipse. His brother Tecumseh, veteran of the Battle of Fallen Timbers in 1794, now capitalized on his brother Tenskwatawa's success to rekindle dreams of a pan-Indian confederation.

Tecumseh argued that no tribe had the right to sell land, because the lands belonged to all Indians. After whiskey-influenced tribal chiefs ceded three million acres at the Fort Wayne, Indiana, "whiskey treaty" in 1809, Tecumseh, too, drew many follow-

ers, and the brothers represented a serious threat to U.S. expansion.

President Thomas Jefferson (served 1801–1809) had purchased the vague, huge area of Louisiana from the French in 1803 and indicated U.S. policy toward Native people east of the Mississippi River in a letter to William Henry Harrison, Indiana Territory governor and future president. Jefferson suggested that the ceding of Native lands should be promoted by encouraging Indian leaders to incur debt to trade houses and then accepting land as payment. Indians would be forced to settle on smaller plots and would either become like U.S. farmers or would be removed beyond the Mississippi River.

Thus, in 1811 General Harrison led a U.S. preemptive attack on Tippecanoe while Tecumseh was rallying support from such southern tribal leaders as Alexander McGillivray of the Creek. The prophet Tenskwatawa lost prestige after he predicted victory but was turned back and his village burned. Tecumseh was then unable to convince the southern Indian tribes to join the united front and had to look again to British alliance in the War of 1812.

Tecumseh and British General Isaac Brock captured the frontier posts Detroit, Dearborn (Chicago), and Michilimackinac, but British distractions with Napoleon kept British troops occupied elsewhere. British General Henry Proctor, Native commander Tecumseh, and U.S. General Harrison then engaged in siege and fort warfare in the Northwest Territory, with neither side able to remove the other. The United States remained firmly entrenched at Fort Wayne, the British at Fort Detroit, and the Native tribes controlled the lands between. The tide turned with an American naval victory on Lake Erie on September 9, 1813; Proctor abandoned western British posts for Canada, fearing he could not be supplied by British ships on the Great Lakes. Tecumseh and his Indian allies were appalled but had no choice but to accompany Proctor into Canada, as Harrison approached with more than three thousand troops. The retreat and pursuit turned into a pitched battle on October 5, 1813, on the Thames River near Moraviantown north of Lake Erie. Harrison outnumbered Tecumseh and Proctor three to one and broke the alliance center with a mounted charge by Kentucky Riflemen. Tecumseh, fighting on the flank with five hundred Indians, was surrounded and killed.

Tecumseh died trying to put up a north-south continental line of European and Indian power against the American advance west. His effort was the last real attempt that had any chance of success. The Treaty of Ghent in 1814 that ended the war represented the complete loss of power by Native people east of the Mississippi River. Forced removal of the Cherokee and the Plains Indian Wars would follow.

Chris Howell

See also Battle of Fallen Timbers, 1794; Battle of Horseshoe Bend (Tohopeka), 1814; Fort Wayne, Indiana; Harrison, William Henry; Indian Removal; Jefferson, Thomas; McGillivray, Alexander; Michilimackinac, Michigan; Right of Occupancy/Right of Soil; Tippecanoe River, Indiana; Wabash River, Indiana.

References and Further Reading

McConnell, Michael. 1992. *A Country Between: The Upper Ohio Valley and Its Peoples, 1724–1774.* Lincoln: University of Nebraska Press.

Starkey, Armstrong. 1998. *European and Native American Warfare, 1675–1815.* Norman: University of Oklahoma Press.

Steele, Ian K. 1994. *Warpaths: Invasions of North America.* New York and Oxford: Oxford University Press.

Tebbel, John, and Keith Jennison. 2003. *The American Indian Wars.* Edison, NJ: Castle Books. Originally published 1960 by Harper and Brothers, New York.

Utley, Robert M., and Wilcomb E. Washburn. 1977. *Indian Wars.* Boston: Houghton Mifflin.

Battle of Horseshoe Bend (Tohopeka), 1814

The Battle of Horseshoe Bend on March 27, 1814, was a crushing military defeat for the Southeast Indian alliance during the War of 1812. These Muscogee Creek Red Stick warriors represented the last bastion of Native power east of the Mississippi River, but their fate had been sealed long before battle with the inability to form alliance with Tecumseh, the great Shawnee leader of Northwest Territory Indians.

From the American Revolution (Treaty of Paris in 1783) to the War of 1812 (Treaty of Ghent in 1814), American Indians east of the Mississippi River lost power to the exploding United States. The Iroquois League in New York, the Northwest Territory confederacy of 1795, Tecumseh's Indian confederacy, and the Cherokee Nation in the southeast lost their lands.

However, while some Native people turned to spiritual prophets like the Iroquois Handsome Lake and the Shawnee Tenskwatawa, others leaders like the Creeks Alexander McGillivray and William McIntosh negotiated with local states, settlers and the U.S. federal government. Armed resistance was also turned to as in the case of Tenskwatawa's brother, Tecumseh, who attempted to capitalize on his brother's power and the southeast Indian quarrels by campaigning for a pan-Indian alliance from the Great Lakes to New Orleans. However, the loss of prestige by his brother at the Battle of Tippecanoe in 1811 and splits within the southeast Indian tribes meant Tecumseh started the War of 1812 with the British and not the Muscogee Creek militants or Red Sticks as his allies.

Chickasaws, Choctaws, and Cherokees in particular would not commit to Tecumseh's alliance even though the treaty of 1790 between Creek leaders and the U.S. government proved useless in guaranteeing Creek lands. The Shawnee and Creek

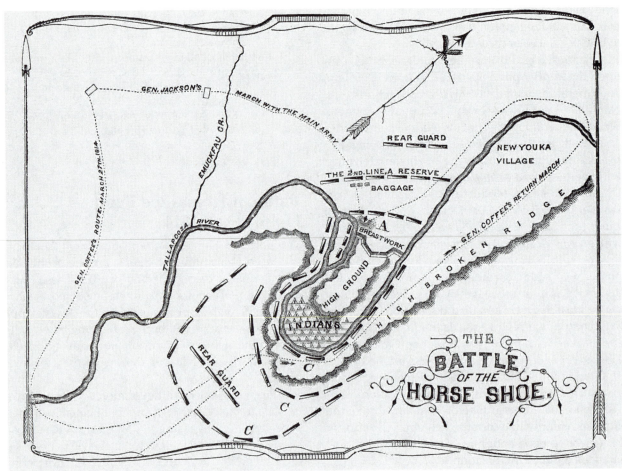

The Battle of Horseshoe Bend ended the fighting in the Creek War of 1813, and resulted in the deaths of over 900 Creeks led by Chief Menawa. Major General Andrew Jackson and John Coffee defeated the Red Stick Creek at the Horseshoe Bend of the Tallapoosa River near Tohopeka on March 27, 1814. This led to the Treaty of Fort Jackson with the ceding of 20 million acres of Creek land. (North Wind Picture Archives)

were old enemies unable to unite against the U.S. settlers.

The militant Creek would have to fight the War of 1812 alone and suffered devastating losses as a result. In what is called the Creek War of 1813–1814, U.S. forces under General and future President Andrew Jackson decimated the Creek confederacy. At the Battle of Holy Ground on December 23, 1813, about 750 Red Stick warriors were killed as American forces adopted Indian ways of frontier warfare with increasing success in the southeast.

Muscogee Creek warriors retreated to a heavily fortified peninsula on the Tallapoosa River to await the final onslaught of Jackson's forces. On March 27, 1814, Jackson's American troops, some 2,500 in number, along with 500 Cherokee and Creek allies

attacked. The Indian allies swam across the river and stole the escape canoes of the militant Red Stick Creek before attacking them from the rear. In the end over 800 Creek were killed out of 1,000 in the fortified village. Muscogee Creek power was broken in the southeast, and the death of Tecumseh and retreat of the British in the north at the Battle of the Thames in 1813 completed the collapse of Indian and British military resistance in North America east of the Mississippi River.

Tens of thousands of Native people had been killed and forcibly uprooted from their homelands in the Creek War and the War of 1812. The Treaty of Fort Jackson on August 9, 1814, followed with Creek loss of land to the U.S. Finally, the Treaty of Ghent on December 24, 1814, between the British and the

Americans ended all hopes of Native power in the east. Removal of Indian tribe remnants west of the Mississippi River presented the only solution acceptable to a land hungry U.S. population now approaching ten million people.

Chris Howell

See also Battle of Fallen Timbers; Battle of Horseshoe Bend; Harrison, William Henry; Indian Removal; Jackson, Andrew; McGillivray, Alexander; Tippecanoe River

References and Further Reading
LaFeber, Walter. 1994. *The American Age: U.S. Foreign Policy at Home and Abroad, 1750 to the Present.* New York: W.W. Norton and Co.
McConnell, Michael. 1992. *A Country Between: The Upper Ohio Valley and Its Peoples, 1724–1774.* Lincoln: The University of Nebraska Press.
Starkey, Armstrong. 1998. *European and Native American Warfare, 1675–1815.* Norman: University of Oklahoma Press.

Treaty of Ghent, 1814

The signing of the Treaty of Ghent in Belgium on December 24, 1814, signified the diplomatic termination of hostilities between the United States and the British Crown and ended the War of 1812. However, unlike the peace treaty signed in 1783 between the United States and Great Britain, the Treaty of Ghent did contain a specific article addressing tribal nations that were involved in the war.

The body of the treaty addressed issues that arose before and during the War of 1812. The treaty called for the ending of hostilities on both sides and for the return of prisoners or property taken during the war; it affirmed the two countries' mutual desire to promote the abolition of slavery, and it redefined, reconfirmed, and established territorial boundaries between the two governmental powers in accordance with either the Treaty of Paris of 1783 or the new claims in the 1814 treaty. However, as with the Treaty of Paris of 1783, no Indian nations were signatories.

Article 9 of the Treaty of Ghent applied directly to Indian tribes or nations that had been involved in the war. The article required both the United States and the British Crown to cease hostilities against the tribes or nations after the ratification of the treaty; it also required the tribes or nations to cease hostilities against the United States and Great Britain. The treaty called for both governments to restore all the possessions, privileges, and rights enjoyed by the tribes or nations before the outbreak of hostilities in 1811.

The Treaty of Ghent was openly contested by the United States. The treaty was not received well by General Andrew Jackson because of Article 9's explicit direction to return lands and other possessions to the Indians. At issue, for Jackson, was a huge cession of land comprising large portions of Alabama and Georgia that had been gained during the Creek Indian War of 1813–1814.

In 1814, the United States, along with several Indian allies, defeated the Red Stick Creeks at Horseshoe Bend in Alabama, ending the Creek Indian War. The defeat resulted in the Treaty of Fort Jackson in 1814. The treaty called for peace, for several concessions by the Creeks, and for the cession of more than 23 million acres of Creek land in payment for the war against the United States.

Jackson refused to accede to Article 9 of the Treaty of Ghent and return the Creek lands. In the face of Jackson's adamant refusal to return the land, neither the United States nor Great Britain insisted on compliance. Thus, due to inaction on both governments, the land cession of the Treaty of Fort Jackson stood.

The Treaty of Ghent greatly reduced Britain's influence with the Indian nations. Subsequently, from 1815 to 1817, twenty-one treaties between the United States and numerous midwestern Indian nations expressly mentioned the provisions of peace and the end of hostilities as provided by Article 9 of the Treaty of Ghent. These tribal nations were the Potawatomi, Piankashaw, Teton, Sioux of the Lakes, Sioux of St. Peter's River, Yankton Sioux, Omaha, Kickapoo, Wyandot (Delaware, Seneca, Shawnee, Miami, Chippewa, and Ottawa), Osage, Sauk, Fox, Iowa, Kansa, Winnebago, Menominee, Otoe, and Ponca.

Michael A. Stewart

See also Battle of Horseshoe Bend (Tohopeka), 1814; Harrison, William Henry; Jackson, Andrew; Tecumseh.

References and Further Reading
Kappler, Charles J., ed. 1972. *Indian Treaties 1778–1883.* Matituck, NY: Ameron House.
Prucha, Francis Paul. 1994. *American Indian Treaties The History of a Political Anomaly.* Los Angeles: University of California Press.
St. German, Jill. 2001. *Indian Treaty-Making Policy in the United States and Canada 1867–1877.* Lincoln: University of Nebraska Press.

Johnson v. M'Intosh, 1823

Johnson v. M'Intosh stands as one of the U.S. Supreme Court's most significant Indian law opinions. It justified a lesser status for Indian title to land through the related doctrine of discovery and the right of conquest. Chief Justice John Marshall argued for the Court that "[i]t has never been doubted, that either the United States, or the several States, had a clear title to all the lands . . . subject only to the Indian right of occupancy."

Neither the plaintiffs nor the defendants in the *Johnson v. M'Intosh* dispute were Indians or tribes; rather, they were whites competing for the same land. The plaintiffs argued that, as holders of a deed from the Piankeshaw Indians, they were entitled to the land. Marshall's opinion, however, sided with the defendants, ruling that the plaintiffs had no right to the land before the U.S. judiciary. The case was recognized as significant at the time it was heard, for it helped resolve the status of land purchased from Indians. The case's importance has not declined: "*Johnson v. M'Intosh* is at the root of title for most real property in the United States" (Bobroff 2001).

The European nations and the United States, stepping into Europe's shoes through independence, had independent rights to land that other European nations needed to respect through the doctrine of discovery. Chief Justice John Marshall wrote, "This principle was, that discovery gave title to the government by whose subjects, or by whose authority, it was made, against all other European governments, which title might be consummated by possession." Furthermore, Marshall wrote, the Indians, though "the rightful occupants," possessed "impaired" rights to the land "and their power to dispose of the soil at their own will, to whomsoever they pleased, was denied by the original fundamental principle, that discovery gave exclusive title to those who made it."

Johnson v. M'Intosh insisted that the doctrine of discovery gave the United States a claim to the land against other European nations, which, when coupled with the right of conquest, ensured that the United States, not the Indians, held the final rights to land. Marshall explained, "Conquest gives a title which the Courts of the conqueror cannot deny, whatever the private and speculative opinions of individuals may be, respecting the original justice of the claim which has been successfully asserted." Though his writing at times appears to be apologetic, concerned with the original justice of the claim, Marshall does "find some excuse, if not justification, in the character and habits of the people whose rights have been wrested from them."

The rationalization for the doctrine of discovery and the right of conquest contained in *Johnson v. M'Intosh* is found in racial imagery and a sense of the inevitable. Marshall writes, "[The] Indians inhabiting this country were fierce savages, whose occupation was war, and whose subsistence was drawn chiefly from the forest . . .they were as brave and as high spirited as they were fierce. . . . Frequent and bloody wars, in which the whites were not always the aggressors, unavoidably ensued. European policy, numbers, and skill, prevailed."

The outcome of the case is based in part on a sense that "[u]nalterable facts [of conquest] gave rise to mandate" (Robertson 1997). Thus, *Johnson v. M'Intosh* would become the legal precedent that permitted differing treatment of Indian land rights and clothed in judicial robes the maxim "Might makes right."

Ezra Rosser

See also Aboriginal Title; Doctrine of Discovery; Right of Conquest; Right of Occupancy/Right of the Soil.

References and Further Reading

Bobroff, Kenneth H. 2001. "Symposium: Indian Law in Property: *Johnson v. M'Intosh* and Beyond," 37 *Tulsa Law Review* 521.

Frickey, Philip P. 1993. "Marshalling the Past and Present: Colonialism, Constitutionalism, and Interpretation in Federal Indian Law," 107 *Harvard Law Review* 381.

Johnson v. M'Intosh, 21 U.S. 543, 8 Wheat 543 (1823).

Kades, Eric. 2001. "History and Interpretation of the Great Case of *Johnson v. M'Intosh*," 19 *Law and History Review* 67.

Robertson, Lindsay G. 1997. "John Marshall as Colonial Historian: Reconsidering the Origins of the Discovery Doctrine," 13 *Journal of Law and Politics* 759, 761.

Indian Removal Act, 1830

The Indian Removal Act was promoted by President Andrew Jackson (served 1829–1837) and passed on May 28, 1830. The act aimed "to provide for an exchange of lands with the Indians residing in any of the states or territories, and for their removal west of the river Mississippi" (*U.S. Statutes at Large*, 1830). The amount of $500,000 was allocated to support the land negotiations. Its main purpose was to acquire more land for white settlements in states east of the Mississippi River while guaranteeing Indian rights to western land. To this end, Congress set the Indian Territory (encompassing land west of Arkansas, Missouri, and east of Mexican territory) under the Indian Intercourse Act (1834).

Following the Louisiana Purchase of 1804 by President Jefferson, opportunities for settlements west of the Mississippi swelled. Arkansas Territory was established in 1819, Missouri in 1821. Meanwhile, the Committee on Indian Affairs was created (1824) within the War Department. The constant flow of settlers into Indian land led to numerous battles (the Creek War of 1813 in Alabama, the Seminole War of 1817–1818 in northern Florida, the Red Bird War of 1827 in Wisconsin). Eventually, each conflict resulted in defeat for the Indians, who ceded more land to the U.S. government through treaties.

By the 1820s, it had become clear that pioneers were not willing to tolerate cohabitation with Indians. Moreover, land speculators perceived the Indians as an impediment to territorial expansion. Ultimately, Georgia challenged the Cherokees to leave the state. However, the Cherokee—one of the Five Civilized Tribes, along with the Choctaw, Creek, Chickasaw, and Seminole—adopted a formal constitution (1827) asserting the tribe's sovereignty and its protection solely under the U.S. government. The Georgia legislature argued, in turn, that the Cherokees were merely renting the land, as the United States had been established after Great Britain's sovereign possessions. These ongoing tensions led President Jackson to view the removal of all Indians from pioneers' land as the only viable solution. The Removal Act passed in the House of Representatives by a small majority, 102 to 97 (Cave 2003).

Northern tribes, including the Potawatomi, were resettled in western lands after signing eighty-six removal treaties between 1829 and 1851 (Prucha 1994). Although the act seemingly precluded "violation of any existing treaty between the United States and any of the Indian tribes" (*U.S. Statutes at Large*, 1830), it nonetheless was a direct abuse of Indian sovereignty. In the South, after the Choctaws agreed to their removal in the Treaty of Dancing Rabbit Creek of 1830, some tribes who were most rooted to the land through farms and trade practices fought the removals in violent uprisings. The Cherokees refused to sign a removal treaty and challenged it before the Supreme Court in *Cherokee Nation v. Georgia* (1831) and *Worcester v. Georgia* (1832). Despite his

acknowledgment that Georgia had no jurisdiction over Cherokee territory and no claim to their lands, Chief Justice John Marshall declared that Indian tribes were "domestic dependent nations" rather than sovereign nations (Prucha 1994). This decision paved the way for the enforcement of the removal policy and eventually for subsequent litigation affecting Indians. A minority of Cherokees signed the Treaty of New Echota (1835), ceding all their land for $5 million. They were given two years to move voluntarily to Indian Territory. Some Seminoles, refusing to sign the removal Treaty of Payne's Landing (1832), fought in the Second Seminole War (1835–1842). Certain Creeks, as well, rejected the removal treaty of 1832, resulting in the Creek War (1835–1836). Finally, the Cherokees who defied removal were coerced by the U.S. military to march to Indian Territory. During the fall and winter of 1838–1839, about four thousand Cherokees died in the appalling conditions on the infamous "Trail of Tears." Indian Territory had a quasi-autonomous government until the creation of Oklahoma in 1907.

Whereas the proponents for removal believed this was a humanitarian act preventing Indians from disappearing, opponents—including the Whig Party and Jeremiah Evarts, a Christian missionary—sharply criticized the government's greed for cheap land, as well as the corruption and fraud that swayed the negotiations and the application of removal treaties. In a message to Congress in 1829, President Andrew Jackson declared that "our conduct toward these people" reflected on "our national character" (Cave 2003).

Céline Swicegood

See also Aboriginal Title; *Cherokee Nation v. Georgia*, 1831; General Allotment Act (Dawes Act), 1887; Indian Removal; *Johnson v. M'Intosh*, 1823; *Mitchel v. United States*, 1835; Trail of Tears; *Worcester v. Georgia*, 1832.

References and Further Reading

Cave, Alfred. 2003. "Abuse of Power: Andrew Jackson and the Indian Removal Act of 1830." *Historians* 65(6): 1330–1353.

Prucha, Francis Paul. 1994. *American Indian Treaties: The History of a Political Anomaly*. Berkeley: University of California Press.

Remini, Robert. 2001. *Andrew Jackson and His Indian Wars*. Viking.

Rogin, Michael. 1975. *Fathers and Children: Andrew Jackson and the Subjugation of the American Indian*. New York: Alfred A. Knopf.

United States Statutes at Large. 1830. 21st Congress, 1st Session, 28 May.

Cherokee Nation v. Georgia, **1831**

In *Cherokee Nation* v. *Georgia* (1831), the Supreme Court denied that the Cherokee constituted a sovereign nation and effectively made the tribe into wards of the United States. The case evolved out of attempts by the state of Georgia to assert jurisdiction over Native American lands that were protected by a federal treaty; ultimately, it involved the question of the power of the federal judiciary to review state legislative decisions. The decision, a landmark in federal Indian law, defined the status of all Native American tribes within the United States.

By the 1830s, the Cherokee Nation had lost a tremendous amount of power. Warfare, treaties, federal trade policies, and assimilation had served to weaken Cherokee society significantly. The tribe had fallen back into the mountains of northern Georgia and western North Carolina, onto land guaranteed to them in 1791 by a treaty with the United States. To the state of Georgia, however, the Cherokee remained a problem. When Georgia ceded its western lands in 1802, it obtained a promise from the federal government that all Indian territorial rights within the state would be terminated. State legislators committed themselves to the removal of the Cherokee through an official policy of harassment. In 1828, Georgia passed a law stipulating that, after June 1, 1830, the authority of state law would extend over the Cherokee living within its boundaries. In 1829, the discovery of gold in Cherokee territory gave additional impetus to the drive to extinguish Indian title to Georgia land.

Georgia attempted to extend state jurisdiction over the Cherokee through laws that specifically targeted the Indians with the aim of destroying the political, economic, and social structure of their nation. This legislation, which easily passed, set out to nullify all Cherokee law, to prohibit meetings of the tribal council, and, perhaps most importantly, to claim and redistribute the lands of the Cherokee to Georgians. Georgia also established a police force, the Georgia Guard, to patrol Cherokee lands. The police devoted their energies to attacking the Cherokees, arresting Principal Chief John Ross, and destroying a Cherokee printing press. The Cherokee protested that Georgia had violated treaties between the Native Americans and the U.S. government that acknowledged tribal sovereignty. To maintain control of their republic, the Cherokee resolved to battle Georgia through the legal system.

According to Article III of the U.S. Constitution, the Supreme Court is assigned to hear disputes arising between a state and a foreign power. The Cherokee Nation, as a foreign power, petitioned the Court in 1831 to invoke its jurisdiction and grant an injunction barring enforcement of Georgia's jurisdiction laws within Cherokee territory. Two highly distinguished white attorneys, John Sergeant and William Wirt, represented the Cherokee when oral arguments before the Court began on March 11, 1831. Georgia officials, bearing in mind that Article VI of the Constitution forbids any state law that supersedes federal treaties, denied that the Cherokee had any right to stand before the Court. The Georgians refused to acknowledge the papers served on them by John Ross and did not speak in oral arguments before the Court. They did attempt to weaken the power of the federal judiciary by seeking congressional support for a bill limiting the Supreme Court's power to review state legislative decisions.

The Supreme Court sought to craft a compromise that preserved the rule of law while maintaining the right of Americans to conquer lands. In *Cherokee Nation v. Georgia,* Chief Justice John Marshall stated that the Supreme Court had no jurisdiction to hear a Cherokee request to enjoin Georgia's efforts. Writing for the majority, he defined the Cherokee as a "domestic, dependent nation" rather than a sovereign nation for purposes of Article III of the U.S. Constitution. The deeply divided Court never addressed the Cherokee argument that Georgia had violated treaty agreements and the Constitution.

Despite the dozens of international treaties signed over the course of many years by the United States and various Indian nations, the Supreme Court decided that Native Americans could not form a foreign nation. The decision resulted in the creation of a continent-wide real estate law that favored the federal government while diminishing the rights of Native Americans.

Caryn E. Neumann

See also Sovereignty; Treaty; Trust Doctrine; *Worcester v. Georgia,* 1832.

References and Further Reading

Aaseng, Nathan. 2000. *Cherokee Nation v. Georgia.* San Diego: Lucent Books.

Norgren, Jill. 1996. *The Cherokee Cases: The Confrontation of Law and Politics.* New York: McGraw-Hill.

Wilkins, Thurman. *Cherokee Tragedy: The Ridge Family and the Decimation of a People*. 2nd ed. Norman: University of Oklahoma Press.

Worcester v. Georgia, 1832

In *Worcester* v. *Georgia*, the United States Supreme Court voided Georgia laws that restricted activities within Cherokee territory on the grounds that such legislation violated the terms of federal treaties as well as the contract and commerce clause of the U.S. Constitution. This court case, an attempt by the Cherokees to maintain sovereignty in the wake of the *Cherokee Nation* v. *Georgia* loss, formed part of the Cherokee resistance to removal.

Eager to acquire Cherokee lands, the state of Georgia had determined to force the Cherokees to agree to removal. As part of its campaign of harassment against the Native Americans, Georgia passed a law on December 22, 1830, that required all white men to take an oath and obtain a special permit from the state to live in Cherokee territory. The legislation targeted educators and missionaries who supported the rights of the Native Americans. The Cherokee Nation, recognized in federal treaties as a sovereign nation, had its own system for regulating commerce and visitations with non-Indians residing in Georgia. Accordingly, the Cherokees strongly objected to the attempt of Georgia to ignore Cherokee sovereignty and impose its own regulations.

Three Protestant missionaries from the large and prominent American Board of Commissioners for Foreign Missions who had been active in recording and preserving Cherokee culture refused to submit to the new law. Friendly to the Cherokees, these men announced their opposition to Cherokee removal, and the Georgia militia promptly entered Cherokee territory to arrest them. The men, who included group spokesperson Reverend Samuel Austin Worcester and Reverend Elizur Butler, were released when they claimed protection as federal employees. The administration of President Andrew Jackson indicated its support for Georgia's position by terminating the mens' jobs, including Worcester's position as postmaster. The militia returned and arrested ten missionaries on July 15, 1831, on charges of "residing in the Cherokee Nation without licenses." They were beaten, chained, and forced to march thirty-five miles a day to the Gwinnett County jail. Eight ministers gained pardons when

Samuel A. Worcester (1798–1859) was born at Peacham, Vermont. He served as a missionary to the Cherokee Nation and refused to follow Georgia law, resulting in the court case, Worcester v. Georgia, *1832. (Library of Congress)*

they agreed to abide by Georgia's laws, but Worcester and Butler refused to submit to the state. Both clergymen were tried in Gwinnett County Superior Court on September 15, 1831, in *State* v. *Missionaries* and were found guilty. Sentenced to four years at hard labor in the state penitentiary at Milledgeville, they began serving their sentences while the Cherokees hired attorney William Wirt to appeal their cases. Wirt, who had served as U.S. attorney general under Presidents James Monroe and John Quincy Adams, petitioned the Supreme Court for redress.

As it had in *Cherokee Nation v. Georgia*, the state insisted that the Cherokees had no standing in federal court and refused to participate in oral arguments before the Supreme Court. On March 3, 1832, the Court ruled against Georgia by deciding that Worcester and Butler had been arrested and imprisoned under an unconstitutional law. Chief Justice John Marshall, in a majority opinion that declared all of Georgia's anti-Cherokee legislation illegal, concluded that Georgia had violated the authority of the United States and the political rights of the Cherokees. The Court declared that the 1785 Treaty of

Hopewell and 1791 Treaty of Holston explicitly acknowledged the right of the Cherokees to self-government. It issued a mandate to the Georgia Superior Court ordering it to reverse its decision and free the missionaries. The decision affirmed American recognition of Native American sovereignty as well as the right of Indian nations to occupy their territory and control the transfer of their lands, but it was a Pyrrhic victory.

Georgia would not tolerate a sovereign Cherokee nation within its boundaries and ignored the Supreme Court's ruling. Governor Wilson Lumpkin declared that he would rather hang the missionaries than release them. (He eventually discharged them.) Georgia court officials insisted that the federal court had overreached its authority and refused to reverse their decision. President Jackson, no friend of Native Americans, weighed in on the dispute by purportedly saying privately that Marshall had made his decision and he (Marshall) could now enforce it. Jackson refused to take any action to help the Cherokees. Under the circumstances, the Indians had few other options except to sign a removal treaty, which they did in 1835. By 1838, the majority of Cherokees had departed on the "Trail of Tears" to Oklahoma.

Caryn E. Neumann

See also *Cherokee Nation v. Georgia,* 1831; Indian
 Removal; Sovereignty.
References and Further Reading

Norgren, Jill. 1996. *The Cherokee Cases: The
 Confrontation of Law and Politics.* New York:
 McGraw-Hill.
Reid, John Philip. 1970. *A Law of Blood: The Primitive
 Law of the Cherokee Nation.* New York: New York
 University Press.
Woodward, Grace Steele. 1963. *The Cherokees.*
 Norman: University of Oklahoma Press.

Mitchel v. United States, **1835**

In *Mitchel v. United States,* the U.S. Supreme Court affirmed that aboriginal title has force in U.S. law and that claims succeeding from the transfer of that title, when licensed by the proper governing official, will be deemed legally valid. Specifically, *Mitchel* stands for the proposition that U.S. rights of ownership to Indian lands are subject to the right of occupation of those tribes to lands in their continuous possession and use, and that this right can only be extinguished when the tribe, with federal approval, voluntarily alienates that land.

Like *Johnson v. M'Intosh* (21 U.S. 543; 5 L. Ed. 681, 1823), which is cited as precedent in *Mitchel,* the underlying issue involves a dispute between the United States and a private party over lands purchased from tribes in territory that had been under foreign colonial rule.

In this case, the petitioners (Colin Mitchel and others) had purchased 1.2 million acres of land from an English company that had originally been granted the land from the Creek and Seminole tribes in 1804 and 1806 in sales confirmed by the Spanish governor of the Florida Territory. These sales were valid under Spanish law and were intended to discharge the debts owed to the company for losses the company incurred while doing trade with the tribes.

The U.S. government objected to the legality of the petitioners' claims on various grounds, among them that the tribes had no title, under Spanish law, that they could have transferred to the company. The government argued that any right of occupation that the tribes may have had was extinguished by the Treaty of Picolata in 1765, into which the tribes entered with Great Britain when it took possession of the Florida Territory, and that this extinguishment carried forward when Spain acquired Florida via its treaty of 1783 with Britain. Moreover, the United States claimed, even if the tribes did retain title in occupancy, the original sales of 1804 and 1806 were invalid because the governor of the Florida Territory did not possess the authority under Spanish law to confirm that sale. Thus, the United States argues that, when it acquired the Florida Territory in the Adams-Onís Treaty of 1819 with Spain, it took clear title to all the lands claimed by Mitchel and his fellow petitioners.

Pursuant to a congressional act in 1828 to settle Florida private land claims, Mitchel and others petitioned the Superior Court of Middle Florida to hear their case. In 1830, the court found that their claims were not based on a valid transfer of title and dismissed their petitions. The petitioners appealed this decision to the U.S. Supreme Court, which entered the appeal in January 1831.

The Supreme Court reversed the Florida court's decision. In its opinion, Justice Henry Baldwin points to the long recognition, under English law, of an aboriginal right of occupation held by Indian tribes to lands they possessed under British colonial rule, and the continuation of that right under Spanish law. The opinion reads, "[O]ne uniform rule seems to have prevailed . . . that friendly Indians were protected in the possession of the lands they occupied . . . that their right of occupancy is considered as sacred as the fee simple to the whites" (34 U.S. 711, 746–747). Moreover, because the possessory rights of the tribes were recognized as valid by the Spanish officers who publicly confirmed their sale to the English company, they were deemed sufficiently notorious to have put the United States on notice of their existence when it entered into the treaty of 1819 with Spain. As such, the federal government's claims could not supersede the claims of the petitioners, whose title to the lands was purchased in 1811 from the English company.

It may be argued that this case speaks less to the status of aboriginal title under U.S. law and rather more to the requirement that government officials must authorize any effort by Indian tribes to alienate that title. At the same time, the case explicitly recognizes the extent to which a tribe's aboriginal right to occupation "could not be taken without their consent . . . until they abandoned them, made a cession to the government, or an authorized sale to individuals" (34 U.S. 711, 746). Whatever force this opinion may still have, it is nonetheless true that unless "recognized" in a federal treaty or statute, federal extinguishment of aboriginal title without the consent of the tribe will not give rise to a right of compensation under the Fifth Amendment (*Tee-Hit-Ton Indians v. U.S.*, 348 U.S. 272; 99 L. Ed. 314, 1955).

Justin B. Richland

See also Aboriginal Title; *Cherokee Nation v. Georgia*, 1831; Indian Removal Act; *Johnson v. M'Intosh*, 1823; Sovereignty.

References and Further Reading

Missal, John, and Mary Lou Missal. 2004. *The Seminole Wars: America's Longest Indian Conflict.* Gainesville, Tallahassee, Tampa, Boca Raton, Pensacola, Orlando, Miami, Jacksonville and Fort Myers: University Press of Florida.

Mitchel v. United States, 34 U.S. 711; 9 L. Ed. 283 (1835).

Norgreen, Jill. *The Cherokee Cases: Two Landmark Federal Decisions in the Fight for Sovereignty*. 2003. Norman: University of Oklahoma Press.

Smith, Jean Edward. 1996. *John Marshall: Definer of a Nation*. New York: Henry Holt.

Trail of Tears

Also known as "the trail where they cried," the Trail of Tears refers to the removal of the Cherokee Indians from their homes in Tennessee, Georgia, and North Carolina along a forced march to the newly organized Indian Territory (present-day Oklahoma) in 1838. It is generally accepted that approximately four thousand Cherokees perished in the long journey, although some scholars have suggested that the number could well have been twice that (Anderson 1991, 75–95). Ordered by President Martin Van Buren, the removal effort that came to be known as the Trail of Tears was a direct result of Andrew Jackson's policy of removal and the Indian Removal Act passed by Congress in 1830. This general act required individual treaties to be signed with each tribe, and in the case of the Cherokee, it was the blatantly fraudulent Treaty of New Echota in 1835 that led to their eventual removal. Despite facing stiff resistance in Congress, the treaty was eventually passed by a slim margin; upon its ratification, the United States assumed title to the entire Cherokee Nation. Ostensibly, removal was to be voluntary, but by 1838 only two thousand of the estimated eighteen thousand to twenty thousand members of the Cherokee Nation had left of their own volition. President Van Buren's patience soon ran out, leading him to order a forced removal effort under the direction of General Winfield Scott. All Cherokees who remained in their eastern homes were rounded up, corralled in military stockades, and then forced westward in a march that began in October 1838. To make matters worse, the limited funds promised to provide food and supplies for the Cherokee were often never delivered or were subject to graft on the part of officials and suppliers charged with those responsibilities. In the end, disease, hunger, exhaustion, and freezing temperatures took their toll, resulting in the deaths of thousands in the camps and during the migration.

The tragedy suffered by the Cherokee was representative of the fate that befell a number of other Southeastern tribes during the 1830s and 1840s—many of which endured their own versions of the Trail of Tears. The term itself actually originated with the removal of the Choctaw from their homes in Mississippi following the passage of the dubiously executed Treaty of Dancing Rabbit Creek in 1830. In a series of forced removals from 1831 to 1833, approximately twelve thousand to thirteen thousand Choctaws were marched west to new homes in the Indian Territory; more than two thousand perished along the way due to repeated epidemics of dysentery and cholera, meager supplies and funding, and freezing temperatures (Green 1978, 8–9). In 1837, the Chickasaws were removed from their territory in Alabama; the Creeks and Seminoles would also

Ordered by the American government to leave their homelands after the passage of the Indian Removal Act, Cherokee made the long trek from the southeastern United States to the Indian Territory (present-day Oklahoma) during 1838–1839. Approximately 4,000 died of exhaustion, illness, and starvation along the way, prompting the Cherokee to name the forced march the Trail of Tears. (Woolaroc Museum, Bartlesville, Oklahoma)

eventually be removed following their own struggles with the federal government. As grievous as each of these events was, however, it was the Cherokee removal that burned the name "Trail of Tears" into the psyches of Americans, and it is the Cherokee experience that is so often associated with the infamous expression.

The tragic scale of the Trail of Tears has made it one of the most widely studied events in the history of American Indian policy and its effects on Native peoples. Interpretations of the policies, treaties, and ideologies that led to the Trail of Tears have ranged from charges of outright genocide to relatively apologetic characterizations of the motivations driving Andrew Jackson and other removal proponents as lamentably misguided benevolence. To be sure, avowed removal proponents such as Michigan's governor Lewis Cass echoed social theorists of the time with protestations that the only way to save Indians from extinction was to move them beyond the reach of unscrupulous whites. This paternalistic

beneficence preached by Cass and others saturated much of Andrew Jackson's speeches on removal, but it would be naïve to believe that altruism alone was at the heart of removal efforts. Ultimately, the discovery of gold in northern Georgia fueled the already insatiable hunger for Indian lands, while issues of states' rights vis-à-vis Indian sovereignty polarized the debates over removal even further. For the Cherokee in particular, these issues combined to create a climate that ultimately rendered moot a petition signed by approximately sixteen thousand Cherokees declaring that the Treaty of New Echota was not representative of their desires, the considerable public support that arose out of the debates, and a favorable Supreme Court decision (*Worcester v. Georgia*), which ruled Georgia's removal laws illegal. All of these efforts went for naught, and the Trail of Tears thus became the defining event of a notorious chapter in the history of white-Indian relations.

Bradley J. Gills

References and Further Reading

Anderson, William L., ed. 1991. *Cherokee Removal:
Before and After.* Athens: University of Georgia
Press.

Green, Len. 1978. "Choctaw Removal Was Really a
'Trail of Tears.'" *Bishinik: The Official Publication
of the Choctaw Nation,* November, 1978: 8–9.

McLoughlin, William G. 1993. *After the Trail of Tears:
The Cherokees Struggle for Sovereignty,
1839–1880.* Chapel Hill: University of North
Carolina Press.

Perdue, Theda, and Michael D. Green, eds. 1995.
*The Cherokee Removal: A Brief History with
Documents.* New York: St. Martins Press.

Wallace, Anthony F.C. 1993. *The Long, Bitter Trail:
Andrew Jackson and the Indians.* New York: Hill
& Wang.

Treaty of Guadalupe Hidalgo, 1848

The Treaty of Guadalupe Hidalgo, negotiated for the United States by diplomat Nicholas Philip Trist (1800–1874), ended the Mexican-American War and was signed at the village of Guadalupe Hidalgo near Mexico City on February 2, 1848. Article IX of the treaty outlined the protection of civil rights extended to Mexican citizens living in the newly conceded area, thus making them a part of the United States.

The treaty granted the United States more than five hundred thousand square miles of territory, or nearly half of the Republic of Mexico. Along with the Gadsden Purchase (1853), the ceded area eventually became the states of California, Nevada, Arizona, New Mexico, Utah, and parts of Colorado, Wyoming, Nebraska, and Oklahoma and granted the U.S. demand that Mexico recognize the Río Grande as the southern border of Texas.

Mexican officials negotiated furiously with Trist to win concessions to protect the rights of Mexicans living in the region. Article IX attempted to extend further the civil rights of Mexican citizens living in the area by giving them the option to return to Mex-

ico with their property or to remain in the United States as U.S. citizens.

Many Anglos in the United States felt that the citizenship provisions in the treaty were too liberal, as they provided U.S. citizenship to a rather large percentage of people living in the territories during a period when U.S. law limited naturalization to free "white" immigrants. Some argued that those remaining in the newly acquired territories required further action by Congress to become citizens. This ambiguous citizenship status became especially glaring after the discovery of gold in California. Suddenly, thousands of people rushed to the area, directly competing against the Native-born miners for the best mining locations. Lynching, harassment, and other abuses of those not considered citizens forced several countries, including the Republic of Mexico, to lodge formal diplomatic protests against the U.S. government. Mexico often referred to Article IX in those protests, citing the formal citizenship granted to its former citizens. Most people in the United States did not view Mexicans living in the California territory as citizens; as Mexico viewed them as citizens of another country. They often lived without the juridical protection of either government.

While those of Spanish ancestry suffered under the new treaty, Indians suffered even more abuse. Since 1812, Mexico had offered citizenship to "civilized" Indians, and the Mexican Constitution of 1824 extended full citizenship to them. While Article IX plainly granted U.S. citizenship to all Mexican citizens living in the transferred territories, it was not long before states began to enact constitutions that excluded blacks and Indians while recognizing some Mexicans. During these years, American states determined their own requirements for citizenship and often exercised this power to exclude minorities from citizenship. Those without the right to actively participate in the political arena seldom enjoyed the benefit of civil rights, and under U.S. laws Indians and "half-breeds" were not considered citizens. Indians were given neither citizenship nor the protections listed in Articles VIII or IX of the treaty.

Although the Treaty of Guadalupe Hidalgo ended the war between the United States and the Republic of Mexico, it failed to ensure the status and rights of Mexicans and Indians living in the territory conceded to the United States. Indeed, it can be argued that these populations have yet to gain full citizenship.

Robert O. Marlin IV

See also Gadsden, James; Plenary Power;
    Sovereignty; Treaty.
References and Further Reading
Griswold del Castillo, Richard. 1990. *The Treaty of
    Guadalupe Hidalgo: A Legacy of Conflict*. Norman:
    University of Oklahoma Press.
Mahin, Dean B. 1997. *Olive Branch and Sword: The
    United States and Mexico, 1845–1848*. Jefferson,
    NC: McFarland.
United States. "Treaty of Peace, Friendship, Limits
    and Settlement with the Republic of Mexico."
    February 2, 1848. U.S.-Mex., *United States
    Statutes at Large* 9, pt. 922.

California, Eighteen Unratified Treaties, 1851–1852

Many scholars and Indian activists have used the eighteen unratified treaties made in California to demonstrate how shoddily the state treated its indigenous population after the American gold rush. Negotiated in good faith, the treaties faced tremendous opposition from mining and agricultural interests in the state and died in a "secret session" of Congress. Even though the end result may have been more procedural than deliberately malicious, the eighteen unratified California treaties stand as an example of a turbulent period in the state's history and tell us much about how non-Indians viewed the state's Native population.

The year 1848 brought innumerable changes to California. The Treaty of Guadalupe Hidalgo ended the Mexican-American War and added the American Southwest to the United States. This included California, with its history of missions and ranchos, where California Indians lived with and worked for Spanish and Mexican settlers. That same year, the discovery of gold on the American River touched off an international and domestic migration to the state. At first, Indians found opportunities to mine for themselves in the gold rush; more frequently, they worked in gangs mining for wealthy landowners such as John Sutter and John Bidwell. This violation of free labor sensibilities, along with the fear of Indians on the part of many miners (generated on the Overland Trail) and Indian attacks in Oregon, prompted miners and state militias to begin a campaign to eradicate California Indians from the mines. Surely something had to be done to protect the state's Indian population.

In 1850, the U.S. Senate dispatched three agents to California. From the outset, these three men—

Oliver Wozencraft, George Barbour, and Redick McKee—had conflicting orders. The Senate appropriations bill that authorized their expedition did not specifically permit them to make treaties; later, the secretary of the interior authorized them to do so. The trio traveled throughout the state and consummated eighteen treaties with California Indians. Wozencraft stayed in southern California, Barbour worked in central California, and McKee made the arduous journey to northern California. The treaties resembled those of the 1850s: They provided a land base for California Indians out of their existing homelands, and Indians agreed to move to these areas. They provided instruments of assimilation (domesticated livestock, teachers, farm implements, etc.), and the Natives recognized the United States as their protector. In the end, these eighteen treaties reserved 7.5 million acres for California Indians. Once California Indians signed the treaties, many moved to what they thought were their new homes.

Almost immediately, non-Indian Californians protested the treaties. They objected to the amount of land set aside for Indians and warned that it might take too much potential agricultural and mining land out of the hands of productive, white citizens. Also, they argued that California's unique history—in which Indians and non-Indians lived and worked together—made removing Indians to a reservation unnecessary, if not destructive of the state's agricultural economy. Finally, opponents cited shady dealings between the agents and those who were supposed to provide food and supplies to the reservations. For instance, McKee signed a contract with his son to provide cattle for Indians, and Barbour made a dubious cattle contract with John C. Frémont. The U.S. Senate acceded to these complaints. In 1852, the Senate retired to executive session, debated the treaties without public input, and tabled the documents, effectively killing them.

Without treaties, California Indians were in a precarious position, at the whim of state citizens who cared little about them and a state government that ensured their virtual enslavement. In 1850, California passed the nefarious Act for the Government and Protection of the Indians. Amended later, the act allowed for the forced indenture of Indian children. After the Senate killed the treaties, the federal government created a number of temporary military reservations. These lands were temporary (if whites wanted them in the future, they could evict the Indians); they were voluntary for Indians, and they were to be self-sustaining through Indian labor. Between

1853 and 1858, federal Indian commissioners Edward F. Beale and Thomas J. Henley created seven temporary Indian reservations throughout the state. These suffered from a lack of funding, corruption on the part of Beale and Henley, and the heinous actions of non-Indians living on the reservation's borders. Although some of these reservations were indeed temporary, others, such as the Round Valley Reservation, were recognized by executive order and received full standing with reservations established by treaty.

The unratified treaties in California left a lasting impact on the state's Indian population. Although not necessarily unique in that the Senate rejected the treaties (many treaties signed with Indians in Oregon, Washington, Texas, Arizona, and New Mexico were similarly rejected), they created a situation in which most California Indians lived off reservations. Until the early twentieth century, the state and federal government wrestled with this population. Moreover, the treaties stand as a reminder that the state and federal governments virtually ignored and exploited the state's Indian population.

William Bauer

See also California, Hawaii, and the Pacific
       Northwest; Treaty of Guadalupe Hidalgo, 1848;
       United States v. Kagama, 1886.

References and Further Reading

Hurtado, Albert L. 1988. *Indian Survival on the
       California Frontier*. New Haven, CT: Yale
       University Press.

Kelsey, Harry. 1973. "The California Indian Treaty
       Myth." *Southern California Quarterly* 55(Fall):
       225–238.

Phillips, George Harwood. 1997. *Indians and Indian
       Agents: The Origins of the Reservation System in
       California, 1848–1852*. Norman: University of
       Oklahoma Press.

Rawls, James. 1984. *Indians of California: The Changing
       Image*. Norman: University of Oklahoma Press.

Long Walk, 1864

In the summer of 1863, Brigadier General James Henry Carleton—General Edward Richard Sprigg Canby's successor as head of Union forces in New Mexico—caused great change in the Native Southwest. He ordered Christopher Houston Carson, commonly known as "Kit," an experienced trapper, trader, army scout, and Indian agent in the Rocky Mountain West to amass and remove the *Diné* (the Navajos) from their Native homeland in northwestern New Mexico and northeastern Arizona. They

were moved to a remote reservation on the Pecos River in eastern New Mexico known as the Bosque Redondo. Carson's campaign against the Navajos culminated in the Long Walk—a forced march consisting of several episodes of compulsory removal that began as early as 1863 and ended in 1866.

Soon after his appointment as commander of the Department of New Mexico, Carleton, who was determined to bring an end to Native resistance in the area, unleashed an aggressive crusade against the Mescalero Apaches and Navajos in an effort to isolate, remove, and incarcerate the two tribes—traditional enemies—together on a reservation.

The Diné, in retaliation for perceived wrongs enacted against them, raided other tribes—primarily the Pueblos—and non-Indian settlers, including Mexicans and newly arrived European Americans, for decades before Carleton demanded their riddance. In addition to the seeming Navajo menace, Carleton wished to eliminate any obstacle that could potentially threaten mining aspirations in the Southwest.

Although Kit Carson did not lead the three-hundred-mile trek to the Bosque Redondo, he successfully breached the Navajo stronghold at Canyon de Chelly in January 1864 (after effectively subjugating a number of Mescaleros) and launched a scorched-earth campaign that resulted in little loss of life but nevertheless wreaked havoc on the Navajos, compelling them to surrender. Prior to the Canyon de Chelly expedition, Carson reported little success in his quest to round up the Navajos. Instead, members of the tribe typically evaded capture and escaped to distant areas of *Diné Bikéyah*, such as the canyon gorge behind Navajo Mountain that is known today as Glen Canyon. Although Carson's 1863 campaign sent some Navajos to *Hwéeldi*—also referred to as the Bosque Redondo—his accomplishments in 1864 at Canyon de Chelly turned the tide in favor of the United States and resulted in the removal of several thousand Diné.

The Long Walk consisted of a series of removals that lasted for three years and became a pivotal event in the history and culture of the Navajo, like the Cherokee's Trail of Tears, which occurred thirty-four years earlier. The trip to Hwéeldi followed different routes but typically began at Fort Wingate, near present-day Gallup, New Mexico, moved west toward Albuquerque and then southeast to the flat, barren, treeless plains of the Pecos River valley near the army outpost of Fort Sumner. Navajo oral accounts and soldiers' reports detail the hardships endured by the Diné during the three-hundred-mile, journey on foot to the Bosque Redondo. Many stories recount the harsh environmental conditions, including cold weather, heavy snow, and little or no water. Participants in the Long Walk also suffered from starvation and disease brought about by contaminated food. Furthermore, government testimonies and Navajo histories tell of problems with Mexican citizens whose hatred for the Navajos turned into violence as the Diné marched across New Mexico. In addition to exposure, lack of food, sickness, and hostilities from neighboring peoples, the Navajos suffered injustices at the hands of the soldiers. Gus Bighorse, a Navajo warrior who fought against Kit Carson's troops but was removed to Hwéeldi with Manuelito in 1865, told his children, "People are shot on the spot if they say they are tired or sick or if they stop to help someone. If a woman is in labor with a baby, she is killed. . . . They are heartbroken because their families die on the way" (Bighorse 1990, 28–35). If they survived the trek across New Mexico, life at the Bosque Redondo proved to be just as dismal. Upon the Navajos' arrival at their new home, the Diné fought with their traditional Apache enemies, who were already there, and suffered tremendously from hunger and disease.

Carleton's idea of settling the Navajos (and Mescaleros) on a faraway reservation proved to be consistent with mid-nineteenth-century paternalistic theories of the best way to deal with hostile tribes. During the early 1860s, many Americans, including government officials and humanitarians, believed that reservations would segregate and assimilate Indian peoples, helping them to achieve the ultimate goal of "civilization"—a sedentary lifestyle firmly rooted in education, Christianity, and agriculture. Ironically, reservations sometimes developed into cultural enclaves that enabled Native peoples to maintain their languages and cultivate strong tribal identities. The Long Walk and life at the Bosque Redondo encouraged the Navajos, traditionally divided into clans, to develop a common identity based upon their haunting experiences as a tribe.

Recognizing its failed attempt to turn the Navajos into Christian farmers, the U.S. government allowed the tribe to return to its homeland in 1868. The several thousand Navajos who had evaded capture and remained on the western and northwestern fringes of Diné Bikéyah strengthened the tribes' claims to the area and permitted the Navajos to extend their land base in the Treaty of 1868.

Sonia Dickey

See also Barboncito; Canyon de Chelly, Arizona; Carson, Kit; Fort Sumner, New Mexico; Manuelito; Treaty with the Navajo–June 1, 1868.

References and Further Reading
Bailey, Lynn R. 1964. *The Long Walk: A History of the Navajo Wars, 1846–1868*. Los Angeles: Westernlore Press.
Bighorse, Tianna, and Noel Bennett., eds. 1990. *Bighorse the Warrior*. Tucson: University of Arizona Press.
Dunlay, Tom. 2000. *Kit Carson and the Indians*. Lincoln: University of Nebraska Press.
Iverson, Peter. 2002. *Diné: A History of the Navajos*. Albuquerque: University of New Mexico Press.
Roessel, Ruth, and Broderick H. Johnson, eds. 1973. *Navajo Stories of the Long Walk Period*. Tsaile, AZ: Navajo Community College Press.

Connolly v. Woolrich (Canada), 1867

Connolly v. Woolrich (1 *Canadian Native Law Cases* 70–243) is one of the earliest judgments in Canada that examines the validity and effect of aboriginal custom and law—in this case the customs of the Cree Nation on the institution of marriage.

The judgment of the Quebec Superior Court was rendered in July of 1867 and that of the appellate court in 1869. The case was appealed to the Judicial Committee of the Privy Council in England but was settled out of court before it was heard by that judicial body. The most interesting judgment is that of the Quebec Superior Court, which in essence was approved by the appellate court.

The facts giving rise to this landmark case arose in the early part of the nineteenth century. In 1803, William Connolly, a trader born in the area of Montreal, traveled west to the Northwest Territories, an area which today forms part of northern Manitoba. He was seventeen years old. William Connolly married a Cree girl named Suzanne according to the customs and laws of the Cree Nation and lived with her in an exclusive relationship. They had six children. Together, in 1831, they moved back to the Montreal area with some of their children.

In 1832, William Connolly left his Cree wife Suzanne and married Julia Woolrich in a ceremony performed according to the laws in force in Lower Canada. He died in 1849, and in his will he bequeathed all of his property to Julia Woolrich and their two children; he left nothing to Suzanne or the children he had had with her. Suzanne, who had never accepted his marriage to Julia, had moved back to the area of her birth, and had taken refuge in a convent, died in 1862.

The case was instituted by John Connolly, William's son by his wife Suzanne. John argued that William Connolly's marriage to his (John's) mother was valid and that it had created a community of property between them that entitled Suzanne to half of William's estate, as she had been alive at the time of his death. As one of her six children, he claimed his share of her half of the estate.

The key question before the court was whether the marriage, which had been solemnized according to Cree custom, was valid and enforceable. The lawyers for Woolrich argued that it was English law that was and had been in force in the Northwest Territories for more than a century and that, because the marriage had not been solemnized according to English law, it was not valid. Woolrich relied on the granting of the Hudson's Bay Company Charter by the King of England in 1670 as evidence of the primacy of English law in the Northwest Territories, which were part of the territory governed by this charter.

Justice Samuel Monk of the Quebec Superior Court concluded that English law did not prevail in the region where William married Suzanne in 1803 and that the "customs of the Cree Indians relative to marriage were in force there at that time" (1 C.N.L.C. at p. 81). He noted that, before being conquered in Canada by the British, the French had conducted a long-term trading relationship with the Cree and other First Nations inhabiting the Northwest Territories, and that during two hundred years of trading the French had never tried to "subvert or modify the laws and usages of the aboriginal tribes, except where they had established colonies and permanent settlements, and then only by persuasion" (1 C.N.L.C. at p. 77).

William Connolly's marriage to Suzanne was valid because the territorial rights, political organization, laws, and usages of the Indian tribes were not modified by the arrival and establishment of European traders (1 C.N.L.C. at p. 79). Therefore, William's subsequent marriage to Julia Woolrich was ruled a nullity.

This conclusion was upheld by the majority judges of the appellate court, and the matter was settled between the parties before it was heard by the Judicial Committee of the Privy Council.

Although the judgment is dated in its use of language. it remains relevant today for its recognition of

the force, validity, and legitimacy of aboriginal customs, institutions, and laws.

For many years, this judgment received little attention from Canadian courts and lawyers. More recently, it was referred to in detail by the Royal Commission on Aboriginal Peoples in its report, *Aboriginal Peoples, Self-Government, and the Constitution*. At page 7 of this report, the commission concluded that one of the lessons to be drawn from the judgments in *Connolly v. Woolrich* is that sources of law and authority in Canada "include the common laws and political systems of Aboriginal nations."

Anjali Choksi

References and Further Reading
Connolly v. Woolrich, 1 Canadian Native Law Cases 70 (Quebec Superior Court).
Johnstone et al. v. Connolly, 1 Canadian Native Law Cases 151, also reported at (1869), 17 R.J.R.Q. 266, (Quebec Queen's Bench).
Royal Commission on Aboriginal Peoples. 1993. *Partners in Confederation: Aboriginal Peoples, Self-Government, and the Constitution*. Ottawa: Canada Communication Group.

Constitution Act (Canada), 1867

The Constitution Act of 1867 was formerly referred to as the British North America Act. This is the British legislation that created the Dominion of Canada, effective July 1, 1867. Of greatest relevance to the treaties with Canada's various Native peoples are Articles 91 and 92, which distribute powers between the federal and provincial governments. The distribution of powers in these articles has also been a significant source of legislative difficulty in terms of determining which level of government is responsible for and has control over various aspects of Native life that are regulated by previous treaties.

According to Article 91.24, the Crown provides exclusive legislative authority to the federal government in Canada in the area of "Indians, and Lands reserved for the Indians." In Article 92.5, the Crown provides exclusive legislative authority to provincial governments in Canada in the area of "(the) Management and Sale of the Public Lands belonging to the Province and of the Timber and Wood thereon." This exclusive legislative division between the federal and provincial governments thus did not provide for a governing role for First Nations in Canada. As all Native populations in Canada were under the exclusive jurisdiction of the federal government, they did not have the same guaranteed rights as other peoples in Canada. Furthermore, whatever rights they did have were potentially subject to extinguishment by acts of legislation, administration, or treaty. Thus, the Constitution Act of 1982 was not able to recreate Native rights that had been eliminated between 1867 and 1982, only to protect and guarantee those rights that still existed.

According to later legal decisions on the terminology of the Constitution Act, Canada's Inuit are to be included in the meaning of the term *Indians*. The same cannot necessarily be said of Canada's Métis population. Recognition of Métis has generally been accomplished not through the Constitution Act but rather through the Manitoba Act of 1870 and the Dominion Lands Act of 1879. Furthermore, some Métis who lived with non-Métis Indians became "treaty Indians" under the Indian Act of 1886, particularly if the mother was Native and the father was not Native.

An underexamined and highly complex facet of the Constitution Act is the delineation of "Lands reserved for Indians." This is of particular importance in determining the complete extent of Rupert's Land, the territory given to the Hudson's Bay Company (HBC) by the English Crown in 1670. This land was subsequently transferred to the Canadian government in 1870 under the Rupert's Land and Northwestern Territory Order, according to terms laid out in Section 146 of the Constitution Act. Through the provisions of the HBC's surrender of territory to the Canadian government, with the land transfer was responsibility for the protections and compensation, where necessary, of the Natives in those territories as well as the responsibility to settle the claims of these Natives. The problems arise from the fact that the HBC was surrendering to the Canadian government only the lands over which it had jurisdiction—Rupert's Land, not the Northwestern Territories, which fell outside its jurisdiction. Thus, the obligations to protect the Native populations outside Rupert's Land and in the Northwestern Territories could be interpreted as bearing only a moral, not a legal, obligation for the Canadian government. As such, the Canadian government needed only to settle claims of compensation for lands required for settlement, in conformity with equitable principles that have been the practice of the British Crown in previous dealings with Native populations.

The interplay between the jurisdictional rights of the federal and provincial governments as they relate to the governance of Natives and Native legal issues is evident in a number of areas. These areas include employment law and marriage law, wherein the bulk of legislative control is with the provincial governments. Due to the division of powers, social services has been a contentious area, with numerous disputes over responsibility occurring between the levels and involving complex issues of finances, culture, history, and constitutionalism. Generally, the provinces have refrained from financial responsibility for these services on reserve land but have legal rights to regulate and deliver these services on reserves. It is also an issue in the use of nonreserve lands, Crown land, which the government holds in guarantee for Natives. The issue of jurisdiction has arisen as a result of the provincial government, which has jurisdiction over the sale and use of public lands (as these guaranteed lands are), coming into conflict with the concept of Native title to these lands, as it is the government that has guaranteed to protect these lands on behalf of the Natives, who had no guaranteed legislative jurisdiction over themselves. In important legal decisions in the late nineteenth century, this issue tended to be settled in favor of the provinces.

Donald R. Bennie

See also Constitution Act (Canada), 1982; Métis; Sovereignty; Trust.

References and Further Reading

Harring, Sidney L. 1998. *White Man's Law: Native People in Nineteenth Century Canadian Jurisprudence*. Toronto: Osgoode Society.

McNeil, Kent. 1982. *Native Claims in Rupert's Land and the North-western Territory: Canada's Constitutional Obligations*. Saskatoon: University of Saskatchewan Native Law Centre.

Reiter, Robert. 1994. *The Law of Canadian Indian Treaties*. Edmonton: Juris Analytica.

Manitoba Act (Canada), 1870

The Manitoba Act of 1870 created the province of Manitoba, reserved 1.4 million acres of land for the Métis, guaranteed the equality of the French and English languages, and established separate schools for Protestants and Roman Catholics. The Manitoba Act was subsequently confirmed by the British Parliament with the passage of the British North America Act of 1871. The creation of Manitoba signified the federal government's desire to control western

Louis Riel (1844–1885) was a Métis leader and led the Northwest Rebellion. He was hanged for treason on November 16, 1885 at Regina, Saskatchewan. (Corbis)

development and expansion and is the first attempt by Canada to deal with Métis rights.

After confederation in 1867, Canadians looked to the west as a natural extension of Canada; they wanted a nation that stretched from sea unto sea. With this in mind, the Canadian politicians negotiated with the Hudson's Bay Company (HBC) to purchase Rupert's Land. In 1868, the HBC agreed to sell Rupert's Land to Canada for £300,000. The HBC kept one twentieth of its lands, which included land for agricultural purposes and the land surrounding trading posts. The actual transfer was planned to take place in December 1869 but was delayed until July 1870. Once the sale was completed, the entire area became known as the Northwest Territories.

Angered by British denials of their requests for crown colony status and the lack of consultation concerning the sale, and fearful that their way of life would be destroyed by ethnocentric English newcomers, the Métis decided to resist Canadian imperialism. After preventing incoming lieutenant governor William McDougall from entering Red River, the

Métis, led by Louis Riel, assumed control of Fort Garry, the HBC post, and declared a provisional government in October 1869. Negotiators were dispatched to Ottawa with a list of Métis grievances, concerns, and demands. Politicians in Ottawa, buffeted by anti-French and anti-Native sentiments, passed the Manitoba Act, which was based on national political concerns and Métis demands.

The act created the new province's governmental structures. Manitoba's government would consist of a lieutenant governor appointed by Ottawa, an appointed upper house, and an elected lower house. The province would receive two appointed senators at the federal level and would be allowed to elect four members to Parliament. Provincial crown lands remained under the control of the federal government. There were also financial considerations designed to help the province establish and run the government (Canada, 1870). Its small size and square shape led to Manitoba's nickname, the Postage Stamp Province.

Sections 31 and 32 of the Manitoba Act concerned Métis lands. Section 31 reserved 1.4 million acres of ungranted lands for the Métis and their children. It also gave the government the right to determine the location of the grant and the eligibility of individuals to receive land. Section 32 recognized individuals' titles to the land they already occupied. Finally, both sections referred to the need to extinguish Indian claims to the land (Canada, 1870).

Under the terms of Section 31 the government of Canada established a system of awarding land to the Métis. Essentially, eligible Métis would receive scrip, a certificate redeemable for a quarter section of land, that could be used to preempt land anywhere in Manitoba or the Northwest Territories, provided it had been surrendered by the Indians and surveyed. The administration of Section 31 through the scrip process, and the recognition of existing titles through Section 32, created problems. The general historical consensus is that the government managed the entire process badly through fraud and negligence. According to the Royal Commission on Aboriginal People, "[I]t took from 1877 until 1900 to complete the process and more than 90 per cent of the land was diverted . . . to persons other than Métis children." There is evidence that some Métis received scrip for land that they already occupied, which was contrary to the provisions of Section 32. Thomas Flanagan, political scientist and former policy advisor to the Reform Party of Canada, maintains that, despite both documented and oral evidence, the government followed the spirit and intent of Sections 31 and 32 (Flanagan 1991). Moreover, he concludes that protests concerning the injustice and rampant corruption since 1874 had little to do with the Métis and more to do with the interests of speculators (Flanagan 1991, 179).

In 1996, the Royal Commission on Aboriginal People reported that, although the courts can determine legal liability, the government of Canada is "morally obliged to enter negotiations with Métis representatives to correct this injustice." The Manitoba Métis failed to receive what was promised in 1870, and Canada "fell inexcusably short of its moral obligation to treat Manitoba Métis equitably" (Canada 1991, Ch. 5, App. 5C). The Métis are still seeking justice.

Karl S. Hele

See also Canada; Métis; Riel, Louis.
References and Further Reading
Canada. 1870. Manitoba Act. Constitution of Canada.
Canada. 1991. *Report on the Royal Commission on Aboriginal Peoples*, vol. 4, *Perspectives and Realities*. Ottawa: Canada Communication Group.
Dickason, Olive Patricia. 2002. *Canada's First Nations: A History of Founding Peoples from Earliest Times*. Toronto: Oxford University Press.
Flanagan, Thomas. 1991. *Métis Lands in Manitoba*. Calgary, AB: University of Calgary Press.
Friesen, Gerald. 1987. *The Canadian Prairies: A History*. Toronto: University of Toronto Press.
Sprague, D. N. 1980a. "Government Lawlessness in the Administration of Manitoba Land Claims, 1870–1887." 10 *Manitoba Law Journal* 415–441.
Sprague, D. N. 1980b. "The Manitoba Land Question, 1870–1882." *Journal of Canadian Studies* 15: 74–84.
Stanley, George F. G. 1960. *The Birth of Western Canada: A History of the Riel Rebellions*. Repr., 1992. Toronto: University of Toronto Press.

Indian Appropriations Act, 1871

The Indian Appropriations Act passed by the U.S. Congress on March 3, 1871, contained a simple clause that repudiated the process of making treaties with American Indian tribes: " . . . That hereafter no Indian nation or tribe within the territory of the United States shall be acknowledged or recognized as an independent nation, tribe, or power with whom the United States may contract by treaty . . ." (16 *Stat.* 566). The treaty-making process originated in the U.S. Constitution, in Article I, Section 8 of which Indian tribes were explicitly identified along with foreign nations as entities with whom Congress would regulate commerce. The commerce clause, which encapsulated the economic ambitions of the new American nation, was the basis on which the federal government established its relationships with Indian tribes. Indians controlled furs and food as the basis for trade, and they possessed the land that the American government needed for its expansion. Through the long and complicated process of treaty making, Indian tribes gave up most of their land and accepted the ostensible protection of the U.S. government. In the treaty-making process, the executive branch of the government appointed commissioners to treat with tribes. Commissioners made promises to tribal leaders, which the U.S. Senate had to ratify and which the House of Representatives had to fund in the annual appropriations bill for the Office of Indian Affairs. The annual appropriation act became the main vehicle for implementing federal Indian policy. Congress was preoccupied with how much Indians were costing the government rather than how the government was carrying out its responsibility to Indians under treaties.

Ely Parker, commissioner of Indian affairs and himself a Seneca Indian, in his annual report in 1870 made clear the government's position with regard to Indian tribes and treaties. Arrangements between tribes and the government "*should not be of a treaty nature. . . . A treaty involves the idea of a compact between two or more sovereign powers, each possessing sufficient authority and force to compel a compliance with the obligations incurred. . . . The Indian tribes of the United States are not sovereign nations, capable of making treaties, as none of them have an organized government of such inherent strength as would secure a faithful obedience of its people in the observance of compacts of this character.*" Parker reiterated the notion that tribes were "wards of the government" and that their claims to lands were "a mere possessory one." The treaty process had given them a false impression of "national independence." He called for an end to "the cruel farce of thus dealing with its helpless and ignorant wards" (Parker 1869, 6).

Debate over the appropriations bill for 1871 revealed this sentiment. Congressman Fitch of Nevada declared that "all the money that is expended in the State of Nevada for . . . paying salaries of Indian agents and purchasing blankets for

Indians is uselessly expended" (*Congressional Globe* 1871, 1821). Indian tribes were considered totally dependent on the federal government and totally subject to congressional control. The general tenor of the debate in Congress was to slash payments to carry out provisions of Indian treaties. A rumor was also circulating in Congress that a new federal policy was in the offing that would give responsibility for Indian agencies to various religious denominations (Priest 1969, 96–102). Congress would thus be able to pass its responsibilities on to these organizations. Congress also adopted the policy that its statutes took precedence over treaties as the supreme law of the land. There were no Indian voices to contest the act. Congress simply dismissed the idea of tribes as sovereign nations capable of dealing with the federal government.

Clara Sue Kidwell

See also Bureau of Indian Affairs (BIA); Parker, Ely
    S. (Donehogawa); Sovereignty; Treaty; Trust.
References and Further Reading
Congressional Globe, 41st Congress, 3rd Session,
    January 25, 1871, p. 730; March 1, 1871, p. 1821.
Parker, E. S., to Hon. J. D. Cox, Washington City,
    DC, December 23, 1869, *Report of the*
    Commissioner of Indian Affairs, Made to the
    Secretary of the Interior, for the year 1869.
    Washington, DC: Government Printing Office,
    1870.
Priest, Loring Benson. 1969. *Uncle Sam's*
    Stepchildren: The Reformation of United States
    Indian Policy, 1865–1887. Lincoln: University of
    Nebraska Press.

Cherokee Tobacco **Case, 1870**

In 1870, the Supreme Court ruled that the Cherokee Nation was not exempt from taxation on tobacco manufacture, despite the existence of an 1866 treaty specifically guaranteeing them exemption. In a violation of the U.S. Constitution's treaty clause, the Court based its ruling on the grounds that a law of Congress supersedes the provisions of a treaty.

In the *Cherokee Tobacco* suit, two Cherokee nationals, Elias Boudinot and Stand Watie, challenged the imposition of an 1868 federal tax law on their tobacco factory, which had been established in the Cherokee Nation under provisions of the Cherokee Treaty of 1866.

Article 10 of the 1866 treaty stated that Cherokee citizens had the right to sell any product or merchan-

dise without having to pay "any tax thereon which is now or may be levied by the U.S." In 1888, Congress enacted a general revenue law that imposed taxes on liquor and tobacco products "produced anywhere within the exterior boundaries of the United States." Justice Noah Swayne, speaking for the Court, said that the case was simple because it came down to which of the two laws—treaty or general domestic—was superior. He developed the term the "last-in-time" rule, which in effect said that whichever document is latest in time stands, whether treaty or statute (Kappler 1904).

This was a significant precedent for Native Americans, specifically the Cherokee. The treaty termination law, attached as a rider to the Indian Appropriations Act of March 3, 1871, had closed the door on Indian treaties, although some preexisting ratified treaties were still honored by the United States. This law effectively froze tribes in political limbo. They were no longer recognized as nations capable of treating with the federal government, but they remained separate sovereignties outside the pale of the U.S. Constitution.

As a result of this decision, Native American tribes were virtually deprived of legal and political protection. Hereafter, the federal government explicitly or implicitly could abrogate treaty provisions, and Native American tribes had little recourse but to return to the Congress that had enacted the annulled legislation. The Supreme Court generally deferred to the political branches on Native American matters, saying that "the act of Congress must prevail as if the treaty were not an element to be considered" (*U.S. v. Cherokee,* 1870).

This opinion ignored the historical and political reality that the Cherokee Nation was a separate and autonomous political entity not subject to general domestic laws unless they had given their express consent. The opinion denied the fact that Congress (itself) had not explicitly stated in the law of 1868 that the revenue act applied to Indian Territory. In fact, it disavowed the general principle that specific laws, such as treaties, which create special rights, are not to be held "repealed by implication by any subsequent law couched in general terms" (*U.S. v. Cherokee, 1870*).

Even with earlier U.S. guarantees of the sanctity of treaty rights, *Cherokee Tobacco* announced that those hard-won rights, often secured at the cost of great amounts of tribal land and the loss of other rights, could be destroyed by mere implication.

Fred Lindsay

See also Bureau of Indian Affairs (BIA); Sovereignty; Treaty; Trust; *Worcester v. Georgia*, 1832.

References and Further Reading

Filler, Louis, and Alan Guttmann. 1962. *The Removal of the Cherokee Nation: Manifest Destiny or National Dishonor?* Lexington, MA: D. C. Heath.

Kappler, Charles J., ed. 1904. *Indian Affairs: Laws and Treaties*, vol. 2, *Treaties*. Washington, DC: Government Printing Office.

United States v. Cherokee Tobacco, 78 U.S. 616 (1870) (Wall.).

Wardell, Morris L. 1938. *A Political History of the Cherokee Nation 1838–1907*. Norman: University of Oklahoma Press.

Wilkins, David. 1997. *American Indian Sovereignty and the U.S. Supreme Court: The Masking of Justice*. Austin: University of Texas Press.

Indian Act of Canada, 1876

The Indian Act of Canada is a legislated act of the Canadian government that has had a profound impact on the lives of aboriginal peoples since its enactment in 1876. The Indian Act regulates most aspects of the lives of aboriginal peoples who reside on Indian reserves. At the individual level, it sets forth a legal definition of who is eligible to be considered a status Indian under the act and defines their rights. At the collective level, it defines the structure, rights, and responsibilities of band councils in relation to reserve lands and resources. The band council is an elected system of local government that replaced traditional forms of governance when the Indian Act was imposed. Under the Indian Act, final decision-making power for all matters concerning Indian people and reserve lands rested with the federal government. Indian peoples did not own reserve lands. All reserve lands were held in trust by the Canadian government. Although the Indian Act has undergone several revisions since it was first passed in 1876, it has fundamentally remained unchanged. It continues to reflect the Canadian government's paternalistic attitude toward aboriginal peoples.

The origin and content of the 1876 Indian Act arose out of the historic realities of the late nineteenth century and the ideologies of the Canadians of European descent. Aboriginal peoples were no longer needed as military allies, and their vital roles in the fur trade economy were lessening with the decline of that industry. The Canadian government had also begun the process of signing treaties with aboriginal nations in central Canada as a means of opening up lands for settlement and resource extraction. In the minds of the non-aboriginal people, Indians needed to be civilized. The Indian Act was enacted to provide the political and legal force necessary to bring about the cultural and social changes that would lead to the inevitable assimilation of aboriginal peoples into European Canadian society.

The Indian Act set out the rules by which a status Indian lost status and became enfranchised. A status Indian woman who married a non-status man, Indian or non-Indian, lost her Indian status and was no longer considered an Indian under the act. The children from this marriage were not considered Indian under the act. Status Indians who earned university degrees or entered professions would also lose their status.

The potlatch, the central institution of the peoples of the West Coast, became illegal in 1884 when an amendment was added to the Indian Act. This was followed in 1895 by another amendment that outlawed the sun dance among the Plains peoples. A further amendment in 1927 prohibited Native organizations from raising money or retaining lawyers to pursue any claims they had to their traditional lands. The last major revision of the Indian Act occurred in 1951. The laws prohibiting the potlatch, the sun dance, and other ceremonies, as well as the right to pursue a land claim, were repealed. It was not until 1960, under the Canadian Bill of Rights, that status Indians gained their full rights as citizens and were allowed to vote in federal elections.

In 1985, the Indian Act was revised by Bill C-31. The rules changed regarding the loss of status that occurred when status Indian women married non-status men. Women who had lost their status, and their children, could apply for reinstatement under the Indian Act. Under the new regulations, status Indian women and men maintain their status when marrying nonstatus individuals, as do their children. However, in this situation, Indian status is not continued into the next generation. Based on existing marriage patterns, this will result in a steady decline in the number of status Indians registered under the Indian Act.

The overall objective of the Indian Act, the assimilation of aboriginal peoples, was never accomplished. Though aboriginal people's lives have been drastically affected by the Indian Act, they have maintained their distinct cultures and identities and continue to fight for the right to practice self-governance.

Ross Hoffman

See also Canada; Canadian Bill of Rights, 1960; Constitution Act (Canada), 1867; Modern Treaties/Comprehensive Land Claim Agreements (Canada); Self-Government Agreements (Canada).

References and Further Reading

Frideres, James S., and René R. Gadacz. 2001. *Aboriginal Peoples in Canada: Contemporary Conflicts.* 6th ed. Toronto: Prentice Hall.

Native Law Centre. 1993. *The Indian Act and Amendments, 1970–1993: An Indexed Collection.* Saskatoon: University of Saskatchewan Native Law Centre.

Venne, Sharon Helen, comp. 1981. *Indian Acts and Amendments 1868–1975: An Indexed Collection.* Saskatoon: University of Saskatchewan Native Law Centre.

Ex Parte Crow Dog, 1883

Ex Parte Crow Dog was a landmark 1883 Supreme Court case. In it, the Court's opinion affirmed tribal jurisdiction while opening the door to increased Congressional oversight. The case, which centered on the high-profile killing of a Lakota chief by another Indian, ultimately prompted the passage of federal legislation that limited tribal sovereignty and provided the basis for later judicial interpretations granting Congress full legal authority over American Indians.

On August 5, 1881, Spotted Tail, a principal chief of the Sicangu (Brulé) Lakota, was shot and killed while returning from a tribal council. His killer, Crow Dog, was another influential Sicangu leader, a former head of the Rosebud agency police force and Spotted Tail's cousin. Historians disagree on Crow Dog's precise motive, but the killing was most likely the result of political rivalry—both aggravated and shaped by the influence of U.S. officials on traditional power relations in Sicangu society.

Though U.S. Indian agents were free to interfere in tribal politics, they were prohibited from enforcing American laws on the reservation. As a national policy, the United States left the prosecution of internal crime—offenses committed by Indians upon other Indians—to the individual tribes to adjudicate in accordance with local custom. Consequently, when news of Spotted Tail's killing reached the nearby Rosebud agency, officials there summoned a tribal council. In traditional Lakota society, the killing of another person was classified as a personal conflict—a matter to be settled by the participants

Crow Dog (c. 1835–1910), a Lakota leader, killed a rival, Spotted Tail, in 1881. This led to a landmark Supreme Court opinion in 1883 that affirmed tribal jurisdiction while opening the door to increased Congressional authority over native peoples. (Library of Congress)

and their immediate families. But this was a high-profile event that threatened tribal unity. Eager to avoid a protracted feud among existing tribal factions, the assembled council took measures to facilitate the resolution process and dispatched envoys to both families. In keeping with Lakota custom, Crow Dog was obliged to pay blood money to compensate Spotted Tail's family. After payment of $600, eight horses, and a blanket, the tribe considered the matter resolved.

Average Americans who followed these events were reportedly appalled by the monetary settlement. The agency clerk at Rosebud, ostensibly in response to a public demand for justice, ordered Crow Dog's arrest on the basis that the federal statutes applied to Indian country under the Federal Enclaves Act of 1817 and through provisions of an 1868 U.S. treaty with the Sioux. Crow Dog was transported to Deadwood, Dakota Territory, where he was tried in federal court, convicted, and sentenced to death.

The case might well have ended there had a federal marshal not inexplicably released Crow Dog to settle affairs at home. No one expected Crow Dog to return voluntarily to custody for his execution. When he did, newspapers praised his return as heroic and honorable, and public sentiment shifted in his favor. Amid this publicity, several attorneys volunteered to appeal the conviction, and a petition to review the constitutionality of the government's case was ultimately presented to the Supreme Court on Crow Dog's behalf.

In the resulting opinion, *Ex Parte Crow Dog*, 109 U.S. 556 (1883), the Supreme Court upheld the U.S. government's long-standing policy of yielding jurisdiction to Indian nations over all crimes committed by and against American Indians in Indian country. The Court, however, additionally determined that federal jurisdiction over Indians was dependent upon the expression of intent by Congress to exercise such jurisdiction. Because Congress had never expressed such intent, the Court overturned the conviction and released Crow Dog.

Though favorable, the opinion proved a disastrous precedent for American Indian sovereignty: Congress was now constitutionally free to limit tribal authority by demonstrating its intent through legislation. The unpopular decision additionally galvanized many other Americans who felt that Crow Dog had escaped punishment. This case, they believed, demonstrated that Indians were incapable of governing themselves. Under a prevailing social climate that favored assimilation, the public pressured the government to extend its jurisdiction to encompass Indian reservations.

In 1885, advocates of this reform were rewarded with the Major Crimes Act, a brief piece of legislation that granted the federal government criminal jurisdiction on reservation lands over Indians accused of any of the seven serious crimes of murder, manslaughter, rape, assault with intent to kill, arson, burglary, or larceny. The push for reform also led to the establishment, in 1883, of governmentally appointed and approved "courts of Indian offenses" to deal with lesser crimes. These changes signaled a reversal in federal Indian policy that eroded tribal sovereignty and significantly altered the legal and constitutional status of Indian nations and peoples.

Caoimhín Ó Fearghail

See also Plenary Power; Sovereignty; Spotted Tail; *United States v. Kagama*, 1886.

References and Further Reading

Clow, Richmond L. 1998. "The Anatomy of a Lakota Shooting: Crow Dog and Spotted Tail, 1879–1881." *South Dakota History* 28(4): 209–227.

Harring, Sidney L. 1994. *Crow Dog's Case: American Indian Sovereignty, Tribal Law, and United States Law in the Nineteenth Century.* Cambridge: Cambridge University Press.

Wilkins, David E., and K. Tsianina Lomawaima. 2001. *Uneven Ground: American Indian Sovereignty and Federal Law.* Norman: University of Oklahoma Press.

Elk v. Wilkins, 1884

In *Elk v. Wilkins*, 112 U.S. 94 (1884), the United States Supreme Court held that Indians were not protected by the Fourteenth Amendment of the Constitution. The Fourteenth Amendment granted citizenship through one of two methods: birth or naturalization. In the *Elk v. Wilkins* case, the Court emphatically denied Elk's claim on both issues. Therefore, neither those Indians still living on reservations or those who had severed all ties to their tribes and had assimilated themselves into the dominant culture held the right to become citizens or to vote.

In 1881, John Elk, an English-speaking farmer living in Omaha, Nebraska, attempted to register to vote but was denied by city council officials on grounds that he was an Indian. Elk argued that he was a citizen of the United States, that he had lived in Omaha for several years, had assimilated himself into the dominant culture, and had broken all ties to his original tribe. However, the majority opinion of the Supreme Court ruled against him. Justice Horace Gray addressed the issue of whether the Fourteenth Amendment of the Constitution applied to Indians born in U.S. territory who had voluntarily separated themselves from their tribes and who lived, worked, and paid taxes among the white citizens of the country.

After denying Indians protection under the Fourteenth Amendment, based on the argument that their place of birth did not grant them that protection, the Court addressed the issue of naturalization. The Court also denied Indians the right to become naturalized citizens of the United States. The Court further argued that the plaintiff's having surrendered himself to the United States did not mean that "the United States accepted his surrender, or that he has ever been naturalized . . . or in any way recognized or treated as a citizen" (*Elk v. Wilkins*, 1884).

Although the majority decision of the Court went against Elk, Associate Justice Marshall Harlan dissented, arguing that provisions of the Civil Rights Act of 1866 did apply to a portion of the Indian population. Justice Harlan maintained that, because the 1866 act specifically excluded "Indians not taxed," it therefore included Indians who had left their tribes and assimilated themselves into the dominant culture.

In response to the *Elk v. Wilkins* decision, Senator Henry Dawes of Massachusetts argued that the Indians needed to become more independent and less reliant upon tribal relations. To accomplish this goal of greater independence, Dawes authored the General Allotment Act of 1887, also known as the Dawes Act.

Robert O. Marlin IV

See also Allotments; Assimilation;
    Guardianship/Wardship; General Allotment
    Act (Dawes Act), 1887.
References and Further Reading
Elk v. Wilkins, 112 U.S. 94 (1884).
Martin, Jill E. 1990. "Neither Fish, Flesh, Fowl, Nor
    Good Red Herring: The Citizenship Status of
    American Indians, 1830–1924," *Journal of the
    West*, 29(3): 75–87.
Pommersheim, Frank. 1995. *Braid of Feathers:
    American Indian Law and Contemporary Tribal Life*.
    Berkeley: University of California Press.
Zelden, Charles L. 2002. *Voting Rights on Trial: A
    Handbook with Cases, Laws and Documents*. Santa
    Barbara, CA: ABC-CLIO.

United States v. Kagama, 1886

In *United States v. Kagama*, 118 U.S. 375 (1886), the Supreme Court enunciated a "superior position" of the federal government vis-à-vis Native nations (a doctrine that came to be known as plenary power) as it upheld the Major Crimes Act of 1885. The Court was upholding the federal trust responsibility against erosion by the states. The Court said that "the people of the states . . . are often [the Indians'] deadliest enemies." This case was the first Supreme Court decision to directly address the legality of federal jurisdiction over both Indians and non-Indians in Indian country.

A year after the Major Crimes Act was passed, attorneys for Kagama argued that it was unconstitu-

tional. The Supreme Court ruled that the commerce clause of the Constitution did not authorize Congress to regulate the internal affairs of Indian nations and their members. However, the Court held that, because the states had no legal authority over Indians living on reservations, the role of sovereign must be played by the United States. Native American conceptions of sovereignty were omitted from this legal formulation.

The facts of the case concerned two Indians, Kagama and Mahawaha, who killed another Indian on the Hupa Reservation in California. They were arrested, tried, and convicted in federal court on grounds that the commerce clause of the Constitution gave the government jurisdiction on the Hupa Reservation. The U.S. Supreme Court, following John Marshall's opinions in *Cherokee Nation v. Georgia* (1831) and *Worcester v. Georgia* (1832), held that Indian lands did not constitute foreign nations. "These Indian tribes are the wards of the nation," ruled the Court. "They are communities dependent on the United States . . . From their very weaknesses and helplessness, so largely due to the course of dealing of the federal government with them and the treaties in which it has been promised, there arises the duty of protection and with it the power." The Court also held that "[t]he Indians owe no allegiance to a state within which their reservation may be established, and the state gives them no protection."

Justice Samuel Miller, writing for the Court majority, said that the government had always regarded Native nations as semi-sovereign entities, "not as states, not as nations, but as separate people, with power of regulating their internal relations and thus not brought into the laws of the Union or the States within whose limits they resided."

Bruce E. Johansen

See also *Cherokee Nation v. Georgia*, 1831; Sovereignty;
    Treaty; Trust.
References and Further Reading
Kickingbird, Kirke. 1983. *Indian Jurisdiction*.
    Washington, DC: Institute for the Development
    of Indian Law.
United States v. Kagama 118 U.S. 375 (1886).
Wilkins, David E., and K.Tsianina Lomawaima. 2001.
    *Uneven Ground: American Indian Sovereignty and
    Federal Law*. Norman: University of Oklahoma
    Press.
Williams, Robert A., Jr. 1997. *Linking Arms Together:
    American Indian Treaty Visions of Law and Peace,
    1600–1800*. New York and Oxford: Oxford
    University Press.

General Allotment Act (Dawes Act), 1887

Enacted on February 8, 1887, the General Allotment Act (also known as the Dawes Act after its sponsor, Henry L. Dawes) provided for the allotment of tribal lands in severalty and for the cession of surplus land for white settlement. Reservation lands were divided into parcels deeded to individual tribal members, with proceeds from the sale of surplus land going to fund Indian education and agricultural development. Two contradictory impulses motivated supporters of allotment. Philanthropic "friends" of the Indian intended to hasten "assimilation" into white society by weakening tribal structures and encourag-

ing Indians to become "civilized," independent, landholding farmers, while simultaneously protecting Indian land from illegal encroachment by white settlers. Paradoxically, however, the legislation also provided a mechanism for the legal divestment of "surplus" Indian land to white settlers and was thus also supported by western land grabbers. Between 1887 and 1934, when the Indian Reorganization Act formally ended the policy of allotment, approximately 90 million acres of land, two-thirds of the original Indian landholding of 138 million acres, had passed out of Indian ownership (Downes 1945, 332).

The principal provisions of allotment were as follows: (1) Each family head was allocated a land grant of 160 acres, with each single person over the

The General Allotment Act of 1887 surveyed and assigned individual allotted lands to members of Indian tribes. Surplus lands following tribal allotments were often opened to white settlement. On September 16, 1893, over 6 million acres of the Cherokee Outlet in Oklahoma Territory were opened for settlement. (Bettmann/Corbis)

age of eighteen and each orphan under the age of eighteen receiving 80 acres and each single person under the age of eighteen receiving 40 acres. Married women were excluded from allotment benefits. (2) Following implementation of allotment, a period of four years commenced during which allottees could select their own land. If allottees failed to select land by the end of this period, the secretary of the interior could instruct the Indian agent to undertake selection on their behalf. (3) Subject to the approval of the secretary of the interior, each allottee would be issued with a patent in fee holding their lands in trust for twenty-five years for the sole use and benefit of the allottee and his or her heirs, during which period the land could not be alienated or encumbered. (4) On expiry of the trust period (which the president had the discretion to extend) the allottee would receive the land in fee simple and become a U.S. citizen, subject to the civil and criminal laws of the state in which the allottee was resident.

The central aim of allotment was to "civilize" Indians by transforming them into independent farmers and citizens and diminishing the bonds of tribal culture. It was thought that individual property ownership would act as an incentive to Indians for self-improvement and that the distribution of white settlers onto unallotted land across reservations would provide Indians with examples of the key "American" values of industriousness and individualism to which to aspire. By dispersing tribal members across the reservation onto individual family farms, it was also hoped that the practice of "heathen" customs, rituals, and religions would be inhibited.

In practice, allottees were frequently poverty-stricken through poor land choice or limited agricultural skills, and millions of acres of allotted land were eventually lost to white settlers through fraud or sold to pay taxes, leading to a checkerboard pattern of ownership of tribal lands. The divestment of land was hastened by an 1891 amendment to the act allowing for the leasing of "unalienable" lands under certain circumstances, for example, where an allottee was unable to occupy and improve land due to age or infirmity.

A number of tribes were exempt from allotment, including the Cherokee, Creek, Choctaw, Chickasaw, Seminole, Osage, Sac and Fox, Miami, Peoria, a portion of Sioux land in Nebraska, and the Seneca Nation of New York State, although later legislation, such as the Curtis Act of 1898 dealing with the so-called Five Civilized Tribes, eventually nullified most of these exemptions.

Annie Kirby

See also Allotments; Assimilation; Collier, John; Curtis Act, 1898; Dawes, Henry Laurens; Dawes Commission; Indian Reorganization Act, 1934; Meriam Report, 1928.

References and Further Reading

Carter, Kent. 1999. *The Dawes Commission and the Allotment of the Five Civilized Tribes, 1893–1914.* Orem, UT: Ancestry.com Incorporated.

Downes, Randolph C. 1945. "A Crusade for Indian Reform, 1922–1934." *The Mississippi Valley Historical Review* 32(3): 331–354.

Otis, D. S. 1973. *The Dawes Act and the Allotment of Indian Lands.* ed. Francis Paul Prucha. Norman: University of Oklahoma Press.

Washburn, Wilcomb E. 1986. *The Assault on Indian Tribalism: The General Allotment Law (Dawes Act) of 1887.* Malabar, FL: Robert E. Krieger.

St. Catherine's Milling & Lumber Company v. The Queen (Canada), 1887

This case involved the Ojibway of Treaty 3 (1873), the province of Ontario, and the federal government of Canada. It was heard before the Judicial Committee of the Privy Council, a committee of law lords based in the United Kingdom, which at the time was the highest court of appeal for Canada. It concerned the logging interest of a private company and the status of Crown lands reserved for Indians by the Dominion of Canada, and whether this was consistent with the rights of the province of Ontario to these lands. It is a leading Canadian decision on aboriginal land rights and the division of federal-provincial legislative powers over aboriginal lands. It is the first Canadian case in which the existence of aboriginal land rights is recognized.

The province of Ontario challenged the logging company's federal permit to a timber berth on Lake Wabigoon, and the challenge succeeded in all the lower courts. The federal government of Canada appealed to the Privy Council. It argued that, under Treaty 3 and its legislative authority under Section 91(24) of the Constitution Act of 1867, which grants the federal government authority to make laws in relation to "Indians, and Lands reserved for the Indians," it was entitled to administer all treaty lands. The province counter-argued that section 91(24) only extended to lands that were "Indian reserves," which in the pre-confederation legislation referred to small tracts of land allotted to various tribes, and not treaty lands.

In its decision, the Privy Council referred to the Royal Proclamation of 1763, which provides for the protection of aboriginal land rights, and ruled that Parliament had authority to legislate in respect of "all lands reserved, under any terms and conditions, for Indian occupation," including those covered by the proclamation. The area in dispute was within the proclamation's reservation of hunting grounds, and the Indians had, prior to treaty, an aboriginal or Indian title to those lands. For the purposes of Section 109 of the Constitution Act of 1867, Indian title was defined as "an interest other than that of the Province." Once that interest was ceded under Treaty 3, however, the Province had full and unencumbered beneficial interest of the Crown, subject to the administration and control of the provincial legislature. This meant that the federal government of Canada had no property right in the disputed area. Also, Treaty 3 did not indicate that the Indians were intended to have beneficial interest in timber revenues. For these reasons, the federal government's appeal failed.

Although the Privy Council did not rule on the precise nature of Indian interest, it made several important observations about it. The Privy Council held that Indian possession of lands "can only be ascribed to the general provisions made by the Royal Proclamation in favour of all Indian tribes then living under the sovereignty and protection of the British Crown." It also held that, under the Royal Proclamation of 1763, "the tenure of the Indians was a personal and usufructuary right, dependent upon the good will of the Sovereign."

Judge John Gwynne described the Royal Proclamation of 1763 as the "Indian Bill of Rights," which specifically guaranteed Indian rights: " . . . Nations or Tribes of Indians . . . should not be molested or disturbed in the Possession of such Parts of Our Dominions and Territories as, not having been ceded to or purchased by Us, are reserved to them . . . as their Hunting Grounds . . . We do . . . strictly enjoin and require, that no private Person do presume to make any purchase from the said Indians of any Lands reserved to the said Indians . . . ; but that, if at any Time any of the said Indians should be inclined to dispose of the said Lands, the same shall be Purchased only for Us, in our Name, at some public Meeting or Assembly of the said Indians . . . "

Although *St Catherine's* represents a historic decision in terms of providing the impetus for continuing recognition of aboriginal peoples and their land rights, the decision restricted the nature of any land rights by suggesting that they are contingent on Crown grant or recognition. This meant that, upon acquisition of sovereignty by conquest or cession, private property rights or preexisting customary land rights ceased to exist and could only be enforced if subsequently recognized by legislation or executive action.

Özlem Ülgen

See also Aboriginal Title; Canadian Indian Treaty 3–October 3, 1873; Constitution Act (Canada), 1867; Royal Proclamation of 1763.
References and Further Reading
Harring, Sidney L. 1998. *White Man's Law: Native People in Nineteenth-Century Canadian Jurisprudence.* Chapter 6. Toronto: University of Toronto Press.
McNeil, Kent. 1997. "The Meaning of Aboriginal Title." In *Aboriginal and Treaty Rights in Canada: Essays on Law, Equality and Respect for Difference,* ed. Michael Asch. Vancouver: University of British Columbia Press.
Slattery, Brian. 1987. "Understanding Aboriginal Rights," 66 *Canadian Bar Review* 727.
St. Catherine's Milling and Lumber Co. v. The Queen, 13 S.C.R. 577 (1887).

Atoka Agreement, 1897

The noted Atoka Agreement occurred between the Chickasaw and Choctaw Nations and the U.S. government. This agreement involved the creation of tribal rolls pursuant to the Dawes Act and allotment of the two tribes' lands into residential, municipal, commercial, and trust property. The agreement also detailed the process for selling the "excessive holdings" that remained after the allotments had taken place, outlined some mineral rights of the nations, and provided lands and rights for the freedmen of African descent who had been slaves of the Chickasaw and Choctaw from the late 1700s in Mississippi, through removal to Indian Territory in 1837, and until 1866 when the Civil War ceased (Kappler 1904, vol. 1, 646–656).

After hostilities between the North and South ended, both the Choctaw and Chickasaw, who had allied with the South, signed the treaty of 1866 at Fort Smith, Arkansas. Although the United States had broken treaties by not providing protection to any of the five tribes whose territory had been encroached upon by the Confederates, the government held the Choctaw and Chickasaw, as well as the Cherokee, Muscogee (Creek), and Seminole, totally responsible for the tribe members who had sided with the South. In addition to providing amnesty for the Chickasaw and Choctaw tribes who had broken their peace agreements with the U. S. government by signing total alliances with the Confederates, the treaty of 1866 organized the two tribal governments and began the mapping process of the nations for roads, incorporation of towns, and, ultimately, allotment to tribal citizens. The treaty of 1866 also directed the two tribes to give all persons of African descent or their descendants residency in the nations, forty acres, $100.00, and full voting rights (Kappler 1904, vol. 2, 918–931). The Choctaw eventually fulfilled these requirements by 1886, whereas the Chickasaw opposed the document with regard to the freedmen and refused to allot the freedmen any land in the Chickasaw Nation.

The federal government proved no better at resolving the situation. The responsibility of the United States under the treaty of 1866 included moving the freedmen to land previously ceded by the Chickasaw and Choctaw known as the leased district, just west of the Chickasaw Nation (Morris, Goins, and McReynolds 1986, Map 26). However, the U.S. government never enforced the movement of the freedmen to the lands on which the Wichita, Kiowa, Comanche, and Plains-Apache (known contemporarily as the Apache tribe of Oklahoma) were already living when the United States awarded the land to the Chickasaw and Choctaw in the 1830 Treaty of Dancing Rabbit Creek. Still not pleased about that land cession being accomplished without their consent, the Plains tribes of southwestern Oklahoma presented potentially inhospitable hosts for the freedmen—or anyone else, for that matter.

Compounding the problem between the Chickasaw and the freedmen was the large number of freed slaves who came into the nation from other places, such as Texas, Arkansas, and Louisiana. The Chickasaw's firm ideological stance remained that every freedman did not have a claim to part of the Chickasaw Nation solely by virtue of location or Indian blood (Gibson 1971, 291). As a result, the Chickasaw delayed adhering to the demands of the treaty of 1866 by lengthy legal maneuverings and typically slow, tribal bureaucratic malaise. Therefore,

"freed" slaves of African descent actually had no legal civil rights, property rights, or federal government support in the Chickasaw Nation from after the Civil War through Oklahoma's statehood in 1907 (Littlefield 1980, 220–227).

Even though Chickasaw voters refused to pass the Atoka Agreement when it was first submitted to them in the spring of 1898, the passage of the Curtis Act by the U.S. Congress that summer, and the refusal of Congress to accept the negative vote of the Chickasaw people, effectively convinced the Chickasaws that they should pass the agreement. They did this with some minor adjustments in August 1898. When the Chickasaw rolls were finally completed, according to the requirements of the General Allotment Act, on January 1, 1906, the names of 6,319 citizens were listed: 1,538 full bloods, 4,146 mixed bloods, 635 intermarried whites, and 4,670 "Negroes" or freedmen (Gibson 1971, 306–307). Although all enrolled Chickasaw freedmen did receive an average forty-acre allotment in the Chickasaw Nation, the freedman found an even more hostile society in the new state of Oklahoma. All-black towns thrived in the forthcoming new state of Oklahoma, and it offered African Americans opportunities unmatched anywhere in the South. Ironically, Oklahoma enacted segregationist Jim Crow laws in 1907 as its first legislative action upon obtaining statehood.

Along with the General Allotment Act and the Curtis Act, the Atoka Agreement sealed the U.S. government's plan to dissolve the Chickasaw and Choctaw Nations. By 1906, the tribe had lost control of its collectively held lands through the allotment process and witnessed its laws and government abolished. The federal government appointed chiefs for the tribes until 1970, when Congress passed legislation to allow the Choctaw, Chickasaw, Cherokee, Muscogee (Creek), and Seminole to elect their own officers (Chickasaw Commission 1975).

Hugh W. Foley, Jr.

See also Curtis Act, 1898; General Allotment Act (Dawes Act), 1887; Indian Removal Act, 1830; Indian Territory; Reconstruction Treaties with the Cherokee, Choctaw, Chickasaw, Creek, and Seminole–1866; Treaty with the Choctaw–September 27, 1830.

References and Further Reading

Akers, Donna L. 2004. *Living in the Land of Death: The Choctaw Nation, 1830–1860.* East Lansing: Michigan State University Press.

Chickasaw Commission. 1975. *Laws of the Chickasaw Nation, I.T., Relating to Intermarried and Adopted Citizens and the Rights of Freedmen.* Wilmington, DE: Scholarly Resources.

Gibson, Arrell. 1971. *The Chickasaws.* Norman: University of Oklahoma.

Kappler, Charles J., ed. 1904. *Indian Affairs: Laws and Treaties,* 2 vols. Washington, DC: Government Printing Office.

Littlefield, Daniel F., 1980. *The Chickasaw Freedmen.* Westport, CT: Greenwood Press.

Morris, John W., Charles R. Goins, and Edwin C. McReynolds. 1986. *Historical Atlas of Oklahoma.* 3rd ed. Norman: University of Oklahoma Press.

Curtis Act, 1898

The Curtis Act of 1898 (30 *Stat.* 495, ch. 517) was a piece of allotment-era legislation that attempted to destroy tribal governments and communities in the Indian Territory, particularly among the Five Civilized Tribes. The act overturned numerous treaty rights by allotting tribal lands, invalidating tribal laws, abolishing tribal courts, and giving the secretary of the interior control over tribal revenues as well as mineral leases on Indian lands.

In the late 1890s, the "pulverizing engine" of the General Allotment Act had stalled relative to several of the tribes in the Indian Territory, and many of them refused to negotiate new agreements that would essentially abrogate solemn promises made to them earlier. Chief Isparhecher, a full-blood Muscogee Creek, noted the "alarming disregard for the terms of treaties already in existence. . . . What good is there to come of future treaties with the United States when she has no respect for those already existing between us?" (Carter 1999, 30). Ultimately, the inevitability of allotment became apparent, and some of the tribes attempted to negotiate the best terms they could with the Dawes Commission. When some of those agreements were presented to the tribal membership, however, they were often voted down. One such agreement with both the Choctaws and Chickasaws, the Atoka Agreement, was rejected by the Choctaws in December 1897.

In Washington, D.C., members of Congress were growing increasingly impatient with the progress of allotment in the Indian Territory under the Dawes Commission. On February 24, 1898, Representative Charles Curtis, himself one-eighth Kaw, introduced "An Act for the Protection of the People of the Indian Territory, and for other purposes," and President William McKinley signed the bill into law on June 28, 1898. Despite its benevolent-sounding title, the only people protected by this legislation were non-Indians. In effect, what the Dawes Commission had been unable to achieve through negotiation, the Curtis Act now attempted through legislative fiat.

The portions of the act that immediately affected the tribes dealt with enrollment. Tribal resistance had stymied the Dawes Commission's attempts to collect rolls of citizens, and allotment could not proceed until satisfactory rolls were generated. The act specified that the commission "shall have access to all rolls and records of the several tribes, and the United States court in Indian Territory shall have jurisdiction to compel the officers of the tribal governments and custodians of such rolls and records to deliver same to said commission, and on their refusal or failure to do so to punish them as for contempt" (Section 21).

Once a citizenship roll was completed and tribal lands were surveyed, Section 11 authorized the commission to proceed with allotment. Mineral rights on allotted land, however, were not distributed. Section 13 gave the secretary of the interior exclusive control over those rights.

As if allotment itself were not sufficient to destroy the tribal collective, the Curtis Act also attempted to starve tribal governments financially. Section 19 specified that "no payment of any moneys on any account whatever shall hereafter be made by the United States to any of the tribal governments or to any officer thereof for disbursement." Instead, the secretary of the interior was now in charge of tribal funds, which subsequently would be distributed only to individual tribal members.

In addition to the monetary restrictions, the Curtis Act attacked the legal infrastructure of the tribes. Section 26 specified that "the laws of the various tribes or nations of Indians shall not be enforced at law or in equity by the courts of the United States in the Indian Territory." Section 28 went even further, decreeing that "all tribal courts in Indian Territory shall be abolished, and no officer of said courts shall thereafter have any authority whatever to do or perform any act theretofore authorized by any law in connection with said courts, or to receive any pay for same."

The Curtis Act also incorporated two of the agreements that had been negotiated by the Dawes Commission. Section 29 repeated the terms of the

Atoka Agreement of April 23, 1897. Section 30 repeated the terms of the agreement reached with the Creek Special Commission on September 27, 1897. These two sections imposed a December 1, 1898, deadline on all three tribes to ratify the agreements. If they did so, the terms of the Curtis Act would apply to those tribes only in instances in which the terms of the act did not conflict with the provisions of the prior negotiated agreements.

Gavin Clarkson

See also Atoka Agreement, 1897; General Allotment Act (Dawes Act), 1887; Indian Territory.
References and Further Reading
Burton, Jeffrey. 1997. *Indian Territory and the United States: 1866–1906, Courts, Government and the Movement for Oklahoma Statehood.* Norman: University of Oklahoma Press.
Carter, Kent. 1999. *The Dawes Commission and the Allotment of the Five Civilized Tribes, 1893–1914.* Orem, UT: Ancestry.com.
Debo, Angie. 1961. *The Rise and Fall of the Choctaw Republic.* 2nd ed. Norman: University of Oklahoma Press.
Debo, Angie. 1940. *And Still the Waters Run: The Betrayal of the Five Civilized Tribes.* Princeton, NJ: Princeton University Press. Repr., University of Oklahoma Press.
Hoxie, Frederick E. 1984. *A Final Promise: The Campaign to Assimilate the Indians, 1880–1920.* Lincoln: University of Nebraska Press.
McDonnell, Janet A. *The Dispossession of the American Indian, 1887–1934.* Bloomington: Indiana University Press.
Washburn, Wilcomb E. 1975. *The Assault on Indian Tribalism: The General Allotment Law (Dawes Act) of 1887).* Philadelphia: Lippincott.

Lone Wolf v. Hitchcock, 1903

The Treaty of Medicine Lodge in 1867 was signed between the United States and the Kiowa, Comanche, and Plains Apache. This treaty designated reservation lands but was reversed in 1892 by a congressional commission. Lone Wolf brought suit in the Supreme Court to halt the sale of reservation lands. The Supreme Court denied his claim, determining that Congress had the power to change promises formed through treaties.

During the mid-nineteenth century, the Kiowa Indians inhabited the southern plains of the United States. By 1853, the Kiowa allowed military forts and roads into their region and began to accept federal annuities. A treaty was signed between the United

States and the Kiowa, Comanche, and Plains Apache in 1867 at Medicine Lodge Creek (15 *Stat.* 581, 589) The tribes agreed to relinquish 90 million acres in exchange for a 2.9 million-acre reserve. The treaty promised the Indians "absolute and undisturbed use and occupation" of their reserve. Article 12 of the treaty required consensus of three-fourths of the male adult members for further cession of their lands. In 1892, the Jerome Commission was sent by the federal government to obtain Native consent to change the treaty of 1867, in anticipation of obtaining a portion of the reserve for settlement.

The agreement reached with the tribes came under dispute, which centered on the necessary three-fourths consent of male tribal members. The validity of the signatures obtained was controversial and did not amount to the obligatory number; nevertheless, the agreement was submitted to Congress. After several critical changes to the document, Congress approved the revised arrangement. The Act of June 6, 1900, took possession of 2,991,933 acres of the Kiowa, Comanche, and Plains Apache Reservation. The federal government paid tribal members only 93 cents per acre—a considerably lower price than that paid for adjacent Native land.

In 1901, A-Kei-Quodle, a Kiowa band chief known as Lone Wolf, requested an injunction against secretary of the interior Ethan Allen Hitchcock to terminate the sale of ceded reservation lands. The Supreme Court would address the issue of treaty-based property rights and the powers Congress retained in relationship to the tribes. It took one year before the Supreme Court would hear this case, and they decided against Lone Wolf. The Supreme Court ruled that a congressional statute superseded an earlier treaty, legitimizing the breaking of the Treaty of Medicine Lodge of 1867. The Supreme Court's final opinion declared, "Plenary authority over the tribal relations of the Indians has been exercised by Congress from the beginning . . . not subject to be controlled by the judicial department of the government . . ." (187 U.S. 553 [1903] at 565). It was not a judiciary decision to invalidate this form of congressional legislation. The issue of plenary power, the absolute power that Congress holds unrestrained by the Constitution, was recognized as legal over the other controversial issues of this case. The Supreme Court redefined plenary power to grant the federal government the unrestricted ability to modify or extinguish existing Native rights. The Supreme Court ignored the issue of fraudulent signatures and presumed that Congress had acted in good faith in their dealings with the Indians. The Native Americans remained dependent wards of the federal government who could not be safeguarded by their previous treaty rights.

The implications of the Supreme Court's decision in *Lone Wolf* demonstrated that treaty-based property rights were no longer protected if congressional legislation chose not to recognize them. The Supreme Court ruling implied that congressional powers had always existed, even retroactively, when affirmed by legislation; consent between the federal government and the tribes was no longer a legal requirement. Supporters of allotment in severalty applauded the Supreme Court's decision as an affirmative judgment to further continue the division of tribal lands. Federal power over tribal lands and Native rights became more abstruse after *Lone Wolf;* subsequent cases cite *Lone Wolf* as the basis of congressional plenary power. Recent court rulings have curtailed some aspects of congressional plenary power, demanding no future revocation of treaty rights without "just compensation." *Lone Wolf* remains one of the most influential Supreme Court decisions in the last one hundred years, and it continues to influence Native American law.

Susan Sánchez-Barnett

See also Aboriginal Title; Curtis Act, 1898; *Elk v. Wilkins,* 1884; *Ex Parte Crow Dog,* 1883; Plenary Power; Supremacy Clause; *United States v. Kagama,* 1886.

References and Further Reading
Clark, C. Blue. 1999. *Lone Wolf v Hitchcock: Treaty Rights and Indian Law at the End of the Nineteenth Century.* Lincoln: University of Nebraska Press.
Lone Wolf v. Hitchcock, 287 U.S. 553, 1903.
Wilkins, David E., and K. Tsianina Lomawaima. 2001. *Uneven Ground: American Indian Sovereignty and Federal Law.* Norman: University of Oklahoma Press.

Winters v. United States, 1908

The premise of this case concerned whether settlers (appellants) could construct and maintain dams and reservoirs on the Milk River in Montana that would affect the flow of water to the Fort Belknap Reservation. The reservation for the Gros Ventre and Assiniboine tribes was established by an act of Congress on April 15, 1874, and ratified by a subsequent act of Congress on May 1, 1888, but it was silent on tribal water rights. The Supreme Court had to consider whether the tribe had ceded its water rights with the cessation of the land. Justice Joseph McKenna delivered the opinion of the Court. The Court held that the Federal Act of 1888 establishing the reservation reserved tribal water rights. Three issues were important in the decree (opinion). First, treaty and agreement ambiguities were interpreted in favor of the tribes, as they could not have known all terms that would have rendered the agreement void. Second, the tribal grant ceding lands to the United States in exchange for arid reservation lands was not predicated on the premise of losing constant use of the river. The tribe depended on the river to irrigate arid lands that were used for agriculture, farming, and cultivation. Third, upon Montana's entry into the Union under the "equal footing doctrine," the federal government reserved and did not extinguish tribal water rights.

The history that led to the case was examined by the Court. In 1889, houses were built on the river, and the occupants (settlers) relied on the water for agricultural purposes. In 1900, the settlers built large dams and reservoirs above the point at which the federal government and the tribes diverted their water. This resulted in the deprivation of water for both the tribes and the United States. The settlers had no notice of claim by the United States or the tribes over the river and were oblivious to the reservations' reliance on the river. Moreover, they believed that, under U.S. law, the river water could be used contemporaneously with the land. Thereafter, many thousands of people and communities were reliant on the river for irrigation and cultivation; without the water, the land would become useless, and communities would dissipate.

The Supreme Court first addressed the issue of jurisdiction. A decree was entered against all acts perpetuated by the settlers, and the motion to dismiss the claim was denied. The case turned on the agreement of May 1888 pursuant to the establishment of the reservation. The reservation was a small part of land with a dependency on the river which was exchanged for copious amounts of land.

The question remained whether the tribe retained the use of waters or whether cession diminished tribal water rights. The Court ruled that the tribes had not ceded their water rights with land cessation, and thus they continued to enjoy the land

and the waters. This conclusion was based on the canon that treaty and agreement ambiguities are interpreted and resolved in favor of the tribes. The Court decreed that it was unthinkable that, at the time of the agreement, the tribes were attentive to all terms and words that could defeat the purpose of an agreement or treaty. Moreover, Congress would not have rendered the agreement void a year after the establishment of the reservation, as it was federal policy to induce the "civilization and improvement" of the tribes.

The appellants put forward five defenses, all of which were nullified by the Supreme Court: first, that land cessation contemporaneously ceded tribal water rights to the river; second, that large numbers of springs were situated on the reservation and could sustain the tribe; third, that it was not the intention of the government to reserve any tribal water rights; fourth, that the appellants' claim was antecedent to that of the United States and the tribes; and fifth, that the reservation was repealed by the admission of Montana into the Union on February 22, 1859, under the equal footing doctrine.

The Supreme Court held that the power of government could reserve waters and exempt them from appropriation under state law; therefore, the waters were reserved and were to continue for the tribes. Moreover, the Congressional Act of 1888, which established the reservation, implied and contemporaneously reserved tribal rights to an undiminished quality and volume of water. If the water rights were not reserved, the federal government would have reneged on its policy of advocating the reform of tribal tradition with the issuance of essential resources for the tribe's existence. The state and its people did not thus gain rights over Milk River to dispose of it and the land at will under U.S. law.

Dewi I. Ball

See also Government-to-Government Relationship; Plenary Power; Reserved Rights Doctrine; Sovereignty.

References and Further Reading

Canby, William C. 1998. *American Indian Law in a Nutshell.* St. Paul, MN: West Group.

Colby, Bonnie G., John E. Thorson, and Sarah Britton. 2005. *Negotiating Tribal Water Rights: Fulfilling Promises in the Arid West.* Tucson: University of Arizona Press.

Pevar, Stephen L. 2002. *The Rights of Indians and Tribes.* 3rd. ed. Carbondale: Southern Illinois University Press.

Meriam Report, 1928

The Meriam Report details the conditions of Indians in the 1920s and includes some discussion of treaty rights and claims. The report, officially published as *The Problem of Indian Administration,* is the compilation of material gathered at the request of the Bureau of Indian Affairs (BIA) by the Institute for Government Research (IGR). The Meriam Report provided the blueprint for the administration of Indian affairs for decades to come, including the establishment of the Indian Claims Commission.

Since the intent of the Meriam Commission was to investigate the social and economic status of Indians and to evaluate how the BIA's services to Indians compared to services provided to non-Indians, treaty issues were not a major consideration of the report. Lewis Meriam (an IGR employee) and his group of investigators spent seven months visiting ninety-five schools, hospitals, agencies, and other BIA facilities. Ray A. Brown, a University of Wisconsin law professor, was in charge of investigating legal issues. His observations are provided in Chapter 13, "Legal Aspects of the Indian Problem." This chapter considers issues such as state versus national jurisdiction, citizenship, and court access.

Chapter 13 of the report also considers treaty rights. Brown and the others recognized the validity of the treaties and of the federal government's role as trustee, but they also believed that the treaties were outdated and that they unnecessarily complicated Indian law. The document explains that, up until 1871, the process of treating with Native American tribes was the same process used in negotiations with foreign countries. The result was a different legal foundation for each of the tribes, which the federal government was still forced to deal with. Brown and the others suggested that the BIA consider whether or not allowing this complicated system to continue was wise. The report further postulated that a commission could be appointed to "terminate" treaty rights and to create a Native American law code that did away with the "archaic provisions" that applied to certain tribes (Meriam 1928, 750). As an example, the document reprinted part of the 1794 Treaty of Canandaigua with the Iroquois to show how some annuity payment systems were still in force.

Brown and the rest of the commission were very much aware, however, of the long-standing claims based on treaty rights that many tribes had against the federal government. The report warns that no law code could be created until these claims were extinguished. Until tribes felt that claims have been settled, the document stated, they would not cooperate with the creation of a new law code and would expect a large cash settlement. Without congressional approval, however, tribes could not sue the United States in the court of claims. The haphazard process of getting an act through Congress and then actually marshalling forces for the suit were, Brown and the others felt, extremely cumbersome and ineffectual. To streamline the process, the report suggests that the secretary of the interior gather a staff specifically to look into the outstanding tribal claims and to draft legislation where warranted to obtain congressional approval.

While the compiled Indian law code never materialized, the long-term impact of the report's recommendations on legal aspects may be the Indian Claims Commission (ICC). Although not the first to explain such a court (Commissioner of Indian Affairs Francis Leupp proposed a similar solution in 1910), the report was the most influential document to make such a suggestion. The report's recommendation to extinguish tribal claims met with approval, and Congress debated the issue through the 1930s. In 1946, Congress created the ICC, which acted as a court and awarded more than $800 million to tribes across the country (Rosenthal 1990, 266–267). Although the Meriam Report did not equate termination of the treaty obligations with termination of the trustee relationship, many in Congress who voted for the ICC did and subsequently supported the termination bill H.R. 108. In this matter, then, as in all others, the long-term effect of the Meriam Report is mixed.

Angela Firkus

See also House Concurrent Resolution 108, 1953; Indian Claims Commission Act, 1946; Indian Claims Commission (ICC); Termination.

References and Further Reading

Meriam, Lewis, et al. 1928. *The Problem of Indian Administration: report of a survey made at the request of Hubert Work, Secretary of the Interior, and submitted to him, February 21, 1928.* Baltimore: Johns Hopkins Press.

Philp, Kenneth R. 1977. *John Collier's Crusade for Indian Reform 1920–1954.* Tucson: University of Arizona Press.

Rosenthal, Harvey D. 1990. *Their Day in Court: A History of the Indian Claims Commission.* New York: Garland.

Indian Reorganization Act, 1934

The Indian Reorganization Act (IRA) of 1934, also known as the Wheeler-Howard Act, was the cornerstone of Commissioner of Indian Affairs John Collier's package of reforms, known collectively as the Indian New Deal. The legislation, although wide ranging, consisted of two principle features: it prohibited the future allotment of communally held Indian lands to individual tribal members in severalty, and it provided for the establishment of limited forms of tribal government and property management.

The IRA formally terminated the process of allotment begun under the General Allotment Act of 1887, which had resulted in some two-thirds of tribally owned land passing into white ownership. Existing periods of trust on already-allotted land were extended indefinitely, and the act prohibited the further allotment of reservation land to individuals. Surplus land that had been opened for sale was withdrawn and returned to tribal control, and up to $2 million dollars per annum was made available for the acquisition of land, water, and surface rights (Deloria and Lytle 1984, 269).

The second major objective of the act was to remodel tribal governments as self-governing municipal authorities. Collier's original plan was for tribes to adopt written constitutions and bylaws reflecting traditional tribal decision-making and leader selection methods. A team of consultant anthropologists was employed to facilitate this process, but Congress refused funding and the unit was disbanded. As a result, tribal constitutions were largely drawn up in Washington, based on European American political conventions, and presented to Indian leaders unfamiliar with European American legal jargon. Tribes, rather than subtribal groups such as clans, bands, and families, were made the basis of the new political structures. The resulting constitutions, many of which were virtually identical regardless of the specifics of tribal traditions, made little provision for consensus-based decision making or for the role of spiritual leaders. The new constitutions were required to be ratified by a majority of adult members of a tribe through secret ballot. About 77 out of 258 tribes voted against accepting the act, perhaps reflecting a deep-seated distrust of the Bureau of Indian Affairs (BIA) (McNickle 1993, 94).

In addition to the cessation of allotment and the adoption of tribal constitutions, the IRA also established a $10 million revolving credit fund to provide loans to Indian chartered corporations for promoting the economic development of tribes. A further sum of $250,000 per annum was made available for the payment of tuition and other expenses for vocational and trade schools, with not more than $50,000 allocated to high school and college students (Deloria and Lytle 1984, 144–145). The act also provided for the preferential hiring of suitably qualified Indians within the BIA.

The IRA was part of a wider body of policies that constituted the Indian New Deal, including the Indian Arts and Crafts Board Act of 1936, which expanded the market for Indian-made arts and crafts and protected them with a government trademark. The constitutional right to freedom of religion for Indians was reaffirmed, and the revival of traditional dances and ceremonies was also encouraged. The Oklahoma Indian Welfare Act and the Alaska Native Reorganization Act, both of 1936, extended provisions similar to those contained in the IRA to the Oklahoma tribes (with the exception of the Osage) and Alaska Natives.

Some scholars have argued that the rejection by Congress of certain key elements initially contained within Collier's proposals, such as a tribal court system and the adequate provision for the transfer of responsibilities from the BIA to tribal communities, resulted in the effective retention of colonial rule, with power concentrated in the hands of the secretary of the interior and federal bodies. Despite its limitations, the IRA represented a major divergence from the assimilationist impulse that had previously dominated federal policy regarding Native Americans.

Annie Kirby

See also Allotments; Bureau of Indian Affairs (BIA); Collier, John; General Allotment Act (Dawes Act), 1887; Indian New Deal; Meriam Report, 1928.

References and Further Reading

Collier, John. 1948. *Indians of the Americas: The Long Hope.* New York: Mentor Books.

Deloria, Vine, Jr., and Clifford Lytle. 1984. *The Nations Within: The Past and Future of American Indian Sovereignty.* New York: Pantheon Books.

McNickle, D'Arcy. 1973. *Native American Tribalism: Indian Survivals and Renewals.* Repr., New York and Oxford: Oxford University Press, 1993.

Taylor, Graham D. 1980. *The New Deal and American Indian Tribalism, The Administration of the Indian Reorganization Act, 1934–45.* Lincoln: University of Nebraska Press.

Washburn, Wilcomb E. 1984. "A Fifty-Year Perspective on the Indian Reorganization Act." *American Anthropologist,* 86(2): 279–289.

United States v. Creek Nation, 1935

This case was a lawsuit by the Muscogee Creek Nation/tribe of Indians against the United States to recover compensation for certain lands of that tribe charged to have been appropriated by the United States.

From 1826 to 1840, the Muscogee Creek Indians, some voluntarily and some forcibly, left their homes in the East and relocated in Indian Territory in what is now the state of Oklahoma. Pursuant to a treaty dated February 14, 1833, the Creek Nation acquired a patent awarding the nation fee simple title to a part of the Indian Territory. Over time, the white population in Indian Territory outnumbered the Native American population.

By a treaty of 1866, the Muscogee Creeks ceded to the United States the westerly half of that tract but expressly retained the easterly half. The United States stipulated that it would cause a north and south line separating the ceded from the unceded lands to be surveyed under the direction of the commissioner of Indian affairs and guaranteed the Creeks quiet possession of their unceded lands.

In 1871, the commissioner of Indian affairs had the divisional line surveyed. A controversy arose as to whether the line was surveyed too far to the east and thereby encroached on unceded lands of the Creeks; but that controversy, if not terminated before, was put to rest and the line effectively recognized by an agreement made between the Muscogee Creek tribe and the United States in 1889. Combined with other surveys, including one made for another Native American tribe, the United States erroneously treated the strip of unceded Creek land by allotment to the other tribe. The error amounted to more than five thousand acres of land.

The case finally came before the Supreme Court in 1926. It was agreed that the Creek tribe was entitled to compensation, but the parties were not agreed respecting the time as of which the value should be ascertained. The tribe contended for the value in 1926, when the suit was brought. The government argued for the value at time of appropriation, which it insisted was in 1873, when the survey was approved by the commissioner of Indian affairs or its alternative, at the time the lands were disposed of under the act of 1891.

When the Muscogee Creek demanded compensation for this lost land a century after the mistake was made, government lawyers argued that the Creek should have corrected the survey or complained earlier.

In the majority opinion of *United States v. Creek Nation*, the Supreme Court disagreed, giving the Creek Fifth Amendment compensation from the government. According to the Court, "The tribe was a dependent Indian community under the guardianship of the United States . . . at the time, and as such it was entitled" to rely on the United States, its guardian, for needed protection of its interests.

Although the United States had broad powers and wide discretion in managing Indian tribes' affairs, it remained "subject to limitations inhering in such a guardianship," including an obligation of care in handling Indian property, the Court said, and the case was dismissed.

Fred Lindsay

See also Indian Removal; Indian Territory; Treaty; Treaty with the Creek–June 14, 1866.
References and Further Reading
Debo, Angie. 1941. *The Road to Disappearance: A History of the Creek Indians.* Norman. University of Oklahoma Press.
Green, Donald E. 1973. *The Creek People.* Phoenix, AZ: Indian Tribal Series.
Green, Michael D. 1982. *The Politics of Indian Removal: Creek Government and Society in Crisis.* Lincoln and London: University of Nebraska Press.

Indian Claims Commission Act, 1946

Signed into law by President Harry S Truman on August 13, 1946, the Indian Claims Commission Act established a commission empowered to hear the claims of American Indian communities against the federal government. The new commission consisted of a chief commissioner and two associate commissioners who heard claims from Indian communities based on issues of law and equity. Claimants could base their cases on the U.S. Constitution, laws, and executive orders, but most cases involved land transfers agreed upon through treaties. Although the law claimed to create a commission, the new agency functioned like a court. The law allowed the government to use all possible defenses against Indian claims and to establish offsets reducing claim payments based on goods and services already provided by the government. The commission's process for appeals involved both the court of claims and the Supreme Court.

The act marked a shift in federal Indian policy from the Indian New Deal of the 1930s to the termination policy of the 1950s. Many supporters of the Indian Claims Commission argued that the commission offered compensation to Indian communities unfairly treated by the government; even the National Congress of American Indians, founded by American Indian leaders in 1944, endorsed the idea. However, other supporters of the commission viewed it as a first step to terminating the trust relationship between the federal government and Indian communities. These individuals believed that, until the government settled all Indian claims, federal involvement with Indian affairs could not end.

Before the Indian Claims Commission heard Indian complaints against the government, the United States Court of Claims handled them. Congress established the court of claims in 1855 to hear suits against the federal government, but eight years later, in 1863, it prohibited the court from hearing claims based on treaties with Indian nations. In 1881, Congress granted the Choctaws the right to present their claims to the court, reopening an avenue for Indian complaints against the government but only through the difficult process of gaining permission from Congress for each individual case. Use of these special jurisdictional acts proved inefficient. Native communities filed 219 complaints with the court of claims before 1946; however, the court granted only thirty-five awards.

Criticism of the system for Indian claims began as early as the 1890s. By the twentieth century, Commissioner of Indian Affairs Francis Leupp recommended the creation of a new court to hear only Indian claims, and in 1928, the Meriam Report suggested the creation of an Indian Claims Commission. The government continued to study various plans to settle Indian claims until passage of the Indian Claims Commission Act in 1946. Commissioner of Indian Affairs John Collier tried to include an Indian claims court in his Indian Reorganization Act of 1934, and legislative efforts to create an Indian claims commission began in 1935. After 1935, Congress focused on the commission structure to handle claims, considering a number of bills before proposing H.R. 4497 in October of 1945. This bill, intro-

Photographed after the signing of the Indian Claims Commission Act are President Harry S Truman, seated, and from left to right, Senator Joseph C. O'Mahoney of Wyoming; Reginald Curry of the Ute Tribe; Julius Murray of the Uintah Ute Tribe; and Oscar Chapman, acting Secretary of the Interior. The Indian Claims Commission operated for 32 years, adjudicating the long-standing land and accounting claims of Native Americans against the federal government. (Bettmann/Corbis)

duced by Representative Henry M. Jackson of Washington, ultimately became the Indian Claims Commission Act, or Public Law 726 under the Seventy-Ninth Congress.

The new law created a temporary agency empowered to hear claims for only ten years, but Congress maintained the court for thirty-two years, granting extension acts in 1956, 1961, 1967, 1972, and 1976. Despite the extended time frame, the commission did not settle all outstanding claims, forcing the court of claims to handle the remaining work. Overall, the commission decided 549 claims and awarded approximately $800 million during its existence, leaving the court of claims sixty-eight unresolved dockets after its dissolution on September 30, 1978.

Jay Precht

See also Cohen, Felix S.; Collier, John; Indian Claims Commission (ICC); Indian Reorganization Act, 1934; Leupp, Francis Ellington; Meriam Report, 1928; Termination; Watkins, Arthur V.

References and Further Reading

Fixico, Donald L. 1986. *Termination and Relocation: Federal Indian Policy, 1945–1960.* Albuquerque: University of New Mexico Press.

Iverson, Peter. 1998. *"We Are Still Here": American Indians in the Twentieth Century.* The American History Series. Wheeling, IL: Harlan Davidson.

Prucha, Francis Paul. 1984. *The Great Father: The United States Government and the American Indians,* vol. 2. Lincoln and London: University of Nebraska Press.

Rosenthal, H. D. 1990. *Their Day in Court: A History of the Indian Claims Commission.* New York and London: Garland.

House Concurrent Resolution 108, 1953

House Concurrent Resolution (HCR) 108 represented the beginning of official U.S. termination policy regarding Native Americans. Termination is an important aspect of twentieth-century federal Indian policy. It both drove and reflected the actions of federal officials throughout the 1950s and 1960s. HCR 108 indicated that all Indians within the United States were to assume all the rights and responsibilities of being American citizens. This included being subject to the same U.S. laws that applied to other Americans (*House Report* no. 841). The driving force behind HCR 108 was the idea of assimilation. The government concluded that Indians must be assimilated into the dominant culture in order to become real Americans.

Federal officials formulated HCR 108 to end federal responsibility to Indian tribes and also to terminate the unique trustee relationship between tribes and the federal government. Senator Arthur Watkins of Utah, who also chaired the Senate Subcommittee on Indian Affairs, and Senator Henry M. Jackson of Washington State both adamantly believed that termination was the course to equality for Native Americans. Jackson introduced HCR 108 during the 83rd Congress, and on August 1, 1953, Congress adopted it. Congressional recognition did not make it law, but recognition did mean that Congress agreed with the fundamentals of the bill and that it supported a termination policy for Indian tribes (Fixico 1986, 97).

The government had determined that many tribes were already nearly assimilated, and these groups were the first targets of termination. HCR 108 specified that federal supervision be removed from tribes in California, Florida, New York, and Texas. It additionally named the Flathead tribe in Montana, the Klamath tribe in Oregon, the Menominee tribe in Minnesota, the Potawatami tribes in Kansas and Nebraska, and the Turtle Mountain Chippewa tribe in North Dakota as tribes who could survive well without federal supervision. The secretary of the interior expected a report on these tribes, and legislation relating to terminating them, by January 1, 1954, a mere four months after HCR 108 was approved (*House Report* no. 841).

Although HCR 108 did not actually terminate tribes, it served as the legislative foundation for the government to carry out termination. The 84th Congress witnessed a flood of termination bills, and new termination legislation would continue until President Richard Nixon formally repealed the termination laws within HCR 108 in 1970. HCR 108 also paved the way for Public Law 280, a law that allowed several states to take jurisdictional control over some reservation services.

Laurie Arnold

See also Assimilation; *Menominee Tribe of Indians v. United States, 1968;* Public Law 280, 1953; Termination; Watkins, Arthur V.

References and Further Reading

Burt, Larry W. 1982. *Tribalism in Crisis: Federal Indian Policy, 1953–1961.* Albuquerque: University of New Mexico Press.

Fixico, Donald L. 1986. *Termination and Relocation: Federal Indian Policy, 1945–1960.* Albuquerque: University of New Mexico Press.

House Concurrent Resolution 108. 1953. 67 *U.S. Statutes at Large* B132; House Report no. 841, 83-I, serial II666.

Philp, Kenneth R. 1999. *Termination Revisited: American Indians on the Trail to Self-Determination, 1933–1953.* Lincoln and London: University of Nebraska Press.

Prucha, Francis Paul. 1995. *The Great Father: The United States Government and the American Indians.* Lincoln: University of Nebraska Press.

Public Law 280, 1953

Passed by Congress in 1953, Public Law (PL) 280 provided for the jurisdictional transfer of criminal and civil matters from Indian tribal control to state control. Congress approved PL 280 to work in concert with a larger movement by the government to terminate Indian tribes. Termination, as described in House Concurrent Resolution (HCR) 108, meant the end of federal supervision of Indian tribes and the end of Indians' trustee status. PL 280 was an aggressive move by the government to discontinue tribal control over offenses committed on Indian lands. The law applied to Indian lands in California, Minnesota, Nebraska, Oregon, and Wisconsin. PL 280 did allow some tribes within these states to retain jurisdictional control, however. The Red Lake Reservation in Minnesota, the Warm Springs Reservation in Oregon, and the Menominee Reservation in Wisconsin were all excluded from PL 280 (Prucha 1995, 1044). PL 280 was amended later by Congress to include Alaska.

PL 280 emerged as a policy from the federal government, not as a request from Indian tribes. In fact, PL 280 did not require consultation or consent from the Indian tribes facing the new policy. President Dwight Eisenhower supported the foundations of PL 280, but when he signed off on the legislation, he asked Congress to amend the resolution when it reconvened. Eisenhower wanted to include requirements for consultation with tribes. Congress did write an amendment calling for consent from Indians, but the Interior Department opposed it, and terminationist senator Arthur Watkins wrote a vehement minority report against the consent amendment. Ultimately, the amendment failed (Prucha 1995, 1046).

Decentralization of the Bureau of Indian Affairs (BIA) comprised another aspect of PL 280. The law assumed that states would be able to handle efficiently their new responsibilities and jurisdiction, thus the BIA could close offices in the states of transfer. Determining which offices to close meant defining who was Indian, in order to count how many people would need services. This activity was also undertaken without consulting Indians (Fixico 1986, 112–113). The reason consultation proved to be such a contentious issue for the government, especially for the Department of the Interior, was simply that the government remained intent on terminating Indian tribes. The government did not wish to negotiate with groups who would, for the government's intents and purposes, no longer exist after termination legislation obtained congressional approval.

PL 280 remains emblematic of governmental assimilation policies in the postwar era. It was a fundamental building block of later termination legislation, and it illustrated the government's concerted efforts to integrate Indians into the broader U.S. population.

Laurie Arnold

See also Assimilation; House Concurrent Resolution 108, 1953; *Menominee Tribe of Indians v. United States;* Termination; Watkins, Arthur V.

References and Further Reading

Burt, Larry W. 1982. *Tribalism in Crisis: Federal Indian Policy, 1953–1961.* Albuquerque: University of New Mexico Press.

Fixico, Donald L. 1986. *Termination and Relocation: Federal Indian Policy, 1945–1960.* Albuquerque: University of New Mexico Press.

House Concurrent Resolution 108. 1953. 67 *U.S. Statutes at Large* 588–590; House Report no. 848, 83-I, serial II666.

Prucha, Francis Paul. 1995. *The Great Father: The United States Government and the American Indians.* Lincoln: University of Nebraska Press.

Philp, Kenneth R. 1999. *Termination Revisited: American Indians on the Trail to Self-Determination, 1933–1953.* Lincoln and London: University of Nebraska Press.

Tee-Hit-Ton Indians v. United States, 1955

The United States purchased Alaska from Russia through the Treaty of 1867, but Native land rights were not mentioned in this treaty. The Tee-Hit-Ton band of the Tlingit Indians inhabited lands in Alaska that would later be established as the Tongass National Forest. In 1951, Congress sold timber from the Tongass National Forest to a private lumber company, and the Tee-Hit-Ton sued the United States for compensation under the Fifth Amendment. In 1955, in *Tee-Hit-Ton Indians v. United States* (348 U.S. 272), the Supreme Court decided against the Tee-Hit-Ton, affirming that, since Congress had never acknowledged the Tee-Hit-Ton and their land rights, then none existed.

The United States acquired Alaska in 1867 from Russia, attaining 365,000 acres of land inhabited by thirty-one thousand Native Peoples and nine hundred white settlers. No treaties between the federal government and Native groups were concluded either before or after the Alaskan purchase. Federal policy regarding Alaskan Natives' rights to land was mentioned in the Organic Act of 1884, which provided that "Indians or other persons in said district [Alaska] shall not be disturbed in the possession of

any lands actually in their use or occupation or now claimed by them, but the terms under which such persons may acquire title to such lands are reserved for future legislation by Congress" (Organic Act, 1984)

In 1947, Congress instructed the secretary of the interior to sell timber from the Tongass National Forest "notwithstanding any claim of possessory rights" (61 *Stat.* 920). The resolution defined that the receipts from the timber sale be placed in a special U.S. Treasury account until the timber and Native land rights had been defined. A private company was contracted to harvest all saleable timber from a section of the Tongass National Forest. The Tee-Hit-Ton, a band of the Tlingits, claimed aboriginal title of this land and proprietary interest in any timber sold.

The Tee-Hit-Ton filed suit in the court of claims requesting recompense from the United States for the timber sale. The basis of their claim was the question of aboriginal land ownership and equitable rights under the Fifth Amendment. The court of claims ruled that the Tee-Hit-Ton did possess original Indian title or Indian right of occupancy, but because this was not stated in the Treaty of 1867 when Alaska was purchased, the Tee-Hit-Ton case was dismissed (128 Ct. Cl., at 92, 120F).

The Tee-Hit-Ton appealed to the Supreme Court, which had previously heard cases concerning Native land issues, and Justice Stanley Reed submitted the final opinion that denied the claim. The Supreme Court declared two important points in their denial of the Tee-Hit-Ton claim. The first was that Congress did not acknowledge Native title to this land, illustrated by the sale of the timber from the Tongass National Forest. If Congress had never acknowledged the Tee-Hit-Ton's right to occupy the forest, then the Native Peoples could not have held title and therefore did not have proprietary interest in the timber. The second point was the Court's corroboration of the legal concept of the conqueror's sovereignty over and ownership of Native lands. Justice Reed wrote that "every American schoolboy knows that the savage tribes of this continent were deprived of their ancestral ranges by force and that, even when the Indians ceded millions of acres by treaty . . . it was not a sale but the conqueror's will that deprived them of their land" (348 U.S. 272 [1955] at 289–290). The Supreme Court determined that Congress could extinguish Indian occupancy at its own judgment without recompense, quoting from *Johnson v. M'Intosh* (8 Wheat. 543, p. 587), "that discovery gave an exclusive right to extinguish the

Indian title of occupancy, either by purchase or by conquest."

Although Alaska was purchased by the United States in 1867, no treaty or agreement with any Alaskan Native group was ever accomplished. Without this recognition of their ancestral lands by the federal government, the Alaskan Natives were at a disadvantage for recognition of their sovereignty and rights. Under the reserved rights doctrine, tribal nations have tried to keep all powers, rights, and resources not expressly surrendered to the federal government. As the Alaskan Natives had never relinquished their rights under the Organic Act of 1884, it was reserved by Congress to grant them title.

Susan Sánchez-Barnett

See also Reserved Rights Doctrine; Sovereignty; Supremacy Clause.

References and Further Reading

Newton, Nell Jessup. 1980. "At the Whim of the Sovereign: Aboriginal Title Reconsidered," 31 *Hastings Law Journal* 1215–1285.

Organic Act. 1884. 23 *U.S. Statutes at Large* 24, Sec. 8.

Sutton, Imre. 1985. *Irredeemable America: The Indians' Estate and Claims.* Albuquerque: University of New Mexico Press.

Wilkins, David E., and K. Tsianina Lomawaima. 2001. *Uneven Ground: American Indian Sovereignty and Federal Law.* Norman: University of Oklahoma Press.

Williams v. Lee, 1959

Williams v. Lee is a seminal case in federal Indian law because the Supreme Court uses it to articulate what later became known as the infringement test—which works to protect the right of Indians to govern themselves. In other words, *Williams* was an important victory for tribal sovereignty against state power and remains so today.

The plaintiff in *Williams* was a non-Indian who operated a general store within the Arizona portion of the Navajo Reservation. The defendants were Indians who had not paid for goods sold to them on credit. The store owner sued in state court to collect, which resulted in a judgment in his favor—dismissing the defendant Indians' motion to transfer the case to tribal court as the proper jurisdiction. The Arizona Supreme Court affirmed, holding that Arizona state courts had proper jurisdiction over civil suits brought by non-Indians against Indians, even though the underlying transaction occurred on the reservation, because Congress had not expressly forbidden state courts from exercising such jurisdiction.

The U.S. Supreme Court disagreed with this presumptive interpretation. Indeed, arriving at the opposite conclusion, Justice Hugo Black, writing for the majority, noted that, ever since the Court's decision in *Worcester v. Georgia* (1832) to deny effect to laws from the state of Georgia into Cherokee land, "when Congress has wished the States to exercise this power it has expressly granted them the jurisdiction which *Worcester v. Georgia* had denied" (Williams 1959). Consequently, states should be precluded from reading into congressional silence any implied power to regulate Indian affairs on Indian land.

Justice Black also interpreted an 1868 treaty signed by General William T. Sherman and several Navajo chiefs and headmen as containing terms that implicitly led to the understanding that exclusive jurisdiction over the internal affairs of the Indians existed in whatever tribal government manifested itself. Moreover, against the weight of implied congressional intent, which Justice Black found in other sources, and the treaty, Arizona could not point to a federal grant of jurisdiction because it had not accepted such responsibility available to it under Public Law 280.

In reversing the Arizona Supreme Court, Justice Black then articulated the terms and application of the Court's infringement test: "[T]o allow the exercise of state jurisdiction here would undermine the authority of the tribal courts over Reservation affairs and hence would infringe on the right of Indians to govern themselves. It is immaterial that respondent is not an Indian. He was on the Reservation and the transaction with an Indian took place there. The cases in this Court have consistently guarded the authority of Indian governments over their reservations. Congress recognized this authority in the Navajos in the Treaty of 1868, and has done so ever since. If this power is to be taken away from them, it is for Congress to do it" (Williams 1959).

Interestingly, the *Williams* decision was delivered during the height of the government's termination-era policies. This occurred when the Eisenhower administration and the attendant Congress were busily dismantling tribes and reservations in a misguided effort to assimilate Indians into the dominant white society. Although it is speculative to find a connection between Indian termination policies and other minority-related federal initiatives (such as public school integration) during this time, the government's vision of solving the problems of the country's diverse groups by blending them into the mainstream group is nonetheless evident.

Michael J. Kelly

See also Assimilation; Public Law 280, 1953; Termination; Treaty with the Navajo–June 1, 1868; *Worcester v. Georgia, 1832.*

References and Further Reading

Anderson, Terry L. 1995. *Sovereign Nations or Reservations? An Economic History of American Indians.* San Francisco: Pacific Research Institute for Public Policy.

Thorington, Nancy. 2000. "Civil and Criminal Jurisdiction over Matters Arising in Indian Country: A Roadmap for Improving Interaction among Tribal, State and Federal Governments," 31 *McGeorge Law Review* 973–1042.

Wilkins, David E., and K. Tsianina Lomawaima. 2001. *Uneven Ground: American Indian Sovereignty and Federal Law.* Norman: University of Oklahoma Press.

Williams v. Lee, 358 U.S. 217 (1959).

Worcester v. Georgia, 31 U.S. 515 (1832).

Canadian Bill of Rights, 1960

The Canadian Bill of Rights is a piece of federal legislation adopted by Prime Minister John Diefenbaker's government on August 10, 1960. Its provisions acknowledge an individual's right to liberty, life, assembly, association, and other key human rights. A landmark legal decision in 1970 decided under the bill resulted in the elimination of a discriminatory section of the Indian Act. It thus paved the way for equal treatment of Indians before the law.

John Diefenbaker began to push for increased governmental protection of human rights shortly after he became a member of Parliament in 1945. The human suffering experienced by many during World War II appalled Diefenbaker. He was particularly critical of the federal government's wartime decision to intern Japanese Canadians and seize their property. This was done under the assumption that Japanese individuals could pose a threat to national security given that Canada was at war with Japan. The harshness of the decision angered many Canadians; they believed that the equality of Canadian citizens was being trampled upon. Diefenbaker was among those who believed that the government should guarantee certain rights and freedoms to all

Canadians, thus protecting them from rash governmental decisions based on political expediency, race, or even common approval. He and his supporters were not alone in their call for universal human rights and equality. The newly formed United Nations adopted the now famous Universal Declaration of Human Rights on December 10, 1948. As a member nation, Canada endorsed the declaration, but there were increased calls for similar domestic legislation within Canada. It would be twelve years in coming.

In 1957, Diefenbaker's Progressive Conservative Party won a landslide victory in the federal election. As leader of the party, Diefenbaker became Canada's next Prime Minister. He was free to pursue his goal of creating a uniquely Canadian version of the Universal Declaration of Human Rights. It took a number of years to determine the structure and function of the legislation. There were many disagreements among various levels of government.

The ultimate step to ensure equality rights for Canadian citizens would be to entrench such rights within the constitution itself. Unfortunately, Diefenbaker's federal government could not agree with the provincial governments on a suitable way to amend the constitution to include a declaration of rights. Ultimately, the federal government unilaterally adopted the legislation on August 10, 1960. It was entitled the Canadian Bill of Rights. Its provisions did not apply to provincial laws because it was a piece of federal legislation and not a part of the constitution. Nevertheless, Diefenbaker believed that the bill's moral authority would encourage the provinces to follow suit and that provincial dissention would be politically, if not legally, difficult.

The Canadian Bill of Rights acknowledges an individual's right to life, liberty, personal security, and equality before the law. It also protects an individual's freedom of religion, speech, association, and assembly. Furthermore, the bill protects the freedom of the press. Laws must be crafted in accordance with these rights, and any infringement is permitted only by due process of law. The bill, therefore, sought to replace the excesses of rash decisions with sober thought and sound judgment. However, since the bill did not apply to provincial laws and did not override other legislation, it was difficult to tell how effective the Canadian Bill of Rights would be.

Courts were hesitant to base their rulings on the bill because it was not enshrined in the constitution and thus was difficult to use to expand rights or strike down legislation. Many courts used the bill as a simple interpretive aid. Nevertheless, the Canadian Bill of Rights would be cited in a landmark legal decision. This was the case of *The Queen v. Drybones.*

In 1967, a status Indian named Joseph Drybones was arrested for intoxication at the Old Slope Hotel in Yellowknife, capital city of the Northwest Territories. He was charged under Section 94 of the Indian Act, a piece of federal legislation that defines the rights and obligations between the Canadian government and Indians. Section 94 of the act made it illegal for an Indian to be intoxicated while off a reservation. Drybones argued that his punishment was discriminatory because it was not illegal for non-Indians to be intoxicated in a public place. Such discriminatory laws were inconsistent with the Canadian Bill of Rights, which guaranteed equality before the law. In 1970, the Supreme Court ruled six to three that Section 94 of the Indian Act was indeed discriminatory and rendered it inoperative. It was later removed from the Indian Act. *The Queen v. Drybones* became the landmark case decided under the Canadian Bill of Rights and was an important step in ensuring the equal treatment of Indians before Canadian law.

Although the bill is still in effect, most of its provisions today are included in the Canadian Charter of Rights and Freedoms. This charter was entrenched in the Canadian constitution in 1982 and applies to both federal and provincial levels of governments.

Gordon Stienburg

See also Indian Act of Canada, 1876.

References and Further Reading

Diefenbaker, John. 1976. *One Canada: Memoirs of the Right Honorable John G. Diefenbaker: The Years of Achievement, 1956 to 1962.* Toronto: Macmillan of Canada.

Isaac, Thomas. 2004. *Aboriginal Law: Commentary, Cases, and Material.* 3rd ed. Saskatoon: Purich.

McMillan, Alan. 2004. *First Peoples in Canada.* Vancouver: Douglas and McIntyre.

Smith, Denis. 1995. *Rogue Tory: The Life and Legend of John G. Diefenbaker.* Toronto: Macfarlane, Walter and Ross.

Federal Power Commission v. Tuscarora Indian Nation, 1960

In 1809, the Tuscarora Indian Nation acquired title in fee simple to 4,329 acres of land purchased from the Holland Land Company near the town of Lewiston, New York. Previously, the Tuscarora Nation had been removed in 1775 from their lands in North Carolina and sent to reside with the Oneidas in central New York. In the twentieth century, the town of Lewiston, situated just below the Niagara Falls, came to be viewed as a prime location for the development of a hydroelectric project because of the high volume of water flowing down the Niagara River and over the falls. In 1958, the New York Power Authority (NYPA) applied for a license from the Federal Power Commission to begin development of a hydroelectric project in the Lewiston area. This application also included a request to expropriate 1,383 acres of Tuscarora lands for the construction of a storage reservoir associated with the project.

The Tuscarora challenged the license application of the NYPA on the basis that the NYPA did not have the authority to take the Tuscarora lands. Despite these objections, the commission granted the license on January 30, 1958. The Tuscarora applied for a rehearing on the basis that the lands in question were part of their reservation lands and could not be taken away in the absence of a finding by the commission that the license would not interfere or be inconsistent with the purpose for which such said reservation was created or acquired.

The commission, however, denied the application for a rehearing and held that the lands were not part of the reservation and were the best location for the reservoir. The Tuscarora then filed a petition for review with the court of appeals. The court of appeals held that the Tuscarora lands in question were in fact part of the reservation within the meaning of Sections 3(2) and 4(e) of the Federal Power Act and remanded the case to the commission. The case once again worked its way up to the court of appeals, where the court approved the license but instructed the commission specifically to exclude the power of the NYPA to condemn the lands of the Tuscarora for reservoir purposes.

The U.S. Supreme Court granted certiorari and entered a judgment on this matter on March 7, 1960. The two main issues before the Court were (1) whether the lands owned in fee simple by the Tuscarora were to be considered part of the reservation as defined under the Federal Power Act (16 U.S.C., s. 791[a] et seq.) and (2) whether such lands could be expropriated by the NYPA under the eminent domain powers conferred by Section 21 of the Federal Power Act.

A majority of the Supreme Court held that the Tuscarora lands held in fee simple were not part of the reservation as defined under the Federal Power Act. This act specifically defined reservations as "lands and interests in land owned by the United States and withdrawn, reserved, or withheld from private appropriation and disposal under the public land laws, and lands and interest in lands acquired and held for any public purpose." The Court thus distinguished the Tuscarora lands held in fee simple (land in which the United States did not have an interest) from the reservation lands as defined under the act (land in which the United States did have an interest).

On the second issue, the Supreme Court held that general acts of Congress apply to all persons, including Indians and their lands. The Court stated that the Federal Power Act, a law of general and broad application, was intended to apply to lands owned by any person, including Indians, and that the act even specifically included and defined reservations. Therefore, the Court held that, because the act did apply to Indians and lands owned by Indians, a licensee (such as NYPA) could take, by the exercise of the right of eminent domain, the lands it required if it paid just compensation to the owner (the Tuscarora).

In dissent, three justices of the Supreme Court held that the Tuscarora lands at issue were within the definition of reservations under the Federal Power Act. As such, the act did not authorize the taking of such a large tract of land, as the taking would interfere with the purpose for which the reservation was created: a permanent home for the Tuscarora.

Lysane Cree

See also Commerce Clause and Native Americans; Federal Policy and Treaty Making: A Federal View; Indian Removal Act, 1830; Indian Removal and Land Cessions, 1830–1849; Indian Treaty Making: A Native View.

References and Further Reading
Burton, Lloyd. 1991. *American Indian Water Rights and the Limits of Law.* Lawrence: University Press of Kansas.
Federal Power Act. 1920. 16 U.S.C., s. 791(a) et seq. (last amended 1995).
Federal Power Commission v. Tuscarora Indian Nation (1960) 362 U.S. 584, 80 S. Ct. 858 (U.S.S.C.).
Hauptman, Laurence M. 1988. *Formulating American Indian Policy in New York State, 1970–1986.* Albany: State University Press of New York.
Witt, Shirley Hill. 1972. *The Tuscaroras.* New York: Crowell-Collier Press.

Alcatraz Occupation, 1964 and 1969

Although commonly known as a rocky island in the San Francisco Bay that once served as a prison and is now a tourist attraction, to Native peoples Alcatraz represents political empowerment. In an attempt to seize control of their futures through social activism, Natives occupied and took control of the island three different times during the 1960s: on March 9, 1964; on November 9, 1969; and on November 20, 1969. For Native Americans, the occupations resulted in positive changes and advancements in the face of overwhelming government resistance.

Although seventy-two other federal facilities were occupied by Indian people, Alcatraz is considered the most important. It was a success in that the U.S. government policy of termination (HR 108, 1953) ended and a policy of Indian self-determination became official several years later, in 1975. In the early 1970s, President Nixon returned forty-eight thousand acres of land to the Taos Indians, and occupied lands near Davis, California, became a Native American university.

According to local tribal oral history, "The Rock" was home to the Costanoan and Ohlone peoples, who lived in the coastal area between Point Sur and the San Francisco Bay ten thousand to twenty-one thousand years before the arrival of Spanish and Portuguese explorers. Alcatraz was originally used by Natives as a camping and food-gathering location, as a penal colony for those who violated social taboos, and also as a hideout for Indians fleeing from the California mission system.

Due to government termination policy during the last half of the twentieth century, tribes found themselves dissolved, no longer existing as legal entities. In an attempt to smooth over the resulting upset and displacement, President Dwight Eisenhower promoted the government's post–World War II relocation program by offering financial assistance to Natives to move to cities targeted by the program. Thousands of Indians moved from reservations into the San Francisco, Oakland, and San Jose areas looking for employment and a better life. Indian identity was challenged when Indians were forced to adjust

A tipi is erected on Alcatraz to symbolize the claim to native lands during the Native American occupation of the island in November 1969. A group called the Indians of All Tribes occupied the island until 1971, residing in abandoned buildings and living off food ferried over from mainland San Francisco. The protest was one of the more dramatic events of the ongoing Native American rights movement. (Bettmann/Corbis)

to living in urban communities, particularly when the new situation scattered them in poor neighborhoods throughout the Bay Area. After eighteen years of relocation, sixty-seven thousand Indians, many from tribes in other states, resided in the Bay Area (De La Torre, 2001, 12).

The new urban Natives found solidarity while battling the experiences of racism, discrimination, and disillusionment, incurred when relocation propaganda did not live up to its promises. As multitribal identity formed, churches, student groups, Indian centers, and other associations began to grow during the civil rights movement of the 1960s. Newly enacted educational opportunity programs found Natives enrolling at the University of California, Berkeley; University of Minnesota; and San Francisco State University. These schools developed the first Native American studies programs in the country.

On March 9, 1964, the federal government discontinued the use of Alcatraz as a federal penitentiary. Allen Cottier, president of the American Indian Council, organized a plan for five Sioux Indians to take possession of the island. Led by Richard McKenzie, the group attempted to buy title to Alcatraz by offering the federal government 47 cents per acre, demanding the island be used for a cultural center and an Indian university. Four hours later, they were removed from the island—but the seed was planted that American Indians could and would collectively regain control of their own destinies.

Encouraged, American Indian students at SFSU formed the Student Council of American Natives (SCAN), which offered support and dialogue about their concerns. SCAN evolved into the Student Kouncil of Intertribal Nations (SKINS), led by Richard Oakes, who became instrumental in subsequent occupations of Alcatraz. Students at UCB also formed an organization, the United Native Americans, to promote self-determination. The two groups, coordinated by LaNada Boyer, asserted a plan to develop student activism. Red Power was born, supported, and nourished by the political unrest percolating and pouring forth in the Bay Area during the 1960s.

On November 9, 1969, Alcatraz was seized and occupied by fourteen Native American college students, who for nineteen hours laid symbolic claim to the island. Led by Richard Oakes, the group called themselves Indians of All Tribes. Although the Fort Laramie treaty of 1868 referred to government land in the northern plains, not California, those in the group who were from tribes that were party to the treaty used it as justification to file for a homestead on the island. They left Alcatraz fueled by the momentum and support they received from the Bay Area intertribal community that had witnessed and had been victims of the federal seizure of Native lands.

Realizing that a prolonged occupation was not only possible but necessary to stop the attempted dissolution of Native Americans into the urban melting pot, Richard Oakes again led an occupation of Alcatraz, this one lasting from November 20, 1969, until June 10, 1971. Oakes was joined by approximately one hundred Indians, who immediately began organizing. They put a council into place and assigned jobs to everyone on the island, such as security, sanitation, and schooling. All decisions were made by unanimous consent of the people.

After insisting that the island be vacated, the federal government attempted to barricade it, without success. Eventually, the government agreed to negotiate with the Indian council but insisted that the Indians could not establish a university, a cultural center, or a museum, let alone ownership of the island. At one point, occupiers were offered a portion of Fort Miley in San Francisco but chose to hold out for full title to Alcatraz. Electrical power to the island was shut off, and the freshwater barge was shut down. Three days later, several historic buildings were destroyed when fire broke out. Further damage to buildings occurred when copper wiring and tubing were stripped and sold to gain money for food.

By early 1970, Indian organization on Alcatraz became fragmented. Two groups rose in opposition to Richard Oakes and as students returned to school; they were replaced by urban people who had not been involved from the beginning of the occupation, including hippies and members of the drug culture. Oakes left the island after his thirteen-year-old daughter fell three floors down a stairwell and died; thereafter, each group tried to assert itself as leader, which not only ignited confusion and disarray but ruptured the unity of the protest and deflated commitment to the cause.

Even though it was determined that the collision of two tankers had not been caused by lack of a light or foghorn on Alcatraz, on June 10, 1971, President Richard Nixon issued the order that federal marshals, FBI agents, and Special Forces swarm the island and remove the five women, four children, and six unarmed Indian men who remained there. The occupation was over.

Denise Lajetta

See also American Indian Movement (AIM); Oakes, Richard; Sovereignty; Treaty; Treaty with the Sioux, Etc., and Arapaho–April 29, 1868.

References and Further Reading

De La Torre, Joely. 2001. "From Activism to Academics: The Evolution of American Indian Studies at San Francisco State 1968–2001." *Indigenous Nations Studies Journal*, 2(1): 11–20.

Johnson, Troy R. 1996. *Occupation of Alcatraz Island: Self-Determination and the Rise of Indian Activism.* Urbana: University of Illinois Press.

Johnson, Troy R., and Joane Nagel, eds. 1994. "Alcatraz Revisited: The 25th Anniversary of the Occupation, 1969–1971." Special Edition. *American Indian Culture and Research Journal*, 18(4).

Warren Trading Post Co. v. Arizona Tax Commission, 1965

This case concerned whether the State of Arizona could levy a tax on the "gross proceeds of sales, or gross income" of 2 percent on a retail trading business with a trading license from the Commissioner of Indian Affairs operating on the Navajo Reservation. The 1868 Navajo treaty enjoined tribal jurisdictional exclusivity over the land and the use of the land and precluded state jurisdiction and authority therein. Warren Trading Post Company presented two defenses. First, state tax levied on income taken from a reservation was invalid as a consequence of the commerce clause—Article I, Section 8, clause 3 of the U.S. Constitution, which vested in Congress the unilateral power to regulate commerce with the tribes. Second, state tax contravened the congressional meaning of the commerce clause, which enabled Congress to regulate traders and trade with the tribes and allowed the tribes to govern themselves within their reservations. The state supreme court upheld the tax. The U.S. Supreme Court ruled that, through statutes and regulations, Congress had assumed the authority to levy taxes on traders operating within reservations. Consequently, the State of Arizona could not levy taxes on traders within a reservation or enforce extra burdens on the traders or the tribes. Justice Hugo Black delivered the opinion of the Court.

The U.S. Supreme Court stated that the treaty with the Navajo in 1868 had created a reservation that was a permanent home set apart for the tribe. From the establishment of the reservation, Congress did not interfere with Navajo internal affairs, and thus the tribe controlled their own affairs free of state control. Before the 1868 Navajo treaty, the tribe had governed themselves free of state restriction, and this was a continuation of that policy. The Court cited Chief Justice John Marshall in *Worcester v. Georgia* (1832) and stated that Native Americans were treated as distinct nations, under the protection of treaties and completely separated from the jurisdiction of the states. Moreover, the federal government had enacted statutes and treaties that provided a plethora of controls over people wishing to trade with Native Americans.

The Supreme Court proceeded to examine the history of federal control and authority over tribal commerce. The Court stated that Congress had enacted statutes from 1790, whereby traders were obliged to obtain a trading license from federal officials, to 1901, whereby the commissioner of Indian affairs prescribed trade regulations with Native American tribes. Under the statutes, the commissioner of Indian affairs had the sole right to issue licenses to traders wishing to trade with the tribes; the commissioner could also establish regulations upon them.

The Supreme Court's examination of the historical development of congressional regulation and statutes regarding commerce with Native American tribes elucidated that Congress had provided for the right of the trader to trade with the Navajo; the Court further found that the State of Arizona lacked the authority and jurisdiction to impose taxes upon the trader within the Navajo Reservation. The statutes relied upon by the Court were ruled to bar states from taxing traders on their sales, as granted by a license from the commissioner, on reservation lands.

The Court held that, from the evaluation of statutes and the historical assessment of the treaty of 1868, the right of the State of Arizona to enforce its taxing authority on federal traders on the Navajo Reservation (which was set aside by treaty) was invalid and without authority. Congressional purpose provided that no burden would be imposed upon traders wishing to trade on Native American reservations except as enacted by Congress.

The Supreme Court held that to allow state taxation on reservations would impose financial burdens on both the tribe and the traders. Furthermore, it would fracture the congressional statutory plan to protect Native Americans against unfair prices. Federal legislation did not provide the states with any control within the Navajo Reservation and thus did not sanction the use of state taxes therein. Taxing the sales of a federally licensed trader on reservation lands could not apply, and thus the judgment of the supreme court of Arizona was reversed. Federal statutes barred the imposition of taxes in this case, but the U.S. Supreme Court did not rule on whether the tax was barred under the argument that the commerce clause gave Congress power to regulate commerce with the tribes.

Dewi I. Ball

See also Commerce Clause; Government-to-Government Relationship; Indian Territory; Sovereignty; Treaty; Treaty with the Delaware–September 17, 1778; Treaty with the Navajo–June 1, 1868; *Worcester v. Georgia*, 1832.

References and Further Reading

Pevar, Stephen L. 2002. *The Rights of Indians and Tribes.* Carbondale: Southern Illinois University Press.

Wilkins, David E., and K. Tsianina Lomawaima. 2001. *Uneven Ground: American Indian Sovereignty and Federal Law.* Norman: University of Oklahoma Press.

Wilkinson, Charles F. 1987. *American Indians, Time, and the Law: Native Societies in a Modern Constitutional Democracy.* New Haven, CT: Yale University Press.

Indian Civil Rights Act, 1968

The Indian Civil Rights Act (ICRA, 25 U.S.C. §§ 1301–1333) was enacted on April 11, 1968, and is like the Bill of Rights in that it guarantees to Native peoples personal freedoms against actions of the federal government. The act was born out of necessity. Public Law 280, passed in 1954, transferred civil and criminal jurisdiction of reservation Indians to six states (Alaska, California, Minnesota, Nebraska, Oregon, and Wisconsin). Public Law 280 created a certain amount of lawlessness and reduced federal programs to Indian citizens, for example, welfare, health, education, and law enforcement programs in California. Other examples include allegations of maltreatment or lack of protection by law enforcement officers because reservations have no tax base, or because in many instances the response time (several miles) makes law enforcement almost nonexistent. Because Indian tribes were not subject to the Bill of Rights and other constitutional protections, the Indian Civil Rights Act was passed in response to lawlessness before as well as after the passage of PL 280 and in response to other issues pertaining to crime in Indian country. The ICRA is divided into seven titles: Title I is the act itself. Title II encompasses the definition of an Indian tribe, self-government, tribal courts, and Indian rights. Title III establishes the model code governing courts of Indian offenses. Title IV covers jurisdiction over criminal and civil actions (PL 280). Title V is an amendment to the United States Code, Section 1153 of Title 18. Title VI deals with the employment of legal counsel by Indian tribes. Title VII deals with materials relating to the constitutional rights of Indians and authorizes the secretary of the interior to make available certain documents, manuscripts, and opinions relating to Indian law and to republish these documents. The documents include *Indian Affairs Laws and Treaties*, Volumes 1 and 2, and *Federal Indian Law*.

The most important title, Title II, defines an Indian tribe, self-government, and the tribal court, as well as the constitutional rights provided by the act and *habeas corpus* (release from unlawful restraint). The constitutional rights provided in Title II of the ICRA are as follows:

No Indian tribe in exercising powers of self-government shall (1) make or enforce any law prohibiting the free exercise of religion, or abridging the freedom of speech, or the press, or the right of the people peaceably to assemble and to petition for a redress of grievances; (2) violate the right of the people to be secure in their persons, houses, papers, and effects against unreasonable searches and seizures, nor issue warrants, but upon probable cause, supported by oath or affirmation, and particu-

larly describing the place to be searched and the person or thing to be seized; (3) subject any person for the same offense to be twice put in jeopardy; (4) compel any person in any criminal case to be a witness against himself; (5) take any private property for a public use without just compensations; (6) deny to any person in a criminal proceeding the right to a speedy and public trial, to be informed of the nature and cause of the accusation, to be confronted with the witnesses against him, to have compulsory process for obtaining witnesses in his favor, and at his own expense to have the assistance of counsel for his defense; (7) require excessive bail, impose excessive fines, inflict cruel and unusual punishments, and in no event impose for conviction of any one offense any penalty or punishment greater then imprisonment for a term of one year or a fine of $5,000, or both; (8) deny to any person within its jurisdiction the equal protection of its laws or deprive any person of liberty or property without due process of law; (9) pass any bill of attainder or ex post facto law; or (10) deny to any person accused of an offense punishable by imprisonment the right, upon request, to a trial by jury of not less than six persons. (Getches, Wilkinson, and Williams 1998, 506)

Kurt T. Mantonya

See also Indian Country; Public Law 280, 1953.
References and Further Reading
Clarkin, Thomas. 2001. *Federal Indian Policy: In the Kennedy and Johnson Administrations 1961–1969.* Albuquerque: University of New Mexico Press.
Deloria, Vine, Jr., and Clifford M. Lytle. 1983. *American Indians, American Justice.* Austin: University of Texas Press.
Getches, David H., Charles F. Wilkinson, and Robert A. Williams, Jr. 1998. *Cases and Materials on Federal Indian Law.* St. Paul, MN: West.
Johnson, Troy R., ed. 1999. *Contemporary Native American Political Issues.* Walnut Creek, CA: Altamira Press.

Menominee Tribe of Indians v. United States, 1968

The 1968 Supreme Court decision on hunting and fishing rights for the Menominee tribe of Wisconsin had its roots in the policy of termination that

A protestor wrapped in a U.S. flag dances before a police roadblock during the takeover of the Alexian Brothers Novitiate by the Menominee Warrior Society on January 1, 1975. The Warrior Society had objected to the slow reorganization of the Menominee Tribe after federal services were restored. (Corbis/Bettmann-UPI)

dominated federal Indian legislation during the 1950s and 1960s. The goal of termination was the ending of the trust relationship that existed between the tribes and the federal government. This was to be accomplished by the federal government's divestiture of all of the assets it held for the tribes either to individual Indians or to tribal corporations, thus making Indian assets taxable and ending federal treaty responsibilities. This would facilitate what had been the main goals of many bureaucrats since the Dawes Act: the end of Indian tribal sovereignty and the complete assimilation of American Indians into mainstream American society.

After the passage of House Concurrent Resolution 108 in 1953, Bureau of Indian Affairs (BIA) officials set to work to determine which tribes were most economically ready for the discontinuation of

federal services and supervision. The Menominee tribe already had a successful lumber operation on its reservation, which the BIA believed would be a viable basis of support for the tribe. Adding to this was the fact that, in 1951, the tribe had won a sixteen-year battle with the federal government over the mismanagement of Menominee forest resources, resulting in an $8.5 million award, which Utah senator and termination proponent Arthur V. Watkins made clear was tied to the tribe's acceptance of their termination, which was set forth in Public Law 399.

For the remainder of the decade, the tribe struggled with making termination happen with as little impact on the tribal population as possible. All tribal property was to be transferred to a new corporation, Menominee Enterprises, Inc., in which all tribal members were shareholders. The reservation land was to become Menominee County. All this was finally accomplished by 1961, but the poverty that has constantly plagued Indian peoples only intensified with the withdrawal of federal oversight. Tribal assets, including the lumber operation, became subject to state taxes, and the once-prosperous reservation became the state's newest and poorest county.

The issue of hunting and fishing rights came to the fore as a result of termination. Only a year after termination was accomplished, the state of Wisconsin took the position that termination had ended the provisions of the Treaty of Wolf River, which had guaranteed the tribe hunting and fishing rights on the reservation. Even before termination, Public Law 280 (1953) had given state and local authorities jurisdiction over Indian land. The state prosecuted three Menominees for violating state gaming regulations.

The tribe brought suit in the court of claims to recover damages from the loss of hunting and fishing rights, and their claims were upheld. The case was appealed to the Supreme Court, and in its decision, Justice William O. Douglas argued, "[I]t is therefore argued with force that the Termination Act of 1954, which became fully effective in 1961, submitted the hunting and fishing rights of the Indians to state regulation and control. We reach, however, the opposite conclusion." Further, he stated, "We find it difficult to believe that Congress, without explicit statement, would subject the United States to a claim for compensation by destroying property rights conferred by treaty, particularly when Congress was purporting by the Termination Act to settle the Government's financial obligations toward the Indians."

In essence, the Court declared that the doctrine of reserved rights, the idea that tribes retain rights to their land's resources until such rights are specifically ceded—rights that previously applied mainly to land, water, and mineral rights—applied to hunting and fishing rights as well. Even though the Menominee Reservation was terminated, their right to practice their treaty-protected lifeways related to that land was not.

Steven L. Danver

See also Deer, Ada E.; House Concurrent Resolution 108, 1953; Public Law 280, 1953; Reserved Rights Doctrine; Sovereignty; Watkins, Arthur V.

References and Further Reading

Hosmer, Brian. 1997. "Reflections on Indian Cultural 'Brokers': Reginald Oshkosh, Mitchell Oshkenaniew, and the Politics of Menominee Lumbering." *Ethnohistory* 44:(3).

Hosmer, Brian. 2002. "Blackjack and Lumberjack: Economic Development and Cultural Continuity among Twentieth Century Menominees." In *Peoples of Persistence*, ed. R. David Edmunds. Bloomington: Indiana University Press.

Ourada, Patricia K. 1979. *The Menominee Indians: A History.* Norman: University of Oklahoma Press.

Prucha, Francis Paul. 1995. *The Great Father: The United States Government and the American Indians.* Lincoln: University of Nebraska Press.

Puyallup Tribe v. Department of Game of Washington, 1968

The premise of the case concerned whether the Puyallup and Nisqually tribes could assert rights to take fish under Article 3 of the Treaty of Medicine Creek of 1854, ". . . at all usual and accustomed grounds . . . in common with all citizens of the territory. . . ." Also involved were the conservation measures adopted by the state of Washington with regard to its territorial waters. The conservation measures concerned the use of tribal set nets to catch salmon and steelhead, anadromous fish that were covered by treaty rights. The case addressed two central issues. First, the construction of the Treaty of Medicine Creek of 1854 was interpreted liberally in favor of the tribes but did not give tribal members the exclusive right to fish off reservation. Second, the constitutional implication of conservation measures adopted by Washington State was deemed a valid basis for extinguishment of treaty rights, and state regulation could be imposed upon the tribes. Fur-

thermore, the state supreme court held that treaty fishing rights could be regulated by Washington State. Mr. Justice Douglas delivered the opinion of the U.S. Supreme Court. The Court held, first, that the state could regulate tribal off-reservation fishing, in accordance with "all citizens of the territory"; second, that the use of set nets at various locations was remanded to the trial court to determine whether it was a "reasonable and necessary" measure.

Washington State had prescribed regulations pertaining to fishing within its territorial waters, and these included the time, the areas, the tools, and the means by which fish could be caught. The Court had to decide whether, under the aegis of the treaty of 1854, the Puyallup and Nisqually could use set nets on the rivers in question. The tribes fished both commercially and for subsistence; these facts, in turn, had to be examined against the legality or illegality of the use of set nets, if Washington State laws were upheld.

The U.S. Supreme Court cited *United States v. Winans* (1905), in which the Yakima tribe relied on treaty rights to protect the taking of fish in areas used with other citizens. In that case, private individuals had bought land, obtained state fishing rights, and sought to exclude Native Americans from the land. The Court ruled that a change in ownership of the river borders did not revoke the treaty rights, for they were "continuing" rights. This was due to the importance of the covenant entered into by both the tribes and the United States.

Douglas stated that the treaties were to be interpreted liberally in favor of the tribes. The court proceeded to address, first, whether set nets were allowed under the auspices of the treaty. It was assumed at the time of the treaty that the use of the nets and commercial fishing were customary, but the treaty did not stipulate the purpose, mode, or manner of fishing. Second, the Court addressed whether the terms of the treaty to fish "at all usual and accustomed places" was applicable to the tribes. The right to fish at the respective places was not exclusive but one "in common with all citizens of the Territory." State citizens were thus regulated, and it followed that the tribe could also be regulated in the interest of conservation, provided that regulations met the appropriate standards and did not discriminate against the tribes.

Similar treaty language was cited by the U.S. Supreme Court in *Tulee v. Washington* (1942), which held that the tribe retained the treaty right to fish off reservation on ". . . all usual and accustomed grounds. . . ." and that this right could not be impinged upon by the state. The issue was "the time and manner of fishing," and this was not defined by the treaty. Thus, nondiscriminatory measures of conservation were imposed on the tribe. A similar opinion was decreed in this case.

The tribe retained treaty rights to fish off reservation but were dependent on state regulation and measures of conservation. Thus, certain practices were prohibited to citizens and Native Americans alike, and this included the use of set nets in freshwater. Conversely, state regulation permitted citizens and thus Native Americans the use of purse seines and other nets in salt water for commercial fishing. The former was justified for reasons of conservation because fishing by hook sustained the numbers of fish, in contrast to set nets, which greatly reduced the numbers of fish. The U.S. Supreme Court remanded to trial court the question of whether the prohibition of set nets used in freshwater was a "reasonable and necessary" conservation measure; the findings had to address equal protection for both tribes and citizens with relevance to the phrase "in common with."

Dewi I. Ball

See also Medicine Creek, Washington; *Mille Lacs Band v. Minnesota,* 1999; *Puyallup Tribe Inc. v. Department of Game of Washington,* 1977; Treaty; Treaty with the Nisqually, Puyallup, Etc.–December 26, 1854.

References and Further Reading

Canby, William C. 1998. *American Indian Law in a Nutshell.* St. Paul, MN: West.

Pevar, Stephen L. 2002. *The Rights of Indians and Tribes.* 3rd. ed. Carbondale: Southern Illinois University Press.

Wilkins, David E., and K. Tsianina Lomawaima. 2001. *Uneven Ground: American Indian Sovereignty and Federal Law.* Norman: University of Oklahoma Press.

Sohappy v. Smith and *United States v. Oregon,* 1969

Federal district court judge Robert Belloni's combined ruling in *Sohappy v. Smith* and *United States v. Oregon* generally receives less recognition than the famous Boldt Decision of 1974 (*United States v. Washington*), which was the culmination of nearly a century of litigation over Northwest Indian treaty fishing. As even Judge George Boldt acknowledged, however, the *Sohappy* opinion paved the way for his own by firmly establishing the right of four Columbia River treaty tribes to take "a fair and equitable share" of the salmon passing through their "usual and accustomed places." Although Belloni's ruling permitted state regulation of Indian fishing, it also limited state regulatory powers and offered the tribes a meaningful role in the rule-making process. Thus, despite some unresolved questions and angry objections from both sides, the *Sohappy* decision represented a landmark victory for tribal sovereignty and an important step toward co-management of the resource.

The case revolved around conflicting interpretations of the treaty of 1855 between the United States and the confederated tribes and bands of the Yakama Indian Nation. In Article 3 of the agreement, the Indians had reserved "the right of taking fish at all usual and accustomed places, in common with the citizens of the Territory. . . ." The precise meaning of that phrase became increasingly controversial as salmon runs declined due to overfishing, dam building, and the destruction of spawning habitat by logging, grazing, and irrigation projects. In the early twentieth century, the states of Oregon and Washington began to pass conservation laws that often discriminated against Indian methods or fell most heavily on the terminal fisheries (rivers and tributary streams) where Indians traditionally caught salmon. State authorities insisted that Indians fishing off the reservation possessed only the "in common" right of ordinary citizens and therefore had to obey state laws. To the treaty tribes, however, state regulation represented a violation of their sovereignty as well as a threat to the cultural, spiritual, and economic well-being of Indian fishing families.

The state-tribal conflict on the Columbia River peaked in the late 1960s. By 1966, the Yakama, Umatilla, and Nez Perce tribes had passed their own ordinances to regulate tribal fishing, but the states ignored them and continued to arrest Indians for violating state laws. In 1968, David and Richard Sohappy, enrolled members of the Yakama Nation, spent four days in jail for illegal fishing. After receiving suspended thirty-day sentences and $250 fines, they joined twelve other Yakama in a lawsuit against Oregon Fish Commission chairman McKee A. Smith and a slate of Oregon fish and game officials. The plaintiffs asked the court to define their treaty fishing rights and the extent to which the state could regulate them. Because sovereign immunity prevented them from suing the state directly, U.S. assistant regional interior solicitor George Dysart pushed for a separate federal action that could bind the state government. Although the Yakama tribal council had some doubts about the case, it chose to intervene in *United States v. Oregon* along with the Nez Perce tribe, the confederated tribes of the Umatilla Reservation, and the confederated tribes of the Warm Springs Reservation.

Judge Robert Belloni merged *Sohappy v. Smith* with *United States v. Oregon* in his decision of April 1969, which held that Oregon's restrictions on treaty fishing were invalid and discriminatory. Although the state could regulate the off-reservation Indian fishery, its powers were limited by certain conditions and standards, which Belloni spelled out in his written opinion and decree. Specifically, he ruled that state regulations must be proven "reasonable and necessary for conservation," must be the least restrictive possible, and must not discriminate against Indians, who could potentially fish at times and with gear prohibited to non-Indians. The tribes must be given the opportunity for meaningful participation in the regulatory process, and they had a right to "a fair and equitable share" of the catch. Belloni did not define "fair share" or consider the issue of tribal self-regulation, leaving them for Boldt to address five years later.

The *Sohappy/Oregon* ruling received mixed reviews from Indians and non-Indians alike. Some tribal leaders felt that it conceded too much to the states, whereas Native fishers like the Sohappys continued to insist that neither the tribes nor the states could regulate them. Non-Indian commercial and sport fishermen also considered the ruling unfair and detrimental to their interests, and Washington officials refused to implement it until 1979. By continuing his jurisdiction in the case, however, Belloni ensured that the plaintiffs could "seek timely and effective judicial review." Moreover, his "meaningful participation" standard would help shape fishery management practices as the tribes and the states gradually moved from litigation to cooperation.

Andrew H. Fisher

See also Boldt Decision (*United States v. Washington*), 1974; Sohappy, David, Sr.; Treaty with the Nisqually, Puyallup, Etc.–December 26, 1854; Treaty with the Yakama–June 9, 1855.

References and Further Reading
Berg, Laura. 1995. "Let Them Do As They Have Promised: A History of *U.S. v. Oregon* and Four Tribes' Fight for Columbia River Salmon." *Hastings West-Northwest Journal of Environmental Law and Policy* 3(1): 7–18.
Parman, Donald L. 1984. "Inconstant Advocacy: The Erosion of Indian Fishing Rights In the Pacific Northwest, 1933–1956." *Pacific Historical Review* 53 (May): 163–189.
Ulrich, Roberta. 1999. *Empty Nets: Indians, Dams, and the Columbia River.* Corvallis: Oregon State University Press.

Nixon's Message to Congress, July 8, 1970

President Richard Nixon repudiated the termination era and officially transitioned U.S. Indian policy toward tribal self-determination on July 8, 1970, with the delivery of his Special Message to Congress on Indian Affairs. The message reaffirmed the U.S. responsibility to Indians but did so in a way that called for giving Indians a greater role in controlling the programs that affected them. The message formed the basis for the subsequently enacted Indian Self-Determination and Education Assistance Act and helped establish Nixon as "arguably the most ardent supporter of Indian sovereignty" (Clarkson 2002).

Nixon's special message forms the line used by most scholars to separate the termination era from the present self-determination period. Nixon called for a rejection of termination as an unfair and ineffective policy. He stated, "Both as a matter of justice and as a matter of enlightened social policy . . . [t]he time has come to break decisively with the past and to create the conditions for a new era in which the Indian future is determined by Indian acts and Indian decisions." Nixon saw termination as retarding Indian initiative because all experimentation was potentially very costly, as it had to be set against "the threat of eventual termination." Nixon rejected the "burgeoning Federal bureaucracy" in favor of the new goal, "to strengthen the Indian's sense of autonomy without threatening (through termination) his sense of community."

Through nine related policy suggestions for Congress, Nixon was attempting not simply to transfer control over to Indian hands but also to provide more resources for Indians. The message's first two goals, rejecting termination and the [tribal] right to control and operate federal programs, were in keeping with the general focus on shifting control. Nixon argued that the right to assume control over federal programs, as well as the right of retrocession, belonged with the tribes and was not dependent on the will of the U.S. government. However, the message significantly included the notion that the United States must respond "to just grievances which are especially important to the Indian people," which Nixon used to further the particular case for the restoration of certain sacred lands. Additional funding was the focus of three of the nine goals: economic development legislation, more money for Indian health, and helping urban Indians. The economic development legislation goal, for example, called for a tripling of the lending for Indian development projects. Finally, two goals—establishment of an Indian trust counsel authority and an assistant secretary for Indian and territorial affairs—were directed at improving the internal ability of the U.S. government to meet its responsibilities to tribes.

Aspects of the 1970 message's idea of self-determination can be found in the presidencies and Indian policies of both John F. Kennedy and Lyndon B. Johnson (Bielski 2000). However, as attested to by a 2000 U.S. congressional resolution, Nixon's special message generally is credited with "[setting] forth the foundation for a new, more enlightened Federal Indian policy grounded in economic self-reliance and political self-determination" (U.S. Congress 2000). Most studies of the shifts in federal policy between assimilation and isolation rightly highlight Nixon's special message and express the opinion that "Indian tribes, members of Congress, and the Administration started again down the road which had initially been paved by the Indian Reorganization Act. The legislation that occurred as a result of Nixon's message of 1970 became the foundation for federal Indian policy for the remainder of the century" (Johnson and Hamilton 1995).

Ezra Rosser

See also Alaska Native Claims Settlement Act, 1971; American Indian Self-Determination and Education Act of 1975; Government-to-Government Relationship; Sovereignty; Termination.

References and Further Reading

Bielski, John R. 2000. "Judicial Denial of Sovereignty for Alaskan Natives: An End to the Self-Determination Era," 73 *Temple Law Review* 1279, 1282.

Clarkson, Gavin. 2002. "Not Because They Are Brown, But Because of EA: Why the Good Guys Lost in *Rice v. Cayetano,* and Why They Didn't Have to Lose," 7 *Michigan Journal of Race and Law* 317, 332.

Johnson, Tadd M., and James Hamilton. 1995. "Symposium Rules of the Game: Sovereignty and the Native American Nation: Self-Governance for Indian Tribes: From Paternalism to Empowerment," 27 *Connecticut Law Review* 1251, 1262.

Message from the President of the United States Transmitting Recommendations for Indian Policy [Special Message to Congress on Indian Affairs], H.R. Doc. No. 91–363, 91st Cong., 2d Sess. (July 8, 1970).

U.S. Congress. Senate. Resolution, "Commemorating the 30th Anniversary of the Policy of Indian Self-Determination." S Res. 277 IS 106th Cong., 2d sess. (March 23, 2000).

Alaska Native Claims Settlement Act, 1971

Indigenous peoples of Alaska are commonly known as Alaska Natives. These include Aleut, Inuit, Tlingit, Haida, and Athapascan. Much reduced in number by disease and social pathologies common to the social suffering wrought by colonialism, after the Alaska Native Claims Settlement Act of 1971 (ANCSA) came into effect, approximately eighty thousand Alaska Natives were enrolled as shareholders in thirteen regional corporations.

"They said go out and save who we are." This was the basic instruction of Alaska indigenous elders to young leaders of the Alaska Federation of Natives negotiating the Alaska Native Claims Settlement Act. When Russia sold Alaska to the United States in 1867, indigenous peoples' rights and land ownership remained unresolved. When Alaska was granted statehood in 1959, the state began to impose laws and regulations on Alaska Natives; it also began to select the 104 million acres it had been granted by the U.S. government as a condition of statehood. Pressures quickly mounted associated with lack of consultation regarding activities that promised to massively encroach on indigenous people's lands and resources. These included an experimental nuclear explosion to create a deep-sea port at Point Hope, a migratory birds protection treaty with Canada and Mexico, and a proposed oil pipeline across indigenous lands. During the 1960s, the diverse indigenous peoples of the state drew together, forming the Alaska Federation of Natives to fight dispossession and exploitation. In 1966, the federation called for a moratorium on development until indigenous peoples' land rights and ownership were recognized. Discovery of oil reserves at Prudhoe Bay in 1968 played a major role in motivating a land and rights agreement. The federal government was keen to develop domestic oil resources, the state was anxious for economic development and its benefits, and oil companies sought to profit from their discoveries. Faced with massive resource development in an environment of long-unresolved aboriginal rights and title, conditions for reaching an agreement were favorable.

ANCSA created twelve regional corporations (and later an additional corporation for Natives residing outside of Alaska). Its provisions included ownership of forty-four million acres of land and $962.5 million to compensate Alaska Natives for extinguishing their aboriginal rights. This transformed the relationship between Alaska Natives and their homelands. Ownership did not rest with tribal governments; instead, land title was held by the twelve regional corporations and approximately 220 local village corporations. Indigenous or tribal governments were bypassed, for ANCSA contained no specific provisions for internal self-government or tribal government development. Membership was open to people recognized as one-fourth degree or more Native ancestry, born on or before December 18, 1971.

The model chosen by negotiators departed from the reservation system south of the 48th parallel. The ANCSA model placed land and monetary compensation largely with village and regional corporations. At the time, the model was viewed as a structure securing land ownership and as a sound base for economic participation through for-profit corporations. Implementing the ANCSA as it was originally written proved problematic; as a result, ANCSA provisions causing social and political tension were amended. For example, restricting membership to Alaska Natives born before a certain date effectively excluded those born after that date ("afterborns") from participation. Legislative amendments allowed Natives born after December 1971 to participate, although at the discretion of shareholders of individual corporations. Loss of land assets as a result of bankruptcy and the forced exploitation of resources by corporations were addressed by further amendments in 1991, under which undeveloped land cannot be taxed or taken

The Trans-Alaska pipeline snakes across a vast expanse of land. The pipeline has the capacity to move 2 million barrels of oil each day. The Alaska Native Claims Settlement Act allows Alaska natives to receive a portion of the profits from the oil sales as a part of the agreement of $962.5 million and 44 million acres of land. (Corel)

through adverse possession, creditors, bankruptcy, or dissolution. Major concerns arose over the fact that stock in the corporations was made available for sale after a set time period, potentially fulfilling goals of termination by allowing nonindigenous buyers and by increasing nonindigenous participation not only in land ownership but also in corporate decision making serving both economic and cultural goals. Additional amendments therefore stipulated that stock restrictions could remain in force unless shareholders voted to remove them. Basic elements of ANCSA's corporate structure were almost immediately at odds with indigenous peoples' view of the agreement as a way to strengthen communities, culture, and identity, and as a basis for their continued existence as indigenous peoples. Fortunately, legislative remedies for difficulties in implementation have been made available.

Stephanie Irlbacher-Fox

See also Indian Claims Commission (ICC).
References and Further Reading
Berger, Thomas R. 1985. *Village Journey: The Report of the Alaska Native Review Commission.* New York: Hill and Wang.

Case, David S. 2002. *Alaska Natives and American Laws*. 2nd ed. Fairbanks: University of Alaska Press.

Castile, George Pierre. 1998. *To Show Heart: Native American Self-Determination and Federal Indian Policy, 1960–1975.* Tucson: University of Arizona Press.

Trail of Broken Treaties, 1972

The Trail of Broken Treaties was a protest organized by Native American activists in 1972. Leaders of the protest included Dennis Banks and Russell Means of the American Indian Movement (AIM) and Hank Adams, an organizer of the fish-in protests in the Pacific Northwest. The protest, which consisted of a caravan of protestors crossing the country from the West Coast to Washington, D.C., was intended to call attention to the issues affecting Native Americans; it made treaty rights a major focus of their rhetoric and demands.

The caravan left the West Coast in October 1972 and was joined along the way by more protestors. Upon arrival in Minneapolis, the caravan issued a series of demands known as the Twenty Points. The caravan moved on to Washington, D.C., arriving there in the final week of the 1972 presidential campaign, where many of the protestors occupied the Bureau of Indian Affairs building for six days. They asked the government to recognize the Twenty Points as the basis of any negotiation. The building was ransacked and government files stolen; the protestors claimed that government infiltrators were responsible for much of the damage. The situation was resolved peaceably by the government's assurance that the protestors' demands would be considered, and the protestors were granted immunity

Dennis Banks (left), an Ojibwa and national leader of the American Indian Movement (AIM), and preacher Carl McEntire during the 1972 "Trail of Broken Treaties" occupation of the Bureau of Indian Affairs building in Washington, D.C. (Bettmann/Corbis)

from prosecution. However, the government subsequently rejected the demands, and this led to further violent protest (most notably the occupation of Wounded Knee in 1973).

The Twenty Points proposed a new framework for considering the status of Native American tribes and the relationship between these tribes and the federal government (Deloria 1974, 48). The key demands were repeal of the 1871 law that had ended treaty making with Native American tribes, the establishment of a treaty commission to sign new treaties, Senate ratification of past unratified treaties, and passage of a law giving Indians the right to issue a declaration on treaty rights and other rights that would be binding on courts (Prucha 1994, 412–413). Other demands included restoration of a land base for Native Americans, consolidation of natural resources, and the addressing of health, housing, employment and education issues. These points were never seriously considered by the government, which declared that the 1871 law could in no way be reconsidered and that complete sovereignty for Native Americans was impossible.

The Trail of Broken Treaties was part of a radical social protest movement and politics that characterized the 1960s and 1970s, although many of its demands had a profound historical basis. It was based on a common "pan-Indian" politics, and its rhetoric about treaties was based on the universal rather than particular. In making the demands general, the intent was also to "define one status for all Indian people" (Deloria 1974, 50). Treaties were seen as symbolic of the relationship between the U.S. government and Native American people, a relationship that had been betrayed over two centuries. Sovereignty and the restoration of the treaty relationship were held up by some Native American protestors as the essential step toward Native American self-determination and political power. As the preamble to the Twenty Points expressed it, such recognition would allow "a reconstruction of an Indian future in America." Self-determination continued to be important to Native American political demands and was to some extent granted by the U.S. government, but not through any acknowledgment of treaty rights.

The radical demands of organizations such as the American Indian Movement (AIM) and protests such as the Trail of Broken Treaties played an important role in calling public attention to the issue of treaty rights and the condition of Native American peoples. Although treaty rights were

never addressed by the U.S. government, they continue to be an issue for debate. In this, the Trail of Broken Treaties was an important and influential protest in the history of Native American treaties.

Amanda Laugesen

See also American Indian Movement (AIM); Banks, Dennis; Means, Russell; Sovereignty.

References and Further Reading

Deloria, Vine, Jr. 1974. *Behind the Trail of Broken Treaties: An Indian Declaration of Independence.* New York: Delacorte Press.

Nagel, Joane. 1996. *American Indian Ethnic Renewal: Red Power and the Resurgence of Identity and Culture.* New York: Oxford University Press.

Prucha, Francis Paul. 1994. *American Indian Treaties: The History of a Political Anomaly.* Berkeley and Los Angeles: University of California Press.

Calder v. Attorney-General of British Columbia (Canada), 1973

This case involved the Nisga'a of British Columbia and the Province of British Columbia and was heard before the Supreme Court of Canada. The court assessed historical and anthropological evidence regarding the Nisga'a claim to aboriginal title. The Nisga'a community on the coast of British Columbia requested a declaration that they possessed unextinguished aboriginal title and control of the Nass River Valley in northern British Columbia. The Nisga'a claim had been rejected in the lower courts, so they appealed to the Supreme Court. The Court recognized that aboriginal title exists in Canadian law, regardless of any recognition by government. However, the court split evenly on the derivation of aboriginal title and whether the Nisga'a aboriginal title had been extinguished by colonial legislation prior to British Columbia's entry into the confederation.

Justices Ronald Martland, Wilfred Judson, and Roland Ritchie held that the Royal Proclamation of 1763, which the Nisga'a claimed applied to the disputed territory and entitled them to protection, was not applicable to aboriginal title in British Columbia. They found that, when the Colony of British Columbia was established in 1858, the Nisga'a territory became part of it. Also, a series of proclamations delivered by Governor James Douglas between 1858 and 1863 and subsequent ordinances revealed the intention to exercise absolute sovereignty over all the lands of British Columbia. Such sovereignty would be inconsistent with any conflicting interest, including aboriginal title. Thus, aboriginal title, if it did exist, had been effectively extinguished by subsequent legislation.

However, Justice Judson later recognized the source of aboriginal title as historical occupation of land: "[T]he fact is that when the [European] settlers came, the Indians were there, organised in societies and occupying the land as their forefathers had done for centuries." This represents a significant change in judicial interpretation of the source and nature of aboriginal title in recognizing that title derives from the factual and physical occupation of lands by aboriginal peoples, prior to the arrival of Europeans, rather than from Crown grant or legislative recognition.

Justices Emmett Hall, Wishart Spence, and Bora Laskin rejected the idea that, after conquest or discovery, aboriginal peoples have no rights except those granted or recognized by the conqueror or discoverer. They pointed to existing Canadian common law, which affirms aboriginal rights to possession and enjoyment of lands. Aboriginal title is not dependent on recognition by the Crown, whether by treaty, executive order, or legislation. They held that the Nisga'a title continued. Justice Hall also noted the importance of the Royal Proclamation of 1763 to aboriginal peoples in Canada: "Its force as a statute is analogous to the status of the Magna Carta which has always been considered to be the law throughout the Empire."

Ultimately, the Nisga'a appeal failed on a technical legal point. The actual decision of the seventh justice, Louis-Philippe Pigeon, did not address the merits of either position of the split court but ruled simply that the Nisga'a action failed due to lack of consent of the Crown to permit an action against it. The question of the existence of Nisga'a aboriginal title was left unresolved until 1999.

This is a landmark case because it recognized for the first time that aboriginal title exists under Canadian common law and does not derive from Crown grant or recognition, as previously held in *St. Catherine's Milling Co. v. The Queen* (1887). Before this case, there had been limited recognition of aboriginal rights to land either under treaty or under Canadian common law.

The case was also an impetus for change in federal government policy toward aboriginal title claims. After the Supreme Court's confirmation that aboriginal title exists in Canadian law, the federal government announced it would reverse its policy of refusing to enter into treaties with aboriginal groups. It was willing to assume responsibility for protection of aboriginal land interests as stated in the Royal Proclamation of 1763 and to commence negotiations to reconcile their interest with the Crown's underlying title to all lands in Canada. The government introduced the comprehensive land claims process, whereby negotiation of aboriginal title claims would eventually lead to a treaty settlement.

The Nisga'a claim was eventually settled under a treaty negotiation process leading to the Nisga'a Final Agreement (1999), between the Nisga'a First Nation, the Province of British, and the Government of Canada.

Özlem Ülgen

See also Aboriginal Title; Nisga'a Final Agreement–April 27, 1999; Royal Proclamation of 1763; *St. Catherine's Milling and Lumber Company v. The Queen* (Canada), 1887.

References and Further Reading

Calder v. Attorney General of British Columbia. 1973. 1 S.C.R. 313.

McConnell, W. H. 1974. "The *Calder* Case in Historical Perspective," 38 *Saskatchewan Law Review* 88.

McClanahan v. Arizona State Tax Commission, 1973

The premise of the case concerned whether the State of Arizona had jurisdiction to impose a personal income tax on individual members of the Navajo tribe while said individuals resided in, and whose income was exclusively derived from, the reservation. The U.S. Supreme Court relied on the test derived from *Williams v. Lee* (1959): whether the imposition of a state tax infringed on the tribe "to make their own laws and be ruled by them." The Court relied on tribal treaty rights and on the historic presumption that tribes have always governed themselves on reservations. Three factors influenced the opinion of the Court. First, federal preemption had primacy over Native American inherent sovereignty; the latter was described as providing a "backdrop" to the reading of the treaties and statutes. Second, the Court invoked the canon of interpretation, according to which treaty ambiguities are resolved in favor of the tribes, and thus the Navajo treaty of 1868 was validated to preclude state taxation. Third, the Court affirmed the Navajo position following an examination of the relevant statutes, which included the Buck Act (Title 25 U.S.C. 1322 [a]) and the Arizona Enabling Act. Justice Thurgood Marshall delivered the unanimous opinion. The U.S. Supreme Court held that Arizona did not have the jurisdiction to impose a personal income tax on income earned exclusively by a tribal member on a reservation.

The case concerned an enrolled member of the Navajo tribe who lived within the Navajo reservation. In 1967, the tribal member paid $16.20 in taxes, which was withheld by his employer, and $11.84 of this was termed "tax liability." At the end of the tax year, the tribal member filed a protest against the collection of the state tax and sought a refund. The Arizona Superior Court dismissed the action, and the Arizona court of appeals affirmed.

The question decided by the U.S. Supreme Court was a narrow one and concerned whether a state may tax a reservation tribal member for income earned exclusively on the reservation. Marshall cited *Worcester v. Georgia* (1832) and stated that the general tenet extended to disallowing state taxation and jurisdiction within the reservation. Despite the evolution of Native American sovereignty, the tribe traditionally has retained jurisdiction over the reservation, primarily governing themselves free from state interference except at the issuance of an express act of Congress. Moreover, the Court held, Native American inherent sovereignty had been supplanted by federal preemption as a bar to state jurisdiction, and modern-day cases rely on treaties and statutes to circumscribe state authority.

Marshall proceeded to examine the Navajo treaty of 1868 and the applicable statutes. The treaty of 1868 established an exclusive reservation for the Navajo Nation. Marshall stated that, although the treaty failed explicitly to mention whether the Navajo were free from state law or exempt from state tax, it was not a simple contract between two parties of equal bargaining power. Thus, the canon— according to which ambiguous expressions are construed in favor of the tribes—was invoked. The canon, the tradition of tribal independence, and the treaty that established exclusive sovereignty over reservation lands under federal supervision all preempted state law.

Marshall proceeded to address the relevant statutes. First, the Arizona Enabling Act was not silent on tax immunity, but its equivocal language was interpreted in favor of the tribes. Second, the Buck Act and its legislative history also justified this position, as it and the enabling act prevaricated as to

whether or not reservation members were to be taxed. Third, Title 25 U.S.C. 1322 (a) was negated, as tribal consent was not obtained by the state. The treaty of 1868 and the sovereign history of the tribe were read in a manner where Congress would not have circumscribed Navajo jurisdiction within the reservation and on the contrary, granted the tribe tax-exempt status.

Arizona's defense relied on *Williams v. Lee* (1959) and intimated that taxing individuals does not impinge on tribal self-government. Marshall stated that the *Williams* test did not apply to these circumstances, in which a Navajo member was earning income on a reservation protected by treaty and federal statutes. Under the *Williams* test, if tribal government had not been infringed upon, and a tribe accepted state law concurrent within the reservation, state tax would still not bind the tribe or its members. Moreover, tax could not be imposed upon the income, the lands, or the individual members of the reservation, as federal statutes gave individual rights to tribes, which are entities composed of individuals. The Court held that Arizona had interfered with matters arising from Native American and federal government provenance.

Dewi I. Ball

See also Government-to-Government Relationship; Sovereignty; Treaty; Treaty with the Navajo–June 1, 1868; *United States v. Kagama*, 1886; *Warren Trading Post Co. v. Arizona Tax Commission*, 1965; *Williams v. Lee*, 1959; *Worcester v. Georgia*, 1832.

References and Further Reading

Canby, William C. 1998. *American Indian Law in a Nutshell*. St. Paul, MN: West.

Pevar, Stephen L. 2002. *The Rights of Indians and Tribes*. 3rd. ed. Carbondale: Southern Illinois University Press.

Wilkins, David E., and K. Tsianina Lomawaima. 2001. *Uneven Ground: American Indian Sovereignty and Federal Law*. Norman: University of Oklahoma Press.

Wounded Knee Occupation, 1973

Undoubtedly, the most renowned episode in the history of Indian activism in the latter half of the twentieth century was the American Indian Movement's takeover of Wounded Knee, South Dakota, on February 27, 1973. This incident and the government's subsequent seventy-one-day siege of the community

Wounded Knee takeover by the American Indian Movement (AIM) at the Pine Ridge Reservation in South Dakota in 1973. (UPI/Bettmann/Corbis)

drew national attention—albeit briefly—to the issue of Indian sovereignty and treaty rights. Organized by American Indian Movement (AIM) leaders Russell Means and Dennis Banks (and sanctioned by traditional elders and local activists on the Pine Ridge Reservation), the occupation of the historic site was the result of mounting opposition to the reservation's partisan tribal government.

Led by Chairman Richard "Dick" Wilson, the Oglala Sioux Tribal Council developed a reputation for corruption and repression in the early 1970s. Wilson's favoritism toward his family, Bureau of Indian Affairs (BIA) employees, and mixed-blood supporters around the town of Pine Ridge rankled the rural, traditional, full-blooded members of the tribe, who were more concerned with the maintenance of Lakota culture than with economic gain. Likewise, his outspoken animosity toward AIM was at odds with the organization's growing influence on Pine Ridge—especially in the aftermath of the February 1972 death of Raymond Yellow Thunder at the hands of white racists in Gordon, Nebraska. AIM's

swift efforts to seek justice for the Yellow Thunder family stood in stark contrast to the inactivity of the tribal council. As participants of the Trail of Broken Treaties caravan filtered back to South Dakota in late November that year, Wilson stood poised to stifle outside agitators, whom he deemed fanatical and lawless.

The event that triggered the occupation of Wounded Knee occurred in the early morning hours of January 22, 1973. Darld Schmitz, a white man, stabbed to death Wesley Bad Heart Bull, a Lakota from the Pine Ridge Reservation, outside a bar in Buffalo Gap—a reservation border town approximately fifty miles south of Rapid City. Charged only with second-degree manslaughter, Schmitz was released on $5,000 bail. For many Indians, the case exemplified the discrimination they regularly faced from the state and local governments in South Dakota. In response to a request from the victim's mother, AIM leaders Russell Means and Dennis Banks led protestors to the Custer County Courthouse on February 6, determined to reverse the injustice. The demonstration turned into a riot, resulting in the arrest of nineteen Indians, including Means and Banks. Subsequent efforts by officials in nearby Rapid City to redress Indian grievances collapsed as a result of further violence.

For Dick Wilson, AIM was the common denominator of the centers of violence and disruption. Determined to keep AIM and other outside agitators off his reservation, the tribal chairman, with the aid of a $62,000 grant from the BIA, organized an auxiliary police force dubbed the Goon Squad by his enemies (which his supporters turned into an acronym for Guardians of the Oglala Nation), and secured a tribal court order preventing AIM leaders from proselytizing at public events on the reservation. The Goon Squad quickly became Wilson's private militia and served to enforce the dicta of the chairman. By mid-February, Wilson's efforts to guarantee order on Pine Ridge were reinforced by seventy-five federal marshals from the government's Special Operations Group.

Wilson's traditionalist opponents formed the Oglala Sioux Civil Rights Organization (OSCRO) and tried unsuccessfully to impeach the chairman. Unwilling to accept the continuance of Wilson's authoritarianism on the reservation, OSCRO leaders met with Means and Banks in the Calico Hall Community Center on February 27, 1973, to request their assistance. Chief Frank Fools Crow suggested that AIM draw attention to their plight by making a stand at Wounded Knee—a small village inhabited by fewer than a hundred people and the site of the massacre of Chief Big Foot's band of Minneconjou Lakota by the U.S. Seventh Cavalry in 1890. To this the activists readily assented and proceeded to lead two hundred supporters in a convoy of fifty-four cars to the village that night. Arriving at 7:30 in the evening, members of AIM and their followers seized the Wounded Knee trading post, where they took its owners, the Gildersleeves, hostage and, after confiscating weapons and supplies, established a command post at nearby Sacred Heart Catholic Church, the cemetery of which contained the mass grave of the victims of the massacre of 1890. The occupiers then issued a statement declaring that they were operating under the provisions of the Fort Laramie Treaty of 1868 and were only demanding what was rightfully theirs—sovereignty.

As news of the takeover at Wounded Knee spread over Pine Ridge, the BIA police, federal marshals, FBI agents, and Wilson's Goon Squad sealed off the roads leading into the village. Within forty-eight hours, more than two hundred law enforcement officials were on hand equipped with armored personnel carriers, automatic weapons, and .50-caliber machine guns. Helicopters and F-4 Phantom jets flew overhead, in part for reconnaissance but also for purposes of intimidation. It was soon clear, however, that unlike the circumstances almost eighty-three years earlier, there would be no attack on the inhabitants of Wounded Knee. Both sides settled down for a siege.

Proclaiming an independent Oglala Nation on March 11, the occupiers of Wounded Knee busied themselves with the construction of bunkers for protection from sniper fire. Food and medical supplies slipped through the government's permeable perimeter via supporters who, responding to the extensive media coverage of the standoff, journeyed to the reservation from around the nation. Civil rights groups, Vietnam veterans against the war, quixotic college students, and various church organizations strove to provide aid to the besieged activists. Efforts to negotiate a settlement failed repeatedly. In addition to reforming the tribal government, AIM's demands expanded to include congressional investigations into the BIA and the Department of the Interior as well as governmental acknowledgment of treaty violations. During the first few weeks of the siege, both of South Dakota's senators as well as negotiators from the attorney general's office met with AIM leaders but were unsuccessful in gaining dispossession of the village. On April 5, a breakthrough in the stalemated talks appeared imminent, but a last-minute impasse again nullified all hope of an immediate resolution.

Throughout the seventy-one-day siege, AIM activists and government forces continued to harass each other with sporadic sniping. On March 26, during a particularly heavy exchange of gunfire, U.S. Marshal Frank Grimm was wounded in the chest and subsequently paralyzed from the waist down. Almost a month later, on April 25, a ricocheting .50 caliber bullet hit Frank Clearwater, a Cherokee, in the head while he slept on a cot inside a church. The next day, Lawrence "Buddy" Lamont, a Lakota Vietnam veteran, died after being shot through the heart. Both fatalities, combined with other injuries and growing deprivations among the Wounded Knee occupants, led Chief Fools Crow to press AIM to intensify their efforts to bring about an end to the standoff. On May 6, Lakota elders accepted the Nixon administration's promise to investigate Wilson's regime on Pine Ridge, to meet with traditionalists on the reservation to discuss the violations of the treaty of 1868, and to ensure fair handling of the Wounded Knee activists. In turn, the occupiers agreed to disarm and dispossess the village.

The ten-week siege of Wounded Knee ended May 8. Few of AIM's leaders remained in the vicinity to see its conclusion. Russell Means left on April 5 for an ultimately unproductive meeting with White House officials in Washington, D.C. He spent the remainder of the month traveling the country, lobbying for support. Dennis Banks, fearing imminent arrest, left Wounded Knee on May 7 and became a fugitive. On the day of the stand-down, 147 men and women were on hand to surrender to their besiegers. In the end, despite the national media attention and public sympathy generated by the standoff, little changed in its aftermath. Dick Wilson continued his reign as tribal chairman and spent the next two years solidifying his control of the reservation. White House officials did travel to Pine Ridge on May 17 but offered little in the way of political or economic concessions. For AIM, the siege represented the high-water mark of the organization. During the years that followed, long and costly legal battles depleted its resources while its membership succumbed to bitter factionalism.

Alan C. Downs

See also American Indian Movement (AIM); Banks, Dennis; Means, Russell.

References and Further Reading

Banks, Dennis, and Richard Erdoes. 2004. *Ojibwa Warrior: Dennis Banks and the Rise of the American Indian Movement.* Norman: University of Oklahoma Press.

Cornell, Stephen. 1988. *The Return of the Native: American Indian Political Resurgence.* New York: Oxford University Press.

Josephy, Alvin, Jr., ed. 1971. *Red Power: The American Indian's Fight for Freedom.* New York. McGraw-Hill.

Josephy, Alvin, Jr., Joane Nagel, and Troy Johnson, eds. 1999. *Red Power: The American Indian's Fight for Freedom.* Lincoln and London: University of Nebraska Press.

Means, Russell, and Marvin J. Wolf. 1995. *Where White Men Fear to Tread: The Autobiography of Russell Means.* New York: St. Martin's Griffin.

Smith, Paul Chaat, and Robert Allen Warrior. 1996. *Like a Hurricane: The Indian Movement from Alcatraz to Wounded Knee.* New York: New Press.

Boldt Decision (*United States v. Washington*), 1974

Better known as the Boldt Decision, *United States. v. Washington* marked the legal turning point in the Northwest Indian fishing rights controversy. In Phase I (1974), U.S. District Judge George Boldt decreed that the treaty tribes' reserved right to fish "in common" entitled them to 50 percent of the harvestable salmon entering their "usual and accustomed places." He also held that the tribes could regulate their share of the fishery, but non-Indian protests and state resistance obstructed his ruling until the U.S. Supreme Court affirmed it in 1979. In Phase II (1980), Boldt's successor ruled that the tribes had rights to hatchery fish and to protection of the salmon from environmental degradation. Although many problems remain unresolved, the Boldt Decision set an enduring standard for allocation and helped revive the moribund tribal fishing economy in the Pacific Northwest.

The case was the culmination of more than a century of conflict and litigation over off-reservation fishing rights. In 1854–1855, the Indians of Puget Sound had signed five treaties that ceded most of their aboriginal territory but explicitly reserved "the right of taking fish at all usual and accustomed places, in common with the citizens of the Territory." Although federal officials assumed that Indians would eventually abandon their subsistence practices and assimilate into American society, tribal representatives believed that their fishing rights had been guaranteed in perpetuity. They would not have signed the treaties without such promises, and they did not anticipate future restrictions on their rights. As anthropologist Barbara Lane later testified at trial, "the most likely Indian interpretation of the 'in common' language would be that non-Indians were to be allowed to fish without interfering with continued pursuit of traditional Indian fishing" (Lane 1977, 4).

By the early twentieth century, however, non-Indian commercial fishing and habitat destruction had decimated salmon populations, leading Washington State to impose regulations on tribal fishing in ceded territory. State officials argued that Indians should obey the same restrictions as non-Indians, even though those rules often discriminated against Indians, violated their treaty rights, and undermined both their economic self-sufficiency and cultural traditions. Six fishing rights cases reached the U.S. Supreme Court prior to 1974. The Court upheld the

Native Americans protest violations of tribal fishing rights along the Columbia River in Washington State in 1971. (Corbis)

treaties every time, but it also refused to preclude state regulation of tribal fishing rights. Consequently, Washington State continued to harass Indian fishers despite the fact that, by the late 1960s, their share of the salmon harvest had fallen to less than 5 percent. Tribal activists such as Hank Adams, Robert Satiacum, and Billy Frank, Jr., responded with "fish-ins" to challenge state law and provoke a test case. Following a series of violent police raids that attracted national media attention, the federal government finally agreed to pursue legal action on behalf of fourteen treaty tribes.

Judge Boldt hoped that *United States v. Washington* would settle the matter once and for all. Considering both contemporary dictionary definitions and the Indian understanding of the treaties, he construed the words "in common" to mean that the treaty tribes had a right to half of the allowable harvest. In addition, he held that the treaty tribes could regulate off-reservation fishing by their members, whereas the state could only regulate them for "reasonable and necessary" conservation purposes.

Although his decision built on existing precedents, it shocked many non-Indians and triggered waves of protest, including extensive outlaw fishing and numerous countersuits. Washington State also appealed and refused to enforce the ruling until the Supreme Court affirmed it in 1979.

The controversy did not end there. In 1980, shortly after Boldt's retirement, Judge William Orrick heard Phase II of the case. He ruled that the tribal share included hatchery fish and that the treaties implied the right to have salmon habitat protected from environmental threats. Two years later, however, a circuit court review overturned his opinion on the latter issue. The tribes continue to press for environmental protection, but they face strong opposition from regional politicians and business interests as well as lingering intertribal differences over allocation. Even so, the Boldt Decision helped to revitalize their fishing economies and gave them a meaningful role in the management of Northwest salmon fisheries.

Andrew H. Fisher

See also *Puyallup Tribe v. Department of Game of Washington*, 1968; *Puyallup Tribe Inc. v. Department of Game of Washington*, 1977; Reserved Rights Doctrine; *Sohappy v. Smith* and *United States v. Oregon*, 1969.

References and Further Reading

Bentley, Shannon. 1992. "Indians' Right to Fish: The Background, Importance, and Legacy of *United States v. Washington*." *American Indian Law Review* 17: 1–35.

Cohen, Fay G. 1986. *Treaties on Trial: The Continuing Controversy over Northwest Indian Fishing Rights*. Seattle: University of Washington Press.

Lane, Barbara. 1977. "Background of Treaty Making in Western Washington." *American Indian Journal* 3 (April): 2–1.

Morton v. Mancari, 1974

In deciding *Morton v. Mancari*, 417 U.S. 535 (1974), the U.S. Supreme Court held that that tribal Indians were "members of quasi-sovereign tribal entities" and that Indian status was thus "political rather than racial in nature" (Canby 1998, 553–554). Given that unique classification, Indian preferences in hiring and promotion at the BIA were upheld.

The case arose wherein non-Indian employees of the Bureau of Indian Affairs (BIA) brought a class action lawsuit to invalidate Indian hiring and promotion preferences at the BIA that were part of the 1934 Indian Reorganization Act (IRA). The IRA directed the secretary of the interior to develop standards for hiring Indians to fill positions maintained by the Indian Office, which administered tribal affairs. The IRA gave such qualified Indians preference when vacancies in the BIA were to be filled. In 1972, the policy was expanded to incorporate an Indian preference at the initial hiring stage as well as for promotions. In the subsequent lawsuit, the non-Indian BIA employees claimed that the preference was a violation of the Equal Employment Opportunity Act (EEOA) of 1972 and also constituted invidious racial discrimination in violation of the due process clause of the Fifth Amendment.

Because the complaint sought to enjoin the enforcement of a federal statute as unconstitutional, a special three-judge federal district court was convened to decide the matter. After a brief trial, the district court concluded that the hiring preference for Indians was implicitly repealed by EEOA, which proscribed discrimination in most federal employ-ment on the basis of race. Having made such a determination, the district court did not rule on whether the hiring preference violated the due process clause of the Fifth Amendment. The district court also enjoined federal officials "from implementing any policy in the Bureau of Indian Affairs which would hire, promote, or reassign any person in preference to another solely for the reason that such person is an Indian" (ibid., 540).

The Supreme Court reversed the district court's ruling, holding that the Indian hiring preference was not repealed by the EEOA. Writing for a unanimous majority, Justice Harry Blackmun wrote that the Indian preference does not constitute invidious racial discrimination. In fact, the Indian preference did not constitute "racial discrimination" or even "racial" preference but was, rather, an employment criterion designed to further the cause of Indian self-government and to make the BIA more responsive to the needs of its constituent groups.

Furthermore, the Constitution itself explicitly and implicitly grants Congress the authority to deal with the special problems of Indians. Article I, Section 8, clause 3 gives Congress the power to "regulate Commerce . . . with the Indian Tribes," and thus "singles Indians out as a proper subject for separate legislation" (ibid., 552).

Justice Blackmun also noted that the federal government had had an Indian hiring preference as far back as 1834 and that, since then, Congress has repeatedly enacted additional Indian hiring preferences. According to the legislative history cited by Justice Blackmun, the purpose of these preferences "has been to give Indians a greater participation in their own self-government; to further the Government's trust obligation toward the Indian tribes; and to reduce the negative effect of having non-Indians administer matters that affect Indian tribal life" (ibid., 542–543).

Separately, Justice Blackmun pointed out that literally "every piece of legislation dealing with Indian tribes and reservations, and certainly all legislation dealing with the BIA, single out for special treatment a constituency of tribal Indians living on or near reservations" (ibid., 552). "If Indian preference laws, which were derived from historical relationships and explicitly designed to help only Indians, were deemed invidious racial discrimination, an entire Title of the United States Code (25 U. S. C.) would be effectively erased and the solemn commitment of the Government toward the Indians would be jeopardized" (ibid.).

Although *Morton v. Mancari* involved the BIA's hiring preference for Indians, the Court extended its holding to other areas of Indian policy as "long as the special treatment can be tied rationally to the fulfillment of Congress' unique obligation toward the Indians" and as long as the policy "is reasonable and rationally designed to further Indian self-government" (ibid., 555).

Gavin Clarkson

See also Commerce Clause and Native Americans; Indian Reorganization Act, 1934; *Rice v. Cayetano*, 2000.

References and Further Reading
Anderson, Terry L. 1995. *Sovereign Nations or Reservations? An Economic History of American Indians.* San Francisco: Pacific Research Institute for Public Policy.
Canby, William C., Jr. 1998. *American Indian Law in a Nutshell.* 3rd ed. St. Paul, MN: West.
Pommersheim, Frank. 1995. *Braid of Feathers: American Indian Law and Contemporary Tribal Life.* Berkeley: University of California Press.
Wilkins, David E., and K. Tsianina Lomawaima. 2001. *Uneven Ground: American Indian Sovereignty and Federal Law.* Norman: University of Oklahoma Press.

American Indian Self-Determination and Education Act of 1975

The American Indian Self-Determination and Education Act of 1975 (P.L. 93–638) was the culmination of efforts by the U.S. government to end the paternalistic relationship between Indian tribes and the federal government by directing federal funding from governmental agencies to tribal governments. Several factors contributed to the evolution of this act.

As early as 1824, the U.S. government began the process of forced assimilation with the education of the American Indian in government-operated schools and the seizure of Indian land. When the Bureau of Indian Affairs (BIA) was created as a part of the War Department in 1842, it included the operation of thirty-seven Indian schools. By 1870, $100,000 was authorized to fund and operate federal schools for Indians. In 1918, the "quantum degree of Indian blood" criteria was established to determine who could attend the government-regulated Indian schools.

In 1921, Congress passed the Snyder Act, which established government services for Indian peoples through the BIA. In 1928, the Merriam Report recognized that the quality of education in reservation schools was not equivalent to the quality of education in the public school systems.

The Roosevelt administration passed the Indian Reorganization Act in 1934, which granted more tribal autonomy and self-reliance with less dependency on the federal government. The Johnson O'Malley Act, also passed by Congress in 1934, provided incentives for the state's public school systems to become involved in Indian education. This law authorized the secretary of the interior to contract for Indian educational services with state-supported schools, colleges, and universities through available grants rather than building separate schools.

In 1960, President John F. Kennedy hastened the effort to provide schools for all Indian children through the operation of Indian schools on reservations. Congress passed the Elementary and Secondary Education Act in 1965, which serviced all the disadvantaged youth in the United States, along with an amendment to Title I that stressed the inclusion of the BIA. In addition, Titles III and IV of this act made it possible to provide more programs for Indian students.

The National Indian Education Advisory Committee, established by the BIA in 1967 during the Johnson administration, facilitated the 1969 publication of *Indian Education: A National Tragedy—A National Challenge* (also referred to as the Kennedy Report). This report recommended increased Indian control of education, a good federal school system, and the establishment of the National Indian Board of Education. Formed in 1970, the National Indian Board of Education was a combination of Indian teachers, educators, and scholars. That same year, President Richard Nixon announced a new era of Indian self-determination, that is, control over all decisions affecting Indians, including education. Tribally controlled community colleges began to form in 1971. The U.S. government strengthened its commitment to Indian self-determination with the passage of the Indian Education Act of 1972. This act enabled the U.S. Department of Education to provide direct funds for the special needs of all Indian students in public school systems that have ten or more Indian students (now known as Title IX Indian Education). The National Advisory Council on Indian Education was established to monitor the provisions of the law, prioritize programs, and evaluate Indian education throughout the federal system and to begin active work with the Indian community colleges.

Congress passed the Indian Self-Determination and Education Assistance Act, P.L. 93–638, in 1975. This act recognized Indian tribes as sovereign nations with control over their educational programs. Educational improvements followed the implementation of this act, with additional money for Native schools, cultural programs in white public schools, incorporation of tribal cultures and Native languages into the curricula, English as a second language (ESL) instruction, and Indian parent support and involvement for students. Early childhood education initiatives were an important part of this law.

Amendments to the public law have included the establishment of the American Indian Policy Review Commission, the Indian Child Welfare Act for Indian child custody cases, and the elevation of tribal governments to the same level as state governments.

Helen M. Krische

See also American Indian Policy Review Commission; American Indian Self-Determination and Education Act of 1975; Bureau of Indian Affairs (BIA); Indian Reorganization Act, 1934.

References and Further Reading

Cahape, Patricia, and Craig B. Howley, eds. 1992. *Indian Nations At Risk: Listening to the People.* Summaries of Papers Commissioned by the Indian Nations At Risk Task Force of the U.S. Department of Education. Charleston, WV: ERIC Clearinghouse on Rural Education and Small Schools Appalachia Education Laboratory.

Castile, George Pierre. 1998. *To Show Heart: Native American Self-Determination and Federal Indian Policy, 1960–1975.* Tucson: University of Arizona Press.

Wilkinson, Charles. 2005. *Blood Struggle: The Rise of Modern Indian Nations.* New York and London: W.W. Norton.

People v. LeBlanc, 1976

People v. Leblanc was a landmark case involving the fishing rights affected by the treaty of 1836. According to the treaty, the Chippewa Indians reserved the rights to fish in all waters adjoining the lands that were ceded by the treaty. However, these rights were relinquished in the treaty of 1855.

Those rights reserved under the treaty of 1836 were intended to be temporary. The treaty of 1855 thus provided for payments in lieu of claims for land. The intentions were that the Chippewas would not continue their traditional way of life and would assimilate into white society (*7 Stat.* 491 [1836], 11 *Stat.* 621 [1856]).

Albert B. LeBlanc, a Chippewa Indian, was convicted in the 91st District Court of fishing without a commercial license and fishing with a gill net. The Chippewa circuit court affirmed. The defendant admitted the acts as charged but asserted that to convict him would conflict with a federal treaty guaranteeing to all Chippewa Indians living on the Bay Mills Indian Reservation the right to fish in the Whitefish Bay area of Lake Superior, including Pendills Bay, where he was fishing when he was arrested. The court of appeals reversed the conviction of fishing without a license and remanded the cause to the district court for a determination as to whether the statutory ban on gill nets was necessary to prevent a substantial depletion of the fish supply, in which case the second conviction would be affirmed. Both parties appealed.

Both LeBlanc and Judge Nicholas J. Lambros of the district court ruled that the Chippewas held reserve fishing rights in Pendills Bay according to the treaty of 1836. These rights were not surrendered in the treaty of 1855, although Pendills Bay was not a part of the Bay Mills Reservation. Furthermore, the defendant was not fishing on a reservation but had off-reservation rights based on the treaty of 1836, and therefore the conviction of fishing without a commercial license was not legal. According to the court, any ambiguity in interpretation was to be decided in favor of the Chippewa.

Because fishing was a lifeway of the Chippewa in the 1830s, the Chippewa had the right to fish off reservation. The Supreme Court of Michigan agreed: "Justice [James] Ryan voted to affirm the convictions because he agreed with Justice [Lawrence] Lindemer that Article Thirteen of the Treaty of 1836 must be interpreted to mean that settlement of the land of the Upper Peninsula terminates all usual privileges of occupancy associated with the land. He agreed with Justice Mennen G. Williams the decisions of the U.S. Supreme Court regarding the construction of Indian treaties required the conclusion on this record that the Treaty of 1855 did not extinguish any of the fishing rights granted the Chippewa's in the Treaty of 1836" [55 Mich App 684; 223 NW2d 305 (1974) affirmed].

In October 1974, the court of appeals ruled in favor of the defendant based on rights dealt with in the treaty of 1836. Both sides applied for leave to appeal to the Supreme Court, and this was granted. On May 7, 1979, in *United States v. State of Michigan,* the fishing rights of the Chippewa were recognized by the Court; proper steps were to be taken by the secretary of the interior to protect Chippewa fishing rights, thereby preempting the state's authority to regulate fishing by tribal members (*United States v. State of Michigan,* 1981).

In 1985, a consent agreement for managing conservation was worked out between the Bay Mills Indian Community, the Sault Ste. Marie tribe of Chippewa Indians, the Grand Traverse band of Ottawa/Chippewa Indians, and the State of Michigan. In July 2000, a Chippewa Ottawa Resource Authority (CORA) charter was established for conservation management and supervision of the treaty fishing rights established in 1836. On August 31, 2000, CORA established fishing regulations for the Chippewa in Lakes Superior, Huron, and Michigan.

Jean Bedell-Bailey

See also Boldt Decision (*United States v. Washington*), 1974; *Lac Courte Oreilles Band of Chippewa Indians v. Voigt et al.,* 1983; Treaty with the Chippewa–May 9, 1836; Treaty with the Chippewa–July 29, 1837; Treaty with the Chippewa–February 22, 1855; Treaty with the Nisqually, Puyallup, Etc.–December 26, 1854.

References and Further Reading
Bressett, Walter, and Rick Whaley. 1994. *Walleye Warriors: An Effective Alliance Against Racism and for the Earth.* Philadelphia: New Society.
Lac Courte Oreilles Band of Chippewa Indians et al., v. Lester P. Voigt et al. 1983. 700 F. 2d 365.
Satz, Ronald. 1991. "Chippewa Treaty Rights: The Reserved Rights of Wisconsin's Chippewa Indians in Historical Perspective." *Transactions, Wisconsin Academy of Sciences, Arts and Letters,* 79(1).

Puyallup Tribe Inc. v. Department of Game of Washington, 1977

The case concerned whether the Puyallup tribe could invoke tribal sovereign immunity against state regulatory jurisdiction over tribal fishing activity—which included limiting the number of steelhead fish caught by the tribe—on and off the reservation. The tribe intimated that limiting the number of steel-

head was an unnecessary conservation measure. Justice John Stevens delivered the opinion of the U.S. Supreme Court. The Court based its opinion on four issues. First, tribal sovereign immunity could be invoked to protect the rights of the tribe, but from the decree (opinion) of *Puyallup I* in 1968, the state court held jurisdiction over individual members of the tribe. Second, allotment had diminished tribal exclusivity over reservation lands granted within the Treaty of Medicine Creek of 1854. Consequently, the tribe could not exclusively take steelhead passing through the reservation, and the state assumed regulatory capacity over on- and off-reservation activity, subject to conservation measures. Third, the trial court held that, pursuant to a remand from the U.S. Supreme Court in *Puyallup II* (1973), the limitation placed on the tribe regarding steelhead numbers was a reasonable conservation measure. And fourth, the tribe was advised to provide voluntarily a list of members who could fish under treaty rights and provide statistics to ensure against erroneous state regulatory enforcement.

The Department of Game of Washington State filed a complaint in trial court against tribal members who claimed immunity from state conservation laws when fishing with set and drift nets for steelhead in the Puyallup River. The tribe stated that it had an exclusive right to fish in the river as a property right under the treaty of 1854 and that tribal sovereign immunity precluded state jurisdiction.

The U.S. Supreme Court ruled, pursuant to *Puyallup I* of 1968, individual members of the tribe who fished off reservation were held to be under state jurisdiction, and sovereign immunity did not apply. Moreover, the tribe contended, the state could not regulate tribal fishing, notwithstanding state civil and criminal jurisdiction within the reservation for most purposes. The Court ruled that, under Article 3 of the treaty of 1854, tribal members could fish "at all usual and accustomed places," but only concomitant with "in common with all citizens of the Territory." Treaty exclusivity was negated, and under state conservation measures, the tribal manner of fishing could be regulated as long as it did not discriminate against tribal members.

Tribal sovereign immunity was applied following *Puyallup II* (1973) when the state court had to determine, first, the number of steelhead the tribe could catch while net fishing in the river running through the reservation; second, the identity of members permitted to fish under the treaty; and third, the weekly reporting of steelhead numbers caught by the tribe. Washington State could not impose jurisdiction over a tribe without tribal or congressional consent but could limit the number of steelhead caught by an individual tribal member.

The tribe asserted, relying on the treaty of 1854 and federal preemption, that it and not the state had jurisdiction over on-reservation fishing, as previous Puyallup decisions had decided only off-reservation issues. The U.S. Supreme Court ruled that tribal exclusivity had been extinguished pursuant to the alienation of reservation land and all land adjoining the river. Moreover, nonmembers who fished within the reservation were under state warden supervision.

The issue of imposing limitations on tribal catches was introduced in *Puyallup II* (1973). This case directed the state court to devise limits for catching steelhead between tribal member net fishing and nonmember sport fishing. Limits had to be "fairly apportioned." The U.S. Supreme Court ruled that fair apportionment could not exist if the tribe had authority to take unlimited numbers of fish within the reservation and the treaty did not allow the tribe to take every last fish.

The limitation, which was necessary to determine steelhead numbers for subsequent years and to enforce laws if quotas were exceeded, was based on the numbers of steelhead caught every season and was applied to all members of the tribe. The Supreme Court stated that the tribe did not have to provide information to the state court regarding the tribal members enjoined to fish under treaty rights and the size of the catch. It was suggested that the tribe provide the necessary information voluntarily to prevent the risk of an erroneous state enforcement act.

Dewi I. Ball

See also Allotments; Medicine Creek, Washington; Puyallup Tribe v. Department of Game of Washington, 1968; Reserved Rights Doctrine; Sovereignty; Treaty; Treaty with the Nisqually, Puyallup, Etc.–December 26, 1854; Williams v. Lee, 1959.

References and Further Reading

Canby, William C. 1998. *American Indian Law in a Nutshell.* St. Paul, MN: West.

Pevar, Stephen L. 2002. *The Rights of Indians and Tribes.* 3rd ed. Carbondale: Southern Illinois University Press.

Wilkins, David E., and K. Tsianina Lomawaima. 2001. *Uneven Ground: American Indian Sovereignty and Federal Law.* Norman: University of Oklahoma Press.

Longest Walk, 1978

The Longest Walk was a march organized in 1978 by American Indian Movement (AIM) leader Dennis Banks to protest congressional legislation that threatened to abrogate Indian treaty rights. The marchers left Alcatraz, California, in February and arrived in Washington, D.C., in mid-July with a contingent of more than twenty-five hundred people. In addition to protesting anti-Indian legislation, the walk was intended to commemorate the forced removal of American Indians from their homelands and to raise awareness of past and present injustices suffered by Indian people.

For American Indian activists, the Longest Walk was the last in a series of protests that began with the occupation of Alcatraz Island in 1969–1971 and included the 1972 Trail of Broken Treaties, the takeover of the Bureau of Indian Affairs (BIA) headquarters in Washington, D.C., and the 1973 occupation of Wounded Knee. In 1977, AIM broadened its outreach and, with its "international arm," the International Indian Treaty Council (IITC), helped bring together representatives of ninety-eight indigenous nations from across the Americas for a hearing on the rights of American Indians held before the United Nations Commission on Human Rights in Geneva, Switzerland. This event galvanized Indian activists to take action when lawmakers in Congress moved to enact legislation that threatened Indian treaty rights.

Washington representative Lloyd Meeds, a member of the American Indian Policy Review Commission, was the leader of the movement to terminate Indian treaty rights and sovereignty. Meeds opposed the 1975 Indian Self-Determination Act and held that Indian people should no longer be regarded as sovereign people. In 1977 and 1978, Meeds and his fellow congressman from Washington, Jack Cunningham, introduced a series of bills that directed the president to abrogate all treaties with Indians within a year, subjected Indians to state jurisdiction, abolished tribal tax immunities, and extinguished Indian hunting and fishing rights protected by past treaties—a matter of particular importance to commercial fishing interests in the Pacific Northwest.

In response to this proposed legislation, Dennis Banks (Chippewa) organized the Longest Walk. Unlike previous AIM protests, the Longest Walk was a peaceful event. On July 25, the organizers held a mass rally at the Washington Monument, during which they delivered a manifesto entitled "Affirmation of the Sovereignty of the Indigenous People of the Western Hemisphere." The manifesto, which was read into the *Congressional Record* by California representative Ron Dellums, called for the recognition of all indigenous peoples as nations and demanded that the United States respect the treaties it had made with Indian peoples and the sovereignty of American Indian tribes.

The Longest Walk, and the attention it drew to Indian issues, helped prevent passage of the legislation of Meeds and Cunningham. The movement also succeeded in raising the consciousness of Indian people and in winning public recognition of Indian peoples' rights to self-determination. However, after the Walk the influence of AIM declined, as legal actions and FBI persecution drove many of the movement's leaders into hiding.

Anne Keary

See also American Indian Movement (AIM).
References and Further Reading
Banks, Dennis, and Richard Erdoes. 2004. *Ojibwa Warrior: Dennis Banks and the Rise of the American Indian Movement.* Norman: University of Oklahoma Press.
Castile, George Pierre. 1998. *To Show Heart: Native American Self-Determination and Federal Indian Policy, 1960–1975.* Tucson: University of Arizona Press.
Cornell, Stephen. 1988. *The Return of the Native: American Indian Political Resurgence.* New York: Oxford University Press.
Robbins, Rebecca L. 1988. "American Indian Self-Determination: Comparative Analysis and Rhetorical Criticism," *Issues in Radical Therapy/New Studies on the Left,* 13: 48–58.
Smith, Paul Chaat, and Robert Allen Warrior. 1996. *Like a Hurricane: The Indian Movement from Alcatraz to Wounded Knee.* New York: New Press.

Oliphant v. Suquamish Indian Tribe, 1978

This Supreme Court case deviated from long-standing federal-Indian jurisprudence and opened the door for subsequent decisions to further abrogate tribal sovereignty. Well over a century and half of federal-Indian legal precedent established that tribes possess inherent, territory-based powers that are subject to divestment only by specific, unambiguous acts of Congress. In *Oliphant*, the Supreme Court strayed from this doctrine by declaring that tribes do not maintain criminal authority over non-Indians because it is "in conflict with the interests of the overriding sovereignty" and is inconsistent with a tribe's "dependent status." The Court's decision in *Oliphant* effectively turned on its head the fundamental inherent sovereignty principle of federal-Indian law. The result of this decision, and of the many to follow, was the piecemeal destruction of Indian sovereignty.

In *Oliphant*, two non-Indian residents of the Port Madison Reservation were arrested by tribal police after they crashed into a police vehicle, assaulted a tribal officer, and evaded arrest. The defendants were released and arraigned by the tribal court. Following arraignment, defendants sought a writ of habeas corpus asserting that the tribal court lacked criminal jurisdiction over non-Indians. This petition was denied by the federal district court and the U.S. court of appeals. The Supreme Court reversed the Ninth Circuit court's decision and held that tribal courts do not have criminal jurisdiction over non-Indians who commit crimes on Indian reservations. The Court determined that federal [and state] sovereignty interests outweigh Indian sovereignty interests, and that tribal criminal jurisdiction over non-Indians was inconsistent with their "dependent status."

The *Oliphant* Court advanced its holding by concluding that criminal jurisdiction over non-Indians posed a fundamental conflict with individual rights guaranteed by national citizenship. In reaching this decision, the Court employed its own "implicit divestiture" stating, "While Congress never expressly forbade Indian tribes to impose criminal penalties on non-Indians, we now make express our implicit conclusion of nearly a century ago that Congress consistently believed this to be the necessary result of its repeated legislative actions."

The *Oliphant* decision has been highly criticized. For example, according to many, the Court disregarded well-established precedent and was curiously selective about the cases it chose, some of which had no bearing at all. Another recurring criticism is that the Court made sweeping, unsupported generalizations regarding congressional intent in the area of tribal jurisdiction over non-members and cited dubious sources for support.

Oliphant marked a stark departure from the one-hundred-fifty-year presumption that Indian nations possess inherent power over their territories, subject to divestment only by a specific act of Congress.

Unlike previous Supreme Court cases, *Oliphant* paved the way for future courts to imply that tribal power exists only where Congress has expressly granted it. This is quite problematic for Indian nations, as it poses a direct threat to tribal governmental power. Because tribal powers had presumptively been inherent for so long, Congress had little need to expressly grant tribes the power to maintain authority over those within its borders. Therefore, areas that tribes traditionally have assumed to be clearly within their authority are now, following *Oliphant* and its progeny, subject to divestment by the Court.

Montana v. United States provides a striking example of how *Oliphant* has influenced future Courts. In *Montana,* the Supreme Court extended its *Oliphant* reasoning and held that, absent a congressional statute creating a particular tribal sovereign right, Indian nations lacked regulatory authority over the conduct of nonmembers on the reservation unless one of two narrow exceptions was satisfied. Over the past twenty-five years, the Court has consistently utilized the *Oliphant-Montana* rule to limit significantly other forms of tribal authority over non-Indians as well.

Oliphant has had profound practical effects on Indian nations, too. For one, it added to the complexity surrounding criminal jurisdiction over crimes committed on Indian reservations. Following *Oliphant,* states maintain criminal jurisdiction over certain crimes occurring on some reservations, the federal government has jurisdiction over others, and tribes retain authority to prosecute a limited number of crimes committed by Indians. Moreover, by not having criminal jurisdiction over non-Indians, tribes have lost their ability to effectively enforce their laws, and the perception that tribal law enforcement is powerless has become all too common.

Through *Oliphant* and its progeny, the Court has systematically dismantled tribal sovereignty. Thus, what used to be a presumptive authority, that of a sovereign over its respective nation, has now been significantly undermined, if not destroyed. Accordingly, the ability of Indian nations to be recognized as viable and legitimate entities capable of self-rule remains in a state of flux.

Ryan L. Church

See also Allotments; American Indian Self-
    Determination and Education Act of 1975;
    Cherokee Nation v. Georgia, 1831; Domestic
    Dependent Nation; General Allotment Act
(Dawes Act), 1887; Public Law 280, 1953;
    Sovereignty; *United States v. Wheeler,* 1978.

References and Further Reading
Getches, David H. 1979. *Cases and Materials on Federal Indian Law.* St. Paul, MN: West.
Prucha, Francis Paul. 1984. *The Great Father: United States Government and the American Indians.* Lincoln: University of Nebraska Press.

United States v. Wheeler, 1978

The premise of the case was whether the Navajo tribal court was an extension of the United States federal court and justice system. The question examined and discussed in this case was whether, under the double jeopardy clause of the Fifth Amendment, a tribal member could be brought before a federal court under the Major Crimes Act of 1885 following the imposition of a tribal court sentence. Three issues defined this case: first, the primary role of tribal inherent sovereignty over the imposition of federal authority in dictating tribal affairs; second, whether a treaty enabled the tribal court to assume jurisdiction and to impose a sentence that was less punitive than under United States law; and third, whether, if the tribal court was an extension of federal law, the Fifth Amendment would bar a retrial under the double jeopardy rule. Justice Potter Stewart delivered the opinion of a unanimous Supreme Court. The Court ruled that tribal inherent authority had precedence over a federal delegation of authority. The Navajo tribal court had jurisdiction to punish the tribal member, as the tribal court was held to be an independent forum, not one originating from the Constitution or from the U.S. justice system. Moreover, the tribe had never abandoned its authority to punish tribal members, and the double jeopardy clause did not apply, for the Navajo Nation was a separate sovereign entity.

A member of the Navajo Nation was arrested on October 16, 1974, by tribal police at the Bureau of Indian Affairs High School in Many Farms, Arizona, on the Navajo Reservation. The tribal member was charged with disorderly conduct in violation of Title 17, 351 of the Navajo Tribal Code 1969 and with contributing to the delinquency of a minor in violation of Title 17, 321 of the Navajo Tribal Code 1969. The tribal court sentenced the tribal member to fifteen days in jail or a fine of $30 on the first charge and to sixty days in jail or a fine of $120 on the second; the jail terms were to be served concurrently. Thereafter, on November 19, 1975, the district court for Arizona charged the tribal member with statutory rape. The tribal member filed to remove the charge, stating that the matter had been dealt with in tribal court, that the court was within the remit of federal authority, and that this barred a retrial under the Fifth Amendment. The district court dismissed the indictment, and the Court of Appeals for the Ninth Circuit affirmed.

The U.S. Supreme Court stated that a tribe's authority to punish tribal crimes was a consequence of its inherent or retained sovereignty, not of federal delegation. Inherent sovereignty thus had not been removed by treaty or federal statute and was reconcilable with their dependent status. This affirmation came sixteen days after the ruling in *Oliphant v. Suquamish Indian Tribe* (1978), which categorically revoked the notion of tribal inherent sovereignty. The Supreme Court ruled that the authority of the Navajo to punish its own members in tribal court was founded in treaties and in its inherent sovereignty.

The Court declared that a Navajo decree in tribal court was an act of a separate and independent sovereign and not an extension of the federal justice system. Thus, the Court explicitly stated that a tribal court is wholly separate from the federal system, and opinions by separate sovereigns fail to bar federal prosecution under the double jeopardy clause of the Fifth Amendment.

The ultimate source of authority to try members in tribal court is based on inherent sovereignty and not on federal power. Thus, inherent authority was not created by, and does not arise from, the Constitution of the United States; the tribes' power is extra- and pre-constitutional. Treaties prescribed that tribes retained the right to punish tribal members, and thus tribes have the right to self-government and to law enforcement through criminal procedures. Moreover, *United States v. Wheeler* was the first case since *Talton v. Mayes* (1896) to be based unequivocally on Native American inherent sovereignty. The Supreme Court further declared that Native American tribes were distinguishable from cities, states, federal territories, and nations.

Dewi I. Ball

See also Canyon de Chelly, Arizona; *Oliphant v. Suquamish Indian Tribe,* 1978; Plenary Power; Sovereignty; Treaty; Treaty with the Navajo–June 1, 1868; *United States v. Kagama,* 1886.

References and Further Reading

Canby, William C. 1998. *American Indian Law in a Nutshell*. St. Paul, MN: West.

Wilkins, David E., and K. Tsianina Lomawaima. 2001. *Uneven Ground: American Indian Sovereignty and Federal Law*. Norman: University of Oklahoma Press.

Wilkinson, Charles F. 1987. *American Indians, Time, and the Law: Native Societies in a Modern Constitutional Democracy*. New Haven, CT: Yale University Press.

Hamlet of Baker Lake v. Minister of Indian Affairs and Northern Development (Canada), 1980

This is the first case after *Calder v. Attorney-General of British Columbia* (1973) that confirms the common-law basis of aboriginal title in Canada. In this case, the aboriginal group sought to establish substantive land rights, including aboriginal title, through the courts by identification and confirmation of principles. The case was heard before the Federal Court of Canada Trial Division and involved the Inuit of the Baker Lake area of the Northwest Territories, the federal government of Canada, and several mining companies carrying out mining exploration activities in the area.

The Inuit asserted an existing aboriginal title over an undefined area of the Northwest Territories of Canada, including approximately seventy-eight thousand square kilometers around the community of Baker Lake. Although the government conceded that the Inuit had occupied and used the area since time immemorial, the mining companies disputed the existence of aboriginal title in the contemporary Inuit community or in their ancestors. Both Canada and the mining companies argued that, even if aboriginal title did exist, it had been extinguished either by the Royal Charter of 1670, which granted Rupert's Land to the Hudson's Bay Company, or by subsequent legislation incorporating Rupert's Land into Canada. The Inuit argued that the mining activities were "unlawful invasions" of their rights under Inuit aboriginal title and, in particular, that their right to hunt caribou had been gravely impaired.

Justice Patrick Mahoney held that the Inuit had an occupancy-based aboriginal title to the Baker Lake area and that it was recognized by the common law, subject to legitimate legislative infringements.

He outlined certain elements necessary for the establishment of aboriginal title before the courts: (1) organized society: aboriginal claimants and their ancestors must show that they were members of an organized society; (2) specific territory: the organized society must have occupied the specific territory over which aboriginal title is claimed; (3) exclusivity: the occupation of the specific territory must have been to the exclusion of other organized societies; and (4) factual occupation: the occupation of the specific territory must have been an established fact at the time the British Crown asserted sovereignty over Canada.

The Baker Lake community met all these requirements, and the court confirmed the existence of their aboriginal title. Justice Mahoney concluded, "The fact is that the aboriginal Inuit had an organized society. It was not a society with very elaborate institutions but it was a society organized to exploit the resources available on the barrens [lands west of Hudson Bay] and essential to sustain human life there. That was about all they could do: hunt and fish as their ancestors did." He continued, "[A]t the time England asserted sovereignty over the barren lands west of Hudson Bay, the Inuit were the exclusive occupants of the portion of barren lands extending from the vicinity of Baker Lake north and east toward the Artic and Hudson Bay to the boundaries of the Baker Lake R.C.M.P. detachment area . . . An aboriginal title to that territory, carrying with it the right freely to move about and hunt and fish over it, vested at common law in the Inuit."

The only question that remained was whether aboriginal title had been extinguished, either by the transfer of the lands to the Hudson's Bay Company or by the subsequent admission of Rupert's Land into Canada. Justice Mahoney held that neither had had the effect of extinguishing the Inuit's aboriginal title, because the Crown had not shown clear and plain intention to extinguish aboriginal rights. He explained that, "the extinguishment of their aboriginal title was plainly not in Parliament's mind in 1950. The barren lands were not, for obvious reasons, being opened for settlement and so there was no reason to extinguish the aboriginal title . . . Extinguishment of the Inuit's aboriginal title is not a necessary result of legislation enacted since 1870. The aboriginal title in issue has not been extinguished." The decision was not appealed.

Some of the *Baker Lake* requirements were modified after *Delgamuukw v. British Columbia* (1997). For example, the exclusivity principle is no longer so strict. More than one aboriginal group may occupy the same territory, in which case they may be able to establish shared exclusive occupancy, allowing joint title to the land to the exclusion of all other groups.

Although compensation was not sought by the Inuit in this case, Justice Mahoney did indicate that aboriginal peoples may be entitled to compensation where mining laws, used to grant private companies permits to undertake exploration activities on aboriginal lands, diminish aboriginal rights. This was also an indication of how aboriginal title and aboriginal rights may coexist with settlement or development by nonaboriginal peoples.

Özlem Ülgen

See also Aboriginal Title; Canada; Canadian Indian Treaties; *Calder v. Attorney-General of British Columbia* (Canada), 1973; *Delgamuukw v. British Columbia* (Canada), 1997; Inuit.

References and Further Reading

Asch, Mark, ed. 1997. *Aboriginal and Treaty Rights in Canada: Essays on Law, Equality and Respect for Difference.* Vancouver: University of British Columbia Press.

Borrows, J. 1997. "Frozen Rights in Canada: Constitutional Interpretation and the Trickster," 22 *American Indian Law Review* 37.

Hamlet of Baker Lake v. Minister of Indian Affairs and Northern Development. 1980. 1 F.C. 518.

Maine Indian Claims Settlement Act of 1980

The Maine Indian Claims Settlement Act of 1980 (MICSA), signed into law by President Jimmy Carter on October 10, 1980, was the largest Indian claim and the first to include provisions for land reacquisition. Proclaimed by many at the time as a success story for the Wabanaki peoples of Maine, this controversial settlement has ignited debates about tribal sovereignty versus state jurisdiction in land use, tribal courts, environmental protection and enforcement, and educational funding. *Wabanaki* is an all-inclusive term that refers to the easternmost confederation of tribes, which consists of the Penobscot, Passamaquoddy, Maliseet, and Mi'kmaq. Although MICSA recognized aboriginal claim to 60 percent of Maine, or 12.5 million acres with 350,000 people, it extinguished aboriginal title to that land and compensated the Passamaquoddy tribe, the Penobscot Nation, and the Houlton band of Maliseet with $81.5

President Jimmy Carter signs the 1980 Maine Indian Claims Settlement Act, using an eagle feather from the Penobscot Nation as Maine state officials and members of the nation look on. (Steve Cartwright/Wabanaki Alliance)

million (American Friends Service Committee [AFSC] 1989, D-98–D-102).

Although tribal land claims in Maine surfaced in the 1940s, the settlement originated in 1957, when Passamaquoddy leader John Stevens discovered a copy of the tribe's 1794 treaty with Massachusetts that clearly defined reservation lands, including the twenty-three-thousand-acre Indian Township, the largest reservation in New England. In 1964, when William Plaisted, a non-Indian Princeton resident, added to his previously acquired reservation land from a poker game and began to build summer cabins, tribal members from Indian Township staged a peaceful sit-in to halt construction efforts. This incident raised awareness of more than six thousand acres of Indian land that were alienated from tribal ownership. In 1968, the tribe filed a lawsuit against Massachusetts asking $150 million in damages. After several delays, the Passamaquoddy tribe filed suit in federal district court against the U.S. Department of the Interior. In *Passamaquoddy v. Morton* (1975), the court recognized that the Passamaquoddy tribe and

the Penobscot Nation had title to federal services provided to other Indian tribes and that Maine possessed no authority to interfere with tribal government (Brodeur 1985, 69–141; Ghere 1984, 249).

Attorney Thomas N. Tureen argued that the Trade and Intercourse Act of 1790, which stipulated that Congress must approve the purchase of Indian land, applied to Maine and that, therefore, several treaties between Wabanaki people and Massachusetts and Maine were invalid (Brodeur 1985, 82; O'Toole & Tureen 1971, 1–39; for treaties, see Deloria & DeMallie 1999, 1094–1095). During the settlement negotiation, Wabanaki peoples experienced a harsh backlash from Maine citizens. After years of negotiation, the Maine Indian Claims Settlement Act of 1980, which was settled outside of court, acknowledged that the Trade and Intercourse Act of 1790 applied to Maine and that almost two-thirds of the state was Indian land. From the $81.5 million compensated to the tribes, $54.5 million, of which the Penobscot and Passamaquoddy each received $26.8 million, permitted each of the two tribes to purchase one hundred fifty-thousand acres of unorganized territory in Maine, to be held in trust with the federal government. A trust fund of the remaining $27 million was divided between the Penobscot and Passamaquoddy, and each tribe would invest $1 million for their elders. After MICSA's passage, the two tribes chose different ways to utilize the settlement funds. Whereas the Passamaquoddy turned their attention to economic development, the Penobscot focused on land acquisition (AFSC 1989, B-142–B-160, D-101–D-102; U.S. Congress 1980).

The Association of Aroostook Indians achieved the inclusion of the Houlton band of Maliseet in MICSA. During the claims negotiation in 1979, the Maliseet, whose homeland encompasses the valley of the Saint John River and its tributaries, protested that the Penobscot claims overlapped with their family hunting territory near Houlton, Maine. MICSA provided $900,000 to finance the purchase of a five-thousand-acre reservation but did not include trust money for the Maliseet (U.S. Congress 1980; Wherry 1981, 10–11). MICSA excluded the Mi'kmaq of Maine, who later received federal recognition by the 1991 Aroostook Band of Micmac Settlement Act. It established the same compensation for the Maliseet in MICSA and provided a $50,000 property fund (Prins 1996, 7–17, 213–214).

Although the tribes as a whole maintain mixed feelings about what MICSA has brought to them, individual family members tend to make decisions based first and foremost on the needs of their families. Per capita payments distributed to tribal members were thought to be a forced acceptance of the agreement. Therefore, some tribal opponents of the settlement refused to accept the payments. Critics of the settlement felt that it did not respect Wabanaki tribes as sovereign people and reduced reservations' status to that of municipalities. MICSA's language is subject to interpretation, and the act's ambiguity on several key points seems to have obscured the settlement's meaning for some tribal voters. Other tribal people viewed the act as a step toward self-determination and believe that the settlement's outcome was unforeseeable.

MICSA created the Maine Implementing Act (MIA), enacted by the Maine legislature, to define the tribal-state relationship by establishing specific laws concerning Wabanaki peoples and Indian land. The MIA formed the Maine Indian Tribal-State Commission (MITSC) to serve as a mediator between Wabanaki communities and Maine. Composed of state officials, tribal leaders, and appointed members, MITSC strives to cultivate a tribal-state relationship "based on open communications and mutual respect" (MITSC 1997, 13–15). Tribal governments do not interpret MICSA as a limitation of sovereign rights. Although some tribal people have expressed concern over the commission, MITSC continues the legacy of the Wabanaki peoples' unique relationship with Maine.

Micah Pawling and John Bear Mitchell

See also Aboriginal Title; Government-to-Government Relationship; Nonrecognized Tribes; Sovereignty; Trust Land.

References and Further Reading

American Friends Service Committee. 1989. *The Wabanakis of Maine and the Maritimes: A Resource Book about Penobscot, Passamaquoddy, Maliseet, Micmacs, and Abenaki Indians.* Bath, ME: Maine Indian Program.

Brodeur, Paul. 1985. *Restitution: The Land Claims of the Mashpee, Passamaquoddy, and Penobscot Indians of New England.* With afterword by Thomas N. Tureen. Boston: Northeastern University Press.

Deloria, Vine, Jr., and Raymond J. DeMallie, ed. 1999. "Treaty Between the Penobscot and Massachusetts, August 8, 1796." *Documents of American Indian Diplomacy: Treaties, Agreements, and Conventions, 1775–1979,* vol. 2, 1094–1095. Norman: University of Oklahoma Press.

Ghere, David L. 1984. "Assimilation, Termination, or Tribal Rejuvenation: Maine Indian Affairs in the 1950s." *Maine Historical Society Quarterly,* 24(2): 239–264.

Maine Indian Claims Settlement. 1979. Title 30, Chapter 601. Accessed July 11, 2007, at http://janus.state.me.us/legis/statutes/30/title 30ch601.pdf.

Maine Indian Tribal-State Commission. January 17, 1997. "At Loggerheads: The State of Maine and the Wabanaki." Maine Indian Tribal-State Commission. Accessed July 11, 2007, at http://www.mitsc.org.

O'Toole, Francis J., and Thomas N. Tureen. 1971. "State Power and the Passamaquoddy Tribe: A Gross National Hypocrisy?" *Maine Law Review* 23(1): 1–39.

Prins, Harald E. L. 1996. *The Mi'kmaq: Resistance, Accommodation, and Cultural Survival.* Fort Worth, TX: Harcourt Brace.

U.S. Congress. 1980. "Maine Indian Claims Settlement and Land Acquisition Funds in the U.S. Treasury." US Code, Title 25, Chapter 19, Subchapter II, 1724. Accessed July 11, 2007, at http://www.law.cornell.edu/uscode/html/ uscode25/usc_sec_25_00001724———000-.html.

United States v. Sioux Nation, 1980

Although for Indians it was a legal victory that upheld compensable property interests, the *Sioux Nation* case may be considered a Pyrrhic victory at best. At issue in the case was the Native American claim to the Black Hills of South Dakota and the uncompensated confiscation of the Black Hills by the U.S. government. The legal basis for the claim rested in a 112-year-old treaty.

The Treaty of Fort Laramie in 1868 was concluded at the culmination of the Powder River Wars, a series of military engagements between the U.S. Army and various Sioux tribes led by Red Cloud. Article 2 of the treaty established the Great Sioux Reservation, including the Black Hills, for exclusive occupation and use by the Indians. And Article 12 mandated that no subsequent treaty could cede any of the land reserved unless it was approved by three-fourths of all the adult Sioux males occupying the land.

However, gold was discovered in the Black Hills six years later, and pressure became intense to open the areas reserved for the Sioux to exploration and mining. Frustrated by the refusal of the Sioux to accept the government's offer of $6 million or an annual rental of $400,000 for the Black Hills, the secretary of the interior classified those who had temporarily left the reservation to hunt as "hostile" and turned management of the Sioux over to the War Department. The army's campaign against the Indians culminated in the slaughter of General Custer's 7th Cavalry detachment at Little Big Horn by Sitting Bull's warriors, which in turn led to inevitable victory by the army and return to the reservation by the Sioux.

In August 1876, Congress attempted to force the issue by enacting an appropriations measure withholding subsistence funds to the Sioux, who were by that time dependent on the government, unless they ceded the Black Hills. A federal commissioner was dispatched to secure this trade, and another treaty was presented to the Sioux and signed by 10 percent of the adult males—far short of the three-fourths required by Article 12 of the Fort Laramie treaty. Nevertheless, Congress passed the 1877 act implementing the new agreement, thereby legitimizing settlement of the Black Hills by non-Indians.

Before the 1980 Supreme Court case, the Sioux Nation sought twice to secure compensation for Congress's taking of the Black Hills. In 1920, a special jurisdictional act allowed the Sioux to take their case to the court of claims; however, that case was dismissed in 1942 as representing merely an uncompensable moral, rather than legal, claim. Four years later, upon establishment of the Indian Claims Commission, the Sioux brought their case again, and the commission found that the 1877 act had constituted a taking of property that required compensation under the Fifth Amendment. The commission ruled that the Indians were entitled to $17.5 million for the land and gold taken. But the court of claims overturned this ruling on appeal, holding that the case had been decided in 1942 and could not be brought again.

In 1978, Congress enacted a law removing the *res judicata* bar—allowing the Sioux's case to move forward. Subsequently, the court of claims agreed with the commission's finding and determined that the tribe was entitled to the principle sum with 5 percent annual interest, to be calculated from 1877. Justice Harry Blackmun, writing for the majority of the Supreme Court, agreed in its 1980 review of the case, holding the government's good-faith defense when dealing with the Indians insufficient to bar an inquiry into the factual circumstances surrounding the taking of Indian lands.

In a vigorous dissent, Justice William Rehnquist emphasized the culpability of the Sioux, which he said received scant attention in the majority's factual inquiry and which had been equal to that of the government in the 1870s. Quoting white settlers' accounts of Indian savagery against them in the Black Hills, Rehnquist also warned against judging past events by the light of current revisionist historians.

Although the Supreme Court's *Sioux Nation* decision found a compensable taking for land confiscated subject to recognized Indian title, the ruling in the *Tee-Hit-Ton* case, which found no compensable taking for land confiscated subject to unrecognized aboriginal title, still stands. Although the *Sioux Nation* case accords the tribe a legal right to compensation for the Black Hills, the Sioux have consistently refused to accept their money—holding out their wish to get the land back instead. Thus, the Black Hills claim remains unresolved.

Michael J. Kelly

See also Fort Laramie, Wyoming; *Lone Wolf v. Hitchcock*, 1903; Red Cloud (Makhpiya-Luta);

Tee-Hit-Ton Indians v. United States, 1955; Treaty with the Northern Cheyenne and Northern Arapaho–May 10, 1868.

References and Further Reading

LaVelle, John P. 2001. "Rescuing Paha Sapa: Achieving Environmental Justice by Restoring the Great Grasslands and Returning the Sacred Black Hills to the Great Sioux Nation." *Great Plains Natural Resources Journal* 5: 40–101.

New Holy, Alexandra. 1998. "The Heart of Everything That Is: Paha Sapa, Treaties, and Lakota Identity." *Oklahoma City University Law Review* 23: 317–352.

Fixico, Donald L. 1998. *The Invasion of Indian Country in the Twentieth Century: American Capitalism and Tribal Natural Resources.* Niwot, CO: University Press of Colorado.

Lazarus, Edward. 1991. *Black Hills/White Justice: The Sioux Nation Versus the United States, 1775 to the Present.* HarperCollins.

United States v. Sioux Nation of Indians, 448 U.S. 371 (1980).

Constitution Act (Canada), 1982

Canada ceased to be a colony of Britain in 1931, but it was not a truly independent country before 1982, when Canada "repatriated" its constitution from Great Britain. Before 1982, the Canadian constitution was a British statute and subservient to the British Parliament. The Constitution of 1982 contained, for the first time, a Charter of Rights (similar to the U.S. Bill of Rights) and a recognition of the rights of aboriginal people.

Section 35, paragraph 1 of the Constitution states, "The existing aboriginal and treaty rights of the aboriginal peoples of Canada are hereby recognized and affirmed." The second paragraph defines *aboriginal* as including "Indian, Inuit, and Métis peoples of Canada."

In Canada, Indian people are usually referred to as First Nations people. Also, the term *Eskimo* is no longer an acceptable characterization of the indigenous peoples of the Far North, who prefer to be referred to as the Inuit. The Métis are the third group of aboriginal people recognized by the Canadian constitution; loosely translated, *métis* means simply "mixed-blood" and is used to designate the descendants of intermarried indigenous and European peoples, but only if those peoples can demonstrate that theirs is a culture that is distinct from that of mainstream Canada.

There was some debate in Canada over the characterization of the Métis as aboriginal people, which was most often used to describe the people indigenous to the continent before European contact. The Canadian Supreme Court answered this question in 2003 when it ruled in favor of two Métis men from Sault Ste. Marie, Steve and Roddy Powley (father and son) who were arrested for killing a moose "out of season." The Powleys claimed an aboriginal right under the constitution to hunt for subsistence; the Court upheld that right but ruled that it applied only to the Métis in the Sault Ste. Marie area. Other Métis groups would have to seek to define their own set of "aboriginal rights" in the courts.

Others have been doing exactly that. In a very important case for aboriginal peoples in the Maritimes, the Canadian Supreme Court recognized an aboriginal right to access the area's natural resources to "secure a moderate living." The case centered around Donald Marshall, a Mi'kmaq, who was arrested for catching eels "out of season" and without a license. Marshall claimed that a 1760 treaty with the British granted him such a right and that the constitution guaranteed that right. In a 1999 decision, the Canadian Supreme Court agreed. The *Marshall* case, as it has come to be known, set the stage for another constitutional challenge when Joshua Bernard, another Mi'kmaq man, was arrested for harvesting logs from Crown land in New Brunswick. Although his rights have been upheld in New Brunswick's highest court, the province appealed to the Canadian Supreme Court, which ruled in July 2005, that commercial logging could not be seen as an extension of the trading in which aboriginal people engaged before European contact, a right that was upheld in the *Marshall* case.

The *Bernard* case, while standing somewhat in contradiction to *Marshall* (as they both claimed rights under the same treaty of 1760), reflects an earlier (2001) case in which the Canadian Supreme Court also failed to recognize aboriginal rights that were upheld in the lower courts. In this earlier "pre-contact trade case," the Court denied Chief Mike Mitchell and other Mohawks of the Akwesasne Reserve—which straddles the U.S.-Canada border where New York, Ontario, and Quebec meet—a claimed aboriginal right to bring personal goods into Canada without paying a duty for those goods.

In the *Mitchell* case, the claim of an aboriginal right to "import" (for trade and personal use) goods duty-free was upheld by the lower courts, but the

Canadian Supreme Court, while agreeing that the Mohawks had this specific aboriginal right, determined that the granting of duty-free importation of goods to the Mohawks of Akwesasne would abrogate the sovereign right of the Canadian government to impose duties on imported goods. This was something the Court could not do, regardless of the validity of the "recognized and affirmed" rights of the Mohawks.

According to some analysts, the *Mitchell* and *Bernard* cases "recognize and affirm" only those aboriginal rights that can be shown to be subservient to the rights that the Canadian government has derogated unto itself, making a mockery of those rights that the indigenous people freely exercised before the arrival of Europeans, rights seemingly guaranteed to them in Section 35 (1) of the Canadian constitution.

Phil Bellfy

See also Métis; Sault Ste. Marie, Michigan and Ontario; Sovereignty; Treaty; Trust.

References and Further Reading

Asch, Michael. 1984. *Home and Native Land: Aboriginal Rights and the Canadian Constitution.* Toronto: Methuen.

Cardinal, Harold. 1977. *The Rebirth of Canada's Indians.* Edmonton: Hurtig.

Dickason, Olive Patricia. 1992. *Canada's First Nations: A History of Founding Peoples from Earliest Times.* Norman: University of Oklahoma Press.

Morse, Bradford, ed. 1985. *Aboriginal Peoples and the Law: Indian, Métis and Inuit Rights in Canada.* Ottawa: Carleton University Press; Don Mills, ON: distributed by Oxford University Press.

Lac Courte Oreilles Band of Chippewa Indians v. Voigt et al., 1983

Lac Courte Oreilles Band of Chippewa Indians v. Voigt et al. is a landmark 1983 federal appeals court decision that affirmed the treaty rights of six bands of Wisconsin Chippewa (hereafter Wisconsin Ojibwe) to hunt, fish, and gather on off-reservation public lands in the territories they ceded to the United States in the treaties of 1837 and 1842. Often referred to as the Voigt Decision, this legal controversy between the state of Wisconsin, the Lac Courte Oreilles, and five other Wisconsin Ojibwe bands began in 1974, when two brothers from the Lac Courte Oreille Ojibwe band were arrested by the Wisconsin Department of

Natural Resources for illegally fishing outside the borders of their northern Wisconsin reservation. The two brothers, Fred and Mike Tribble, deliberately challenged the state's authority to regulate their off-reservation hunting and fishing. In 1978, a federal district court found that the tribe had relinquished its off-reservation treaty rights when it accepted a reservation in the treaty of 1854 with the United States. The appellate court reversed this decision, finding that, when the Ojibwe negotiated treaties with the United States in 1837 and 1842, they understood that their off-reservation usufructuary rights would be relinquished only if they harassed non-Indian settlers. The court found no evidence that the Ojibwe had not lived up to their side of the treaty bargain. The judges determined that the tribe's treaty rights had not been extinguished by the treaty of 1854 between the Ojibwe and the United States or by a presidential removal order of 1850. The court ruled that the removal order, which required the Ojibwe to vacate their Wisconsin homelands, was illegal and that there had been no explicit language in the treaty of 1854 terminating the tribe's treaty rights. The U.S. Supreme Court denied Wisconsin's appeal of this decision.

Following the Supreme Court's refusal to hear the state's appeal, the appellate court ordered the district court to define the nature of the treaty right and the ability of the state to regulate the exercise of the treaty right. From 1984 to 1991, the district court issued a series of decisions on the nature of the treaty right. Based on an examination of the historical record, the court ruled that the Ojibwe could harvest a large variety of plants and animals on public lands in the ceded territory, using any methods and technologies available at the time of the treaties or developed since that time. The treaty harvest could be used for subsistence, or the harvest could be traded and sold to non-Indians. The court ruled that, if the Ojibwe enacted their own hunting, fishing, and gathering rules in accordance with court decisions, then the state could not regulate Ojibwe hunters and fishers off reservation. In accordance with this ruling, the Ojibwe established a natural resource organization called the Great Lakes Indian Fish and Wildlife Commission. Other district court decisions determined the harvest levels of fish and white-tailed deer on lakes and public lands of the ceded territory. The court ruled that the treaty right did not involve a right to harvest commercial timber and that sovereign immunity protected the state from Ojibwe claims for millions of dollars compensation for the loss of their treaty rights from the 1880s until 1983.

In reaction to the Voigt Decision and the Ojibwe exercise of their off-reservation treaty rights, anti-Indian treaty rights groups emerged in northern Wisconsin during the 1980s. Groups such as Equal Rights for Everyone, Protect American's Right and Resources, and Stop Treaty Abuse organized large, sometimes violent protests at the off-reservation boat landings where Ojibwe spearfishers launched their boats during their spring spearfishing season. The organized protests ended in the early 1990s, and today the Ojibwe exercise their treaty rights in a relatively quiet and routine manner. In the spring of 2003, the Wisconsin Ojibwe spear-fished 27,522 walleye from 175 ceded territory lakes. They also speared 220 muskellunge. In 2002, they harvested 1,019 white-tailed deer. In addition to their harvest of game fish and deer, the Ojibwe harvest bear, fur-bearing animals, waterfowl, turkey, various wild plants, maple syrup, firewood, and balsam.

Steven E. Silvern

See also Great Lakes Indian Fish and Wildlife Commission; Reserved Rights Doctrine.

References and Further Reading

Bressett, Walter, and Rick Whaley. 1994. *Walleye Warriors: An Effective Alliance Against Racism and for the Earth.* Philadephia: New Society.

Lac Courte Oreilles Band of Chippewa Indians et al. v. Lester P. Voigt et al. 1983. 700 F. 2d 365.

Satz, Ronald. 1991. "Chippewa Treaty Rights: The Reserved Rights of Wisconsin's Chippewa Indians in Historical Perspective." *Transactions, Wisconsin Academy of Sciences, Arts and Letters,* 79(1).

Silvern, Steven. 1999. "Scales of Justice: Law, American Indian Treaty Rights, and the Political Construction of Scale." *Political Geography* 18(6): 639–668.

United States v. Dion, 1986

The 1986 Supreme Court decision in *United States v. Dion* stands for the proposition that American Indians may continue to rely on rights secured to them in treaties with the United States, even if those rights were secured two hundred years ago, unless there is clear evidence that Congress actually considered the right implicated in the treaty and affirmatively chose to abrogate that portion of the treaty with a later statute.

The defendant in this case, a member of the Yankton Sioux tribe, was convicted for shooting four bald eagles on the reservation, in violation of the Endangered Species Act and the Eagle Protection Act. The defendant relied on a treaty in 1858 between the Yankton Sioux and the United States which ceded all but four hundred thousand acres of land to the United States and removed the Yankton to a reservation in exchange for the federal government's guarantee of the Indians' continued quiet and undisturbed possession of their reserved land and an annual stipend. No restriction was placed on hunting rights of the Yankton Indians, and all parties to the litigation agreed that the treaty vested an exclusive right in them to hunt and fish on their land.

However, Justice Thurgood Marshall, writing for the majority, did not accept the view that prior treaty rights were impervious to later statutory abrogation. After noting that statutes and treaties are coequal articulations of federal law under Article VI of the Constitution and that, in general, the later in time controls, Justice Marshall explained that, in special regard to Indian treaties (as opposed to foreign treaties), a higher standard of subsequent statutory abrogation is required. Specifically, Congress's intent to abrogate Indian treaty rights must be clear and plain, although it need not be expressly stated in the statutory language itself. "What is essential is clear evidence that Congress actually considered the conflict between its intended action on the one hand and Indian treaty rights on the other, and chose to resolve that conflict by abrogating the treaty" (*U.S. v. Dion* 1986).

The Eagle Protection Act of 1962 establishes a blanket prohibition on killing bald eagles, making such action a federal crime. However, the act also contains an elaborate permitting scheme, whereby American Indians can apply to the Department of the Interior for a permit to take bald eagles for religious purposes. The secretary of the interior may issue such permits on a discretionary basis. Absent such a permit, the taking of a protected eagle by an American Indian, even for an ostensibly religious purpose, remains illegal.

The Court found that the existence of this permitting scheme in the act was itself clear evidence that Congress believed that it was abrogating Indian treaty rights to take eagles and that the scheme was designed to solve the problem of the act's application to Indians. The Court also decided that, because the Endangered Species Act of 1972 was silent regarding Indian hunting rights but prohibited exactly the same conduct for the same reasons, it did not need to be analyzed but in fact worked together with the Eagle Protection Act to abrogate the earlier Indian treaty rights to take bald eagles.

Thus, the Court concluded, "Dion here asserts a treaty right to engage in precisely the conduct that Congress, overriding Indian treaty rights, made criminal in the Eagle Protection Act. Dion's treaty shield for that conduct, we hold, was removed by that statute, and Congress' failure to discuss that shield in the context of the Endangered Species Act did not revive that treaty right" *(U.S. v. Dion* 1986).

Seven years later, in *United States v. Bourland,* Justice Clarence Thomas, writing for the majority, used the standard in *Dion* to conclude that Congress had abrogated the Cheyenne River Sioux tribe's original treaty rights to regulate hunting and fishing by non-Indians on Indian land when those lands were essentially taken for a federal water project under the Flood Control Act—which provided for general recreational use of the water bodies by the public. Justice Thomas's reasoning was that hunting and fishing were recreational uses and, therefore, Congress intended non-Indians to avail themselves of that use equally with Indians.

Justices Harry Blackmun and David Souter vigorously dissented, accusing the majority of misapplying the *Dion* standard and pointing to a clear lack of evidence that Congress had considered the conflicting treaty rights and decided to abrogate them. Consequently, although the correct interpretation of the *Dion* standard remains in doubt (narrow or broad), judges continue to find the basic premise of its test useful.

Michael J. Kelly

See also Plenary Power; Treaty.
References and Further Reading
 Diekemper, Tracy A. 1995. "Abrogating Treaty Rights Under the Dion Test: Upholding Traditional Notions that Indian Treaties Are the Supreme Law of the Land." *University of Oregon Journal of Environmental Law & Litigation* 10: 473–497.
South Dakota v. Bourland, 508 U.S. 679 (1993).
United States v. Dion, 476 U.S. 734 (1986).

Indian Gaming Regulatory Act, 1988

In October 1988, President Ronald Reagan signed into a law the Indian Gaming Regulatory Act (IGRA). Although many observers believe that IGRA granted Native nations new rights and unfair advantages, in fact the act constrained their sovereignty as it introduced novel regulatory schemes. The legislation responded to the *Cabazon* decision, which allowed tribes to operate card games, and it became the foundation of IGRA.

Gambling has ancient roots in Native America, serving important economic, social, and recreational functions in many communities. During the more than five hundred years in which Native Americans have interacted first with Europeans and later with European Americans, non-Native religious and political leaders have looked down upon indigenous games of chance. Gradually, in response to dwindling federal funding during the second half of the twentieth century, some American Indian tribes began to conceive of gambling as a means of economic development and social survival. They turned first to such games as bingo and later experimented with cards, lotteries, and parimutuel. Although these developments were small-scale and varied among tribes, they often conflicted with state laws and put Native American operations into competition with an increasingly lucrative gaming industry. Consequently, attorneys general and legislators worked to curtail Indian operations, despite the fact that such efforts ran contrary to established roles and relationships between states and tribes. Court decisions in the late 1970s and early 1980s did little to ease the rising tensions, affirming the capacity of tribes to establish gaming while prompting states to seek more favorable federal intervention.

In the early 1980s, Congress began to formulate a legislative compromise, emphasizing initially the control of tribal operations. After years of debate and lobbying, IGRA was passed, which displeased states, tribes, and the gaming industry precisely because it sought to balance competing interests.

IGRA envisioned gambling as a promising opportunity that would at once encourage "economic development, self-sufficiency, and strong tribal government." The act endeavored to make tribal communities the primary beneficiaries of gambling enterprises. It instructed that revenues be spent on public services, charitable endeavors, or per capita distributions. The act also contained provisions to protect tribal gaming from organized crime. It created the National Indian Gaming Commission (NIGC) to oversee the implementation of its intricate rules and ambitious objectives.

Casino advertising on the Morongo Indian Reservation, near Cabazon, California. In 1987, California v. Cabazon Band of Mission Indians *led to the Indian Gaming Regulatory Act. (Bob Rowan; Progressive Image/Corbis)*

IGRA outlined three types of gambling that required distinct forms of regulation. Class I games, or traditional games played in association with social and ceremonial occasions for prizes of limited value, fell under the exclusive jurisdiction of tribal governments. Class II games included bingo, lotto, and related games of chance and were controlled by the tribes and the NIGC. Class III gaming, or casino gaming, included slot machines and table games and were subject to joint tribal and state regulation, provided that a tribal government could negotiate a compact with a state government granting them permission for such operations. If states balked, tribes could sue them in federal court, compelling them to participate in negotiations in good faith or submit to mediation.

The compromises central to IGRA, particularly its efforts to balance states' rights and sovereignty, diminished the capacity of tribal government to exercise self-rule. In fact, in many ways IGRA asserts that indigenous claims to dominion and self-determination were less significant than the claims advanced by individual states. Furthermore, it affirmed a long paternalist tradition that renders tribes dependents and wards of the state rather than independent, equal, and empowered nations.

In the wake of IGRA, gambling has become an increasingly powerful force in Indian country and American culture. It has fostered the establishment of numerous gaming operations, encouraging economic development and cultural preservation. It has also exacerbated social problems while contributing to anti-Indian sentiments. Moreover, IGRA has diminished tribal sovereignty. On the one hand, the act has furthered popular resentment toward and misunderstandings of sovereignty, in which the act is seen as an entitlement that gives Native Americans unfair advantages and inappropriate rights not available to all Americans. On the other hand, judicial decisions have undermined the tribal rights even more. In 1996, the Supreme Court, in a five-to-four decision, ruled that tribes could not sue states in court, limiting the capacity of tribes to compel states to open compact negotiations to appeals to the secretary of the interior, while granting states the ability to override tribal decisions and desires. In a very real sense, IGRA typifies recent policy shifts that both affirm the reality of sovereignty but work to limit it.

C. Richard King

See also Sovereignty; Statutes as Sources of Modern Indian Rights: Child Welfare, Gaming, and Repatriation; Treaty; Trust Doctrine; Trust Responsibility.

References and Further Reading

Eadington, William R., ed. *Indian Gaming and the Law.* Reno, NV: Institute for the Study of Gambling and Commercial Gaming.

Light, Steven Andrew, and Kathryn R. L. Rand. 2005. *Indian Gaming and Tribal Sovereignty: The Casino Compromise.* Lawrence: University Press of Kansas.

Mason, W. Dale. 2000. *Indian Gaming: Tribal Sovereignty and American Politics.* Norman: University of Oklahoma Press.

Native American Graves and Repatriation Act, 1990

Thousands of American Indian human remains and funerary objects passed into the collections of non-Indian museums and federal agencies during the course of America's westward expansion. Much of that assemblage occurred pursuant to looting and grave desecration. Native Americans, in general, accord great spiritual significance to the bones of their ancestors; consequently, efforts were made during the height of the Indian rights movement in the 1980s to reclaim this lost heritage. The Native American Graves and Repatriation Act of 1990 (NAGPRA) was the culmination of the Phoenix Dialogue, a series of discussions among Native Americans, museum officials, anthropologists, antiquities dealers, and government agencies that sought to restore American Indian skeletons and burial objects to their respective tribes for reinternment.

NAGPRA, therefore, mandates return of these items to culturally affiliated tribes, whether the items exist in federally funded museums or government agencies or are newly discovered on federal or tribal land. Museums and agencies are tasked with cataloging, identifying, and then repatriating the human remains and funeral objects in their holdings. Moreover, remains and objects newly uncovered—for instance, due to new construction or inadvertent discovery—must be identified and repatriated as well.

Penalties for noncompliance are severe. Those who knowingly traffic (sell, purchase, use for profit, or transport for sale or profit) in Indian human remains or cultural items can be fined and imprisoned for up to a year. Subsequent violations carry prison terms up to five years. The penal provisions of NAGPRA have been upheld against individual traders by federal courts.

Until 1996, NAGPRA encountered very little resistance from the scientific community in either its terms or application. Most human remains and burial items were only a couple of centuries old, were easily traceable to living lineal descendants as grandparents or great grandparents or their personal items, and could be returned and reburied in a respectful manner. However, a discovery in that year on the banks of the Columbia River in Kennewick, Washington, changed this dynamic.

A skeleton recovered there by local anthropologist Jim Chatters was first analyzed under direction of the county medical examiner according to the assumption that it was a one-hundred-and-fifty-year-old white pioneer—due to the skull's distinctive Caucasoid, rather than Native American, physical traits. Then, Chatters found a stone spear point embedded in the pelvis. This raised the issue of age. Carbon dating determined that Kennewick Man, as he came to be known, was actually 9,300 years old. Consequently, the new question became, What was a person with Caucasoid physical traits doing in that part of North America almost ten thousand years ago?

The scientific community very much wanted this question answered. However, the Native American community did not, and they had NAGPRA on their side. Because Kennewick Man was discovered on aboriginally occupied land (areas historically occupied by Indians), a coalition of local tribes led by the Umatilla Indians were able to lay claim to the bones under NAGPRA. The federal government, which had custody of the skeleton because it was found in a navigable waterway, complied and agreed to turn over the remains for reburial.

Acting quickly to forestall this loss to science, a group of eight anthropologists filed suit in Oregon's federal district court to enjoin the government's handover. After six years of legal wrangling, the judge overturned an administrative decision by Interior Secretary Bruce Babbitt affirming the earlier agency decision to repatriate the bones based on the oral history of the local tribes—that they had occupied that land forever, and therefore this must be one of their ancestors, regardless of his physical characteristics.

The judge's decision allowing the scientists to study the remains before repatriation, however, was stayed pending appeal of the case to the Ninth Circuit Court of Appeals. That case is unresolved as of this writing, and the status of Kennewick Man remains in limbo. For American Indians, the spiritual importance of returning their ancestors to the ground, no matter how far removed, cannot be overstated. Neither can one casually undermine science's ability to use such remains to unlock ancient mysteries of the peopling of North America.

NAGPRA fails to resolve this inherent conflict in its application to ancient remains, and it offers little concrete guidance to federal judges whose task it is to arrive at a just solution. Nevertheless, NAGPRA continues to be regarded as successful when applied to relatively recent human remains and funeral objects.

Michael J. Kelly

See also American Indian Movement (AIM); Federally Recognized Tribes; Indian Country; Supremacy Clause.

References and Further Reading
Bonnichsen v. United States, 217 F. Supp. 2d 1116 (Dist. Ct. Or. 2002).
Kelly, Michael J. 1999. "A Skeleton in the Legal Closet: The Discovery of 'Kennewick Man' Crystalizes the Debate over Federal Law Governing Disposal of Ancient Human Remains." *University of Hawaii Law Review* 21: 41–67.
Ragsdale, John W. 2001. "Some Philosophical, Political and Legal Implications of American Archeological and Anthropological Theory." *UMKC Law Review* 70: 1–53.
United States v. Corrow, 941 F. Supp. 1553 (Dist. Ct. N.M. 1996).
United States v. Kramer, 168 F.3d 1196 (10th Cir. 1999).

Self-Government Agreements (Canada)

Beginning in 1993, the government of Canada negotiated and established for the first time constitutionally protected self-government treaties with several of Canada's First Nations, treaties that affirmed the right of these aboriginal groups to govern themselves and restored to them the power to pass laws and make decisions on issues that were internal and integral to these culturally distinct communities.

For thousands of years prior to European settlement, Canada's aboriginal peoples practiced their own forms of government. However, with the arrival of European settlers to the continent, everything changed. Assimilationist colonial policy, aimed at integrating Canada's First Nations into Canadian colonial society, contributed to the erosion of aboriginal governments and placed aboriginals under the rule of colonial governments. Historic agreements such as the Numbered Treaties and the Indian Act (1867) denied sovereignty and self-government to Canada's aboriginal peoples.

Though there has always been opposition from both aboriginal and nonaboriginal peoples to the state's denial of aboriginal sovereignty, the post–World War II period in Canada was marked by intense struggle for aboriginal self-government. The postwar period saw renewed emphasis on technological, ecological, and infrastructural development in Canada. In many instances, these attempts to develop the nation placed the government in direct conflict with groups of aboriginal peoples who demanded recognition of their rights to land and title as well as sovereignty and self-government. Although the right to self-government was regularly denied to aboriginal peoples across the country, a few self-government agreements were approved. These include those for the Cree, Nakaspi, and Inuit of Northern Quebec under the James Bay and Northern Quebec Agreement (1975) and the Northeastern Quebec Agreement (1978); the Sechelt Indian Band of British Columbia under the Sechelt Indian Band Self-Government Act (1986); and the seven Yukon First Nations under the Final Umbrella Agreement of 1993.

Importantly, none of these self-government treaties was explicitly covered by Section 35 of the Constitutional Act, 1982, the section pertaining to the rights of aboriginal peoples in Canada. In 1995, on the basis of promises made during the 1993 election campaign, the governing Liberal party established the Inherent Right to Self-Government policy, which affirmed that the right to sovereignty and self-government was, indeed, an existing right within Section 35 of the Constitution Act. The policy determined that Canada's aboriginal peoples were to be given authority and/or jurisdiction in all matters considered internal and integral to aboriginal groups, and any matters deemed essential to maintaining these aboriginal governing bodies. Aboriginal governments, however, would not be granted sovereignty in the sense of sovereign independent states; they would work in conjunction with the government of Canada, which would continue to assume jurisdiction over matters pertaining to Canadian sovereignty, defense, external relations, and anything considered to be a national matter. Ideally, self-government agreements would be negotiated in relation to land claims and would involve the participation of both federal and provincial governments and aboriginal peoples, and each of them would contribute financially to the negotiated aboriginal governments. This policy was important because it clearly defined self-government as a constitutionally protected right of aboriginal peoples, and constitutional protection provided a considerable roadblock to those who might challenge this right. Indeed, only the government of Canada can amend Section 35 and thus deny aboriginals the right of self-government.

The first direct implementation of this constitutionally protected right of aboriginal self-government occurred in 1998 with the Nisga'a Final Agreement, which covered the Nisga'a of British Columbia and was ratified by all parties in 2000. Framework agreements (agreements pertaining to issues to be discussed during negotiations) and agreements-in-principle (nonratified agreements) have been established with many aboriginal groups, and final agreements (those which are ratified and ready to be made effective through federal and provincial legislation) have been established with the Ta'an Kwach'an Council of the Yukon (2002), the Tlicho of the Northwest Territories (2002), the Kluane First Nations of the Yukon (2003), the Anishnaabe (2004), and the Kwalin Dun First Nation of the Yukon (2005). The first stand-alone self-government agreement was concluded in 2003 by the Westbank First Nation of British Columbia.

Robyn Bourgeois

See also Canadian Indian Treaties; Modern Treaties/Comprehensive Land Claims Agreements (Canada); Nacho Nyak Dun Final Agreement–May 29, 1993; Nisga'a Final Agreement–April 27, 1999; Northeastern Quebec Agreement–January 31, 1978; Sovereignty; Tribal Government Authority versus Federal Jurisdiction; Vuntut Gwitchin Final Agreement–May 29, 1993.

References and Further Reading

Asch, Michael. 1984. *Home and Native Land: Aboriginal Rights and the Canadian Constitution.* Toronto: Methuen.

Cardinal, Harold. 1977. *The Rebirth of Canada's Indians.* Edmonton, AL: Hurtig.

Russell, Dan. 2000. *A People's Dream: Aboriginal Self-Government in Canada.* Vancouver: University of British Columbia Press.

Cobell Case, 1996

On June 10, 1996, Elouise Cobell, a member of the Blackfeet tribe, led a group to file a class action lawsuit against the U.S. government. Originally known as *Cobell v. Norton*, subsequently as *Cobell v. Babbitt*, and finally as *Cobell v. Kempthorne*, the plaintiffs alleged that the federal government had made a series of enormous mistakes, failing in its responsibility to keep accurate records of American Indian accounts held in trust by the United States.

This is the largest law suit brought by Native peoples against the United States to date. The plaintiff claimed that Indian trust accounts affect an estimated 250,000 American Indians. Cobell has also claimed that the amount of money affected is estimated at anywhere from $50 billion to perhaps as high as $176 billion. Although the amount has yet to be determined, the case is important because it is premised on the federal government's broad-scale negligence in its handling of the monies of Native Americans.

Based on the 374 treaties signed between American Indian tribes and the U.S. government, a trust responsibility of the highest degree is to be maintained by both sides of a treaty. Hence, the federal government holds accounts for Indian tribes and individual Indian people based on treaties that were signed years ago.

In 1778, the U.S. government negotiated its first treaty with an Indian tribe, the Delaware. Nearly four hundred treaties and agreements were made before an appropriations act passed in 1871 stopped the treaty-making process, although agreements were made thereafter. The treaties and agreements were official only after ratification by Congress.

Since its filing in 1996, the *Cobell* case has encountered name changes, changes of judges, and political criticism in the media. As of 2007, the case is still in the federal court with no decision in the near future. It is certain to be a landmark decision in federal-Indian relations, and measures will need to be put in place for the safekeeping of American Indian trust accounts.

Donald L. Fixico

See also Indian Appropriations Act, 1871; Treaty; Treaty with the Delaware–September 17, 1778; Trust.

References and Further Reading

Pommersheim, Frank. 1995. *Braid of Feathers: American Indian Law and Contemporary Tribal Life.* Berkeley, Los Angeles, and London: University of California Press.

Prucha, Francis Paul. 1994. *American Indian Treaties: The History of a Political Anomaly.* Berkeley, Los Angeles, and London: University of California Press.

St. Germain, Jill. 2001. *Indian Treaty-Making Policy in the United States and Canada 1867–1877.* Lincoln and London: University of Nebraska Press.

R. v. Van der Peet (Canada), 1996

This case was part of a trilogy of cases (the other two were *R. v. N.T.C. Smokehouse Ltd.* [1996] 2 S.C.R. 672 and *R. v. Gladstone* [1996] 2 S.C.R. 723) relating to aboriginal commercial fishing rights in British Columbia that were decided before the Supreme Court of Canada.

In this case, Dorothy Marie Van der Peet, from the Sto:lo community, was charged with selling ten salmon caught under the authority of an Indian food fish license, contrary to British Columbian provincial legislation prohibiting the sale or barter of fish caught under such a license. The lower courts found against her, and she then appealed to the Canadian Supreme Court. She claimed an aboriginal right to sell fish and that the provincial legislation infringed this right, which was constitutionally protected under Section 35(1) of the Constitution Act of 1982, which states, "The existing aboriginal and treaty rights of the aboriginal peoples of Canada are hereby recognised and affirmed."

Delivering the decision for the majority of justices on August 22, 1996, Chief Justice Antonio Lamer dismissed Van der Peet's claim to an aboriginal right to sell. The evidence was insufficient to establish a network of Sto:lo trade in fish prior to contact with Europeans. The court accepted that fishing for food and ceremonial purposes was a significant and defining feature of the Sto:lo culture, to which Van der Peet belonged. However, this was not sufficient to demonstrate that the exchange of salmon was an integral part of Sto:lo culture. Van der Peet had to prove that the exchange itself was integral to Sto:lo culture. The exchange of salmon as part of interaction of kin and family was not of suffi-cient independent significance to establish an aboriginal right to exchange fish for money or other goods. Therefore, it was not an aboriginal right protected under Section 35(1).

Although the claim to an aboriginal right to commercial fishing failed in this particular case, the possibility of its existence in other aboriginal communities was not ruled out. The court developed the "integral to distinctive culture" test, which requires an aboriginal group to prove that a particular practice, custom, or tradition is integral to their culture in order for it to be recognized as an aboriginal right protected under the Canadian constitution. Where it is difficult for a group to prove aboriginal title, which would allow them exclusive occupation and use of land for a variety of purposes, they may be able to show the existence of aboriginal rights to land and resources under the "integral to distinctive culture" test. One of the factors that courts must take into account in applying the test is the perspective of aboriginal peoples, including their oral history.

The court also outlined some important principles in the general adjudication of aboriginal rights cases. The intent and and purpose of Section 35(1) of the Constitution Act of 1982 is recognition and reconciliation. It recognizes the prior occupation of North America by aboriginal peoples and seeks to reconcile the preexistence of aboriginal societies with the Crown's sovereignty. The court clearly identified aboriginal title and rights as arising from the existence of distinctive aboriginal communities occupying "the land as their forefathers had done for centuries," a finding reached earlier in *Calder v. Attorney-General of British Columbia*. The Chief Justice explained that aboriginal rights are "distinctive" because of aboriginal prior occupation of lands, "and this fact, above all others, separates aboriginal peoples from all other minority groups in Canadian society and which mandates their special legal and constitutional status." Also, the Crown has a fiduciary obligation toward aboriginal peoples and must act honorably and in good faith. This obligation extends to all aboriginal peoples whether or not on reserves or aboriginal title lands.

The case has been criticized for taking a "frozen rights" approach to aboriginal rights in requiring precontact evidence of a practice, custom, or tradition integral to the group's culture. But the court did not rule out the possibility of aboriginal rights containing a commercial aspect to them, and this depends on the evidence presented at court in each case. Thus, aboriginal fishing rights, including aboriginal commercial fishing rights, if they exist on the facts of the case, have not been extinguished in British Columbia, as was held in *R. v. Gladstone*.

Özlem Ülgen

See also Aboriginal Title.

References and Further Reading

Asch, Michael. 1984. *Home and Native Land: Aboriginal Rights and the Canadian Constitution*. Toronto: Methuen.

Barsh, Russel Lawrence, and James Youngblood Henderson. 1997. "The Supreme Court's *Van der Peet* Trilogy: Naïve Imperialism and Ropes and Sand," 42 *McGill Law Journal* 994.

Borrows, John. 1997. "Frozen Rights in Canada: Constitutional Interpretation and the Trickster," 22 *American Indian Law Review* 37.

Cardinal, Harold. 1977. *The Rebirth of Canada's Indians*. Edmonton, AL: Hurtig.

Dickason, Olive Patricia. 1992. *Canada's First Nations: A History of Founding Peoples from Earliest Times*. Norman: University of Oklahoma Press.

R. v. Van der Peet (1996) 2 S.C.R. 507.

Delgamuukw v. British Columbia (Canada), 1997

On December 11, 1997, the Supreme Court of Canada issued its landmark decision in *Delgamuukw v. British Columbia*. The critical issue was whether the Gitksan and Wet'suwet'en people had aboriginal title to the vast tracts of land comprising their territory in British Columbia. It is the leading Canadian case on aboriginal title, marking the beginning of Canada's definitive judicial recognition of aboriginal title, its source and content.

The actual court hearing took 356 days, included oral testimony from aboriginal peoples, and was the culmination of several years of litigation in the lower courts. The court did not actually decide the nature and content of the Gitksan and Wet'suwet'en aboriginal title because there were evidentiary problems in establishing its existence in any part of their territory. However, the court gave a strong indication that it favored resolution of the matter through negotiations undertaken in good faith by all parties.

Importantly for future aboriginal claimants, the court identified several requirements for the proof of aboriginal title, including its content and nature: (1) historical occupation—the aboriginal claimant group must show that it occupied the land at the time the Crown asserted sovereignty over it; (2) physical occupation—the claimant group must show physical occupation of the land through factors such as dwellings, cultivation or enclosure of fields, regular use of definite tracts of land for hunting, fishing, or exploitation of resources; (3) continuity—where it is difficult to show pre-sovereignty occupation of the land, the claimant group may rely on present occupation so long as they can show substantial connection between the people and the land; and (4) exclusivity—the claimant group must show intention and capacity to retain exclusive occupation and control over the land.

For the first time in legal history, the court outlined the source and content of aboriginal title. Aboriginal title is defined as the right to exclusive use and occupation of land for a variety of purposes, which need not be aspects of those aboriginal practices, customs, and traditions that are integral to distinctive aboriginal cultures. This allows for different forms of development activity, including mineral rights, nontraditional uses of land, and commercial exploitation. The court confirmed that the source of aboriginal title is prior occupation of lands by aboriginal peoples, and preexisting systems of aboriginal law: "The first is the physical fact of occupation, which derives from the common law principle that occupation is proof of possession in law . . . [because possession was before the assertion of British sovereignty] . . . this suggests a second source for aboriginal title—the relationship between the common law and pre-existing systems of aboriginal law."

The court also outlined an "inherent limitation" to aboriginal title: lands cannot be used "in a manner that is irreconcilable with the nature of the attachment to the land which forms the basis of the group's claim to aboriginal title." For example, land used mainly as hunting grounds cannot be used for strip-mining, as this would destroy the land's value. This recognizes the continuing importance of land to aboriginal groups and their value systems. As trustees of the land, they preserve its use and resources for future generations. The court clearly stated that this limitation is not intended as a "legal straitjacket on aboriginal peoples who have a legitimate legal claim to the land."

Another restriction on aboriginal title is its inalienability, that is, it cannot be sold, transferred, or surrendered to anyone other than the Crown: "[A]lienation would bring to an end the entitlement of the aboriginal people to occupy the land and would terminate their relationship with it . . . the inalienability of aboriginal lands is, at least in part, a function of the common law principle that settlers in colonies must derive their title from Crown grant and, therefore, cannot acquire title through purchase from aboriginal inhabitants. It is also, again only in part, a function of a general policy 'to ensure that Indians are not dispossessed of their entitlements'."

In balancing the needs of aboriginal and non-aboriginal peoples, the court also discussed the possibility of legitimate Crown infringement on aboriginal title lands where there is a valid legislative objective with a compelling and substantial purpose: "[T]he development of agriculture, forestry, mining and hydroelectric power, the general economic development of the interior of British Columbia, protection of the environment or endangered species, the building of infrastructure and the settlement of foreign populations to support those aims, are kinds of objectives that are consistent with this purpose [reconciliation] and, in principle, can justify the infringement of aboriginal title."

Özlem Ülgen

See also Aboriginal Title; Nisga'a Final
    Agreement–April 27, 1999.

References and Further Reading

Delgamuukw v. British Columbia. 1997. 3 S.C.R. 1010.

Elliott, D.W. 1998. "Delgamuukw: Back to the
    Court?" 26(1) *Manitoba Law Journal* 97.

McNeil, Kent. 1998. "Defining Aboriginal Title in the
    90's: Has the Supreme Court Finally Got It
    Right? Twelfth Annual Roberts Lecture, March
    25, York University, Toronto, Ontario.

Ülgen, Özlem. 2000. "Aboriginal Title in Canada:
    Recognition and Reconciliation," 47 *Netherlands
    International Law Review* 146.

Mille Lacs Band v. Minnesota, 1999

The premise of this case was whether an 1837 treaty that guaranteed hunting, fishing, and gathering rights for the Mille Lacs Band (Chippewa) was extinguished through three separate but interlinked decisions. The first decision was an executive order issued by President Zachary Taylor in 1850 abrogating the usufructuary rights—a special property right according to which one party (Mille Lacs Band) has the right to utilize and enjoy the profits and advantages of something belonging to another (United States), so long as the property is not damaged or altered in any way. The second decision was an 1855

treaty purporting to abrogate the usufructuary rights of the treaty of 1837. The third was Minnesota's admission to the Union in 1858 under the Minnesota Enabling Act, which claimed to extinguish the usufructuary rights of the Chippewa established in the treaty of 1837. The U.S. Supreme Court ruled that Article V of the 1837 treaty, which guaranteed usufructuary rights of the Chippewa, were not abrogated on the land ceded to the United States. The Court was divided five to four in favor of the Chippewa, and Justice Sandra Day O'Connor delivered the opinion of the Court.

On July 29, 1837, a treaty was signed by several Chippewa bands, including the Mille Lacs band, ceding land in present-day Minnesota and Wisconsin. The treaty conveyed land to the United States in return for twenty annual payments of money and goods. The integral part of the treaty for this particular case was Article 5, which guaranteed the Chippewa the right to hunt, fish, and gather on ceded lands at the pleasure of the president of the United States. Thereafter, pressure mounted for the removal of the Chippewa from the ceded lands, and on February 6, 1850, President Zachary Taylor issued an executive order commanding the Chippewa to move from the ceded lands and revoked their hunting, fishing, and gathering rights guaranteed under the treaty of 1837. Land acquisition was fundamental to the United States, and in the treaty of 1855 it acquired land from the Chippewa and set aside a reservation for the tribe. In 1858, Minnesota joined the Union, and it was believed that, under the "equal footing doctrine" and the Minnesota Enabling Act, its entry extinguished all Native American rights guaranteed by treaty.

In 1990, the Mille Lacs band and several members sued Minnesota, its officials, and the Department of Natural Resources. In the mid-1990s, other Wisconsin bands of Chippewa joined the suit. The district court held that the Chippewa retained their usufructuary rights under the treaty of 1837 and resolved several resource allocation and regulation issues. The Court of Appeals for the Eighth Circuit affirmed.

The Supreme Court held that the president did not have the authority to issue the removal order, because it did not arise from the Indian Removal Act of 1830, he failed to obtain Chippewa consent, and the executive order did not evolve from the Constitution or an act of Congress. Furthermore, the removal order of 1850 issued by the president was inseverable from the section of the order purporting to abrogate Chippewa usufructuary rights, and thus it was invalidated. The court stated that the treaty of 1837 did not authorize the removal order, it did not mention or make provisions for removal, and the issue was not discussed during treaty negotiations. Thus, the primary purpose of the executive order of 1850 was the removal of the Chippewa and not the abrogation of usufructuary rights.

The Supreme Court held that the treaty of 1855 did not extinguish the usufructuary rights guaranteed under the treaty of 1837. The Court's reasons were that the treaty of 1855 did not mention the treaty of 1837 or usufructuary rights, and its purpose was only to cede land to the United States and not to extinguish the usufructuary rights guaranteed in 1837.

Furthermore, the Supreme Court ruled that the Chippewa did not relinquish their usufructuary rights on Minnesota's entry into the Union in 1858. The Court's reasons were that Congress had not clearly expressed the abrogation of usufructuary rights and that Minnesota's Enabling Act had failed to mention the rights. The Supreme Court ruled that a tribe's treaty rights to hunt, fish, and gather on state land can coexist with state natural resources management and are not implicitly terminated at statehood, and the Senate did not intend to terminate the rights guaranteed under the treaty of 1837 when Minnesota was admitted to the Union.

The Supreme Court issued a decision that protected the fishing, hunting, and gathering rights of the Chippewa guaranteed to them in the treaty of 1837. Moreover, this is the first Supreme Court decision to protect Native American treaty rights since *New Mexico v. Mescalero Apache Tribe* (1983), and the Chippewa were vindicated in pursuing a judgment in favor of their treaty rights, originally guaranteed to them more than 162 years ago.

Dewi I. Ball

See also Dodge, Henry; Indian Removal Act, 1830; *Puyallup Tribe v. Department of Game of Washington*, 1968; Sandy Lake, Minnesota; Sovereignty; Treaty.

References and Further Reading

Danziger, Edmund, Jr. 1979. *The Chippewas of Lake Superior.* Norman: University of Oklahoma Press.

Fixico, Donald L. 1998. *The Invasion of Indian Country in the Twentieth Century: American Capitalism and Tribal Natural Resources.* Niwot, CO: University of Colorado Press.

Satz, Ronald N. 1991. *Chippewa Treaty Rights: The Reserved Rights of Wisconsin's Chippewa Indians in Historical Perspective.* Madison, WI: Wisconsin Academy of Sciences, Arts and Letters.

Bureau of Indian Affairs (BIA) Public Apology, 2000

On September 8, 2000, Kevin Gover, assistant secretary of the interior for Indian affairs, made history. In his capacity as the highest federal official directly in charge of federal-Indian affairs, Gover made a public apology to American Indians in a ceremony recognizing the 175th anniversary of the establishment of the Bureau of Indian Affairs (BIA), which was founded as the Office of Indian Affairs. The Bureau of Indian Affairs received its current name in 1947.

At present, Kevin Gover, a Pawnee, is a lawyer and a professor of law at Arizona State University. Under the Clinton administration, Gover was appointed to serve as assistant secretary from 1997 to January 2001.

In his statement, Gover made it clear that he did not speak for the U.S. government but only for the Bureau of Indian Affairs, for which he was empowered to speak. He pointed out that the Indian Office was started during a time when the United States was at war with Indians, and that the agency had set out to destroy Native peoples; Sand Creek, for example, illustrated the deliberate actions taken to harm Indians. Gover advised that the beginning of the twenty-first century represented a prime time for reconciliation and for showing greater respect for Indian tribes and their people. Such past atrocities would never happen again, according to Gover.

In retrospect, Assistant Secretary Gover's apology was the first of its kind and an extraordinary ending to 175 difficult years of BIA paternalism toward American Indians. American Indians had endured war, suffering, and poor health conditions while the U.S. government often worked against Indian communities. In the end, Indian people and their tribal governments did more than just survive; they now prosper in a period known as the era of Indian self-determination.

Donald L. Fixico

See also Black Kettle; Indian Self-Determination; Trust; Trust Responsibility.

References and Further Reading

Dippie, Brian. 1982. *The Vanishing American: White Attitudes and U.S. Indian Policy.* Lawrence: University Press of Kansas.

Iverson, Peter. 1998. *"We Are Still Here": American Indians in the Twentieth Century.* Wheeling, IL: Harlan Davidson.

Tyler, S. Lyman. 1973. *A History of Indian Policy.* Washington, DC: United States Department of the Interior, Bureau of Indian Affairs.

Wilkinson, Charles. 2005. *Blood Struggle: The Rise of Modern Indian Nations.* New York: W.W. Norton.

Rice v. Cayetano, 2000

In *Rice v. Cayetano*, 528 U.S. 495 (2000), the Supreme Court invalidated the State of Hawaii's definition of "Native Hawaiian" for purposes of voting in an election of the board of trustees of the Office of Hawaiian Affairs (OHA). OHA administers programs benefiting two subclasses of Hawaiian citizenry: Hawaiians and Native Hawaiians. The Hawaiian state constitution limited the right to vote for the nine OHA trustees and the right to run in the statewide election for the position of OHA trustee to those two subclasses. The court held that, because the definitions of these subclasses were racial rather than political in nature, the voting restrictions violated the Fifteenth Amendment.

At first glance, it appears that the rights of yet another group of indigenous inhabitants of this nation were trampled upon. A closer inspection of the case reveals, however, that the Native Hawaiians were, instead, victims of a constitutionally faulty remedial infrastructure that was based on their race rather than their inherent sovereignty as indigenous people. The crux of the majority opinion was that the voting restrictions were both racially defined and imposed by the state and thus were constitutionally impermissible. Although the majority opinion did not elucidate acceptable alternatives, it implies that, had the voting restrictions been based on membership in a Native Hawaiian political entity, and had that entity, rather than the State of Hawaii, been the administrator of the resources controlled by OHA, it is likely that the outcome would have been favorable to the Native Hawaiians. The constitutional defect identified by the majority was not an attempt to provide a measure of self-determination for Native Hawaiians; rather, the defect was a faulty infrastructure that attempted to promote such self-determination as a function of race under the auspices of the state.

Until 1893, the Kingdom of Hawaii was a separate sovereign nation and entered into a number of treaties with the United States, first in 1826 and subsequently in 1849, 1875, and 1887 (Clarkson 2002). It is important to note that all of the treaties between the United States and the Kingdom of Hawaii treated Native Hawaiians as a collective political entity, not as an ethnic group.

With tacit assistance from the United States, the monarchy was illegally overthrown by nonindigenous settlers in 1893, and in 1898 Hawaii was annexed as part of the United States. At the moment of annexation, all former Crown and government lands were ceded to the United States. As with the Indians on the mainland, the United States also assumed a trustee relationship over the Native population, with similarly disastrous results. By 1920, it was clear that Hawaii's Native population was not faring well.

Rather than restoring the land base to a Native Hawaiian political entity, however, Congress enacted the Hawaiian Homes Commission Act (HHCA), whereby two hundred thousand acres of former Crown lands were set aside for the purpose of leasing homesteads to individual Native Hawaiians for a nominal fee. Similar in purpose and effect to the General Allotment Act, the well-intentioned HHCA was overwhelmed by the ambitions of others who coveted the lands. As with allotment, much of the land given to the Native Hawaiians was of poor quality.

Hawaii became a state in 1959, and Congress ceded its trust responsibility to the state, along with 1.2 million acres intended for, among other things, the betterment of the conditions of the Native Hawaiians. In 1978, Hawaii established the OHA to implement its trust obligation. Unfortunately, the OHA was not the result of a government-to-government relationship with a Native Hawaiian political entity but was instead based on racial definitions of "Native Hawaiian" or "Hawaiian." These particular race-based classifications would be the linchpin in the case against the racially exclusive system of election of the OHA board of trustees.

Harold "Freddy" Rice descended from preannexation residents of the islands, but because he was neither "Native Hawaiian nor "Hawaiian," his application to vote in the OHA election was denied. Rice sued Governor Ben Cayetano, arguing that the voting restriction violated the Fifteenth Amendment.

The state argued that Native Hawaiians were just as "Native" as Indians on the mainland and had a similar trust beneficiary relationship, and thus the Court's prior rulings, specifically *Morton v. Mancari*, would allow for special programs for Native Hawaiians, such as OHA. The district court agreed, as did the Court of Appeals for the Ninth Circuit. Voting seven to two, however, the Supreme Court reversed the Ninth Circuit, holding that the OHA voting restriction violated the Fifteenth Amendment.

The aftermath of *Rice v. Cayetano* was twofold. The non-Native interests in Hawaii initiated litigation to further erode the trust responsibility and infrastructure of the State of Hawaii, while certain Native Hawaiian groups sought a legislative remedy that would finally establish a government-to-government relationship with the United States.

Gavin Clarkson

See also General Allotment Act (Dawes Act), 1887; *Morton v. Mancari*, 1974.

References and Further Reading

Clarkson, Gavin. 2002. "Not Because They Are Brown, but Because of It: Why the Good Guys Lost in *Rice v. Cayetano*, and Why They Didn't Have to Lose." *Michigan Journal of Race and Law* 2: 318–362.

Cohen, Felix S., and Rennard Strickland, eds. 1982. *Felix S. Cohen's Handbook of Federal Indian Law.* Charlottesville, VA: Michie.

Kapilialoha MacKenzie, Melody. 1991. *Native Hawaiian Rights Handbook.* Honolulu: University of Hawaii Press.

Sand Creek Massacre Site Return, 2002

On May 6, 2002, by federal legislation, the U.S. government returned the Sand Creek Massacre site to the Cheyenne and Arapahoe tribes. The historic site is located in southeast Colorado. This legislation was introduced by Senator Ben Nighthorse Campbell of Colorado, a Cheyenne and the only American Indian in Congress in 2002.

This infamous incident happened during the early morning on November 29, 1864. It was not an act of misunderstanding but a deliberate decision to inflict suffering and death on Indians in the same area where Colorado settlers harbored ill feelings toward Native peoples. Cheyenne and Arapahoe warriors defended their homeland against white settlers who desired their land. Colonel John Chiving-

ton, the territorial governor, raised a local militia and planned the attack on the Indians.

The result was a devastating assault on the Cheyenne and Arapahoe, who were led by Peace Chief Black Kettle of the Cheyenne and Chief White Antelope of the Arapahoe. The two tribes were directed to camp near Fort Lyon in southeast Colorado, where they were regarded as peaceful Indians. On that winter morning, the Indian encampment under a white flag of truce was attacked by Chivington and his men. They killed and then mutilated the bodies of almost the entire camp, slaughtering women and children as well.

The Cheyenne and Arapahoe responded in revenge, leading to more bloodshed between Indians and whites. Initially, Chivington was exalted locally as a hero, but realists viewed the attack as a massacre of peaceful Indians. This infamous event became a main point in the correction of wrongs against Native people, as noted by historians and also acknowledged in Assistant Secretary Kevin Gover's apology to American Indians on behalf of the Bureau of Indian Affairs in 2000.

Donald L. Fixico

See also Black Kettle; Chivington, John Milton; Treaty with the Cheyenne and Arapaho–October 28, 1867.

References and Further Reading

Berthrong, Donald J. 1976. *The Cheyenne and Arapaho Ordeal: Reservation and Agency Life in the Indian Territory, 1875–1907.* Norman: University of Oklahoma Press.

Berthrong, Donald J. 1963. *The Southern Cheyenne.* Norman: University of Oklahoma Press.

Hatch, Thom. 2004. *Black Kettle: The Cheyenne Chief Who Sought Peace but Found War.* John Wiley.

Vestal, Stanley, ed. 1934. *Early Days among the Cheyenne and Arapahoe Indians.* Norman: University of Oklahoma Press.

National Museum of the American Indian, 2004

The result of a massive effort, the National Museum of the American Indian (NMAI) opened in Washington, D.C., on September 21, 2004. NMAI is a part of the Smithsonian Mall and displays Native American history and cultures representing the entire Western Hemisphere. The collections at NMAI comprise an estimated eighty thousand artifacts of Native peoples.

Rick West, a Cheyenne attorney, was the founding director of NMAI. West was successful in raising funding for the new museum, and he promoted NMAI in the media very well. His leadership proved to be invaluable in getting NMAI off the ground and in building positive relationships with tribal museums and other museums throughout the country. As of this date, West is retiring from the directorship, and NMAI is off to a strong start.

The National Museum of the American Indian enjoys a national and international reputation as an increasing number of people in the United States and the world become interested in Native peoples. In the early years of the twenty-first century, scholars in Finland, England, New Zealand, Australia, Germany, and Japan have exhibited impressive scholarly knowledge of American Indians and have sent visitors and college students to NMAI to learn about Indian people and their diverse cultures.

Donald L. Fixico

See also Bureau of Indian Affairs (BIA); Native
    American Graves Protection and Repatriation
    Act, 1990; Sacred Sites; Sovereignty; Treaty.
References and Further Readings
Jacobson, Lisa, ed. 2006. "Review Roundtable: The
    National Museum of the American Indian." *The
    Public Historian: A Journal of Public History*, 28(2):
    47–90.
Messenger, Phyliss Mauch, ed. *The Ethics of Collecting
    Cultural Property: Whose Culture? Whose
    Property?* Albuquerque: University of New
    Mexico Press.
Nagel, Joane. 1996. *American Indian Ethnic Renewal:
    Red Power and the Resurgence of Identity and
    Culture.* New York and Oxford: Oxford
    University Press.

Indian Tribal Energy and Self-Determination Act, 2005

In August 2005, President George W. Bush signed into law the Energy Policy Act. Title V of this law is known as the Indian Tribal Energy and Self-Determination Act. After several delays, Congress enacted this timely legislation.

The Indian Tribal Energy and Self-Determination Act focuses on improving relations between tribes and the federal government, giving tribal governments more control over the development of tribal lands. Energy resource management is essential to the tribes as accelerating climate change increases the importance of all energy resources on the continent.

In addition to its tribal focus, the Council of Energy Resource Tribes (CERT) will play an important role in the development of tribal resources. Founded in Denver in 1975 by twenty-five tribes holding such energy resources as coal, oil, uranium, timber, and water, CERT presently has a membership of fifty-three tribes, including a few Canadian First Nations groups.

Indian tribes hold more than one-third of the coal in the West on reservation lands, as well as large amounts of oil, especially in Wyoming and Oklahoma. Timber-rich areas are in Wisconsin, Oregon, and Washington. As the largest coal-producing tribe, the Navajos are particularly affected by this legislation, followed by the Crow, the second-largest coal-producing tribe. The Blackfeet of Montana develop fifty million barrels of oil per year. In 2004, holdings of the Ute and Southern Ute in northeast Utah accounted for nearly 36 percent of oil sold from Indian leases, and Shoshone and Arapaho holdings in Wyoming accounted for 21.54 percent. The Osage in Oklahoma continue to hold impressive amounts of oil under their lands. The Colville Confederated Tribes maximize timber resources and are one of the top tribal groups harvesting timber. The Warm Springs of Oregon own and operate Warm Springs Power Enterprises, the largest hydropower company in Oregon, and the Flathead tribes of Montana (Confederated Salish and Kootenai Tribes) have timber industry sales.

The Indian Tribal Energy and Self-Determination Act will have major impact on all 562 federally recognized tribes, and nearly sixty tribes possess energy resources that the nation needs. An important part of the self-determination development includes water, especially in the West and Southwest. Finally, the act will profoundly affect the development of Indian sovereignty and tribal governance.

Donald L. Fixico

See also Indian Water Rights and Treaties; Property:
    Land and Natural Resources; Treaty.
References and Further Readings
Ambler, Marjane. 1990. *Breaking the Iron Bonds: Indian
    Control of Energy.* Lawrence: University Press of
    Kansas.
Fixico, Donald L. 1998. *The Invasion of Indian Country
    in the Twentieth Century: American Capitalism and
    Tribal Natural Resources.* Niwot, CO: University
    Press of Colorado.

Wilkinson, Charles. 2004. *Blood Struggle: The Rise of Modern Indian Nations.* New York and London: W.W. Norton.

Seminole Tribe of Florida Purchase of Hard Rock Café, 2007

On April 7, 2007, the Seminole tribe of Florida bought Hard Rock International Restaurants for $965 million. In doing this, the Seminoles became the owners of the chain of Hard Rock Cafés, which are spread throughout the United States. This business transaction made the Seminoles a tribe with nation-wide investments.

By purchasing this restaurant chain, the Florida Seminoles became a national mega-casino tribe operating in more than one state. By 2005, the total profit made by tribes involved in Indian gaming was more than $20 billion. Of the more than two hundred tribes involved in gaming, only 20 percent are considered mega-casino tribes—tribes that earn about 80 percent of the total revenue generated by gaming. The Florida Seminole are now among them.

The Seminoles of Florida started the Indian gaming industry, which began in the late 1970s with a bingo operation in the southern tip of the state. In the *Butterworth* court case, the State of Florida unsuccessfully sued the Seminole for operating illegally. The court decided in favor of the Seminole, finding that the tribe's operation of a bingo game on their treaty reservation was immune from state regulations and laws. Unregulated bingo as an industry then spread to other tribes, such as the Pequot of Connecticut, who visited the Florida Seminoles for advice.

Unregulated Indian gaming led to the introduction of legislation during the same time that the Cabazon tribe of southern California became involved in a lawsuit, which they won. Again, Indian sovereignty was protected by a court ruling, which compelled Congress to pass legislation pro-tecting the tribes from organized crime; and the Indian Gaming Regulatory Act (IGRA) became law in 1988.

The Indian gaming industry remains in an upward-spiraling growth pattern as more tribes open casinos. The Florida Seminoles remain a leader in this capitalistic endeavor, and this has benefited the small tribe with much internal programmatic development. It is indeed a time of Indian self-determination for the Seminoles, who, ironically, numbered as few as 350 after the Third Seminole War (1855–1858). Although the majority of the tribes-people were removed to Indian Territory to become the Oklahoma Seminoles, those who fought to remain in Florida have prospered impressively.

Donald L. Fixico

See also American Indian Self-Determination and Education Act of 1975; Indian Country; Indian Gaming Regulatory Act, 1988; Sovereignty; Statutes as Sources of Modern Indian Rights: Child Welfare, Gaming, and Repatriation; Treaty.

References and Further Readings

Ambrose I. Lane, Sr. 1995. *Return of the Buffalo: The Story Behind America's Indian Gaming Explosion.* Westport, CT: Bergin and Garvey.

Eadington, William R. 1990. *Indian Gaming and the Law.* Reno, NV: Institute for the Study of Gambling and Commercial Gaming.

Eisler, Kim Isaac. 2001. *Revenge of the Pequots: How a Small Native American Tribe Created the World's Most Profitable Casino.* New York: Simon & Schuster.

Kersey, Harry A., Jr. 1996. *An Assumption of Sovereignty: Social and Political Transformation among the Florida Seminoles, 1953–1979.* Lincoln: University of Nebraska Press.

Light, Steven Andrew, and Kathryn R. L. Rand. 2005. *Indian Gaming and Tribal Sovereignty: The Casino Compromise.* Lawrence: University Press of Kansas.

Mason, W. Dale. 2000. *Indian Gaming: Tribal Sovereignty and American Politics.* Norman: University of Oklahoma Press.

Northrup, Jim. 1997. *The Rez Road Follies: Canoes, Casinos, Computers and Birch Bark Baskets.* New York: Kodansha America.

Adair, William P.

(1829–1880)

William P. Adair was an assistant chief of the Cherokee Nation during the Civil War. He led a band of Native Americans in the Confederate Army and fought at the Battle of Pea Ridge, but, most important, he was a negotiator of treaties for the Cherokee Nation in selling, saving, and acquiring Cherokee land.

From the 1840s until the 1860s, Cherokees sought compensation from Texas for lands lost in 1839. In the mid-1850s, the tribe sent William P. Adair to Washington, D.C., to petition Congress for permission to sue the state of Texas for the return of one and a half million acres in East Texas. For the next hundred years, the Cherokee periodically renewed their claim against the state of Texas but without success.

The Civil War was a major event in the lives of the southern Indians, who had been removed to Indian Territory in the antebellum period. Early attempts to remain neutral crumbled under pressure from their Arkansas and Texas neighbors, clever Confederate diplomacy, and indifference from the United States because of other problems. By the fall of 1861, the Five Civilized Tribes of Indian Territory had signed Confederate treaties and had organized military companies to serve as a home guard.

As the Civil War neared, neutrality appeared unlikely for the Choctaw, Chickasaw, Seminole, Creek, and Cherokee of Indian Territory. Their relations with both the southern states and the federal government had been unpleasant, as both had forced the tribes' removal from the lower South.

Washington authorities controlled the investments of the tribes. The tribes knew that, if they changed their allegiance, all their investments would be lost, so they consented to the will of the Confederacy. In May 1861, the Confederate government authorized three Native American regiments to fight in the war, one of which was the Cherokee regiment.

During the war, William P. Adair became the commander of a brigade of Native Americans organized by General Albert Pike. He gained a measure of fame as a result of the Confederate defeat in the Battle of Pea Ridge and the Battle of Poison Springs (Arkansas) in1864, but he always envisioned the reacquisition of his tribal land.

When it was realized that the South was losing the war, Chief Stand Watie sent Adair and other members of the Ridge Party (Cherokees with white heritage) to meet with General Francis Herron to negotiate terms of surrender for the Confederate Cherokees, and a new, postwar era began.

The Ridge Party believed that it was in the best interests of the Cherokee to seek favorable terms from the U.S. government to get their land back before squatters and state governments made matters worse. The reacquisition of the Cherokee's land became Adair's life's work. In 1869, Adair and Clement N. Vann were appointed commissioners on behalf of the Cherokee Nation to meet with the Osages in council, to remove them from Cherokee land. Adair continued to fight for the Cherokee Nation until his death in Washington, D.C., on October 23, 1880.

Fred Lindsay

See also Pike, Albert; Treaty with the
    Cherokee–December 29, 1835; Watie, Stand.
References and Further Reading
Conley, Robert J. 2005. *The Cherokee Nation: A History.* Albuquerque: University of New Mexico Press.
Everett, Dianna. 1990. *The Texas Cherokees: A People Between Two Fires, 1819–1840.* Norman: University of Oklahoma Press.
King, Duane K. 1979. *The Cherokee Indian Nation: A Troubled History.* Knoxville: University of Tennessee Press.

Adams, Hank

(1943–)

Hank Adams is an Assiniboine-Sioux political activist, leader, and organizer who was important in the struggle over Indian fishing and treaty rights in the Northwest section of the United States during the 1960s and 1970s.

Although the activism of Adams dates to his high school days, he began to be noticed when he became involved with the Democratic Party in the early 1960s. A supporter of John F. Kennedy and a campaign worker for Robert Kennedy's presidential bid in 1968, it was Adams's work with citizens' rights advocate Ralph Nader that gave him access to

Marlon Brando (left) gives 40 acres of land to Hank Adams (1943–), an Assiboine-Sioux and head of the Survival of American Indians Association in 1974. Adams, a participant in the fish-ins of the 1960s and the Trail of Broken Treaties in 1972, has helped to protect Native American rights in legislatures and the courts. (Bettmann/Corbis)

U.S. senators, whom he acquainted with Native American issues.

It was also in the 1960s that Adams became involved in the Red Power Movement and became a member of the National Indian Youth Council. As an advocate, he played a crucial role at the "fish-ins" in the Northwest, fighting for Indian fishing rights protesting Washington State's policies regarding them.

Adams was born on the Fort Peck Indian Reservation in Montana at a place known as Wolf Point, which was commonly referred to as Poverty Flats. He was very active in Moclips High School in Montana, where he was student body president, editor of the school newspaper, and a member of both the football and the basketball teams. His interest in politics was emphasized after his graduation from high school and his move to California, but his activist career began in April 1964, when he refused induction into the U.S. Army until Indian treaty rights were recognized. His attempt failed, and he ultimately served in the army, but this helped authenticate his political commitment. After serving in the army, Adams joined the fight for Indian fishing rights in the Northwest. As chairman of the National Indian Youth Council's Washington State Project, Adams organized fish-ins and demonstrations protesting the state's policies on Native American fishing rights. In the early 1960s, Adams and other Native Americans claimed that the treaties signed in the 1850s guaranteed them the right to fish at traditional sites. State officials, sport fishermen, and commercial fishermen disagreed, and this led to serious confrontations over fishing rights.

In 1964, Adams helped organize a march on the Washington State capitol in Olympia. The march included a thousand Native Americans and the actor Marlon Brando. This demonstration captured the public's attention and was followed by other marches and fish-ins. In 1968, Adams became the director of the Survival of American Indians Association, a local western Washington organization concerned primarily with Native American fishing rights.

The struggle for the recognition of Indian treaty fishing rights was strengthened with a decisive victory when federal judge George Boldt ruled in favor of the Native Americans in a landmark Supreme Court case, *United States v. Washington*, in 1974. The judge ruled that treaty Indians were entitled to 50 percent of the commercially harvested catch in Washington State. The Boldt Decision, as it is called, forced the state of Washington to recognize Native American treaty fishing rights.

Although he was not always in the limelight, Adams was given credit for developing the Twenty Points that were presented to the White House at the tragic Trail of Broken Treaties in 1972; he also served as a negotiator between the White House and the Freedom Fighters of Wounded Knee.

Adams has had numerous articles published in newspapers and journals, and his views have also been communicated in film and on television. He has been involved in monitoring and lobbying the Washington State legislature and twice entered primary elections as a congressional candidate.

Fred Lindsay

See also Boldt Decision *(United States v. Washington)*, 1974; Trail of Broken Treaties; Wounded Knee Occupation, 1973.

References and Further Reading

Blue Cloud, Peter, ed. 1972. *Alcatraz Is Not an Island*. Berkeley, CA: Wingbow Press.

Brand, Johanna. 1993. *The Life and Death of Anna Mae Aquash*. Toronto: James Lorimer.

Cahn, Edgar S. 1975. *Our Brothers' Keeper: The Indian in White America*. New York: New American Library.

Caldwell, E. K. 1999. *Dreaming the Dawn: Conversations with Native Artists and Activists*. Lincoln: University of Nebraska Press.

Chaat, Paul, and Robert Warrior. 1996. *Like a Hurricane: The Indian Movement From Alcatraz to Wounded Knee*. New York. New Press.

Churchill, Ward, and Jim Vander Wall. 1988. *Agents of Repression: The FBI's Secret Wars against the Black Panther Party and the American Indian Movement*. Boston: South End Press.

Cohen, Fay G. 1986. *Treaties on Trial: The Continuing Controversy over Northwest Indian Fishing Rights*. Seattle: University of Washington Press.

Cornell, Stephen. 1988. *Return of the Native: American Indian Political Resurgence*. New York: Oxford University Press.

Fortunate Eagle, Adam. 1992. *Alcatraz! Alcatraz! The Indian Occupation of 1969–1971*. Berkeley, CA: Heyday Books.

Johnson, Troy R., ed. 1994. *Alcatraz, Indian Land Forever*. Los Angeles: University of California American Indian Studies Center.

Johnson, Troy. 1996. *The Occupation of Alcatraz Island: Indian Self-Determination and the Rise of Indian Activism*. Urbana: University of Illinois Press.

Johnson, Troy, Joane Nagel, and Duane Champagne, eds. 1997. *American Indian Activism: Alcatraz to the Longest Walk*. Urbana: University of Illinois Press.

Josephy, Alvin, Jr., Joane Nagel, and Troy Johnson, eds. 1999. *Red Power: The American Indian's Fight for Freedom*. Lincoln and London: University of Nebraska Press.

Kahn, Edgar S. 1969. *Our Brother's Keeper: The Indian in White America*. New York: New Community Press.

Steiner, Stan. 1968. *The New Indians*. New York: Delta Books.

Stern, Kenneth. 1994. *Loud Hawk: The United States versus The American Indian Movement*. Norman: University of Oklahoma Press.

American Indian Movement (AIM)

The American Indian Movement (AIM) was formed in 1968 in Minneapolis, Minnesota, to protest police brutality. Founders of AIM included Clyde Bellecourt, Dennis Banks, and George Mitchell. The movement became one of the most important and prominent Native American protest organizations,

Members of the American Indian Movement (AIM) beat a drum in support of their cause during the 1973 occupation of Wounded Knee, South Dakota. AIM's flag is displayed behind the group. (Corbis/Bettmann-UPI)

campaigning on many issues affecting Native Americans. The honoring of treaty rights was foremost among their demands.

AIM began as an urban organization in response to urban issues. It was part of the social protest movements of the 1960s insofar as its tactics and some of its rhetoric and concerns were inspired by other civil rights movements. Most significantly, it was inspired by the African American protest organization the Black Panthers, which called for "Black Power." "Red Power" became an important part of the rhetoric and ideology of AIM.

AIM was most prominent and influential in Native American affairs in the early 1970s. Some of the important and high-profile campaigns organized by or participated in by AIM included the occupation of Alcatraz Island in 1969, the Trail of Broken Treaties in 1972, and the occupation of Wounded Knee in 1973. After the controversial and violent

Wounded Knee, membership and interest in AIM declined. AIM's confrontational style and radical demands alienated some and also led to significant repression by the government.

One of the most important concerns of AIM, especially in the 1970s, was the honoring of treaty rights. The Trail of Broken Treaties protest, organized largely by AIM, specifically sought to call public attention to the history of broken treaties between the U.S. government and Native American tribes. The occupation of Wounded Knee by AIM members, while concerned with complicated tribal politics on the Pine Ridge reservation in South Dakota, also called for the honoring of the 1868 treaty between the United States and the Lakota Sioux, placing the breaking of the treaty in a context of the breaking of some 371 others. The result of the breaking of the 1868 treaty, AIM declared, was "that our water has been stolen, our minerals have been stolen, and our land has been stolen. All this must be paid for retroactively and in perpetuity" (AIM Statement on Wounded Knee, November 1973). In general, however, much of the rhetoric of AIM's campaigns was more universal than particular. Rather than calling for the honoring of any particular treaty, AIM called for a return to the treatment of Native American tribes and nations as sovereign people. This reflected the pan-Indian nature of AIM as it evolved. The social protest movement of the younger generation of Native Americans who were represented in AIM tried to construct an "American Indian" identity based on a history shared across tribes of poor treatment and the continual breaching of treaty rights. AIM also fostered cultural pride and celebrated Native American culture and heritage.

In calling for treaty rights, AIM envisioned complete sovereignty for Native Americans and the return of confiscated lands. Their radicalism made the U.S. government decidedly uncomfortable and even hostile. Nor was AIM's view shared by all Native Americans. In response to the Trail of Broken Treaties, the Nixon administration declared that treaty making between the U.S. government and Native Americans had been forbidden by Congress in 1871. The Native American demand for self-determination—the right of Native Americans to run the programs that affected their lives and to participate in shaping government policies—was addressed by the federal government in the American Indian Self-Determination and Education Act of 1975. Rather than sovereignty, self-determination has continued to be the more persistent and more prominent demand of Native Americans.

Since the 1970s, AIM has continued to function as an important Native American political organization, although perhaps more locally than nationally. AIM has campaigned for civil rights and other issues affecting local Native American communities, for example, education, stereotypes of Native Americans in the media, job training, and fishing rights. Yet AIM's concern to bring treaty rights and the sovereignty issue to public attention has been and continues to be an important part of the history of Native American political activism.

Amanda Laugesen

See also American Indian Self-Determination and Education Act of 1975; Sovereignty; Trail of Broken Treaties; Wounded Knee Occupation, 1973.

References and Further Reading

American Indian Cultural Support. AIM and Wounded Knee II Documents, 1973–1983. Accessed February 8, 2005, at http://www .aics.org/WK/index.html (c.1999).

Castile, George Pierre. 1998. *To Show Heart: Native American Self-Determination and Federal Indian Policy, 1960–1975.* Tucson: University of Arizona Press.

Cornell, Stephen. 1988. *The Return of the Native: American Indian Political Resurgence.* New York: Oxford University Press.

Smith, Paul Chaat, and Robert Allen Warrior. 1996. *Like a Hurricane: The Indian Movement from Alcatraz to Wounded Knee.* New York: New Press.

American Indian Policy Review Commission

In 1973, Senator James Abourezk (South Dakota) introduced Senate Joint Resolution 133, a bill providing for the establishment of a federal commission to review all aspects of U.S. policy, law, and administration relating to the affairs of American Indian tribes. Congress passed the resolution on January 2, 1975, creating the American Indian Policy Review Commission. Congress charged the commission with reviewing federal policy toward Indians and reporting their findings. Specifically, Congress directed the commission to analyze "the historical and legal developments underlying the Indians' relationship with the Federal Government and . . . the nature and scope of necessary revisions in the formulation of policy and programs for the benefit of Indians."

The commission consisted of eleven officers: three senators, three congressmen, and five American Indian representatives—three from federally recognized tribes, one from a non-federally recognized tribe, and one representing "urban Indians." The commission established eleven different task forces. Each task force conducted extensive review of particular federal policy areas, such as the federal-tribal relationship, tribal governments, Indian education, Indian health, and reservation and resource development and protection, then reported its findings to the Policy Review Commission. As the commission's work progressed, the need became clear for a full Senate committee with oversight and legislative authority to receive the commission's report and act on its recommendations. In fact, one of the commission's final recommendations was the creation of a special Indian affairs committee in the Senate. Accordingly, the Committee System Reorganization Amendments of 1977 included a provision to establish a temporary Select Committee on Indian Affairs having jurisdiction over all proposed legislation and other matters relating to Indian affairs.

The Indian Policy Review Commission submitted its major recommendations to Congress in May 1977. The commission proposed replacement of the Bureau of Indian Affairs (BIA) with an independent Indian agency, and that the new agency contract directly with tribes for the same services then provided by the BIA. Although experts and policymakers continue to debate the commission's legacy, the two-year review did substantially increase the participation of congressional legislators in Indian affairs. Moreover, the review initiated a process limiting the role of the BIA and did more to promote the concept of sovereignty—that is, tribal self-governance—than anything since the Nixon administration's development of a plan to strengthen tribal autonomy and economic development in 1970. Nixon's plan led eventually to the passage of the American Indian Self-Determination and Education Act on January 4, 1975. The Policy Review Commission also felt that procedures should be "established so that all tribes will be guaranteed their unique relationship with the United States." The report then recommended specific criteria for the formal recognition of tribes not then recognized by the federal government.

Two critical developments arose immediately from the commission's recommendations. First, in 1977, the Senate established the Committee on Indian Affairs, making it a temporary select committee set to disband at the close of the 95th Congress. However, following several term extensions, on June 6, 1984, the Senate voted to make the committee permanent. This committee has full authority to study the unique issues facing American Indian, Native Hawaiian, and Alaska Native peoples and to propose legislation to deal with these issues. Essentially following the Policy Review Commission's task forces, these issues include, but are not limited to, Indian education, economic development, land management, trust responsibilities, health care, and claims against the United States. Second, in 1978 Congress outlined and adopted a set of specific criteria for federal recognition and created a subagency within the BIA to accept and address formal petitions for recognition.

However, aside from laying the foundations for the Senate Select Committee on Indian Affairs and the current federal recognition process in 1978, Congress did not enact the commission's recommendations. This failure was in some measure due to the departure of key legislative sponsors, such as Senator James Abourezk, as well as to a backlash from several western legislators who feared that their constituencies would feel threatened by greater tribal sovereignty. Nevertheless, certain commission recommendations gradually influenced policymakers. For instance, by the late 1980s Congress had authorized the Tribal Self-Governance Demonstration Project, which transferred significant administrative functions (as well as funding) from the BIA to selected federally recognized tribes. In essence, the self-governance project implemented some of the commission's original views. Thus, despite lacking many immediate results in 1977, the American Indian Policy Review Commission set forth a new vision of the federal-Indian relationship, a vision that continues to attract increased political support.

C. S. Everett

See also American Indian Self-Determination and Education Act of 1975; Bureau of Indian Affairs (BIA); Federally Recognized Tribes; Nixon's Message to Congress, July 8, 1970; Sovereignty.

References and Further Reading

American Indian Policy Review Commission. 1977. *Final Report Submitted to Congress, May 17, 1977.* [Microfilm]. Washington, DC: Government Printing Office.

American Indian Policy Review Commission. 1977–1978. *Meetings of the American Indian Policy Review Commission.* [Microfilm.] Washington, DC: Government Printing Office.

Brown, Anthony D. 1979. *New Directions in Federal Indian Policy: A Review of the American Indian Policy Review Commission.* Los Angeles: University of California American Indian Studies Center.

Castile, George Pierre. 1998. *To Show Heart: Native American Self-Determination and Federal Indian Policy, 1960–1975.* Tucson: University of Arizona Press.

Aquash, Anna Mae Pictou
(1945–c. 1975)

Anna Mae Pictou Aquash was one of the leading women of the American Indian Movement (AIM) in the early 1970s. Anna Mae Aquash was a staunch advocate for American Indian rights. Despite her many endeavors as an activist, however, she is often remembered for her untimely and mysterious murder on the Pine Ridge Reservation in South Dakota.

Born to Mi'kmaq parents on March 27, 1945, near Shubenacadie, Nova Scotia, Anna Mae, along with her two older sisters and younger brother, spent much of her youth in poverty. Her father, Francis Thomas Levi, left the family before Anna Mae's birth. Her mother, Mary Ellen Pictou, married Noel Sapier four years later, and the family moved to Pictou Landing, a Mi'kmaq reserve in Nova Scotia. Sapier practiced traditional craftwork and instilled into his stepdaughter a sense of her heritage and culture. While at Pictou Landing, Anna Mae contracted ocular tuberculosis, which ultimately spread to her lungs and, although treated, left her temporarily weakened and in ill health. Sapier died in 1956, and Mary Ellen Pictou abandoned her children to marry another man. Anna Mae's insecure family life, combined with the racial taunts from her non-Indian schoolmates, had a detrimental effect on her secondary school grades. She attended Milford High School but dropped out at the end of the ninth grade.

In 1962, Anna Mae journeyed to Maine to work the potato and berry harvest and then moved to Boston with Jake Maloney, another Mi'kmac Indian. She secured a job at the Elvin Selow sewing factory, while Jake opened a karate school. In June 1964, the couple had their first child, Denise, followed by Deborah seventeen months later. Desiring to raise their daughters in a more traditional setting, Anna Mae and Jake moved to New Brunswick, Canada, where they formally married at Richibucto and settled on the Mi'kmac reserve.

In 1969, the couple's marriage ended, and Anna Mae returned to her job at the sewing factory. She also did volunteer work at the Boston Indian Council, an organization she helped to create. Among other things, the council strove to help the city's Indian population avoid alcohol abuse, a problem with which Anna Mae, too, struggled in the aftermath of her marital difficulties. In 1970, Anna Mae heard about the American Indian Movement's planned national day of Indian mourning at the 350th anniversary celebration of the arrival of the Pilgrims in Plymouth, Massachusetts. Choosing to participate in the protest that November, her interest in Indian activism was piqued as she listened enthusiastically to Russell Means's oratory. Anna quit her job at Elvin Selow and moved to Bar Harbor, Maine, where she taught in the Teaching and Research in Bicultural Education School Project (TRIBES) until its funding expired. In 1971, she returned with her daughters to Boston and entered the New Careers program at Wheelock College. Anna Mae began teaching at the experimental Ruggles Street Day Care in the district of Roxbury, a predominantly black community in the city. Offered a scholarship to Brandeis University, she chose instead to continue her work with urban Indians and helped initiate the Boston Indian Council's job placement program with the General Motors plant in Framingham, Massachusetts.

During this period in Boston, Anna Mae met and established a relationship with Nogeeshik Aquash, an Ojibwa artist from Walpole Island in Ontario, Canada. The two traveled to Washington, D.C., with members of the Boston Indian Council to participate in the final stage of the Trail of Broken Treaties. In March 1973, she and Nogeeshik left for the Pine Ridge Reservation in South Dakota to help the besieged Indian activists at Wounded Knee. There, Anna Mae smuggled supplies past the government roadblocks at night and aided in the construction of protective bunkers for the beleaguered Indians. On April 12, Wallace Black Elk married Anna Mae and Nogeeshik in a traditional Lakota ceremony. Thirteen days later, the Aquashes were detained and released by the FBI as they attempted to leave Wounded Knee. Returning first to Boston in an unsuccessful attempt to start an AIM survival school in the city, the couple then moved to Ontario to set up a display of Indian art and culture at the National Arts Centre. The exhibit spawned an interest in traditional Mi'kmaq ribbon shirts, and Anna Mae foresaw the sale of these colorful shirts as a fund-raising enterprise for AIM.

With the conclusion of her exhibit in May 1974, Anna Mae, now separated from her husband, moved to the Twin Cities of Minnesota, where she made ribbon shirts and worked for the Red School House, the AIM survival school in St. Paul, and for AIM's central office in Minneapolis. There, Anna Mae became closely associated with Dennis Banks and soon became a national AIM leader. In the fall, she traveled to Los Angeles to help establish an AIM office on the West Coast. In January 1975, along with two fellow workers from the Los Angeles office, Dino Butler and his future wife, Nilak (Kelly Jean McCormick), Anna Mae journeyed to Gresham, Wisconsin, to aid the Menominee Warrior Society in their short-lived takeover of an unused abbey (the society hoped to convert the building into an Indian health center). After leaving Gresham, she organized a benefit concert in St. Paul for AIM survival schools before moving briefly to Rosebud, South Dakota, and then to Oglala on the Pine Ridge Reservation near Tent City, the AIM encampment on the property of the Jumping Bull family. AIM members were there in reaction to growing tensions on the reservation between tribal chairman Dick Wilson and Lakota traditionalists. Anna Mae became involved in community work with local women and began to develop plans for a comprehensive cultural history of the Indian peoples of North America.

In early June 1975, Anna Mae accompanied her compatriots at Tent City to the annual AIM convention in Farmington, New Mexico. Upon their return to Pine Ridge, on June 26 the activists were involved in a shoot-out on the Jumping Bull property with two FBI agents. Both agents died, along with one member of AIM. The reservation immediately became the focus of a massive manhunt as the FBI attempted to apprehend the individuals responsible for the death of their agents. As far as the government was concerned, Anna Mae's presence implicated her as either a suspect or a witness. Finally located on the Rosebud Reservation at the home of AIM's spiritual leader, Leonard Crow Dog, on September 5 she was charged with unlawful possession of explosives and firearms and taken to Pierre, South Dakota. Released on bond, Anna Mae chose to flee rather than stay and face trial. Recaptured by the FBI on November 14 on the Port Madison Reservation in Washington, she returned to South Dakota to stand trial on the Rosebud charges. Released again prior to the day of her trial, Anna Mae left her Pierre motel room on the evening of November 24 and went into hiding in Colorado.

On February 24, 1976, a rancher discovered Anna Mae's decomposed and frozen body in a ravine near Wanblee, South Dakota. Unable to identify the body, the pathologist removed her hands for possible later identification and ruled that exposure was the cause of death. On March 3, "Jane Doe" was buried in the cemetery at the Holy Rosary Mission (Red Cloud Indian School) at Pine Ridge. That same day, the FBI lab identified the severed hands as belonging to Anna Mae Aquash. Her family asked for a second autopsy and had the body exhumed on March 10. An independent pathologist discovered that she had been murdered—shot in the back of the head at close range with a .32-caliber weapon. Four days later, her body was reburied at the Wallace Little Ranch in Oglala, where it remained for twenty-eight years. On June 21, 2004, Anna Mae's family returned her remains to the Mi'kmaq reserve in Nova Scotia.

What happened to Anna Mae following her November 24 flight from Pierre until her death in December 1975 (or possibly early January 1976) is conjecture. There is compelling evidence that she fled to Denver and was there kidnapped and taken to South Dakota by some members of AIM who falsely suspected her of being an FBI informant. She was subsequently killed, according to this theory, to rid the organization of a government spy. Although approached several times in the past by the FBI in hopes of employing her services, Anna Mae openly denied any allegations that she was on the FBI's payroll. The FBI also stated that there was no truth to the assertions. Other members of AIM believed she was killed by a faction of the organization who thought that she could identify those responsible for the June 26 deaths of the two FBI agents on the Jumping Bull property. Although efforts continue to bring Anna Mae's killers to justice, the case remains unresolved. On March 20, 2003, Fritz Arlo Looking Cloud and John Graham were indicted for the murder of Anna Mae Pictou Aquash. Their cases continue at this date.

Alan C. Downs

See also American Indian Movement (AIM); Banks, Dennis; Bellecourt, Clyde.
References and Further Reading
Brand, Joanna. 1993. *The Life and Death of Anna Mae Aquash.* Toronto: James Lorimer.

Cornell, Stephen. 1988. *The Return of the Native: American Indian Political Resurgence.* New York: Oxford University Press.
Matthiessen, Peter. 1991. *In the Spirit of Crazy Horse.* New York: Penguin Books.
Smith, Paul Chaat, and Robert Allen Warrior. 1996. *Like a Hurricane: The Indian Movement from Alcatraz to Wounded Knee.* New York: New Press.

Aupaumut, Hendrick
(c. 1757–1830)

Hendrick Aupaumut was a Mahican chief who became a significant cultural broker between the United States and Indians of the Ohio Valley and Great Lakes region. A resident of the blended Indian village of Stockbridge in Western Massachusetts, Hendrick Aupaumut was educated under the tutelage of John Sargeant, a Congregational minister appointed by the Society for the Propagation of the Gospel in Foreign Parts. With other Stockbridge Indians, he joined the colonists at war with England. In June 1775, he volunteered for William Goodrich's company and was assigned to the regiment of Colonel John Patterson. Thus, he was likely present when Patterson's men fortified the redoubt on Prospect Hill, protecting Cambridge Road from British incursion during the battle of Bunker Hill.

Aupaumut later enlisted with approximately thirty Stockbridge Indians in the service of Captain Abraham Nimham's company of Indians and fought at the battle of White Plains. George Washington rewarded Apaumat's service to the fledgling nation with a commission of captain. His most significant contribution to U.S.-Indian relations was his role as informal ambassador to western tribes for the United States. Designs of the nascent government to use him in such a capacity were broached as early as 1781, when Colonel Daniel Broadhead, the commanding office at Fort Pitt (present-day Pittsburgh), asked Samuel Huntington, president of the Continental Congress, to encourage the Native peoples still on the American side to come to Fort Pitt and speak to the tribes there. Aupaumut's first journey west was at the behest of secretary of war General Henry Knox in 1792 following St. Clair's defeat the previous fall.

Aupaumut viewed his mediation in tribal relations in keeping with his people's traditional role and their kinship ties to many western tribes. His journey, however, was fraught with difficulties. The Miami and Delaware leaders with whom he met were determined by their military victories over Generals Josiah Harmar and Arthur St. Clair to resist further encroachments by American settlers on their land. They accused Aupaumut of being a spy for the United States. Aupaumut also fell ill during the trip and was unable to rendezvous at the appointed hour with General Rufus Putnam at Fort Jefferson. Putnam assumed the worst and reported that Aupaumut's negotiations had failed and that the Stockbridge sachem was probably dead. Though very much alive, Aupaumut's reputation as a mediator was at stake. Upon hearing continued rumors that the U.S. government was displeased with his efforts, Aupaumut prepared a full account of his actions in a report nearly seventy pages long. This document is a rare Native perspective on negotiations with tribes from the Ohio Valley. Aupaumut accompanied U.S. commissioners the following year and interpreted their speech to the Delaware. When the talks failed over boundary issues between Indian and American territory (the western Indians insisted on the Ohio River), and Anthony Wayne was ordered to engage the Indians, Aupaumut served as his negotiator and interpreter.

That same year, Aupaumut helped negotiate three separate treaties between the United States and the Seneca Nation, the Oneida, Tuscorora, and Stockbridge Nations, and the collective Six Nations. Before the War of 1812, Aupaumut met again with the western tribes, hoping to persuade them to turn away from Tecumseh and his dream of a pan-Indian alliance against the United States. Aupaumut had his own plans for a pan-Indian community, but he failed in his efforts to secure land along the White River in Indiana for the Stockbridge and other Christian Indians. Aupaumut's reputation as negotiator remained strong, however. Jedidiah Morse, who served as government agent for the Indian Office, sought out the Stockbridge leader to accompany him on yet another round of Indian removal negotiations. But Aupaumut stayed in New Stockbridge in western New York to help his own tribe find a better home. He eventually represented his Stockbridge band of Mahican Indians in successful negotiations for Menominee Indian land in the Wisconsin Territory, where he died in 1830. Hendrick Aupaumut's extensive writings provide a rare window on the complex intertribal relationships in the early decades of the American republic and highlight the difficulties of Native Americans who sought the middle ground between peoples of diverse cultures and agendas.

John Savagian

See also Fort Pitt, Pennsylvania; St. Clair, Arthur; Treaty with the Delaware–September 17, 1778; Wayne, Anthony.

References and Further Reading

Aupaumut, Hendrick. 1827. "A Short Narration of My Last Journey to the Western Country," *Memoirs of the Pennsylvania Historical Society*, vol. 2 (23 October 1827): 61–131.

Rhonda, Jeanne, and James P. Ronda. 1979. "'As They Were Faithful': Chief Hendrick Aupaumut and the Struggle for Stockbridge Survival, 1757–1830." *American Indian Culture and Research Journal* 33: 43–55.

Taylor, Alan. 1996. "Captain Hendrick Aupaumut: The Dilemmas of an Intercultural Broker." *Ethnohistory* 43: 431–457.

Bagot Commission (Canada)

The Bagot Commission, launched in 1842 by British North American governor general Sir Charles Bagot, was a comprehensive investigation of Indian affairs in Canada East and Canada West. As such it established the fundamental elements of colonial policy that guided Indian affairs for more than a century (Leslie 1982, 31; Miller 2000, 132). Canada West's civil secretary, Rawson W. Rawson, former Crown lands commissioner John Davidson, and registrar of the court of chancery William Hepburn served as commissioners. Released in 1844, the final report contained one hundred appendices listing Indian populations, expenditures, department accounts, testimony, and proceedings of Indian councils. The report concluded that the Indians in both Canadas faced similar problems: squatters, land loss, intemperance, lack of progress in education and agriculture, and poor accounting of band funds. Indians' right of occupancy, their right to compensation for surrendered lands, protection of reserve boundaries, and the Royal Proclamation of 1763 were recognized as important policy planks. Reforms were proposed that would improve education and lead to the elimination of Native land use patterns as well as establish the government's financial, political, legal, and moral obligations while promoting assimilation through civilization (Leslie 1982, 31, 38–39).

As Indian acceptance or cooperation was not required to reform the Indian Department, it was the first to be reorganized. Offices were moved from Kingston to Montreal, a chief clerk was placed in charge of all records, the chief superintendent became an advisory position to the governor general, resident superintendents now corresponded directly with the civil secretary, and three positions known as Indian Visitors were created—two in Canada West and one in Canada East (Leslie 1982, 48–49). Accounting practices would also be reformed to give Indian leaders a proper accounting of their funds and to protect the government from accusations of fraud or mismanagement.

Recommendations were also made concerning Indian land, its surrender, and its administration. The report acknowledged the Indians' right of occupancy and right to compensation for land surrenders as outlined in the Royal Proclamation of 1763. Once the land had been surrendered and reserves surveyed, the government encouraged individual ownership of land rather than collective ownership. Despite Native resistance, this idea influenced Canadian Indian policy for generations.

As a result of the commission, a census of the Indian population of Canada West and Canada East would be undertaken. Presents or gifts, which previously had been distributed to all Indians, would be distributed only to those listed on the census. Also, individuals deemed sufficiently educated would be refused presents. Natives, who viewed the annual distributions as an important symbol of their continuing relationship with the British Crown, strenuously resisted the stoppage of presents. Nonetheless, by the end of the 1850s present distribution had ceased.

The commissioners also recognized that education was vital for Native survival and civilization. The report claimed that day schools plagued with poor attendance and parental influence hindered children's education. It proposed that £3000 be set aside to establish four Indian boarding schools with attached farms. The schools would instruct children in farming, animal husbandry, mechanical trades, and domestic economy. All crops and animals raised on the farm would be used to reduce the operating expenses of the schools. Finally, the commission endorsed the idea that all religious denominations should receive support and cooperation from the Indian Department in implementing all educational policy. Initially, Indians cooperated with and supported the boarding schools; however, they never accepted the assimilationist intent behind the policy (Leslie 1982, 40–41; Miller 2000, 133–135).

Two land acts—"An Act for the Better Protection of the Indians of Upper Canada [West] from Imposition, and the Property Enjoyed by them from Trespass and Injury, 1850" and "An Act for the Better

Protection of the Lands and Property of the Indians of Lower Canada [East], 1851"—drew on recommendations of the Bagot Commission. In Canada East, a commissioner was placed in charge of Indian lands who held the power to lease or sell while protecting Indian interests. The act of 1851 also created the first legal definition of the term *Indian*, which largely reflected the Bagot Commission's recommendations. Although the act of 1850 did not include a definition of *Indian*, it enacted strict laws relating to trespass and resource use. It also appointed Indian superintendents and Crown lands officials as justices of the peace to enforce the new law (Dickason 2002, 228–229; Leslie 1982, 51). Additionally, these laws made it illegal for Indians to pawn goods for liquor and exempted Indians from property taxes on reserves, as well as from the seizure of property in lieu of debts unless an Indian owned £25 or more in fee-simple land. Thus, five years after the Bagot Commission's report, the essential elements of Indian legislation were in place that eventually formed the first federal Indian Act in 1871 (Leslie 1982, 51; Miller 2000, 132–133; and Dickason 2002, 228–231).

Karl S. Hele

See also Royal Proclamation of 1763.

References and Further Reading
Canada. "Report on the Affairs of the Indians of Canada." 1844–1845. App. EEE. *Journals of the Legislative Assembly of Canada.* [Appendix is not paginated].
Canada. "Report on the Affairs of the Indians of Canada." 1847. App. T. *Journals of the Legislative Assembly of Canada.* [Appendix is not paginated].
Dickason, Olive Patricia. 2002. *Canada's First Nations: A History of Founding Peoples from Earliest Times.* Toronto: Oxford University Press.
Leslie, John. 1982. "The Bagot Commission Developing a Corporate Memory for the Indian Department." *Historical Papers/Communications historiques,* 31–52.
Miller, J. R. 2000. *Skyscrapers Hide the Heavens: A History of Indian-White Relations in Canada.* 3rd ed. Toronto: University of Toronto Press.

Banks, Dennis
(1937–)

Dennis Banks, an Anishinabe born on Leach Lake Reservation in northern Minnesota, cofounded the American Indian Movement (AIM) with Clyde Bellecourt and George Mitchell in 1968. AIM's goals

Dennis Banks (1937–) an Anishinabe from Leeck Lake Reservation in northern Minnesota, was a co-founder of the American Indian Movement (AIM) in 1968 in Minneapolis. (Bettmann/Corbis)

were to initiate lawsuits to protect Native rights guaranteed in treaties, sovereignties, laws, and the U.S. Constitution. In 1970, the organization created a court advocacy program, persuaded the National Convention of Churches to provide more funding for their Indian programs, established an Indian school system, and eliminated some racist textbooks. To elevate national awareness of AIM's goals, Banks and his constituents also interrupted a Plymouth, Massachusetts, Thanksgiving celebration and a Jesuit pageant honoring Christianity in Sault Ste. Marie, Michigan.

With AIM chapters in forty-three states, Banks orchestrated protests to bring Indian priorities to the attention of the media. In 1972, he led the takeover of the federal Bureau of Indian Affairs (BIA) building in Washington, D.C. The protest, known as the Trail of Broken Treaties, began in San Francisco as a caravan traveling to the nation's capital to meet with congressional leaders. When government representatives refused to meet with the group, the protestors occupied the BIA building for eight days. Following his plan to bring Indian issues to national consciousness, Banks supplied the media with BIA records that contained information about questionable management practices. President Richard Nixon finally agreed to hear the group's Twenty Points solution paper and gave them $66,000 to return to their homes.

Not everyone celebrated Banks's role in elevating Indian priorities. When he and other demonstrators went to the Pine Ridge Reservation in South Dakota to celebrate their BIA victory, tribal chair Richard Wilson removed Banks from the reservation. The controversy surrounding Banks's activities escalated in 1973, when a white man killed Wesley Bad Heart Bull. During the protest against the judicial system, the Custer, South Dakota, courthouse burned to the ground. Shortly thereafter, Banks and Russell Means led the occupation of Wounded Knee, South Dakota, based on land claims in the 1868 Treaty of Fort Laramie. Protesting the 1890 massacre of 150 unarmed Sioux, Banks and his associates demanded the resignation of Richard Wilson and a Senate investigation of four hundred broken treaties and of BIA management practices. The standoff ended on May 8, after seventy-one days of national press coverage. However, Banks left Wounded Knee the night of May 7 and went to the Northwest Territories in Canada to avoid arrest. He and Means faced trial in 1974 for their activities at Wounded Knee. Judge Alfred Nichol eventually dismissed all charges. Shortly thereafter, Banks was again a defendant, this time for charges based on the Custer courthouse incident. Avoiding prison under California Governor Jerry Brown's protection until 1983, Banks continued to organize protests and rallies such as the Great Jim Thorpe Longest Walk, a spiritual run from New York to Los Angeles. He also served as the first American Indian chancellor at an Indian-controlled institution, Deganawida Quetzecoatl (DQ) University. In 1985, he surrendered to South Dakota authorities and served eighteen months in prison. He currently directs the Sacred Run Foundation, which sponsors international running and cultural events. His recent autobiography, *Ojibwa Warrior*, was published in 2004. Banks has actively reshaped his image from one of militancy to gentle concern and continues to bring public awareness to Native American issues.

Clara Keyt

See also American Indian Movement (AIM); Bellecourt, Clyde; Bureau of Indian Affairs (BIA); Means, Russell; Trail of Broken Treaties, 1972; Wounded Knee Occupation, 1973.

References and Further Reading

Banks, Dennis, and Richard Erdoes. 2004. *Ojibwa Warrior: Dennis Banks and the Rise of the American Indian Movement.* Norman: University of Oklahoma Press.

Cheatham, Kae. 1997. *Dennis Banks: Native American Activist.* Springfield, NJ: Enslow.

Barboncito

(1820–1871)

Barboncito was born in 1820 in lower Canyon de Chelly in present-day Arizona to a woman of the Ma'iidesgizhnii (Coyote Pass or Jemez clan) and an unknown father. His warrior name was Hashke Yich'i'adehyilwod, "He Ran Down Toward the Enemy in Anger." Like other Diné or Navajo headmen, he was versed in ceremonies such as the Blessingway and the Enemyway. He is perhaps best known by the name given to him by the Mexicans, Barboncito. Extant references to other Navajo leaders with similar names, including Barbon and El Barbon, make the identity of some leaders uncertain. However, Barboncito had become known as a prominent headman by the 1850s. Today, Navajos remember their leader as a man who used his knowledge and skill as a warrior on behalf of his people, for his oratorical power was a significant factor in the Americans' decision to allow the Navajo people to return to their homeland in 1868. After the Navajos' return to their homeland, Barboncito remained a leader who served until his death in 1871.

During Barboncito's lifetime, the Diné (the People, or Navajo) faced American expansion, which began in 1846. Although white settlers coming West and seeking land became a problem eventually faced by the Diné, the major reason for cycles of conflict and peace between Navajos and New Mexican settlers was slave raiding, the targets of which were Navajo women and children. Reports of valuable natural resources in Navajo country also began to circulate. Barboncito participated in the resistance when the American military laid claim to Navajo land and then with Navajo defeat in 1863, and journeyed with his people to the Bosque Redondo prison in southeastern New Mexico, where he encouraged his people to keep their courage and faith.

In 1851, the American military established a fort in the heart of Navajo country. This post was a site first of contention and then of war between the Navajos and the U.S. military as Navajos pressed their claims to the land. In 1860, after a series of clashes with the soldiers, Navajo warriors led by Manuelito and Barboncito attacked the fort at dawn. Although one thousand warriors attacked the fort, they were unable to take it, largely because of superior U.S. firepower.

The conflicts between the Navajos, and the New Mexican settlers continued almost unabated. In the fall of 1862, Brigadier General James H. Carleton assumed command of the Department of New Mexico. Carleton, following established U.S. policy for dealing with Native peoples, conceived a plan to remove Indians that were considered a threat to white interests, which included mining and settlement. Mescalero Apaches and Navajos were to be removed and relocated from their homelands to Bosque Redondo, a reservation near Fort Sumner, New Mexico. There, they would be subjected to assimilation policies.

In 1863, under Carleton's orders, Kit Carson waged a war against the entire Navajo Nation. The People retreated before Carson's men, who burned their hogans, destroyed cornfields and peach trees, and slaughtered livestock. Leaders such as Barboncito protected their people as best as they could during this suffering. Eventually, as the burn-and-scorch campaign continued, destitute and starving Diné began to surrender at the American forts. By the end of 1864, thousands of Navajos were forced to walk from their beloved homeland to Bosque Redondo, near Fort Sumner, New Mexico, a journey of more than three hundred miles, where they were to begin new lives.

A peace leader, Barboncito was one of the first to surrender and take his people to the prison camp. He found the living conditions deplorable and escaped twice, but if conditions at the prison camp were impossible, Navajos in their homeland faced constant harassment and deprivation in their homeland. The Diné endured nightmarish conditions at the prison camp. Attempts to farm failed as drought conditions prevailed and cutworms destroyed cornfields. They lived in holes dug into the ground. Forced to walk as far as twenty miles in search of firewood, Navajo women and children were easy prey for raiders who waited for them. They were constantly hungry and cold.

After four years, from 1864 to 1868, Carleton's "experiment" was acknowledged a failure. Because the U.S. government was no longer willing to pay for the upkeep of Navajos at Bosque Redondo, military officials considered another plan for assimilating the Navajos. In the spring of 1868, Navajo leaders met with U.S. officials to discuss conditions at the reservation and to consider alternatives. For the Navajos, the opportunity to return home seemed a strong possibility, even though military leaders were considering sending them to Indian Territory. Talking among themselves, the Diné selected Barboncito to present their case to the Americans. Barboncito, already known as an eloquent and persuasive speaker, would once again prove effective as he presented the Navajo case for return to their homeland.

Meeting with Samuel F. Tappan, who had served with the Colorado Volunteers, and William Tecumseh Sherman, a general who had waged a successful campaign against the Confederates during the Civil War, the Navajos, led by Barboncito, negotiated for two days. Sherman asked why the Navajos had not prospered at the reservation. Barboncito explained that life had been harsh at Bosque Redondo. He declared that Navajos already had a home, that they should not live outside of the four sacred mountains.

With many issues discussed during these negotiations—including land, Navajo slavery, and assimilation of Navajos into the American mainstream—the leaders eventually came to an agreement. For the Diné, the negotiations were successful because they were to return to their homeland, albeit a decidedly smaller land base than what they had previously claimed. Finally, the U.S. officials capitulated to Navajo pleas.

On June 1, 1868, the Navajo leaders and U.S. representatives signed the treaty. Although the agreement later would be ratified by Congress and then signed by the president of the United States, the Navajos began their journey home on June 18. Coming generations of Navajos would remember their ancestors' ordeal and the roles that leaders such as Barboncito played to ensure the survival of the People. Through stories passed down through the generations, the Navajo people are reminded of the power of the human spirit to overcome incredible obstacles.

After the Navajo return to Dinétah, Barboncito remained an important leader recognized by both Navajos and U.S. officials. Because the Navajo population was always too large for the diminished land base, it soon spilled into regions designated as public domain. The Navajos' use of the lands for grazing was contested by white settlers, including Mormons, on the northwestern boundaries of Navajo land; in the ensuing disputes, both Navajos and whites were killed. Barboncito worked to quell the disturbances and to keep the peace between Navajos and whites. Today, Barboncito is remembered as an important peace leader of the Navajos who proved courageous and faithful when war was inevitable. His ability to speak eloquently and powerfully served the purpose of bringing the People back to their sacred homeland.

Jennifer Nez Denetdale

See also Fort Sumner, New Mexico; Manuelito; Treaty with the Navajo–June 1, 1868.

References and Further Reading

Bailey, Lynn R. 1964. *The Long Walk: A History of the Navajo Wars, 1846–1868*. Los Angeles: Westernlore Press.

Dunlay, Tom. 2000. *Kit Carson and the Indians*. Lincoln: University of Nebraska Press.

Iverson, Peter. 2002. *Diné: A History of the Navajos*. Albuquerque: University of New Mexico Press.

Roessel, Ruth, and Broderick H. Johnson, eds. 1973. *Navajo Stories of the Long Walk Period*. Tsaile, AZ: Navajo Community College Press.

Bearskin, Leaford

(1921–)

In 1983, Leaford Bearskin was elected chief of the Wyandotte Nation, known since the 1500s in American history as part of the Hurons as well as the Keepers of the Council Fire for the Old Northwest (Delaware) Confederacy. In this capacity, he led the Wyandotte into the twenty-first century after a long career as a military officer and civilian employee of the U.S. Air Force. Among his accomplishments as chief, Bearskin helped the tribe achieve economic self-sufficiency with several business ventures that have benefited both the tribe and local communities. Through his leadership, the Wyandotte have enhanced health care, education, nutrition services, employment opportunities, and emergency services for tribal members. Magnified by his history as a bomber pilot in World War II, an airlift squadron commander during the Berlin Blockade of 1948, and an air base group commander, Bearskin also initiated several Veterans' Day events in northeastern Oklahoma and established a Wyandotte Color Guard to represent the tribe at nationwide events.

Bearskin was born in a log cabin on a hundred and forty acres of allotment land along Sycamore Creek in the hills northeast of Wyandotte, Oklahoma, where he attended public school. The family lost the land after his older brother was stricken with polio. Bearskin's parents borrowed money from the local bank to get medication. Subsequently, a land speculator came through town and bought several mortgages from the bank, including the Bearskins', and then foreclosed on them.

After graduating from high school, Bearskin wanted to attend college, but he lacked the financial means to do so. Because he also harbored a secret desire to fly an airplane, Bearskin joined the Army Air Corps in 1941. Assigned to an air base in Alaska when the Japanese bombed Pearl Harbor, Bearskin applied for flight school when the corps revised the minimum requirements for pilot training to a high school diploma. Thus began a highly distinguished career in which Bearskin was awarded such military honors as the Distinguished Flying Cross, the Asiatic Campaign Medal (with four major battle stars), the National Defense Medal, the United Nations Service Medal, and the Air Force Longevity Service Award (with three bronze oak-leaf clusters). After numerous outstanding efficiency ratings and many commendations, Bearskin retired from the Air Force in 1960. Following his retirement, Bearskin spent another twenty years working for the air force as a civil servant in the areas of missile weapons systems, logistics, and headquarters operations.

Beginning with his election as chief in 1983, Bearskin has made voluminous contributions to the Wyandotte Nation and the surrounding communities of northeastern Oklahoma. Bearskin rewrote the tribal constitution, obtained a grant for the tribe's first economic development project (the Wyandotte convenience store complex), and returned the Wyandotte Nation offices to tribal land. He also led a $5.7-million settlement of Wyandotte land claims in Ohio with the U.S. government. Additional tribal programs Bearskin instituted include a senior citizens' nutrition program, a food delivery program to local shut-ins, the construction of a tribal social activities center, the creation of a tribal library, and the establishment of a health clinic also available to non-Indian members of the community on a space-available basis. Educationally, the Wyandotte Turtle Tots preschool was recognized as the best preschool in the United States in 1995 and 1996 by the U.S. Department of Education.

Also impacting communities nearby, such as Wyandotte, Fairland, and Miami, Oklahoma, Bear-

skin oversaw the creation of a cemetery for anyone in the area, Indian or non-Indian, who needed a place to be buried. Under his watch, the Wyandotte Nation also significantly enhanced local public services. The tribe helped the City of Wyandotte create twenty-four-hour law enforcement, which helped reduce crime in the area. The tribe also supports the city's fire department, emergency medical services, and flood management control, and it supervises and funds several regional transportation projects, building or improving roads and bridges to benefit the whole of Ottawa County. Chief Bearskin also ensured that the tribe's wellness center is available to the entire community. Nationally, Bearskin oversaw the tribe's purchase of six technical schools across the United States that teach highly employable vocational subjects such as court reporting, medical records maintenance, and other skills.

Chief Bearskin instigated the establishment of the Wyandotte Cultural Center, and he directed a cultural committee to revive an annual powwow that had not taken place since the early 1960s. Since its rebeginning in 1991, the annual intertribal event draws as many as four thousand people to the Wyandotte Nation in early September and has a dramatic impact on the service-oriented businesses of the area. Chief Bearskin also instituted a Wyandotte language program that is ongoing; throughout his career, he has traveled extensively, speaking about the Wyandottes, their lifeways and concerns. In 2005, Bearskin led the Wyandotte Nation in establishing a gaming complex in Wyandotte County, Kansas.

Hugh W. Foley, Jr.

See also Allotment; Indian Claims Commission Act, 1946; Indian Gaming Regulatory Act, 1988.
References and Further Reading
Bearskin, Leaford. 1998. Interview by author, October 18.
Wyandotte Nation of Oklahoma. "Chief Leaford Bearskin." Accessed May 24, 2005, at http://www.wyandotte-nation.org.

Bellecourt, Clyde
(1936–)

Along with Dennis Banks, George Mitchell, and Edward Benton Banai, Clyde Bellecourt was one of the founding members of the American Indian Movement (AIM). He rose to fame for his leadership

Clyde Bellecourt (1936–), an Ojibwa of White Earth Indian Reservation in northern Minnesota, was one of the founding members of the American Indian Movement (AIM) in 1968. (Bettmann/Corbis)

in the 1972 cross-country trek known as the Trail of Broken Treaties, which culminated in the takeover of the Bureau of Indian Affairs (BIA) building in Washington, D.C. Bellecourt was one of the most outspoken and adamant proponents of Indian sovereignty and rights in the late twentieth century.

The son of a World War I veteran, Bellecourt was born on May 8, 1936, on the White Earth Ojibway Indian Reservation in Minnesota. He and his eleven siblings grew up in a cramped, government-built home and subsisted on their father's meager disability checks. Young Clyde was educated at a local Benedictine missionary school but often found himself in trouble with his teachers. Eventually, he was shipped off to a reform school in the city of Red Wing. When he was sixteen, Clyde and his family moved to Minneapolis as part of the BIA's new relocation program.

The move to the big city led only to further problems with the law. Through the 1960s, Bellecourt was in and out of jail for burglary and robbery. In 1966, while serving a two-to-fifteen-year sentence in the state penitentiary at Stillwater, he met Edward

Benton Banai, who encouraged Bellecourt to embrace Ojibway culture and spirituality. The two teamed up with fellow convict Dennis Banks and began to discuss how they could advocate Indian rights. Their ultimate solution was the formation of the Indian Patrol in 1968. Freshly released from prison, they took a page from the Black Panthers and began monitoring police brutality of Native peoples in the Twin Cities.

Eventually, the Indian Patrol evolved into the American Indian Movement as the organization began to expand its activities. As AIM's first chairman, Bellecourt targeted negative stereotypes of Indians in the media and in schools, advocated sovereignty, and called for a return to Native values, customs, and spiritual beliefs. After the occupation of Alcatraz in 1969–1971, AIM adopted the takeover tactic as the best way to get its message across. Accordingly, Bellecourt, along with Banks, Russell Means, Hank Adams, and several others, decided to occupy the BIA building after the Trail of Broken Treaties. Renaming the building the Native American Embassy, AIM insisted that the federal government recognize Indian sovereignty, respect its treaties, protect Indian religious freedom, restore terminated tribes, and replace the BIA with an "Office of Federal Indian Relations." Though Bellecourt and his organization did not succeed in obtaining their main demands, they did get widespread media attention. The takeover of the BIA was followed by several other occupations in the 1970s, most notably Wounded Knee on the Pine Ridge reservation in South Dakota.

In the 1980s, Bellecourt helped establish the International Indian Treaty Council, as AIM became increasingly involved in issues facing indigenous peoples throughout the Americas. Much of the new organization's attention was focused on the civil war in Nicaragua, where the Marxist Sandinistas battled the right-wing Contras. The conflict, however, caused a fracture in AIM's leadership. Bellecourt favored the Sandinistas, whereas Russell Means supported the Native Miskito people, who were allied with the Contras. By 1993, AIM had split into two organizations—Bellecourt's National American Indian Movement and Means's International Autonomous Confederation of the American Indian Movement. Nevertheless, in 1999, the two leaders were able to put their differences aside and join together to protest the murder of two Indians in White Clay, Nebraska.

Bellecourt has continued to work for Indian rights in the twenty-first century. He and his brother Vernon are active in the National Coalition on Racism in Sports and the Media as well as numerous other causes. In 2005, Heart of the Earth, Inc., established in Clyde's name a $60,000 scholarship for Indian youth. Upon completing their degrees, recipients of the scholarship are to return to their reservations to teach Indian languages, culture, and history. The scholarship provides an excellent opportunity for young high school graduates while also putting into practice what Bellecourt has advocated since those long, dark days in Stillwater prison.

Bradley Shreve

See also American Indian Movement (AIM); Banks, Dennis; Wounded Knee Occupation, 1973.
References and Further Reading
Caldwell, E. K. 1999. *Dreaming the Dawn: Conversations with Native Artists and Activists.* Lincoln: University of Nebraska Press.
Churchill, Ward, and Jim Vander Wall. 1988. *Agents of Repression: The FBI's Secret Wars against the Black Panther Party and the American Indian Movement.* Boston: South End Press.
Johnson, Troy, Joane Nagel, and Duane Champagne, eds. 1997. *American Indian Activism: Alcatraz to the Longest Walk.* Urbana: University of Illinois Press.
Josephy, Alvin, Jr., Joane Nagel, and Troy Johnson, eds. 1999. *Red Power: The American Indian's Fight for Freedom.* Lincoln and London: University of Nebraska Press.
Warrior, Robert Allen, and Paul Chaat Smith. 1996. *Like A Hurricane: The Indian Movement from Alcatraz to Wounded Knee.* New York: New Press.

Black Hawk

(1767–1838)

Black Hawk, also known as Makataimeshekiakiak, was born a few years after the Sauk and Fox tribes moved down from the Wisconsin River to Illinois country to establish Saukenuk on the Rock River where it led into the Mississippi (present-day Rock Island, Illinois). Black Hawk grew to manhood following the valor of his great grandfather and father and often demonstrated his courageous drive to keep his nation on tribal land. Descended from the first chief, Nanamakee or Thunder, Black Hawk led and returned from battles and wars with proofs of his courage as a war leader.

When his father, a medicine man of the Sauk, died after a battle with the Cherokees, Black Hawk took the great medicine bag of the tribe, carrying the sacred continuity of the nation. He sought to ensure the continuation of the ways of his people despite the increasing encroachments of the United States through treaties.

Though the Sauk (Sac) and Fox wished to be recognized by the United States as a nation through a treaty, the combined tribes believed they would be dealt with as they always had been by the British—that is, that they would be offered gifts but would not be required to cede land. The first of the American treaties, known as the Treaty of St. Louis with the Sauk [Sac] and Fox, which raised Black Hawk's rancor, came about in November 1804 through a misunderstanding following the arrest and delivery of a young warrior for the murder of settlers in the Louisiana Territory. William Henry Harrison, governor of Indiana Territory, was in St. Louis to reorganize the government of the territory following the Louisiana Purchase when he decided it would be an opportune time to treat with those few members of the Sac who were in St. Louis to deliver the young warrior. The Sacs asked for redress after offering to

Black Hawk (1767–1838) a Sauk, also known as Makataimeshekiakiak, was the war leader of the Black Hawk War of 1832 against U.S. expansion that consumed the tribal homeland of Saukenuk on the Rock River, near present-day Rock Island, Illinois. He died October 3, 1837, in Iowaville on the Des Moines River, Southeast Iowa. (Library of Congress)

turn over one of their own for the murders of the settlers. Willing to deal, Harrison tied land cession into the bargain of allowing the prisoner to go free pending a pardon from President Jefferson. Later, those who signed the treaty claimed they were misled and/or made to drink, to confirm what they had done: signed away their entire geographic boundaries from the Wisconsin River in the north to the Fox River (Illinois) on the east, down to the Illinois; from the west at the Gasconade on the Missouri to the Mississippi. For this cession of land, the Sac and Fox received $2,234.50 in goods and a $1,000 annuity, also in goods, to be divided between the Sac and Fox. When news of this agreement arrived at Saukenuk, Black Hawk refused to acknowledge the treaty, and over the next twenty-eight years, his disavowal sowed the seeds of his downfall.

In the years leading up to the War of 1812, Black Hawk and his tribe continued to acknowledge the British as their white father and made raids against the Osage. In 1808, the Americans came up the Mississippi to build Fort Madison above the Des Moines River; Black Hawk and his warriors intimidated the soldiers as they built their fort, taking the soldiers' guns by stealth while they chopped timber for buildings and then giving them back. This did not endear Black Hawk to the Americans, nor did he desire it. When the war commenced, he sided with the British. In July 1814, on the Mississippi at Campbell's Island above Saukenuk, Black Hawk and his warriors attacked U.S. gunboats under the command of Lieutenant John Campbell, who had been sent to the relief of Prairie du Chien. Following the end of the war, Black Hawk continued to raid white settlements and other Native nations. He refused to attend the treaty of 1815 at Portage des Sioux, which sought to end hostilities between the United States and tribes that had been on the side of the British. About this time, Black Hawk's tribe earned the nickname "the British Band" for continued allegiance to the British. Not until May 1816 did Black Hawk finally come to the treaty table and "touch the quill" to make his mark with the Americans and to acknowledge the land cessions of the treaty of 1804.

Over the ensuing years, Black Hawk's power was usurped by a young, untried member of the tribe named Keokuk, who was made a war chief over Black Hawk. Keokuk, known for his oratorical skill, understood that the Americans were not going away, and he tried to make peace by accommodating them and giving up more land. As Black Hawk saw the land, including his own village, being signed over time and again in the treaties of 1819, 1824, 1825, and 1830, he grew angry and concerned about the future. Unable to bear the treaties' requirement to relocate across the Mississippi from his beloved Saukenuk, Black Hawk undertook a most dangerous course.

In late spring of 1832, with the support of a civil chief, Neapope, and the guidance of the Winnebago prophet Wabekieshiek, Black Hawk took his people back over to the east side. General Edmund P. Gaines arrived with regulars to demand that Black Hawk return. He warned the Native leader that refusal bore grave consequences. During the night, Black Hawk and his tribe left, but they did not return to the west side of the river. Rather, they began a trek, which brought about the battle that forever ended his career as a war leader. With reassurances from the prophet that the British would come to his aid and that other tribes would support him, Black Hawk moved into Wisconsin Territory seeking the support he thought was a given. Trailing along with his half a thousand warriors and women, children, and the elderly, Black Hawk failed to find assistance; at the same time, he refused to turn back and cross over the Mississippi. Growing hungry, the warriors assaulted American settlers to the south, raiding stores, while the remaining band hid out. Along the Mississippi, north of where the Wisconsin River empties into it, the Sac were decimated as they pursued troops led by General Henry Atkinson and militia under Colonel Henry Dodge. Fewer than two hundred survived what is now known as the Battle of Bad Axe. Black Hawk was taken prisoner along with the others.

Another treaty evolved in the later part of the summer of 1832; it strictly prohibited Black Hawk, his two sons, and other warriors of his band from taking leadership roles in the future. The rest of the surviving band was to be redistributed among the other bands of Sac and Fox to prevent them from ever rising up again.

While yet a prisoner, Black Hawk was taken east with others of his band to be handed over to the War Department and to have a meeting with President Andrew Jackson, during which he had the opportunity to recount his side of the affair. After a tour of the capital, Black Hawk and his party were imprisoned for a short time at Fort Monroe, Virginia. Soon allowed to return home, the group stopped over in Philadelphia, where they became objects of entertainment for the citizens. Upon his return to the West, Black Hawk was turned over to Keokuk. Reunited with his wife and children, he lived a quiet life, although he made one more trip to Washington, in 1837. A newspaperman, J. P. Patterson, expressed interest in recording Black Hawk's account of his life. It was later published as the *Life of Makataimeshekiakiak or Black Hawk*. Blackhawk died on October 3, 1838, following an illness.

Sally Colford Bennett

See also Chouteau, Auguste; Clark, William; Dodge, Henry; Forsyth, Thomas; Gaines, Edmund Pendleton; Harrison, William Henry; Jackson, Andrew; Prairie du Chien, Wisconsin; St. Louis, Missouri; Treaty with the Sauk and Fox–November 3, 1804.

References and Further Readings
Hagan, William T. 1958. *The Sac and Fox Indians.* Norman: University of Oklahoma Press.
Jackson, Donald, ed. 1955. *Black Hawk, an Autobiography.* Urbana: University of Illinois Press.
Kappler, Clarence J., ed. 1904. *Indian Affairs: Laws and Treaties,* vol. 2, *Treaties.* Washington, DC: Government Printing Office.
Nichols, Roger L. 1992. *Black Hawk and the Warrior's Path.* American Biographical History Series. Arlington Heights, IL: Harlan Davidson.
Temple, Wayne C. 1987. *Indian Villages of the Illinois Country.* Vol. 2, part 2 of *Illinois State Museum Scientific Papers.* Springfield: Illinois State Museum.

Black Kettle
(1803/07–1868)

The southern Cheyenne leader Black Kettle was the most noted peacemaker of the Cheyenne, well known for his effort to guide his people through the years of frontier conflict in the 1860s and to ensure a future of honor for them. Black Kettle embodied the code of conduct given to peace chiefs by Sweet Medicine, the Cheyenne cultural hero. Peace chiefs are to avoid any violence, even if they or their families are in imminent danger, but must always stand firm against opponents of their people.

In Cheyenne, Black Kettle's name was spelled in various documents as Moke-tav-a-to, Mo-ta-vato, Moke-ta-ve-to, Moke-to-ve-to, Moka-ta-va-tah, and Mo-ko-va-ot-o. He belonged to the Suthaio band. Although as a young man Black Kettle was a renowned war leader who fought the Kiowa, Kiowa-Apache, Comanche, Ute, Delaware, and Pawnee, he never approved of war against European Americans. He became a principal Cheyenne chief in the 1850s. At that time, Cheyenne bands migrated over present-day Montana, South Dakota, Wyoming, Nebraska, Colorado, and Kansas.

In 1861, Black Kettle was the first to sign the Treaty of Fort Wise (Kansas) for his people. This treaty assigned them a small reservation in southeastern Colorado, encompassing Sand Creek. Black Kettle made every attempt to make peace with the United States, including journeys to Washington and Denver. He kept preventing his warriors from fighting the army even when the army began shooting them. In addition, Black Kettle secured the release of many European American captives by purchasing them at his own expense.

In 1864, Black Kettle's people were promised protection at Fort Lyon in Colorado, but after they had established their village at Sand Creek, they were massacred by troops under Colonel John Chivington on November 29. Black Kettle survived the massacre, and even though he fell into disgrace among his own people because he had led them into such a betrayal, he continued to counsel peace when the Cheyenne wanted to strike back. In 1865, Black Kettle attended the council on the Little Arkansas in Kansas that discussed compensation for the Sand Creek massacre. The treaty signed there assigned the Cheyenne, together with the Arapahoe, to an alternative reservation in the northern part of Indian Territory (present-day Oklahoma).

In 1867, Black Kettle was invited by Colonel Jesse Leavenworth to represent the Cheyenne at another peace council, this time along with the Arapahoe, Comanche, Kiowa, and Plains Apache, that was to be held at Medicine Lodge Creek in southern Kansas. Because of the extensive European American intrusion into the Plains Nations' land, which culminated during the Colorado gold rush of 1859, the uneasiness between American Indians and European Americans was mounting and being expressed through reprisals on each side. The proposed Medicine Lodge treaty was to be negotiated with the largest of the Southern Plains Indian nations and represented the last diplomatic effort of the United States to approach the land issue. The treaty marked the beginning of the reservation period for the Plains Indian nations. They were removed from their land, thus also from the pathways of commerce and settlement, and confined to reservations, where they would be assimilated.

The Dog Soldiers, the militant Cheyenne band, did not want peace and unsuccessfully tried to prevent Black Kettle from attending the treaty councils. After Black Kettle arrived at the site, leaders of the Dog Soldiers named Tall Bull and Gray Head demanded that Black Kettle explain the importance of signing the treaty during the upcoming ceremonies of Sacred Arrows Renewal. The Treaty of Medicine Lodge stipulated that the Cheyenne give up all their land for a reservation in Indian Territory between the Arkansas and Cimarron rivers, where they were supposed to adopt the European American pattern of civilization. After Black Kettle signed, the Dog Soldiers chiefs joined in signing the Treaty of Medicine Lodge on October 28, 1867.

The U.S. government was slow to meet the stipulations of the treaty that promised provisions to the Cheyenne living on their reservation, however. Young warriors thus grew increasingly restless and uncontrollable, joining the fighting parties on their raids. Following a trail left by one such party, the Seventh Cavalry under Colonel George Custer attacked Black Kettle's village, encamped at the Washita River. Together with many of his people (estimated at as many as twenty men and forty women and children), Black Kettle and his wife were killed at dawn on November 27, 1868. When the *New York Times* reported this massacre, it described Black Kettle, the greatest Cheyenne peace chief, as one of the most warlike characters of the plains.

Antonie Dvorakova

See also Assimilation; Chivington, John Milton; Treaty with the Cheyenne and Arapaho–October 28, 1867.

References and Further Reading
Berthrong, Donald, J. 1963. *The Southern Cheyennes.* Norman: University of Oklahoma Press.
Hoig, Stan. 1980. *The Peace Chiefs of the Cheyennes.* Norman: University of Oklahoma Press.
Jones, Douglas C. 1966. *The Treaty of Medicine Lodge: The Story of the Great Council as Told by Eyewitnesses.* Norman: University of Oklahoma Press.

Blondin-Andrew, Ethel Dorothy
(1951–)

Throughout her political career with the government of Canada, Ethel Blondin-Andrew has served as a strong and representative voice for the views of aboriginal people living in northern Canada, bringing their concerns to national prominence. Blondin-Andrew is an advocate for aboriginal people, youth, persons with disabilities, and the environment.

Born on March 25, 1951 in Fort Norman (Tulita), Northwest Territories, Canada, Ethel Blondin-Andrew is a Treaty Dene of the Dene Nation, and she is fluent in English and Dene-Slavey.

Blondin-Andrew earned a bachelor's degree in education from the University of Alberta before returning to teach at the elementary school level in several communities in the Northwest Territories, including Tuktoyaktuk, Deline, and Fort Providence. She was one of the first accredited aboriginal teachers in northern Canada. She went on to work as an aboriginal language and curriculum specialist as well as a college instructor. Furthermore, she became acting director of the Public Service Commission of Canada, national manager of Indigenous Development Programs, and assistant deputy minister of culture and communications for the government of the Northwest Territories.

On November 12, 1988, Blondin-Andrew became the first aboriginal woman to be elected to the House of Commons of the government of Canada as a member of Parliament for the Western Arctic. She is affiliated with the Liberal Party of Canada. Blondin-Andrew has since been reelected four times as member of Parliament, most recently on June 28, 2004.

As a member of Parliament, Blondin-Andrew encouraged the House of Commons to pass a bill for the establishment of an aboriginal languages foundation, an organization that would facilitate the acquisition, preservation, enhancement, maintenance, retention, and use of First Nations languages across Canada. Although this was a laudable objective and was much needed by First Nations, the bill was defeated by a vote in the House of Commons.

On November 4, 1993, Blondin-Andrew was named secretary of state (training and youth) and was, again, the first aboriginal woman to become a member of the Privy Council and the Cabinet.

In 1997 she was named secretary of state (children and youth). In this position, Blondin-Andrew tackled some tough issues, including fetal alcohol syndrome, a problem that affects many First Nations communities. In addition, Blondin-Andrew was involved with the creation of the National Expert Advisory Committee on the Centres of Excellence for Children's Well-Being. The government of Canada contributed $20 million over a period of five years for the development of the five existing centers, which bring together professors, scientists, and government officials to address issues affecting children across Canada (for example, early childhood development, child welfare, and children with special needs).

Blondin-Andrew received an honorary doctorate from Brock University in Ontario, Canada, in June 2001 as an acknowledgement of her ongoing work and efforts for Canada's aboriginal communities. In 2002, Blondin-Andrew received the Aboriginal Women in Leadership Distinction Award for her work in political leadership and children's issues.

Ethel Blondin-Andrew was named minister of state (northern development) for the government of Canada on July 20, 2004. As minister, Blondin-Andrew has been supportive of the recent Canada-Aboriginal Peoples Roundtable, which marked the beginning of a renewed dialogue between First Nations leaders from across the country and the Canadian government.

As a single mother of three children, a Dene woman from northern Canada, and a member of parliament with the government of Canada, Ethel Blondin-Andrew has had a unique opportunity to travel across the country and raise awareness about issues specific to northern Canada as well as First Nations issues in general. She has opened doors for other First Nations people who may want to have a career in politics with the government of Canada, and she brings a new perspective to the House of Commons.

Lysane Cree

See also Canada; Constitution Act (Canada), 1867; Constitution Act (Canada), 1982; Sahtu Dene and Métis Comprehensive Land Claim Agreement–September 6, 1993.

References and Further Reading
Asch, Michael. 1984. *Home and Native Land: Aboriginal Rights and the Canadian Constitution.* Toronto: Methuen.
Cardinal, Harold. 1977. *The Rebirth of Canada's Indians.* Edmonton: Hurtig.
Dickason, Olive Patricia. 1992. *Canada's First Nations: A History of Founding Peoples from Earliest Times.* Norman: University of Oklahoma Press.

Blount, William
(1749–1800)

William Blount was one of the first United States superintendents of Indian affairs. Born into a distinguished family of merchant-planters in Bertie County, North Carolina, Blount grew up disparaging the rough-hewn, backcountry colonial settlers. Not surprisingly, Blount was an opponent of the Regulators, a loose organization of western populists seeking greater economic, political, and social parity with the eastern planters through election, tax, and judicial reforms. By May 1771, Regulator demands grew into physical confrontation, and Blount served in the loyalist militia that confronted and crushed a force of two thousand Regulators. These opposing groups eventually allied, though, when Britain reaffirmed protection of Indian lands, closing off western settlement, and the eastern seaboard planter elite resisted Britain's attempts to reassert control over local affairs, handled by the colonial assembly for nearly a century. There was some reform after the Regulator movement, both groups having representation in the assembly. The increasing tension

William Blount (1749–1800) of Windsor, North Carolina was a senator from Tennessee and served as one of the first U.S. Superintendents of Indian Affairs. He died in 1800, in Knoxville, Tennessee. (Buckner, Melton F., The First Impeachment: The Constitution's Framers and the Case of Senator William Blount, *1998.)*

between that body and the royal governor led the colony to support the movement for independence from Britain. William Blount emerged as a powerful but moderate Revolutionary War leader.

For three years, William Blount was involved in recruiting and provisioning forces to support George Washington's army in the north and local military operations in the southern states, and in commanding a unit serving under General Horatio Gates, which engaged, and was defeated by, General Cornwallis at Camden, South Carolina. Blount was also a paymaster for North Carolina and issued vouchers to Tuscarora Indians in the revolutionary cause. After the war, Blount moved west to Rocky Mount, a cabin near present-day Johnson City, Tennessee.

Blount served in North Carolina's state assembly from 1780–1784 and 1788–1790, and was a North Carolina delegate to the Continental Congress from 1783–1784 and 1786–1787. William Blount also represented North Carolina in its dealings with the Cherokee.

In 1790, President Washington appointed Blount governor of the newly formed territory south of the Ohio River. It was during his tenure as territorial governor that Blount also served as superintendent of Indian affairs for the Southern District. He negotiated the 1791 Treaty of Holston—also called the Blount Treaty—with the Cherokee Nation. More than twelve hundred Cherokee attended the negotiations, and forty-two tribal leaders signed the treaty, acknowledging Cherokee defeat in 1779 in support of the British during the Revolution. The Cherokee surrendered all claims to land lying east of the Clinch River and north of a line running through Kingston to the North Carolina border. The treaty redrew national boundaries and opened up significant land to American settlement.

Blount also oversaw the organization of the territorial militia but cautioned against its deployment except in a purely defensive capacity to deal with nontreaty Indians. In 1795, Blount called a constitutional convention to organize part of the territory into a state, and Tennessee entered the Union the next year. Meanwhile, Blount's speculation in western lands led him into financial difficulties, and he seems to have formed a tentative plan to conquer for Britain—not the United States—the Spanish provinces of Florida and Louisiana, using the combined warriors of the Cherokee and Creek Nations, frontier militias, and British naval forces. President Adams intercepted a letter Blount wrote alluding to the plan—thereafter called Blount's Conspiracy—and turned it over to the Senate on July 3, 1797. Blount's Conspiracy involved the corruption of two U.S. officials and would have breached Article V of the Treaty of San Lorenzo el Real (signed October 27, 1795) between the United States and Spain, by which each power agreed not to incite Indian nations to attack the other.

The House of Representatives impeached Blount on July 7, 1797, and the Senate expelled him the following day for guilt of a "high misdemeanor" inconsistent with his public trust and duty as a senator. The House of Representatives adopted articles of impeachment on January 17, 1798, but the Senate later decided that it had no jurisdiction, as Blount was no longer a member of the Senate and had never been a civil officer of the United States within the meaning of the Constitution. The case is significant because it was the first impeachment brought before the Senate. Britain disavowed the conspiracy, although evidence suggests its tacit approval. However, the rough-hewn, backcountry settlers welcomed Blount back to Tennessee a hero, and he became the presiding officer of the state Senate.

William Blount played an integral role in pushing the United States past the southern Appalachian range and propelling the nation ever westward through constant negotiation and renegotiation of treaties with Native nations. Blount died at Knoxville on March 21, 1800.

C. S. Everett

See also Treaty with the Cherokee–July 2, 1791.
References and Further Reading
Kappler, Charles J., ed. 1904. *Indian Affairs: Laws and Treaties,* vol. 2, *Treaties.* Washington, DC: Government Printing Office.
Masterson, William. 1954. *American National Biography; Dictionary of American Biography: William Blount.* Repr., New York: Greenwood Press, 1969.
Melton, Buckner F., Jr. 1998. *The First Impeachment: The Constitution's Framers and the Case of Senator William Blount.* Macon, GA: Mercer University Press.

Boudinot, Elias

(1800–1839)

Coward and traitor, or realist and pragmatist? Elias Boudinot continues to be a controversial figure in Cherokee history. Born Gallegina (Buck) Watie in 1800, he was educated at the Moravian missionary school near his home in present-day Georgia, where he learned the new written Cherokee language that he would use to publish the tribe's first bilingual newspaper. Boudinot was to become a respected Cherokee leader who supported his people's relocation to present-day Oklahoma. Taking a position against Chief John Ross and the rest of the Cherokee tribe, he violated the tribal law forbidding anyone to sign treaties to cede Cherokee lands.

While traveling to study at the American Board School in Connecticut, the young Buck Watie visited with two former presidents at their homes: Thomas Jefferson in Monticello and James Madison in Montpelier, Virginia. Watie's most significant visit was to Burlington, New Jersey, where he met Dr. Elias Boudinot, a statesman, poet, and writer who would become his benefactor. Watie would adopt Boudinot's name in appreciation of his financial support.

The American Board sponsored an eastern states speaking tour by Boudinot (formerly Watie), during

which he solicited donations for a daily Cherokee-language newspaper as well as an academy and library. The bilingual *Cherokee Phoenix* was established in 1827 in New Echota, Georgia, with Boudinot as editor. The first edition was delivered on February 21, 1828. Missionary Samuel Worcester worked with Boudinot publishing Cherokee-language religious texts and hymns. Cherokee chief John Ross disagreed with the editorial position of the newspaper on the question of Indian removal, maintaining that relocation was not a viable solution to the land dispute between the Cherokee and the federal government. Despite Boudinot's insistence on the freedom to print his viewpoint, he was forced to resign his editorship.

Boudinot's house was the meeting place for the signing of the Treaty of New Echota in December 1835. Nearly one hundred of the Cherokee signers felt that the U.S. federal government could not be stopped in its takeover of Cherokee-owned land. By agreeing to this treaty, they believed that they were guaranteeing a selection of quality land and repayment of moving expenses to present-day Oklahoma.

Ironically, in 1829 both Boudinot and fellow Treaty Party leader John Ridge supported a law that called for the death penalty for releasing Cherokee land to white settlers. Rival party members used this law to justify the execution of Ridge and Boudinot, who were killed in 1839 by unidentified assailants in the new Cherokee Nation.

Pamela Lee Gray

See also *Cherokee Nation v. Georgia,* 1831; Indian Removal Act, 1830; Ridge, John Rollin; Ridge, Major; Ross, John; New Echota, Georgia; Watie, Stand; Trail of Tears; Treaty with the Cherokee–December 29, 1835; *Worcester v. Georgia,* 1831.
References and Further Reading
Gabriel, Ralph Henry. 1941. *Elias Boudinot, Cherokee, and His America.* Norman: University of Oklahoma Press.
Hoig, Stanley W. 1998. *The Cherokees and Their Chiefs in the Wake of Empire.* Fayetteville: University of Arkansas Press.
McLoughlin, William G. 1993. *After the Trail of Tears: The Cherokees Struggle for Sovereignty, 1839–1880.* Chapel Hill: University of North Carolina Press.
Perdue, Theda, and Michael D. Green, eds. 1995. *The Cherokee Removal: A Brief History with Documents.* New York: St. Martins Press.
Sturm, Circe. 2002. *Blood Politics: Race, Culture, and Identity in the Cherokee Nation of Oklahoma.* Berkeley, Los Angeles, and London: University of California Press.

Wallace, Anthony F. C. 1993. *The Long, Bitter Trail: Andrew Jackson and the Indians.* New York: Hill and Wang.

Brant, Joseph
(1742–1807)

Joseph Brant is revered by many historians for his compliant acceptance of colonial society and the ability to effectively interact with government officials. Yet oral tradition and recent histories are less tolerant of Brant for the role he played in pursuing the profits associated with assimilating into colonial society, which necessitated the sale of Mohawk lands and his abandonment of traditional ways.

Born in March 1742 on the banks of the Ohio River to Peter and Margaret, Brant, whose given name was Thayendanegea ("He Places Two Bets"), was the stepson of Brant Canagaraduncka, an influential Mohawk leader. Following Brant's birth, his family returned to upstate New York, where his sister Molly met and married Sir William Johnson, the British superintendent of the northern Indians of Canada, in 1753. Brant later served in the French and Indian Wars under Johnson's command and became a favorite of the British commander, who arranged for him to attend the Indian Charity School in Lebanon, Connecticut, where he learned to speak English while studying Western history.

He left school after a year to work as a translator for the Anglican Missionary, and in 1765 he married Christine, the daughter of an Oneida chief, and had two children. He also worked as an interpreter for Johnson following Christine's death from tuberculosis in 1771. In 1773, he married his wife's sister Susannah, who also died of tuberculosis a few months later. In 1774, Brant was appointed secretary to Johnson's successor, Guy Johnson.Brant quickly became the most reliable interpreter in the region, and he played an important role in Mohawk-British relations. A fierce British ally, in 1775 he was received by King George III, became a Freemason, and was appointed to the rank of captain. Many Native leaders were cautious about his allegiance to the Crown. Even so, he led four of the Six Nations for the British side during the Revolutionary War. When the war ended, however, the Mohawk territory was formally yielded to the United States, forcing the removal of Brant and his followers to the Grand River valley in Ontario, Canada.

Mohawk sachem Joseph Brant (1742–1807), also known as Thayendanega, was a significant native leader during the American Revolution. Brant allied himself with the British against the American colonists. He died in 1807 at his estate near Brantford, Ontario. (National Archives)

Cognizant of the Mohawk role in the war, in 1784 General Frederick Haldimand rewarded the Mohawks with a tract of land six miles on either side of the Grand River in Ontario, which amounted to 675,000 acres, in return for territory lost to the Americans in New York State. The Mohawks and Brant moved to the Grand River basin, where they made their settlement at present-day Brantford, Ontario. Brant also received a pension and a parcel of land at the Head of the Lake (Burlington). Brant and the Six Nations chiefs signed a formal deed in 1787 that extended several thousand acres of land to European settlers for farming, milling, and other trades to avoid the land's usurpation by squatters. This was an important decision that is still a source of community debate.

Clearly, Brant viewed becoming Europeanized as the primary means of long-term survival of the Mohawk, and he encouraged his followers to adopt European technologies and lifestyles. He was among the first generation of Mohawks to own land individually rather than maintaining communal ties, and he adopted European ways; for example, he owned two black slaves and developed a fondness for roast beef and organ music.In the end, it was in part his allegiance to Britain that led to the loss of territories in the United States. In addition, Brant's failure to obtain firm title to the Haldimand lands and the Grand River reserve lands has led a number of contemporary historians to conclude that Brant's presence was divisive and led to the ruination of the Six Nations.

Joseph Brant lived his remaining days with his third wife, Catherine Croghan, spending the majority of his time trying to establish the Mohawks' legal title to the land. In addition to raising his seven children, he also worked on translating the Bible into Mohawk. On November 24, 1807, Brant died at age 65 in the home he built at Grand River, Ontario. He was buried at the Episcopal church that he also constructed.

Yale D. Belanger

See also Battle of Fallen Timbers, 1794.
References and Further Reading
Jakes, John. 1969. *Mohawk: The Life of Joseph Brant.* New York: Crowell-Collier Press.
Kelsay, Isabel. 1984. *Joseph Brant, 1743–1807: Man of Two Worlds.* Syracuse, NY: Syracuse University Press.
Robinson, Helen. 1986. *Joseph Brant: A Man for His People.* Toronto: Dundurn Press.
Thomas, Howard. 1973. *Joseph Brant (Thayendanegea).* New York: Prospect Books.

Buffalo

(1759–1855)

Chief Buffalo, also known as Kechewaishke, Beshkike, and Le Boeuf, was principal chief of the Lake Superior Ojibwe and signer of the 1837, 1842, and 1854 treaties. In 1850, President Zachary Taylor signed an executive order removing the Ojibwe to Minnesota. Two years later, at the age of 93, Buffalo led a delegation to Washington, where he met with Taylor's successor, Millard Fillmore. Buffalo persuaded Fillmore to rescind the removal order and establish permanent homelands for the Ojibwe. Buffalo was chief architect of the 1854 treaty, which created four of the six Ojibwe reservations in Wisconsin. He died a year later at his home in La Pointe on Madeline Island in Wisconsin.

Buffalo was born at La Pointe and distinguished himself in his early years as a powerful war chief. In 1842, he orchestrated a brilliant victory against the Sioux at the Brule River. Far outnumbered, on the night before the battle he ordered fires built along the river to trick the Sioux into thinking his numbers were greater than they were. Later, he became a powerful orator and a skillful negotiator. In 1854, he insisted that U.S. negotiators state explicitly in the treaty that the Ojibwe retained their hunting, fishing, and gathering rights to the land they were giving up.

Buffalo is best known for his highly successful 1852 journey to Washington, D.C., and meeting with the president, in which the removal order relocating the Ojibwe to Sandy Lake, Minnesota, was reversed. Along with O-sho-ga and interpreter Benjamin Armstrong (his nephew by marriage and adopted son), Buffalo walked and traveled by canoe, steamboat, and train to Washington, where his efforts to meet with Luke Lea, the commissioner of Indian affairs, were rebuffed. Lea told Armstrong to take the Ojibwes with him on the next train and that he did not want to hear from him again.

Buffalo's delegation attracted a lot of attention in Washington. The members were invited to the homes of prominent individuals and besieged by dozens of people who gathered outside their hotel, forcing them to occasionally slip away through a back door. While in the dining room one day, the delegation was approached by several Whig Party officials. The Whigs arranged an audience with their president, Fillmore, who smoked a peace pipe with the old chief. Buffalo told Fillmore about the disastrous annuity payment at Sandy Lake two years earlier, when U.S. officials had tried to lure the Ojibwe into permanently relocating to Minnesota. About four hundred Ojibwe had died from disease, starvation, or cold while trying to collect their treaty payments. Buffalo told the president that the Ojibwe were more resolved than ever not to relocate. He said there was universal disappointment over the failure of the U.S. government to live up to promises made in the 1837 and 1842 treaties. Buffalo told the president that he was particularly concerned that he might not be able to control the young warriors of his tribe. Two days later, Fillmore rescinded the removal order and ordered that the annuity payments be distributed from La Pointe as before.

The historic meeting also set up the 1854 treaty, the third and final land cession treaty, in which Ojibwe reservations in Michigan, Minnesota, and Wisconsin were established. Buffalo insisted that the Ojibwe bands not give up the last of their lands without receiving an assignment of land as a new home. The chief added that he wanted annuities to be paid to his people at LaPointe instead of at Sandy Lake. The old LaPointe chief demanded that the government's interpreter be replaced with one of his own people, because he did want any trickery as in the past.

Buffalo's health began to fail. He was too sick to attend the council meetings that took place during the 1855 annuity distribution. On September 7, 1855, two days after being baptized a Catholic, Buffalo died. He was buried in the Catholic cemetery at LaPointe on Madeline Island. However, according to some oral accounts, his remains were moved to an undisclosed location on the mainland.

Patricia A. Loew

See also Bureau of Indian Affairs (BIA); *Lac Courte Oreilles Band of Chippewa Indians v. Voigt et al.*, 1983; Treaty with the Chippewa–July 29, 1837; Treaty of 1855 with the Chippewa–February 22, 1855; Bureau of Indian Affairs.
References and Further Reading
Armstrong, Benjamin. 1892. *Early Life among the Indians.* Ashland, WI: Press of A. W. Bowron.
Loew, Patty. 2001. *Indian Nations of Wisconsin: Histories of Endurance and Renewal.* Madison: Wisconsin Historical Society Press.
Satz, Ronald N. 1991. *Chippewa Treaty Rights: The Reserved Rights of Wisconsin's Chippewa Indians in Historical Perspective.* Madison: Wisconsin Academy of Sciences, Arts, and Letters.

Bureau of Indian Affairs (BIA)

Before the American Revolution, Native Americans enjoyed some protection from treaties made with the English; however, with war looming, the first Continental Congress created the Department of Indian Affairs. The function of this organization was to obtain treaties and ensure tribal neutrality during the upcoming war. Created in 1775, the department was divided into northern, central, and southern divisions. After the war, the United States War Department was officially formed, and one of its responsibilities was Indian relations. The view of most politicians in the late 1700s and early 1800s was that the Indian and American culture were incompatible; however, they believed that Natives had the basic skills required to evolve culturally. To this end, Congress passed four Trade and Intercourse Acts, which dealt exclusively with Indian affairs. These acts established a factory system in which trade goods were provided at a fair price so that Indians would remain close to trading posts and maintain trade relations.

President Thomas Jefferson (1801–1809), along with those in Indian affairs, believed that the factory system was not a permanent solution, because the Indians would continue to be a hunter-gatherer state and thus would never be truly civilized. In 1822, the factory system was terminated. Two years later, John C. Calhoun, the secretary of war, established the Bureau of Indian Affairs. By this action, the War Department was relieved of all responsibility concerning Indian affairs but retained its authority in them. Calhoun appointed Thomas McKenney, a former superintendent of Indian affairs, as the head of this new office. McKenney and two assistants inherited the job of approving vouchers for expenditures, allocating funds for civilizing Indians, settling disagreements between Natives and white settlers over land, and handling all correspondence normally directed to the War Department concerning Indian affairs.

McKenney quickly realized that, in order to carry out his new responsibilities, he must have the authority to enforce the actions of the department. On March 31, 1826, he presented to Congress a bill that would establish an office of Indian affairs independent of the secretary of war (the names Bureau of Indian Affairs and Office of Indian Affairs were interchangeable). Because Calhoun had established this division of the War Department with out congressional authorization, he retained all authority. This bill would make the Office of Indian Affairs an official body, which, although still serving under the secretary of war, would have the authority to act and to enforce the actions. Congress failed to approve the bill twice, and it was not until 1931 that the Bureau of Indian Affairs was officially recognized and formed.

The formation of an official Bureau of Indian Affairs (BIA), it was hoped, would bring to a close an era of confusion in the handling of Indian policy. The opinion that Indians could be assimilated into white culture was abandoned, and the new consensus was to force the tribes off land desired by the U.S. government. This removal policy was formally adopted in 1825 and, in the hands of the BIA, was fully implemented by the 1830s. With a concerted effort on the part of the BIA and the U.S. government, huge numbers of Indians were forced off their lands and pushed west. The results were particularly devastating in the Southeast, where the Cherokee, Chickasaw, Creek, and Seminole were moved hundreds of miles to their new homes. The most infamous incident involving these removals involved the Cherokee.

Traditionally located in present-day Virginia, western Virginia, Kentucky, Tennessee, western North Carolina, South Carolina, northern Georgia, and northeastern Alabama, the Cherokee were a large tribe thriving in a hunter-gatherer state. The Cherokee had by any standards assimilated white civilization. They had developed a written language, had their own newspapers, had adopted the Christian religion, and had even adopted their own constitution. In an attempt to solve their dilemma legally, the Cherokee brought their case to the Supreme Court, where they unexpectedly won a decision favoring their ownership of their ancestral land. The decision reached by Chief Justice John Marshall said, "The Cherokee nation, . . . is a distinct community, occupying its own territory, . . . in which the laws of Georgia can have no force . . ." (*Worcester v. Georgia*, 1832, 6 Peters, 534–536, 558–563). Unfortunately, the rest of the United States did not share the sentiments held by the Supreme Court. President Andrew Jackson, not an Indian sympathizer, refused to enforce the rulings. The Cherokee were forced to move, many times at gunpoint, and thousands died. The harsh conditions and cruel treatment of the BIA and the U.S. government during the removal caused eight thousand Indian deaths. This one-thousand-mile march west became known as the Trail of Tears because the Indian way of life was all but erased.

In 1849, Congress moved the Bureau of Indian Affairs to the Department of the Interior, which by 1867 had allowed the BIA to become more involved with the affairs of the Indians. By this time, the BIA had in effect become the governmental body presiding over the Indian territories, and it took full liberty in brutalizing their way of life. The agency forbade any language but English to be spoken, outlawed all Indian religious ceremonies, and forbade Indians any form of traditional government. The biggest injustices presided over by the BIA were felt by Indian children. Put into boarding school to "civilize" them, these young Indians were abused physically, emotionally, and spiritually in an attempt to make them ashamed of who they were. The treatment of Indians and the shaming they endured caused suicide, alcoholism, and depression to become normal characteristics of Indian societies.

For its entire duration as a government institution, the BIA invoked the will of the people in destroying the Native Americans' lifeways. It was not until the early twentieth century, when federal policy began to stop trying to destroy Indian culture and instead began to protect it, that the BIA developed into an institution dedicated to helping the Indian cause. In 1928, the Meriam Report was published, which detailed the shortcomings of the services provided for the reservations. This report sparked an era in which the BIA and the government worked hard to improve Indian life socially, economically, and psychologically. By 1960, the BIA's services were expanded to include forestry, agricultural extension service, range management, and land acquisition in an effort to improve the Indians' plight. This was the peak of the BIA's range of responsibilities; shortly thereafter, the government allocated the education of Indian children to the state and health care to the Department of Health, Education, and Welfare.

In the 1970s, Congress proceeded to pass a series of laws that helped better the situation of Native Americans. Some of these include the American Indian Self-Determination and Education Act of 1975, the Indian Health Care Improvement Act of 1976, and the Indian Child Welfare Act of 1978. The BIA of today is attempting to change its position from one of management of tribes to one of assistance. One of the most important aspects of the modern BIA is that, of its more than ten thousand employees, 95 percent are Native American. Although Indians' position toward the BIA is tentative, both sides hope that the BIA can truly move to a position of assistance instead of a dictator of policies. In September 2003, when the head of the BIA publicly apologized for the agency's "legacy of racism and inhumanity," it was seen by all as admission of past misdeeds and a commitment to a better future. The closing words of this apology express the desires and hopes of the BIA and Native Americans in years to come: "The Bureau of Indian Affairs was born in 1824 in a time of war on Indian people. May it live in the year 2000 and beyond as an instrument of their prosperity."

Arthur Holst

See also American Indian Self-Determination and Education Act of 1975; Sovereignty; Termination; Treaty; Trust Doctrine.

References and Further Reading

Kvasnicka, Robert M., and Herman J. Viola, eds. 1979. *The Commissioners of Indian Affairs, 1824–1977.* Lincoln: University of Nebraska Press.

Prucha, Francis Paul. 1984. *The Great Father: The United States Government and the American Indian.* Lincoln and London: University of Nebraska Press.

Prucha, Francis Paul. 1994. *American Indian Treaties: The History of a Political Anomaly.* Berkeley: University of California Press.

Burke, Charles H.

(1861–1944)

Charles H. Burke was commissioner of Indian affairs during 1921–1929 and one of the last overt supporters of the forced assimilation of American Indian peoples. The decade during which Burke oversaw the Bureau of Indian Affairs (BIA) witnessed the beginnings of a battle waged between the so-called obscurantists, such as Burke and interior secretaries Albert B. Fall and Hubert Work, and the "Red Progressives," led by John Collier and Gertrude Bonnin.

Before he became the head of the BIA, Burke's tenure as a Republican congressman from South Dakota had earned him a long-established record as an assimilationist. In 1906, he had authored the Burke Act, which sought to change the terms of the Dawes Act of 1887, which had begun the process of alienating treaty-guaranteed land from the tribes. Burke's act allowed a shortening of the twenty-five-year period before reservation land allotted to individual Indians lost its federal trust protection. All Indians judged by the government to be competent to handle their property independently could have the trust restrictions waived, opening the way for the sale of the land. This resulted in yet more land passing from Indian to non-Indian hands. During Burke's tenure, the BIA and its parent body,

Secretary of the Interior Hubert Work and Commissioner of Indian Affairs Charles Burke (left) with Chief Red Eagle and Chief Bacon Rind. During Burke's service as commissioner, he worked to improve health conditions among Native Americans. (Library of Congress)

the Department of the Interior, pursued a policy of opening reservation lands to non-Indian settlement and reservation petroleum and mineral resources to business.

Probably the most overt example of land grabbing against all law during Burke's tenure as commissioner occurred in 1922, when he and Secretary Fall were able to persuade New Mexico senator Holm Bursum to propose a bill to legitimize the land claims of squatters who had illegally settled on land held by the New Mexico Pueblos. By September, the Bursum Bill had caught the attention of numerous other national and local groups working for reform in Indian affairs. John Collier's articles against the bill were published in *Sunset* magazine, bringing the obscurantist-progressive debate into many middle-class homes.

Organized by Collier and numerous Pueblo leaders in response to the threat posed by the Bursum Bill to Pueblo Indian lands, water, and, by extension, their entire way of life, a meeting took place on November 5, 1922, at Santo Domingo Pueblo. In attendance were more than one hundred representatives from all the pueblos of New Mexico. Although each pueblo governs and advocates for itself in most matters, a pueblo-wide council meeting to address a threat posed by a non-Indian government was not without precedent, as the Spaniards would have known since the Pueblo Revolt of 1680. Owing to the efforts of the Indian peoples of the Southwest and much of the informed public, the bill was defeated.

Burke continued the government's long-established policy of suppressing Indian culture, relying on off-reservation schools to accomplish his assimilationist agenda. Immediately upon taking office, Burke set about suppressing Indian religion by increasing enforcement of the Religious Crimes Codes, even personally ordering several religious leaders from Taos Pueblo jailed. In the case of the Sun Dance, he argued that, because the ceremony would require Indians to travel from a wide area for an extended period, to the neglect of their crops, it was not acceptable and could be punished under the Indian Offense Laws (Prucha 1984).

Most of Burke's term as commissioner was consumed by continuing criticism and activism by the Red Progressives, culminating in the release of the Meriam Report in 1928, which took the BIA to task for the poor living and working conditions and educational opportunities for Indians. The report concluded that the imposition of white culture and government by the BIA and the continuing depletion of tribal lands (most of which were guaranteed by treaty), the specific agenda that Burke pushed during his tenure, were the causes of most of the problems Indians faced.

Steven L. Danver

See also Bureau of Indian Affairs (BIA); Southern Plains and the Southwest; Treaty of Guadalupe Hidalgo, 1848.

References and Further Reading

Fixico, Donald L. 1998. *The Invasion of Indian Country in the Twentieth Century: American Capitalism and Tribal Natural Resources.* Niwot, CO: University Press of Colorado.

Kelly, Lawrence C. 1979. "Charles Henry Burke (1921–29)." In *The Commissioners of Indian Affairs, 1824–1977,* eds. Robert M. Kvasnicka and Herman J. Viola, 251–261. Lincoln: University of Nebraska Press.

Philp, Kenneth R. 1981. *John Collier's Crusade for Indian Reform, 1920–1954.* Tucson: University of Arizona Press.

Prucha, Francis Paul. 1984. *The Great Father: The United States Government and the American Indians.* Lincoln: University of Nebraska Press.

Caldwell, Billy
(1780–1841)

Billy Caldwell was a man of Mohawk-Irish descent who rose to a position of influence within the United Band of Ottawa, Chippewa, and Potawatomi Indians over the course of the early nineteenth century. After working for much of the early 1800s in the Indian Department of the British government, Caldwell used trade and kinship connections to rise to a position of power within the United Band community. In the late 1830s, he moved west with this band and served as an important intermediary and leader for them until his death in 1841.

Billy Caldwell was the son of an officer in the British army and a Mohawk woman. Raised among the Mohawk people until the age of eight, he spent his remaining childhood years with his father's second family near Detroit. Caldwell went to a Jesuit school, where he learned both French and English. In his late teens, he began to work for local fur traders, Robert and Thomas Forsyth, and by 1803 had assumed the position of clerk at their Chicago trading post. Over the course of the next decade, he ventured into trading operations of his own, although he never left the umbrella of the Forsyth firm. Dur-

ing this period, Caldwell also created a personal connection with the Potawatomi communities that resided on the St. Joseph River in southern Michigan by marrying La Nanette, the daughter of Wabinema, or White Sturgeon. Following her death, he married the mixed-descent daughter of Robert Forsyth and an Ojibwa woman. Through both his work and his marriages, by 1812 Caldwell had established himself as a valued middleman and broker among the British, American, and Indian communities in the region. At the outbreak of the War of 1812, Caldwell sided with the British, and in 1813 he obtained the rank of captain in the Western Division of the British Indian Department. During his service, he interacted primarily with Potawatomi warriors, who had also allied with the British. After the American victory, Caldwell's fortunes declined within the British service, and he received his discharge in the fall of 1816. Failing to establish a career in the years following his discharge, Caldwell returned to Chicago in 1820 at the age of forty and reconnected with his former employers, the Forsyths. During this time in Chicago, Caldwell returned to his intermediary position among the diverse communities in the Great Lakes region. He often served as an interpreter for U.S. government agents, and his experience and standing in the community even garnered him a nomination for the office of justice of the peace in 1826.

As a result of his affiliation with the Forsyths, his work for the American government, and his connections to the Potawatomi Indians in the region, Caldwell became a prominent figure in U.S.-Potawatomi relations. Based primarily on the initiative of Indian agent Alexander Wolcott, Caldwell, as a named Potawatomi chief, negotiated and signed the 1829 treaty that ceded lands claimed by the United Band in and around the Rock River in northern Illinois. He also signed the treaty of 1833 in Chicago, which ceded approximately five million acres of land in northern Illinois and southern Wisconsin and paved the way for the removal of the United Band to lands west of the Mississippi River. Yet in the years between this last treaty and his death, Caldwell worked solely on behalf of the United Band. He moved west with them and set up his home near Council Bluffs in Iowa Territory. During his brief tenure in the West, Caldwell helped to represent the Indians' interests in all negotiations and interactions with American officials and gained the trust and allegiance of such leaders as Abtekizhek, or Half Day.

Billy Caldwell died on September 27, 1841, one of the many victims of a cholera epidemic that hit the region. Only a few years later, the comments of Potawatomi leaders during treaty negotiations testified to Caldwell's legacy. The first of many demands was that the United States officially acknowledge the community of Indians formerly known as the United Band as "The Prairie Indians of Caldwell's Band of Potawatomies."

John P. Bowes

See also Forsyth, Thomas; Indian Removal Act, 1830; Treaty with the Chippewa, Etc.–September 26, 1833.

References and Further Reading
Clifton, James A. 1978. "Personal and Ethnic Identity on the Great Lakes Frontier: The Case of Billy Caldwell, Anglo-Canadian." *Ethnohistory*, 25(1): 69–94.
Clifton, James A. 1977. *The Prairie People: Continuity and Change in Potawatomi Indian Culture 1665–1965.* Lawrence: Regents Press of Kansas.
Edmunds, R. David. 1979. *The Potawatomis: Keepers of the Fire.* Norman: University of Oklahoma Press.

Canassatego

(c. 1690–1750)

Canassatego was *tadadaho* (speaker) of the Iroquois Confederacy in the middle of the eighteenth century and a major figure in diplomacy with the French and English colonists. His advice that the colonies should form a union on the Iroquois model may have influenced Benjamin Franklin's plans for colonial union as early as 1754 at the Albany Congress. Some scholars disagree with the idea of a congress coming from the Iroquois model.

In 1744, Pennsylvania officials met with Iroquois sachems in a treaty council at Lancaster, Pennsylvania. This meeting was one of a number of significant diplomatic parlays between British colonists, the Iroquois, and their allies that preceded and helped shape the outcome of the French and Indian War. At the meeting, Canassatego and other Iroquois complained that the colonies, having no central authority, had been unable to restrain invasion of Iroquois lands. In that context, Canassatego advised the colonists to form a union like that of the Iroquois.

Richard Peters, delegate from Pennsylvania, described Canassatego at Lancaster as "a tall, well-made man" with "a very full chest and brawny limbs, a manly countenance, with a good-natured [*sic*] smile. He was about 60 years of age, very active, strong, and had a surprising liveliness in his speech" (Grinde and Johansen 1991, 94).

At the time of the Lancaster Treaty Council, Franklin, then a Philadelphia printer, was publishing the transcripts of Indian treaty councils as small booklets that enjoyed a lively sale in the colonies and in England. The Lancaster Treaty was one of several dozen treaty accounts published by Franklin between 1736 and 1762. Franklin read Canassatego's words as they issued from his press and as he became an advocate of colonial union by the early 1750s, when he began his diplomatic career as a Pennsylvania delegate to the Iroquois and their allies. Franklin urged the British colonies to unite in emulation of the Iroquois Confederacy in a letter to his printing partner James Parker in 1751 and as he drew up his Albany Plan of Union in 1754.

After he advised colonial leaders to form a federal union at the Lancaster Treaty Council of 1744, Canassatego also became a British literary figure, the hero of John Shebbeare's *Lydia, or, Filial Piety*, published in 1755. The real Canassatego died in 1750. With the flowery eloquence prized by romantic novelists of his time, Shebbeare portrayed Canassatego as something more than human—something more, even, than the "noble savage" that was so popular in Enlightenment Europe. Having saved the life of a helpless English maiden from the designs of a predatory English ship captain en route, once in England Canassatego became judge and jury for all that was contradictory and corrupt in mid-eighteenth-century England.

Disembarking, Shebbeare's Canassatego meets with a rude sight: a ragged collection of dwellings, and men rising from the bowels of the earth dirty, broken, and degraded. Asking his hosts for an explanation, Canassatego is told that the men have been digging coal. The Iroquois sachem inquires whether everyone in England digs coal for a living and reflects that he is beginning to understand why so many English have fled to America.

In 1775, Canassatego's thirty-one-year-old advice was recalled at a treaty between colonial representatives and Iroquois leaders near Albany. The treaty commissioners told the sachems that they were heeding the advice Iroquois forefathers had given to the colonial Americans at Lancaster, Pennsylvania, in 1744. Although some may be skeptical of the Iroquois influence on the founding of the U.S. government, there are interesting parallels in that both are based on a democratic representation of their peoples.

Bruce E. Johansen

See also Albany Conferences of 1754 and 1775.
References and Further Reading

Boyd, Julian. 1981. "Dr. Franklin, Friend of the Indian." In *Meet Dr. Franklin*, ed. Ray Lokken, Jr. Philadelphia: Franklin Institute.
Grinde, Donald A., Jr., and Bruce E. Johansen. 1991. *Exemplar of Liberty: Native America and the Evolution of Democracy*. Los Angeles: University of California.
Van Doren, Carl, and Julian P. Boyd, eds. 1938. *Indian Treaties*. Printed by Benjamin Franklin 1736–1762. Philadelphia: Historical Society of Pennsylvania.
Wallace, Paul A. W. 1961. *Indians in Pennsylvania*. Harrisburg: Pennsylvania Historical and Museum Commission.

Canonicus
(c. 1562–1647)

The name Canonicus (also Cananacus, Conanicus, and various other variations) might be a Latin derivation of Qunnoune (Drake 1880, 118). He was the sachem of the Narragansetts, a native North American nation established in what is today Rhode Island. Although "he never fully trusted the English" (Hodge 1912, I, 202), mostly because of their aggressive ways, Canonicus always remained friendly to them. He gave Roger Williams the tract of land where Providence, Rhode Island, now stands. Long after his death, Canonicus was still remembered as a great sachem, as evidenced by the U.S. Navy naming four ships after him. He should not be confused with Canonchet, a later Narragansett sachem.

The earliest Narragansett sachem that the English had heard about was Tashtasick, who is sometimes referred to as Canonicus's father. But the tradition also reports that Wessonsuoum and Keneschoo, his son and daughter, were the parents of Canonicus (Drake 1880, 118). He spent his life in a village called Narragansett, north of what is now Kingston, Rhode Island. Following the two-sachem rule, the Narragansetts had Canonicus as their home sachem, while Miantonomi, his nephew, dealt with other matters, such as war parties.

Unlike other nearby nations, the Narragansetts largely avoided the diseases that carried off New England's native population in 1617–1619. This situation strengthened Canonicus's power and authority, in part because numerous refugees from other nations joined his people. Although he fought the Wampanoags, Canonicus remained at peace with his English neighbors. In the spring of 1636, Roger Williams went to the Narragansett country after he was banished from Massachusetts. Tradition reports that he was greeted by Canonicus with the words, "What cheer, nétop [my friend]" (Simmons 1978, 194). They soon established a good relationship, and Canonicus later gave some land to Williams, who was involved in the diplomatic efforts to stop the Narragansett war against the Wampanoags.

It was also under Williams's influence that Canonicus decided, in 1637, to help the Puritans and their Mohegan allies in their war against the Pequots.

After the Pequot Nation's dispersal following that devastating war, Mohegans and Narragansetts agreed to a treaty that would erase old enmities. The treaty was broken in 1643 when Sequasson, an allied sachem, was attacked by Uncas, sachem of the Mohegans. Miantonomi asked the English if he could retaliate, and they answered that they would not intervene. Unfortunately, Miantonomi was captured by Uncas in a raid soon afterward. Despite the £40 ransom sent by Canonicus, Uncas handed Miantonomi over to the English, who sentenced him to death secretly under Uncas's rule. The Narragansetts sought revenge for the disrespect of the ransom custom. On April 19, 1644, after having been under Puritan pressure for a long time, the Narragansetts surrendered themselves and their lands voluntarily to King Charles I for protection. Canonicus refused to explain his decision and suffered a loss of esteem among his people as a result. Canonicus signed a surrender treaty on August 28, 1645, in which he acknowledged various misdeeds, and he agreed to cede the Pequot country (Simmons 1978, 92). Canonicus never regained his full authority. He died on June 4, 1647, at the age of roughly eighty-five (Drake 1880, 119).

Philippe Charland

See also Aboriginal Title; Colonial and Early Treaties, 1775–1829; Northeast and the Great Lakes; Right of Conquest; Williams, Roger.

References and Further Reading

Drake, Samuel. 1880. *Drake's Indians of North America*. New York: Hurst.

Hodge, Frederick Webb, ed. 1912. *Handbook of North American Indians*, vols. 1 and 2, *North of Mexico*. Washington, DC: Government Printing Office.

Simmons, William S. 1978. "Narragansett." In *Handbook of North American Indians*, vol. 15, *Northeast*, ed. Bruce G. Trigger, 190–197. Washington, DC: Smithsonian Institution.

Captain Jack
(c. 1837–1873)

Kintpuash, a Modoc, later called Captain Jack by European American colonists of California, played a major role as a leader in the Modoc War of 1872–1873. Born at the Wa'chamshwash village on the Lower Lost River near the California-Oregon border, Kintpuash's father was ambushed and slain by whites during the Ben Wright Massacre of 1846. Little is known of his life before age twenty-five. We do know that his Modoc name, Kintpuash, meant "He Has Water Brash [Psoriasis]."

The Modocs had little contact with the immigrants until the advent of the 1849 California gold rush. Around this time, Kintpuash acquired the nickname Captain Jack because he wore a uniform

Captain Jack, also known as Kintpuash, was a key leader in the Modoc War. (Library of Congress)

coat with brass buttons, which had been given to him by a U.S. Army officer. Although the Modocs opposed European American expansion into their lands, Captain Jack counseled peace and encouraged trade with the settlers living near Eureka, California, during the 1840s. He had taken two wives by this time.

The gold rush intensified tensions and hostilities in the 1850s until Schonchin John, a Modoc chief, signed a treaty removing his band to a reservation in Oregon in 1864. The area was also the traditional homeland of the Klamaths, however, who resented the Modoc intrusion. Realizing that the land in Oregon was insufficient, Captain Jack and his followers returned to California and requested a reservation there. The federal and state authorities denied their request.

Settlers soon began to insist on the forced removal of Modocs. On November 28, 1872, forces invaded Captain Jack's camp and coerced him into consenting to removal. As tensions mounted at the meeting, violence broke out. Scarfaced Charley, a Modoc leader angered by the army's behavior, refused to give up his gun, and shots were fired during the ensuing struggle. When the fighting stopped, eight soldiers and fifteen Modocs were dead.

Fearing reprisals, the Modocs under Captain Jack fled to the Lava Beds nearby, believing that they would be safe there. However, this was not the case. Hooker Jim and his Modocs, encamped on the other side of the Lost River, were attacked by settlers; while retreating to the Lava Beds, they killed twelve whites in revenge. Within this hostile environment, the Modoc leaders—Captain Jack, Schonchin John, and Hooker Jim—prepared for an attack in the vast, largely inaccessible volcanic area. But Captain Jack still counseled peace and negotiation, arguing that the government would ultimately win. However, more militant factions under Hooker Jim and Schonchin John outvoted him.

On January 13, 1873, troops moved into the Lava Beds to quell the Modoc uprising. On February 28, Captain Jack's cousin Winema (married to a white man named Frank Riddle) and a peace delegation began talks with the rebellious Modocs. Hooker Jim and Schonchin John thought Captain Jack a coward for consenting to the talks, so they insisted that Captain Jack kill General Edward S. Canby, the head of the delegation. The Modoc militants also believed that U.S. resolve would be damaged by the death of Canby.

Reluctantly, Captain Jack agreed to their terms only if the Modocs were refused amnesty and a return to their California homeland. At a meeting on April 11, Captain Jack shot Canby. The Reverend Eleazar Thomas was also killed, and Albert Meachum, the Indian superintendent, was severely wounded. Winema and her husband managed to escape with the remaining members of the peace party. Quickly, the government fielded more troops and heavier weapons.

The rugged lava rock terrain worked to the Modocs' advantage at first, but dissension among the Modoc leaders and harsh conditions weakened their position. Captain Jack surrendered in late May. After a military trial, in which Hooker Jim testified for the prosecution, Captain Jack, Boston Charley, Black Jim, and Schonchin John were hanged on October 3, 1873. Since the administration of President Ulysses S. Grant had instituted its Peace Policy toward Indians, the American people were stunned by the uprising and the consequent inhumanity and insensitivity of the pursuit and hanging of the Modocs.

In the final analysis, white prejudice, Indian betrayal, greed, and an opportunistic press made a deplorable situation far worse. Employing more than a thousand soldiers to fight a Modoc force that never numbered more than fifty-three, the army incurred losses of seven officers, thirty-nine soldiers, two scouts, and sixteen civilians. The Modoc dead numbered eleven women and seven men. An enormous human and financial cost was endured to capture and remove 155 Modocs to Indian Territory.

A melodrama entitled *Captain Jack* was staged for a brief time in 1873, but it failed to fully capitalize on the tragic bloodletting. A second group of grisly entrepreneurs were more successful. On the day after Captain Jack's execution, robbers excavated his grave, embalmed his body, and put it on display in a carnival sideshow that toured profitably across many eastern cities.

In 1909, fifty-one of the Oklahoma Modocs were permitted to return to their reservation in Oregon.

Bruce E. Johansen

See also California, Hawaii, and the Pacific Northwest; Indian Territory.

References and Further Reading

Hagen, Olaf T. No date. "Modoc War Correspondence and Documents, 1865–1878." May 1942. Typescript, Office of Archeology and Historic Preservation, National Park Service. [Approximately 1,780 pages of documents selected from records in the National Archives,

War Department, Presidio of San Francisco, University of California (Berkeley) Library, and the Applegate Collection.]

McCarthy, Michael. No date. "Journal of Michael McCarthy." Library of Congress. Accessed at http://www.cr.nps.gov/history/online_books/labe/biblio.htm.

Miller, Colonel William Haven. No date. "Incidents of the Modoc War." [Narrative made available to Dr. Ron Rickey by Miller's grandson, Captain Charles F. Humphrey, Vallejo, California. Miller was a second lieutenant in Troop F, First Cavalry, during the Modoc War.]

Carson, Kit

(1809–1868)

Christopher Houston Carson, called Kit, served in the American West as a mountain man, expedition guide, Indian agent, and soldier from 1829 until his death in 1868. Although best known as an Indian fighter, Carson contributed to the development of the nascent United States as a guide in John Charles Frémont's expeditions into the western territories and as a messenger and soldier under the leadership of General Stephen Watts Kearny in California in 1846 and General Edward Richard Sprigg Canby in New Mexico during the Civil War. Carson's most infamous role befell him in 1863, when he was ordered to amass and remove the Diné (Navajos) from northeastern Arizona to the Bosque Redondo in eastern New Mexico—a series of events that culminated in the Long Walk.

Born on December 24, 1809, in Boonesborough, Kentucky, but raised near Franklin, Missouri, Carson was the sixth child of Rebecca Robinson Carson and her husband Lindsey. Kit quit school upon his father's death in 1818 and spent the majority of his youth working odd jobs that did not require the adolescent to read and write. In 1824, Carson's mother placed her fifteen-year-old son in a formal apprenticeship with David Workman, a saddle and harness maker. Two years later, Kit broke his contractual agreement with Workman and eventually made his way via the Santa Fe Trail to Taos, New Mexico, an important supply base and convenient marketplace for trappers and traders located seventy miles north of Santa Fe. Here, an illiterate Carson learned to speak Spanish fluently and found work as a cook for Ewing Young, a master trapper from Tennessee who earlier had participated in the overland trade with Santa Fe.

Scout Christopher "Kit" Carson (1809–1868) was renowned as a frontiersman, but also has a controversial legacy for his treatment of native people. (Library of Congress)

Carson first accompanied Young on a trapping expedition to California's central valley in August 1829, returning as Young's most dependable lieutenant in April 1831. While serving in this capacity, Carson fought, negotiated, and traded with the Zuni, Mojave, and Apache. Carson's association with Young launched his extended career as a fur trapper and brought him into contact with Thomas "Broken Hand" Fitzpatrick and the Rocky Mountain Fur Company. His exploits under the leadership of Fitzpatrick, beginning in the fall of 1831, led Carson down the Platte, Green, Columbia, and Salmon rivers—some of the most spectacular and beaver-rich areas in the Rocky Mountains. Carson spent the next decade trapping beaver in the American West, where he became intimately familiar with the cultures, languages, and traditions of several Indian tribes—experiences that later served him well as a federal Indian agent to the Ute in northern New Mexico.

As the beaver trade waned during the late 1830s and early 1840s, William Bent employed

Carson as a post hunter at Bent's Fort on the Arkansas River. While visiting family in Missouri in 1842, Carson met John C. Frémont, a western surveyor, explorer, and cartographer who later became a California senator and Republican Party presidential candidate, on a riverboat headed up the Missouri River from St. Louis. Frémont recruited Carson as a guide for his first expedition across the Great Plains on the Oregon Trail and into the Rocky Mountains, where they penetrated the Wind River Range in Wyoming and ascended a summit later christened Fremont Peak. Over the next several years, Carson escorted Frémont to Oregon, California, the central Rocky Mountains, and the Great Basin. Frémont's popular reports, actually written by his wife Jessie, sensationalized Carson's tenure as an expedition guide, transforming the temperate Missourian into a hero of gun duels, bear hunts, and wilderness adventures.

Carson's notoriety as an effectual mountain man and scout coincided with the adoption of Manifest Destiny by the United States as an axiom for western expansion. His third and final expedition occurred when Frémont asked him in August 1845 to serve as a guide to California. This scientific foray collided with international politics. President James Knox Polk's aspiration to acquire Mexican-controlled California and the New Mexico territory led to war with Mexico from 1846 to 1848. The Mexican government ultimately ceded much of the Southwest to the United States.

During the Mexican-American War, Carson served as a dispatch rider for the U.S. Army under the leadership of General Stephen Kearny. Stationed in California, Carson twice carried urgent messages to Washington, D.C., including news of the discovery of gold. These duties kept Carson away from his Taos home and his wife, Maria Josefa Jaramillo. Carson also missed the 1847 Taos Rebellion, in which Charles Bent, governor of New Mexico, lost his life while protecting members of Kit's family from a mob. Concern for his family's safety convinced Carson to quit his itinerant life.

In 1853, Carson accepted an appointment in Taos as federal agent for the Ute Indians. Carson remained an Indian agent until the outbreak of the Civil War, at which time he accepted a position as lieutenant colonel of the First New Mexico Volunteers. Promoted to colonel in September 1861, Carson actively participated in General Edward Canby's unsuccessful attempt to repel Confederate forces at the Battle of Valverde on February 21, 1862. A brief assignment at Fort Craig in southern New Mexico cost Carson the opportunity to participate in the Union victory at Glorieta Pass.

Owing to Carson's familiarity with southwestern tribes, General James Henry Carleton, Canby's successor as head of Union forces in New Mexico, next selected Carson to lead a military campaign against the Apaches in an effort to relocate the tribe to the Bosque Redondo. In June 1863, after successfully subjugating the Apaches, Carson left Fort Sumner, marched westward with seven hundred men, and launched three arduous scouting expeditions into the heart of Navajoland—a forty-five-thousand-square-mile swath of land in northwestern New Mexico and northeastern Arizona—to round up the Diné in preparation for their trek to the Bosque Redondo. Unable to locate more than a handful of Navajos at any given time, Carson grew frustrated but continued his pursuit of the tribe. Breaching the Navajos' stronghold at Canyon de Chelly that winter, Carson practiced a scorched-earth policy that resulted in little loss of life but compelled the Navajos to surrender.

In March 1865, Carson was promoted to brigadier general and accepted an appointment as commander of Fort Garland, Colorado. The following October, Carson participated in a treaty council with the Cheyenne, Arapaho, Comanche, Kiowa, and Kiowa-Apache in south-central Kansas at the confluence of the Little Arkansas and Arkansas Rivers. These negotiations resulted in the establishment of a reservation as outlined in the Treaty of the Little Arkansas River signed between the United States and the Cheyenne and Arapaho on October 14, 1865. His health failing, Carson left military service in 1867 and assumed the position of superintendent of Indian affairs for Colorado. While serving in this capacity, Carson accompanied a Ute delegation to Washington, D.C., to negotiate the establishment of a permanent reservation for the Colorado and Utah Utes. On May 25, 1868, almost immediately following his return to his beloved West and one month after the death of his wife, Carson passed away at Fort Lyon, Colorado. Buried in the old Taos cemetery, resting peacefully beside his wife, Carson irrevocably abandoned his roving way of life.

Sonia Dickey

See also Canyon de Chelly, Arizona; Fort Sumner, New Mexico; Long Walk; Treaty with the Cheyenne and Arapaho–October 14, 1865.

References and Further Reading

Carter, Harvey L. 1968. *"Dear Old Kit": The Historical Christopher Carson*. Norman: University of Oklahoma Press.

Dunlay, Tom. 2000. *Kit Carson and the Indians*. Lincoln: University of Nebraska Press.

Guild, Thelma S., and Harvey L. Carter. 1984. *Kit Carson: A Pattern for Heroes*. Lincoln: University of Nebraska Press.

Roberts, David. 2000. *A Newer World: John C. Frémont, Kit Carson, and the Claiming of the American West*. New York: Simon & Schuster.

Sabin, Edwin. 1995. *Kit Carson Days: Adventures in the Path of Empire*. Rev. ed. 2 vols. Lincoln: University of Nebraska Press.

Simmons, Marc. 2003. *Kit Carson and His Three Wives: A Family History*. Albuquerque: University of New Mexico.

Cass, Lewis

(1782–1866)

Lewis Cass served as governor of Michigan Territory. In that capacity, he led expeditions in the 1820s to secure millions of acres in land concessions from Native nations. As a territorial governor, a U.S. senator, secretary of state, secretary of war, and a presidential candidate, Cass was a fervent supporter of territorial expansion.

Born in New Hampshire and educated at Exeter Academy, Cass moved to Ohio in 1799 and began a career in law and politics. During the War of 1812, he attained the rank of brigadier general, and in 1813 he was appointed governor of Michigan Territory by President James Madison. He would hold this position until 1831, which made him the longest-serving territorial governor in the history of the United States.

Cass considered Indian affairs to be his major responsibility as a territorial governor, and he pursued this endeavor with enthusiasm. Beginning in 1820, he embarked on an expedition around the Great Lakes to secure land concessions from Native nations; in more than twenty treaties negotiated by Cass, tens of millions of acres of land were secured for the United States. Land and federal payments were also secured for Cass's negotiating partners, which included Cass's private secretary, his personal assistant, and his physician. On his negotiating team, Cass also included Henry Schoolcraft, whose vivid descriptions of the land ceded by Native nations contributed to westward settlement by U.S. citizens.

Lewis Cass (1782–1866), who served as President James Buchanan's secretary of state, secured millions of acres of Indian land while negotiating treaties. (Library of Congress)

Among the notable treaties negotiated by Cass are the Treaty of St. Mary's (1818), the Saginaw Treaty (1819), and the Treaty of Sault St. Marie (1820). One of his greatest accomplishments as a negotiator, however, was not a land cession treaty but a "peace" treaty negotiated among Native nations. With the express purpose of ending conflict among Native peoples, Cass and William Clark assembled representatives of the "Sioux and Chippewa, Sacs and Fox, Menominie, Ioway, Sioux, Winnebago, and a portion of the Ottawa, Chippewa, [and] Potawattomie" tribes at Prairie du Chien in 1825. There, the Native nations agreed for the first time to live within certain set boundaries, in effect "clearing the title" to real estate in Wisconsin, Minnesota, Iowa, and other present-day states. Within twenty years, virtually all of this land had been purchased (or taken) from individual tribes.

Because of his reputation as an Indian expert, Cass was called upon for testimony before the

Supreme Court when the Cherokee Nation claimed sovereign jurisdiction over their territory in the late 1820s. Cass supported the position of the State of Georgia in that case, arguing that, for their own good, the Cherokee people should be removed west of the Mississippi. The Cherokee people won the case, but Andrew Jackson refused to enforce the outcome of the litigation.

In 1831, President Andrew Jackson appointed Cass secretary of war. As "Indian affairs" became more a matter of war than of diplomacy, Cass remained a leader in land acquisition for the United States. In 1832, for instance, at the request of superintendent of Indian affairs William Clark, Cass signed the order of extermination in the Black Hawk War.

From 1836 to 1842, Cass served as the American ambassador to France. He was elected to the U.S. Senate from Michigan in 1845 and in 1848 was nominated for the presidency by the Democratic Party. In that election, Martin Van Buren split the party by running as a third-party candidate, garnering barely enough votes to secure the election for Cass's Whig opponent, Zachary Taylor. Cass continued to hold his Senate seat until 1857, when he was appointed secretary of state by James Buchanan. He resigned in 1860 to protest the lack of reinforcements at Charleston forts prior to the beginning of the Civil War. Cass died peacefully at his home in Michigan in 1866.

Martin Case

See also Black Hawk; Clark, William; Jackson, Andrew; Prairie du Chien, Wisconsin; Schoolcraft, Henry Rowe; Treaty with the Sioux, Etc.–September 17, 1851.

References and Further Reading

Prucha, Francis Paul. 1967. *Lewis Cass and American Indian Policy.* Detroit, MI: Wayne State University Press.

Prucha, Francis Paul. 1962. *American Indian Policy in the Formative Years: The Indian Trade and Intercourse Acts 1790–1834.* Lincoln: University of Nebraska Press.

Wallace, Anthony F. C. 1999. *Jefferson and the Indians: The Tragic Fate of the First Americans.* Cambridge, MA, and London: Belknap Press of Harvard University Press.

Chivington, John Milton

(1821–1894)

John Chivington was a minister, Civil War hero, Indian fighter, and politician. A Methodist preacher turned military commander, Colonel John Milton Chivington won fame for his contributions to the Union victory at Glorieta Pass, a battle that is credited with saving the West for the Union. The luster of his historic service subsequently was tarnished by often-inaccurate accounts of his role as commander of the Third Colorado Volunteer Cavalry at the Battle of Sand Creek, labeled by eastern newspapers and philanthropists "the Sand Creek Massacre."

Standing six foot four inches, possessing a barrel torso, a thick neck, a full beard, and piercing eyes, the 260-pound Chivington was a formidable figure both in the pulpit and in uniform, but his insistence on strict discipline and obedience to his orders made his parishioners view him as being excessively rigid and his soldiers to unfavorably characterize him as a martinet.

Throughout 1864, Cheyenne warriors under Chief Black Kettle had been terrorizing cities and settlements in the Colorado Territory, disrupting lines of communications, and slaying residents. By late summer, Denver had been virtually sealed off, leading territorial governor John Evans to request military assistance. General Samuel R. Curtis, commander of the Department of Kansas, ordered Colonel Chivington and the Third Colorado Volunteer Cavalry, who were nearing the conclusion of an uneventful one-hundred-day enlistment, to quell the Indian threat in the Denver region. Following a fresh, bloody trail, the troops arrived at Fort Lyon, whereupon Chivington was informed by both the post commandant, Major Scott Anthony (brother of suffragist Susan B. Anthony), and Indian agent Samuel G. Colley, that Black Kettle's warriors were encamped at Sand Creek. The two urged him to launch an immediate offensive.

Assured of the hostile nature of the encampment, at dawn on November 29, 1864, Chivington began to attack the camp, and in the ensuing engagement approximately two hundred warriors and fifty women and children, some active participants in the fighting, were slain.

Despite his acclaim throughout Colorado as a hero and savior, Chivington was decried as a mass murderer in eastern newspapers, which cited stories by witnesses of dubious veracity who asserted that Sand Creek was a peaceful winter camp under the protection of the U.S. government, and that the village at the time of the attack had even flown an American flag as a sign of peace.

Three investigative hearings were held into Chivington's conduct during the battle at Sand

On November 29, 1864, Methodist minister and soldier Colonel John M. Chivington (1821–1894), seated, led a force of Colorado Volunteers in a surprise attack on a peaceful Cheyenne village at Sand Creek, Colorado. More than half of the camp's inhabitants, mostly women and children, were killed. The attack put Chivington in a storm of controversy and he spent the remainder of his life defending his actions. (North Wind Picture Archives)

Creek, none of which was impartial or fair to Chivington. One was chaired by Lieutenant Colonel Samuel F. Tappan, a personal enemy of Chivington, who refused to admit many of Chivington's objections to testimony; another was chaired by the Committee on the Conduct of the War, infamous for its questionable ethical practices and legal abuses while assailing the record of officers it wanted removed. In each hearing, witnesses supporting Chivington's claim that no American flag was visible in the village, that fresh scalps were found in the lodges, that Major Anthony had given him written orders to attack what had been described as a hostile encampment, and that he had done his best to maintain discipline and prevent mutilation of Indian corpses were summarily dismissed. Instead, credence was given to self-serving testimony by fur traders who

had lost valuable pelts stored in the camp during the battle and by Edward Wynkoop, an ambitious officer and pacifist who sought to replace Anthony as commander of Fort Lyon and who, without any official authorization, had led Black Kettle to believe that Sand Creek would be considered a safe haven. Even after these biased hearings, evidence against him was so weak that Chivington was mustered out of the army without receiving any punishment for the alleged crimes at Sand Creek.

His reputation slandered, an embittered Chivington moved to Denver, steadfastly maintaining the propriety of his actions at Sand Creek. Chivington spent the remainder of his life holding local political offices and serving on various editorial boards, including that of *The Christian Advocate.* His death in October 1894 was marked by the largest funeral in

Colorado's history; thousands of mourners paid homage to the man they considered one of their state's greatest heroes.

Bruce A. Rubenstein

See also Black Kettle.
References and Further Reading
Craig, Reginald. 1959. *The Fighting Parson*. Los Angeles: Westernlore Press.
Hoig, Stan. 1961. *The Sand Creek Massacre*. Norman: University of Oklahoma Press.
Mendoza, Patrick M. 1993. *Song of Sorrow*. Denver: Willow Wind.
U. S. Congress. Senate. "Report of the Joint Committee on the Conduct of the War," 38th Cong., 2nd sess. Senate Document 142, Vol. 3. Washington, DC: Government Printing Office, 1865.
U. S. Congress. Senate. "Report of the Secretary of War," 39th Cong., 2nd sess. Senate Executive Document 26. Washington, DC: Government Printing Office, 1867.

Chouteau, Auguste

(1749–1829)

From fur trader and clerk to explorer and treaty negotiator, Auguste Chouteau's influence over the Upper Louisiana Territory and the West has been the inspiration of legends and novels. Though born in New Orleans to Marie Therese Bourgeois and Rene Auguste Chouteau, Chouteau was raised by his mother's common-law husband, Pierre Leclede, who also mentored him in the fur trade. By age fourteen, Chouteau assisted Leclede in the founding of St. Louis, Missouri. There, he and his family built a fur trade empire by establishing trading posts up the Missouri River and its tributaries. His younger brother Pierre, sometimes referred to as Peter, was also involved in Indian and trading affairs.

Besides operating his fur trading business, Chouteau also served as a judge and as a lieutenant colonel in the local militia. Chouteau is said to have owned thousands of acres of land, as well as the most impressive library west of the Mississippi, containing more than six hundred volumes of books. His prosperity and confident knowledge of both Indian affairs and the fur trade made him a valuable asset to Americans taking over the territory. Chouteau came to the attention of Thomas Jefferson following the Louisiana Purchase.

In 1804, William Henry Harrison arrived at St. Louis to be the guest of Chouteau. His purpose was to make a treaty with the Sac and Fox. Chouteau offered his expertise. In the course of that negotiation, Chouteau, who owned extensive lands, kept Harrison from invalidating the Spanish land grants in place prior to the Louisiana Purchase of 1803 by inserting an article into the treaty for that purpose, thereby protecting Chouteau's own lands.

As early as 1813, while the War of 1812 raged, the Missouri *Gazette* called upon President James Madison to consider appointing August Chouteau and William Clark as treaty commissioners to oversee a treaty involving the Indians. In 1815, following the end the War of 1812, Chouteau was indeed appointed treaty commissioner to assist in negotiations with former warring Indians, particularly those who were situated near the Mississippi and Missouri rivers. Missouri territorial governor William Clark and Illinois territorial governor Ninian Edwards were the other two commissioners for the treaty that came to be known as the Treaty of Portage des Sioux. The site of the treaty was north of St. Louis, Missouri Territory, along the Missouri River where it empties into the Mississippi River.

Part of Chouteau's duties involved directing reliable men to travel to various Indian settlements to invite and influence them to attended the treaty. At least nineteen tribes arrived during the summer of 1815, including the Big and Little Osage, Iowa, Sac (Sauk) and Fox, Potawatomi, Shawnee, Delaware, Piankashaw, Kaskaskia, Kickapoo, Maha, Ponca, and Sioux. The commissioners made extensive preparations, including the construction of a council house and a large arbor for shade. The government supplied three companies of American infantry from nearby Fort Bellefountain, and on the river sailed gunboats. All were intended to show that the United States was intent on peace. An excessive array of presents, which had cost thousands of dollars, were spread out to be offered to the headmen of each tribal nation, everything from blankets and cloth to rifles and tobacco. The intention was to prove the wealth and superiority of the Americans by giving such trade goods in order to induce an offer to live at peace. There was no talk of land cession in this treaty, which had been a concern of many of the Indians. Of all the commissioners present, Chouteau is reported to have made quite a stir in a scarlet coat with gold lace and buttons.

Meeting with individual tribes, the commissioners smoothed out problems among the tribes. Almost all seemed willing to lay aside their war talk and treat for peace, all but the Sac and Fox, who

8

challenged the validity of the treaty of 1804. According to the Americans, they boldly attempted to intimidate the commissioners, informing them that they had raiding parties out that very moment. But later, according to the Sac and Fox leader Lemoite, the Americans had guns aimed at him and the members of his delegation. Refusing to go along with the treaty, the Sacs quit the place during the night. They would not return to negotiations for nearly a year. In the meantime, the other attendees agreed and the Treaty of Portage Des Sioux was ratified on December 26, 1815.

Chouteau spent the remaining years of his life at St. Louis overseeing his extensive holdings and serving the government when called upon.

Sally Colford Bennett

See also Black Hawk; Clark, William; Treaty with the Potawatomi–July 18, 1815, through Treaty with the Kickapoo–September 2, 1815.

References and Further Reading

Cunningham, Mary B., and Jeanne C. Blythe. 1977. *The Founding Family of St. Louis.* St. Louis, MO: Midwest Technical Publications.

Fisher, Robert L. 1933. "The Treaty of Portage Des Sioux." *Missouri Valley Historical Review,* 19(4): 495–508.

Gregg, Kate L. 1939. "The War of 1812 in the Missouri Frontier, Part II." *Missouri Historical Review* 33(2): 184–202.

Gregg, Kate L., ed. 1937. *West with Dragoons: The Journal of William Clark on his Expedition to Establish Fort Osage, August 25 to September 22, 1808.* Fulton, MO: Ovid Bell Press.

Hagan, William T. 1958. *The Sac and Fox Indians.* Norman: University of Oklahoma Press.

Clark, William

(1770–1838)

Born the ninth of ten children to John and Ann (Rogers) Clark on August 1, 1770, on a plantation in Caroline County, Virginia, William Clark led a full life as a soldier, explorer, Indian agent, Missouri territorial governor, and superintendent of Indian affairs at St. Louis. While Clark was a teenager, his family relocated to a new plantation called Mulberry Hill near present-day Louisville, Kentucky. Clark joined the Kentucky militia, and then, in 1792, President George Washington commissioned Clark a lieutenant of infantry. During General Anthony Wayne's Ohio River Indian campaigns, Clark fought at the Battle of Fallen Timbers. He resigned his commission

A capable and energetic soldier, William Clark (1770–1838) became one of the United States' most able Indian agents after his exploration of the Louisiana Purchase with Meriwether Lewis. (Library of Congress)

shortly after the Treaty of Greenville to return home and care for his parents and the family estate.

In 1803, Clark agreed to co-command an expedition with Meriwether Lewis to explore the Louisiana Purchase and establish a commercial route to the Pacific. Lewis and Clark met with Indian leaders, distributed trade goods, delivered speeches, solicited Indian delegations to travel to Washington, and conducted negotiations for peace, friendship, and trade. They announced U.S. sovereignty and left calling cards of empire (medals, flags, certificates). Clark gained an appreciation for the tremendous diversity of Indian cultures and was the more skillful diplomat of the two.

Following the expedition's return, President Thomas Jefferson appointed Clark Indian agent. From 1807 to 1838, Clark served as the federal government's representative to the Indian nations in the West, personally signing thirty-seven treaties (one-tenth of all ratified treaties). Clark's first treaty was concluded at Fort Osage during the summer of 1808. The Osages present agreed to a land cession in exchange for a trading post and military protection from their enemies. Other Osages who were not present demanded that the treaty be modified, and then they, too, accepted it.

During the War of 1812, President James Madison commissioned Clark as Missouri's first territorial governor, a position Clark occupied from 1813 to 1820. Clark also acted as an ex officio superintendent of Indian affairs. To keep Missouri's frontier settlements safe, he authorized a string of frontier blockhouses and mounted ranger patrols to keep the peace. He also took the offensive against British forces and their allies at Prairie du Chien. The Treaty of Ghent established peace with Britain but not with their Indian allies. Clark presided at the Portage des Sioux peace council in 1815 and within a year had negotiated peace and friendship treaties with the Iowa, Kansa, Kickapoo, Omaha, Osage, Piankashaw, Potawatomi, Sac and Fox, Sioux, and Winnebago tribes.

Governor Clark conducted treaties of trade and friendship for tribes farthest from settlement, and treaties calling for land cessions and removal for those located within the Missouri and Arkansas territorial boundaries. Whether conducted at his council house in St. Louis—with the Kansa, Kickapoo, Osage, Otoe, Ponca, Pawnee, Quapaw—or at Washington—with the Iowa, Sac and Fox—Clark acquitted himself as a competent diplomat at councils. He also supervised Indian agents, including Pierre Chouteau, Nicholas Boilvin, Lawrence Taliaferro, and Thomas Forsyth.

After Alexander McNair defeated Clark in Missouri's inaugural gubernatorial election, President James Monroe appointed Clark superintendent of Indian affairs headquartered at St. Louis in 1822. Most treaties made before 1820 had sought peace and friendship to undermine European rivals, or trading relationships to promote the fur trade and provide manufactured goods. Those made after 1820 generally involved land cessions and removal. Clark exercised jurisdiction over western tribes and eastern nations being removed west of the Mississippi River. He expressed great sympathy for those removed tribes and promoted their interests as he understood them. Nevertheless, Clark agreed with and helped implement Indian removal. His ethnocentrism caused him to dismiss the notion that Indians could maintain their identity and culture within the advancing U.S. frontier.

As superintendent, Clark conducted twelve treaties at places like Fort Atkinson, Fort Leaven-worth, Prairie du Chien, St. Louis, and Washington. Most of these treaties involved land cessions by tribes including the Delaware, Iowa, Kansas, Kickapoo, Osage, Piankashaw, Sac and Fox, and Shawnee. When not involved in treaties, Clark issued trading licenses and aided eastern tribes undergoing removal. He presided at the peace treaty at Prairie du Chien in 1825 and negotiated with Black Hawk and Keokuk during and after the Black Hawk War.

Perhaps it was in the realm of policymaking that Clark made his greatest contributions. Clark was the most experienced and knowledgeable government official in the trans-Mississippi West. From the government's perspective, Clark served as an able administrator of federal policy who offered helpful suggestions in fine-tuning policy to match frontier realities. In a time of expanding bureaucratic control, he helped modify the Indian Civilization Act of 1819. Clark and Michigan territorial governor Lewis Cass filed a report in 1829 that changed the laws and regulations governing Indian affairs, contributed to the Indian Removal Act of 1830, revised the Trade and Intercourse Laws, and culminated in the reorganization of the entire Indian Bureau in 1834. That year, Clark retained his influential position in St. Louis despite being in his sixties.

Jay H. Buckley

See also Battle of Fallen Timbers, 1794; Black Hawk; Cass, Lewis; Chouteau, Auguste; Forsyth, Thomas; Greenville, Ohio; Indian Removal Act, 1830; Jefferson, Thomas; Lewis, Meriwether; Prairie du Chien, Wisconsin; St. Louis, Missouri; Treaty of Ghent, 1814; Treaty with the Sioux, Etc.–August 19, 1825; Treaty with the Wyandot, Etc.–August 3, 1795; Wayne, Anthony.

References and Further Reading

Bakeless, John. 1947. *Lewis and Clark: Partners in Discovery.* New York: William Morrow.
Ronda, James P. 1984. *Lewis and Clark among the Indians.* Lincoln: University of Nebraska Press.
Steffen, Jerome O. 1977. *William Clark: Jeffersonian Man on the Frontier.* Norman: University of Oklahoma Press.

Cochise

(c. 1810–1874)

One of the greatest Indian leaders of the nineteenth century, Cochise led the Chiricahua Apache in a protracted war of survival against both the encroaching Mexicans and Americans. Cochise successfully

guished himself in these raids and was honored for his ability and bravery.

In the 1830s, Cochise engaged in conflicts with Mexican settlers. The raids and counterraids turned what would later become the American Southwest into a dangerous and violent place. The bloodshed continued into the 1840s, as Cochise became one of the principle Chokonen war leaders. During that time, Mexicans killed his father, which only led to further escalation of the fighting. Moreover, his father's death fostered a deep antagonism and hatred for Mexicans, sentiments Cochise held for the rest of his life.

After the United States and Mexico signed the Treaty of Guadalupe Hidalgo, Americans began pouring into the New Mexico territory, or, from Cochise's standpoint, the Apachería. Indeed, for the Chiricahua these new immigrants were nothing short of invaders who were competing for scarce resources in the harsh desert environment. Inevitably, this new white settlement led to conflict. Matters were aggravated when the son of a white settler was kidnapped. Territorial officials immediately—and erroneously—blamed Cochise and his Chokonen band. In February 1861, Lieutenant George Bascom, who was posted at Fort Buchanan, called Cochise in to parley. Once in the American camp, the Chiricahua leader was apprehended and charged with abduction of the young boy.

Under heavy guard, Cochise managed to cut his way out through the back of the tent where he was held prisoner and escape into the nearby hills. Unfortunately, five others, including his two nephews and one of his brothers, did not make it to safety. In retaliation for Bascom's treachery, Cochise and his men attacked a wagon train, killing all the Mexicans and kidnapping four Americans. He held the men hostage, offering to free them only if his brother and nephews were released. Bascom refused. In response, Cochise executed his four prisoners. Bascom, in turn, hanged all five of the Chiricahuas, leaving the corpses dangling from an oak tree for weeks. The hatred Cochise reserved for Mexicans was now extended to the Americans, leading to a state of all-out war that would last more than a decade.

As the fighting between the Chiricahua and the United States roared on, President Ulysses S. Grant appointed General Oliver Otis Howard as chief peace commissioner in the Southwest. Though Howard was a respected military man, he was also a Christian humanitarian who believed that negotiation, rather

A master of hit-and-run tactics, Chochise (c. 1810–1874) became a feared Native American warrior in the Southwest. Cochise was the predecessor to Geronimo, leading the Chiricahua Apache during the 1860s and early 1870s. He died June 8, 1874, on the reservation near Apache Pass, Arizona. (Bettmann/Corbis)

evaded capture and staved off American forces throughout the 1860s. His strategic genius, fearlessness, and sheer stamina enabled the Chiricahua chief to eventually broker a treaty that met his demands rather than those of the United States.

No one knows exactly when Cochise was born, but most historians believe it was around 1810. He was the son of Pisago Cabezón, a great leader in his own right of the Chokonen band of the Chiricahua Apache. Cochise was the eldest of three brothers, all of whom were steeped in traditional Chokonen ways. At the age of fifteen, he began training to become a warrior, at which he quickly excelled; he was fast, disciplined, and an excellent marksman with the bow and arrow. Soon he was accompanying the older warriors on horse raids. Cochise distin-

than brute force, was a better means of ending conflict. He took extraordinary steps to court Cochise and bring the bloody war with the Apache to an end. In October 1872, Howard and his first lieutenant, Joseph Sladen, headed into the Dragoon Mountains of eastern Arizona to broker a treaty with the Chiricahua. Howard acquiesced to nearly all Cochise's demands, carving out a reservation in southeastern Arizona along the Mexican border. For his part, Cochise kept the peace and halted all fighting in the United States, though he continued to raid in Mexico. The peace, however, ended with the death of the great Apache leader in 1874.

Bradley Shreve

See also Southern Plains and the Southwest; Treaty of Guadalupe Hidalgo, 1848.

References and Further Reading

Aleshire, Peter. 2001. *Cochise: The Life and Times of the Great Apache Chief*. New York: John Wiley.
Sweeney, Edwin R. 1991. *Cochise: Chiricahua Apache Chief*. Norman: University of Oklahoma Press.
Sweeney, Edwin R., ed. 1997. *Making Peace With Cochise: The 1872 Journal of Captain Joseph Alton Sladen*. Norman: University of Oklahoma Press.

Cohen, Felix S.

(1907–1953)

Felix Solomon Cohen played an instrumental role in bringing an end to the allotment era and in creating the legal structure for meaningful tribal self-governance that continues to be worked out to this day. Cohen is best known as the author of the 1941 *Handbook of Federal Indian Law*, a pioneering work that insists that Indian tribes possess all aspects of sovereignty except those which Congress has taken away. Additionally, Cohen helped craft two of the most significant pieces of Indian legislation of the twentieth century: the Indian Reorganization Act of 1934 (IRA) and the Indian Claims Commission Act of 1946 (ICCA).

Felix Cohen was hired as assistant solicitor for the Department of the Interior in 1933. He joined John Collier, commissioner of Indian affairs, in working to bring an end to the allotment policies and ushering in Theodore Roosevelt's New Deal to Indian communities. Originally without experience relating to Native Americans, Cohen began his government service with a strong educational background: a Ph.D. in philosophy from Harvard (1929) and a law degree from Columbia (L.L.B. 1931). Cohen's influence and his ability to craft innovative legislation and arguments aiding Indians were partly due to the combination of his educational background and his respected non-Indian scholarship.

Cohen's first task with the Department of the Interior was to draft the Wheeler-Howard Act, which has since become known as the Indian Reorganization Act. Cohen's IRA aimed to facilitate the development of western-style tribal governments. It allowed tribes to establish governments that would be recognized as such by the U.S. government. Cohen is criticized for his establishment of a corporate structure of tribal governance rather than a more flexible framework that would allow greater adherence to traditional ways of governing. Additionally, the inability to include in the final version of the IRA the consolidation of allotted lands in tribal government hands, due to opposition from allottees, was seen by Cohen as a weakness of the IRA. "Still, from Cohen's perspective . . . the IRA was an act of liberation," freeing tribes to begin the work of developing their own strong governments (Dalia 2001).

Felix Cohen's organization of diverse judicial opinions and federal practices into the handbook reflects Cohen's commitment to legal scholarship, a commitment that incorporates more than merely what judges write by also including a deep understanding of the historical and social background underlying Indian policies. The handbook's significance, however, extends well beyond this single passage; "in recognition of Cohen's genius, vision, and hard work," it was retitled *Felix S. Cohen's Handbook of Federal Indian Law* when it was revised in 1982 (Martin 1998–1999, 165–166).

Prior to resigning from the Department of the Interior in December 1947, Cohen helped write the Indian Claims Commission Act of 1946. Although the ICCA failed to allow tribes to get their land back, and the total dollar amounts available under the ICCA were well below the true damage amounts, the law enabled tribal suits to recover damages for their lost land. Cohen's last years before his untimely death were spent teaching at Yale Law School and the City College of New York and in private practice, largely working on behalf of Native Americans.

Ezra Rosser

See also Collier, John; Government-to-Government Relationship; Indian Claims Commission (ICC); Indian Claims Commission Act, 1946; Indian New Deal; Indian Reorganization Act, 1934; Sovereignty.

References and Further Reading

Cohen, Felix S. 1941. *Handbook of Federal Indian Law.*
Repr., Albuquerque: University of New Mexico
Press, 1971.

Cohen, Lucy Kramer, ed. 1960. *The Legal Conscience:
Selected Papers of Felix S. Cohen.* New Haven, CT:
Yale University Press.

Martin, Jill E. 1998–1999. "The Miner's Canary: Felix
S. Cohen's Philosophy of Indian Rights," 23
American Indian Law Review 165, 166.

Tsuk, Dalia. 2001. "The New Deal Origins of
American Legal Pluralism," 29 *Florida State
University Law Review* 189, 239.

Collier, John

(1884–1968)

John Collier, commissioner of Indian affairs
(1933–1945), is best known as the architect of the
Indian New Deal. Collier sought to end the policy of
assimilation, instead proposing a culturally plural-
istic approach that encouraged ethnic pride and
acknowledged the value of Indian cultures to white
society. Collier's most significant legislative achievement was the Indian Reorganization Act of 1934,
which abandoned the policy of allotment and provided for the establishment of limited forms of tribal
government and property management.

Collier's rejection of assimilation was grounded
in his experiences as a social worker in New York in
the early twentieth century. Collier believed that the
industrial age manifested a breakdown of community values and, concluding that the preservation
and nurture of ethnic values was essential to reversing this trend, focused on the development of social
and ethnic communities, encouraging ethnic pride,
unity, and self-responsibility among local immigrant
groups. Collier left New York in 1919, frustrated by
the post–World War I drive to "Americanize" immigrants; following a short period as head of California's adult education program, he relocated to Taos,
New Mexico. Here, Collier was introduced to the

John Collier (1884–1968) of Atlanta, Georgia, served as the U.S. Indian Affairs Commissioner from 1933 to 1945. (Library of Congress)

Indian pueblo at Taos and realized that, in Pueblo culture, he had discovered the embodiment of his utopian vision of a socially integrated, community-centered ethnic group that provided a template for the redemption of a selfish, materialistic, and fragmented American society.

Taking up residence in the colony of writers and artists in Taos, Collier became a prominent member of the crusade to protect and restore Indian culture. Collier was an active opponent of the proposed Bursum Bill, which sought to legislate rights for white squatters on Pueblo lands. The defeat of the Bursum Bill led to the formation in 1923 of the American Indian Defense Association, of which Collier was executive secretary. The association provided legal aid services, opposed allotment, and called for an investigation into and reorganization of the Indian bureau. Many of the association's proposals were to form the basis for legislation eventually enacted by Collier during his tenure as commissioner of Indian affairs. Collier's vision of a "New Deal" for American Indians, born out of his utopianism and romanticized view of Pueblo Indians, was intended to preserve Indian cultures by encouraging religious and social freedom, promoting tribal arts and self-government, and restructuring education so that it encouraged rather than suppressed tribal loyalties.

Collier was appointed commissioner of Indian affairs on April 21, 1933, and immediately embarked on a radical program of reform. The Board of Indian Commissioners was abolished and replaced with a consultant group of social scientists advising on arts and crafts, education, natural resources, law, and cultural anthropology. The influence of Christian missionaries in Indian day schools and boarding schools was curtailed, and the constitutional right to freedom of religion for American Indians was reaffirmed. The Indian Reorganization Act (IRA) of 1934 repealed the policy of allotment and provided for the restoration of tribal political structures and the incorporation and operation of property by tribes. Other reforms implemented by Collier included the preferential hiring of Indian employees in the Bureau of Indian Affairs, the creation of a revolving credit fund to provide loans for agricultural and educational purposes, and the establishment of the Indian Arts and Craft Board Act.

In 1940, Collier attended the Inter-American Conference on Indian Life in Patzcuro, Mexico, a gathering that internationalized the policies of the Indian New Deal and led to the creation of the Inter-American Indian Institute, of which Collier served as president until 1946. Wishing to focus on the development of his international ethnic policies, Collier's resignation as commissioner of Indian affairs was accepted by President Franklin D. Roosevelt on January 22, 1945.

Annie Kirby

See also Bureau of Indian Affairs (BIA); General Allotment Act (Dawes Act), 1887; Indian New Deal; Indian Reorganization Act, 1934; Meriam Report, 1928.

References and Further Reading

Collier, John. 1948. *Indians of the Americas: The Long Hope.* New York: Mentor Books.

Deloria, Vine, Jr., and Clifford Lytle. 1984. *The Nations Within: The Past and Future of American Indian Sovereignty.* New York: Pantheon Books.

Holm, Tom. 2005. *The Great Confusion in Indian Affairs: Native Americans and Whites in the Progressive Era.* Austin: University of Texas Press.

Philp, Kenneth R. 1972. "John Collier and the American Indian, 1920–1945." In *Essays on Radicalism in Contemporary America*, ed. Leon Borden Blair, 63–80. Austin and London: University of Texas Press.

Commission to the Five Civilized Tribes.

See Dawes Commission.

Cooper, Douglas H.
(1771–1879)

Douglas H. Cooper served as U.S. agent to the Choctaw and Chickasaw Nations and played an important role in the negotiation of treaties between those nations and the U.S. government. He was born in Virginia in 1771, a scion of a well-established family with Baptist affiliations. His first foray into public life was when he was licensed to preach in 1793; he went on to establish churches in South Carolina, Georgia, and Mississippi. Upon his father's death, he became a property owner in Mississippi and studied law. His family home, Mon Clava, was situated on Choctaw land ceded by the Treaty of Dancing Rabbit Creek in 1830. He served in the Mexican-American War, distinguishing himself in the battles of Buena Vista and Monterey. He played an active role in Mississippi politics and was rewarded with an appointment as U.S. agent to the Choctaw in 1853.

In 1855, the Choctaw and Chickasaw negotiated a treaty that was intended to consolidate their outstanding claims against the U.S. government for the fulfillment of treaty provisions and to put their relationship with the federal government on a new footing. To this end, they enlisted the services of Albert Pike, a Washington lawyer, to assist in formulating the treaty language. Pike took the case on a contingency basis for 25 percent of the payment for the lands east of the Mississippi ceded in the Treaty of Dancing Rabbit Creek. Cooper accompanied the Choctaw delegation to Washington and took part in the treaty negotiations. He received a share in the portion of Pike's fee that he, Cooper, rebated to the Choctaw delegation for the opportunity to represent the tribe.

In his role as U.S. agent, Cooper provided a summary of the amount due to the Choctaw Nation under the provisions of the new treaty. He also advised the delegation that they could profit by leasing their western lands for the settlement of the Wichita tribe, which Congress was anxious to move out of the way of territorial expansion. The treaty provided for that lease of Choctaw lands west of the 98th meridian.

In March 1856, Cooper was appointed U.S. agent for the Chickasaw as well as the Choctaw and was stationed at Fort Washita to serve both tribes. He also oversaw the final payment to Choctaws in Mississippi, who had tried to take land claims in that state under the fourteenth article of the Treaty of Dancing Rabbit Creek. When the Choctaws received a favorable judgment from Congress in 1859 on their claims under that treaty, Cooper was charged with overseeing the purchase of corn for Choctaws, who were suffering the effects of a major drought in the Choctaw Nation.

Cooper's southern sympathies coincided with those of Choctaw leaders as the United States moved inexorably toward civil war. The Choctaw leadership declared for the Confederacy and signed a treaty with Albert Pike, now the Confederacy's agent to the tribes of Indian Territory. Cooper raised troops for the Confederacy while still in the service of the U.S. government. He served as an officer in the Confederate army, ultimately serving as commander in charge for the Indian Territory.

With the Confederate defeat, the Choctaws had to negotiate yet another treaty to reestablish their relationship with the federal government. Cooper accompanied the Choctaw delegation to Washington, D.C., to negotiate that treaty. He introduced the delegates to his brother-in-law, John Latrobe, with whom they contracted to serve as their agent in the treaty negotiations. The Choctaw general council approved an advance of $100,000 to Latrobe, and he rebated 5 percent to the Choctaw delegation and to Cooper. Despite his Confederate service, Cooper witnessed the signing of the treaty of 1866 in his capacity as U.S. agent.

Douglas Cooper was an active player in treaty negotiations between the Choctaw Nation and the United States in 1855. He profited from rebates of lawyers' fees to facilitate that treaty. He was a key figure in the Confederate government's relations with the tribes in Indian Territory during the Civil War, and he profited again from the negotiations surrounding the treaty of 1866. As an agent of the U.S. government, he worked as much for his own self-interest he did for the Choctaw whose interests he was charged to protect. He died at Old Fort Washita on April 30, 1879.

Clara Sue Kidwell

See also Indian Territory; Opothleyahola; Pike, Albert; Reconstruction Treaties with the Cherokee, Choctaw, Chicasaw, Creek, and Seminole–1866.

References and Further Reading

Abel, Annie Heloise. 1992. *The American Indian in the Civil War, 1862–1865*. Lincoln: University of Nebraska Press.

Cottrell, Steve, and Andy Thomas. 1995. *Civil War in Indian Territory*. New York: Pelican.

Fischer, LeRoy. 1974. *The Civil War Era in Indian Territory*. Los Angeles: Lorin L. Morrison.

Spencer, John. 2006. *The American Civil War in Indian Territory*. Oxford: Osprey.

Taylor, Ethel Crisp. 2005. *Dust in the Wind: The Civil War in Indian Territory*. Westminster, MD: Heritage Books.

Wright, Muriel H. 1954. "General Douglas H. Cooper, C.S.A." *The Chronicles of Oklahoma*, 32(9): 142–184.

Cornplanter

(c. 1730–1836)

Known as Kaintwakon by his people, Cornplanter was born to his Seneca mother and Dutch trader father sometime between the mid-1730s and the early 1750s. Although he was raised by his mother's people as a Seneca and apparently never learned to speak English, Cornplanter would become an

Seneca sachem Cornplanter (c. 1730–1836) took part in negotiating the treaties signed at Fort Stanwix in 1784 and Fort Harmar in 1789. However, he did not actually sign either document. He died at Cornplantertown, Pennsylvania, in 1836, perhaps more than 100 years old. (Getty Images)

important diplomat and maker of peace between the Iroquois and the English.

Information on Cornplanter's youth is sketchy, but evidence suggests he fought as a skilled and respected young warrior against the British in the French and Indian War. Some scholars place him specifically at the defeat of British general Edward Braddock in 1755. By the beginning of the Revolutionary War, Cornplanter had assumed an important position among the Seneca. At first, both the British and American rebels urged the Iroquois Confederacy to remain neutral in the conflict, but secretly both sides hoped to obtain Indian assistance for their cause.

Eventually, the British gave promises of goods and rum to the confederacy in exchange for an alliance. As was the practice, representatives of the Six Nations met to discuss this possibility at Oswego, New York, in July 1777. Cornplanter and his uncle Kiasutha were the representatives for their group, the Chenussio Senecas. Although both men resisted the alliance at first, they eventually agreed and led an attack on the Americans at Fort Stanwix.

By the time the Revolution was over, Cornplanter was a principle war chief of the Seneca and a respected warrior and field commander. When the British lost the war, however, Cornplanter immedi-

ately advocated cooperation with the new American nation. To Cornplanter, the British had made false promises and then abandoned their allies to the enemy. Survival would now depend on working with the United States and giving up what he considered the foolish resistance of other Iroquois such as Red Jacket.

In 1784, Cornplanter agreed to large land cessions in exchange for peace with the United States in the Treaty of Fort Stanwix. The Fort Harmar Treaty in 1789 ceded even more Iroquois land, and Cornplanter's support of both treaties made him unpopular among some of the less conciliatory Senecas. However, Cornplanter continued to work for peace and accommodation with the United States, which he believed necessary to preserve his people. In the early 1790s, Cornplanter served as a mediator between Indians and the Americans. In 1791, President George Washington sent Cornplanter to negotiate peace between the Indians of Michigan and Ohio and the United States.

Although unsuccessful, Cornplanter did manage to keep the Iroquois out of the conflicts. He began to travel to various cities in the Northeast to talk about his people and their needs. In 1797, Cornplanter signed another treaty, ceding more land to a private land company. In exchange for his cooperation, the State of Pennsylvania granted him private ownership of about fifteen hundred acres. Although he eventually lost two-thirds of the land, he did maintain ownership of 750 acres.

Red Jacket and others who refused to sign the cession considered Cornplanter a traitor to his people. Cornplanter believed, however, that the Seneca needed to adapt to American ways in order to survive. During some of his travels as an emissary of peace, Cornplanter met with and was very impressed with the Quakers in Pennsylvania. He admired their teachings of peace and sent his oldest son to a Quaker school. Eventually, in 1798, Cornplanter invited the Quakers to come and teach his people, to build schools and missions.

However, Cornplanter eventually became very disillusioned with the United States and felt ashamed of his accommodationist policies. Sometime after the War of 1812, according to some accounts, he publicly burned his military uniform, destroyed his medals, and ordered all the missionaries out of his land. In his later years, he advocated a return to Seneca traditions and rejection of white ways. This change of heart helped him regain the respect of those Seneca who felt he had betrayed them in the past. He died in 1836 at his home. His descendants continued to live on what was known as the Cornplanter Tract until the completion of the Kinzua Dam in 1964, which placed the entire tract under water.

Today, Cornplanter is remembered as an important peacemaker and leader of the Seneca people. Even though his cooperation with the United States and land cessions led to significant losses for his people, the Iroquois and Seneca now remember and respect his role as mediator and celebrate the spirit of peace with which he lived his life.

April R. Summitt

See also Treaty with the Six Nations–January 9, 1789; Treaty with the Six Nations at Fort Stanwix–November 5, 1768.

References and Further Reading

Abler, Thomas S. 1989. *Chainbreaker: The Revolutionary War Memoirs of Governor Blacksnake.* Lincoln: University of Nebraska Press.

Deardorff, Merle H., and Harold L. Myers. 1994. *Chief Cornplanter.* Harrisburg: Pennsylvania Historical and Museum Commission.

Francello, Joseph A. 1998. *Chief Cornplanter of the Senecas.* Allentown, PA: Glasco.

Swatzler, David, and Henry Simmons. 2000. *A Friend among the Senecas: The Quaker Mission to Cornplanter's People.* Mechanicsburg, PA: Stackpole Books.

Symes, Martha. 1995. "Cornplanter." In *Notable Native Americans*, ed. Sharon Malinowski. New York: Gale Research.

Costo, Rupert
(1906–1989)

From the 1930s to the 1950s, Rupert Costo, a Cahuilla, was active in national and tribal politics, serving both as a vocal critic of the Indian New Deal in the 1930s and as tribal chairman of the Cahuillas in the 1950s; later, Costo became an important figure in Native American publishing.

As a football player in the 1920s at Haskell Institute and Whittier College (where he played with future president Richard M. Nixon), Rupert Costo early in life demonstrated his athletic and intellectual aptitudes to the Indian and non-Indian world.

During the 1930s, California was a major center of opposition to Collier's Indian New Deal, and Costo was one of the principal leaders of the opposition. Costo believed that the Indian New Deal was a device to assimilate the American Indian; he believed that the Indian Reorganization Act was being used to colo-

nize Native Americans because, in his view, genocide, treaty making and treaty breaking, substandard education, disruption of Indian culture and religion, and the General Allotment Act (Dawes Act) had failed. Costo knew that partial assimilation already had taken place in Native societies through the use of "certain technologies and techniques," but he knew that total assimilation, which meant fading into the general society with a complete loss of culture and identity, was another thing altogether. Costo called the IRA "the Indian Raw Deal" (Mails 1990, 146).

For most of his working life, Costo was employed by the state of California as an engineer in the Highway Department. Upon his retirement, Costo and his wife, Jeannette Henry Costo (eastern Cherokee), founded the San Francisco-based American Indian Historical Society in 1964. The organization was often in the forefront of American Indian issues, such as the protection of American Indian cemeteries and American Indian human remains, as well as the correction of American Indian textbooks. The Costos sought to develop publications that accurately reflected the historical role of Indians in American society.

Initially, the American Indian Historical Society published three journals: *Wassaja*, a national Indian newspaper; *The Indian Historian*, a respected academic journal; and the *Weewish Tree*, a national magazine for young Indian people. Rupert Costo coedited all three publications with his wife. In 1970, the society founded another publication arm, the Indian Historian Press, an American Indian-controlled publishing house that published fifty-two titles. Some of the well-known titles were *Textbooks and the American Indian* (1970; Rupert Costo, ed.) and *The Iroquois and the Founding of the American Nation* (1977; Donald A. Grinde, Jr. [Yamasee]).

Through his editorial column in *Wassaja*, Costo advocated increased sovereignty for Native rights. He also worked tirelessly for the protection of American Indian civil, social, and religious rights.

At the end of his life, Costo endowed the Rupert Costo Chair in American Indian History at the University of California, Riverside. Costo and his wife also established the Costo Library of the American Indian at the University of California, Riverside, one of the most comprehensive collections of American Indian books in the United States. In 1994, the University of California, Riverside, renamed its Student Services Building Costo Hall in honor of the outstanding contributions of both Costos to the university.

Bruce E. Johansen

See also Alcatraz Occupation 1973; Sovereignty;
Statutes as Sources of Modern Indian Rights:
Child Welfare, Gaming, and Repatriation.

References and Further Reading
Johansen, Bruce E. 2005. *Native North America: A
History.* Westport, CT: Praeger.
Champagne, Duane and Jay Stauss, eds. *Native
American Studies in Higher Education: Models for
Collaboration between Universities and Indigenous
Nations.* Walnut Creek, Lanham, New York, and
Oxford: Atlamira Press.

Crazy Horse (Tašunka Witko)

(c. 1840–1877)

Crazy Horse was an Oglala Lakota leader of armed resistance to U.S. encroachment upon tribal lands, and he is a symbol of independence among contemporary American Indians. He was born around 1840 in South Dakota to an Oglala Lakota father, who was also named Crazy Horse, and a Miniconjou Lakota mother called Rattling Blanket Woman. The family included a sister, whose name is unknown, and a half brother, Little Hawk.

Crazy Horse may have witnessed the Grattan Massacre of 1854, in which Lieutenant John L. Grattan and his thirty-man command were killed during an unprovoked attack on a Lakota village near Fort Laramie, Wyoming. This event is often cited as pivotal in the formation of his negative perception of non-Indians and their intentions.

Crazy Horse's bravery in war with the United States and other tribes (principally the Crow and Shoshone) earned him high status, and in 1865 he was declared a "shirt wearer" (leader) among his people. During the Red Cloud War (1866–1868), he fought along the Bozeman Trail, which cut across Lakota territory from Wyoming to Montana's gold fields. He served as one of the decoy riders who led Captain William Fetterman's eighty-man command out of Fort Phil Kearny into a devastating ambush known as the Fetterman Massacre (December 21, 1866) and participated in the Hayfield and Wagon-Box fights the following year.

In 1870, Crazy Horse eloped with Black Buffalo Woman, wife of a Lakota named No Water. During a confrontation between the two men, No Water shot Crazy Horse in the face with a pistol. Crazy Horse lost his shirt-wearer position as a result of this scandal; around the same time, whites killed his half-brother Little Hawk. Within a year, Crazy Horse married Black Shawl, mother of his only child, a daughter called They Are Afraid of Her, who died around 1874, possibly a cholera victim.

When the government set a deadline of January 31, 1876, for Lakotas to report to reservations, Crazy Horse joined Sitting Bull in defying the order. When the army launched an offensive against "hostiles," Crazy Horse provided leadership in two epic Montana battles: he helped defeat General George Crook at the Battle of Rosebud (June 17), and he crushed Lieutenant Colonel George Custer's 7th Cavalry at the Battle of the Little Bighorn (June 25). These victories proved Pyrrhic, for the army relentlessly pursued Lakotas through the winter of 1876–1877. On May 8, 1877, Crazy Horse and his followers surrendered at Fort Robinson, Nebraska. Crazy Horse never mastered the subtleties of Lakota politics, but he appeared to accept the inevitable and during his brief stint as a reservation dweller married Nellie Larrabee (or Laravie), the daughter of a French trader and a Cheyenne or Lakota woman.

On September 5, 1877, unaware that a decision had been made to place him under arrest, Crazy Horse appeared at Fort Robinson to dispel rumors about whether he intended to remain a government opponent. Indians and soldiers escorted him to the guardhouse where, suddenly realizing he faced imprisonment, Crazy Horse pulled back from the doorway. A fracas broke out, and a soldier stabbed Crazy Horse in the back with his bayonet. That night, Crazy Horse died.

During his life, many of Crazy Horse's contemporaries viewed him as an inspiring, albeit enigmatic, leader of their resistance to foreign domination. After his death, Crazy Horse was transformed into the leading figure in a tragedy in which the visionary hero is doomed to suffer martyrdom, a victim of the malevolent machinations of oppressors from outside his culture and collaborationist traitors from within. Given the time that has elapsed and the fact that he came from a culture that maintained records through drawings and oral history, separating the Crazy Horse of historic reality from the Crazy Horse of hagiography seems an impossible task.

Ron McCoy

See also Red Cloud (Makhpiya-Luta); Treaty of
Fort Laramie with the Sioux, Etc.–September
17, 1851.

References and Further Reading

Hardorff, Richard G., ed. 1998. *The Death of Crazy Horse: A Tragic Episode in Lakota History.* Spokane, WA: Arthur H. Clark.

Riley, Paul D., ed. 1976. "Oglala Sources on the Life of Crazy Horse: Interviews Given to Eleanor H. Hinman." *Nebraska History,* 57 (Spring): 1–51; also in *The Nebraska Indian Wars Reader 1865–1877,* ed. Eli S. Paul. Lincoln: University of Nebraska Press, 1998, 180–216.

Sandoz, Mari. 1942. *Crazy Horse: The Strange Man of the Oglalas.* New York: Alfred A. Knopf.

Crowfoot

(c. 1830–1890)

Crowfoot is considered by many to be the greatest warrior and peacemaker in the story of the settlement of western Canada, and he is perhaps best known for his belief that he and his people could live peaceably alongside white men. Yet Crowfoot's reign as chief occurred during a tumultuous period highlighted by the Blackfoot's removal from traditional territories, forcing the complete transformation of their lifestyle.

Born in 1830 to Blood Indians Istowun-eh'pata (Packs a Knife) and Axkyahp-say-pi (Attacked Toward Home), Crowfoot's father died during a horse raid against the Crow when Crowfoot was still a boy. Upon returning to Packs a Knife's camp, Crowfoot's mother fell in love with a Blackfoot warrior, Akay-nehka-simi (Many Names); following their marriage, she and her two sons were adopted by the Blackfoot. Crowfoot managed to survive epidemics of diphtheria (1836) and smallpox (1837) and, as a young man, earned a reputation as a warrior and leader following a series of daring raids. Wounded six times in nineteen battles, he also gained the admiration of his own and neighboring communities for single-handedly killing a grizzly bear and for his skills as an orator.

Crowfoot took ten wives during his life, securing his position in Blackfoot society, although only four of his children reached maturity. When his son was killed by a Cree war party, he adopted Pito-kanow-apiwin ("Poundmaker"), a Cree who shared his father's belief in working for peace with non-Native settlers, a peace accomplished mainly through the establishment of commercial relationships with Hudson's Bay Company employees. Trading guns, iron kettles, beads, and woollens for buffalo hides, horses, and dried meats, Crowfoot

regularly interacted with white settlers until the time of his death. By the early 1870s, however, encroachment of westward-moving settlers had reached levels significant enough to disturb Blackfoot social and economic patterns. The introduction of whiskey, smuggled across the international border by American traders, also had a disastrous effect upon the Blackfoot, leading to alcohol-induced internal feuds. Responding to western concerns, politicians in Ottawa dispatched the Northwest Mounted Police in 1873 to aid in defusing the situation and to establish a paramilitary presence in the West.

The arrival of the Mounties resulted in the removal of whiskey peddlers, although this was followed by an influx of settlers, which in turn forced the initiation of treaty negotiations. Acting as the Blackfoot's main chief, Crowfoot was one of a coalition of chiefs to negotiate and sign Treaty 7 in September 1877, which formalized the Blackfoot-Canadian government relationship. The Crowfoot-led Blackfoot Confederacy ceded fifty thousand acres of traditional territory in return for tracts of reserve land considered impervious to settler encroachment and a variety of provisions including but not limited to a yearly stipend, rations, police protection from American bootleggers, ammunition, and rations. Crowfoot was also commended by Queen Victoria of England for his refusal to ally with Sioux leader Sitting Bull during the wars between the Plains Indians and the U.S. Cavalry.

Despite government promises to aid in protecting the Blackfoot traditional lifestyle, soon after signing Treaty 7 Crowfoot and his people faced starvation and for several winters chose to reside in Montana in search of buffalo. Upon their return to Canada and their allotted reserves, Crowfoot and his people did their best to survive on government rations and hunting. In spite of such hardships, Crowfoot resisted joining forces with Métis leader Louis Riel, who attempted to form a provisional government in 1885, although the Blackfoot leader did instruct his people to assist Cree or Métis rebels passing through their territory. Crowfoot's choice appeared apt in hindsight, considering the rebellion's demise.

In his later years, Crowfoot watched helplessly from the confines of his reserve as the Blackfoot were reduced from great buffalo hunters of the northwest plains to dependency upon the Canadian government for their survival. Crowfoot became an intermediary, working with the federal government in an attempt to improve the condition of his people, traveling to Montreal and Ottawa to meet with government officials and the prime minister, only to return home to and die in his tipi on April 5, 1890.

Yale D. Belanger

See also Black Kettle; Canadian Indian Treaty
7–September 22, December 4, 1877; Métis; Riel,
Louis; Sovereignty; Trust.

References and Further Reading

Champagne, Duane. 1994. *Native America: Portrait of the Peoples.* Detroit: Visible Ink Press.
Dempsey, Hugh. 1989. *Crowfoot: Chief of the Blackfeet.* Norman: University of Oklahoma Press.
Waldman, Carl. 1990. *Who Was Who in Native American History.* New York: Facts on File.

Dawes Commission (Commission to the Five Civilized Tribes)

The Commission to the Five Civilized Tribes, popularly known as the Dawes Commission, worked in Indian Territory between 1893 and 1906 to further the U.S. policy of allotment and assimilation.

All removal treaties made in the 1830s with the nations that became known as the Five Civilized Tribes—Cherokees, Choctaws, Creeks, Chickasaw, and Seminole—guaranteed that the new land titles in Indian Territory would be perpetual and that no government would ever be forced upon them. After the Civil War, the Five Civilized Tribes ceded half their territory. The ceded portion was partially used for repatriating western tribes, and the rest was opened to white settlers in 1889. In large part due to the "openings," a steady stream of white and black settlers moved into the territory and established towns over which tribal governments had no authority. By 1890, there were approximately 70,000 tribal citizens and between 140,000 and 250,000 nontribal residents (estimates vary).

The territory remaining to the Five Civilized Tribes included valuable agricultural and timber lands, extensive coalfields, and gold deposits, which citizens developed. Each tribe had its own constitution and infrastructure, including a school system, a general council, and a system of courts. Some became wealthy, whereas others lost control over their land due to intermarriage or leasing to noncitizens. All tribes, however, practiced communal land tenure and limited the size of holdings and leasing practices. Until 1890, the federal government hesitated to break pledges it had made with the Five Civilized Tribes.

In 1869, the newly formed Board of Indian Commissioners recommended that communal land tenure be replaced by individual ownership. Cultural assimilation was the goal. Even reformers who had recently advocated that all treaties be honored followed suit in calling for allotment and assimilation, including the most influential campaigner for this bill, Senator Henry Dawes.

The Dawes Severalty Act was passed in 1887. It provided for individual allotments to Native Americans out of reservation lands; so-called surplus land would revert to the government. The Five Civilized Tribes were not exempt from the Dawes Act, but they were not exempt from the policy; the Dawes Commission was established in 1893 (27 *Stat.* 645) to carry out the policy among them. President Grover Cleveland appointed Henry Dawes, Meredith H. Kidd, and Archibald S. McKennon as its original commissioners.

The work of the Dawes Commission was slow for the first few years. The tribes resisted by organizing international councils to establish policy, appointing tribal commissions, and otherwise struggling to safeguard their cultures. In 1894, the Cherokee National Council wrote a response to the Dawes Commission annual report and traveled to Washington, D.C., to present their arguments before Congress.

In 1895, a reconstituted Dawes Commission asked Congress to impose a territorial form of government on Indian Territory. Congress declined, but in 1895 the commission was given the authority to survey tribal lands and determine citizenship status. After three years of publishing annual reports, appearing before congressional committees, and giving public speeches inside and outside of Indian Territory, the commission brought the Choctaws to the bargaining table, and an agreement was signed in 1896. Due to these factors as well as to pressure exerted by the railroad companies, resistance to the Dawes Commission further softened in 1897. The Creek, Chickasaw, and Seminole Nations had signed by 1898. A big blow to tribal autonomy came in 1898, when the Curtis Act effectively ended tribal governance by abolishing tribal courts and enforcing allotment. It also stipulated the creation of an authoritative citizenship roll that became known as the Dawes Roll.

After the tribal officials were deprived of authority by the Curtis Act, the Cherokee Nation was forced to enter negotiations with the Dawes

Commission. In 1902, an agreement was ratified, and the rolls closed with approximately forty-five thousand names listed. Each enrollee was entitled to forty acres of average land, inalienable and nontaxable for up to twenty-one years, and an additional amount of land equaling $325.60. Cherokee tribal government was terminated in 1906, and the next year Oklahoma became a state.

The work of the Dawes Commission did more than break up a system of communal land tenure; it destroyed the often-fragile connections that held tribes together. As a result, a class structure definitively replaced tribal social structures.

In the 1970s, the Dawes Roll, which had played such a crucial part in dissolving the tribes, was used to build them up again.

Deborah Gilbert

See also Allotments; Curtis Act, 1898; Dawes, Henry Laurens; General Allotment Act (Dawes Act), 1887; Indian Removal; Indian Territory; Jackson, Andrew; Trail of Tears.

References and Further Reading

Debo, Angie. 1940. *And Still the Waters Run.* Princeton, NJ: Princeton University Press.

Gibson, Arrell M. 1978. "Indian Land Transfers." In *Handbook of North American Indians,* vol. 4, ed. William C. Sturtevant, 211–229. Washington, DC: Smithsonian Institution.

Hagan, William T. 1978. "United States Indian Policies, 1860–1900." In *Handbook of North American Indians,* vol. 4, ed. William C. Sturtevant, 51–65. Washington: Smithsonian Institution.

Wardell, Morris L. 1938. *A Political History of the Cherokee Nation: 1838–1907.* Norman: University of Oklahoma Press.

Dawes, Henry Laurens

(1816–1903)

Henry Laurens Dawes lived during a time of great change and development in the early period of the United States. The nineteenth century was also a time of confusing changes for the Indians in this country. The non-Indian population was growing rapidly and pushing westward. The desire for more farmland, the discovery and exploitation of rich natural resources, the discovery of silver and gold in the West, and the building of the transcontinental railroad were all factors pressuring the young government to open up to everyone the hundreds of millions of acres on the Indian reservations.

Senator Henry L. Dawes (1816–1903) of Massachusetts served as chairman of the Dawes Commission and he supported the General Allotment Act of 1887. (Library of Congress)

Henry L. Dawes was born in Cummington, Massachusetts, on October 30, 1816, the son of a farmer, Mitchell Dawes, and Mercy Burgess. He graduated from Yale in 1839. His first position after graduation was in teaching. In 1841, he taught at the Sanderson Academy, an girls' school in Ashfield, Massachusetts. It was here that he met his future wife, Electa Allen Sanderson, a student at the academy and six years his junior. His next undertaking was as editor of the *Greenfield Gazette;* later, he edited the *Adams Transcript* in Greenfield. During this time, he also studied law in the firm of Wells and Davis. He was admitted to the Massachusetts bar in 1842. Henry and Electa were married in Ashfield on April 12, 1844, and settled in North Adams. They lived in North Adams for twenty years before moving to Pittsfield, their final home.

Dawes went into private law practice for a few years and in 1848 was elected to the Massachusetts State House of Representatives. He was reelected in 1849 and 1852. He served in the State Senate in 1850 and was a member of the state constitutional convention of 1853. He was district attorney for the western district of Massachusetts from 1853 to 1857 and served as a Republican member of the House of

Representatives from 1857 to 1875 and Senator from 1875 to 1893. While in the House, he served on several committees: Ways and Means, Appropriations, and Elections. While in the Senate, he served on numerous committees, including the Committee on Buildings and Grounds, as a member of which he was instrumental in the completion of the Washington Monument, and the Committee on Indian Affairs.

During most of the nineteenth century, many members in Congress and people throughout the country felt that it would be in the Indians' best interests to be brought into mainstream society. This, they felt, could only be done by breaking up the tribal affiliations and the reservations. Dawes was a great proponent of this strategy because he thought it was the most humanitarian solution for the Indians, who would then become self-sufficient farmers on their allotted lands and assimilate into the "civilized" society, and, in time, the reservation system would disappear altogether. The surplus land could then be sold for agrarian use and other development.

Several attempts at this had failed, when in 1879 Senator Richard Coke of Texas introduced yet another allotment bill to Congress. Although not successful at first, the bill was finally passed in 1887 as the General Allotment Act, or the Dawes Severalty Act after Henry L. Dawes, who sponsored it at the time of passage. The fact that Coke introduced this bill is all but forgotten.

Dawes retired from the Senate in 1893, but his retirement was short lived. Two years later, in 1895, President Grover Cleveland appointed him chairman of the Commission to the Five Civilized Tribes, which became known as the Dawes Commission. The Five Civilized Tribes (Cherokee, Chickasaw, Creek, Choctaw, and Seminole) were initially exempt from the General Allotment Act of 1887 because of their unyielding opposition to it, but now the government insisted on breaking up their tribal governments and lands too. Dawes was chairman of the commission for ten years, until the time of his death.

His wife, Electa, died on April 15, 1901; Henry died on February 5, 1903, at the age of 86. The Daweses had five children, only three of whom survived to adulthood: Anna Laurens, born in 1851; Chester Mitchell, born in 1855; and Henry Laurens, born in 1863. Both of Dawes's sons became lawyers; Chester settled in Chicago, Illinois, and Henry remained in Pittsfield. Anna also lived out her days in Pittsfield, where she wrote several books, including a biography of Senator Charles Sumner in 1892. She died in 1938. It was Anna who donated her father's papers to the Library of Congress in Washington, D.C.

Gayle Yiotis

See also Assimilation; Dawes Commission; General Allotment Act (Dawes Act), 1887.

References and Further Reading

Dawes, Henry Laurens. *Papers*. Washington, DC: Library of Congress.

Debo, Angie. 1940. *And Still the Waters Run: The Betrayal of the Five Civilized Tribes*. Princeton, NJ: Princeton University Press. Repr., New York: Gordian Press, 1966.

Howes, Frederick G. 1910. *History of the Town of Ashfield, Franklin County, Massachusetts from its Settlement in 1742 to 1910*. Ashfield, MA: Town of Ashfield.

Hoxie, Frederick E. 1984. *A Final Promise: The Campaign to Assimilate the Indians, 1880–1920*. Lincoln: University of Nebraska Press.

McDonnell, Janet A. *The Dispossession of the American Indian, 1887–1934*. Bloomington: Indiana University Press.

Moore, William F. 1898. *Representative Men of Massachusetts, 1890–1900*. Everett: Massachusetts Publishing.

U.S. Bureau of the Census. 1930. *Fifteenth Census of the United States*. Washington, DC: Department of Commerce.

Washburn, Wilcomb E. 1975. *The Assault on Indian Tribalism: The General Allotment Law (Dawes Act) of 1887)*. Philadelphia: Lippincott.

De La Cruz, Joseph Burton
(1937–2000)

Born in 1937, Joseph De La Cruz became one of the leading American Indian activists in the United States. He was particularly concerned with the white exploitation of native-owned resources within the boundaries of reservation lands. On his own tribal lands, De La Cruz became well known for pulling his truck onto a bridge to prevent logging trucks from crossing over onto reservation lands. He did this to protest the misuse of tribal lands by the Bureau of Indian Affairs (BIA) for the profit of logging companies and to protect tribal rights to the lumber, shellfish, and other fishing industries, an act that later led to compensation paid to the Quinault tribe for their lumber.

De La Cruz served as president of the Quinault Nation from 1970–1994 on the 211,000 acres of Washington State's rainforest region. He was also president of the National Congress of American Indians from 1980 until 1985, president of the National Tribal Chairman's Association, and president of the Affiliated Tribes of Northwest Indians; he also served in many other native rights and health organizations. He was the recipient of the Chief George Manuel Leadership Award and was the first person to hold the distinguished Joe Tallakson Chair for Public Policy at the Center for World Indigenous Studies, which he held from 1998 to 2000. With Bruce Babbitt, former attorney general of Arizona and secretary of the interior, De La Cruz was co-chair of the National Council on Tribal State Relations; with former governor Daniel J. Evans, he served as co-chair of the Northwest Renewable Resource Center; and he was the North American representative to the World Council of Indigenous Peoples.

De La Cruz's major concerns were environmental, health, and sovereignty issues among all American Indian nations. He was a staunch supporter of the effort to educate the American public about treaties between American Indian tribes and the U.S. government, and he called for reform in the Bureau of Indian Affairs (which is the oldest federal agency in the United States). He also supported the education of natives and non-natives alike about the cultural aspects of Native Americans. De La Cruz was one of three Indian leaders in the formation of the First Americans Education Project. During a 1989 Senate Committee on Indian Affairs hearing on Senate Concurrent Resolution 76, De La Cruz addressed such major concerns as the public's need for education on American Indian treaties, governments, and cultures; a government-to-government policy that promoted tribal self-government and tribal self-sufficiency; and the need for American Indian tribal governments, the U.S. government, and Congress to work together to restructure the federal administration of Indian affairs. These were items that he addressed many times in governmental hearings. He was not always revered by everyone. He often clashed with Washington senator Slade Gorton, Republican chairman of the Senate Interior Appropriations Subcommittee, on Indian spending.

Joseph Burton De La Cruz was an activist until the end. On April 6, 2000, he was waiting at the Seattle-Tacoma International Airport for a flight to Oklahoma to speak at a Native Health Conference, when he suddenly had a massive heart attack. He died of this heart attack at the age of sixty-two. He left behind his wife, Dorothy; their three daughters,

Gayle, Tina, and Lisa; and two sons, Joe and Steve. At the time of his passing, he had seven grandchildren and two great-grandchildren. Not only the family mourned his loss but the entire state of Washington, as well as all Native Americans the world over. The *Seattle Times* reported his funeral as attended by " . . . a pageant of Pacific Northwest tribal and political leaders." About fifteen hundred people attended the funeral services, which were held in the soon-to-be-opened Ocean Shores Casino. De La Cruz had been instrumental in putting together the package deal for the Quinault Nation. He was buried at Inchelium, the Colville Indian reservation where his wife Dorothy was born (Eskenazi 2000).

Dorothy De La Cruz, Joseph's wife, continues to marshal support for Native American causes. In September 2002, she led the first mile in the cross-country relay race Sovereignty Run, which began in Taholah, Washington, and ended at the steps of the U.S. Supreme Court to bring to light the unjust Court decisions against Native tribes.

Priscilla MacDonald

> See also American Indian Movement (AIM); Boldt
>   Decision (*United States v. Washington*), 1974;
>   Government-to-Government Relationship;
>   Sovereignty.

References and Further Reading

Eskenazi, Stuart. "Northwest Tribes, Leaders Honor a Warrior of Wisdom." *Seattle Times*, April 23, 2000.

Johnson, Troy, Joane Nagel, and Duane Champagne, eds. 1997. *American Indian Activism: Alcatraz to the Longest Walk.* Urbana and Chicago: University of Illinois Press.

Olson, Ronald. 1936. *The Quinault Indians.* Seattle: University of Washington Press.

Parman, Donald L. 1984. "Inconsistency Advocacy: The Erosion of Indian Fishing Rights in the Pacific Northwest, 1933–1956." *Pacific Historical Review*, 53 (May): 163–189.

Dearborn, Henry
(1751–1829)

Henry Dearborn was a physician, a Revolutionary War veteran, a U.S. marshal for the District of Maine, a U.S. congressman, a secretary of war, a War of 1812 veteran, and a minister to Portugal.

Henry Dearborn is a relatively obscure figure in American history. Although his career as an officer in the American Revolution was fairly distinguished,

Henry Dearborn (1751–1829) was a distinguished veteran of the American Revolution who later served capably as the nation's secretary of war during the Thomas Jefferson and James Madison administrations (1801–1809), which oversaw Indian affairs during that time. (Library of Congress)

his tenure as secretary of war under President Thomas Jefferson and his subsequent service in the War of 1812 cast a pall on his reputation.

With a New Hampshire ancestry dating back to 1639, Dearborn was born in North Hampton, on February 23, 1751. He was educated as a physician and, at twenty-four years of age, had an established practice by the outset of the Revolutionary War. Elected captain of the sixty-man militia unit he had organized in 1772, he fought at the rail fence at Bunker Hill (Breed's Hill).

His experience in the war included a steady rise through the officers' ranks. He was involved in most of the major operations of the war, including action against the Iroquois Confederation (Six Nations) and the Battle of Yorktown. He was taken prisoner at Quebec, held for a year, and finally released. He served under most of the well-known officers, including General George Washington, from whom his regiment earned a commendation.

After a brief stint as the U.S. marshal for the District of Maine (1790), Dearborn served two undistinguished terms (1793–1797) representing Mass-

achusetts in the House of Representatives as a Republican.

Dearborn began his service as secretary of war under President Thomas Jefferson in March 1801. At this time, matters concerning Indians rested with the War Department, and the Jefferson administration's policy regarding Indian affairs was one of accommodation and appeasement, which, it was hoped, would end in civilization through acculturation. To this end, there were two approaches: The first was to teach the Indians to use land as whites did, through individual ownership, agriculture, and skilled trades, as a function of which they would soon become civilized—and even intermarry with whites. Given failure or dissatisfaction with this approach, the second approach was voluntary removal, in which the Indians would trade eastern land for some of the newly acquired wilderness west of the Mississippi.

Dearborn appeared to share a belief in this philosophy and attempted to do what was required. During his tenure, thirty-one formal treaties were negotiated, in at least two of which Dearborn was the principal negotiator. However, those upon whom he depended, some of whom were working diligently to promulgate war with Europe, diverted Dearborn's attention. For example, James J. Wilkinson, commanding general of the western frontier and governor of Upper Louisiana, was involved with the expensive and ill-fated 1806 Red River expedition, which caused embarrassment to Jefferson and nearly drew Americans into war with Spain. Next was William Henry Harrison, governor of Indiana Territory, whose military and political ambitions helped to escalate the animosity between Americans and the confederation of tribes enlisted by Tecumseh (Shawnee), still in alliance with the British. Occupying Dearborn's attention further was the continuing political divisiveness over ties with the French. In March 1809, Dearborn resigned, as the newly elected president, James Madison, took office.

In January 1812, Madison appointed Dearborn senior major general in command of the Army's northeast sector, from the Niagara River east to the New England coast. Unfortunately, the years he had spent in Washington—depending on diplomatic solutions to end conflict—resulted in his inability to function effectively in a military capacity. As critics have noted, he was unfit for command both psychologically and physically. His inability to control his troops, his overcautious behavior, his patience with futile negotiation processes, and his ill health (result-

ing from obesity, which demanded the use of a specially designed cart) have all been cited as reasons for the losses of Detroit and several other forts in the Great Lakes region to the British. Unlike his subordinate, General William Hull, commander of Fort Detroit, he was spared a court martial (possibly through political favoritism) and was reassigned to administrative command in New York before being honorably discharged in 1815.

Dearborn married three times: to Mary Barlett (1771), to Dorcas Marble (1780), and to Sarah Bowdoin (1813). His last public service was as U.S. ambassador to Portugal (1822–1824). Henry Dearborn died on June 6, 1829, at his home in Roxbury, Massachusetts.

Deborah Rubenstein

See also Assimilation; Jefferson, Thomas; Harrison, William Henry; Indian Removal; Tecumseh.

References and Further Reading

Lavender, David. 1998. *The Fist in the Wilderness.* Lincoln: University of Nebraska Press.

Sheehan, Bernard W. 1974. *Seeds of Extinction: Jeffersonian Philanthropy and the American Indian.* New York: W.W. Norton.

Wallace, Anthony F. C. 1999. *Jefferson and the Indians: The Tragic Fate of the First Americans.* Cambridge, MA: Belknap Press of Harvard University Press.

A Native American rights activist noted for her fight in overturning the Menominee Termination Act of 1954, Ada Deer (1935–) was appointed as the first woman assistant secretary of the Department of Interior for Indian affairs in 1993. (Corbis)

Deer, Ada E.

(1935–)

Ada Elizabeth Deer was born August 7, 1935, in the town of Keshena on the Menominee Indian Reservation in northeastern Wisconsin. She grew up in a one-room log cabin on the banks of the Wolf River, where she and her family spent the next eighteen years without the benefit of running water and electricity. In this natural environment, Deer, aided by her mother, developed her lifelong commitment to public service. Her mother, Constance Stockton (Wood) Deer is of Scottish-English descent and worked as a registered nurse for the Bureau of Indian Affairs (BIA). Deer's father, Joseph Deer, was a Menominee Indian who worked at the Menominee Indian Mills. He died January 10, 1994, at the age of eighty-five. Both were members of the Rightfully Enrolled Menominee Indians (REMI), an organization that opposed the government's termination policy of the 1950s.

The goal of termination was to withdraw federal support to tribal governments, to end Indians

tribes' status as sovereign nations, and to assimilate them into the American mainstream. The Menominee were among a handful of Indian tribes that the government considered sufficiently prosperous to terminate. Congress passed the Menominee Termination Act in 1954. By 1961, the act was fully in effect. It was the year Deer received a master's degree in social work from Columbia University, the first Native American to obtain the honor. The next decade of her life was spent laying the foundation for what was to become one of the defining moments of her life. While her tribe was falling inevitably into poverty, Deer was gaining valuable experience serving as a social worker, Peace Corps volunteer, and BIA service coordinator. Other service assignments eventually led to the study of law. But after one semester at the University of Wisconsin-Madison Law School, Deer was compelled to withdraw so that she could aid in her people's survival.

Returning to Menominee County (formerly the Menominee Indian Reservation), Deer and others organized a grassroots movement to regain control of tribal interests from Menominee Enterprises, Inc. (MEI), a corporation formed to administer tribal resources. Deer had become involved in 1969, when she and her siblings, Bob and Connie, became concerned over the sale of ancestral lands to pay down rising tribal debt. When a request by Deer to MEI president George Kenote asking for a breakdown of one of the corporation's land sales was met by resistance, the family realized the need for legal assistance. A call by Deer to Wisconsin Judicare, a Madison-based legal service agency funded by the Office of Equal Opportunity (OEO), fortunately resulted in free legal representation. The agency's director, Joseph Preloznik, met with Deer and her family and agreed to begin an investigation into MEI, the land sale, and other tribal problems. But even before this initial meeting, tribal members, uncomfortable with what they felt were actions injurious to the Menominee, were gathering in groups in Chicago, Milwaukee, and Menominee County.

During this time, Ada Deer was active in organizing Milwaukee area Menominee tribal members. She enlisted a Menominee art student, John Gauthier, to help arrange the first meeting. Deer's friends Louise Kitchkume and Georgianna Ignace and anthropologist Nancy Lurie played important roles in the early days of the movement. Spring of 1970 witnessed the coalescence of the Menominee as an independent political entity. Deer's sister, Connie, was responsible for the group's name, Determination of the Rights and Unity of Menominee Shareholders (DRUMS). DRUMS' significance was enhanced by its members, who were better educated and more politically sophisticated than in prior efforts.

Early action by the group often was met with strong opposition. MEI mill hands were deputized to disrupt the first meeting held in Menominee County. Death threats were placed on the cars of tribal members in attendance. Fortunately, Judicare was there to protect the group's First Amendment rights and its right to peaceful assembly. By the summer of 1970, DRUMS was a formidable force in Milwaukee, Chicago, and Menominee County.

Led by Deer, James White and others in the organization capitalized on the social protest movements of the 1970s. A "March for Justice," a letter-writing campaign, and a tribal meeting to discuss the issue were among the strategies DRUMS implemented. As a result of organized protests against the real estate venture, DRUMS members gained seats on the MEI Board of Directors. By 1972, the project

was dead. DRUMS' major goal, the reversal of termination, was achieved a year later. A sympathetic president, Richard Nixon, came out against termination. Congress passed legislation to restore their tribal status. On December 22, 1973, President Nixon signed the bill ending the disastrous experiment.

Charles W. Buckner

See also Federally Recognized Tribes; House Concurrent Resolution 108, 1953; *Menominee Tribe of Indians v. United States*, 1968; Nonrecognized Tribes; Termination; Watkins, Arthur V.

References and Further Reading

Bataille, Gretchen M., ed. 1993. *Native American Women*. New York: Garland.
Ourada, Patricia K. 1979. *The Menominee Indians: A History*. Norman: University of Oklahoma Press.
Peroff, Nicholas C. 1982. *Menominee Drums: Tribal Termination and Restoration, 1954–1974*. Norman: University of Oklahoma Press.

Deloria, Vine, Jr.
(1933–2005)

In the 1960s, a thirty-one-year-old Hunkpapa Sioux from the Standing Rock Reservation with a long family heritage of social, political, and spiritual leadership stepped forth on the national scene as executive director of the National Congress of American Indians (NCAI). Vine Deloria, Jr., served three years as executive director of the NCAI, an experience that profoundly impacted his view of the *tipi sapa*, or sacred black lodge, that his great-grandfather had seen in a vision a century earlier. Shocked by what he saw in Indian country—and by how American Indians were perceived—Deloria realized that new tactics were needed if tribal people were to survive the "chaotic and extreme individualism" of America (Deloria 1985, 20). Over the next four decades, Deloria's prolific pen would profoundly impact the way Americans and the world viewed American Indians.

Little known outside national tribal leadership and scarcely known among the masses in Indian country, Deloria "seized the nation by its lapels" with a series of provocative and insightful books in the late 1960s and 1970s. Until that time, many Indians had been viewed "as ciphers rather than as contemporary people facing issues such as education, jobs, healthcare and civil rights." Although Indians were suitable for wall decorations, to adorn the

Vine Deloria, Jr., a Native American scholar, author, and activist, influenced two generations of leaders, Native and non-Indian. (AP Photo)

nation's coinage, and as foils in Western movies, they were viewed as neither modern nor political. "Indians were an unknown quantity," Deloria once observed. "There was a huge gap in how we were perceived by the average citizen and who we actually were" (Porter 2002, 9).

Deloria poignantly outlined his intellectual and theoretical views in a 1969 book that shook the foundations of academia and religious institutions, challenging worldwide perceptions of American Indians. *Custer Died for Your Sins: An Indian Manifesto* set Deloria on the road to national prominence, calling for Indian self-determination within a political and cultural construct that was unique and separate from the larger American political and social constraints. Peoplehood was impossible, Deloria proclaimed, "without cultural independence, which in turn is impossible without land" (Deloria 1969, 180).

The social and historical context within which Deloria came into prominence was rooted in the eighteenth century. "As long as any member of my family can remember," Deloria stated in 1969, "we have been involved in the affairs of the Sioux tribe." His intellectual and leadership abilities in the strug-

gle for Indian rights came from carrying on "the leadership qualities of his father, grandfather, and great grandfather" and "stem[med] not only from his formal education and academic position but also from an extraordinary family heritage" (Hoover 1997, 28). In reflecting on his family, Deloria once wrote that his great-grandfather (Saswe), grandfather (Philip), and father (Vine, Sr.) "created a family heritage that has been a heavy burden but that could not have been avoided once Saswe chose the red road [of leadership]" (Deloria 2000, 84).

Vine Deloria, Jr., was born on March 26, 1933, in Martin, South Dakota, on the Pine Ridge Reservation. After attending elementary school in Martin, Deloria graduated from St. James Academy in Faribault, Minnesota, before serving a three-year stint in the U.S. Marine Corps and attending Iowa State University, where he earned a bachelor of science degree in 1958. He then earned a master's degree in theology from Augustana Lutheran Seminary in Rock Island, Illinois, in 1963. Although he considered following his father's—and grandfather's and great-grandfather's—footsteps into the ministries of the Episcopal Church, Deloria chose a different path,

one that centered on tribalism and traditional religious expressions.

In 1964, Deloria accepted a position with the United Scholarship Service in Denver, Colorado, to develop a scholarship program for American Indians to attend elite eastern preparatory schools. Later that year at the Sheridan, Wyoming, convention, he found himself elected executive director of the NCAI, a position he later said he was naïve enough to accept. Expected "to solve problems presented by tribes from all over the country," Deloria found the work challenging because of "unscrupulous individuals" who made tasks difficult to solve and accented the "great gap between performers and publicity" (Deloria, 1968). Financial concerns always threatened the NCAI; the organization was more than once on the verge of insolvency. When he left as executive director in 1967, Deloria realized that "other tactics would have to be used to further the cause for Indian rights" (Deloria 1969, 270–273).

Part of the new tactic was to train Indian attorneys who could help tribes understand their rights and responsibilities. With this in mind, Deloria returned to school in 1967 and earned a law degree from the University of Colorado in 1970. While still in law school, Deloria wrote *Custer Died for Your Sins*, a book that became his best seller and parlayed his family heritage and legacy of leadership into national prominence. From 1970 to 1972, Deloria taught at Western Washington State College, from 1972 to 1974 at the University of California at Los Angeles, and from 1978 to 1990 at the University of Arizona, where he established an Indian policy studies program within the Political Science Department and an American Indian studies program in 1982. Between 1990 and 2000, he was a professor at the University of Colorado, Boulder, where he retired from academia.

Putting action together with his desire to help tribes understand their rights, Deloria was one of three Indian attorneys to establish the Institute for the Development of Indian Law in 1970. This organization provided training and training materials for tribes and educational institutions around the country. He also served in organizations such as the Citizens Crusade against Poverty, the Council on Indian Affairs, the National Office for the Rights of the Indigent, the Indian Rights Association, and the Intertribal Bison Council. He was also a founding trustee on the board of the National Museum of the American Indian. As the preeminent scholar of protection

of sacred lands, enforcement of treaty rights, and repatriation of cultural patrimony and burial remains, Deloria won numerous awards both in and outside of Indian country.

Among the accomplishments of Vine Deloria, Jr., is a truly extraordinary event that shifted the foundation of an entire academic discipline and, in the process, created a more favorable view of American Indians and Indian tribes. The event was the publication of *Custer Died for Your Sins*, in which Deloria indicted anthropologists and put them on alert that American Indians refused to be imprisoned in their words and writings. In the process, Deloria gave voice to a whole generation of American Indians for the development of a distinct academic discipline of American Indian studies in which Indians themselves would define what was important.

In 1989, the American Anthropological Association convened a session entitled "Custer Died for Your Sins: A Twenty-Year Retrospective on Relations Between Anthropologists and American Indians." Its purpose was to explore the changes that had occurred in Indian-anthropologist relations since *Custer* was first published. Out of this session came *Indians and Anthropologists: Vine Deloria, Jr., and the Critique of Anthropology*, which initiated "a new period in relations between American Indian people and anthropologists in particular, between Indians and non-Indians in America generally, and between colonized peoples and the metropolis globally" (Biolsi and Zimmerman 1997, 4).

Easily the "most influential polemicist" of the latter half of the twentieth century, Deloria "exceeded all others with similar motives" by using the social upheavals of the sixties as his forum to "represent a voice of outrage on behalf of Native Americans" (Hoover 1997, 31). Those tutored under and influenced by Deloria's scholarship have built into their thinking new ethics and morality because of *Custer* and Deloria's subsequent writings. Anthropologist Murray L. Wax once credited "the shapeshifting Deloria—lawyer, priest, political scientist, prophet, educator, and satirist"—with shifting the orientation of the anthropologist from that of a "detached observer" to that of a "committed and engaged participant, linked to the local community" (Wax 1997, 59).

Deloria acknowledged that progress was made. "Scholars better understand their skills and the degree to which they can assist Indians," Deloria opined. "We have certainly not found paradise, but we have seen considerable light brought to bear on problems, and we can now make choices we could not make before." Nonetheless, the social sciences continue to be "a deeply colonial academic discipline." America has a "state religion," Deloria observed, "and it is called science," which controls the process of information about and interpretation of American Indians and their cultural patrimony. Scholars hiding behind the cloak of science will again "raise their voices" against American Indians in the future, Deloria predicts, because the real battle is "over control of definitions: Who is to define what an Indian *really* is?" (Deloria 1997b, 210–212).

Long committed to the belief of "[getting] knowledge into the hands of ordinary people," Deloria spent a lifetime helping tribes and tribal people understand the basis of their existence, stressing the legal and moral bases of tribal political and social life. In *Tribes, Treaties, and Constitutional Tribulations* (1999), he provided an analysis of the U.S. government and how each branch relates to Indian tribes. In *Of Utmost Good Faith* (1971), Deloria provided an anthology of Indian legal papers, including Supreme Court rulings, treaties and agreements, legislative acts, and tribal speeches. In *American Indians, American Justice* (1983), *American Indian Policy in the Twentieth Century* (1985), *Behind the Trail of Broken Treaties* (1974), and *The Nations Within* (1984), Deloria provided a legal and historical framework of tribes in the United States. In *We Talk; You Listen: New Tribes, New Turf* (1970) and *God Is Red* (1973), he expounded on his theoretical framework that tribalism was the only alternative to modern life.

Deloria's recent books focused on the ideological foundations of Western science and its fallacies. *Red Earth, White Lies* (1995), *For This Land* (1999), *Spirit and Reason* (edited by his wife Barbara Deloria in 1999), and *Evolution, Creation and Other Modern Myths* (2002) all assailed Christianity and the religion of Western science while advocating a return to tribal ways. Tribal philosophies, Deloria theorized, were superior to both Western scientific interpretations and religious dogmas. Believing that the real battle for survival was ideological, Deloria spent a lifetime educating Indians and non-Indians on spiritual matters that define ideology. For these efforts, *Time* magazine recognized Deloria as one of the ten most influential religious thinkers of the twentieth century.

In toto, Deloria's writings provide an insightful, scholarly and, at times, witty view of the nature of tribes and their dealings with the United States, demonstrating how and why at a philosophical level

tribalism and tribal ways are superior to mainstream Western American ways. Tribal groups, Deloria once observed, "recognize the value of relations," which creates "a society of responsibility." To belong to a tribe, one had to "feed the poor," "take care of the orphans," and "provide for the elders." In short, tribalism was relational rather than institutional and hierarchal. American Indians, Deloria wrote in 1997, must "redefine their understanding of leadership to reflect traditional Indian ways." The key to returning to traditional leadership is to return to tribal ways, including the use of storytelling to help young people "feel they belong to something of their own" (Deloria 1997a, 2, 4).

Deloria passed away on November 13, 2005, in Golden, Colorado, at age seventy-two, after surgical complications. University of Colorado professor Charles Wilkinson called him "probably the most influential American Indian of the past century. He was also a wonderful human being, brilliant, bitingly funny, and profoundly warm and compassionate, always willing to lend a hand or raise a spirit" (Johansen 2005, 7-B).

David H. DeJong

See also Alcatraz Occupation, 1964 and 1969; American Indian Movement (AIM); Sovereignty; Statutes as Sources of Modern Indian Rights: Child Welfare, Gaming, and Repatriation; Wounded Knee Occupation 1973.

References and Further Reading

Biolsi, Thomas, and Larry J. Zimmerman. 1997. "What's Changed, What Hasn't." In *Indians and Anthropologists: Vine Deloria Jr., and the Critique of Anthropology,* 3–23. Tucson: University of Arizona Press.

Deloria, Vine, Jr. 1968. *Where Were You When We Needed You?* Washington, DC: National Congress of American Indians.

Deloria, Vine, Jr. 1969. *Custer Died for Your Sins: An Indian Manifesto.* New York: Macmillan.

Deloria, Vine, Jr. 1985. "Out of Chaos." *Parabola* 10(2): 14–22.

Deloria, Vine, Jr. 1997a. *Tribal Sovereignty and American Indian Leadership.* St. Paul, MN: American Indian Policy Center.

Deloria, Vine, Jr. 1997b. "Anthros, Indians and Planetary Realities." In *Indians and Anthropologists: Vine Deloria, Jr., and the Critique of Anthropology,* 209–222. Tucson: University of Arizona Press.

Deloria, Vine, Jr. 2000. *Singing for a Spirit: A Portrait of the Dakota Sioux.* Santa Fe, NM: Clear Light.

Hoover, Herbert T. 1997. "Vine Deloria, Jr., in American Historiography." In *Indians and Anthropologists: Vine Deloria, Jr., and the Critique of Anthropology,* eds. Thomas Biolsi and Larry J. Zimmerman, 27–34.Tucson: University of Arizona Press.

Johansen, Bruce E. 2005. "Indian Country Hero Leaves Lasting Legacy." *Omaha World-Herald,* November 18: 7-B.

Porter, William. 2002. "Longtime Activist Vine Deloria, Jr., to Receive Wallace Stegner Award for His Cultural Contributions." *Denver Post,* October 24.

Wax, Murray L. 1997. "Educating an Anthro: The Influence of Vine Deloria, Jr." In *Indians and Anthropologists: Vine Deloria, Jr., and the Critique of Anthropology,* eds. Thomas Biolsi and Larry J. Zimmerman, 50–60.Tucson: University of Arizona Press.

Deskaheh

(1872–1925)

Born in 1872, elevated to the position of *royaner* (hereditary chief) of the Cayuga Nation under the name Deskaheh in 1917, Levi General died June 27, 1925. He is buried at the Cayuga Longhouse in Sour Springs. Deskaheh is well known for his unsuccessful efforts between 1921 and 1925 to stop Canadian interference in Six Nations affairs by obtaining international recognition, through the League of Nations, of Haudenosaunee (Iroquois) sovereignty.

After 1918, the Canadian government, particularly the Department of Indian Affairs and its director, Duncan Campbell Scott, refused to recognize the sovereignty of the traditional Six Nations' governance system at Grand River, Ontario. Adamant that the 1784 Haldiman treaty had confirmed Haudenosaunee independence, Deskaheh traveled to England in 1921 with a petition for King George V. The petition was received by the colonial secretary, Winston Churchill, who returned the document to Canada.

Deskaheh and his American lawyer, George Decker, then traveled to Geneva in 1923, where they convinced The Netherlands to lay Iroquois grievances before the League of Nations. Deskaheh, as a representative of the Six Nations, approached the Dutch based on a seventeenth-century mutual aid agreement.

On April 26, 1923, The Netherlands requested that the Iroquois petition be placed before the League of Nations Council. Following Britain's and Canada's response, written largely at Scott's direction, the secretariat of the League presented the petition but failed to place it on the agenda for discussion. At this point, The Netherlands withdrew its support. Much to the shock of Canada, Deskaheh twice requested, on August 7 and September 4, 1923, that the league grant the Six Nations formal membership as a state. Without the support of a member nation, however, Deskaheh's application was referred until September 27, when Ireland, Panama, Persia, and Estonia requested that the petition be presented to the league and the case for Iroquoian independence be brought before the International Court. Nonetheless, by 1924 Britain had convinced Deskaheh's supporters to cease interference in an internal Canadian matter.

Meanwhile, in Canada, a federal order-in-council dissolved the Six Nations' Confederacy Council and created a democratically elected government subject to the Indian Act. Once elected, members of the democratic council, at the direction of their Indian agent, Colonel Morgan, proclaimed that Deskaheh was not an official representative. Also in 1924, in a dispute over land tenure between the traditional council and Indian Affairs, an Ontario court ruled in *Garlow v. General* that Deskaheh's lands and possessions were to be confiscated and sold at auction. Colonel Morgan auctioned Deskaheh's goods after the Brant County sheriff refused to interfere because his authority did not extend to the Six Nations.

In the fall of 1924, Deskaheh returned to England to petition the king, an effort that failed. Deskaheh finally left Europe in January 1925, gave his last speech on Iroquois and Indian rights on March 10, and, after learning that his healer had not been allowed to cross the border, died on June 27. His funeral three days later was well attended by Haudenosaunee and the ever-watchful Royal Canadian Mounted Police. Canadian officials hoped that, with the "troublemaker's" death, the sovereignty issue would disappear. At the funeral, according to Iroquois customs, his brother Alexander General was elevated to *royaner* with the name of Deskaheh.

During his visits to Europe, many reporters, diplomats, and visitors were disappointed that Deskaheh failed to live up to their stereotype of a typical Indian chief. Much to Deskaheh's credit, he refused to lower himself by playing Indian. Instead, he usually wore a simple brown suit and kept regular company with his lawyer, although photographs do exist of him in traditional garb.

While seeking to promote his people's sovereignty, Deskaheh's petitions and speeches form a wonderful corpus of material on indigenous rights and their trammeling by colonial powers. The most readily available materials by Deskaheh are the *Redman's Appeal for Justice* and his final speech on March 10, 1925.

Karl S. Hele

See also Northeast and Great Lakes; Treaties with the Six Nations—October 22, 1784, January 9, 1789, November 11, 1794.

References and Further Reading

Rostowski, Joëlle. 1987. "The Redman's Appeal for Justice: Deskaheh and The League of Nations." In *Indians and Europe: An Interdisciplinary Collection of Essays,* ed. Christian F. Feest, 435–453. Aachen, Germany: Rader Verlag.

Woo, Li Xiu (Grace Emma Slykhuis). No date. "The Truth About Deskaheh: Part II, III, IV." *Eastern Door.* Accessed August 1, 2004, at www.easterndoor.com/9–10/9–10–4.htm and www.easterndoor.com.

Woo, Li Xiu (Grace Emma Slykhuis). 1999. "Canada v. the Haudenosaunee (Iroquois) Confederacy at the League of Nations: Two Quests for Independence." Ph.D. dissertation, M. en droit international—Université du Québec à Montréal.

An experienced Indian fighter, Henry Dodge (1782–1867) commanded the army's first cavalry regiment after the War of 1812 and he is noted for his service during the Black Hawk War in 1832. (North Wind Picture Archives)

Dodge, Henry

(1782–1867)

Henry Dodge was born on October 12, 1782, in Vincennes, Northwest Territory (present-day Indiana). Born and raised in frontier Indiana and Kentucky, Henry Dodge shared most westerners' hunger for land and their belief that, in the long run, American citizens should not have to coexist peacefully with sovereign Indian peoples. After his father settled the family in the Ste. Genevieve District of Spanish Louisiana (later Missouri) in 1796, Henry assisted him and their slaves in building wealth through salt making, distilling, farming, and lead mining. Dodge became Ste. Genevieve County's sheriff in 1805 and held office until 1821. He commanded mounted Missouri militiamen in defending American settlements from Indians during the War of 1812 and witnessed the postwar peace treaties concluded by William Clark, Ninian Edwards, and Auguste Choteau with

Teton and Yankton leaders at Portage des Sioux on July 19, 1815.

In the summer of 1827, Dodge moved his household up the Mississippi to establish lead mining and smelting operations on Ho-Chunk (Winnebago) lands in what is now southwestern Wisconsin. Dodge quickly built a following among like-minded miners by commanding a hundred of them as mounted militia in harassing Ho-Chunks during "Red Bird's War" during that first summer. He then established lead works near today's Dodgeville and by mid-February headed a settlement of some 130 fully armed miners. The U.S. government eventually yielded to the invading miners and insisted that any Indians who claimed lands in or near the lead mining region east of the Mississippi—which included subgroups of Ojibwe, Potawatomi, and Ottawa as well as Ho-Chunk—sell them to the United States. The cessions were formalized through two treaties signed at Prairie du Chien on July 29 and August 1, 1829. Dodge witnessed both, directed a memo of appreciation to Congress, and eventually owned more than one thousand acres in the region.

Dodge furthered the U.S. conquest of southern Wisconsin in 1832, commanding mounted militiamen with deadly effectiveness against Black Hawk's fleeing Sauk and Mesquakie (Fox) followers. President Jackson rewarded him with command of the U.S. Mounted Rangers, and Major Dodge witnessed the two treaties dictated by Winfield Scott and John Reynolds to Sauk, Mesquakie, and Ho-Chunk at Fort Armstrong in the wake of Black Hawk's defeat. The first (September 15, 1832) was meant to hasten Ho-Chunk removal west of the Mississippi; the second (September 21) appropriated to the United States roughly six million acres of Sauk and Mesquakie land in eastern Iowa.

In 1834 and 1835, as colonel of the First U.S. Dragoons (forerunners of the U.S. Cavalry), Dodge led expeditions west to council with Comanche, Kiowa, Wichita (Toyash), Pawnee, Arikara, Arapahoe, Cheyenne, and other peoples. Among other things, the government hoped to stop these groups from warring with the eastern Indians resettled by the United States on the eastern Plains. Dodge's expeditions set the stage for the formal peace treaty that 186 Comanche, Wichita, Cherokee, Muscogee (Creek), Choctaw, Osage, Seneca, and Quapaw representatives signed with U.S. commissioners at Camp Holmes on August 24, 1835. The treaty would not end violence on the plains, but it allowed increased trade between Americans and western Indians.

Dodge became the Wisconsin Territory's first governor and superintendent of Indian affairs on July 4, 1836, and served as the lone U.S. commissioner for four separate land cession treaties during the next thirteen months. The first, signed with Oshkosh and other Menominee leaders at Cedar Point on September 3, 1836, yielded the United States some four million acres, mostly pinelands north of Green Bay, in exchange for $700,000. Later that month, Dodge signed two treaties with Sauk and Mesquakie leaders near Rock Island, further reducing their land holdings west of the Mississippi.

His final treaty, signed with leaders of diverse upper Mississippi Ojibwe groups at St. Peter's Agency (by Fort Snelling) on July 29, 1837, was in American eyes among the most impressive ever negotiated. In exchange for $870,000, the United States claimed some twelve million acres, including most of northwestern Wisconsin. Ojibwes from the ceded lands long disputed the U.S. interpretation of the treaty, correctly recalling that their chosen spokesman, Majigabo (Great Speaker, or *La Trappe*), negotiated the treaty as a pineland lease, not a cession. Moreover, Dodge had improperly rushed the negotiations and violated numerous other Ojibwe diplomatic protocols. Dodge omitted such details in his report, and the Senate ratified the treaty, just as it had his others.

The popular Dodge, along with other westerners, advised the government to force further Wisconsin land cessions in 1837. That fall, U.S. officials brought Dakotas and Ho-Chunks to Washington, where they successfully pressured each delegation to sell all of their remaining lands east of the Mississippi, which included most of southwestern Wisconsin.

Dodge remained politically active until 1857, serving as Wisconsin's territorial governor until 1841 and again from 1845 to 1848; from 1841 to 1845 he was the territory's delegate to Congress. When Wisconsin became a state in 1848, Dodge entered the U.S. Senate, where he remained until 1857. He died in Burlington, Iowa, in 1867.

Chad Ronnander

See also Black Hawk; Treaty with the Chippewa–July 29, 1837; Treaty with the Menominee–September 3, 1836.

References and Further Reading

Clark, James I. 1957. *Henry Dodge, Frontiersman*. Madison: State Historical Society of Wisconsin.

Pelzer, Louis. 1911. *Henry Dodge*. Ames: State Historical Society of Iowa.

Salter, William. 1890. *The Life of Henry Dodge, from 1782 to 1833*. Burlington, IA: press unknown.

Satz, Ronald N. 1991. *Chippewa Treaty Rights: The Reserved Rights of Wisconsin's Chippewa Indians in Historical Perspective*. Madison: Wisconsin Academy of Sciences, Arts and Letters.

Smith, Alice. 1973. *The History of Wisconsin*, vol. 1, *From Exploration to Statehood*. Madison: State Historical Society of Wisconsin.

Dodge, Henry Chee

(c. 1857–1947)

Henry Chee Dodge (Hastiin Adiits'a'ii, "Man Who Interprets") was an influential leader of the Navajo Nation for more than half a century, serving as the reservation government's chairman from 1923 to 1928 and from 1942 to 1946. Fluent in both English and Navajo when few were, Dodge played an influential role as a translator and political leader and worked to expand the size of the Navajo Nation.

Dodge was born shortly before the Navajos' Long Walk to Fort Sumner, and his mother and father died when he was very young. Upon Dodge's return from the Long Walk, Indian agent W. F. M. Arn took an interest in the young man, for Arn believed that Dodge was the son of a former Indian agent, Henry Dodge. It is more likely, however, that his father was a captive Mexican. Upon returning from Fort Sumner, Dodge attended school for a short time in Fort Defiance. By 1882, he was serving as the official agency interpreter, and, having shown courage several times, he was put in charge of the Navajo police force and named head chief by the Indian agent. Dodge also made the first of eight trips to Washington, D.C., accompanying a delegation of Navajos to Grover Cleveland's inauguration in 1884. On his last trip, in his eighties, he asked for more schools, hospitals, land, and irrigation facilities for the Navajos.

In 1890, Dodge invested in a partnership and bought the Round Rock Trading Post, which he co-managed. In 1892, when Indian agent David Shipley was surrounded and beaten at Round Rock while recruiting students for the Fort Defiance Boarding School, Dodge helped rescue him, defending him for three days until soldiers came to the rescue. During the 1890s, Dodge also became a successful rancher at Crystal, New Mexico, and by 1907 he was a wealthy, prominent Navajo headman.

In 1914, Dodge wrote to the secretary of the interior stressing the need for more schools so that Navajo children could learn to speak English. He also stated that the allotment of the Navajo Reservation would hurt most Navajos and that state governments had no interest in helping Navajos. In 1940, Dodge criticized day schools and the teaching of the Navajo language and asked for more boarding schools.

In 1922, Dodge was appointed a member of a three-man Navajo business council to sign oil leases by the U.S. government, and in 1923 a twelve-member Navajo council was elected and chose Dodge as chairman. He worked to get the money from the oil leases to benefit all Navajos, even those living off the reservation, rather than just those from the region where the oil was located.

Indian agents for the Navajo called for stock reduction because of overgrazing as early as the 1880s. The increasing Navajo population and their livestock impinged on their neighbors, including the Pueblo Indians. Dodge worked to get more land for the Navajo by cooperating with the demands of the federal government. In the 1920s, Jacob Morgan rose to prominence as Dodge's opponent, representing young, assimilated, Christian Navajos educated in boarding schools. Morgan questioned whether Dodge was really a Navajo and, as a fundamentalist Protestant, opposed Dodge's sympathy toward Catholics, the Native American Church, and traditional Navajo religion. Another strike against Dodge was his practice of the Navajo tradition of polygamy for wealthy Navajos, having over his lifetime eight wives, four of whom were sisters, and six children.

Dodge's son Thomas, an attorney, became tribal chairman in 1932, and in 1935 he was appointed assistant superintendent for the Navajo agency in an attempt to gain Navajo support for the Indian Reorganization Act, which the Navajos voted against. When John Collier became commissioner of Indian affairs in 1933, he pressured Thomas to implement stock reduction to protect Navajo lands from eroding and filling up the newly built Boulder (now Hoover) Dam on the Colorado River. Increasing Navajo discontent with stock reduction and the council's complicity led Thomas to resign the chairmanship in 1936.

Riding the antistock reduction sentiment of most Navajos, Morgan became tribal chairman in 1938 but was defeated by Dodge in 1942. Dodge's son Ben and his daughter Annie Wauneka, a respected health educator, also served on the Navajo tribal council.

Jon Reyhner

See also Fort Sumner, New Mexico; Long Walk, 1864; Treaties with the Navajo—September 1849, June 1, 1868.

References and Further Reading

Brugge, David M. 1985. "Henry Chee Dodge." In *Indian Lives: Essays on Nineteenth- and Twentieth-Century Native American Leaders*, eds. L. G. Moses and Raymond Wilson, 91–112. Albuquerque: University of New Mexico Press.

Iverson, Peter. 2002. *Diné: A History of the Navajos.* Albuquerque: University of New Mexico Press.

Niethammer, Carolyn. 2001. *I'll Go and Do More: Annie Dodge Wauneka, Navajo Leader and Activist.* Lincoln: University of Nebraska Press.

Doolittle Committee

The work of the Doolittle Committee in the mid-1860s represented a profound shift away from the prevailing philosophy of military control of Indian affairs toward a more paternalistic approach aimed at forestalling the supposedly inevitable extinction of American Indians. The committee, whose official name was the Joint Special Committee to Inquire into the Condition of the Indian Tribes, was convened in March 1865 and named for its congressional sponsor and chairman, Senator James R. Doolittle of Wisconsin. The mix of senators and representatives then spent the next year and a half surveying the conditions of Indian tribes throughout the western United States. Their final report, presented in January 1867, painted a stark picture of the condition of America's Indians, projecting a bleak opinion of their future and delivering a scathing indictment of their treatment at the hands of whites. But even as the report detailed numerous transgressions and castigated the actions of the many U.S. agents, civilians, and military officials then in charge of Indian affairs in the West, it was also imbued with a customary bias that painted the western tribes as hopelessly indolent and fated to become extinct unless a more enlightened federal Indian policy could be implemented. These misguided conclusions and the attitudes promoted by the Doolittle Committee proved to be a watershed for a movement of paternalistic reformers and Indian advocates that dominated policy debates throughout the remainder of the nineteenth century.

The Sand Creek Massacre, along with numerous other violent skirmishes between Indians and whites across the Great Plains, inspired the call for an investigation into the conditions of the Indian tribes and the conduct of the civilians and military officials that governed them. Once the committee was approved and the members were appointed, the seven congressman split into three groups assigned to designated territories west of the Mississippi. Senators Lafayette S. Foster of Connecticut and Edmund G. Ross of Kansas joined Doolittle in surveying conditions in Kansas, the Indian Territory (present-day Oklahoma), Colorado, New Mexico, and Utah. Senator James W. Nesmith of Oregon and Congressman William Higby of California were assigned to the states of California, Oregon, and Nevada, along with the territories of Washington, Idaho, and Montana, and Congressmen William Windom of Minnesota and Asahel W. Hubbard of Iowa covered the state of Minnesota and the territories of Nebraska, Dakota, and Montana. In order to supplement their direct observations, the committee sent out questionnaires to various agents and others who dealt with the tribes, to get their opinions on various aspects of Indian life, education, handling of annuities, and their general impressions of the operations of the Indian Bureau. The responses to these queries detailed two primary conclusions: that fraud and corruption were rampant within the system of Indian affairs and that Indian populations were declining everywhere. The 532-page appendix to the report detailed the questionnaire responses and was riddled with charges of corruption and depredations perpetrated by lawless white men. Some of these allegations were certainly true, but many contained dubious assertions and little proof in support of the charges. Nevertheless, it should be remembered that conclusions of the Doolittle Committee were composed to serve a purpose, and that purpose was to effect a change in the way the United States dealt with American Indians.

To that end, the committee's report offered a number of suggestions for various reforms in both the structure and the administration of the Bureau of Indian Affairs. Yet, in keeping with the ethnocentric bias so prevalent among paternalistic reformers of the nineteenth century, the overarching context of the committee's conclusions was colored by a belief that the "lower" race of Indians was fated to become extinct. Despite ascribing significant blame to unscrupulous whites for the many Indian wars that wreaked havoc on Indian communities, officials also continued to argue that it was the inherent inferiority of Indian people that edged them toward extinction. Thus, even as they acknowledged the devastation of warfare on Indian populations, the committee and its respondents concomitantly attributed the additional afflictions of intemperance, disease, and hunger to the inferiority of Indian peoples and their tendency to adopt "all the vices and none of [the] virtues" of the whites among them (U.S. Congress 1867, 5). Predictably, this attitude ultimately meant that their proposed solutions for overhauling the administration of Indian affairs did little to actually effect any direct improvement in the lives of Indian peoples. But the Doolittle Committee's greatest significance lies not in their lack of success in cultivating real policy changes but in the spirit of reform they brought to public debates that inspired a new era of paternalism in federal Indian affairs.

Bradley J. Gills

See also Bureau of Indian Affairs (BIA); Indian Rights Association (IRA).

References and Further Reading

Keller, Robert H., Jr. 1983. *American Protestantism and United States Indian Policy, 1869–1882.* Lincoln: University of Nebraska Press.

Prucha, Francis Paul. 1976. *American Indian Policy in Crisis: Christian Reformers and the Indian, 1865–1900.* Norman: University of Oklahoma Press.

Prucha, Francis Paul. 1984. *The Great Father: The United States Government and the American Indian.* Abr. ed. Lincoln: University of Nebraska Press.

Trennert, Robert A., Jr. 1975. *Alternative to Extinction: Federal Indian Policy and the Beginnings of the Reservation System, 1846–1851.* Philadelphia: Temple University Press.

United States Congress Joint Special Committee to Inquire into the Condition of the Indian Tribes. 1867. *Condition of the Indian Tribes. Report of the Joint Special Committee, Appointed under Joint Resolution of March 3, 1865. With an Appendix.* Washington DC: U.S. Government Printing Office.

Dull Knife

(c. 1810–1883)

The harrowing march of Dull Knife and his Cheyenne compatriots from U.S. Army captivity toward their homeland in present-day Wyoming is described in Mari Sandoz's *Cheyenne Autumn* (1953). Dull Knife, as he was called by the Lakota, also was called Morning Star by the Cheyennes. Dull Knife, with Little Wolf, led the trek after their exile to Indian country (Oklahoma today) late in the 1870s and 1880s.

Dull Knife and Little Wolf were among the Cheyennes who allied with the Lakota and other Native nations who defeated George Armstrong Custer at the Little Bighorn on June 25, 1876. The army, reinforced with fresh troops, then pursued the Lakota and their allies. By 1877, U.S. Army troops had chased Dull Knife into the Bighorn Mountains near the head of the Powder River. The Cheyenne were then arrested and sent to Oklahoma, where, during the next several months, many of them died.

During mid-August 1878, the Cheyennes asked Indian agent John Miles to let them leave Oklahoma for home. On superiors' orders, Miles refused. The Cheyennes, who lacked food, took matters into their own hands, escaping homeward

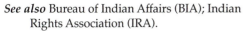

Dull Knife and fellow chief Little Wolf led several hundred of their people in an epic march from Oklahoma toward their homelands in Montana during 1878. (National Archives and Records Administration)

on foot. Early the next day, three hundred surviving Cheyennes started a march to their homelands in the Powder River Country several hundred miles away. The next day, cavalry caught up with them on the Little Medicine Lodge River. The Cheyennes refused to surrender and continued their trek, repelling other attacks. They crossed the Arkansas and South Platte rivers. At White Clay Creek, Nebraska, they split into two groups. Dull Knife led 150 people to the Red Cloud agency, where they surrendered. Little Wolf and another 150 people hid in the Nebraska Sand Hills.

Little Wolf's band surrendered to Lieutenant W. P. Clark and an army unit of Cheyenne and Lakota scouts the following March.

Back in Nebraska, Dull Knife's band arrived at the Red Cloud agency and found it abandoned, so they marched to Fort Robinson. Dull Knife's band

lived at the fort for two months. Officers at the fort then were ordered by superiors to force the Cheyennes back to Oklahoma. Dull Knife refused to go; Captain Oscar Wessells, the commanding officer, locked the Cheyennes in a freezing barracks with no food or water for three days. They refused to surrender.

On January 9, 1879, the Cheyennes broke out again. Fifty of them died that evening under fire by troops; twenty more died of wounds and exposure. Most of the fewer than a hundred who survived were directed back to Fort Robinson under guard.

Dull Knife and his wife and son then escaped once again, traveling eighteen nights on foot and resting by day, to Pine Ridge. They ate bark and their own moccasins to survive. At the Pine Ridge agency, Bill Rowland, an interpreter, housed the family. Thirty-one other warriors also escaped Fort Robinson. Troops followed them to Hat Creek Bluffs, where they called upon the warriors to surrender. The Cheyennes answered the command with their last three bullets. More shooting followed, killing twenty-eight Cheyenne. The last three survivors stood up, using their empty rifles as clubs, and charged the three hundred soldiers, who killed them.

John Ford, the well-known director of Western movies, released a film version of *Cheyenne Autumn* in 1964, his last Western film. Some reviewers believed that Ford's film was an apology for the excessive cruelty displayed toward Native peoples in his earlier films. Set in 1887, the film recounts the defiant migration of three hundred Cheyennes from their reservation in Oklahoma Territory to their original home in Wyoming. They have done this at the behest of Chiefs Little Wolf (played by Ricardo Montalban) and Dull Knife (played by Gilbert Roland), who are portrayed as "peaceful souls who have been driven to desperate measures because the U.S. government has ignored their pleas for food and shelter." In the *New York Times*, reviewer Bosley Crowther described the film as "a cinematic elegy—not only for the beleaguered Cheyennes, but for John Ford's fifty years in pictures" (Crowther, n.d.).

The bones of the dead Cheyennes later were turned over to the U.S. Army Medical Museum for scientific study. On October 8, 1993, the remains were returned to a delegation of sixteen Cheyennes in Washington, D.C., for reburial under the Native American Graves Protection and Repatriation Act of 1990.

Bruce E. Johansen

See also Indian Removal; Indian Territory; Southern Plains and the Southwest; Treaty with the Apache, Cheyenne, and Arapaho–October 14, 1865; Treaty with the Cheyenne and Arapaho–October 28, 1867.

References and Further Reading
Crowther, Bosley. No date. "Movie Details: *Cheyenne Autumn.*" *New York Times.* Accessed November 1, 2005, at http://movies2 .nytimes.com/gst/movies/movie.html ?v_id=9133.
Little Eagle, Avis. 1993. "Remains of Dull Knife's Band Make Final Journey Home." *Indian Country Today,* October 14.
Sandoz, Mari. 1953. *Cheyenne Autumn.* Lincoln, NB: Center for Great Plains Studies. Repr., Lincoln: University of Nebraska Press, 1992.
Wiltsey, Norman B. 1963. *Brave Warriors.* Caldwell, ID: Caxton.

Dumont, Gabriel
(1837–1906)

Born in 1837 at Red River, Rupert's Land (Manitoba), Gabriel Dumont, a Métis, died May 19, 1906 at Bellevue (St.-Isidore-de-Bellevue), Saskatchewan. Dumont is best known for his role as a military leader in the 1885 Riel Rebellion. Prior to 1885, he was a community leader, a bison hunter, a ferry operator, a store owner, and a farmer. After 1885, Dumont seasonally worked in Buffalo Bill's Wild West Show (1886–1888), became a symbol for Quebec nationalists (1888–1889), and returned in 1893–1894 to Batoche, Saskatchewan. Dumont married Madeline Wilkie at St. Joseph (Walhalla, North Dakota) in 1858. Madeline died in North Dakota in the spring of 1886. The couple had no children.

Dumont grew up on the plains with his parents and extended family. He was involved in the 1851 battle between the Métis and Yankton Dakota at Grand Coteau. By the 1860s, Dumont had risen to the position of hunting leader in the Fort Carleton region (Saskatchewan). In 1872, Dumont opened a ferry service and store on the Fort Carleton Trail. He was elected head of a council of eight in 1873. This council sought to govern the St. Laurent Métis community until the Northwest Territorial government established itself. In 1874, the Northwest Mounted Police (NWMP) investigated the council after the Fort Carleton Hudson's Bay Company factor charged the Métis government with sedition. Although the NWMP cleared it of the

allegations, the council ceased to function. From 1877 to 1884, Dumont supported Métis petitions that requested land surveys and grants and representation on the Northwest Territories governing council, as well as assistance for schooling and farming.

In 1878–1879, the river lot and square lot systems were surveyed in St. Laurent. Dumont and others demanded a resurvey according to the traditional river lot system. The Métis river lot system, drawn from their French heritage, consisted of narrow strips of land that fronted a river and extended inland. The house, constructed beside the river at the front of the lot, allowed easy access to the river and gave the Métis access to farm land as well as a wood lot at the back. The square lot system, derived from the standard grid pattern township surveys, would arbitrarily cut across the river lots. The proposed solution to the issue, through the subdivision of the square lots into smaller sections that could then be pieced together to match the river lots, was complicated, confusing, and appeared unnecessary to the Métis, who already had a viable system of land allotment. Instead, after delaying the decision, the Canadian government in Ottawa offered an awkward method of legal subdivision of the square lots to mimic the river lot layout.

By 1884, survey and treaty issues in Saskatchewan had created a tense atmosphere; non-Native immigrants, Indians, and Métis were dissatisfied with the Canadian government. While discussing further petitions in March 1884, Dumont suggested that Louis Riel be asked for assistance because of his success in negotiating with the Canadian government during the 1869–1870 Red River incident. Dumont and four others returned with Riel from North Dakota in July 1884. After eight months of lobbying Ottawa, Dumont and Riel concluded in February 1885 that Métis concerns would never be addressed. Dumont's unwavering support of Riel convinced many Métis to support the declaration of a provisional government and armed rebellion.

Hostilities commenced at Duck Lake when a Métis force led by Dumont defeated approximately one hundred NWMP and two hundred English-speaking settler volunteers who were attempting to arrest rebel leaders. Dumont forced Major-General Frederick Middleton to halt his advance toward Batoche for two weeks, after a battle at Fish Creek. Following this engagement, the Métis withdrew to defensive positions at Batoche, where they were defeated after a four-day battle (May 9–12). Upon hearing of Riel's surrender, Dumont fled to the United States on May 27. American authorities arrested and later released Dumont after he crossed the border. While in North Dakota, Dumont attempted to raise money and a force to liberate Riel from the jail in Regina, Saskatchewan.

While working in Buffalo Bill's Wild West Show, Dumont met members of New York's French community and began speaking about the 1885 rebellion. After giving a single lecture in Quebec, which shocked the nationalist French Canadian audience with its anticlerical tone, Dumont's planned speaking tour was cancelled. He remained in Quebec until the 1890s and dictated his rebellion experiences during the winter of 1889. In 1893, Dumont applied for scrip in Winnipeg and resettled at his Batoche homestead. His death in 1906 while visiting a favorite nephew (Alexis Dumont) passed unnoticed by Canada.

Dumont's role in the 1885 rebellion has been represented by scholars as either secondary or equal to Riel's. Historians basing their work on Dumont's dictation of his experiences have focused on Riel's interference in military matters to explain why the Métis lost. According to Roderick C. Macleod (2000), documents and events indicate that neither Dumont nor Riel sought a far-reaching military campaign and engaged Canadian forces only when they entered Métis lands. Moreover, the Métis eventually would have been defeated regardless of Dumont's military acumen.

Karl S. Hele

See also Canada; Canadian Indian Treaties; Métis; Riel, Louis.

References and Further Reading
Macleod, Roderick C. 2000. "Dumont, Gabriel." *Dictionary of Canadian Biography Online.* Accessed December 30, 2004, at http://www.biographi.ca/EN/ShowBio.asp?Biold=40814&query=Dumont.
Stanley, George F. G. 1992. *The Birth of Western Canada: A History of the Riel Rebellions.* Toronto, ON: University of Toronto Press.
Woodcock, George W. 2003. *Gabriel Dumont.* Peterborough: Broadview Press.
Woodcock, George W. "Dumont, Gabriel." *The Canadian Encyclopedia.* Accessed December 30, 2004, at http://www.thecanadianencyclopedia.com/index.cfm?PgNm=TCE&Params=A1ARTA0002444.

Emathla, Charley

(c. 1790–1835)

Born a Creek in Georgia, Charley Emathla moved to Florida during the late 1820s, where he would become identified with the Seminole as an opponent of Osceola. Although many of the Georgia Creeks were forcibly relocated west of the Mississippi, Emathla settled on a small farm near Fort King (near Tampa, Florida) with a herd of cattle. He subsequently assumed a leadership role among the Seminoles. As a signatory of the Treaty of Payne's Landing in 1832, Emathla agreed to relocate to Indian Territory (later called Oklahoma). While accompanying a Seminole delegation to inspect the new lands promised in Indian Territory, he also signed the 1833 Treaty of Fort Gibson.

In June 1835, Indian agent Wiley Thompson imprisoned Osceola, a leader of the Seminoles who opposed relocation. Having decided to resist the plans of Emathla and his supporters to leave for Oklahoma, Osceola pretended to change his position. He asked Emathla to intercede for him. Emathla, convinced of Osceola's sincerity, agreed to help. Osceola was released only after he promised to use his influence in favor of emigration.

Instead, Osceola met with other chiefs who were hostile to the move, and all agreed that death was the only appropriate penalty for any Seminole who sold his stock or otherwise prepared to leave. At this news, four hundred and fifty Indians who had agreed to emigrate fled to Fort Brooke for protection. Emathla continued to defy Osceola and openly sold his possessions. As Emathla was returning from the sale with his money, on December 18, 1835, he was ambushed and killed by Osceola's band. Some accounts say that Osceola threw the cattle money over Emathla's dead body as he awaited burial. Others say that he scattered the money to the four winds.

Osceola's faction then killed Agent Thompson on December 28, while another party massacred a military command under Major Francis Dade, after whom Dade County, Florida, is named. Their actions provoked the Second Seminole War (1835–1842).

Bruce E. Johansen

See also Indian Removal; Indian Territory; Osceola; Treaty with the Creek–February 14, 1833; Treaty with the Seminole–May 9, 1832.
References and Further Reading
Bland, Celia. 1994. *Osceola, Seminole Rebel.* New York: Chelsea House.
Covington, James W. 1993. *The Seminoles of Florida.* Gainesville: University of Florida Press.
Mahon, John K. 1967. *History of the Second Seminole War, 1835–1842.* Gainesville: University of Florida Press.

Emathla, a Creek chieftain, was killed by Seminole Chief Osceola. (Library of Congress)

Erasmus, George Henry

(1948–)

George Henry Erasmus, born in 1948 in Rae-Edzo, Northwest Territories, is widely known as a Canadian crusader for Native rights and self-government. Erasmus, who holds seven honorary doctorate degrees, came into public prominence in Canada during the early 1970s as the leader of the Indian Brotherhood of the Northwest Territories. He went on to become the president of the Dene Nation, the national chief of the Assembly of First Nations, and co-chair of the historic Royal Commission on Aboriginal Peoples. All his life he has fought for the rights of Native peoples to control their own lives and their own lands.

As a Dene raised in Yellowknife, Erasmus witnessed the impoverished plight of his people and has fought to break the cycle of alcoholism, poverty, and dependence on government handouts by advocating political sovereignty. Erasmus became a leader in the NWT Indian Brotherhood; at twenty-eight, he become president of the Dene Nation, a position he held for seven years. He voiced crucial environmental and land title concerns on behalf of the Dene people during the Berber pipeline inquiry in 1974, when a pipeline was being proposed to carry oil through the Mackenzie River valley in the Northwest Territories. In 1975, Erasmus advocated for the historic Dene Declaration, which declared the sovereignty of the Dene Nation.

In 1985, Erasmus was elected national chief of the Assembly of First Nations, Canada's largest Native organization. The Assembly of First Nations was born out of the National Indian Brotherhood and represents 630 First Nations communities in Canada. His goals were to unite the First Nations of Canada with the Métis and Inuits and to negotiate with the provincial and federal governments on behalf of all Native peoples in the country.

As national chief, Erasmus participated in the First Ministers Conferences on constitutional matters directly affecting aboriginal peoples of Canada. He became known there as Canada's "eleventh premier." At the final conference, in 1987, the federal and provincial governments unanimously failed to recognize the inherent right of self-government for aboriginal peoples. Despite this roadblock, Erasmus and the Assembly of First Nations won support from some of the provinces and accomplished a heightened awareness of issues affecting Native peoples. Under Erasmus, the public profile of the AFN rose to new heights.

Erasmus was reelected national chief in 1988 and served until 1991. During this time, he brought many aboriginal issues to the attention of the Canadian public. In one speech, he expressed the frustration and anger of Native peoples toward government inaction. He warned that, if politicians did not seek peaceful solutions with his generation of leaders, the next generation might resort to violent political action. In 1990, his warning was realized in the Oka crisis, a violent political standoff between Native peoples and the government over a proposed golf course expansion on Mohawk burial grounds.

In 1991, Erasmus was appointed co-chair of the Royal Commission on Aboriginal Peoples, along with Judge René Dussault, to hear from aboriginal peoples in Canada and recommend solutions to ongoing problems. After five years of hearings and studies, the commission's recommendations included formation of a distinct body of aboriginal government within the Canadian government, granting of province-like power to aboriginal nation governments, and abolition of the Department of Indian and Northern Affairs and its replacement with a Department of Aboriginal Relations and a Department of Indian and Inuit Services. Critics in the Canadian government rejected the recommendations as too costly and unrealistic.

Despite government inaction on issues he advocates, Erasmus is a highly respected leader. He was made an officer of the Order of Canada in 1999, after being appointed a member in 1987. He has also been the Canadian delegate to the World Council of Indigenous Peoples.

In 1998, Erasmus became the head of a new organization, the Aboriginal Healing Foundation. The multimillion-dollar fund for the foundation was the result of a contribution from the Canadian government in acknowledgment of its role in inflicting damage on Native peoples through the residential school system. The purpose of the foundation is to address the legacy of physical and sexual abuse suffered by the students of the residential schools.

Aliki Marinakis

See also Canada; Canadian Indian Treaties.

References and Further Reading

CBC Archives. No date. "George Erasmus: Native Rights Crusader." Accessed March 13, 2005, at http://archives.cbc.ca/300i.asp?id=1-73-516.

Indian and Northern Affairs Canada. 2004. Aboriginal People Profiles. "George Erasmus–Chief." Accessed May 15, 2005, at http://www.ainc-inac.gc.ca/ks/3108_e.html.

Indian and Northern Affairs Canada. 2005. "Royal Commission on Aboriginal Peoples." Accessed May 5, 2005, at http://www.ainc-inac.gc.ca/ch/rcap/index_e.html.

McNab, David T. 2001. "Of Beads and a Crystal Vase, Michael Dorris's *The Broken Cord and Cloud Chamber.*" *West Virginia University Philological Papers* 47: 109–119.

Richardson, Boyce, ed. 1989. *Drumbeat: Anger and Renewal in Indian Country.* Toronto, ON: Summerhill Press.

Eskiminzin

A leader of the Arivaipa Apache band in the late nineteenth century, Eskiminzin guided his people through the turbulent first years of American colonialism in southern Arizona. Known by various

names, including Es-kin-in-zin and Skimmy, *Eski-minzin* is an approximation of the Apache name, Haské Bahnzin (Anger Stands Beside Him). Haské Bahnzin lived a remarkable and difficult life, not only as a leader of a Native community threatened from every corner but also as a farmer, warrior, husband, diplomat, rebel, father, and prisoner.

Although Haské Bahnzin was born into the Pinal band of western Apaches, he married into the closely related Arivaipa band, or *tcéjìné* (Dark Rocks People), who farmed and gathered along Arivaipa Creek and the San Pedro River in southern Arizona. Even decades after his death, Haské Bahnzin was remembered as a generous man who welcomed relatives to gather in the San Pedro Valley. Despite the abundance of the land, Apache lifeways were not entirely tranquil. Haské Bahnzin certainly participated in the violence of war and raiding that pitted Apaches against the Mexican and American empires throughout the 1800s.

In February 1871, after an especially harsh winter, Haské Bahnzin arrived at Camp Grant, a U.S. Army installation on the San Pedro River, asking for peace. Several months later, more than four hundred Apaches had surrendered to the army and were living peacefully at *gashdla'á cho o'aa* (Big Sycamore Stands There), five miles from Camp Grant. Nearby Chiricahua Apaches continued raiding, and Tucson leaders mistakenly believed those camped at *gashdla'á cho o'aa* were responsible. In a surprise attack on *gashdla'á cho o'aa*, the Tucsonans and their Tohono O'odham allies killed more than one hundred Apaches and took close to thirty children as slaves. Haské Bahnzin lost most of the Arivaipa band as well as his own wife and children in the Camp Grant massacre.

In the wake of the massacre, Haské Bahnzin returned to a life in the mountains. During the months that followed, people accused him of committing murders and attacks; however, none of these accusations have been convincingly proven. In 1872, he and his fellow tribesmen returned to Camp Grant, this time to have peace talks with government authorities, Tucson businessmen, and Tohono O'odham leaders. From these discussions, he agreed to move north and settle along the San Carlos River.

Life at San Carlos was not altogether uneventful for Haské Bahnzin. In 1874, he was arrested as a prisoner of war. Later released, he began a farm and continued to mediate among Apaches and government officials. John P. Clum, an Indian agent at San Carlos, befriended Haské Bahnzin and took him across the continent to Washington, D.C., in 1876. He made the trip east again in 1888 to meet President Grover Cleveland.

In 1877, Haské Bahnzin moved to *nadnlid cho* (Big Sunflower Hill), now the town of Dudleyville, in the San Pedro Valley. There he settled down to a successful life as a farmer and rancher. Shortly after he built a home, three or four additional Apache families joined him, also erecting houses and fences and cultivating the land. However, later that year, an Indian agent warned Haské Bahnzin that 150 armed citizens were coming to kill him. With the memory of the massacre at Camp Grant, he fled. He later said Tucsonans stole 513 sacks of grain, 523 pumpkins, and 32 cattle. After his escape, Haské Bahnzin was asked if he might return to San Pedro; he replied, "I would not be safe there and would feel like a man sitting on a chair with some one scratching the sand out from under the legs" (Clum 1929, 22).

Haské Bahnzin went back to San Carlos and tried to begin a new life. Yet, several years later, he was arrested in response to vague accusations of aiding Apache fugitives. Sent in shackles to Mount Vernon Barracks, Alabama, he was eventually released with the help of his old friend, John Clum. But only a year after gaining his freedom, on December 16, 1895, Haské Bahnzin died of chronic stomach pain in obscurity and poverty. The site of his grave remains unknown today.

Chip Colwell-Chanthaphonh

See also Southern Plains and the Southwest.
References and Further Reading
Browning, Sinclair. 2000. *Enju: The Life and Struggles of an Apache Chief from the Little Running Water.* Lincoln, NB: iUniverse.
Clum, John P. 1929. "Es-kin-in-zin." *New Mexico Historical Review* 4(1): 1–27.

Forsyth, Thomas
(1771–1833)

Though born in Detroit under the British flag, Thomas Forsyth demonstrated his loyalty to the United States through often-dangerous service: as a spy during the War of 1812 and later as an Indian agent. His Scotland-born father, William, was a British officer who came to the American colonies about 1760. Sometime after 1763, William Forsyth married the widow of a Scottish military surgeon,

Mrs. Ann McKenzie, whose son by her prior marriage was called John, later known as John Kinzie. After her marriage to William Forsyth, Ann gave birth to six more sons, one of which was Thomas. Young Forsyth followed the fortunes of the Indian trade, learning them from his father, who ran a tavern and trade business.

In 1804 at Chicago, he married Keziah Malotte (or DeMaillot) of Hagerstown, Maryland. He relocated to Peoria, along the Illinois River, building his trading business with his half brother John. They called their venture Kinzie & Forsyth, overseeing clerks and trading posts at Milwaukee and on the Kankakee and Rock Rivers. Kinzie oversaw the post at Chicago, located across the river from Fort Dearborn, and Forsyth continued to manage his site at Peoria. More so than his brother, Forsyth saw himself as an American and offered to keep them informed of movements and intentions along the frontier. Soon, the U.S. government officially appointed him Indian subagent, but Forsyth found the salary wanting in light of the dangerousness of the post.

During the spring of 1812, tensions increased in the Indian country of Illinois Territory, prompting Governor Benjamin Howard of Missouri Territory to write to the secretary of war to encourage an increase in pay to make it worth Forsyth's efforts, deeming "his services so essential." Not only did Forsyth possess a wide knowledge of the tribes of the Old Northwest, he knew the lay of the land and the locations of summer and wintering villages, having extensively traveled the width and breath of the present states of Wisconsin, Illinois, western Indiana, and some of Iowa. This knowledge grew vital as the War of 1812 broke out in the westward country. By mid-August, the secretary of war wrote to Forsyth agreeing to a salary increase.

Fearing the worse, based on intelligence that Fort Michilimackinac had fallen to the British as related by visiting Indians and Billy Caldwell, Forsyth hastened to Chicago, where the fort was under the command of Captain Nathan Heald. But Forsyth arrived a day too late. The garrison had been ordered to evacuate the post for Detroit. They marched out on the morning of August 15, 1812, but made it no more than a mile and a half from the fort. Consisting of fifty-three regulars and fifteen militia, as well as women and children, and accompanied by Miami Indians under the direction of William Wells, the military party was attacked by more than five hundred Indians of numerous tribes including Winnebago, Potawatomi, Sac, Fox, Chippewa, Ottawa, and Sioux. Losing half the regulars, all of the militia, and some of the women and children, Captain Heald surrendered in the hopes of bargaining for the remaining survivors.

When Forsyth arrived late the following morning, he found that many of the prisoners had been divided up among their captors and taken off to Indian villages. In addition, the Wabash Potawatomi had just arrived and realized they were too late for the battle. On learning, shortly before their arrival that morning, that Captain Heald had escaped by boat on Lake Michigan, they sought to overtake him in canoes, but the wind was against them, and they gave up the chase. After Heald arrived in Kentucky to recover from his wounds, Forsyth worked with Heald to assist in recovering the captured prisoners or learning of their fate. Forsyth succeeded in buying off his half brother's son-in-law, Lieutenant Linai T. Helm, and personally accompanied him to St. Louis. Kinzie & Forsyth lost property due to the attack at Chicago.

While Forsyth was at St. Louis, help rode into Peoria on November 9, 1812, in the form of Captain Thomas Craig and the Illinois militia, who, instead of helping the local residents, set fire to some of the residences and stole property. Forsyth lost much, including both household and business goods. Still, Forsyth continued to influence the neighboring Potawatomi, particularly Gomo's band, not to make war on the Americans. In the fall of 1813, this enabled the U.S. Army, the Illinois Rangers, the Missouri Rangers, and the Mounted Missouri Militia, under the command of General Benjamin Howard (former governor of Missouri Territory), to construct Fort Clark at Peoria. Before war's end, Forsyth removed his family to St. Louis, where he received an appointment as Indian agent to the Sac and Fox.

For many years, Forsyth divided his time at both St. Louis and Fort Armstrong (Rock Island, Illinois), working competently at his job as Indian agent. Working with the Sac and Fox proved challenging for Forsyth. The point of disagreement centered on the 1804 treaty, which included land cessions. The Sac and Fox vehemently denied that anyone had the right to sell off their lands. When the Sac and Fox walked out of the treaty of 1815 at Portage Des Sioux, it was over this land cessation as well as a refusal to lay down arms and live peaceably, not only with Americans but with their Indian neighbors as well. The Sac and Fox eventually met in 1816 to treat with Governor Clark. But when the Treaty of Prairie du Chien was being negotiated in 1825, once again they did not show up. Raids on the Sioux were made, and the Sioux retaliated. Forsyth warned Black Hawk, the instigator of the raids, to back down and tried to appease him with offers of horses. Unable to reason with the Sac and Fox, Forsyth contacted the Sioux to let them know what was afoot. Suddenly, Black Hawk dropped his plan.

The United States had had enough. A decision was made for the removal of the Sac and Fox over the Mississippi River into Iowa. Once again, Sac and Fox opposition to the 1804 treaty was brought up. But Forsyth had to remind them that, in the 1816 treaty, they had agreed to the provisions of the 1804 treaty. Still, Black Hawk, opposing Keokuk and the American advisors, reoccupied Saukenuk. Now the United States intended to put those provisions into effect.

In the meantime, William Clark was growing dissatisfied with Forsyth's efforts. Forsyth refused to give up his home at St. Louis and move permanently to Rock Island, where he could be in contact with the Sac and Fox at all times. He preferred to commute back and forth according to the time of year, spending the winter at St. Louis. This did not set well with William Clark. By 1831, Forsyth had been replaced by Felix St. Vrain. Forsyth felt that the Black Hawk War could have been prevented and blamed Clark for its disastrous and most tragic effects upon the Sac and Fox. Within a year of the event, Forsyth died.

Sally Colford Bennett

See also Black Hawk; Clark, William; Harrison, William Henry; Treaty with the Sioux, Etc.–August 19, 1925.

References and Further Reading

Carter, Clarence E. 1934–1962. *Territorial Papers: Louisiana-Missouri Territory.* Washington, DC: U.S. Government Printing Office.

East, Ernest E. 1949. "Lincoln and the Peoria French Claims." *Journal of the Illinois State Historical Society,* Vol. 42(1): 41–56.

Hagan, William T. 1958. *The Sac and the Fox Indians.* Norman: University of Oklahoma Press.

Jackson, Donald, ed. 1955. *Black Hawk, an Autobiography.* Urbana: University of Illinois Press.

Nichols, Roger L. 1992. *Black Hawk and the Warrior's Path.* Arlington Heights, IL: Harlan Davidson.

Quaife, Milo M., ed. 1928–1931. *John Askin Papers, Burton Historical Records,* vol. 1. Detroit: Detroit Library Commission.

Gadsden, James
(1788–1858)

James Gadsden was best known for orchestrating the Gadsden Purchase, in which the United States acquired 29,640 acres of land from Mexico that became the southernmost portions of New Mexico and Arizona in 1853. Gadsden was born in Charlestown, South Carolina, on May, 15, 1788. The grandson of revolutionary figure Christopher Gadsden (1724–1805), James received his bachelor's degree from Yale University in 1806. In 1812, he ended half a decade of mercantile practice in Charlestown when he joined the U.S. Army as a lieutenant of engineers. Gadsden served under General Andrew Jackson in Florida at the time the Seminoles received foreign support. This led to the trial and execution of Alexander Arbuthnot and Robert Ambrister in 1818, two British subjects accused of aiding the Seminole fight against Jackson's militia. The incident severely strained British-American diplomatic relations.

In October 1820, Gadsden became inspector general of the Southern Division. The newly appointed

Following a career as an officer, James Gadsden (1788–1858) accepted an appointment by President James Monroe as a federal commissioner in 1823 to aid the government in the forced removal of the Seminoles from Florida. (Bettmann/Corbis)

colonel organized the occupation and construction of a variety of military posts in the South following the territorial acquisition of Florida. In 1822, after the Senate refused to confirm his appointment as an adjutant general, Gadsden resigned from the military. Following a career as an officer, he accepted an appointment by President James Monroe as a federal commissioner in 1823 to aid the government in the forced removal of Seminole populations throughout the Florida region. Although Gadsden believed he had orchestrated a successful agreement with Seminoles in 1823 that outlined a three-year plan to remove the Indians to lands in present-day Oklahoma, the Seminoles later refused to relocate passively. As a result, conflict erupted between U.S. forces and Indian populations in 1836 in what historians have called the Second Seminole War. During the hostilities, Gadsden served as the quartermaster general of the Florida Volunteers from February to April, 1836. After the military offensive against the Indians, Gadsden returned to South Carolina.

From 1840 to 1850, he served as the president of the Louisville, Cincinnati, and Charleston railroad companies, which later became known as the South Carolina Railroad Company. Throughout his tenure, with the hope of negating economic dependence on the North, Gadsden avidly promoted the construction of a transcontinental railroad that would bind the South to the West. After his engineers advised him that the only practical route would run south of the U.S. border into Mexican territory, Gadsden lobbied the federal government to take the necessary steps to acquire the region from Mexico.

In 1853, Gadsden got his chance. With the assistance of imperial-minded friends such as secretary of war Jefferson Davis, Gadsden was appointed U.S. minister to Mexico by President Franklin Pierce. Gadsden was ordered to "compensate" the financially strapped, fledgling Mexican dictator, Antonio López de Santa Anna, up to $25,000,000 for ownership rights to land that had remained in question since the signing of the Treaty of Guadalupe Hidalgo in 1848.

At the close of the Mexican-American War, Santa Anna had relinquished claim to the United States to over twenty thousand square miles (51,800 square kilometers) of territory that now comprises most of New Mexico, Arizona, California, Nevada, Utah, and Colorado. The official U.S.-Mexican boundary remained in dispute after the treaty. The boundary commissioners found significant errors in the John Disturnell map used in the 1848 negotia-

tions. Public opinion in the United States did not help the situation, as many Americans believed that the land acquired by the United States had been ruthlessly stripped from Mexico. To make matters worse, the territory sought included the region of La Mesilla, a notorious "no man's land" that frequently served as a venue for Indian raiders, and Mexico's Indian claims against the United States remained unresolved.

In 1853, Gadsden was ordered to ascertain the international boundary and address Mexico's Indian claims while conveniently acquiring the necessary territory from Mexico for a railroad that could run to the Gulf of California. "This is a Government of *plunder* and *necessity*" wrote Gadsden of the Mexican dictatorship, realizing he could pay much less for the land in question. The ensuing negotiations led to the Treaty of La Mesilla and eventually to the Gadsden Purchase, signed on December 30, 1853. After being ratified by the Senate on June 30, 1854, the U.S. government agreed to pay Santa Anna $10,000,000 for approximately thirty thousand square miles (77,700 square kilometers) of land south of the Gila River in present-day southern Arizona and southwestern New Mexico. Furthermore, as noted in Article 2 of the Gadsden Purchase, the U.S. government was released from its 1848 obligation to compensate Mexican settlers for damages that had resulted from "her" (that is, American) Indians.

The land acquired in the Gadsden Purchase marked the end of continental expansion in the United States. The relinquished land and Santa Anna's squandering of the received payment left many Mexicans sour and resulted in the eventual overthrow of Santa Anna's regime. As for Gadsden, although Congress had even considered naming the newly acquired territory Gadsonia, he was stripped of his position and recalled in 1856 for meddling too extensively in Mexican politics. He did not live to see the Southern Pacific Railroad built through the purchase that would later bear his name. Gadsden died at Charlestown, South Carolina, on December 25, 1858.

William Campbell

See also Jackson, Andrew; Treaty of Guadalupe Hidalgo, 1848.
References and Further Reading
Devine, David. 2004. *Slavery, Scandal, and Steel Rails: The 1854 Gadsden Purchase and the Building of the Second Transcontinental Railroad Across Arizona and New Mexico Twenty-Five Years Later.* Lincoln, NE: Universe.

Pletcher, David. 1973. *The Diplomacy of Annexation: Texas, Oregon, and the Mexican War*. Columbia: University of Missouri Press.

Stephanson, Anders. 1995. *Manifest Destiny: American Expansionism and the Empire of Right*. New York: Hill and Wang.

Gaines, Edmund Pendleton

(1777–1849)

Edmund Pendleton Gaines embraced the expansionist aims of the United States, which required him to pressure Indians to meet the demands of the treaties they had agreed to. Throughout his career, he spent much of his time occupied with the affairs of the Indians in the various territories and states where he had been ordered to do so, particularly in the South. Whether it was Black Hawk and his followers in Illinois, the Muscogee Creeks displeased with terms of the Fort Jackson treaty, or troubles with the elusive Seminoles in Florida, Gaines found himself on the Indian side of the matter.

Edmund P. Gaines (1777–1849) of Virginia was a capable frontier officer who served the nation for more than half a century in such diverse conflicts as the War of 1812 and the Second Seminole War. (Frick Art Reference Library)

Born in Virginia into humble circumstances, his educating wanting, Gaines spent his youth in North Carolina and then in eastern Tennessee. In his teens, he gained military experience in forays against the Cherokees. Receiving an appointment as ensign in the U.S. Army in 1799, Gaines moved up over the years, attaining the rank of colonel by 1812. He excelled in leadership during the War of 1812 and was rewarded for his gallantry with the rank of brigadier general.

In the years immediately after the War of 1812, Gaines welcomed assignment to serve under General Andrew Jackson, who directed him to implement the boundaries of the Treaty of Fort Jackson. This treaty fueled resentment toward the U.S. government among the "friendly" Creeks, especially those who had supported the United States at Horseshoe Bend in 1814 by attacking other Muscogee Creeks. In late 1824, the Creeks refused to give up their lands and resented the actions of the mixed-blood general and chief William McIntosh, once an ally of Gaines, who, bowing to the pressure of Georgia planters hungry for more land, was rewarded with a reserve of land for agreeing to the terms of a new treaty in December 1824. Furthermore, the Creeks were revolted at the thought not only of giving up their lands but of relocation west of the Mississippi River. Even the Indian agent, John Crowell, would not pressure the Creeks into the treaty. Once drawn up, the treaty was rushed to Washington. By spring, the land was being surveyed with the permission of McIntosh, even though the change in title was not to officially take place until the fall of 1826. Within days, McIntosh was murdered for signing away Creek lands.

Gaines was sent to investigate. The governor of Georgia pressured Gaines, assuming that he and Gaines shared similar beliefs and values; yet Gaines surmised that what Georgia wanted was not what Washington wanted. Gaines attempted to halt the surveying until such time as the actual Indian removal took place; otherwise, a sudden white land grab was sure to make trouble. The governor, greatly disturbed, tried to override Gaines's authority in the matter. Meanwhile, Gaines conducted councils to determine the state of affairs and to make it clear to the Creeks that they had to give up their land and move west. Gaines came to see that it was McIntosh who was at fault, who had violated the trust given him by his people, and who, therefore, had received a suitable reward in his violent demise. In the meantime, the federal government instructed Gaines to use force if necessary to prevent the state of Georgia from surveying the land until the time specified in the treaty. Hence, Gaines was present to protect the Indians from Georgia's encroachment, but in the end, the Creeks were stripped of their lands.

Following the Creek situation, Gaines was placed in charge of Jefferson Barracks at St. Louis, Missouri. In northern Illinois, despite treaties that required the Sac (Sauk) and Fox to move to a reserve in Iowa, the U.S. government was content to allow the tribes to remain on their former land until such time as white settlers were allowed to move in. However, by 1831, whites were encroaching upon the area along the Rock River. Black Hawk, although not a head chief of the Sac, insisted that the treaty of 1805 made by William Henry Harrison stole the land outright by making the treaty with the Sacs, who just happened to be in the area but who had neither the knowledge nor the ability to negotiate on behalf of the tribe, that the Sacs would never have knowingly given up their lands so freely. Once again, Gaines was sent up the Mississippi with troops to sort out the confusion by holding talks with the Sacs. Gaines tried to instruct those present that they had to move over to the Iowa side, and that they needed to consider their own interests. Gaines perceived that Black Hawk, the leader of the so-called British band, which had supported the British even after the War of 1812, was acting independently. When the Sacs refused, Gaines made a show of force, having with him an additional force of sixteen hundred Illinois militia to drive home his point. The military advanced on the villages. During the night, the Sacs quietly returned to Iowa, and violence was prevented. Still, Gaines wanted to have a council with the Sacs to discuss renewing the treaty of 1805. The outcome was a new treaty requiring the British band to acknowledge the authority of Sac tribal leader Keokuk and not to recross the Mississippi River into Illinois. The treaty would fail the following year due to the lack of enforcement on the part of the federal government and thus would bring about the Black Hawk War.

Gaines returned to the South in 1832, just before President Jackson pressed his Indian removal policy upon the Seminoles of Florida. This action ignited a war that lasting into the 1840s and cost the country dearly, not only in money but in lives. For his part, Gaines was involved for a short period, later removing to the western Louisiana border. The matter came about as a result of white demand for land and failure to respect the existing treaties, attributable to the federal government's bowing to local pressure to open up Indian lands for settlement. Following the ratification of the Payne's Landing treaty in 1834, tensions flared in Florida. At a council, Osceola, a Seminole leader, drove his blade into the table at which government officials seated, declaring that the only treaty he would see through was with his knife. Outrage, U.S. officials begged Washington for more help. Then, in December 1835, American troops under the command of General Wiley Thompson were ambushed and routed by a Seminole force, leaving only two wounded survivors. Heeding the call, Gaines amassed a force and headed for Tampa. Upon arriving, he pushed on, discovering the site of Dade's massacre. Gaines and his force were the first whites upon the scene; but it had been some two months since the incident had occurred. Gaines continued on to Fort King, whereupon he discovered supplies lacking. He sent some of his force on to Fort Drane while he turned back for Tampa. On the way, at Withlacoochee River, his force came under fire. After a week of skirmishes, under a white flag the Indians and Gaines worked out an agreement depending upon a peace council that another officer, not Gaines, would lead. Gaines had asked for, and was assured by, the Native-led force of Indians and runaway slaves that they would keep the peace. But infighting and egotism among the U.S. commanders added to the tensions and the breakdown of that peace. General Winfield Scott, assigned to command of Florida, prevented aid from reaching Gaines, preferring Gaines's defeat for interfering with Scott's overall command. Meanwhile, Gaines departed Florida for Texas, where another situation loomed.

Sally Colford Bennett

See also Black Hawk; Chouteau, Auguste; Forsyth, Thomas; Jackson, Andrew; Jesup, Thomas S.; McIntosh, William, Jr.

References and Further Reading

Fredriksen, John C. 1989. *Officers of the War of 1812 with Portraits and Anecdotes: The United States Army Left Division Gallery of Honor.* Studies in Local and Institutional History, vol. 1. Lewiston, NY: Edwin Mellen Press.

Heidler, David S., and Jeanne T. Heidler. 1996. *Old Hickory's War: Andrew Jackson and the Quest for Empire.* Mechanicsburg, PA: Stackpole Books.

Owsley, Frank Lawrence, Jr. 1981. *Struggle for the Gulf Borderlands: The Creek War and the Battle of New Orleans 1812–1815.* Gainesville: University Presses of Florida.

Silver, James W. 1949. *Edmund Pendleton Gaines, Frontier General.* Baton Rouge: Louisiana State University Press.

Geronimo (Goyathlay)

(c. 1825–1909)

This Chiricahua Apache tribal leader, known universally as Geronimo, was arguably the most widely feared and respected Native American of the nineteenth century. His bloody raids caused panic across the desert Southwest. Despite his legendary exploits, however, Geronimo was unable to prevent American military domination of the region. Though he became a media sensation in old age, a "bloodthirsty savage" seen in the flesh by thousands of curious Americans, much of what we know of Geronimo comes from legend, not history. The accepted facts are sketchy.

Geronimo's original name was Goyathlay (alternately Goyakla or Goyahkla), or He Who Yawns. He was born around 1825; accounts vary from 1823 to 1829. Probably in 1858, the Chiricahua encampment, packed with women and children, was surprised by Mexican troops and almost all of Goyathlay's family were killed. Goyathlay and others responded by raid-

Geronimo (c. 1825–1909) was a legendary Bedonkahe Apache war leader and medicine man. (National Archives)

ing along the border with Mexico. Though simple looting held obvious benefits, Goyathlay raided primarily out of revenge; some accounts say he vowed to kill every white man he encountered. Although treaties between the United States and the Apaches, signed in July 1852 and July 1853, secured an Apache promise to cease raids into Mexico, Goyathlay may have seen the raid on his village as an invalidation of those treaties. Certainly, raiding and vengeance were considered honorable actions in his culture.

Goyathlay, a respected shaman or seer but never a hereditary chieftain, fought under Cochise any time actual warfare replaced raiding. He struck in the North or South as opportunities arose, routinely crossing the border for safe haven, leaving pursuers at the international border. Those raided by Goyathlay became increasingly frustrated by the inability to track his Apaches to ground.

Raiding centered on stealing livestock and trade goods, but Goyathlay's raids often included the torture and killing of innocent settlers or merchants. Each raid seemed more sudden and destructive than before, cultivating a fearsome reputation for Goyathlay. Soon, the nickname given by pursuing Mexican soldiers—Geronimo—inspired fear and racial hatred along the border region.

In 1875, the army began to compel all the Apaches to move onto reservations. In 1876, the Chiricahua were moved to arid reservation lands in San Carlos, New Mexico. Geronimo fled but was forced to return in 1877. Living conditions were harsh, rules strict, and confinement hard on this formerly nomadic tribe. Geronimo and some followers broke out in 1881, were recaptured by General George Crook in February 1884, and returned to the reservation.

Geronimo and his warriors, accompanied by their women and children, escaped again in 1885, leading the army on wild chases back and forth across the desert Southwest. Geronimo was eventually coerced into returning once it became clear that his exhausted people could not forever outrun, outwit, and outfight the army. General George Crook, with thousands of troops, corralled him in March 1886, and Geronimo agreed to surrender terms. Two days later, possibly spurred by a whiskey trader spreading dangerous rumors, Geronimo changed his mind and bolted a final time.

In September 1886, troops under General Nelson Miles tracked down Geronimo for the last time. The Apache Wars effectively ended when Geronimo surrendered. The army quickly transported his Chiricahuas to exile in Florida, far from traditional Apache territory. Getting Geronimo away from the "scene of his crimes" figured prominently in the decision. Had the Apaches been confined within the region, protecting them from revenge-seeking citizens would have been problematic. Some reports suggest that, although the surrender stipulated that the Apaches would be exiled for about two years and then allowed to return to the Southwest, the government never intended to comply. Other reports say that Geronimo was induced to surrender by Lieutenant Charles Gatewood with the promise that he would be "reunited with his people," which Geronimo mistakenly understood to mean the Apaches would be given a new homeland. Neither Gatewood nor Miles corrected this misunderstanding. Geronimo joined his people in imprisonment. The group was later moved to Oklahoma once anti-Apache sentiment resided, but it was never allowed to return to tribal homelands.

Geronimo caught the imagination of the American people, captivated by newspaper accounts of his "depredations." Geronimo obliged them with numerous public appearances, touring with a "wild West" show, appearing at the World's Fair of 1904, and riding in President Teddy Roosevelt's inaugural parade. Geronimo died of pneumonia on February 17, 1909, on the Fort Sill Reservation in Oklahoma. He is buried in the Apache cemetery there.

Alexandria E. Casey and Michael S. Casey

See also Cochise; Indian Territory.
References and Further Reading
Adams, Alexander B. 1971. *Geronimo: A Biography.* New York: Putnam.
Debo, Angie. 1976. *Geronimo: The Man, His Time, His Place.* Norman: University of Oklahoma Press.
Faulk, Odie B. 1969. *The Geronimo Campaign.* New York: Oxford University Press.

Great Lakes Indian Fish and Wildlife Commission

The Great Lakes Indian Fish and Wildlife Commission was founded in 1984. It consists of eleven Ojibwe member nations. This Indian organization is led by representatives from each of the eleven-member tribes. The commission oversees treaty rights and conservation issues in Michigan, Minnesota, and Wisconsin. The commission's office is based in Odanah, Wisconsin, on the Bad River Reservation. The commission was established as a result of the struggle for Indian fishing rights and those rights of non-Indians in the western Great Lakes region.

The GLIFWC (pronounced "Gliff-wick") also assists tribal courts, develops plans to conserve resources, provides conservation wardens, and maintains a staff of biologists and technicians.

The commission was formed following the Voigt Decision in 1983, which upheld the nineteenth-century treaties that supported Chippewa rights to hunt and fish on the Great Lakes. These rights were laid out in the treaties of 1836, 1837, 1842, and 1854. The Voigt Decision followed decades of intimidation by white officials and white fishers and hunters. White organizations continue to sue the Ojibwe member nations over their treaty rights.

In light of white challenges and the dangers of despoliation of natural resources, the commission defends treaty rights and supports a staff of biologists devoted to conservation of resources. Federal funding for the commission is modest and dependent on congressional appropriations, which involve annual testimony by the commission's board to request funding.

In Michigan, the member nations consist of the Bay Mills Indian Community, Keweenaw Bay Indian Community, and Lac Vieux Desert Band. In Wisconsin, the members include the Bad River, Red Cliff, Lac du Flambeau, Lac Courte Oreilles, Sokaogan and St. Croix bands. In Minnesota, the Fond du Lac and Mille Lacs tribes complete the membership.

Eric R. Smith

See also Property: Land and Natural Resources; Aboriginal Title; *Mille Lacs Band v. Minnesota,* 1999.
References and Further Reading
Bressett, Walter, and Rick Whaley. 1994. *Walleye Warriors: An Effective Alliance Against Racism and for the Earth.* Philadelphia: New Society Publishers.
Lac Courte Oreilles Band of Chippewa Indians et al., v. Lester P. Voigt et al. 1983. 700 F. 2d 365.
Satz, Ronald. 1991. "Chippewa Treaty Rights: The Reserved Rights of Wisconsin's Chippewa Indians in Historical Perspective." *Transactions, Wisconsin Academy of Sciences, Arts and Letters,* 79(1).
U.S. Congress. House. Department of the Interior and Related Agencies. *Appropriations for 1984, Pt. 4, Hearing by Committee on Appropriations.* 98th Cong., 1st sess., 1984. 728.

Handsome Lake

(1734–1815)

Before he became a visionary, Handsome Lake (Sganyadaí:yoh, Skaniadario) led the life of a typical, well-born Seneca man with family connections to other high-status individuals. His brother (called his half brother by many non-Native scholars) was the Seneca Gaiant'waka (Chief Cornplanter), and his nephew was Sagoyewatha (Red Jacket), the famed Seneca women's speaker to the men's Grand Council. Tradition states that Sganyadaí:yoh was born into the Wolf clan at Conawagas, a Seneca town on the Genesee River in New York located outside modern-day Avon. A sickly child, he was unlikely to have been nominated to any lineage title, because of his poor health. However, the women of the Turtle clan took pity on him and adopted him into their clan, promising titles. Sganyadaí:yoh means "beautiful (i.e., handsome) lake," a reference to Lake Ontario. The term is not a personal name but a position title of one of the Haudenosaunee Grand Council lineage (hereditary) chiefs of the Senecas.

Evolution of a Leader

As a youth, Sganyadaí:yoh became beloved of all, especially the women, whom he tirelessly protected, and the children, for whom he always had a story and a pouch filled with nuts bathed in maple syrup. A young woman quickly singled him out as husband material and asked her mother to arrange their marriage. As a responsible married man, he became even more popular, renowned for his good heart and strength of character. When a lineage sachem of the Wolf clan died, the Wolf clan mothers quickly nominated him as successor, with the joyful permission of the Turtle clan mothers. To the astonishment of the Wolf and Turtle men, Handsome Lake assumed the title of the fabled sachem, Sganyadaí:yoh.

Before this stunning promotion, however, Sganyadaí:yoh was a "young man" (sometimes mistermed "warrior" in non-Native texts), also a position to which men were appointed by the women. Sganyadaí:yoh was selected to participate in the French and Indian War (1754–1763), fighting with the British-League alliance against the French. Immediately after this war, he took part in the Pontiac resistance movement that opposed the British. As more Europeans poured onto the continent, squeezing the original inhabitants, the resultant crowding made for internecine Native strife over who was to occupy the ever-dwindling lands of the East. Sganyadaí:yoh fought with his Seneca brothers against the Cherokees and Choctaws of the South, as the Haudenosaunees and the Algonquins were forced by the non-Native invasion to compete for land.

When the American Revolutionary War broke out in 1776, the Continental Army, knowing that it would not be able to fight on two fronts, urgently courted all eastern Native nations, begging them to remain neutral in this "family fight" with their "bad father," King George III. In the summer of 1777, at the annual meeting of the men's Grand Council in Oswego, Sganyadaí:yoh sided with his brother, Gaiant'waka, in calling for neutrality. Eventually, however, after numerous lethal and unprovoked depredations against them by the colonial militias, the Senecas decided to go to war against the colonists. Sganyadaí:yoh submitted to the consensus, once more fighting for his people.

One morning in 1799, listening to his daughter sing a medicine song as she shelled the beans, Sganyadaí:yoh felt his consciousness slipping away. Staggering to the longhouse door, he collapsed into the arms of his relatives as his spirit wandered out of his body, floating out of the cabin and on to Sky World. Thinking her father dead, his daughter called her uncle Gaiant'waka and the rest of the village. Everyone was saddened by the news. His daughter dressed him in his burial robes, and notice went abroad that he was to be raised up (i.e., his lineage title was to be conferred upon a successor). Just then, a sachem and nephew of Sganyadaí:yoh, Taa'-wonyas (the Awl Breaker), examined the body and refused to believe that Sganyadaí:yoh's spirit had departed for good.

Handsome Lake as Visionary

Around noon the next day, Sganyadaí:yoh came out of his coma, telling his rejoicing relatives that his spirit had been visited by the Four Messengers of Sky World, who brought to him the "four words" (or "matters"): *onega, gutgont, onoityeyende,* and *yondwiniyas swayas.* These four matters became the cornerstone of the Gaiwí:yo, and they consisted of prohibitions on the people. *Onega* means alcohol, the use of which was forbidden. *Gutgont* (*okton*) was the use of the negative spirit power, which, in the hands of the inept, did harm. (It is commonly, though inaccurately, given in English as "witchcraft.") It, too, was outlawed. *Onoityeyende* was said by some to be the practice of poisoning enemies in secret, although others more benignly rendered it "love medicine," while *yondwiniyas swayas* was "cutting the child off in the womb" or the use of birth control techniques, including abortion. These, too, were prohibited by the Gaiwí:yo.

In addition to this foundation, many more teachings came to Sganyadaí:yoh, including the condemnation of Christian missionaries. Notwithstanding this overt unfriendliness to Christian missions, Sganyadaí:yoh incorporated many Christian precepts, values, and attitudes into his Gaiwí:yo, including monotheism, sinfulness and public confession, and the submission of wives to husbands. How many of these ideas he consciously borrowed is unknown, although it is known that Sganyadaí:yoh had learned the mores and precepts of Christianity from his nephew, Henry Obail (Obeal), who had studied the Christian Bible under the Quakers in Philadelphia. However, unlike Jesus, Sganyadaí:yoh made no pretense of being a messiah or "son of God" but rather claimed to be the speaker of "the Creator."

Given the oppressive nature of his message for Haudenosaunee women—who had always controlled their own fertility, held their own councils, filled the majority of the positions as shamans, and owned all the fields and run the clans—it is not surprising that the clan mothers blocked consideration of the Gaiwi:yo by the men's council for almost fifty years. Its initial reception by the people in general was quite negative. Handsome Lake was particularly opposed by Sagoyewatha (the women's speaker) and by his brother, Gaiant¥waka, who heckled his teachings and put as many obstacles in his way as possible. Sagoyewatha, speaking for the clan mothers, denounced Sganyadaí:yoh as an impostor passing off assimilation as tradition. Stung, Sganyadaí:yoh replied that the four messengers had just revealed to him that Sagoyewatha was scheming to sell off more Iroquoian land (an attack on the clan mothers, who owned the land).

From that point, tensions escalated between the clan mothers and the followers of Sganyadaí:yoh. Around this same time, the federal government of the United States granted the Quakers the de facto power to run the New York reservations in an early program of forced assimilation. Under this program, some people gradually became so culturally desensitized to Christian proselytizing that they stopped

recognizing it at the base of the Gaiwí:yo and accepted the teachings as familiar. Others regarded the Gaiwí:yo as the lesser of two evils. It was clear that the missionaries and the occupying government would forcibly prevent the older religions from being practiced, whereas the Gaiwí:yo did retain numerous traditional elements that would otherwise have been lost, such as the annual round of ceremonies, many of the older oral traditions, a masculinized version of the clan kinship, the old marriage rites, the principle (although vitiated) of reciprocity, and ecological concepts with their attendant respect for nature.

The U.S. government had reorganized the councils, installing a new system so that new elections took place. Sganyadaí:yoh was reelected to his position on the Seneca council in 1801. His election having emboldened him, Sganyadaí:yoh set out to destroy his critics, actually accusing Sagoyewatha (and, by implication, the clan mothers) of witchcraft. This foolhardly accusation quickly dashed much of his growing popularity. Along with his opposition to birth control, this tactic greatly outraged the women and their numerous male supporters. Sganyadaí:yoh began losing face among the people. The strength of the reaction to his attack on Sagoyewatha caused Sganyadaí:yoh to backpedal on the issues of birth control and witchcraft, emphasizing, instead, popular issues related to land rights and alcohol issues.

In 1802, Sganyadaí:yoh was among a delegation of Onondaga and Seneca representatives visiting Washington, D.C., to meet President Thomas Jefferson. He lobbied hard for an end to the sale of liquor to the Haudenosaunees, as well as for an end to fraudulent land grabbing. He was far more successful with the administration on temperance than on land retention. Jefferson prompted his secretary of war (the department charged with the oversight of Indian affairs) to write Sganyadaí:yoh a rather patronizing letter of support on behalf of the president on the issue of his temperance work. Sganyadaí:yoh was clearly acceptable to the European American overlords if not to the clan mothers and their supporters.

One of the women's supporters was Gaiant' waka, at whose town (Cornplanter's Town) Sganyadaí:yoh had been living. The people at Cornplanter's Town did not care how many letters of support he had from presidents and Quakers. By 1810, his detractors had become so numerous and the situation so tense that Sganyadaí:yoh was forced to move to Cold Spring, where he continued to alienate people. Early in 1812, he moved to Tonawanda, taking along his chief supporters and his family, among whom was his grandson Sos¥heowa, grandfather of Ely S. Parker, the first Indian commissioner of Indian affairs. Sos¥heowa was to become Sganyadaí:yoh's successor on the Grand Council upon his death in 1815.

Handsome Lake's Final Years

During his four years at Tonawanda, Sganyadaí:yoh reflected on the great hostility that many had shown his teachings; having been kicked out of two towns in rapid succession preyed on his mind. Many say that he turned away from his own teachings during this time. It is certain that he had grown reluctant to tell about his visions or teach any longer, distancing himself and at times seeming to disclaim his own revelations.

In his fourth year at Tonawanda, Sganyadaí:yoh was invited by the Onondagas to describe his "third call," a death song. He was hesitant to comply with this invitation, because his third call was his quivering song. His spirit guides returned to him, however, and advised him to go. Based on this vision, he predicted his death just as he set off for Onondaga. As word spread of his death vision, many joined his trek. Sganyadaí:yoh became increasingly depressed as he approached Onondaga; he seemed almost smitten by fear. Before the assembly he was to address, he broke down, unable to sing and denying that a spiritual meeting was in progress at all. "We are just sitting around the fire," he said (meaning that it was just a family gathering), and refused to teach. To cheer him up, the people played lacrosse, but Sganyadaí:yoh declined to watch and, again insisting that he was about to die, left the field.

His supporters took him to an Onondaga longhouse, forbidding all others to enter and swearing themselves to secrecy concerning events that took place within the longhouse. However, an Onondaga was hiding within and reported that, once inside, Sganyadaí:yoh fell into terrible distress, accusing himself of having been laggard in spreading his message and wishing that he had dared to tell *all* of the visions he had been given. (What those untold visions were, he did not reveal.) His spirit then fell quiet, leaving him once more; four days later, his body-soul followed. At eighty-two, Sganyadaí:yoh was dead.

The Longhouse Religion after Handsome Lake's Death

A half century after his death, Sganyadaí:yoh's legend outstripped his critics' complaints. Elders called a council to gather up his words, which Keepers (oral traditionalists) then committed to memory and knotted into wampum. (Sganyadaí:yoh had, himself, knotted wampum of his Gaiwí:yo.) He began to be called Sedwa¥gowa¥ne, meaning "our great teacher." In 1848, a recital of the the Gaiwí:yo by Sos¥heowa was taken down on paper for the first time at a mourning council in Tonawanda and translated for Lewis Henry Morgan by Donehogä¥wa (Ely S. Parker). In 1851, it was published in the League of the Haudenosaunee. In 1861, the Grand Council heard (accepted) the Gaiwí:yo as legitimate. At the turn of the century, Gawaso Wanneh (Arthur Parker), himself a descendent of Sganyadaí:yoh, published another transcription. In 1994, Chief Jacob Thomas provided yet another version of the code.

Between Sganyadaí:yoh's death in 1815 and 1900, the Longhouse Religion flowered, garnering many supporters. By the turn of the twentieth century—a nadir for all Native groups—Gawaso Wanneh observed that the teachings of Sganyadaí:yoh were on the wane and that "true believers" numbered only a few hundred (Parker 1919, 251). By the mid-twentieth century, however, the Gaiwí:yo was being recited with great frequency on the New York reservations, and, with the general Native renaissance of the 1970s, many young New York Haudenosaunees began looking into it as a way back to their roots.

Barbara A. Mann and Bruce E. Johansen

See also Cornplanter; Parker, Ely S. (Do-He-No-Geh-Weh); Penn, William; Red Jacket.
References and Further Reading
Deardorff, Merle H. 1951. *The Religion of Handsome Lake: Its Origins and Development*. American Bureau of Ethnology Bulletin No. 149. Washington, DC: Bureau of American Ethnology.
Morgan, Lewis Henry. [1851] 1901. *League of the Haudenosaunee, or Iroquois*. 2 volumes. New York: Burt Franklin.
Parker, Arthur C. [Gawaso Wanneh]. 1912. *The Code of Handsome Lake, the Seneca Prophet*. New York State Museum Bulletin 163, Education Department Bulletin No. 530, November 1, 1912. Albany: State University of New York Press.
Parker, Arthur C. [Gawaso Wanneh]. 1919. "Handsome Lake: The Peace Prophet [Speech, 1916]." In *The Life of Ely S. Parker, Last Grand*

Sachem of the Iroquois and General Grant's Military Secretary, 244–251. Buffalo, NY: Buffalo Historical Society.

Shimony, Annemarie Anrod. [1961] 1994. *Conservatism Among the Iroquois at the Six Nations Reserve.* Syracuse, NY: Syracuse University Press.

Thomas, Chief Jacob [Cayuga], with Terry Boyle. 1994. *Teachings from the Longhouse.* Toronto, ON: Stoddart.

Wallace, Anthony F. C. 1970. *The Death and Rebirth of the Seneca.* New York: Alfred A. Knopf.

Harjo, Chitto
(1846–c. 1911)

A full-blooded Muscogee (Creek) leader who valued communal land holdings and traditional ways above the influences of the U.S. government, Chitto Harjo opposed the dissolution of Creek government allotment dictated by the Dawes Commission and the Curtis Act of 1898. He set himself and his allies against progressive mixed-blood Creeks and land speculators.

Chitto Harjo was born Bill Harjo in 1846 near present-day Boley, Oklahoma, in what was then exclusively the Muscogee (Creek) Nation, after the removal of his parents with the Muscogee people from their Georgia and Alabama homelands beginning in 1832. Harjo's name derives from the Muscogee words for *snake* (pronounced "chit-toe") and a word often used as a title for Creek war leaders that is translated loosely as "recklessly brave" or "brave beyond discretion" (pronounced "hah-joe"). His followers came to be called the Crazy Snakes, members of the Crazy Snake Movement (McIntosh 1993).

Beyond his service on the federal side during the Civil War, little is known of Harjo's life until 1899, when he was selected as the speaker of the traditional ceremonial town known as Hickory Ground, a Creek ceremonial center that is still active in the early twenty-first century. Muscogee tradition dictates that a town's chief (or *meeko*) must not speak for himself but must designate someone of status who has the oratorical skills to explain what the chief is thinking or feeling. This status as speaker both confirmed and heightened his status as a leader of, and a speaker for, traditional people.

After the 1898 passage of the Curtis Act, which vastly magnified the powers of the federal government over American Indian affairs, Harjo vocalized the sentiment of many traditional Muscogee people that the U.S. government should uphold the 1832 treaty with the Creeks, which provided the terms for removal and also guaranteed the Creeks eternal sovereignty over their nation. The Curtis Act, however, enacted the process by which the tribe's government and courts would be abolished, as well as distributing the collective Creek land holdings to individual tribal members and then opening up the surplus land for sale.

After Hickory Ground's meeko became ill during a trip to Washington, D.C., Harjo assumed a leadership role and urged resistance to allotment and Muscogee national dissolution. As the Muscogee (Creek) Web site noted in 2005, Harjo's efforts "epitomized the view of all Muscogee people that they possessed an inherent right to govern themselves," and for Harjo, "it was unimaginable that the Nation could be dissolved by a foreign government" (Muscogee [Creek] Nation 2005, 38). In 1900, Harjo began traveling to ceremonial grounds throughout the Creek Nation, openly advocating the formation of a new government and establishing new laws, some of which included the prohibition of commerce of any kind with European Americans. Violators were subject to physical punishment by Snake enforcers.

Chitto Harjo, or Crazy Snake, was a Muscogee (Creek) chief. (Library of Congress)

Alarmed by the rebellious faction, the principal chief of the Creek Nation, Pleasant Porter, alerted the federal government to the Crazy Snake movement and its anarchic implications. Subsequently, in January 1901, Harjo and about a hundred of his followers were arrested by federal troops and imprisoned in Muskogee, but they were freed by a judge who cautioned the Snakes to cease their activities. Harjo continued his outward opposition to allotment, however, and was arrested again in 1902 with nine other Snake leaders. The group was promptly sent to federal prison at Fort Leavenworth, Kansas.

After finishing his two-year sentence, Harjo returned to Indian Territory, where he reiterated, "We do not want our lands divided and each one given one hundred and sixty acres. This is the only land left to the Indians, and once he gives up this small strip of fertile land he will be no more, 1904." In 1905, Harjo traveled to Washington to meet with President Theodore Roosevelt but had no success in convincing Roosevelt to stop allotment. By 1906, a select U.S. Senate committee arrived in Tulsa, Oklahoma, to hear how the Creeks and Cherokees felt about allotment. Harjo made an eloquent but unheeded plea to the senators, urging that the federal government not carve up the earth that was paid for by the relinquishment of Creek lands in Georgia and Alabama (Mann 2001, 228).

Oklahoma statehood in 1907 ended any hope that the Crazy Snake movement would have any lasting effect on Creek politics, because the Creek government was officially abolished upon creation of the forty-sixth state. Continuing to oppose the entire process of allotment, by 1909 Harjo and the Crazy Snakes had created such fear throughout the lower Creek Nation that all sorts of crimes were being attributed to them. In March of that year, Harjo was wounded in a shootout with law officers who had come to arrest him at his home. He escaped, however, and his disappearance led to disagreement about his final resting place. Of several reports, consensus seems to exist that he made it to the Choctaw Nation, where he either died soon thereafter from his wounds or lived for about two more years before being buried in the mountains of southeastern Oklahoma.

Hugh W. Foley, Jr.

See also Allotment; Curtis Act, 1898; Dawes Commission; General Allotment Act (Dawes Act), 1887; Treaty with the Creek–March 24, 1832.

Mann, Barbara Alice, ed. 2001. "'A Man of Misery': Chitto Harjo and the Senate Select Committee on Oklahoma Statehood." In *Native American Speakers of the Eastern Woodlands*, 197–228. Westport, CT: Greenwood Press.

McIntosh, Kenneth Waldo. 1993. *Chitto Harjo, the Crazy Snakes and the Birth of Indian Political Activism in the Twentieth Century.* Ph.D. dissertation, Texas Christian University.

Muscogee (Creek) Nation of Oklahoma. "History." [Web site.] Accessed May 30, 2005, at http://www.muscogeenation-nsn.gov.

"Won't Take Any Part in Matter: Interior Department Not Interested in Election of Chief of the Snake Indians." *The Oklahoman*, January 3, 1904.

Harjo, Suzan Shown
(1945–)

Suzan Shown Harjo is an activist, curator, lecturer, artist, poet, and columnist. She is a leading indigenous voice in a wide range of issues that are important to contemporary American Indian peoples. "There's nothing tedious about my life," she told *Indian Country Today* in 2003.

Harjo was born in 1945 in El Reno, Oklahoma, a former reservation for Cheyenne and Arapaho peoples commonly referred to as the "tribal service area." Through her mother, Susie Rozetta Eades, she is Cheyenne and a citizen of the Cheyenne and Arapaho tribes of Oklahoma. She is Hodulgee Muscogee through her father, Freeland Edward Douglas, a member of the Nuyaka Tribal Town and Wind clan. She is the great-great-granddaughter of Chief Bull Bear, a peace chief, Dog Men Society chief, the first signatory of the Treaty of Medicine Lodge Creek of 1867, and a leader of Cheyenne resistance to the aggressions of nineteenth-century colonization. Harjo follows the example of courage and strength represented by her great-grandfather a century ago.

A witness before congressional committees and a presence in the U.S. capital since 1974, Harjo has worked to develop considerable and noteworthy congressional legislation and appropriations. She served in the Carter administration and was principal author of the 1979 president's report to Congress on American Indian religious freedom. She was executive director of the National Congress of American Indians (NCAI) from 1984 to 1989. Key legislation in which she played a major role includes the 1978 American Indian Religious Freedom Act, the National Museum of the American Indian Act of

1989, the Native American Graves Protection and Repatriation Act of 1990, and the Executive Order on Indian Sacred Sites of 1996. She has been the president and CEO of the Morning Star Institute, a non-profit Indian rights organization. Founded in 1984 and headquartered in Washington, D.C., Morning Star is the sponsoring organization of a lawsuit involving the National Football League franchise in the nation's capital.

Harjo has been curator of the Peabody Essex Museum, as well as for the American Psychological Association in Washington, D.C., and "Visions from Native America" in the rotunda of the U.S. Capitol. She is among the founding trustees of the National Museum of the American Indian.

A Dartmouth College Montgomery Fellow in 1992 and a Stanford University visiting mentor in 1996, Harjo was the Indian Arts Research Center's Eric and Barbara Dobkin Native American Artist Fellow at the School of American Research in Santa Fe for 2004. Her poetry is widely published and anthologized. She led the way in late-twentieth century Native broadcasting as a reporter, producer, and manager for WBAI-FM Radio Station in New York City, where she produced the first regularly scheduled national Indian radio program, *Seeing Red*. She has appeared on *The Oprah Winfrey Show, Larry King Live*, CNN's *Talk Back Live*, and CSPAN's *Washington Journal*. She was American Indian Press Association news director and NCAI communications director in the 1970s and 1980s when Indian journalists broke into major media to tell their own stories and develop their own voices. Since 1999, she has been a featured columnist for *Indian Country Today*, an Indian newspaper with broad circulation in the United States and cyberspace. In 2004, she was the recipient of the Native American Journalists Association award for best column writing.

Name an issue affecting Indian peoples, and Harjo likely has worked on or written about it. In her *Indian Country Today* column, she addresses a variety of issues, including the trust relationship between Indian peoples and the United States, threats to indigenous religious freedoms, repatriation, racism, stereotype-busting in general and mascots that link competitive athletics with qualities associated with Indian peoples in particular, white privilege and supremacy, Indian identity and why it matters, decolonization, partisan politics, the protection of sacred places, and violence against women. The well-being of Indian women, for Harjo, is of particular concern as well as a crucial source of power and

inspiration. "Only the reinstatement of tribal jurisdiction and remedies has a chance of reversing the epidemic levels of violence against Native women," she wrote in a May 2005 column responding to the possibility of congressional reauthorization of the Violence Against Women Act and the reality that the men who assault Native women overwhelmingly are non-Indians and strangers or acquaintances rather than intimate partners and family members. "If Congress fails to act," she wrote, "the reservation streets will remain safe for violent non-Indians—and the Indian women and their children and grand-children will suffer."

Harjo has two children. Her daughter is an artist living in Washington, D.C. Her son is a computer designer and programmer in Portland, Oregon.

D. Anthony Tyeeme Clark (Meskwaki)

See also Native American Graves and Repatriation Act, 1990; Sacred Sites; Statutes as Sources of Modern Indian Rights: Child Welfare, Gaming, and Repatriation.

References and Further Reading

Graef, Christine. 2003. "A Conversation with Susan Shown Harjo: Part Two." *Indian Country Today*, 23: A1.

Harjo, Suzan Shown. 2001. "Respect Native Women: Stop Using the S-Word." *Indian Country Today*, 20: A5.

Harjo, Suzan Shown. 2002. "Native Identity: A Circle of Sovereignty." *Native Americas*, 19: 82.

Harjo, Suzan Shown. 2005. "Congress: Make the Streets Safe for Indian Women, Too!" *Indian Country Today*, 24: A5.

Harrison, William Henry
(1773–1841)

As governor of Indiana Territory, Harrison was responsible for negotiating treaties for land cessions from the local tribes. Harrison's job as territorial governor consisted of constantly balancing disparate tasks. In addition to such duties as administering the territory, meeting with French and British envoys, and overseeing the safety of the population, he served as commissioner of Indian affairs for the vast area under his control. He tried to balance equitable treatment of Native Americans with his assigned task of negotiating treaties for the cession of Indian lands to the United States.

Under President Thomas Jefferson, the official policy of the U.S. government toward Native Americans had several goals: security of settlers, progress

William Henry Harrison (1773–1841) of Virginia, the ninth U.S. president, was elected largely on his reputation as an Indian fighter. (Library of Congress)

of white settlement, guaranteeing Indian allegiance through treaties, facilitating trade, and "civilizing" the tribes and assimilating them into white society by persuading them to become farmers. Jefferson's policies as communicated to Harrison in private, however, lost the veneer of benevolence. In a letter to Harrison in February 1803, Jefferson directed the governor to acquire as much land as he could and as quickly as possible. One technique the president suggested was that, via trade, Harrison should encourage prominent Indians to go into debt, and then use land cessions as the means of paying off the debt. As their lands shrank, the Native Americans would be forced—not persuaded—either to assimilate or to be removed to lands west of the Mississippi.

Harrison was an admirer of Jefferson and wanted to do all he could to carry out the president's wishes. At the same time, he wanted to deal as fairly as possible with the Native Americans. In the final instance, however, he was likely swayed by the idea that Jefferson's policies would ultimately benefit the Native population. In addition, he thought that the British had a counterproductive influence on the Indians, preventing them from seeing the wisdom of the U.S. government's policies.

One source of conflict was that the Native American concept of land use was at odds with the American desire for land ownership. Indians viewed land as equally available to all in their hunting and gathering way of life. The French appreciated the distinction and had tried to understand the Indians' way of life and learn their languages. In contrast, Harrison's main contact with Native Americans was in the form of councils and treaty negotiations, formal and ceremonial occasions that were only possible with translators.

In 1800, when Harrison assumed the governorship, virtually all the land under his jurisdiction was Indian land. The first treaty negotiated by Harrison was at Fort Wayne in June 1803. It was followed by eleven more, which transferred to the United States almost fifty million acres. The last negotiations by Harrison occurred between September and December 1809, when he signed a series of treaties with the Delaware, Potawatomi, Miami, Wea, and Kickapoo in something of a "divide and conquer" strategy; each treaty was tailored to the tribe or tribes involved. Among the reasons for resuming cessions, the last of which had been in 1805, were that the Delaware were ready to move west, and the Potawatomi were in dire need of supplies.

The treaties of 1809 led to conflict with the Shawnee leader Tecumseh and his Indian confederation. Tecumseh's objections included the amount of land involved (nearly three million acres); the fact that negotiations continued to be primarily with chiefs, whom Tecumseh said did not have individual authority to cede lands; and the minuscule amount paid (approximately one-third cent per acre). In council with Harrison in 1810, Tecumseh maintained that he would never accept the cessions as valid. Harrison feared retaliation, so in Tecumseh's absence he attacked the Shawnee village on the Wabash River. The resulting American victory in the Battle of Tippecanoe on November 7, 1811, broke the power of the Indian confederacy and made Harrison a military hero, which led ultimately to his election as president in 1840.

Leigh Darbee

See also Battle of Tippecanoe, 1811; Fort Harrison, Indiana; Jefferson, Thomas; Tecumseh; Tippecanoe River, Indiana; Vincennes, Indiana; Wabash River, Indiana.

References and Further Reading
Baer, M. Teresa. 1999. "Hero and Villain: William Henry Harrison and the Indian Land Treaties." *Traces of Indiana and Midwestern History*, 11 (Fall): 12–23.
Cleaves, Freeman. 1990. *Old Tippecanoe: William Henry Harrison and His Time*. Newtown, CT: American Political Biography Press.
Goebel, Dorothy Burne. 1926. *William Henry Harrison: A Political Biography*. Indianapolis: Historical Bureau of the Indiana Library and Historical Department.
Onuf, Peter S. 1999. "'We Shall All Be Americans': Thomas Jefferson and the Indians." *Indiana Magazine of History*, 95: 103–141.

Hawkins, Benjamin

(1754–1816)

Benjamin Hawkins was chief Indian agent to the tribes of the southeastern United States between 1796 and 1816. His official efforts were directed toward "civilizing" the indigenous people in his jurisdiction by promoting the European American concepts of agriculture, land usage, and industry. His duties also included keeping the president and Congress up to date on the affairs of the Indian nations. Regulating trade between Americans and the tribes was another part of his job.

Before he become chief Indian agent, Hawkins also had a distinguished career. He attended the College of New Jersey (now Princeton University), where he excelled at French. Based on his linguistic skills, during the Revolutionary War Hawkins served on General George Washington's staff as his interpreter. Hawkins served in the North Carolina State House of Commons during 1778–1779 and again in 1784. He was a member of the Continental Congress in 1781–1783 and 1787. From November 27, 1789, to March 3, 1795, Hawkins served in the First United States Congress as a senator from North Carolina. Washington also made Hawkins a colonel.

In 1796, President George Washington appointed Hawkins chief agent for all tribes south of the Ohio River, which included the Cherokee, Choctaw, Chickasaw, and Seminole tribes. He lived among, and spent most of this time period with, the Muscogee Nation, commonly called the Creek. His first major project was to settle land disputes between the Indians and the United States.

Benjamin Hawkins (1754–1816) of North Carolina was appointed by President George Washington to negotiate a treaty with the Creek Nations in 1795 and continued to serve as agent to the Creeks while representing the best interests of the United States. (Library of Congress)

Hawkins represented the United States in numerous treaty negotiations. He was a major contributor to treaties with the Cherokee (1785, 1798), the Chickasaw (1786, 1801), the Choctaw (1786, 1801), and the Creek (1796, 1802, 1805, 1814). These treaties covered such diverse topics as the ceding of certain parcels of lands, the right to build roads through Indian lands, the establishment of military posts, the granting of exclusive trading rights to U.S. agents (thus ending direct trade by the tribes with Spanish or English personnel), the return of prisoners, the cessation of warfare, and "Peace and friendship perpetual." One common treaty provision was for the individual nations to acknowledge they were "under the protection of the United States of America, and of no other sovereign whosoever." The U.S. government would later use this provision to exert their influence over tribal groups.

The longest peace between the Muscogee Creek Nation and the United States occurred during Hawkins's term as Indian agent. Many older tribal leaders held Hawkins in high esteem. Tribal leaders gave him the title "Beloved Man of the Four Nations (Cherokee, Choctaw, Chickasaw and Muscogee Creek)." A rebellious faction among the Muscogee Creek, significantly among younger leaders, led to the Creek War of 1812–1814. Older members of the tribe thwarted an attempt on Hawkins's life by some young warriors.

Hawkins had a paternalistic feeling toward the tribes under his jurisdiction. Although he had a great respect for his charges, he made concerted efforts to get them to adopt more "civilized" ways of life. Along with another of his mentors, Thomas Jefferson, Hawkins felt that the Indians should give up their large tracts of land for smaller plots. It was Hawkins's plan that the Indians should become farmers. Smaller land holdings would help assimilate them into this type of life. Hawkins also advocated the raising of domesticated animals as a source of meat, in place of far-ranging hunting.

Hawkins later clashed with President Andrew Jackson over the treatment of Indians and the seizure of all their lands. Hawkins died not long after the end of the Creek War. During his administration, and often despite his opinion to the contrary, millions of acres of Indian lands in his jurisdiction were seized by federal and local authorities.

Hawkins kept journals about his life among the indigenous people of the southern United States. His observations about Muscogee Creek culture are among the most detailed of the period. His list of indigenous vocabularies was donated to the American Philosophical Society, where it was considered a major contribution.

Hawkins was the first "white man" to settle in Crawford County, Georgia. He maintained a plantation and home there until his death. He considered himself to be a scientific farmer. He shared many of his innovations with the people under his care. He named two of his children after the people he worked with: Muscogee and Cherokee.

For his service to the people of the state of Georgia, Hawkins was honored with a bust that has been placed in the rotunda of the state capitol.

Phil Konstantin

See also Assimilation; Jackson, Andrew.
References and Further Reading
Grant, C. L., ed. 1980. *Letters, Journals and Writings of Benjamin Hawkins.* 2 vols. Savannah, GA: Beehive Press.
Grant, C. L. 1981. "Senator Benjamin Hawkins: Federalist or Republican?" *Journal of the Early Republic,* 1 (Fall): 233–247.
Hawkins, Benjamin. 1947. *Letters of Benjamin Hawkins, 1796–1806.* Spartanburg, SC: Reprint Company.
Henri, Florette. 1986. *The Southern Indians and Benjamin Hawkins 1796–1816.* Norman and London: University of Oklahoma Press.
Kappler, Charles J., ed. 1904. *Indian Affairs: Laws and Treaties,* vol. 2, *Treaties.* Washington, DC: Government Printing Office.

Hendrick
(c. 1680–1755)

Tiyanoga, whom the English called Hendrick, was a major figure in colonial affairs between 1710, when he was one of four Mohawks invited to England by Queen Anne, and 1755, when he died in battle with the French as an ally of the British. In 1754, Hendrick advised Benjamin Franklin and other colonial representatives on the principles of Iroquois government at the Albany Congress.

Hendrick was a Mohawk who developed a relationship with the English colonies led by William Johnson. Hendrick helped keep the Six Nations in the interests of England in its war against France. He is known for his criticism of the English for their failure to defend the Six Nations against the French, and was killed at the Battle of Lake George in 1755. (New York Public Library)

Hendrick, a member of the Wolf Clan, knew both Iroquois and English cultures well. He converted to Christianity and became a Mohawk preacher sometime after 1700. In England, he was painted by John Verelst and called the Emperor of the Five Nations. Hendrick was perhaps the most important individual link in a chain of alliance that saved the New York frontier and probably New England from the French in the initial stages of the Seven Years' War, which was called the French and Indian War (1754–1763) in North America.

Well known as a man of distinction in his manners and dress, Hendrick visited England again in 1740. At that time, King George presented him with an ornate green coat of satin, fringed in gold, which Hendrick was fond of wearing in combination with his traditional Mohawk ceremonial clothing. A lifelong friend of English superintendent of Indian affairs Sir William Johnson, Hendrick appeared often at Johnson Hall, near Albany, and had copious opportunities to rub elbows with visiting English nobles, sometimes as he arrived in war paint, fresh from battle. Thomas Pownall, a shrewd observer of colonial Indian affairs, described Hendrick as ". . . a bold artful, intriguing Fellow and has learnt no small share of European Politics, [who] obstructs and opposes all (business) where he has not been talked to first . . ." (Jacobs 1966, 77).

Hector St. Jean de Crèvecoeur, himself an adopted Iroquois who attended sessions of the Grand Council at Onondaga, described Hendrick in late middle age, preparing for dinner at the Johnson estate, within a few years of the Albany Congress: "[He] wished to appear at his very best . . . His head was shaved, with the exception of a little tuft of hair in the back, to which he attached a piece of silver. To the cartilage of his ears . . . he attached a little brass wire twisted into very tight spirals. A girondole (nose ring) was hung from his nose. Wearing a wide silver neckpiece, a crimson vest and a blue cloak adorned with sparkling gold, Hendrick, as was his custom, shunned European breeches for a loincloth fringed with glass beads. On his feet, Hendrick wore moccasins of tanned elk, embroidered with porcupine quills, fringed with tiny silver bells" (Grinde and Johansen 1991, 104).

By the time Hendrick was invited to address colonial delegates at the Albany Congress in 1754, he was well known on both sides of the Atlantic among Iroquois and Europeans alike. Hendrick played a major role in convening the Albany Congress, in large part because he wished to see his friend John-son reinstated as the English superintendent of affairs with the Six Nations. Without him, Hendrick maintained that the Covenant Chain would rust. It was Johnson himself who conducted most of the day-to-day business with the Indians at Albany.

At the Albany Congress, Hendrick repeated the advice that the Onondaga chief Canassatego had given colonial delegates at Lancaster a decade earlier, this time at a conference devoted not only to diplomacy but also to drawing up a plan for the type of colonial union the Iroquois had been requesting. The same day, at the courthouse, the colonial delegates were in the early stages of debate over the plan of union.

Hendrick was openly critical of the British at the Albany Council and hinted that the Iroquois would not ally with the English colonies unless a suitable form of unity was established among them. In talking of the proposed union of the colonies and the Six Nations on July 9, 1754, Hendrick stated, "We wish this Tree of Friendship may grow up to a great height and then we shall be a powerful people." Hendrick followed that aspiration with an analysis of Iroquois and colonial unity, when he said, "We the United Nations shall rejoice of our strength . . . and . . . we have now made so strong a Confederacy" (Grinde and Johansen 1991, 105, 107). In reply to Hendrick's speech on Native American and colonial unity, Acting Governor James DeLancey said, "I hope that by this present Union, we shall grow up to a great height and be as powerful and famous as you were of old" (Grinde and Johansen 1991, 107). Benjamin Franklin was commissioned to compose the final draft of the Albany Plan the same day.

Hendrick died at the Battle of Lake George in the late summer of 1755, as Sir William Johnson defeated Baron Dieskau. The elderly Mohawk was shot from his horse and bayoneted to death while on a scouting party on September 8.

Bruce E. Johansen

See also Canassatego; Johnson, William.

References and Further Reading

Grinde, Donald A., Jr., and Bruce E. Johansen. 1991. *Exemplar ofLiberty:Native America and the Evolution of Democracy.* Los Angeles: University of California at Los Angeles, American Indian Studies Center.

Jacobs, Wilbur R. 1966. *Wilderness Politics and Indian Gifts.* Lincoln: University of Nebraska Press.

Wallace, Paul A. W. 1946. *The White Roots of Peace.* Philadelphia: University of Pennsylvania Press.

Hitchcock, Ethan Allen

(1835–1909)

As secretary of the interior under Presidents William McKinley and Theodore Roosevelt, Ethan Allen Hitchcock launched an extensive program of reforms, committing himself to the prosecution of land frauds, the conservation of natural resources, the restriction of deforestation, and the improvement of the administration of American Indian affairs within the context of the early twentieth-century policy of Indian Americanization.

From the 1850s through the 1890s, Hitchcock handled successful commercial activities, which made him a talented, wealthy businessman. As a Republican, Hitchcock contributed to the party's financial support and became acquainted with President McKinley, who appointed him Minister to Saint Petersburg in 1897 to promote trade between Russia and the United States. On December 21, 1898, President McKinley called his minister back and appointed him secretary of the interior.

Ethan Hitchcock (1835–1909) of Alabama was the twenty-second secretary of the interior, serving during the administrations of President William McKinley and President Theodore Roosevelt. He was committed to the improvement of the administration of American Indian affairs while supporting the policy of civilizing Indians. (Library of Congress)

In the years Hitchcock was head of the Department of the Interior (1898–1909), federal Indian policy encouraged the education of Indian children and the application of private land ownership principles to Native Americans. Breaking the American Indians' tribal economy had been the main purpose of the 1887 General Allotment Act, also known as the Dawes Severalty Act. During Hitchcock's term, Native Americans were still affected by the disastrous consequences of the Dawes Act, which had brought harsh criticism to bear on the Board of Indian Commissioners. As a result, secretary of the interior Hitchcock had to defend the credibility and authority of the board, with the assistance of commissioners William Jones (1897–1905) and Francis Leupp (1905–1909). The secretary's task also consisted in curbing corruption and managing the administrative inefficiency, thanks to the centralizing of Indian affairs and the increased number of Indian agents in Washington. He was led to reconsider the abrupt transformation of the American Indians' way of life, as implemented in the past. By the beginning of the twentieth century, the former process of quick integration had gradually given way to a policy of turning American Indians into responsible and self-reliant American citizens. In 1901, the Five Civilized Tribes (Cherokee, Seminole, Choctaw, Chickasaw, and Creek) were granted citizenship in the Indian Territory of Oklahoma. In addition, opening lands ceded by allotted Indians under the provisions of the Dawes Act to non-Indians was seen as a means to assimilate Native peoples, whereas Indian land cessions were often the result of the Natives' attempt to improve their miserable living conditions. In this respect, a land cession agreement signed in 1892 triggered a complex controversy in which Secretary Hitchcock appeared as an advocate of Indian rights. The case would go all the way to the Supreme Court, where it was judged in 1903 as *Lone Wolf v. Hitchcock*.

Whereas the Treaty of Medicine Lodge Creek of 1867 stipulated that no part of the Kiowa, Comanche, and Apache Reservation in Oklahoma could ever be ceded without the consent of three-fourths of the adult males of the tribe, Congress enacted a bill on June 6, 1900, which confirmed the 1892 land cession of a Cheyenne and Arapaho group that had ceded reservation lands without the approval of the three-fourths of tribal members as required by the treaty of 1867. An influential Kiowa leader, Lone Wolf, brought suit to prevent the implementation of the land cession bill, with the support of the Indian Rights Association (IRA) and Secretary Hitchcock's concurrence, as "the suit sought to restrain the Interior Department from carrying out the provisions of the allotment act" (Getches, Wilkinson, and Williams 1998, 181). These efforts were to no avail. On January 15, 1903, Justice White asserted the "plenary authority of Congress over Indian relations and its power to pass laws abrogating treaty stipulations" (Prucha 1997, 356). The *Lone Wolf v. Hitchcock* case stands as a turning point in the history of Indian treaties. American Indian peoples were thus denied the implementation of treaty rights and were threatened with seeing their lands disposed of without their consent.

On March 4, 1907, Ethan Allen Hitchcock had to resign from office because of the enmities he had incurred through his inquiries about land and mineral resources frauds.

Anne-Marie Libério

See also Allotment; General Allotment Act (Dawes Act), 1887; Indian Rights Association (IRA); *Lone Wolf v. Hitchcock*, 1903; Plenary Power; Treaty with the Cheyenne and Arapaho–October 28, 1867; Trust Responsibility.

References and Further Reading

Clark, Blue. 1994. *Lone Wolf v. Hitchcock : Treaty Rights and Indian Law at the End of the Nineteenth Century.* Lincoln and London: University of Nebraska Press.

Garraty, John A., and Mark C. Carnes. 1999. *American National Biography,* vol. 10. New York and Oxford: Oxford University Press.

Getches, David H., Charles F. Wilkinson, and Robert A. Williams, Jr., eds. 1998. *Cases and Materials on Federal Indian Law.* 4th ed. St. Paul, MN: West.

Prucha, Francis P. 1997. *American Indian Treaties: The History of a Political Anomaly.* 2nd ed. Berkeley, Los Angeles, and London: University of California Press.

Indian Claims Commission (ICC)

Congress created the Indian Claims Commission (ICC) as a temporary agency in 1946. This agency heard the claims of American Indian communities against the federal government and awarded monetary compensation to successful claimants. The Indian Claims Commission Act (1946), introduced by Representative Henry M. Jackson of Washington, initially granted the ICC only a ten-year life, but extensions in 1956, 1961, 1967, 1972, and 1976 allowed it to function for an additional twenty-two years. Almost all the eligible Indian communities filed claims, and many communities filed more than

one. When the commission's tenure ended in 1978, it had decided 549 claims and awarded approximately $800 million, still leaving sixty-eight unresolved dockets for the court of claims to decide.

Congress created the ICC as a commission to avoid the expense associated with an adversarial process, but despite this effort, the agency functioned as a court. Initially, the president appointed a chief commissioner and two associate commissioners to the ICC, but Congress expanded the number of commissioners to five in 1967. These individuals heard claims based on the U.S. Constitution, laws, and executive orders, but most cases involved land transfers agreed upon through treaties. American Indian communities hired attorneys to represent their interests, and lawyers from the Indian Claims Section of the Lands Division in the Justice Department defended the government against these claims. The government used all possible defenses against Indian claims and established offsets to reduce claim payments based on goods and services already provided by the government. The commission's process for appeals involved both the court of claims and the Supreme Court.

Federal Indian policy changed significantly during the life of the ICC. The early years of the commission witnessed a shift from the Indian New Deal of the 1930s to the termination policies of the 1950s. John Collier tried to include an Indian claims court in the Indian Reorganization Act of 1934, and the National Congress of American Indians, an organization founded by American Indian leaders in 1944, supported the ICC as an agency through which American Indians could gain compensation for land taken without fair payment. However, others supported the ICC because they believed that settling all Indian claims against the government was the first step to ending the federal government's trust responsibility to Indian communities. Arthur V. Watkins, a strong proponent of termination, even served as chief commissioner from 1960 to 1967.

By the mid-1960s, American Indian dissatisfaction with the ICC had intensified. Many critics complained that the ICC offered only monetary compensation. Only Taos Pueblo successfully convinced the ICC to support the return of land as compensation; as a result, Congress placed forty-eight thousand acres in trust for the community. Most communities settled for a monetary award, but others refused to take settlement payments. In one well-known case, eight Lakota communities demanded return of the Black Hills rather than take the money awarded.

The work of the ICC required the contributions of both lawyers and social scientists, leading to some interesting developments. Because the ICC ultimately functioned as a court, communities filing claims needed the services of attorneys. Despite congressional complaints about the attorneys throughout the life of the commission, American Indian communities intensified their use of legal strategies during and after the life of the ICC, granting these lawyers an unprecedented amount of influence. The commission also required the services of expert witnesses. These scholars, primarily historians and anthropologists, combined methods from both disciplines, ultimately contributing to the emergence of ethnohistory. This new methodology, which combined historical research with ethnology to answer anthropological questions, became an important development in the academic study of the American Indian past.

Jay Precht

See also Cohen, Felix S.; Collier, John; Indian Claims Commission (ICC); Indian Reorganization Act, 1934; Leupp, Francis Ellington; Meriam Report, 1928; Termination; Watkins, Arthur V.

References and Further Reading

Fixico, Donald L. 1986. *Termination and Relocation: Federal Indian Policy, 1945–1960.* Albuquerque: University of New Mexico Press.

Iverson, Peter. 1998. *"We Are Still Here": American Indians in the Twentieth Century.* The American History Series. Wheeling, IL: Harlan Davidson.

Prucha, Francis Paul. 1984. *The Great Father: The United States Government and the American Indians,* vol. 2. Lincoln and London: University of Nebraska Press.

Rosenthal, H. D. 1990. *Their Day in Court: A History of the Indian Claims Commission.* New York and London: Garland.

Indian Rights Association (IRA)

The Indian Rights Association (IRA), founded in Philadelphia in 1882 by Herbert Welsh and Henry Pancoast, advocated for the complete assimilation of Indians into American society and dedicated itself to obtaining individual land title, education, civil rights, and citizenship for Indian people. Believing that corruption and mismanagement were in large part to blame for holding Indians back from "civilization," the association also pledged itself to civil service reform in the Bureau of Indian Affairs (BIA).

The reformers of the IRA viewed legislation as the best means to accomplish its goals, and they used a variety of methods to influence Congress and public opinion. They established branch organizations in major cities, conducted field studies to gather information on Indian affairs, and publicized their cause through pamphlets, newspaper articles, and public lectures. The IRA also maintained a full-time lobbyist in Washington who provided reports to members of Congress and pressed for laws the association deemed beneficial to Indians. In addition, the IRA met annually with other Indian reform groups at the Lake Mohonk Conferences in upper New York to discuss solutions to the "Indian Problem."

In the late nineteenth and early twentieth centuries, the IRA saw several of the measures it promoted become federal government policy. The IRA's campaign for individual land title for Indians succeeded in 1887 with the passage of the General Allotment Act (Dawes Act). This act allowed for the breakup of reservation land and the granting of 160 acres to each Indian family head. The association believed that, by encouraging Indians to become farmers on individually owned plots of land, allotment would break the hold of "tribal bonds" and would compel Indians to become self-supporting individuals.

The IRA also successfully influenced Indian education policy. With the backing of the IRA, Thomas Jefferson Morgan, Indian commissioner from 1889 to 1893, implemented a compulsory government school system that integrated reservation schools and off-reservation boarding schools and emphasized the teaching of English, moral instruction, training in agriculture and trades for boys, and training in domestic tasks for girls.

Further, the IRA advocated for the granting of citizenship to Indians and the extension of American laws over Indian people in the belief that the "civilization" of the Indian could not proceed without the guarantee of the law. The association strongly supported the Major Crimes Act of 1885, which extended federal criminal jurisdiction over felony crimes committed by Indians on reservations; the provisions of the General Allotment Act, which made allottees subject to the civil and criminal laws of the state or territory in which they resided; and the Indian Citizenship Act in 1924.

Last, in order to ensure that the laws and policies it promoted were properly implemented, the IRA pushed for the extension of civil service reform legislation to the Bureau of Indian Affairs. In the 1890s, the IRA won its campaign when civil service rules were gradually extended to cover all agency employees below the rank of agent.

Although well intentioned, many of the policies pursued by the IRA were disastrous in practice. The implementation of the Dawes Act ultimately deprived Indian people of more than ninety million acres of their land, and the Indian school system amounted to a major threat to Native American social and cultural life.

On the other hand, it should be noted that many tribes turned to the IRA for assistance and, for their part, the association tried to ensure that Indians retained at least a part of their land and natural resources in the face of American expansionism. For instance, in negotiations for the reduction of the Great Sioux Reservation in the 1880s, the IRA pushed for allotment and a favorable financial settlement for the Sioux. The association also opposed the removal of the Southern Ute from Colorado, campaigned for the rights of the Mission Indians of California to reside on homeland reservations, and tried to secure better terms for the Menominee and Chippewa in their conflicts with the lumber industry.

In the twentieth century, the IRA declined in influence and gradually shifted its position from support for assimilation to support for Indian independence. It opposed the Indian Reorganization Act of 1934, which reversed the policy of assimilation, but in the 1950s the association became critical of the government's termination policy, and in the 1960s it supported the Indian movement for self-determination. The association was later eclipsed by the work of Indian activists, and in 1994 the organization was disbanded.

Anne Keary

See also Assimilation; House Concurrent Resolution 108, 1953; Indian Civil Rights Act, 1968; Indian Reorganization Act, 1934; Termination.
References and Further Reading
Hagan, William T. 1985. *The Indian Rights Association: The Herbert Welsh Years 1882–1904*. Tucson: University of Arizona Press.

Prucha, Francis Paul. 1976. *American Indian Policy in Crisis: Christian Reformers and the Indian, 1865–1900*. Norman: University of Oklahoma Press.

Jackson, Andrew
(1767–1845)

First rising to national prominence on his reputation as an Indian fighter, Andrew Jackson greatly expanded the territory of the United States by wresting vast amounts of land from Native American tribes. As major general of the Tennessee militia, Jackson initially achieved fame for his victory over the Creek Indians at the Battle of Horseshoe Bend, which forced the Creeks to sign away their lands to the United States in the 1814 Treaty of Fort Jackson. Later, as the seventh president, he signed into law

Andrew Jackson (1767–1845), noted Indian fighter, served two terms as president of the United States, founding a new Democratic Party in the process. He argued with Congress and the Supreme Court, used the presidential veto power, and left behind a political legacy known as Jacksonian Democracy. (Library of Congress)

the Indian Removal Act of 1830, which forced thousands of Native Americans in the eastern United States to uproot their lives and relocate to unfamiliar territories west of the Mississippi.

Born in South Carolina, Jackson moved to present-day Tennessee after the Revolutionary War to establish a law practice on the frontier. A rising star in Tennessee politics, Jackson served the state in the U.S. House of Representatives, the U.S. Senate, and the Tennessee Superior Court. Elected major general of the Tennessee militia in 1812 (despite his lack of military experience), Jackson immediately led his troops on a campaign to quell an uprising of the Creek Indians that had erupted during the War of 1812. Soundly defeating the Creeks at the Battle of Horseshoe Bend on March 27, 1814, Jackson forced the Creek Indians to sign the Treaty of Fort Jackson on August 9, 1814. The treaty effectively forced the Creeks off twenty-three million acres of land in present-day Georgia and Alabama, opening the territory to white settlement. The victory at Horseshoe Bend and his subsequent defeat of the British at the Battle of New Orleans cemented Jackson's image as a national hero and won him an appointment as major general in the U.S. Army.

Almost immediately, Jackson was ordered to mount a campaign against the Seminole tribes that were raiding white settlements near the U.S. border with Spanish Florida. In what became known as the First Seminole War, Jackson chased the Seminoles across the border into Spanish Florida (in large measure to seize territory for the United States) on March 15, 1818. Jackson quickly defeated the Seminoles, captured Spanish settlements, and executed two British citizens for supposedly aiding the Native Americans (almost sparking an international incident with both Great Britain and Spain). Ultimately, Spain agreed to cede Florida to the United States in 1819 for $5 million, and President James Monroe named Jackson territorial governor of Florida, empowering him to receive the territory from Spain.

Jackson's military exploits and victories over Native Americans had made him the best-known figure in the United States. Running for the presidency a second time in 1828, Jackson easily won the election and served two terms (1829–1837). In one of his first acts in office, Jackson signed into law the 1830 Indian Removal Act, which forced the so-called Five Civilized Tribes (the Creeks, Cherokees, Choctaws, Chickasaws, and Seminoles) and other tribes to relocate from the eastern United States to

lands west of the Mississippi. Historians debate whether Jackson did this primarily to seize choice lands for white settlers or because he believed he could not protect the tribes from encroaching white squatters and greedy state governments. In either case, Jackson set immediately to work after its passage in his effort to force Native Americans beyond the Mississippi River.

Over the next several years, Native Americans across the eastern United States actively fought their removal to western lands, producing the Second Seminole War and the Black Hawk War. Ultimately, however, the eastern tribes were forced to abandon their homes and march west. Controversial from its inception, the Indian Removal Act opened vast stretches of land for white settlement in the American Southeast, and it also produced the infamous Cherokee Trail of Tears and widespread outrage even among whites. Andrew Jackson spent much of his tenure in office directing the removals and negotiating with tribal leaders. He remained proud of his lifelong record on Indian affairs until his death on June 8, 1845.

Andrew J. Torget

See also Battle of Horseshoe Bend (Tohopeka), 1814; Black Hawk; *Cherokee Nation v. Georgia*, 1831; Indian Removal; Indian Removal Act, 1830; Ross, John; Trail of Tears; *Worcester v. Georgia*, 1832.

References and Further Reading

Remini, Robert. 2002. *Andrew Jackson and His Indian Wars*. New York: Penguin Putnam.
Remini, Robert. 1999. "Jackson, Andrew." In *American National Biography*, eds. John A. Garraty and Mark C. Carnes, 732–737. New York: Oxford University Press.
Wallace, Anthony. 1993. *The Long, Bitter Trail: Andrew Jackson and the Indians*. New York: Hill and Wang.

Jackson, Helen Hunt
(1830–1885)

Helen Maria Fiske, who would become known later in life as Helen Hunt Jackson, was born October 15, 1830, in Amherst, Massachusetts, the daughter of Nathan Welby Fiske, a professor of languages at Amherst College. She was described as "a child of dangerous versatility and vivacity" (Mathes 1990, 21). Variously portrayed as brilliant and something of a pest, the young Helen Fiske learned to read and write earlier than most children, drawing from colle-

A successful and prolific author, Helen Hunt Jackson is best remembered for A Century of Dishonor *(1881) and* Ramona *(1884), books that helped to raise awareness of Native American rights and of their ill treatment at the hands of the U.S. government. (Library of Congress)*

giate surroundings, becoming a young woman "with candid beaming eyes, in which kindness contented with penetration," a "soul of fire," with the ability to "strongly love, to frankly hate" (Mathes 1990, 22).

As a girl, Helen became close friends with the poet Emily Dickinson. Fiske, Dickinson, and Emily Fowler (who was briefly well known as an author in her later life) came to be known as the Amherst girls, a group of talented women born to Amherst faculty members. In her own time, Helen was a better-known poet than Dickinson, who spent much of her own life as a writer in obscurity.

At the age of eleven, Helen Fiske was sent to the first of several boarding schools where she spent her teenage years. By age nineteen, she had been orphaned; both of her parents died of tuberculosis. Early in her life, Helen determined to support herself as an independent woman, not an easy role in a society in which women were defined as men's property. She decided to make her living as a writer.

First known as a romantic poet, she later expanded her scope to include travel articles, short stories, novels, and books for children. Before becoming famous for her Indian reform work late in her life, she had been "an Army wife, mother, and woman of society . . . a literary person, a poet and essayist, writer of travel sketches and short stories" (Banning 1973, xix). She was, according to her biographer Evelyn I. Banning, a woman of contradictions. Although some of her writings laughed at fashion, she dressed elegantly, often beyond the station of the junior army officer, Edward B. Hunt, whom she married at the age of twenty-two. Before the treatment of the Ponca Indians tripped her sense of indignity, Helen Hunt Jackson had been a nearly apolitical person, having taken no published position on women's suffrage or slavery, even as she "burst the bounds . . . [of] the separate sphere assigned to women during the Victorian era" (Mathes 1990, ix).

Within the fifteen years after she married Edward Hunt, Helen gave birth to two sons and lost both of them, one at the age of one year, the other at age nine. Her husband also died, leaving her nearly alone in the world. She assuaged her loneliness by writing poetry, becoming one of the best regarded poets of nineteenth-century America. Ralph Waldo Emerson often carried her poetry in his pocket to show to friends (Banning 1973, xx). In 1875, she married William S. Jackson of Colorado Springs, whose name she carried when her Indian reform work became well known. At the age of forty-nine, she took up the cause of "the Indian" with a fervor that consumed her attention and energies for the last few remaining years of her short life.

Jackson's attention was turned toward the condition of Native Americans during October 1879, shortly after Judge Elmer Dundy had ruled in *Standing Bear v. Crook*. In Boston, Jackson heard a speech describing the travail of Standing Bear and his band of Poncas who, forced off their land in northern Nebraska, had escaped reservation life in Indian Territory. They had trekked five hundred miles northward during the worst of a midcontinental winter to take shelter with the U'mahas (Omahas) near the city of Omaha where, in 1879, Judge Dundy ruled that Standing Bear must be regarded as a human being under the law of habeas corpus.

After the trial, a group of Ponca Indians, included Standing Bear, visited several cities, including Chicago, New York City, Philadelphia, Baltimore, and Boston. It was in Boston, however, that support was greatest; $3,000 of the $4,000 the Poncas thought they would need to pursue their land claim was raised there (Mathes 1989, 46). Henry Wadsworth Longfellow played a crucial role in the success of the Poncas' efforts in Boston. The Poncas stayed in Boston several weeks, from late October into December, and were presented at numerous fund-raisers. In early December, more than a thousand Bostonians gathered at Faneuil Hall to hear Standing Bear speak. After the speeches, more than half the audience crowded the stage to shake hands with him (Mathes 1989, 47).

After hearing their story, Jackson collected funds for the Poncas and encouraged others to take an active part in their struggles. The mayor of Boston joined a fund-raising committee for the Poncas' legal campaign to win back their homeland. Jackson herself joined Standing Bear, Thomas Henry Tibbles, and Suzette "Bright Eyes" LaFlesche on a tour throughout New England. Tibbles credited Jackson's support as being one of the major factors in the Poncas' ultimate victory (Banning 1973, 150).

Jackson's acquaintance with the Poncas started her down a new literary road. Within two years of first hearing the Poncas' heartrending story, Jackson published *A Century of Dishonor*. Three years later, with a pledge to write a novel that would become the Native American version of *Uncle Tom's Cabin*, she published the best seller *Ramona*.

A Century of Dishonor is a factual sketch of broken treaties and corruption in the Indian Bureau; *Ramona* is a fictional account of the abuses suffered by the Mission Indians of California, based on Jackson's travels in that area shortly after *A Century of Dishonor* was published. Both books were among the best sellers of their time, one more indication of just how many non-Indians sympathized with the Native American victims of westward expansion.

Jackson's books may have been so immensely popular during the 1880s because many people in the expanding United States, finding a need to reconcile the taking of a continent with notions of their own civility, sought to deal with the "Indian Problem" in what they believed to be a civilized and humane manner. Thus, cultural genocide (a late twentieth-century phrase) was advanced in the modulated tones of civility, of doing what was believed to be best for "the Indian."

Jackson's books fueled a national debate over what would become of Native Americans who had survived subjugation by immigrant non-Natives. Most of her books combined condemnation of the government's earlier behavior with advocacy of popular solutions to the Indian Problem, such as religious instruction, boarding schools, and allotment.

After *A Century of Dishonor* was published, Jackson sent a copy of it to each member of Congress at her own expense. She then visited each representative personally to emphasize what she thought must be done to remove the stain of the dishonorable century she had described. Jackson had died by the time Congress passed the General Allotment (Dawes) Act in 1887, officially adopting allotment (which she had believed would save Native Americans from extinction), at the same time turning it into a real estate vehicle for homesteaders and corporations (Indians would lose two-thirds of their remaining land base in the fifty years to follow).

Ramona, which was reprinted three hundred times after Jackson's death, was adapted for stage and screen several times. "Every incident in *Ramona* . . . is true," Jackson wrote. "A Cahuilla Indian was shot two years ago exactly as Alessandro is—and his wife's name was Ramona, and I never knew this fact until Ramona was half written" (Mathes 1986, 43).

By the middle 1880s, Jackson was suffering recurring bouts of malarial symptoms and other health problems, which gradually debilitated her. In 1885, on her deathbed, Jackson wrote of her work, "As I lie here, nothing looks to me of any value except the words I have spoken for the Indians" (Banning 1973, 224). Her last letter, dated August 8, was written to President Grover Cleveland: "I ask you to read my *A Century of Dishonor*. I am dying happier in the belief I have that it is your hand that is destined to strike the first steady blow toward lifting the burden of infamy from our country and riting the wrongs of the Indian race . . ." (Banning 1973, 225).

Jackson died on August 12, 1885. Upon hearing of her death, Susette LaFlesche "shut herself into her room and wept all day long," according to her husband, Thomas Henry Tibbles. "For weeks afterward she mourned the loss of this closest of her intimate friends, who had given herself wholeheartedly to save an unhappy race" (Mathes 1986, 44).

Emily Dickinson penned a verse in eulogy of Jackson:

Helen of Troy will die,
but Helen of Colorado, never.
"Dear friend, you can walk"
were the last words I wrote her—
"Dear friend, I can fly"—
her immortal reply (Banning, frontpiece).

Bruce E. Johansen

See also Allotment; General Allotment Act (Dawes Act), 1887; Standing Bear (Mo-chu-no-zhi); Tibbles, Susette La Flesche (Bright Eyes, Inshta Theamba).

References and Further Reading

Banning, Evelyn L. 1973. *Helen Hunt Jackson.* New York: Vanguard Press.

Hayes, Robert G. 1997. *A Race at Bay: New York Times Editorials on the "Indian Problem."* Carbondale: Southern Illinois University Press.

Jackson, Helen Hunt. 1972. *A Century of Dishonor: A Sketch of the United States Government's Dealings with Some of the Indian Tribes.* St. Clair Shores, MI: Scholarly Press. [Originally printed in 1888 Boston: Roberts Bros.]

Mathes, Valerie Sherer. 1986. "Helen Hunt Jackson: A Legacy of Indian Reform." *Essays and Monographs in Colorado History* 4: 25–58.

Mathes, Valerie Sherer. 1989. "Helen Hunt Jackson and the Ponca Controversy." *Montana* 39 (Winter): 42–53.

Mathes, Valerie Sherer. 1990. *Helen Hunt Jackson and Her Indian Reform Legacy.* Austin: University of Texas Press.

Jefferson, Thomas

(1743–1826)

Thomas Jefferson was born in 1743 and died in 1826. As one of the most intellectually curious men to occupy the White House, Thomas Jefferson took an active interest in Native Americans upon assuming the presidency in 1801. Indeed, the third president of the United States embarked upon an arduous compilation of Indian vocabularies while in office, even instructing Lewis and Clark to carefully collect Native linguistic samples on their great expedition westward. Born in Shadwell, Virginia, Jefferson grew up in proximity to American Indians, although not in their direct company. And although he may have occasionally romanticized the American Indian as a "noble savage," he refused to denigrate them and actually defended them as dignified, stoic, strong, happy, and faithful (Burstein 1997).

Thus, it is ironic that Jefferson was fated to sow the "seeds of extinction" against this race he so admired during his tenure in office—ultimately leading to removal of the Native American populations east of the Mississippi River (Ellis 1997). Upon securing the Louisiana Purchase from Napoleon in 1803 and thereby swiftly doubling the size of the United States, Jefferson quickly realized that white settlement of the new land east of the Mississippi

Thomas Jefferson (1743–1826) of Virginia, the third president of the United States, took an active interest in Native Americans upon assuming the presidency in 1801. Ultimately though, his policies proved detrimental to Native Americans. (Library of Congress)

was the most effective way to deal with the burgeoning population of the new country as well as to ensure against future British or French encroachment. However, along with the purchase came many American Indian tribes who already lived there, albeit sparsely.

Consequently, in a letter to William Henry Harrison, then military governor of the Northwest Territory, Jefferson first broached a plan to relocate the tribes west of the Mississippi—into the vastness of open country. Although subsequent administrations actually secured legislation from Congress to carry this out and put the plan into effect, the legacy of the idea traces squarely back to Jefferson. However, it remains unclear exactly to what extent Jefferson meant for this to happen. He was fascinated with the possibility of "civilizing" the Indians, and there is evidence that this was the route he finally settled on pursuing as a way to save the Indians instead of removing them.

In fact, Jefferson's annual State of the Union messages to Congress reflect this notion as his administration's official policy. Specific progress along these lines was reported quite mundanely in Jefferson's Eighth Annual Message to Congress:

With our Indian neighbors the public peace has been steadily maintained. Some instances of individual wrong have, as at other times, taken place, but in nowise implicating the will of the nation. Beyond the Mississippi, the Iowa, the Sac, and the Alabama, have delivered up for trial and punishment individuals from among themselves accused of murdering citizens of the United States. On this side of the Mississippi, the Creek are exerting themselves to arrest offenders of the same kind; and the Choctaw have manifested their readiness and desire for amicable and just arrangements respecting depredations committed by disorderly persons of their tribe. And, generally, from a conviction that we consider them as part of ourselves, and cherish with sincerity their rights and interests, the attachment of the Indian tribes is gaining strength daily. . . . Husbandry and household manufacture are advancing among them, more rapidly with the southern than the northern tribes, from circumstances of soil and climate; and one of the two great divisions of the Cherokee nation have now under consideration to solicit the citizenship of the United States, and to be identified with us in laws and government, in such progressive manner as we shall think best. (Jefferson 1808)

As the author of America's Declaration of Independence, Jefferson made another fateful decision that impacted the legal rights of Native Americans for centuries. The natural rights that Jefferson articulated as inalienable were life, liberty, and the pursuit of happiness. Jefferson relied in part on the philosophy and writings of John Locke as he drafted this critical document for the Continental Congress in 1776. But the original list of basic natural rights written by Locke used the word *property*.

Jefferson, wanting neither to permanently institutionalize the concept of slavery nor legitimize it as a natural right (although he himself was a holder of two hundred slaves), substituted *pursuit of happiness* for *property*. Thus, a major hurdle to colonial unity against the British was avoided. Jefferson could not have known that he simultaneously created a major impediment to Indian property rights that was realized in law forty-seven years later.

In 1823, Chief Justice John Marshall wrote in *Johnson v. McIntosh* that American Indians held no transferable title in land itself. The European countries acquired such title upon either discovery or conquest. Instead of a right to the soil, Indians held the title of occupancy—and whenever they sold their land, this was all the title that the buyer acquired. Arguably, if Jefferson had earlier recognized a natural right in property for all men, Marshall would have found it more difficult to circumscribe Indian property rights later.

Michael J. Kelly

See also Indian Removal, *Johnson v. McIntosh*, 1923; Knox, Henry; Trail of Tears.
References and Further Reading
Burstein, Andrew. 1995. *The Inner Jefferson: Portrait of a Grieving Optimist.* Charlottesville: University Press of Virginia.
Ellis, Joseph. 1997. *American Sphinx: The Character of Thomas Jefferson.* New York: Alfred A. Knopf.
Sheehan, Bernard W. 1973. *Seeds of Extinction: Jeffersonian Philanthropy and the American Indian.* New York: W.W. Norton.

Jemison, Alice Mae Lee
1901–1964

Alice Mae Lee Jemison was an adamant defender of Native American rights who worked as a politician, activist, and journalist. She was considered one of the leading Native American activists during the 1930s.

Born in Silver Creek, New York, on October 9, 1901, near the Cattaraugus Indian Reservation, as a mixture of Seneca and Cherokee she was raised in the traditional, matrilineal society of the Seneca, one of the six tribes of the Iroquois Confederacy. According to the ancient practice of her people, women participated fully in tribal matters, including politics.

A great respect for hard work was instilled in Jemison as a young girl. She was taught to revere the traditions of the Iroquois and to distrust interference by non-Indians in tribal affairs. These beliefs, along with the generally antigovernment views of many residents of western New York at the time, dictated many of her political positions as an adult.

Alice Mae Jemison began her career by aiding in the defense of two young Seneca women who were accused of murdering the wife of an internationally famous sculptor who lived near her residence, in Buffalo. At the time, she was a part-time secretary to Ray Jimerson, the president of the Seneca Nation. The case became sensationalized in hope of swaying public opinion to push it through to a speedy trial and conviction.

Jemison challenged the allegations against the two women by writing her own newspaper stories about the situation, which helped the women gain freedom. She came to the defense not only of the accused but of all Native American people, but as a result of her scintillating newspaper articles against the oppression of "her people," she was hired to write a syndicated column for the North American Indian Newspaper Alliance, which she did from 1932 to 1934, and as a lobbyist for the Seneca Nation in Washington, D.C.

It was in her work as a lobbyist that she attacked and called for the dismantling of the Bureau of Indian Affairs (BIA), the government agency charged with overseeing the official U.S. dealings with Native Americans. Throughout its history, the BIA had accused of corruption, but Jemison blamed it for nearly all the problems of Native Americans. She was a firm believer in the sovereignty of Indian treaty rights, and she strongly believed that the Bureau of Indian Affairs should be abolished.

Alice Lee Jemison is best remembered as an outspoken critic of the Bureau of Indian Affairs and its New Deal program of the 1930s, and as a leader in the ultraconservative American Indian Federation. Her use of inflammatory rhetoric and demagoguery, especially in opposition to New Deal legislation, led some government officials to cast her as an extremist, but her followers would say she that she was complex and misunderstood.

She appeared at more congressional hearings to speak on Indian matters than any other Native American of her time. She fought against the Bureau of Indian Affairs, the Indian Reorganization Act, and the Selective Service Act, which called for young American men to be drafted into the military in preparation for U.S. involvement in World War II; she claiming that the law could not legally be applied to the Seneca. According to past treaties, the Iroquois were a separate nation with a separate government; therefore, she maintained, only the Iroquois Nation could send its citizens to war. She fought wherever she thought there were injustices against the Native American.

To more fully understand Jemison's point of view, it is important to recognize her commitment to preserving Iroquois treaty rights, which she and others believed safeguarded an independent Iroquois sovereignty.

Jemison died on March 6, 1964, of cancer. She was buried at the United Mission Cemetery on the Cattaraugus Reservation. Jemison lives in the memory of her people, who recognize her as a powerful advocate for Indian causes who was instrumental in shaping federal Indian policies during the 1930s and continued to lobby for Indian causes until her death. To some of her contemporaries, she was controversial, but to advocates of Native American rights, she was a hero.

Fred Lindsay

See also Bureau of Indian Affairs (BIA); Domestic Dependent Nation; Indian New Deal; Indian Reorganization Act, 1934; Sovereignty.

References and Further Reading

Abrams, George H. J. 1976. *The Seneca People.* Phoenix, AZ: Indian Tribal Series.

Ballantine, Betty, and Ian Ballantine. 1993. *The Native Americans: An Illustrated History.* Atlanta: Turner.

Hauptmann, Laurence M. 1980. "Jemison, Alice Mae Lee." In *Notable American Women: The Modern Period,* ed. Barbara Sicherman and Carol Hurd Green. Cambridge, MA: Belknap Press of Harvard University Press.

Jerome, David H.

The Cherokee Commission was also called the Jerome Commission, after its chairman, David H. Jerome, a former governor of Michigan and member of the Board of Indian Commissioners. The Jerome was one of more than a dozen commissions created to carry out the goals of the Dawes Severalty Act (1887). The commission's authority came as an attachment to the Indian Service Bill (1889), though the real energy for its creation was the restless force of land seekers who wanted to open Indian lands to white settlement. To fulfill their mission, commissioners would coerce the Indian Territory tribes into allotment in severalty and the sale of their so-called "surplus lands." The nearly twenty tribes with which the Cherokee Commission dealt made it distinctive; most other commissions met with one or a few tribes only. Equally unique was the Cherokee Commission's life span of fifty-two months. Over those years, the commissionership changed, but all members drew upon political patronage. Most of the commission's effectiveness in winning concessions from tribes came under the aggressive direction of David Jerome.

Early on, the commissioners were particularly interested in the Cherokee, who were seen as a special case because the tribe owned the largest territory, a stretch of land between the 96th and 100th meridians that totaled more than six million acres and was called the Cherokee Outlet. Divesting the Cherokee of that land became a "chief purpose" of the commissioners and of secretary of the interior John W. Noble. The commissioners began negotiations with the Cherokee in the fall of 1989, thinking the process would be quick. Instead, the commission found that the Cherokee were well educated about their rights and stalled negotiations repeatedly. Much was at stake. The Cherokee Outlet provided lucrative yearly payments from the Cherokee Strip Live Stock Association for grazing rights. The commissioners realized that the Cherokee's strengthened position was a result of that money. So in order to leverage the Outlet from the Cherokee, the commissioners conspired to make the land valueless by forcing the cattlemen out of the region with a presidential edict. Meanwhile, the Cherokee Commission gained new leadership under David Jerome and, with him, a far more aggressive character. Eventually, the Cherokee lost the Outlet but skillfully gained several conditions from the Cherokee Commission, especially concerning intruders.

Under Jerome's leadership, the Cherokee Commission turned to the smaller tribes that were less able to resist. The Iowa, the Sac and Fox, the Absentee Shawnee, the Citizen band of Pottawatomie, and the Kickapoo soon experienced the commissioners' aggressive and deceitful tactics. The commissioners ran roughshod over these tribes; they grossly underpaid the tribes for their surplus lands while using cunning phrases to convince the tribe otherwise. When some tribes became wise to such actions and sought outside counsel, the commissioners became incensed. The commissioners also ignored the tribes' concerns for future generations and the U.S. legacy of failed promises. For Jerome, these tribes were simply ignorant savages who must accept allotments and give up their lands absolutely. In two months, the commissioners exacted nearly a million acres.

Between 1890 and 1892, the commissioners turned to the western tribes—the Cheyenne, Arapaho, Wichita, Tonkowa, Kiowa, Apache, and Comanche. With time, the commissioners' actions grew more disingenuous. They began to use bribes and payments to gain required signatures. They expanded these tactics, using attorneys to persuade tribes to accept the negotiations—attorneys whose interest should have been with the tribes but who were merely agents of the commissioners paid handsomely out of the tribes' payments for the lands sold. Over time, due in part to pressures from Congress to open land for white settlement, the commissioners became more cynical, more ruthless in their tactics against smaller tribes who resisted allotment and sale of lands.

The Cherokee Commission ended in August 1893 after the last of its five appropriations ran out, which together had totaled $90,000. It acquired 23,595 square miles, nearly fifteen million acres. Almost all this land became available to white settlers and led to the emergence of the state of Oklahoma. This land loss devastated the tribes. It destroyed their practice of holding lands in common, affected their identity, devastated their economic opportunities, and scattered them among an unfriendly white population soon to outnumber them. The commissioners' deceit and abuses would eventually bring tribes before the Indian Claims Commission of the mid-twentieth century, who labeled the Jerome Commission's actions "unconscionable" and eventually compensated Oklahoma tribes with a total of $41,000,000.

S. Matthew DeSpain

See also Aboriginal Title; General Allotment Act (Dawes Act), 1887; Indian Removal; Indian Territory.

References and Further Reading

Hagan, William T. 2003. *Taking Indian Lands: The Cherokee (Jerome) Commission 1889–1893*. Norman: University of Oklahoma Press.

Hoxie, Frederick E. 1984. *A Final Promise: The Campaign to Assimilate the Indians*. New York: Cambridge University Press.

McDonnell, Janet A. *The Dispossession of the American Indian, 1887–1934*. Bloomington: Indiana University Press.

Prucha, Francis Paul. 1994. *The Great Father: United States Government and the American Indians*. Abr. ed. Lincoln: University of Nebraska Press.

Washburn, Wilcomb E. 1975. *The Assault on Indian Tribalism: The General Allotment Law (Dawes Act) of 1887*. Philadelphia: Lippincott.

Jesup, Thomas S.
(1788–1860)

Thomas Sidney Jesup is often referenced as the father of the modern Quartermaster Corps. As a military officer, he served as quartermaster general for forty-two years (1818–1862), holding the record for longest continual service in the same position in U.S. military history. His activities prior to and in this post included the battles of Chippewa and Niagara, oversight of troops during the Second Seminole and

Mexican-American Wars, and strategic planning from his office in Washington, D.C.

Born in Virginia, Jesup's family moved to Kentucky when he was a boy, and his father died shortly after. This left him without a formal education, but that did not hinder him in his pursuit of learning or in finding useful employment. In about 1807, he applied for an appointment as a commissioned officer and was accepted the following year as a second lieutenant in the 7th U.S. Infantry, a unit that would see a good deal of action in the South in years to come. Jesup found advancement more to his liking following the end of the War of 1812. By 1818, he held the rank of brigadier general.

Although Thomas Sidney Jesup carried out his duties as a representative of the U.S. government, he did not always agree with government policies, in particular the removal of the Seminoles from Florida. The final betrayal and arrest of Osceola is often blamed on Jesup.

In May 1837, Osceola had used the white flag as a ruse to obtain supplies for his warriors and followers, telling the government he would surrender himself and his followers to be removed to the West. Taking his word as truth, he was given supplies and allowed to proceed without escort to Tampa for relocation to the West. When Coe Hadjo and his followers offered to also go west in return for supplies, Osceola prevented him from heading to Tampa as agreed. Instead, taking the supplies, he and his followers, as well as Coe Hadjo and his members, made off into the interior.

This use of the white flag forced the Americans to be suspicious. Osceola used it again in the autumn when he asked General Hernandez, under Jesup's command, to come and talk. Jesup allowed Hernandez to go, and to take along a military escort in case of trouble. Jesup drafted a list of pertinent questions for Hernandez to use. These questions were based on a council Jesup had held with another Indian leader, Coe Hadjo, following the white flag incident. Jesup directed Hernandez to arrest the whole group, Osceola included, if the answers proved contrary to Jesup's. On October 21, 1837, Hernandez arrived to find Osceola with a white flag of truce, but his warriors were armed to the hilt. Coe Hadjo was also present. As the talks progressed, word was sent to Jesup that the answers were not what they ought to be. Hernandez took Osceola, Coe Hadjo, and many of their followers prisoner.

Osceola had fallen ill, most likely due to malaria. On horseback, he was taken to Jesup's St. Augustine headquarters, where he informed Jesup that the other Seminoles were ready to emigrate to the West. To confirm this statement, distrusting Osceola's use of a flag of truce, Jesup sent his own messengers out to other Seminole leaders. After weeks of waiting to hear back, word came in that, yes, they would go west. The local whites praised the capture as a sign that their troubles would be soon ending, that slaves would be returned, and that land would be made available. Back in Washington, political critics assailed Jesup for taking Osceola and his followers as a sign of trickery. In the meantime, thousands of Indians had not yet come in to surrender themselves. So Jesup prepared to launch a campaign to bring them in. In late November, a prisoner escaped, prompting Jesup to order all remaining prisoners to be moved to South Carolina where they could be isolated on an island fortress, Fort Moultrie. Osceola was among the prisoners transferred, and he died there in late January 1838. The following month, the Seminoles shipped out for New Orleans, later to be sent to the West.

As Jesup continued to hunt down more of the elusive Seminoles and runaway slaves in the early spring of 1838, he wrote to Washington, asking the administration to alter the course of the removal policy and to recognize the futility and the grave costs of attempting to undertake such a war. He advocated allowing the remaining population to stay in Florida. He asked that the old treaty be set aside in favor of a newer one that reflected such an alteration in removal policy. The removal policy could be said to date back to as early as 1803 under the direction of then-president Jefferson, who sought to remove all the Indians east of the Mississippi and sent them to the territories to the west of it. Later, President Andrew Jackson made removal policy a keystone of his presidency, so that, by 1838, even Martin van Buren considered it a mainstay policy, not to be altered. Jesup would not find any support in the administration. Hence, the war would continue for years to come.

When the war in Florida broke out, Jesup, as quartermaster general, ordered an increased amount of supplies in anticipation that more would be needed. General Winfield Scott had been in command in Florida, and although well supplied and reinforced, he refrained from taking any decisive action. Furthermore, he antagonized General Edmund P. Gaines's promotion of peace by insisting on following the president's mandate to remove the Seminoles and Creeks to the West and return the runaway slaves to their masters. Due to Scott's ineptitude, Jesup replaced him.

In 1839, Jesup resumed his duties as quartermaster general, until the outbreak of the Mexican-American War. At that time, he traveled to the American Southwest to oversee adequate supply and facility distribution to the U.S. military. Due to his tactical abilities to supply and orchestrate an army, his advice was constantly sought after upon his return to Washington. As a result, he remained a prominent figure in the capital until his death in 1860.

Sally Colford Bennett

See also Gaines, Edmund Pendleton; Indian
    Removal; Jackson, Andrew; Osceola.
References and Further Readings
Hartley, William and Ellen. 1973. *Osceola, the
    Unconquered Indian.* New York: Hawthorn
    Books.
Heidler, David S., and Jeanne T. Heilder. 1996. *Old
    Hickory's War: Andrew Jackson and the Quest for
    Empire.* Mechanicsburg, PA: Stackpole Books.
Kiefer, Chester L. 1979. *Maligned General: The
    Biography of Thomas Sidney Jessup.* San Rafael,
    CA: Presidio Press.

Johnson, William
(1715–1774)

Sir William Johnson was probably the single most influential Englishman in relations with the Iroquois and their allies during the French and Indian War. From his mansion near Albany, Johnson accompanied Indian war parties on their forays, painting himself like an Indian and taking part in ceremonial dances. He was a close friend of Hendrick (Tiyanoga), a Mahican-Mohawk leader, with whom he often traveled as a warrior. Joseph Brant fought beside Johnson at the age of thirteen. Because he successfully recruited a sizable number of Iroquois to the British interest, Johnson was made a baronet and awarded £5,000 sterling.

Johnson quickly learned the customs and language of the Mohawks. He had a number of children by Mohawk women, many of them with Mary Brant, a Mohawk clan mother and granddaughter of Hendrick. He generally was well liked among the Mohawks. Hendrick himself had a high regard for the Englishman and expressed his regard when he said, "[H]e has Large Ears and heard a great deal, and what he hears he tells us; he also has Large Eyes and sees a great way, and conceals nothing from us" (Johansen and Grinde 1997, 185).

In June 1760, during the final thrust to defeat the French in North America, Johnson called for men to attack Montreal. About six hundred warriors responded. Many Native warriors living in the Montreal area also responded to his call. Johnson reported he was sending gifts to "foreign Indians" who were switching their allegiance from the sinking French Empire. By August 5, 1760, the Native contingent had reached 1,330.

The defeat of the French and their departure from Canada at the end of the war upset the balance that the Iroquois had sought to maintain. Reluctantly, they attached themselves to the British, but they could no longer play one European power against another. The English now occupied all the forts surrounding Iroquois country. Johnson played a key role in pressing the Crown to limit immigration west of the Appalachians, but land-hungry settlers ignored royal edicts, intensifying conflicts over land. In the meantime, Johnson became one of the richest men in the colonies through land transactions and trade with the Indians.

In his later years, Johnson agonized over whether to side with the British Crown or the revolutionary patriots. At a meeting with the Iroquois on July 11, 1774, at his mansion near Albany, Johnson addressed the Iroquois in the oratorical style he had learned from them, summoning them to the British cause in the coming American Revolution. Suddenly, he collapsed. He was carried to bed, where he died two hours later. The assembly of chiefs was stunned by his sudden death, but Guy Johnson, Sir William's nephew and son-in-law, stepped in to fill the breach left by his elder.

Bruce E. Johansen

See also Brant, Joseph; Hendrick.
References and Further Reading
Flexner, James Thomas. 1959. *Mohawk Baronet.* New
    York: Harper & Row.
Graymont, Barbara. 1972. *The Iroquois in the American
    Revolution.* Syracuse, NY: Syracuse University
    Press.
Grinde, Donald A., Jr. 1977. *The Iroquois and the
    Founding of the American Nation.* San Francisco:
    Indian Historian Press.
Johansen, Bruce E., and Donald A. Grinde, Jr. 1997.
    The Encyclopedia of Native American Biography.
    New York: Henry Holt.
Sullivan, James, et al., eds. 1921–1965. *The Papers of
    Sir William Johnson.* Albany: University of the
    State of New York.

Joseph
(c. 1840–1904)

Chief Joseph became the commander of the Nez Perce uprising of 1877 when his followers responded to the loss of their land through a fraudulent treaty agreement.

Chief Joseph was the statesman-leader of a loosely associated group of Nez Perce, Native Americans who lived in the Wallowa Valley, a mountainous region of Washington, Oregon, Idaho, and Montana. He was also known as Joseph the Younger and Hin-mah-too-lat-kekt (Thunder Rolling in the Mountains). The Nez Perce were once the largest congregation of tribes in the western United States. They represented many different tribes with many cultural differences that existed together peacefully. Generally, they were thought to be one tribe. The Nez Perce were considered valiant warriors. They were given the name Nez Perce (Pierce Nose) by Lewis and Clark because some of their members decorated their noses with shells or pendants.

After gold was discovered in 1859 on the Clearwater River, miners and cattlemen rushed into Chief Joseph's home valley. This onslaught resulted in Native Americans losing their lands and the beginning of conflicts with the Nez Perce, which eventually culminated in war.

Regarded as one of the greatest of Native American strategists, Chief Joseph was a factor in the last phase of the "Indian Wars" in the far West. Born Hinmaton-Yalaktit about 1840, he became Chief of the "non-treaty" Nez Perce upon his father's death in 1873. Refusing to recognize an agreement in 1863 that ceded their lands and confined them to a reservation in Idaho, the Nez Perce and their leader were drawn into a hopeless resistance. However, once Chief Joseph recognized that his two hundred warriors were no match for the U.S. Army, he planned an escape to Canada with women and children. Although Chief Joseph believed initially that the Native American and the white man could live in harmony on the same land, he later became convinced that that was impossible. In June 1877, the Battle of White Bird Canyon broke out. Although they did not lose the battle, the Nez Perce were forced to flee and were pursued by the U.S. Army for eighteen hundred miles.

Chief Joseph led a brilliant, four-month retreat over more than a thousand miles through Montana and Idaho, eluding first one army and then another. When the Nez Perce reached Montana, Chief Joseph decided that he and this people had had enough. He and his chiefs surrendered, and the Nez Perce prisoners were eventually sent to the Indian Territory in Oklahoma.

Although he is generally recognized for his brilliant generalship in leading his people on an eighteen-hundred-mile trek against U.S. forces, Chief Joseph led a twenty-six-year trek to get better treatment for his people. He was considered by many to be a better leader than a warrior. In 1884, officials permitted Chief Joseph and his remaining band to live on the Colville Reservation in Washington. There, the Nez Perce leader spent his remaining years urging the young to pursue education and speaking out against gambling and alcohol abuse.

Often called the Indian Napoleon, Chief Joseph was said to have an obvious appeal as a public speaker. As an advocate for equal rights, Chief Joseph often made speeches for the freedom of his people. Although he is recognized as a symbol of tragedy suffered by nineteenth-century Native Americans, he is still an inspiration to his people. Chief Joseph died on September 21, 1904.

Fred Lindsay

Chief Joseph (c. 1840–1904), Nez Perce, is probably most famous for his leadership during the flight of the Nez Perce from the United States Army in 1877. (Library of Congress)

See also Indian Removal; Indian Removal and Land Cessions, 1830–1849; Indian Treaty Making: A Native View; Lewis, Meriwether; Property: Land and Natural Resources.

References and Further Reading

Beal, Merrill D. 1971. *"I Will Fight No More Forever": Chief Joseph and the Nez Perce War.* New York: Ballantine Books.

Howard, Helen Addison. *Saga of Chief Joseph.* 1978. Lincoln and London: University of Nebraska Press. Orig. pub. 1941 by Caxton Printers.

McWhorter, Lucullus. 1952. *Hear Me My Chiefs: Nez Perce History and Legend.* Caldwell, ID: Caxton Press.

Kicking Bird

(1835–1875)

Best known as head of the peace faction during the Kiowa Wars of the 1870s, Kicking Bird (Kiowa) was the grandson of a Crow captive who had been adopted into the Kiowa Nation. The Kiowas called him Watohkonk, meaning "Black Eagle," as well as Tene-Angpote, "Eagle Striking with Talons" or simply Kicking Bird. Kicking Bird's one wife was called Guadalupe. At the time of his death, Kicking Bird was a staunch proponent of education and had persuaded Thomas C. Battey, the Kiowa Indian agent, to build a school for Kiowa children.

Kicking Bird became a noted warrior as a young man. Growing older, he began to accept the counsel of Little Mountain (a principal chief of the Kiowas), who asserted that a peaceful approach to relations with the whites was better than military actions. In 1865, Kicking Bird signed the Little Arkansas Treaty, which established a Kiowa reservation that was further described in the Treaty of Medicine Lodge in 1867.

With the demise of Little Mountain in 1866, Kicking Bird became the Kiowas' major leader of the peace party, with Satanta representing the war faction. To resolve this split in 1866, the Kiowas turned to Lone Wolf as the compromise choice for principal chief. However, Lone Wolf was unable to unite the opposing forces in his nation. During 1870, at a sun dance on the North Fork of the Red River, Kicking Bird was called a coward. To disprove such allegations, he commanded a war party of about a hundred men against a detachment of U.S. troops in Texas. During the resulting battle, Kicking Bird proved his valor by personally charging into a unit of about fifty soldiers, slaying one of them with his lance.

Kicking Bird still could not assuage his peoples' resentment regarding reservation conditions. Brian C. Hosmer wrote in a biography of him that, by late 1873, the war faction was raiding in Texas and Mexico. During these raids, two young warriors were killed; one was the nephew and the other the son of paramount chief Lone Wolf. Motivated by revenge and angered by the continued slaughter of the buffalo, Kiowa warriors attacked immigrants on the frontier. Kicking Bird kept his followers on the reservation, but some Kiowas, including Bird Bow, White Shield, White Horse, Howling Wolf, and perhaps Satanta and Lone Wolf, joined with Quanah Parker's Quahadi Comanches in the unsuccessful attack on Adobe Walls on June 27, 1874 (Hosmer 2004).

Hosmer continued, describing the end of Satanta's career as a war chief in late 1874 and Lone Wolf's surrender early in 1975. Kicking Bird thus remained the only notable Kiowa leader.

In 1875, to influence the Kiowas, the army gave Kicking Bird the title of principal chief. Hosmer wrote that, as chief and principal intermediary between the tribe and federal authorities, Kicking Bird was placed in charge of the hostile Indians captured during the uprising of 1874 and 1875. This position allowed Kicking Bird to protect some of his followers from danger, but it also placed him under the influence of the Army (Hosmer 2004).

Kicking Bird's cooperation with the army was seen as treason by some of the Kiowas. When officers from Fort Sill gave Kicking Bird a horse, Kicking Bird's reputation as a collaborator was further reinforced. Following Kicking Bird's sudden death on May 4, 1875, at Cache Creek (in Indian Territory), it was widely believed that a cup of coffee he had recently consumed had been poisoned (Hosmer 2004). Several other Kiowas asserted that Kicking Bird had been killed by witchcraft. According to Hosmer, Kiowa lore alleges that Mamanti used his medicinal powers to kill his long-time adversary. Mamanti himself died shortly after hearing of Kicking Bird's death.

Kicking Bird was buried as a Christian at Fort Sill, Kansas, even though he had never been converted. His grave was marked by a simple wooden cross. After the cross decayed, the location of Kicking Bird's remains was forgotten (Hosmer 2004).

Bruce E. Johansen

See also Lone Wolf (Guipähgo); Parker, Quanah; Satanta; Treaty with the Cheyenne and Arapaho–October 28, 1867.

References and Further Reading
Hosmer, Brian C. 2004. "Kicking Bird."Red River Authority of Texas. Accessed January 17, 2007, at: http://www.rra.dst.tx.us/c_t/history /archer/people/KICKING%20BIRD.cfm.
Johansen, Bruce E., and Donald A. Grinde, Jr. 1997. *Encyclopedia of Native American Biography*. New York: Henry Holt.
Mayhall, Mildred. 1971. *The Kiowas*. 2nd ed. Norman: University of Oklahoma Press.
Nye, Wilbur Sturtevant. 1969. *Carbine and Lance: The Story of Old Fort Sill*. 3rd ed. Norman: University of Oklahoma Press.

A major general in the Continental Army, Henry Knox (1750–1806) of Massachusetts helped to establish American artillery as a capable combat arm and later served as secretary of war, at which time he oversaw Indian Affairs for the new government. (National Archives)

Knox, Henry

(1750–1806)

Henry Knox served as secretary of war under the Articles of Confederation and later as first secretary of war under the federal government. In both of these offices, Knox played a role in government handling of Indian issues. He negotiated with Joseph Brant of the Six Nations to settle border disputes regarding the Six Nations territory that remained after the Treaty of Paris. In these talks, Knox assured Brant that the United States wanted nothing more than what was due them under the terms of the treaty. Furthermore, Knox took part in negotiations with the Creek and Cherokee Indians to the south. He was instrumental in organizing the visit of Alexander McGillivray and twenty-nine other chiefs of the Creek Nation to New York City for negotiations, which were concluded successfully.

Henry Knox was very active in settling the frontier conflict with the Wabash and Miami tribes in the Northwest Territory as well. As secretary of war, he helped plan several expeditions against the Indians in the Northwest Territory. One of these was the expedition under General Arthur St. Clair, which failed. The most successful expedition Knox directed was the one headed by General Anthony Wayne. This foray culminated in the Battle of Fallen Timbers, which ended the effective resistance of the Wabash and Miami in the Northwest Territory.

Knox's outlook toward Native Americans was one in which he saw civilization as the key to gener-ating peace on the frontiers of the Republic. By civilization, Knox meant teaching the Indians how to farm and thus bringing them closer to the white culture of the time. Although he believed that promoting assimilation should be voluntary rather than forced, he could take a hard line when necessary. Again, while secretary of war, Knox further advised George Washington to create a series of posts on the borders of Indian Territory that were to remain outside the jurisdiction of the states in order to protect the frontier from incursions by white settlers, as such incursions often resulted in conflicts erupting on the frontier. He further advised Washington not to go to war with the Creeks to the south.

Among his other activities, Knox was a general in the Continental Army and chief of artillery. In fact, he was the only general of the artillery in the history of the U.S. Army.

Early in the War of Independence, Knox greatly enhanced the siege lines at Boston by bringing artillery from Ticonderoga during the winter, which was considered a major feat by contemporaries. Throughout the remainder of the war, he did much to organize and improve the artillery of the army. At the same time, he had the idea that later became the United States Military Academy at West Point. He even put this idea into practice on a limited scale early in 1779, creating a school for the instruction of the officers under his command at Pluckemin, New Jersey. Knox also took part in almost every major action of the war in the North, often personally directing the fire of the guns.

As the war came to a close, Knox was one of the principal founders of the Society of the Cincinnati, an organization designed to function as a fraternity and mutual aid society for the veteran officers of the Continental Army.

Related to his work as secretary of war under Washington, Knox did much. He suggested the organization of the army on the legionary model, which consisted of a combined force of infantry, artillery, and cavalry. This was the model utilized by the army as its standard organizational structure during the early years of the Republic.

Although Knox was very successful both as a military leader and in government, his private dealings were not as profitable. Thus, he resigned his post as secretary of war in 1791 to attend to these private matters.

James McIntyre

See also Battle of Fallen Timbers, 1794; Brant, Joseph; McGillivray, Alexander; St. Clair, Arthur; Wayne, Anthony.

References and Further Reading

Brooks, Noah. 1974. *Henry Knox, A Soldier of the Revolution, Major General in the American Continental Army, Washington's Chief of Artillery, First Secretary of War under the Constitution, Founder of the Society of the Cincinnati 1750–1806.* New York: Da Capo Press.
Callahan, North. 1958. *Henry Knox, George Washington's General.* New York: Rinehart.
Wright, Robert K., Jr. 1986. *The Continental Army.* Washington, DC: Center of Military History, United States Army.

LaDuke, Winona
(1959–)

Having served as Ralph Nader's running mate as the Green Party's vice presidential candidate in 1996 and 2000, Winona LaDuke is arguably North America's most recognizable American Indian activist. LaDuke earned the Green Party nomination by her unstinting support of environmental issues over many years, most often by working with tribes to regain environmental access often guaranteed to tribes by treaty, and to restore a natural balance to reservations that have often been subjected to widespread environmental degradation and resource exploitation.

Born in 1959 in Los Angeles, LaDuke grew up as an "urban Indian." Her father, Vincent LaDuke, was an activist for Native causes and met Betty Bernstein while hitchhiking to Washington, D.C., on one of his publicity campaigns ("Have Blanket, Will Travel"). They married in 1958, and Winona was born the following year. When she was five, her parents divorced, and Winona grew up in Ashland, Oregon, a logging town. In high school, she became an award-winning debater (she placed third in a state competition).

Winona LaDuke is an enrolled member of the White Earth band of Mississippi Chippewa, the homeland of her father. The White Earth Reservation, created by the government in 1867, was originally drawn to contain thirty-six square miles, an entire township. She moved to the reservation after she graduated from Harvard University in 1982 to take a job as principal of the reserve's school. Following in the footsteps of her father, LaDuke became an activist while at Harvard, addressing the United Nations on American Indian treaty issues at the age of eighteen.

The White Earth Reservation to which Winona LaDuke moved was greatly reduced from its original size; by 1982, the tribe had lost control of more than 95 percent of its reserve and controlled less than thirty-five thousand acres. While principal, LaDuke became involved in the reservation controversy surrounding the White Earth Land Settlement Act (WELSA). WELSA was designed to compensate the Anishnaabeg (Ojibway) for the loss of the bulk of the reserve. Although admitting that much of the White Earth Reservation land was lost through fraudulent transactions—mostly to the benefit of logging interests—the legislators who crafted the settlement act were willing to "compensate" the tribe for the loss of its land but made no provisions for the return of any

A leading Native American activist, environmentalist, and author, Winona LaDuke (1959–) works to defend the social, political, economic, and environmental rights of Native Americans. She ran for vice president in 2000 on the Green Party ticket with Ralph Nader. (AP/Wide World Photos)

lands. The tribe was split between those who wanted to accept the $17 million promised by the settlement and those who argued that the money should be rejected and that the tribe should continue its fight to regain control of the state and county lands within the reservation boundaries. LaDuke, although decidedly behind those who wished to regain as much of the lost land as possible, finally came to argue that the settlement should be accepted, the money invested, and the interest used to buy back reservation land from willing sellers.

LaDuke's nonprofit organization, the White Earth Land Recovery Project (WELRP), grew out of this struggle and was bolstered by the receipt of a $20,000 human rights award from Reebok in 1989. Since then, the WELRP has purchased more than fifteen hundred acres—a minute portion of what has been lost, but a significant and symbolic accomplishment nonetheless. LaDuke serves as founding direc-

tor of the White Earth Land Recovery Project, splitting her time between that organization and the Honor the Earth Fund. Winona LaDuke also serves as the program director of this environmental and cultural organization. Honor the Earth works to assist Native organizations and tribes as they work on various environmental issues. On the White Earth Reservation, Honor the Earth helps tribal members grow, harvest, and sell traditional Anishnaabeg foods such as wild rice, maple sugar products, and wild berry jams, as well as organic coffee, books, videos, quilts, and other craft products made by tribal members.

In 1994, Winona LaDuke was named by *Time* magazine one of America's fifty most promising leaders under forty, and in 1997 *MS* magazine named her woman of the year. Among her many other honors, she was awarded the Thomas Merton Award in 1996, the Ann Bancroft Award for

Women's Leadership, and the Global Green Individual Environmental Leadership Award in 1998. She is a former board member of Greenpeace USA and serves as co-chair of the Indigenous Women's Network, an international organization that promotes self-determination for indigenous women in the Americas and the Pacific Basin.

Phil Bellfy

See also American Indian Movement (AIM); Mankiller, Wilma Pearl.

References and Further Reading

LaDuke, Winona. 1997. *Last Standing Woman.* Stillwater, MN : Voyageur Press.
La Duke, Winona. 2002. *The Winona LaDuke Reader: A Collection of Essential Writings.* With foreword by Ralph Nader. Stillwater, MN: Voyageur Press.
Ritter, Peter. "The Party Crasher." *City Pages* (Minneapolis/St. Paul, MN), October 11, 2000.

Lea, Luke

(1810–1898)

Luke Lea helped create the federal reservation system. First appointed Indian agent in 1849, Lea served as commissioner of Indian affairs from July 1, 1850, until March 24, 1853. During his tenure, he played a central role in forging important federal Indian policy.

Lea's family moved from North Carolina to east Tennessee in 1790. Lea's involvement in Indian affairs may stem from his father Luke Lea's service in both the Creek and Seminole wars and his close affiliation with Andrew Jackson.

The elder Luke Lea served in some minor local offices before his election to the 23rd Congress under President Andrew Jackson on the Jacksonian, or Democratic, ticket. Lea gradually came to oppose Jackson, supporting congressional supremacy over the authority of the executive branch. In 1836, Lea supported the Whig Party presidential candidate, Hugh Lawson White. White, author of Jackson's Removal Act of 1830, was opposed to *forced* removal, believing that the Indian nations would voluntarily relocate.

In 1849, Congress, under the administration of Whig president Zachary Taylor, shifted the Office of Indian Affairs—created in 1824 and known from 1947 until the present as the Bureau of Indian Affairs—from the War Department to the newly created Department of the Interior. This structural change ushered in a new federal Indian policy. Early

in August 1849, Lea took up his post as agent at Fort Leavenworth, Kansas. On July 1, 1850, Taylor appointed Lea commissioner of Indian affairs, a position reconfirmed by Taylor's successor, Millard Fillmore. Luke Lea replaced Orlando Brown as the commissioner in the new Office of Indian Affairs. Without credit to Lea's Whig ties, some scholars have portrayed him as the personification of Manifest Destiny and anti-Indian sentiment, but documentation suggests he attempted to protect tribal rights. Under the direction of Lea and his successor, George Manypenny, the Indian Office espoused the "civilization" of Indians through the reservation system. By negotiating treaties of peace and friendship with tribes for their settlement onto special reservations of land, the Indian Office hoped to protect tribes from non-Indian encroachment, exploitation, and conflict and to offer Indians viable alternatives to their traditional lifestyles.

Lea played a significant role in the negotiations of several treaties, including the Treaty of Fort Laramie on September 17, 1851. Lea's name appears as commissioner of Indian affairs on the July 1851 (ratified) treaty with the "See-see-toan" (Sisseton) and "Wah-pay-toan" (Wahpeton) bands of the Dakota or Eastern Sioux Indians, and the August 1851 (ratified) treaty with the Mdewakanton and Wahpekuta bands of the Dakota or Eastern Sioux Indians. These Dakota tribes agreed to sell all the lands they claimed in eastern South Dakota, northern Iowa, and western Minnesota. Lea's contributions to the Fort Laramie treaty influenced federal Indian policy throughout the 1850s and 1860s. Congress ratified the Fort Laramie treaty, with amendments, on May 24, 1852, subject to approval of "the chiefs, headmen, and braves" of the "the Sioux or Dahcotahs, Cheyennes, Arrapahoes, Crows, Assinaboines, Gros Ventre, Mandans, and Arrickaras."

Federal agents procured approval of the treaty's terms from all the tribes by September 1854, when the Crow Nation finally consented. In May 1851, just before the actual negotiations, Lea emphasized to D. D. Mitchell, superintendent of Indian affairs at the Upper St. Louis Agency, that, in entering into the treaty, it was important for the tribes to understand that they lived within fixed boundaries. Lea also advised that each tribe agree not to cross into the reserved land of another tribe without permission from it. Finally, Lea stated that common tribal areas ought to be shared spaces, and the tribes needed to understand that they would have the same rights to use them. Once negotiations were under way, Lea recommended "deportation and absorption" of all the Plains Nations and that the federal government concentrate the Sioux, in particular, on specific "reservations." By purposefully reducing significantly the territory available for hunting, Lea hoped to force the Sioux and others to "change their mode of life" and adopt farming or they would "cease to exist at all."

C. S. Everett

See also Bureau of Indian Affairs (BIA), Indian Removal; Indian Removal Act, 1830; Treaty of Fort Laramie with the Sioux, Etc.–September 17, 1851.

References and Further Reading

Kappler, Charles J., ed. 1904. *Indian Affairs: Laws and Treaties*, vol. 2, *Treaties*. Washington, DC: Government Printing Office.

Kappler, Charles J., ed. 1929. *Indian Affairs: Laws and Treaties*, vol. 4, *Laws*. Washington, DC: Government Printing Office.

Kvasnicka, Robert M., and Herman J. Viola, eds. 1979. *The Commissioners of Indian Affairs, 1824–1977*. Lincoln: University of Nebraska Press.

LeFlore, Greenwood
(1800–1860)

Greenwood LeFlore, a prominent Choctaw chief, signed the Treaty of Dancing Rabbit Creek, which allowed the United States to force the Choctaw people from their homelands in Mississippi. He was one of the wealthiest Native Americans of the nineteenth century; he owned a huge plantation with many slaves and served in the Mississippi State Senate.

LeFlore was the son of Louis LeFleur, a French trader, who married a woman of mixed English and Choctaw heritage named Rebecca Cravat. Cravat was the daughter of an Englishman who entered the Choctaw Nation as a trader after the Revolutionary War. LeFlore was born about 1800 in the Choctaw Nation and was reared among the Choctaws. He became one of the three district chiefs of the Choctaw Nation. In 1830, LeFlore betrayed the Choctaw people by making a secret deal with the United States to support Choctaw dispossession from their ancient homelands in Mississippi and their permanent exile to what was known as the

Malmaison, the antebellum plantation home of Choctaw leader Greenwood Leflore, was built in 1854. (Library of Congress)

Great American Desert—present-day Oklahoma. The U.S. government gave LeFlore money, land, and special treatment so that he would try to take over the Choctaw National government by declaring himself the sole chief. He tried to persuade his fellow Choctaws to sign a removal treaty with the United States. He told his followers that he would lead them to the new land and that it would provide a much better life, away from white intruders, who were causing many problems for the Choctaws in Mississippi. LeFlore never intended to move to the new lands in the West, but his talk caused many people in his district to agree to go. The U.S. government sent negotiators to obtain a treaty with the Choctaws in the fall of 1830. They were instructed by President Andrew Jackson to use every means possible to secure a removal treaty. White Americans, who were prevented from moving onto Choctaw lands by earlier treaties signed by the U.S. government with the Choctaws, wanted the rich Choctaw lands for cotton farms and plantations. The price of cotton on the world market continued to rise steeply, and cotton became a hugely profitable crop.

At the treaty grounds, LeFlore and the U.S. government tricked the majority of the Choctaw Nation into leaving the treaty grounds, telling them that the negotiations were over and that no treaty would be signed because they were almost unanimously opposed to removal. After all the opposition had left, LeFlore and his followers signed the Treaty of Dancing Rabbit Creek, ceding the entire remaining acreage of the Choctaw Nation in Mississippi to the United States. The U.S. negotiators returned to Washington and claimed that the treaty was supported by a large majority of the Choctaws and that the treaty was legally obtained. The U.S. Senate ratified the treaty despite the repeated, vociferous protests of the Choctaws and their white friends. After ratification of the Treaty of Dancing Rabbit Creek, the United States offered the former Choctaw homelands for sale. LeFlore did not emigrate but instead remained in Mississippi and used his ill-gotten gains to further his personal interests as a wealthy, slave-owning planter. He later served as a Mississippi state legislator. He became immensely wealthy, lived a lavish lifestyle, dressed in the latest fashions, and drove beautifully matched horses hitched to a fancy coach driven by slaves dressed in livery. His magnificent antebellum plantation home, Malmaison, was built near Teoc, Mississippi, in 1854 on his fifteen-thousand-acre estate. LeFlore owned more than four hundred slaves. The home burned to the ground in 1942. LeFlore gained his wealth from the Choctaw, from bribes taken from the U.S. government, and, after removal, from speculation in the land that had once been the homelands of the Choctaw Nation.

Donna L. Akers

See also Dancing Rabbit Creek, Mississippi; Indian Removal; Indian Removal Act, 1830; Treaty with the Choctaw–September 27, 1830.

References and Further Reading

Baird, W. David. 1973. *The Choctaw People.* Phoenix, AZ: Indian Tribal Series.

Cushman, H. B. 1999. *History of the Choctaw, Chickasaw, and Natchez Indians.* Norman: University of Oklahoma Press.

Debo, Angie. 1967. *The Rise and Fall of the Choctaw Republic.* Norman: University of Oklahoma Press.

Kidwell, Clara Sue. 1995. *Choctaws and Missionaries in Mississippi, 1818–1918.* Norman: University of Oklahoma Press.

McKee, Jesse O., and Jon A. Schlenker. 1980. *The Choctaws: Cultural Evolution of a Native American Tribe.* Jackson: University Press of Mississippi.

Leupp, Francis Ellington
(1849–1918)

Francis Ellington Leupp was a journalist, a "friend of the Indians," and a commissioner of Indian affairs from 1905 to 1909 who had strong opinions about Indian treaties. He believed in assimilation and advocated breaking down the barriers to Indian acceptance into white society. He considered the treaties to be one of these barriers.

Leupp was Washington's agent of the Indian Rights Association (IRA) from 1895 through 1898 as a Board of Indian Commissioners member from 1896–1897. As commissioner, at times he worked within the treaty system. He believed that some of the treaty rights claims that tribes made were valid. One such case he cited was that of the Klamath Indians, which Congress had resolved efficiently; however, Leupp felt that, whether valid or not, the claims usually were not handled quickly and that unresolved claims were an obstacle to assimilation. To rectify this, in 1910 he suggested the creation of a special court to hear and decide the merits of outstanding grievances.

In general, though, Leupp believed that allegations of violations stemmed from misunderstandings rather than cruelty by the federal government.

Francis E. Leupp was the twentieth commissioner of Indian Affairs, a member of the Indian Rights Association, and the U.S. Board of Indian Commissioners. Leupp was a noted Indian reform advocate who wrote vociferously on the subject. (Indian Craftsman, *April 1909*)

In his book *In Red Man's Land: A Study of the American Indian*, published in 1914, Leupp explained that the treaty negotiations had been complicated by unscrupulous interpreters, by problems of translation between English and the "elemental languages of the Indians," by U.S. negotiators' lack of familiarity with the land, and by the Indians' lack of understanding of the U.S. treaty process (Leupp 1914, 40).

Although Leupp did some work to bring fairness to tribes under the treaty system, more often he supported legislation and programs designed to make the treaties obsolete. Leupp supported the General Allotment Act (Dawes Act) of 1887. He also was in favor of the Curtis Act of 1898, which allotted the Five Civilized Tribes (the Cherokee, Choctaw, Chickasaw, Creek, and Seminole tribes) and replaced tribal governments in Indian Territory with a regular territorial government. Other members of the IRA opposed the Curtis Act because, as the Five Civilized Tribes strongly opposed this new government, the law was a violation of treaty guarantees of some level of autonomy. Leupp later explained that he felt that the "experiment" of self-rule in Indian Territory had failed because of evidence of fraud and chaos.

Furthermore, he believed in treating Indians as individuals, not as members of a tribe. He wrote that a communal system was un-American, had a "stupefying effect" on Indians, and prevented them from becoming enterprising (Leupp 1910, 46–47, 182). While an IRA agent in Washington, he did nothing to try to change the Curtis Act, even though the IRA executive committee passed a resolution instructing him to soften the bill so that it would not adversely affect the tribes.

As commissioner, Leupp continued his work to deemphasize treaty rights and tribal existence. He supported congressional passage of the Burke Act of 1906, which sped up the fee simple process. He also reorganized the Bureau of Indian Affairs by abolishing the regional superintendencies and enhancing the work of teachers and farmers to emphasize service to the individual. To get rid of the "annoying" treaty guarantees of small remunerations (such as a yearly clothing allowance for the Oneida, which at the turn of the century amounted to about 43 cents per person), Leupp obtained permission from Congress to renegotiate these items and capitalize the annuities at a percentage (Leupp 1910, 176–177).

Angela Firkus

See also Allotments; Annuities; Curtis Act, 1898; Dawes Commission; General Allotment Act (Dawes Act), 1887; Indian Rights Association (IRA); Indian Territory.

References and Further Reading

Hagan, William T. 1985. *The Indian Rights Association: The Herbert Welsh Years, 1882–1904.* Tucson: University of Arizona Press.

Leupp, Francis E. 1910. *The Indian and His Problem.* New York: Charles Scribner's Sons; Repr., New York: Arno Press and New York Times, 1971.

Leupp, Francis E. 1914. *In Red Man's Land: A Study of the American Indian.* New York: Fleming H. Revell.

Parman, Donald L. 1979. "Francis Ellington Leupp." In *The Commissioners of Indian Affairs, 1824–1977,* ed. Robert M. Kvasnicka and Herman J. Viola, 221–232. Lincoln: University of Nebraska Press.

Lewis, Meriwether
(1774–1809)

Meriwether Lewis was a soldier, explorer, territorial governor of Upper Louisiana, and ex officio superintendent of Indian affairs. Born on August 18, 1774, he was the eldest son of William Lewis and Lucy Meriwether. Meriwether Lewis grew up on a

serve as his private secretary to help downsize the postwar army.

Jefferson asked Lewis to command an expedition to explore the newly acquired Louisiana Purchase. In addition to the commercial and scientific purposes of the expedition, Lewis was to establish friendly relations with the tribes inhabiting the route from the Mississippi River to the Pacific. He and William Clark met thousands of Indians and were the first U.S. diplomats to visit numerous tribes in the Great Plains region and the Pacific Northwest; the two recorded some of the languages, manners, and customs of the tribes. The British-allied Blackfeet and the Sioux—powerful Missouri middlemen—extended reserved receptions. Others, such as the Nez Perce, Shoshones, and Mandans, offered hospitality in return for trade goods and the promise of more. Lewis and Clark met with Indian leaders, distributed trade goods, delivered speeches, solicited Indian delegations to travel to Washington, and conducted negotiations for peace, friendship, and trade. They announced U.S. sovereignty and left calling cards of empire (medals, flags, certificates). The expedition's only violent act occurred on the return trip, when Lewis and another man killed two Piegan Blackfeet who were stealing their horses and guns.

On March 4, 1807, Jefferson appointed Lewis territorial governor of Upper Louisiana (the Louisiana Purchase north of Louisiana) and ex officio superintendent of Indian affairs. Clark assisted Lewis as principal Indian agent. Post-expedition business and the trial of Aaron Burr prevented Lewis from assuming his post until the following March, however. Lewis tried to govern the territory from the East, which proved impractical and alienated many in St. Louis, especially the territorial secretary, Frederick Bates. Once Lewis arrived in Missouri, things went from bad to worse. Controversies involving Spanish, French, and American land titles, coupled with mining disputes and squatter problems, made dispensing justice difficult.

Lewis did not fare any better in administering Indian affairs. He authorized the construction of Fort Osage on the Missouri and Fort Madison on the Mississippi. He wanted to use trade, not war, as a principal negotiating tool with tribes within his jurisdiction. Clark negotiated a sizable land cession from the Osages in return for trading privileges and protection at the fort in the Osage treaty of 1808. Many Osages who were not present protested the treaty, so Lewis slightly revised it; this was the only

Meriwether Lewis (1774–1809), along with William Clark, led an expedition through the Louisiana Territory and the Oregon Country during 1803–1806 encountering many Native peoples. (Library of Congress)

plantation in Albemarle County, Virginia, near Thomas Jefferson's Monticello and Charlottesville. Lewis joined the Virginia militia at age twenty to help suppress the Whiskey Rebellion. Liking military service, Lewis enlisted as an ensign in the regular army during General Anthony Wayne's Ohio River Indian campaigns and served briefly under Lieutenant William Clark during the summer of 1795. Lewis's military career in the First Infantry progressed rapidly; he received a lieutenant's commission in 1799 and a captain's commission in 1800. President Jefferson, knowing that Lewis had been the army paymaster and therefore knew all the military leaders in the western army, called Lewis to

treaty in the writing of which he actually played a role. Then, he sent the treaty with Osage agent Pierre Chouteau to get Osage approval. To complicate matters, more than six thousand Cherokees settled on Osage lands, and Osage-Cherokee hostilities ensued. Lewis threatened to withhold trade goods from the Osages and to provide the enemies of the Osages with arms and ammunition if the Osages refused to make peace. This kind of talk caused Jefferson and the Department of War to become concerned about Lewis's leadership. Lewis further alienated his superiors by failing to consult with them on implementation of government policies. In addition, the obstacles outside his control prevented him from stopping unlicensed traders, preventing intertribal warfare between the Osages and Cherokees and between the Arikara and Mandan, and failing to return the Mandan Chief Sheheke delegation safely home—all of which contributed to his depression and eventual downfall. Frustrated, Lewis paid the Missouri Fur Company $7,000 to provide an armed escort to protect and transport Sheheke back to the Mandan villages in present-day North Dakota. The government refused to honor additional vouchers connected to this expedition, which destroyed Lewis's credit and reputation.

Lewis embarked for Washington to straighten out his last eighteen months of expenditures and to oversee the publication of the expedition journals. Leaving the Mississippi River at Chickasaw Bluffs (Memphis), he set out along the Natchez Trace in Tennessee, stopping for the evening at Grinder's Stand. On October 11, 1809, he died a violent death that is still shrouded in mystery. Many of his closest friends believed it was suicide, but some anomalies convince others that it was the result of foul play.

Jay H. Buckley

See also Chouteau, Auguste; Clark, William; Jefferson, Thomas; Prairie du Chien, Wisconsin; Treaty with the Wyandot, Etc.–August 3, 1795; Wayne, Anthony.

References and Further Reading

Ambrose, Stephen E. 1996. *Undaunted Courage: Meriwether Lewis, Thomas Jefferson, and the Opening of the American West.* New York: Simon & Schuster.

Bakeless, John. 1947. *Lewis and Clark: Partners in Discovery.* New York: William Morrow.

Dillon, Richard. 1965. *Meriwether Lewis: A Biography.* New York: Coward-McCann.

Ronda, James P. 1984. *Lewis and Clark Among the Indians.* Lincoln: University of Nebraska Press.

Little Crow
(c. 1810–1863)

Little Crow (Cetan Wakan, Santee, or Mdewakanton Sioux), also known as Taoyateduta (His Red Nation), was the leader of Dakota resistance to white invasion during the U.S.-Dakota War of 1862. Born about 1810 in the Bdewakantunwan village of Kapoza (where St. Paul, Minnesota, is today), Taoyateduta came from a line of Dakota chiefs, including the first Little Crow (his great-grandfather), Cetanwakanmani (his grandfather), and Wakinyantanka (his father). Despite the fact that Little Crow was tutored well in Dakota leadership and had earned an impressive war record, when his father was suffering from a fatal accident in 1846, he indicated his support for one of Little Crow's half brothers as his successor when he passed his medals on to him. His family believed Taoyateduta had spent too many years away from Kapoza to effectively assume the chieftainship. Undaunted by this, when the waters

Mdewakanton Santee Sioux Chief Little Crow, who had previously been hospitable and accommodating toward white settlers, led the bloody Minnesota Sioux Uprising in 1862 after many of his people nearly starved in U.S. captivity. The uprising was followed by the largest mass hanging in U.S. history. (Library of Congress)

thawed that spring, Taoyateduta returned to challenge his half brother and in the process was shot by a bullet that traveled through both wrists before passing into his body. Through this act of bravery, he earned the support and sympathy of the villagers; when he recovered from his injuries, his chieftainship was secured.

The mid-nineteenth century was a difficult time to assume Dakota leadership, for the contest over Dakota lands and resources had reached full intensity. From the time the first treaty was signed by Cetanwakanmani in 1805, the pressure to cede Dakota lands and abandon Dakota ways only intensified. A series of land cessions in 1837, 1851, and 1858 severed large chunks for white settlement and eventually confined the Dakota to a narrow strip of reservation land bordering the Minnesota River. Taoyateduta was faced with the difficult challenge of attempting to negotiate justice in the face of repeated treaty violations by the U.S. government, continued white incursions on Dakota land, and constant colonization efforts organized among missionaries, traders, and Indian agents that served to deeply factionalize the Dakotas and undermine Dakota leadership. He consistently sought peaceful solutions to these problems and attempted to maintain good relations with whites in southern Minnesota, tolerating the Christianizing and civilizing efforts and addressing grievances through negotiation. Given the invading settler population, however, peaceful relations were impossible to maintain as long as the Dakotas were committed to maintaining their lands and way of life.

Taoyateduta's peaceful efforts ceased when he agreed to lead the Dakotas in war at the outbreak of the U.S.-Dakota War of 1862. The Dakotas had been pushed beyond their limits in the hot summer of 1862 when they were facing starvation as a consequence of another U.S. treaty violation. When a small group of Dakota warriors killed five white settlers near Acton Township on August 17 and the Dakotas faced the likelihood of a severe backlash, they knew they could not continue to live under those circumstances. The young warriors pleaded with Taoyateduta to lead them in war, and, though he initially refused to engage in what he knew was a futile effort, he reluctantly agreed when they called him a coward. In his famous speech, he finally conceded, "Braves, you are little children—you are fools. You will die like the rabbits when the hungry wolves hunt them in the Hard Moon. Taoyateduta is not a coward: he will die with you!"

On the morning of August 18, the Dakotas began their attack on the Lower Sioux agency, killing most of the whites they encountered and taking others, primarily women and children, as prisoners. These actions threw the Minnesota frontier settlements into a panic, and terrified white settlers fled to the nearby towns and Fort Ridgely. When news of the war spread to St. Paul, Governor Alexander Ramsey commissioned Henry Sibley to lead a regiment of fourteen hundred men on an expedition against the Dakotas. Once the white forces were mobilized, the Dakotas moved to a defensive position, and the war was quelled.

After the final battle was fought at Wood Lake on September 23, 1862, and the release of the 269 white and mixed-blood prisoners was subsequently arranged, Taoyateduta, heartbroken, left his Minnesota homeland. He fled the state, as did thousands of others, to either Dakota Territory or Canada. After spending time farther west attempting to rally indigenous support for continued resistance efforts, Taoyateduta traveled to British Canada to try to build an alliance against the Americans. Without success, in the summer of 1863 he returned to Minnesota with only a small group of Dakotas.

On July 3, Taoyateduta was shot while picking raspberries with his son, Wowinape, by Nathan and Chauncey Lamson, who received bounty payments for their deed. Unfortunately, attacks on him did not end with his death. His body was dragged through the town of Hutchinson, and white boys celebrated the Fourth of July by placing firecrackers in his ears and nose. After he had been scalped, mutilated, and dismembered, his remains were displayed and kept at the Minnesota Historical Society for 108 years before they were finally returned to his family and laid to rest in Flandreau, South Dakota.

From the start of the war to the time of his death, Taoyateduta fought unceasingly for the Dakotas' right to exist in their homeland. He embodies the spirit of indigenous resistance in a struggle that persists today.

Waziyatawin Angela Wilson

See also Northern Plains; Treaty of Fort Laramie with the Sioux, Etc.–September 17, 1851; Treaty with the Sioux–September 29, 1837; Treaty with the Sioux–June 19, 1958.

Reference and Further Reading

Anderson, Gary C. 1986. *Little Crow: Spokesman for the Sioux*. St. Paul: Minnesota Historical Society Press.

Little Turtle
(c. 1752–1812)

Miami leader Little Turtle was responsible for one of the biggest disasters in U.S. Army history. When he realized the futility of continuing to fight, he renounced war and became a loyal ally of the American government.

Little Turtle (Michikinikwa) was born near the Eel River in the vicinity of present-day Fort Wayne, Indiana, around 1752. His father was a chief of the Miamis, but, because his mother was a Mahican, tribal custom dictated that he could not inherit a leadership position. Nonetheless, Little Turtle displayed fine leadership and warrior qualities as a young man, and he was eventually made a Miami chief by the tribal elders. He was pro-British by nature, and in 1780 his warriors attacked and destroyed a French-Illinois expedition under Colonel Augustin de la Balme. After the American Revolution, he became a leading spokesperson for resistance to white encroachment north of the Ohio River and helped to form a loose confederation of Miami, Shawnee, Potawatomi, and Ojibwa Indians. In 1787, Congress guaranteed that the Indians' hunting grounds would be respected. Within a few years, however, a rash of illegal settlements precipitated a fierce border war between the Indians and the frontierspeople. By 1790, when it was apparent the Indians would not accept the squatters, the American government resorted to punitive measures.

The U.S. government initially chose General Josiah Harmar, who had assembled a force of eleven hundred poorly trained Pennsylvania and Kentucky militia, stiffened by three hundred army regulars, to deal with the Indians. Little Turtle by this time was principal war chief of the Miamis, and he ordered his braves to feign retreat, luring the Americans deeper and deeper into the countryside. Harmar met no opposition until he reached Little Turtle's village, where the Indians ambushed and mauled two reconnaissance expeditions in October 1790. Having lost 262 men and accomplished nothing, the white militia withdrew to Kentucky. This victory assured Little Turtle's subsequent leadership over the Maumee Valley tribes, and they united in time to face an even greater onslaught.

In September 1791, the government dispatched General Arthur St. Clair with a force of twenty-three hundred raw regulars and three hundred Kentucky militia against the Indians. Little Turtle commanded a force of similar size, assisted by the Shawnees Blue

Little Turtle, chief of the Miami tribe, led militant opposition to the influx of settlers in the Ohio Country in a conflict known as Little Turtle's War. However, after his defeat at the Battle of Fallen Timbers in 1794, Little Turtle became an ally of the United States. (North Wind Picture Archives)

Jacket and Tecumseh. Desertion soon reduced St. Clair's force to fifteen hundred men, and, encouraged by this weakness, Little Turtle abandoned his usual defensive tactics in favor of a direct assault. This tactic was something that Native Americans had never tried before. On the morning of November 4, 1791, his warriors stormed the American encampment while the soldiers were breakfasting and routed them. St. Clair, gravely ill, roused himself from bed and attempted to rally the survivors before the entire army was annihilated. A bayonet charge enabled five hundred men to escape destruction but at tremendous cost, with more than six hundred soldiers killed and three hundred wounded, and Little Turtle's losses appear to have been negligible. In

November 1792 he also defeated a party of Kentuckians led by John Adair. Fearing that the dreaded "long knives" would attack again, however, Little Turtle spent the next two years shoring up tribal solidarity and soliciting help from the British.

As feared, the Americans appeared once more, this time with General Anthony Wayne at their head. Wayne spent almost two years training and equipping his force of two thousand men and advanced carefully, building forts along the way. Little Turtle respected his professional and energetic preparations, calling him "the chief who never sleeps." The Indians harassed his line of supply with impunity, but when they rashly attacked Fort Recovery in July 1794 and were rebuffed, many grew sullen and returned home. Little Turtle took stock of "Mad Anthony" and counseled other chiefs to seek peace. "We have never been able to surprise him," he warned. "Think well of it. Something whispers to me, listen to peace." Little Turtle was ridiculed and lost command of the Indians to Blue Jacket. On August 20, 1794, Wayne crushed the confederation at the Battle of Fallen Timbers, in which Little Turtle commanded a few Miamis and played a small role. The following year, Little Turtle was a signatory to the Treaty of Greenville, whereby the Indians gave up most of the land that constitutes present-day Ohio. Containing his bitterness, he declared, "I am the last to sign the treaty; I will be the last to break it."

From that time on, Little Turtle remained a friend of the United States, and in 1797 he traveled to Washington, D.C., to meet with President George Washington and Tadeusz Kosciuszko, who presented him with a brace of pistols. Little Turtle was sincere in his quest for peace and made additional land concessions with Governor William Henry Harrison, who built a house for him on the Eel River. He also took the white scout William Wells as his son-in-law and kept the Miamis out of Tecumseh's tribal coalition. Little Turtle succumbed to illness at Fort Wayne on July 14, 1812, and received a military burial.

Steven L. Danver

See also Battle of Fallen Timbers; Harrison, William Henry; St. Clair, Arthur; Tecumseh; Treaty with the Wyandot, Etc.–August 3, 1795; Wayne, Anthony; Wells, William.
References and Further Reading
Carter, Harvey L. 1987. *The Life and Times of Little Turtle: First Sagamore of the Wabash*. Urbana and Chicago: University of Illinois Press.

Edel, Wilbur. 1997. *Kekionga! The Worst Defeat in the History of the United States Army*. Westport, CT: Praeger.

Sword, Wiley. 1985. *President Washington's Indian War: The Struggle for the Old Northwest, 1790–1795*. Norman and London: University of Oklahoma Press.

Lone Wolf (Guipähgo)
(1820–1879)

Lone Wolf, whose Kiowa name was Guipähgo, became a prominent Native leader during the U.S. military invasion and occupation of Kiowa country.

After the death of Dohäsan in 1868, Lone Wolf shared leadership with Ténéangopte, or Kicking Bird, who advocated peace with the U.S. A member of the *on-de* ("first rank") aristocratic caste and the Tsetanma warrior society, Lone Wolf vacillated between strategies of accommodation and resistance. Despite his reputation as a militant, he traveled to Washington, D.C., as early as 1863 in a failed diplomatic effort to obtain a favorable peace policy. Along with other chiefs, he signed the Little Arkansas treaty on Octo-

Lone Wolf (1820–1879), a Kiowa chief, led his people in resistance to the allotment of their reservation during the 1860s. (National Archives)

ber 18, 1865. He attended the Medicine Lodge Council in Medicine Lodge, Kansas, but refused to sign the treaties of October 21, 1867. When hostilities erupted in Indian Territory during 1868, Lone Wolf and other militants agreed to remain on the Kiowa-Comanche reservation near Fort Sill. However, he was neither willing nor able to stop the raiding of war parties. On April 30, 1872, Lone Wolf and his son Tauankia, or Sitting in the Saddle, participated in a raid on a supply caravan at Howard's Wells on the San Antonio-El Paso Road. They clashed with a patrol of the Ninth Cavalry from Fort Concho but returned to the reservation safely.

During the fall of 1872, Lone Wolf was chosen by his tribe as a delegate to accompany special commissioner Henry Alford to Washington, D.C., for a peace conference. After the parley, Lone Wolf used his influence to lobby the government for the release of Satanta, or White Bear, and Addoetta, or Big Tree, from prison. The peaceful feelings disappeared, however, when Tauankia and his cousin, Guitan, were killed by soldiers of the Fourth Cavalry near Kickapoo Springs, Texas, on December 10, 1873. Haunted by his son's death, Lone Wolf organized a war party in May 1874 to recover the bodies for reburial in Kiowa country. After successfully evading army patrols, he buried his son and nephew on a rocky hill. The hill and the nearby stream became known as Lone Wolf Mountain and Lone Wolf Creek.

Still mourning his son and stirred by Mamanti, a holy man whose Kiowa name meant Walks in the Sky, Lone Wolf waged war against the U.S. forces near the Red River. Along with Comanche and Cheyenne parties, he participated in a concerted strike on Adobe Walls on June 27, 1874. On July 12, he led a party against Texas Rangers during the Lost Valley fight. In this particular clash, a warrior named Mamadayte killed ranger David Bailey. The warrior offered the corpse to Lone Wolf, who, after cutting off the ranger's head with a butcher knife, declared his son avenged. Thereafter, he adopted Mamadayte as his new son and gave him the name Guopahko, Lone Wolf the Younger. On September 9, 1874, Lone Wolf's party attempted an unsuccessful raid against Captain Wyllys Lyman's wagon train. To avoid capture, the party hid in Palo Duro Canyon in the Texas panhandle until Colonel Ranald S. Mackenzie's Fourth Cavalry located them and attacked. Abandoning his spirited resistance, Lone Wolf surrendered to authorities at Fort Sill on February 18, 1875, and was placed in irons inside the guardhouse.

Among the Kiowa "ringleaders" taken by Lieutenant Richard Henry Pratt to a prison at Fort Marion, Florida, Lone Wolf remained incarcerated for three years before returning to the reservation in 1878. He died near Fort Sill in the summer of 1879 and was buried on the north slope of Mount Scott, the highest point among the Wichita Mountains in what is now the state of Oklahoma.

Brad D. Lookingbill

See also Indian Territory; Pratt, Richard Henry; Satanta; Sitting Bear (Setangya or Satank); Treaty with the Cheyenne and Arapaho–October 28, 1867; Treaty with the Kiowa and Comanche–October 21, 1867.

References and Further Reading

Haley, James L. 1998. *The Buffalo War: The History of the Red River Indian Uprising of 1874.* Austin, TX: State House Press.

Hoig, Stan. 2000. *The Kiowas and the Legend of Kicking Bird.* Boulder: University Press of Colorado.

Mayhall, Mildred P. 1962. *The Kiowas.* Norman: University of Oklahoma Press.

Mankiller, Wilma Pearl
(1945–)

Wilma Pearl Mankiller became the first female to lead a major Indian nation in the United States when she was elected principal chief of the Cherokee Nation, the second-largest American Indian group in the United States. She was born in rural Rocky Mountain, Oklahoma, on November 18, 1945. The daughter of a Cherokee father and a Dutch-Irish mother, and one of eleven children, she spent her early years close to her people. However, at the age of eleven she and her family relocated to San Francisco as a part of the relocation program of the Bureau of Indian Affairs.

Once in California, Mankiller finished her education despite a difficult adjustment to Hunter's Point, the impoverished, predominantly African American neighborhood in which the Mankillers lived. However, regardless of her personal situation, she managed to create opportunities to work for the good of Indian people wherever she lived. When the issue of American Indian civil rights began to gain the spotlight in the late 1960s, Mankiller was living in the right place to play a vital role in the nascent Red Power movement. After marrying an Ecuadorian named Hugo Olaya at the age of seventeen and having two children, she became director of the

The first woman to become chief of the Cherokee Nation, Wilma P. Mankiller (1945–) is perhaps the best-known modern female tribal leader in the United States. (University of Utah Women's Week Celebration [http://www.diversity.utah.edu])

American Indian Youth Center in East Oakland, California. Although caring for her two children kept her from direct participation when American Indian activists took over the former federal prison on Alcatraz Island in 1969, Mankiller raised money to support the protestors and visited them on Alcatraz.

Although she went through a divorce from Olaya in 1977, Mankiller completed her education that same year, earning her Bachelor of Arts degree from Union College. Mankiller then returned to her Cherokee homeland in Oklahoma, continuing her career of advocacy by addressing two of the most relevant issues to the reservation community: enough water and sufficient housing. At the same time, she did graduate work, earning her Master's degree in community planning from the University of Arkansas in 1979. She volunteered for the Cherokee Nation as an economic stimulus coordinator and became the tribe's program development specialist

in 1979. However, an automobile accident that year left her seriously injured and hospitalized for a lengthy period. Her health problems were compounded when she was diagnosed with systemic myasthenia gravis, a glandular autoimmune disorder, which required surgery and extended her period of recuperation. Despite her health problems, she returned to political life, founding and directing the Cherokee Community Development Department in 1981.

Mankiller's activities in the areas of advocating for treaty rights and better services got her noticed, and her entry into the political structure of the Cherokee Nation came in 1983, when principal chief Ross O. Swimmer asked her to be his running mate. Despite hate mail and death threats because of her gender, she became the first woman elected to the position of deputy principal chief. After Swimmer resigned to become head of the Bureau of Indian Affairs in December 1985, Mankiller was appointed to serve the two years remaining in his term. Once in charge of the more than one-hundred-thousand-member Cherokee Nation, she continued to concentrate on the most vital issues facing her people: unemployment, education, health care, and economic development. Her successes made her popular with her constituents, and she became the first woman elected to lead the Cherokee Nation in 1987, when she validated her appointment by winning the position of principal chief, capturing more than 80 percent of the vote. Despite continued health problems, which resulted in the need for a kidney transplant, she was reelected in 1991 and served as the leader of the Cherokee Nation until the end of her second term in 1995, when she chose not to run for reelection because of persistent health concerns.

Although Mankiller stepped down from her role as head of the Cherokee Nation, she has never stepped down from the political activism that has characterized her life. She continues to live in the capital of the Cherokee Nation, Tahlequah, Oklahoma, with her Cherokee second husband, Charlie Soap. She has received numerous honors, including a special White House ceremony upon the end of her term as principal chief, a Humanitarian Award from the Ford Foundation, induction into the National Women's Hall of Fame in 1993, and the nation's highest civilian honor, the Presidential Medal of Freedom, in 1998. In addition, she has published two books: her best-selling autobiography in 1993, *Mankiller: A Chief and Her People* (with Michael

Wallis), and *Every Day is a Good Day: Reflections of Contemporary Indigenous Women*, which was published in 2004.

Steven L. Danver

See also New Echota, Georgia; Ross, John; Treaty with the Cherokee–December 29, 1835.

References and Further Reading

Champagne, Duane, ed. 1994. *Native America: Portrait of the Peoples*. Canton, MI: Visible Ink Press.

Mankiller, Wilma. 2004. *Every Day Is a Good Day: Reflections of Contemporary Indigenous Women*. Boulder, CO: Fulcrum.

Mankiller, Wilma, and Michael Wallis. 1993. *Mankiller: A Chief and Her People*. New York: St. Martin's Press.

Manuelito

(1818–1894)

Manuelito was born into the *Bit'ahni* clan (Folded Arms People) near Bear Ears, Utah around 1818. Manuelito, as the Mexicans named him, is noted for his resistance to Mexican and American invasions of Navajoland, or *Dinétah*. During his lifetime, Hastiin Ch'iil Hajiin was committed to Navajo sovereignty and endeavored to keep Navajo lands.

Following the teachings from the ancestors, Manuelito trained as a medicine man that followed *hózhó*, the path of harmony and balance to old age, the path that Navajos had been following for generations. Manuelito's marriage to the daughter of the headman Narbona would provide him with the wise leader's insight. In later years, Manuelito would also find his wife Juanita a valuable companion.

Beginning in the late 1500s, Spaniards and then Mexicans came into the Southwest to seek their fortunes and establish colonies. Navajos experienced cultural transformations that made them herdsmen and warriors. With the horse, Navajos ably impeded the foreigners' advances. Manuelito witnessed the shifting relationships of peace and conflict between Navajos and Mexicans. In the 1830s, Mexicans rode into Navajoland determined to break Navajo resistance and to capture women and children for the slave trade. Slavery had been known in the Southwest, but the slave trade intensified with European American invasions. Slave raiders targeted Navajo women and children. In fact, raiding for Navajo slaves reached a peak during the 1860s. In a battle at Copper Pass in the Chuska Mountains, warriors led by Narbona and Manuelito successfully defeated the Mexicans. At that time, Manuelito was but a young man.

By the time the Americans claimed the Southwest in 1846, Manuelito was a respected war chief. The cycle of peace and conflict between Navajos, other tribal peoples, and the Americans began anew. In 1851, the establishment of a fort in Navajoland led to a war that would end in the Navajos' defeat. The conflict began over pasturing lands that lay outside of the newly established fort. In 1858, General William Brooks asserted control of the pastures for army use. In defiance, Manuelito continued to pasture his livestock on the disputed lands, whereupon Brooks ordered the livestock slaughtered. Soon afterward, a Navajo killed Brooks's black slave, and Brooks demanded that the Navajos produce the murderer for U.S. justice. Eventually, Navajos produced a body, most likely that of a Mexican captive. Enraged at what he considered Navajo arrogance, Brooks called for a war. In 1860, Manuelito and one thousand warriors struck at Fort Defiance several times but were unable to take the fort.

The Civil War turned U.S. attention away, and Fort Defiance was abandoned. After the Civil War, white settlement again threatened the Navajos. Manuelito led the resistance and urged his people to have courage. Finding the Navajos obstacles to white expansion, General James H. Carleton ordered their removal to a reservation near Fort Sumner, New Mexico, where the Navajos would learn the arts of civilization.

General Carleton enlisted Indian fighter Kit Carson for the campaign against the *Diné*. Carson and his men literally scorched Navajoland. They destroyed cornfields, peach trees, hogans, and livestock. By 1863, destitute Navajos began surrendering to the Americans. As prisoners, they endured a three-hundred-mile journey to the internment camp. Some Navajo leaders went with their people to encourage them to keep heart. Navajo bodies littered the trail. The old and sick were abandoned if they held up the march. Pregnant women were shot and killed if they could not keep up. Many drowned when they tried to cross the Rio Grande.

At the prison, Navajos barely survived. Manuelito vowed to remain free. The U.S. Army wished to either capture or kill Manuelito, for they feared that he served as inspiration to others who eluded their enemy. In 1865, Navajo leaders, including Herrera, met Manuelito and gave him the army's message to surrender. Manuelito refused, declaring that "his mother and his God lived in the West and

he would not leave them." He would not leave his native home; the United States could kill if they pleased, but he would not leave.

Finally, in 1866, wounded and ill, Manuelito surrendered and was interned at the Bosque Redondo prison. After four years, General Carleton reluctantly admitted that his plan was not working. There was talk of returning the Navajos to their former homes. On June 1, 1868, Manuelito and other leaders signed a treaty so they could return to Dinétah. The treaty stipulated peaceful relationships between Navajos and the United States, defined a boundary for a reservation, and required education for Navajo children. Seventeen days later, more than eight thousand Navajos began the journey home. About three thousand Navajos had died during the war on Navajos.

After his return to Dinétah, Manuelito remained an influential leader who articulated his concerns for the return of his people's land. He was appointed head of the first Navajo police, who would keep order on the reservation. In 1874, he traveled with his wife and other Navajo leaders to Washington, D.C., to meet President Grant. In 1894, Manuelito died from disease and alcoholism. His widow Juanita and his daughters carried on his messages about the importance of land for the coming generations.

Jennifer Nez Denetdale

See also Fort Sumner, New Mexico; Treaty with the Navajo–June 1, 1868.

References and Further Reading

Iverson, Peter. 2002. *Diné: A History of the Navajos.* Albuquerque: University of New Mexico Press.

Kelly, Lawrence. 1970. *Navajo Roundup: Selected Correspondence of Kit Carson's Expedition Against the Navajo, 1863–1865.* Boulder, CO: Purett.

Roessel, Ruth. 1973. *Navajo Stories of the Long Walk Period.* Tsaile, AZ: Navajo Community College Press.

Sundberg, Lawrence D. 1995. *Dinétah: An Early History of the Navajo People.* Santa Fe, NM: Sunstone Press.

Massasoit

(c. 1590–1661/1662)

The name Massasoit is a title meaning "grand sachem" or "great leader." It was bestowed on Ousa Mequin (Yellow Feather), sachem of the Pokanoket and the grand sachem (massasoit) of the Wampanoag Confederation.

Massassoit, leader of the Wampanoag tribe, was able to maintain peaceful relations with English settlers in the area of Plymouth, Massachussetts. He and other Native Americans shared planting and fishing techniques with the colonists and fostered trade and amity between the races. (Library of Congress)

Little is known about Massasoit prior to his contact with the Plymouth Colony in 1621. He was born around 1590 in Montaup, a Pokanoket village near present-day Bristol, Rhode Island, and rose to the leadership of eight large villages. The first documented contact of Massasoit with the English occurred in 1619. In that year, he met with Captain Thomas Dermer following the latter's voyage with Tisquantum (Squanto) to New England. William Bradford, the second governor of Plymouth Colony, described the Pokanoket sachem as "a very lust [sic] man in his best years, an able body, grave of countenance, and spare of speech. . . . His face was painted with a deep red like mulberry and he was oiled both head and face" (Josephy 1994, 211).

Traditionally, Massasoit is remembered for his alliance with the Pilgrims and his efforts to aid the Plymouth Colony. A calculating and skilled diplomat, he established personal relationships with the principal leaders of the colony, including William Bradford and Edward Winslow. Concern about the possibility of conflict with the neighboring Narragansetts led Massasoit to forge an alliance with the colonists at Plymouth in March 1621. The resulting treaty was mutually beneficial, providing security for the colonists and military aid for the Wampanoags in case of hostilities with the Narragansetts. Cemented even further by Edward Winslow's resuscitation of the critically ill sachem in 1632, the alliance also served to keep the Wampanoags out of the Pequot War (1636–1637) and enabled Massasoit to resist Puritan efforts to Christianize his people.

Expanding English settlements around Massachusetts Bay brought pressures on Massasoit to cede land to the English. To this he relented, selling land in the 1650s to the colony in exchange for the maintenance of harmony. Until his death in 1661 or 1662, the Wampanoag bands under Massasoit and the people of the Massachusetts Bay and Plymouth colonies remained at peace.

Alan C. Downs

See also Colonial and Early Treaties, 1775–1829; Metacom; Northeast and the Great Lakes.
References and Further Reading
Axtell, James. 2001. *Natives and Newcomers: The Cultural Origins of North America.* New York: Oxford University Press.
Josephy, Alvin M., Jr. 1994. *500 Nations: An Illustrated History of North American Indians.* New York: Alfred A. Knopf.
Philbrick, Nathaniel. 2006. *Mayflower: A Story of Courage, Community, and War.* New York: Viking.

McGillivray, Alexander
(1759–1793)

Alexander McGillivray, diplomat, merchant, and plantation owner, became the most widely known leader of the Muscogee Creek Nation during the late eighteenth century. Due to his mother's affiliation with the influential Wolf Clan and his father's prominence as a Scottish American trader, McGillivray grew up absorbing the cultural influences of both Native and European American society. He spent much of his youth traveling between Little Tallassee, where his mother's family lived, and colonial Charleston, where he gained a classical education from European tutors.

By the time of the American Revolution, McGillivray had become involved in the regional fur trade and had begun working as an assistant commissary for the British Indian Department, a position that allowed him to expand his influence through the distribution of trade goods and ammunition. Throughout the conflict, he encouraged Creek warriors to attack rebel settlements in the Georgia backcountry and to help defend the British outposts of Mobile and Pensacola in the loyalist colony of West Florida. His efforts led to some minor successes for the British but had little influence on the overall outcome of the fighting. Nevertheless, despite his employer's defeat, McGillivray amassed significant wealth during the 1770s and 1780s, including at least two plantations, dozens of slaves, and a "substantial library" (Saunt 1999, 72). Following the war, he used his riches and bicultural connections to acquire a prominent leadership role in the Creek National Council, a governing body composed of representatives from Creek towns; he was awarded the title Great Beloved Man and served as the entity's principal diplomat in negotiations with both Spanish and U.S. officials. In this capacity, he periodically advocated armed resistance against the steady stream of settlers infiltrating Native lands throughout the Southeast. Hoping to galvanize support from other Indian groups, he held meetings with representatives of the Iroquois, Huron, and Shawnee and sent Creek warriors to fight along side Cherokees as they battled American settlers and illicit traders in present-day Tennessee (Braund 1993, 172).

Although he advocated violence on occasion, McGillivray supported diplomacy to resolve Creek disputes with European Americans as well, his main goal being to pit U.S. and Spanish adversaries against one another while strengthening the negotiating stance of the National Council. As part of this plan, he presided over a treaty of friendship with Spain that was signed in 1784—an agreement that gave the Creek greater access to European manufactured goods and weapons, along with the use of ports on the Gulf of Mexico. McGillivray gained further diplomatic power and historical distinction for his signing of the Treaty of New York in 1790. According to the treaty, the Creek agreed to relinquish part of their territory in northern Georgia to the United States in exchange for repossession of lands further to the west that had been transferred in earlier treaties with state representatives. Additionally, as part of this accord, the United States agreed to guarantee Creek territorial claims against those of the southern states, protect the Creek Nation from settler encroachment, reduce trade restrictions, and supply the Indians with a perpetual $1,500 annuity

(Braund 1993, 176). In his negotiations with both Spanish and U.S. officials, McGillivray personally prospered, gaining a monopoly in what would become Florida, Alabama, and parts of Georgia for Panton, Leslie, and Company, a Scottish American–led trading outfit of which he was a secret partner. At the same time, Spanish officials designated him their principal commissary for distributing gifts to Indians in the region, and the United States secretly appointed him brigadier general in the U.S. Army. Through these positions, McGillivray received more than $4,000 a year in salary from foreign governments, or about two hundred times the amount of money earned by the average Creek hunter during an equivalent period (Saunt 1999, 79). Partly as a result of these happenings, opposition to his influence among the Creeks began to grow, primarily in the Lower Creek towns less loyal to the National Council. William Augustus Bowles, a European American adventurer, and Hoboithle Micco, a Lower Creek headman, separately challenged his authority, priorities, and legitimacy as a nation spokesman and negotiator in foreign affairs. Moreover, factionalism among the Creek in general, which stemmed from both traditional clan-geographical rivalries and newer traditionalist-accommodationist alignments, diminished his support base and brought new leaders to the forefront of Creek government.

Disillusioned and marginalized, McGillivray increasingly spent more time outside Creek territory, eventually moving much of his property to Spanish Florida. Attempting to resurrect his support among the Indians while visiting Pensacola, McGillivray died of an unknown illness on February 17, 1793 (Saunt 1999, 88–89).

Daniel S. Murphree

See also Annuities; Hawkins, Benjamin; Knox, Henry; McIntosh, William, Jr.

References and Further Reading

Braund, Kathryn E. Holland. 1993. *Deerskins and Duffels: Creek Indian Trade with Anglo-America, 1685–1815*. Lincoln: University of Nebraska Press.

Green, Michael D. 1980. "Alexander McGillivray." In *American Indian Leaders: Studies in Diversity*, ed. R. David Edmunds, 41–63. Lincoln: University of Nebraska Press.

Saunt, Claudio. 1999. *A New Order of Things: Property, Power, and the Transformation of the Creek Indians, 1733–1816*. New York: Cambridge University Press.

McIntosh, William, Jr.
(1775–1825)

Known for his orchestration and signing of the Treaty of Indian Springs in 1825 and his ceding of Creek lands in Georgia to the United States, William McIntosh was the most controversial Muscogee Creek Indian leader in the preremoval era.

McIntosh's mother was the son of a Coweta Creek woman of the powerful Wind clan, and his father was an influential Scottish trader. He was also the nephew of several prominent warriors and village chiefs. This helped him initially obtain recognition as a minor war chief. In the early nineteenth century, McIntosh expanded his authority by distributing trade goods such as food, cattle, and cloth to his kinsmen and neighbors.

Because his authority rested on his ability to secure trade goods for redistribution, McIntosh secured alliances with U.S. officials who could assist him. He helped U.S. Indian agent Benjamin Haw-

William McIntosh (1775–1825), Muscogee Creek, was a loyal ally of the United States and rendered useful service during the difficult Creek War of 1813–1814. (Hulton Archive/Getty Images)

kins implement his "civilization plan" and later helped General Andrew Jackson fight Red Stick Creeks and Seminole Indians. He also arranged a series of treaties that often prioritized Anglo-Creek trade relations and his own personal economic interests, to the detriment of the interests of the Creek Nation as a whole. This strategy placed McIntosh at the center of controversy, but it also secured him a spot on the Creek National Council.

McIntosh entered the diplomatic arena in 1805, when he helped orchestrate the Treaty of Washington. This treaty ceded to the United States all of the Muscogee Creek lands between the Oconee and Ocmulgee rivers in Georgia and provided the United States access to a road that connected the Ocmulgee and Mobile, Alabama, a path that cut through the heart of Creek country. In return, the Creeks received a $20,000 annuity and the obligation to provide "houses of entertainment" to cater to Americans who traveled on the intrusive road. McIntosh took advantage of this legal mandate and built an inn, a tavern, and ferries to profit from the road.

McIntosh reemerged in the diplomatic arena during the Creek Civil War (1813–1814), which coincided with the War of 1812. As a Coweta war chief, McIntosh led several hundred Creek warriors into battle against the Red Stick Creek majority and Great Britain. His alliance with the United States, especially with Andrew Jackson, allowed him to help shape the Treaty with the Creeks at Fort Jackson on August 9, 1814. Although the treaty indiscriminately punished the entire Creek Nation for the actions of the Red Sticks, it allowed McIntosh and other "friendly chiefs" to keep their "improvements" and land.

The controversy surrounding McIntosh became even more pronounced in 1821, when he arranged and signed the first Treaty of Indian Springs. In return for supporting this land cession, McIntosh obtained one thousand acres for his own use at Indian Springs and 640 acres for his use around his plantation on the Ocmulgee River. Furthermore, he personally received $40,000 compensation for the assistance he provided in this and earlier treaties.

The Treaty of Indian Springs of 1825 ceded almost all Creek lands in Georgia and much of their land in Alabama. Although fifty-two Creeks signed the treaty, McIntosh was the only member of the Creek National Council and only one of six headmen to sign it. Under this treaty, the Creeks ceded this land, which amounted to more than 6,700 square miles of tribal territory, in return for an equal amount of territory west of the Mississippi River, the cost of removal, and a small annuity.

By arranging and signing the Treaty of Indian Springs, McIntosh violated a recent Creek law that he himself had signed as a member of the National Council. This law, which forbade any cession of Creek lands, called for the death of the Creeks responsible. The Creeks tried and convicted McIntosh in absentia, and on April 30, 1825, executed the war chief at his home.

Andrew Frank

See also Hawkins, Benjamin; Jackson, Andrew; Opothleyahola; Treaty with the Creeks–November 14, 1805; Treaty with the Creeks–August 9, 1814; Treaty with the Creeks–February 12, 1825.

References and Further Reading

Debo, Angie. 1941. *The Road to Disappearance: A History of the Creek Indians.* Norman: University of Oklahoma Press.

Frank, Andrew K. 2005. *Creeks and Southerners: Biculturalism on the Early American Frontier.* Lincoln and London: University of Nebraska Press.

Frank, Andrew K. 2002. "The Rise and Fall of William McIntosh." *The Georgia Historical Quarterly,* 86 (Spring): 18–48.

Green, Michael D. 1982. *The Politics of Indian Removal: Creek Government and Society in Crisis.* Lincoln and London: University of Nebraska Press.

Griffith, Benjamin W., Jr. 1988. *McIntosh and Weatherford: Creek Indian Leaders* Tuscaloosa: University of Alabama Press.

Means, Russell

(1939–)

Russell Means, an Oglala/Lakota born on the Pine Ridge Indian Reservation near the Black Hills, South Dakota, is recognized as one of the liveliest leaders of the American Indian Movement (AIM). Means joined AIM in 1968 and soon formed its first chapter outside Minnesota. He participated in AIM's occupation of Alcatraz Island (November 20, 1969–June 11, 1971), which drew national attention to the cultural, economic, and political needs of American Indians. As the organization's first national director in 1970, Means and his colleague Dennis Banks organized a series of activities promoting AIM's goals: the assertion of Indian self-determination; the protection of rights guaranteed through treaties, sovereignties, laws, and the U.S. Constitution; and the

Russell Means, Native American rights activist, speaks to a crowd of followers in South Dakota in 1974. (Bettmann/Corbis)

years later, he assisted in leading the first U.N.-sponsored international conference concerning the American Indian, held in Geneva, Switzerland. He tried his hand at politics again and ran unsuccessfully for vice-president (1984) and president of the United States (1987), governor of New Mexico (2001), and president of the Oglala Sioux tribe (2001). Means also stood trial twelve times for a variety of charges, including a 1975 murder. He represented himself in all twelve cases, with the help of lawyers from the Wounded Knee Legal Defense/Offense Committee. He served one year in prison for a Sioux Falls, South Dakota, courthouse riot.

Means has garnered international attention for his many "firsts" and continues to remain active as an advocate for Indian priorities. He has served as chief executive officer of the T.R.E.A.T.Y. Fund on the Pine Ridge Reservation since 1983. In 1980, he founded the first Indian-owned, Indian-operated radio station and in 1986, he founded the first independent health clinic on an American Indian reservation, along with several additional Indian advocacy organizations. In 1991, he established the first National Monument to Indian Peoples within the National Park Service system. Means's lecture circuit has included all the major universities in the United States, England, Switzerland, Japan, South Korea, Spain, and Australia.

Clara Keyt

See also Alcatraz Occupation, 1964 and 1969; American Indian Movement (AIM); Banks, Dennis; Bellecourt, Clyde; Bureau of Indian Affairs (BIA); Longest Walk, 1978; Trail of Broken Treaties, 1972; Wounded Knee Occupation, 1973.

References and Further Reading

Means, Russell, and Marvin J. Wolf. 1995. *Where White Men Fear to Tread: An Autobiography of Russell Means*. New York: St. Martin's Press.

Sayer, John William. 1997. *Ghost Dancing the Law: The Wounded Knee Trials*. Cambridge, MA: Harvard University Press.

Stern, Kenneth S. 1994. *Loud Hawk: The United States vs. the American Indian Movement*. Norman: University of Oklahoma Press.

elevation of Native priorities through national media exposure. In 1972, Means and Banks led a group of protestors on the Trail of Broken Treaties, which resulted in an eight-day takeover of the Bureau of Indian Affairs (BIA) office in Washington, D.C. Based on their BIA success, the duo next orchestrated AIM's occupation of Wounded Knee, South Dakota, in 1973, claiming land ceded in the 1868 Fort Laramie Treaty and protesting the 1890 massacre of one hundred fifty unarmed Sioux. The standoff ended on May 8 after seventy-one days of national press coverage. A year later, Means stood trial for his involvement. Five years later, he organized another protest, the Longest Walk, which became the largest peaceful, single-day demonstration in Washington, D.C., up to that time. Participants caravanned from San Francisco to Washington, demanding that the federal government honor its treaty obligations.

Means remained politically active in Indian and national affairs from that time forward. In 1974, he ran unsuccessfully for the presidency of the Oglala Sioux tribe and established the International Indian Treaty Council at the United Nations (U.N.). Three

Metacom
(c. 1637–1676)

Metacom was the son of Massasoit, who had met the first immigrants from England in 1620 in what is now Massachusetts. The English called Metacom

Native American leader Metacom, also known as King Philip, led in King Philip's War (1676). In terms of numbers engaged and casualties sustained in proportion to population, this was one of the bloodiest Indian wars in American history. (Library of Congress)

King Philip. He became grand sachem of the Wampanoags in 1662 and led his people and their allies in a devastating war with the English in 1675 and 1676, dying at its conclusion.

The efforts of Roger Williams, Puritan dissenter and founder of Rhode Island, helped to maintain a shaky peace along the frontiers of New England for nearly two generations after the Pequot War (1636–1637). In 1645, Williams averted another Native uprising against encroaching European American settlements. By the 1660s, however, the aging Williams saw his lifelong pursuit of peace unravel yet again. This time, he felt more impotent than in the past; wave after wave of colonists provided Native peoples with powerful grievances by usurping their land without permission or compensation, and yet Williams continued to believe that neither the Puritans nor any other Europeans had any right, divine or otherwise, to take Indian land. The final years of Williams's life were profoundly painful for a sensitive man who prized peace and harmony above all.

Massasoit, who had maintained peace with the newcomers since 1620, was also aging and becoming disillusioned with the colonists, as increasing numbers of European immigrants drove his people from their lands. Upon Massasoit's death in 1661, Alexander, one of Massasoit's sons, briefly served as grand sachem of the Wampanoags. However, visiting Boston in 1662, Alexander fell gravely ill and died as Wampanoag warriors rushed him into the wilderness. Upon his death, the warriors beached their canoes, buried his body on a knoll, and returned home with rumors that he had been a victim of the English. Metacom became grand sachem after Alexander's death.

Aged about twenty-five in 1662, Metacom distrusted nearly all European Americans, Williams being one of the few exceptions. Metacom also was known as a man who did not forgive insults easily. It was once said that he chased a white man named John Gibbs from Mount Hope to Nantucket Island, about sixty miles, partially over water, after Gibbs insulted his father. Throughout his childhood, Metacom had watched his people dwindle before the English advance. By 1671, about forty thousand non-Native people lived in New England. The Native population, double that of the Europeans before the Pequot War, stood at about twenty thousand. European farms and pastures were driving away game and creating friction over land that the Indians had used without question for so many generations that they had lost count. By 1675, the Wampanoags held only a small strip of land at Mount Hope, and settlers wanted it.

Metacom became more embittered every day. He could see his nation being destroyed before his eyes. He and other people in his nation were interrogated by Puritan officials. Traders fleeced Indians, exchanging furs for liquor. The devastation of alcohol and disease and the loss of land destroyed families and tradition. These were Metacom's thoughts as he prepared to go to war against the English.

As rumors of war reached Williams, he tried to keep the neighboring Narragansetts neutral, as he had done in the past. This time, he failed. Nananawtunu, son of Mixanno, told his close friend Williams that, although he opposed going to war, his people could not be restrained. They had decided the time had come to die fighting rather than to expire slowly as a people. Williams's letters of this time were pervaded with sadness, as he watched the two groups he knew so well slide toward war.

Shortly after hostilities began in June 1675, Williams met with Metacom, riding with the sachem and his family in a canoe not far from Providence. Williams warned Metacom that he was leading his people to extermination. Williams compared the Wampanoags to a canoe on a stormy sea of English fury. "He answered me in a consenting, considering kind of way," Williams wrote, "[saying] [m]y canoe is already overturned" (Giddings 1957, 33).

When Indians, painted for war, appeared on the heights above Providence, Williams picked up his staff, climbed the bluffs, and told the war parties that, if they attacked the town, England would send thousands of armed men to crush them. "Well," one of the sachems leading the attack told Williams, "let them come. We are ready for them, but as for you, brother Williams, you are a good man. You have been kind to us for many years. Not a hair on your head shall be touched" (Straus 1894, 220–224).

Williams was not injured, but his house was torched as he met with the Indians on the bluffs above Providence on March 29, 1676. Williams watched flames spread throughout the town. "This house of mine now burning before mine eyes hath lodged kindly some thousands of you these ten years," Williams told the attacking Indians (Swan 1969, 14). If the colony was to survive, Williams, for the first time in his life, had to become a military commander. With a grave heart, Williams sent his neighbors out to do battle with the sons and daughters of Native people who had sheltered him during his winter trek from Massachusetts forty years earlier. As Williams and others watched from inside a hastily erected fort, nearly all of Providence burned. Fields were laid waste, and cattle were slaughtered or driven into the woods.

Colonists, seething with anger, caught an Indian, and Williams was put in the agonizing position of ordering him killed rather than watching him be tortured. The war was irrefutably brutal on both sides, as the English fought with their backs literally to the sea for a year and a half before going on the offensive. At Northfield, Indians hanged two Englishmen on chains, placing hooks under their jaws. At Springfield, colonists arrested an Indian woman, then offered her body to dogs, which tore her to pieces.

In August 1676, as the Mohawks and Mohegans opted out of their alliance with the Wampanoags, the war ended. The English had exterminated most of the Narragansetts, and nearly all of Metacom's warriors, their families, and friends had been killed or driven into hiding. Metacom himself fled toward Mount Hope, then hid in a swamp. When English soldiers found him, they dragged him out of the mire, then had him drawn and quartered. His head was sent to Plymouth on a gibbet, where it was displayed much as criminals' severed heads were shown off on the railings of London Bridge. Metacom's hands were sent to Boston, where a local showman charged admission for a glimpse of one of them. The remainder of Metacom's body was hung from four separate trees.

In terms of deaths in proportion to total population, King Philip's War was among the deadliest in American history. About one thousand colonists died in the war; many more died of starvation and war-related diseases. Every Native nation bordering the Puritan settlements—those whose members, in happier days, had offered the earliest colonists their first Thanksgiving dinner—was reduced to ruin. Many of the survivors were sold into slavery in the West Indies, which served the colonists two ways: by removing them from the area and by raising money to help pay the colonists' enormous war debts. Metacom's son was auctioned off with about five hundred other slaves following a brief but intense biblical debate over whether a son should be forced to atone for the sins of his father.

Bruce E. Johansen

See also Massasoit; Williams, Roger.
References and Further Reading

Giddings, James L. 1957. "Roger Williams and the Indians." Typescript, Rhode Island Historical Society.

Kennedy, John Hopkins. 1950. *Jesuit and Savage in New France*. New Haven, CT: Yale University Press.

Slotkin, Richard, and James K. Folsom, eds. 1978. *So Dreadful a Judgement: Puritan Responses to King Philip's War 1676–1677*. Middleton, CT: Wesleyan University Press.

Straus, Oscar S. *Roger Williams: 1894. The Pioneer of Religious Liberty*. New York: Century.

Swan, Bradford F. 1969. "New Light on Roger Williams and the Indians." *Providence Sunday Journal Magazine*, November 23: 14.

Vaughan, Alden T. 1965. *New England Frontier: Puritans and Indians, 1620–1675*. Boston: Little, Brown.

Wright, Ronald. 1992. *Stolen Continents*. Boston: Houghton Mifflin.

Oakes, Richard
(1942–1972)

Richard Oakes, a Mohawk who was born on the St. Regis Reservation in New York, helped plan and implement the 1969 American Indian occupation of Alcatraz Island. His eloquence and commanding presence, his pivotal role in the takeover of Alcatraz, his development of a curriculum for the American Indian Studies Department at San Francisco State University, and his involvement in further protests in support of the Pit River and Pomo Indians make

him an important figure in the history of American Indian activism in the 1960s and 1970s.

Oakes spent time in New York City working on high steel structures before moving to California, where he married Anne Marufo. He studied under Louis Kemnitzer at San Francisco State College in the American Indian Studies Department. There, Richard was introduced to the White Roots of Peace and the Third World Liberation Strikes at Berkeley, both inspirations for his activism. While in school, Richard and other students in his program met with Belva Cottier, who, through her own experiences with Alcatraz, helped lay the groundwork for the students' future takeover.

Oakes joined forces with Adam Nordwall, who was also working on plans for an occupation of Alcatraz. Their collaborative group, the Indians of All Tribes, drafted a proclamation to illustrate the grievances of American Indians in cities and on reservations and to list their demands for Alcatraz. Chief among these demands was title to the land and support to build an American Indian Museum, a Center for Native American Studies, a Spiritual Center, and a scientific center for the study of ecology and environmental protection.

November 9, 1969, saw the first attempt to take Alcatraz. Before setting sail, Richard read the proclamation of the IAT to the gathered press, who singled him out as the leader of the movement.

As they approached Alcatraz, Oakes jumped overboard and swam ashore to claim the island by right of discovery. After being removed by the Coast Guard, Oakes and his fellow students made the second attempt to occupy Alcatraz by returning only hours later. That night, the small band of occupants on the island sang songs and danced in celebration. The next day, before the Coast Guard removed them again, Oakes once again stressed the demands of the Indians of All Tribes for title to the land. On November 20, 1969, on a third attempt, eighty-nine American Indians, including Oakes, successfully occupied Alcatraz for an extended period of time.

Oakes believed that the protest on Alcatraz had the power to prove to the federal government and to the American public that American Indians were a vibrant and powerful entity in the late twentieth century, capable of self-determination. He hoped through the media to be able to reveal the vast contributions of American Indians to society and history and to push the federal government to begin acknowledging its massive legal obligations to American Indians.

Opposition to Oakes's growing power in the media created a rift among some of the newer occupiers, who wished for a completely egalitarian society on Alcatraz and saw his image as a threat. On January 5, 1970, Oakes's daughter Yvonne fell down a flight of stairs and was killed. In deep mourning, the Oakes family left Alcatraz, and new leadership factions rose to take his place.

After leaving Alcatraz, Oakes and his family went on to support other activist movements. He took part in the protests against the occupation by the Pacific Gas and Electric Company of the Pit River lands in northern California. In Santa Rosa, California, Oakes helped plan a takeover of a former Central Intelligence Agency (CIA) post, where title to the land was eventually transferred to the Pomo Indians and an American Indian Learning Center was established.

In a tragic end to a brilliant life, Richard Oakes was shot to death on September 20, 1972, by a YMCA camp manager, Michael Oliver Morgan, in Santa Clara, California. Morgan asserted that Oakes had attacked him, whereas Oakes's defenders maintained that he had been assassinated because Morgan objected to Oakes's positions on Native rights issues. Through his efforts on Alcatraz and elsewhere, Richard Oakes helped give an upcoming generation of American Indians a renewed sense of pride and self-respect. His accomplishments in the field of American Indian activism created a new awareness of the important place of American Indians in history and in our modern society.

Vera Parham

See also Alcatraz Occupation, 1964 and 1969.
References and Further Reading
Johnson, Troy R. 1996. *The Occupation of Alcatraz Island: Indian Self-Determination and the Rise of Indian Activism.* Urbana: University of Illinois Press.
Johnson, Troy R., Duane Champagne, and Joane Nagel, eds. 1997. *American Indian Activism: Alcatraz to the Longest Walk.* Urbana: University of Illinois Press.
Oakes, Richard. 1972. "Alcatraz Is Not an Island." *Ramparts* 9 (December): 35–40.

Old Briton

(?–1752)

Old Briton was principal chief of the Piankashaw band of Miami (Twigtwee), located in present-day Indiana. Old Briton, displeased with French hegemony over the Miami as well as their neighbors the Huron, Ottawa, Chippewa, and Wyandotte, strove to break political and economic ties with the French and establish relations with the English in the mid-eighteenth century. In 1747, Old Briton's opportunity came when a pro-British Huron chief, Nicolas, solicited his aid to launch a coordinated attack against Fort Miami, Fort Detroit, and Michilimackinac. The plan called for Old Briton to attack Fort Miami while Nicolas assaulted Fort Detroit and their Chippewa allies struck Michilimackinac. At war with the French, Old Briton moved his people from the lower Wabash River in present-day Indiana to the western portion of present-day Ohio, hoping to secure his people and to replace his old French economic and political partners with Pennsylvania and Virginia. Moreover, he sought to establish his band as middlemen in a lucrative trade network between the English colonies and the western Ohio Indians still under French influence.

Once in the Ohio Valley, Old Briton established a new town, Pickawillany, at the strategic juncture of the Miami River and Loramie's Creek. Anxious to establish relations with the English, Old Briton sent emissaries in the winter of 1747–1748 to the Shawnee, Mingo, and Delaware (located in the vicinity of Logstown, Pennsylvania) and urged them to negotiate with Pennsylvania on his behalf. At the Logstown Conference in April 1748, those tribes persuaded George Croghan, Pennsylvania's representative, to open a "council road" between the two parties. Encouraged, Old Briton sent a delegation headed by his son, Assapausa, to Lancaster, Pennsylvania in 1748. Assapausa succeeded in forging an alliance with the English, the Iroquois Confederacy, and the eastern Ohio Indians.

Bolstered by the new alliance, Old Briton moved to lure the western Ohio Indians away from French interests. Alarmed by Old Briton's actions, the governor of New France, the Marquis de la Galissoniere, sent a force of 245 men under Pierre Joseph de Céloron de Blainville to warn the English off Ohio lands and to arrest Old Briton. De Céloron arrived in Logstown before he reached Pickawillany, giving Old Briton's new allies time to warn him of French intentions. In response, Old Briton called a large number of warriors to Pickawillany and met his French adversaries on an equal footing. To avoid an armed conflict with the Miami, de Céloron negotiated with Old Briton to rejoin the

French. Aware that he could not drive the French from Pickawillany without great cost, Old Briton insincerely pledged to abandon Pickawillany and return to the lower Wabash in the spring. De Céloron, dubious of Old Briton's good faith, woefully departed Pickawillany in September 1749.

Having averted the French assault, in November of 1749 Old Briton encouraged Croghan to build a stockaded trading post at Pickawillany to entice the western Indians to leave the French and resettle in western Ohio. By 1750, Old Briton had convinced more than three hundred Weas and Miamis to migrate to Pickawillany and sign a treaty with the English. In response, the French launched a failed attack against Pickawillany in 1751. Incensed, Old Briton encouraged the western Indians to wage war against New France and began killing French traders and soldiers throughout the Ohio Valley. Additionally, Old Briton forged a coalition against the French that consisted of the Illinois Confederacy, the Shawnee, and the Osages. Fearing that their hold on the Ohio Valley was slipping, the French sent a second expedition consisting of Ottawas and Chippewas against Pickawillany. Unnerved by this potential threat, Old Briton made no preparations to meet the French assault. Thus, he allowed his warriors to go on their annual hunt. With Pickawillany virtually undefended, the French Indians surprised and defeated Old Briton in June of 1752. They then killed the aged Miami chief by boiling and eating his body. With Old Briton's death, the Miami abandoned Pickawillany and resettled near Fort Detroit, thus ending their bid for hegemony over the western portion of the Ohio Valley.

Joseph P. Alessi

See also Battle of Fallen Timbers, 1794; Pontiac; Tecumseh; Treaty with the Wyandot, Etc.–August 3, 1795.
References and Further Reading
Anderson, Frederick. 2000. *Crucible of War: The Seven Years' War and the Fate of Empire in British North America, 1754–1766.* New York: Alfred A. Knopf.
Edmunds, R. David. 1980. "Old Briton." In *American Indian Leaders*, ed. R. David Edmunds. Lincoln, NE: University of Nebraska Press.
White, Richard. 1991. *The Middle Ground: Indians, Empires, and Republics in the Great Lakes Region, 1650–1815.* Cambridge: Cambridge University Press.

Opechancanough
(1545–1644)

In 1607, upon arrival in the lands they would call Virginia, English settlers encountered a highly stratified and densely populated landscape of Algonquian Indian communities under the rule of the Powhatan Confederacy. Led by Chief Powhatan, this confederacy extended throughout the Chesapeake from the Potomac River in the north, south to the James River, eastward to the coast, and westward to the falls of the region's major rivers. An estimated thirty thousand Indians lived under Powhatan's jurisdiction in dozens of allied villages. They subsisted on the region's bountiful fish, shellfish, and game, as well as harvests of corn, beans, and squash.

Powhatan led several small-scale attempts to drive the English out of Jamestown, and in 1617 he abdicated power to his two brothers, Opitchapam and Opechancanough. Powhatan's daughter, Pocahontas, had been married strategically to English

Opechancanough (1545–1644) was a leader of the Powhatan Indians in Virginia and the younger brother of Powhatan, the powerful sachem who ruled the vast Native American empire around Chesapeake Bay. An important negotiator with the English settlers in Virginia during the early seventeenth century, Opechancanough later led raids against them, including the Massacre of 1622. (North Wind Picture Archives)

settler John Rolfe in 1614, but the colonists' constant demand for Indian foods, lands, and resources strained English relations with Virginia's Powhatan communities. The harsh, humid, tropical tidewater also made life hard for Europeans, who expected Native communities to feed and provision their settlers. The effects of European diseases ravaged Indian communities, as the Indians lacked immunities to most major European diseases.

By 1622, Opechancanough had assumed leadership over the Powhatan Confederacy, and for the next two decades he attempted a series of full-scale wars to drive the English from his people's homelands. In the Powhatan Uprising of March 1622, he assumed personal command of an attack on Jamestown that left 347 killed and untold hundreds wounded. Unfortunately for the Powhatans, although their March attack struck terror throughout the English colony, it did not fully dismantle Jamestown; the English counterattacked during the fall harvest, burning Indian crops needed for winter survival. A series of raids and reprisals characterized English-Powhatan relations throughout the 1620s. Finally, in 1632, both sides reached a political agreement that recognized the settlers' right to exist as well as reducing Powhatans' land rights, but this agreement could overcome neither the cycles of vengeance unleashed over the past decade nor the growing engine of European economic expansion.

Jamestown is the oldest English settlement in North America, and Virginia is the oldest colony. Many historians wonder how the English survived in such difficult circumstances, particularly as European servants died in such staggering numbers. Nearly 80 percent of all English servants died during the colony's first decades as the tropical climate killed lower-class Englishmen accustomed to the cooler climate of the North Atlantic.

The answer to the colony's survival, as well as to the eventual demise of Opechancanough's confederacy, is tobacco. Tobacco became the first cash crop of North America, and it generated tremendous profits for the colony's sponsors. Although Opechancanough and his community struggled to adapt to the growing presence of English newcomers in their homelands, they could not withstand the expansion of tobacco production, as the wealth generated by the Virginia colony soon made it the most profitable region of North America.

As tobacco cultivation spread further into interior Powhatan communities, the seeds of violence were also sown. By the end of the 1630s, Englishmen now outnumbered Opechancanough's warriors, as the effects of European diseases and warfare cost the Powhatan their initial demographic advantage. In early 1644, Opechancanough attempted one final push to drive out the English, killing more than four hundred settlers on April 18. Often referred to as the Second Powhatan War, this conflict brought the eventual dispersal of Powhatan villages along the major waterways, forcing Indian survivors to retreat into the interior. Opechancanough was also captured in 1646 and was so old and blind that he needed to be carried on a litter. The English governor proudly paraded his captive around Jamestown, but a disgruntled English soldier shot Opechancanough while he was in prison. With his death came the end of the once-vast Powhatan Confederacy, which had decreased in total numbers by more than 90 percent. By 1669, only two thousand Virginia Algonquians still lived within the confederacy's homelands. Losing nearly all of their land to tobacco farms, the survivors were confined on several small reservations surrounded by colonial towns. Indians suspected of trespassing on colonial farms could be shot by white landowners, and by 1670 more than forty thousand Europeans inhabited the Chesapeake, making it the most profitable and most densely populated portion of the English empire in North America.

Ned Blackhawk

See also Federal Policy and Treaty Making: A Federal View; Government-to-Government Relationship; Powhatan.

References and Further Reading

Hodge, Frederick Webb, ed. 1910. *Handbook of American Indians.* Bureau of American Ethnology Bulletin 30. Washington, DC: Smithsonian Institution.

Rountree, Helen C. 2005. *Pocahontas, Powhatan, Opechancanough: Three Indian Lives Changed by Jamestown.* Charlottesville: University of Virginia Press.

Rountree, Helen C. 1990. *Pocahontas's People: The Powhatan Indians of Virginia through Four Centuries.* Norman: University of Oklahoma Press.

Opothleyahola
(c. 1798–1862)

Opothleyahola was an Upper Muscogee Creek leader and speaker before and after removal and a medicine man, trader, and Union ally during the Civil War. Known for his wisdom, calmness, and eloquence of speech, he rose to prominence prior to Muscogee removal from the current states of Georgia and Alabama.

During the War of 1812, Opothleyahola supported the conservative Red Stick cause, which advocated a renewed sense of Muscogee identity and called for all Indians to return to their traditional ways. He fought under William Weatherford against American troops led by General Andrew Jackson. After the war, he returned to his home in Tuckabatchee in present-day Alabama.

In 1824, the Muscogee people came under heavy pressure to sell their land in the East and remove to Indian Territory. U.S. commissioners met with the Creek National Council at Broken Arrow in December 1824 to discuss removal. Federal officials left the Broken Arrow meeting empty handed but returned in February 1825 to meet with William McIntosh and other Lower Creek headmen. Although the members of the Creek council did not attend the meeting, federal representatives negotiated a treaty with McIntosh. The federal commissioners rushed the treaty back to Washington, arriving just a few days before the Senate was to adjourn for spring recess. The Senate ratified the treaty without examination or discussion; the newly elected president, John Quincy Adams, signed the treaty on March 7, 1825.

The Creek National Council met, declared the Treaty of Indian Springs void, and ordered the execution of McIntosh and three of his accomplices. Then the council sent a group of representatives headed by Opothleyahola to Washington to meet with the president and renegotiate the Treaty of Indian Springs.

Opothleyahola and the other delegates succeeded in getting the McIntosh treaty abrogated, but they soon realized that the federal government still required them to cede all their land in Georgia. Opothleyahola became so distressed by the negotiations and the thought of losing his homeland that he attempted suicide. However, he did survive and thereafter worked diligently to secure the best possible terms for his nation.

The Treaty of Washington City relocated approximately seven thousand Creek from their homes in Georgia to tribal land in Alabama. Unfortunately, the white people of Alabama were not hospitable to the Creek. Living conditions were harsh, and the Creek were constantly harassed. Tension increased between the white settlers and the Indians, and in the spring of 1836 and summer of 1837 the Creek people were forcibly removed to Indian Territory.

Opothleyahola did not want to settle in Indian Territory, so he attempted to purchase land in present-day Texas, but the Mexican government refused to approve the land deal. Once he realized that he would not be able to remove to Texas, he led a group of twenty-seven hundred mostly full-blood, traditional Creeks to Indian Territory. When they arrived in 1836, the group refused to settle in the same area as the McIntosh Creek. He and his followers stayed for a few months near Fort Gibson, and then he led his people south toward the Canadian River. Although this area was set aside for Seminole settlement, Opothleyahola and his followers set up their headquarters there and established North Fork Town. As a result of their geographic separation, Opothleyahola's followers became known as the Canadian Creek, and the McIntosh followers were called the Arkansas Creek because they lived near the Arkansas River. The two factions each set up culturally distinct communities.

When the American Civil War began in 1861, the McIntosh Creek decided to support the Confederacy; Opothleyahola wanted the Creek Nation to remain neutral. As the war began, approximately ten thousand like-minded Indians from various tribes gathered near North Fork Town. As word circulated that the Confederate Creek planned to attack Opothleyahola's camp, he and his followers began traveling north toward Kansas. The refugees were attacked and harassed by Confederate forces all the way to Kansas.

The Loyal Creek endured indescribable horror on their journey to Kansas. Most of the refugees lost all their livestock and personal goods to the Confederates. A late December ice storm caused many of the people to suffer from frostbite, which required amputation of their hands and feet after arrival in Kansas. Unfortunately, after they arrived behind Union lines, neither the people in Kansas nor the federal government were able to provide adequate food, shelter, and clothing to those who survived the trip. Opothleyahola and several hundred of the 7,600 remaining refugees died during their first few months in Kansas from exposure, starvation, and disease.

Joyce Ann Kievit

See also Indian Removal; Indian Removal and Land Cessions, 1830–1849; McIntosh, William; Treaty with the Creek–February 12, 1825; Treaty with the Creek–January 24, 1826.

References and Further Reading

Brockway, Lela Jean McBride. 2000. *Opothleyaholo and the Loyal Muskogee: Their Flight to Kansas in the Civil War.* London: McFarland.

Debo, Angie. 1941. *The Road to Disappearance.* Norman: University of Oklahoma Press.

Fischer, LeRoy H., ed. 1974. *The Civil War Era in Indian Territory.* Los Angeles: L. L. Morrison.

Osceola

(c. 1804–1838)

Osceola was a great Seminole tribal leader who fought the United States against Native American emigration during the 1830s in the Florida swamps and was unconquered in war. Osceola, regarded as a brilliant war strategist, was also known as Asi-Yahola (Assiola)—Black Drink Singer—and Billy Powell. He was raised as a Muscogee Creek in Alabama. His lineage was always in question because of his early name, Billy Powell, and it was thought that he was the son of a white trader. Osceola vehemently denied having white ancestry.

When the Creek War of 1813–1814 began, Osceola and his mother were forced to flee to the Florida peninsula, where Spain claimed the land and the swamps that would prove useful to the survival of the Seminoles. The migration was led by Osceola's uncle, Peter McQueen, a Creek tribal leader. The Creeks joined the Seminole tribe, which was made up of Creeks from earlier migrations as well as other tribes, their black slaves, and Maroons (fugitive black slaves harbored by the Seminoles). Although his natural heritage would always be Creek, Osceola would eventually consider himself a Seminole.

As Osceola grew to manhood, the First Seminole War broke out in 1819 as a result of the white and Indian aggressions along the Georgia-Florida border. This war affected Osceola by making him a fugitive and contributing to his hatred of whites. While continuing his trek to manhood, he served as a medicine man's helper during the annual Creek Corn Dance. During the ceremony, adult titles were given, and the bitter black drink was used to purge and purify the body. It was one of these ceremonies, at the age of eighteen, that Osceola's name was formally changed from Billy Powell to Asi-Yahola (Black Drink Singer) and his future as a leader established.

A Seminole leader, Osceola (c. 1804–1838) achieved his status not as a hereditary chief but rather through his clearly demonstrated skills during the Second Seminole War of 1835–1842 in Florida. (Library of Congress)

In 1826, Osceola moved to an area known as Big Swamp with a growing band of followers. In 1832, the Treaty of Payne's Landing was negotiated, under the terms of which the Seminoles were to remove to a reservation in Arkansas, where they would be reunited with the Creeks, against whom they had fought in the Creek War. In addition, the treaty required all blacks to be turned over to white authorities upon removal. Slaves had been an integral part of the tribe for many years and had even intermarried. This requirement infuriated the Seminoles, including Osceola.

In 1832, Osceola had become a war leader. He was not elected, nor did he inherit his chiefdom; rather, he emerged as a defiant young leader of the Seminoles in their resistance to Indian emigration. He refused to have "his people" sign a treaty that would move the Seminoles from their lands in the Southeast to the unoccupied territory in the West.

Osceola became a guerrilla, an action that precipitated the Second Seminole War (1835–1842), where he used a cat-and-mouse strategy against U.S. troops in the Florida Everglades, costing the federal government an estimated $20 million in damages. Army leaders realized that the only way to stop the Seminoles was to stop Osceola, but as the war raged, he proved to be a formidable opponent and avoided capture.

Osceola became ill with malaria in 1836, however; ultimately, he grew weary of fighting and decided to talk peace. In October 1837, under a flag of truce, Osceola was lured from his hiding place, captured, and imprisoned in South Carolina, where he died.

Fred Lindsay

See also Fort Gibson, Oklahoma; Indian Removal; Jackson, Andrew; Sovereignty; Treaty; Treaty with the Seminole–May 9, 1832.

References and Further Reading

Johnson, Robert Proctor. 1973. *Osceola: The Story of an American Indian.* Minneapolis: Dillion Press.

Missall, John, and Mary Lou Missall. 2004. *The Seminole Wars: America's Longest Indian Conflict.* Gainesville: University Press of Florida.

Wickman, Patricia Riles. 1991. *Osceola's Legacy.* Tuscaloosa: University of Alabama Press.

Oshkosh

(1795–1858)

Oshkosh was grand chief of the Menominee of Wisconsin from 1827 until his death in 1858. He owed his power in part to the treaty process but came to use the system well, serving as a negotiator at all the major Menominee treaty conferences and successfully preventing removal of his people.

In some ways but not all, Oshkosh was destined to be grand chief. A member of the Bear clan, which was traditionally the clan of the first chiefs, this man earned the title Oshkosh (The Brave) at a very early age. Grandson and protégé of powerful chiefs, Oshkosh fought in the War of 1812 and had become the head of the Bear clan by 1821. In the early 1820s, after their old chiefs had died, the Menominee were divided; there was no consensus as to who should lead them or what their future should be. Descendants of the mixed-blood Carron family apparently challenged Oshkosh. The lack of leadership was evident at the boundary-setting negotiations for the Treaty of Prairie du Chien of 1825, at which the Menominee boundaries were left undetermined.

By 1827, Oshkosh had emerged as the leader, and he tried to help the Menominee stave off removal forces for the next thirty years. At the negotiations for another boundary-setting agreement, the Treaty of Butte des Morts, in July 1827, Lewis Cass, governor of Michigan Territory, found that the Menominee still had not chosen a new grand chief. He advised them to resolve this dilemma and, after consulting with them, named Oshkosh to the position and Josette Carron as second chief, or war chief. In addition to a peace and friendship treaty in 1817 and the two boundary-setting treaties, the Menominee were party to six additional treaties. Of these six, only three were both ratified by the Senate and accepted by the Menominee. The Treaty of the Cedars in 1836 was a land cession treaty. In 1848, the Menominee reluctantly ceded all their remaining land in Wisconsin to the federal government. After refusing to remove to their new land in Minnesota, the Menominee signed a new treaty in 1856 that allowed them a reservation in part of their precontact area of northern Wisconsin.

In these negotiations and in other ways, Oshkosh and the rest of the Menominee negotiators proved to be powerful and effective leaders for the Menominee, ultimately preventing removal. At negotiations in 1830, they objected to the translators and negotiators assigned, and the treaty commissioners granted changes. Also in 1830, a delegation of Menominee visited Washington, D.C. At the last minute, Oshkosh purposely decided not to attend so that any treaty forced on the Menominee would have no standing with the tribe. The Menominee subsequently rejected the signed treaty. In the Treaty of the Cedars, they negotiated very favorable terms for the tribe in comparison to other treaties of the time, netting an average of seventeen and a half cents per acre for the land they sold. Patricia Ourada, Menominee history expert, wrote that, at the negotiations, it was obvious that "behind the quiet voice of Chief Oshkosh was a strong will, aided by a shrewd mind" (Ourada 1979, 98).

Because of the 1848 land cession treaty that the tribe had been coerced into signing, all seemed lost, but Oshkosh refused to give up. After inspecting and rejecting the proposed removal site, Oshkosh convinced President Millard Fillmore to allow the Menominee to remain on their land until finally, in 1854, the push for removal had subsided and the people of Wisconsin agreed that the Menominee should be allowed to stay in the state. When Oshkosh died in 1858, his people had weathered removal and

still lived in part of their precontact territory—a claim not many Indian leaders could make.

Angela Firkus

See also Indian Removal; Prairie du Chien, Wisconsin; Treaty with the Chippewa, Etc.–August 11, 1827; Treaty with the Menominee–September 3, 1836; Treaty with the Sioux, Etc.–August 19, 1825.

References and Further Reading

Hoffman, Walter James. 1896. *The Menomini Indians.* United States Bureau of American Ethnology, Fourteenth Annual Report, 1892–93. Washington, DC: Government Printing Office. Repr., New York: Johnson Reprint Corporation, 1970.

Keesing, Felix. M. 1839. *The Menomini Indians of Wisconsin: A Study of Three Centuries of Cultural Contact and Change.* Philadelphia: American Philosophical Society. Repr., Madison: University of Wisconsin Press, 1987.

Ourada, Patricia K. 1979. *The Menominee Indians: A History.* Norman: University of Oklahoma Press.

Turner, Katharine C. 1951. *Red Men Calling on the Great White Father.* Norman: University of Oklahoma Press.

Chief Ouray (1833–1880) of the Southern Ute, served as a spokesman for the seven Ute bands, and as a peacemaker during the Ute War of 1879. (Library of Congress)

Ouray

(1833–1880)

Ouray was born in Taos, New Mexico, in 1833, the son of an Uncompahgre Ute mother and a Jicarilla Apache father named Guera Murah. He grew up to become the best-known of all Ute leaders during the nineteenth century. Upon reaching adulthood, he left northern New Mexico for southern Colorado, where most of the Uncompahgre band of Utes lived. His father, despite his Jicarilla heritage, had become a leader of the band, and Ouray followed in his footsteps. By 1860, with his father's death, Ouray himself had become a leader or chief of the Uncompahgres.

During the early 1860s, the trickle of white settlers and miners into the Southern Utes' territory in the San Juan Mountains of southwestern Colorado became a flood as the search for new sources of gold spread across the West. Although Ouray was unwavering in his protection of Ute lands, he never advocated going to war against the settlers or the U.S. government.

As with many Indian leaders during these years, Ouray had to choose whether to resist relocation and assimilation or accept the federal government's plan for his people. The fact that he is remembered as always befriending whites and federal officials says much about the direction he thought best for his people.

Fluent in four languages (Spanish, his primary language; English; Ute; and Jicarilla Apache), Ouray impressed with his intellect the white officials who were acquainted with him, including Presidents Ulysses S. Grant and Rutherford B. Hayes. His education and his observations of the experiences of other Indian peoples informed his opinion on the futility of war against the whites who were invading Ute territory.

In 1868, Ouray and other Ute leaders negotiated a treaty with Indian agent Kit Carson that gave the Utes fifteen million acres of land in southern Colorado and promised that they would be left alone. In addition, the treaty gave livestock, seed, and farming implements to all Utes wishing to adopt a farming lifestyle. However, the continued influx of miners quickly made the treaty terms moot, forcing a renegotiation of the treaty in 1873, in which the Utes signed over approximately four million acres. Even this proved insufficient when gold was discovered on Ute land in the late 1870s.

Public pressure to remove the Utes from Colorado altogether grew as small parties of Utes reacted by raiding white settlements in 1879. In September, members of the White River band attacked a regiment of some two hundred soldiers sent to protect the local Indian agency, proceeded to set fire to the agency, and killed agent Nathan C. Meeker and ten others. As Ouray might have predicted, the "Meeker Massacre" served only to outrage the white population and prompted an increase in demands for the Utes' removal from the region. Even Ouray could not quell the violence among Ute bands other than his own, and in 1880 the Utes agreed to relocate to a reservation in eastern Utah that, ironically, bears Ouray's name, although Ouray himself did not live to see his people's removal in 1881.

In August 1880, Ouray traveled to the Southern Ute agency at Ignacio, Colorado, to negotiate for more land for his people. Unfortunately, he became ill along the way and died very quickly after his arrival. Upon hearing of his death, the Denver *Tribune* reported on August 24, 1880, "In the death of Ouray, one of the historical characters passes away. He has figured quite prominently. Ouray is in many respects . . . a remarkable Indian . . . pure instincts and keen perception. A friend to the white man and protector to the Indians."

Steven L. Danver

See also Assimilation; Satanta; Sitting Bear (Setangya or Satank); Southern Plains and the Southwest; Treaty of Guadalupe Hidalgo, 1848.

References and Further Reading

Jefferson, James, Robert W. Delaney, and Gregory C. Thompson. 1972. *The Southern Utes: A Tribal History*. Edited by Floyd A. O'Neil. Ignacio, CO: Southern Ute Tribe.

Lyman, June, and Norma Denver, comp. 1969. *Ute People: An Historical Study*. Edited by Floyd A. O'Neil and John D. Sylvester. Salt Lake City: Uintah School District and Western History Center, University of Utah.

O'Neil, Floyd A., and Kathryn L. MacKay. 1979. *A History of the Uintah-Ouray Ute Lands*. American West Center Occasional Papers. Salt Lake City: American West Center, University of Utah.

Stewart, Omer C. 1966. "Ute Indians: Before and After White Contact." *Utah Historical Quarterly* 34: 38–61.

Parker, Ely S. (Do-He-No-Geh-Weh)

(c. 1828–1895)

Ely (pronounced ēlē) Samuel Parker, or Do-He-No-Geh-Weh (Keeper of the Western Door), was a full-blooded Seneca who became the first American Indian to head the Office of Indian Affairs (OIA), or today's Bureau of Indian Affairs (BIA). Parker grew up on a reservation in upstate New York, where he attended the missionary school. He obtained law and engineering degrees before serving as an officer on General Ulysses S. Grant's staff during the Civil War. Parker was the only nonwhite at Robert E. Lee's surrender, for which Parker wrote out the terms.

Ely Samuel Parker came from a distinguished Seneca family that had a significant history of interactions with whites. Red Jacket, the famed Indian orator who obtained his name by allying with the British during the American Revolution, was Parker's tribal grandfather. After the war, the newly formed U.S. government made overtures of peace to the Seneca and Red Jacket. President George Washington presented Red Jacket with a large medal as a

Ely S. Parker, a Seneca and civil engineer, served in the U.S. Grant administration as commissioner from 1869 to 1871. (National Archives)

symbol of friendship and future cooperation. Ely Parker inherited this medal and wore it at all times. His father, William Parker, served during the War of 1812 and was wounded fighting for the Americans.

Born on the Seneca Tonawanda Reservation in upstate New York, Parker obtained his name from Baptist minister Ely Stone, who set up a mission school there. An outstanding student, Parker gained an education and became a practicing Christian while at the local reservation mission school. These attributes helped lay the foundation for his future support of the assimilation of Natives through reservations, education, and Christianity.

Parker's prominence among his own people came early. Before meeting Grant, he served the Seneca by visiting with presidents and congressmen regarding treaty and removal problems. In May 1846, at the age of eighteen, Parker was the interpreter for an American Indian civil rights delegation meeting with President James K. Polk to try to prevent Seneca removal. With the help of Washington politicians, the Seneca Nation successfully resisted removal. During his visit to the capital, Parker met with such notables as Daniel Webster, Henry Clay, John C. Calhoun, Dolley Madison, and Cherokee leader John Ross.

In January 1853, Parker rose to the position of elected chief and representative of the Iroquois Nation. In this role, he negotiated with the government and oversaw legal strategy, which inhibited Seneca removal and reinstated their prior agreements with the government. He knew the threat and damage that removal caused American Indian nations, and he vehemently opposed it. To avoid removal, Parker had to prove that the tribe had made progress toward "civilization." To do so, Parker reported to the government the nation's increased farm production and the significant number of buildings recently built on the reservation.

Parker also obtained a law degree but was banned from taking the bar exam because of his race. He then earned an engineering degree, whereupon he worked on both the Erie Canal and the Chesapeake and Albemarle Canal. In 1857, Grant met Parker while the latter engineered the government's construction of a customs house and maritime hospital in Galena, Illinois.

When Civil War broke out, Parker once again experienced prejudice because of his American Indian heritage. Prohibited from joining the Union Army by Secretary of War William H. Seward, Parker remained determined. After Parker's two years of exhausting efforts to enlist, John Rawlins, also of Galena and a member of Grant's staff, appealed to the War Department on behalf of Parker. Grant, too, wrote the department a praise-filled letter asking that the Seneca be allowed to join the army. Ultimately, in the summer of 1863, the army consented, and Parker enlisted as a captain because of his education. He became one of Grant's most trusted subordinates.

Ely Parker served on Grant's staff from 1863 to 1871, eventually rising to the rank of brigadier general. He remained with Grant from Vicksburg through the first year and a half of Grant's presidency. He served as Grant's point man for Indian affairs from 1865 to 1871. After the war, Parker held the position of commissioner of the OIA (1869–71), helping the president initiate his Peace Policy. Late in life, he renounced many of the assimilation practices he once had practiced and promoted. Parker is buried in Buffalo, New York's Forest Lawn Cemetery, where several monuments are dedicated to his family.

Scott L. Stabler

See also Cornplanter; Government-to-Government Relationship; Northeast and the Great Lakes; Red Jacket; Treaties and American Indian Schools in the Age of Assimilation, 1794–1930.

References and Further Reading

Abrams, George H. J. 1976. *The Seneca People:* Phoenix, AZ: Indian Tribal Series.

Armstrong, William H. 1978. *Warrior in Two Camps: Union General and Seneca Chief.* Syracuse, NY: University of Syracuse Press.

Parker, Arthur C. 1919. *The Life of General Ely S. Parker: Last Grand Sachem of the Iroquois and General Grant's Military Secretary.* Buffalo, NY: Buffalo Historical Society.

Parker, Quanah
(c. 1850–1911)

Commonly cited as the last chief of the Comanche, Quanah (Fragrant or Sweet Smelling) Parker led Comanche resistance to the Treaty of Medicine Lodge of 1867 until the mid-1870s, when he began to encourage Native American assimilation into white society. Although many tribes accepted the treaty, Parker led a renegade band of Quahadi Comanche in defiance of U.S. demands that they resettle onto reservations in the Indian Territory (present-day Oklahoma). Raiding white settlements across the

Quanah Parker (c. 1850–1911) was a Comanche leader and successful rancher. (Library of Congress)

Llano Estacado (Staked Plain) in the panhandle of Texas, Quanah and his followers evaded U.S. Army troops for seven years after the signing of the treaty. Relentless pursuit by the army, however, forced Quanah to surrender his band in 1875. For the rest of his life, Quanah encouraged his people to embrace their new life on the reservation and to assimilate into white society.

Born to Peta Nocona, a Quahadi Comanche chief, and Cynthia Ann Parker, a white woman adopted by the Comanche after being captured in a raid on a white settlement, Quanah's life straddled both the Native American and white worlds. In October 1867, the Arapahoe, Eastern Apache, Cheyenne, Comanche, and Kiowa tribes signed a treaty with the United States along the banks of Medicine Lodge Creek in southern Kansas. In exchange for the tribes' agreement to resettle on reservations in the

Indian Territory and to cease attacking the ever-spreading railroads and white settlements, the U.S. government promised to establish schools to educate Native American children and to provide assistance for the tribes' transition to subsistence farming.

Although many of the Plains Indians acquiesced to the treaty, Quanah led a band of Quahadi Comanches who refused to accept it. They raided white settlements along the Llano Estacado and evaded numerous army expeditions led by Colonel Ranald Mackenzie to capture them. At the same time, spurred by improvements in tanning techniques and the development of new high-powered rifles, white hunters nearly decimated the buffalo herds crucial to the nomadic Comanche way of life. Desperate to fight off the encroaching whites, Quanah and a medicine man named Esa-tai led a coalition of seven hundred warriors in an assault against twenty-eight buffalo hunters at the battle of Adobe Walls in June 1874. Quanah and his followers withdrew after three days of fighting, having killed only three whites but taking heavy casualties themselves. The army continued to pursue Quanah and his band until they finally surrendered at Fort Sill in June 1876.

Once on the reservation, Quanah encouraged his people to embrace much of white culture. He befriended local cattle ranchers, including Charles Goodnight, and began to build a herd of his own, which eventually made him wealthy. Under Quanah's guidance, the Comanche leased out unused reservation land to nearby white ranchers (who were already grazing their cattle on the land in violation of the treaty anyway), which eased tensions with whites and brought money into the reservation. Quanah also promoted formal education among his people at the white-run schools and became active in local affairs, gaining the confidence of white leaders.

By the early 1890s, Quanah was the principal chief of all the Comanche in the Indian Territory. In 1893, he traveled to Washington, D.C., to represent his people in negotiations with the Jerome Commission, which had been formed in 1889 to implement the General Allotment Act. The act proposed to divide up the communal reservation lands into individual allotments, which Quanah opposed because it would prevent the Comanche from leasing unused portions of their lands to cattle ranchers. Eventually, the land was divided, and a contingent of anti-Quanah Comanche (who had always opposed his leadership, in part because of his half-white ancestry) criticized Quanah as an accommodationist.

By the turn of the century, Quanah's life was in decline. His wealth had eroded because of the individual allotment of reservation land, and two of his wives left him. Yet he remained a good friend of many powerful whites and was one of four Native Americans to ride in Theodore Roosevelt's inaugural procession. He died of heart failure on February 23, 1911.

Andrew J. Torget

See also General Allotment Act (Dawes Act), 1887; Indian Territory; Jerome, David H.; Medicine Lodge Creek, Kansas; Treaty with the Kiowa and Comanche–October 21, 1867.

References and Further Reading

Fehrenbach, T. R. 1974. *Comanches: The Destruction of a People.* New York: Alfred A. Knopf.

Neeley, Bill. 1995. *The Last Comanche Chief: The Life and Times of Quanah Parker.* New York: John Wiley.

Weems, John. 1976. *Death Song: The Last of the Indian Wars.* New York: Doubleday.

Penn, William

(1644–1718)

William Penn was an important English Quaker and a voice for religious tolerance in Europe and North America. He founded the Pennsylvania Colony (the state's name is anglicized Latin for "Penn's forest"). The colony's original principles included scrupulous attention to nonviolence (which remains a central tenet of the Quaker creed) as well as fairness in relations with Native Americans, most notably the Leni Lenápes, whom Europeans called the Delawares.

Penn's memory has been a presence throughout Native American history, especially in the Northeast. Quaker influence is particularly notable in the religion of Handsome Lake (known today as the Longhouse Religion) among the Iroquois. Quakers often were invited as trustworthy observers at treaty councils and other crucial events by Native Americans in the Northeast who suspected the motives of other European Americans. As recently as 1990, Quakers were invited to act as observers in clashes between factions on the Akwesasne Mohawk reservation. The Society of Friends, which still maintains its headquarters in Philadelphia, devotes substantial resources to Native American history and relations.

Penn's "holy experiment" was designed to grant asylum to the persecuted under conditions of equality and freedom, at a time when a person

William Penn makes a treaty with Native Americans in Pennsylvania. Penn, a Quaker, campaigned for peace and religious toleration. (Library of Congress)

could be punished severely in Puritan Boston merely for professing Quakerism and when Protestants persecuted Catholics, Catholics persecuted Protestants, and both persecuted Quakers and Jews. The French philosopher Voltaire, a champion of religious toleration, offered lavish praise: "William Penn might, with reason, boast of having brought down upon earth the Golden Age, which in all probability, never had any real existence but in his dominions" (Powell n.d.).

Penn's vision for his colony could be compared in many ways to that of Roger Williams, who had founded Providence Plantations (later Rhode Island) a few decades earlier. Like Penn, Williams was a dissenter from theocracy who welcomed many faiths at a time of deadly religious conflict in England. Williams also practiced very cordial relations with neighboring Native Americans. Like Penn, Williams carried on his campaign for religious tolerance on both sides of the Atlantic.

The most specific description of Penn's mother, Margaret, comes from a neighbor, the acid-tongued diarist Samuel Pepys, who described her as a "fat, short, old Dutch woman, but one who hath been heretofore pretty handsome" (Powell n.d.). She did the child rearing because her husband was seldom at home. His father, William Penn, Sr., was a much-sought-after naval commander because he knew the waters around England, could handle a ship in bad weather, and could get the most from his crew.

William Penn, Jr., was born on October 14, 1644, in London. He developed an early interest in religion, having heard a speech by Thomas Loe, a missionary for the Society of Friends, known by the then-derisive name Quakers. Founded in 1647 by the English preacher George Fox, the Quakers were a mystical Protestant sect that emphasized a direct relationship with God. An individual's conscience, not the Bible, was believed by the Quakers to be the ultimate authority; their doctrine resembled that of the modern-day Unitarians. Quakers had no clergy and no churches. Rather, they held meetings at which participants meditated silently and spoke when moved to do so. They favored plain dress and a simple life (Powell n.d.).

Penn studied Greek and Roman classics and became a religious rebel at Oxford University, where he defied Anglican church officials by visiting John Owen, a professor who had been dismissed for advocating tolerant humanism. Penn also protested compulsory chapel attendance, a position for which he was expelled from Oxford at age seventeen. Penn's parents then sent him to France, where he enrolled at l'Academie Protestante.

Returning to England by 1664, Penn studied at Lincoln's Inn, a prestigious London law school in London. Penn attended Quaker meetings (a criminal act) and was arrested several times. As an aristocrat, he was released, but he insisted that all Quakers be treated equally. Penn was imprisoned six times in England for speaking his mind on matters of religion. While incarcerated, he wrote several pamphlets that provided a theoretical basis for Quakerism, meanwhile attacking intolerance. Penn also devoted considerable time to challenging oppressive government policies in court; one of his cases helped protect the right to trial by jury. Penn used his diplomatic skills and family connections to get large numbers of Quakers out of jail. He also saved many from the gallows (Powell n.d.).

As a result of these activities, the junior Penn's father disowned him. After his release from jail, Penn lived in several Quaker households. When Penn attacked the Catholic and Anglican doctrine of the Trinity, the Anglican bishop had him imprisoned in the infamous Tower of London. Ordered to recant, Penn declared from his cold isolation cell: "My prison shall be my grave before I will budge a jot; for I owe my conscience to no mortal man" (Powell n.d.). In the Tower, Penn wrote several pamphlets defining the principal elements of Quakerism, the best known being *No Cross, No Crown,* which presented a pioneering historical case for religious toleration. During this time, the British Parliament passed the Conventicle Act, which aimed to suppress religious dissent as sedition. Having won his release from prison on legal grounds, Penn challenged the act by preaching Quakerism at public meetings. Penn later used his legal training to prepare an historic defense of religious toleration in court. The jury acquitted all defendants, but the lord mayor of London refused to accept this verdict. He hit the jury members with fines and ordered them held in brutal Newgate prison (Powell n.d.). They sued the mayor for false arrest and won, establishing a major precedent protecting their right of trial by jury.

Convinced that religious toleration was not possible in England, Penn requested a charter for an American colony. On March 4, 1681, realizing that he could rid England of the nettlesome Quakers, Charles II signed a charter for territory west of the Delaware River and north of Maryland. In 1681, from England, Penn sent William Markham as his deputy to establish a government at Uppland (later renamed Chester, now a suburb of Philadelphia) and instructed commissioners to plot Philadelphia (a name derived from ancient Greek, meaning "city of brotherly love"), which was laid out a few miles north of the point where the Delaware and the Schuylkill rivers converge.

The First Frame of Government, which Penn and the initial land purchasers adopted on April 25, 1682, expressed ideals anticipating the Declaration of Independence: "Men being born with a title to perfect freedom and uncontrolled enjoyment of all the rights and privileges of the law of nature. . . . No one can be put out of his estate and subjected to the political view of another, without his consent" (Powell n.d.). This document provided for secure private property, nearly unlimited free enterprise, a free press, and trial by jury, as well as religious toleration. In contrast to the English penal code, which commended the death penalty for roughly two hundred offenses, Penn reserved it for two: murder and treason. Penn also encouraged women's education and participation in public debate (Powell n.d.).

Pennsylvania's legal structure included a humane penal code that (in 1701) extended civil rights to criminals and encouraged the emancipation of slaves, although Penn himself owned human capital. Emancipation did not become official Quaker doctrine until 1758. Even under such a system, however, the representative assembly was left in an inferior position to the executive, which was controlled by the proprietors of the colony.

Penn realized that much of the land his supporters occupied was held by Native Americans, most notably the Delawares (Leni Lenápes), who had never been defeated militarily by the Swedes or the Dutch, who had earlier claimed the area. True to his nonviolent doctrines, Penn refused to fortify Philadelphia, making friendly relations with Native neighbors a practical necessity. Penn also inspired confidence among Native peoples by traveling among them unarmed and without bodyguards.

In 1682, Penn met with the chiefs of the Delaware Nation at the village of Shackamaxon, near the present-day Kensington district of Philadelphia, and signed the Great Treaty, which pledged long-lasting goodwill between the Native Americans and the immigrating Europeans. Philadelphia quickly grew into an urban area of almost twenty thousand people, for a time the largest city in the British colonies. The city retained its reputation as a beacon of freedom for many decades, during which time Benjamin Franklin, for one, moved there from Puritan Boston.

The negotiation of a treaty with the Leni Lenápes also affirmed Penn's claim to the land for his investors, who would have been much less interested in a venture lacking clear title. The treaty also implied diplomatic relations with the powerful Haudenosaunee (Iroquois) Confederacy, of whom the Lenápe were subsidiary allies. Therefore, a chain of friendship (later called the Covenant Chain in frontier diplomacy) was engaged by Penn, although his less scrupulous successors disregarded its provisions in their rush to acquire land. The treaty invoked the rights of both parties to share some areas that European Americans subsequently took for themselves.

Throughout his tenure as chief executive of Pennsylvania, Penn maintained peaceful relations with the area's indigenous peoples, including the Susquehannocks and Shawnees, as well as the Leni Lenápe. His abilities as a sprinter—he could outrun

many Natives—won him respect. He also learned local Native languages well enough to conduct negotiations without interpreters. From the very beginning, Penn acquired Native land through peaceful, voluntary exchange.

Penn was a shrewd businessman who competed with Lord Baltimore, founder of Maryland, for territorial rights. Using his friendly relations with Native peoples, Penn outmaneuvered Maryland agents, a fact that is evident today to anyone who compares the relative sizes of Pennsylvania and Maryland. Most notably, Penn bested Baltimore at acquiring trading rights with the Haudenosaunee Confederacy. Thus, when Benjamin Franklin began his diplomatic career in the early 1750s as Pennsylvania envoy to the Iroquois, he was filling a role first explored by Penn.

By 1701, Penn had returned to England for the rest of his life. He tried to administer his declining estate from a distance until he experienced a debilitating stroke in 1712. Four months later, he suffered a second stroke. After that, Penn experienced difficulty speaking and writing until he died on July 30, 1718.

Bruce E. Johansen

See also Handsome Lake.
References and Further Reading
Dunn, Richard S., and Mary M. Dunn, eds. 1981–1987. *The Papers of William Penn.* Philadelphia: University of Pennsylvania Press.
Dunn, Richard S., and Mary M. Dunn, eds. 1986. *The World of William Penn.* Philadelphia: University of Pennsylvania Press.
Lutz, Norma Jean. 2000. *William Penn: Founder of Democracy.* New York: Chelsea House.
Powell, Jim. No date. "William Penn, America's First Great Champion for Liberty and Peace." *The Freeman: Ideas on Liberty.* Accessed January 20, 2007, at http://www.quaker.org/wmpenn.html.
Watson, John F. 1857. *Annals of Philadelphia and Pennsylvania in the Olden Time.* Philadelphia: E. Thomas.

Pike, Albert
(1809–1891)

Massachusetts-born Albert Pike began his dealings with Native Americans in the West, drawn to the region in the 1830s by adventure and a belief in the opportunities there. Pike became a mountain man in the far Southwest and later published one of the first descriptions of the region and its people. He eventu-

Albert Pike (1809–1891) was a mountain man before becoming a lawyer, leading to many dealings with Native Americans in the West. He was also a brigadier general for the Confederacy and negotiated treaties with Indian tribes for the South. (Library of Congress)

ally settled in Arkansas, practiced law there, supported the Whig Party, and became well known for his writings, oratory, newspaper editing, legal mind, and connections with Indian tribes. During the 1850s, he represented the Creek and the Choctaw and pressed their claims against the U.S. government for unjust and unfulfilled treaty agreements. For the Creek, that meant payment for lands lost under the Treaty of Fort Jackson (1814), and Pike won a substantial claim for the tribe. Mostly, Pike was a lobbyist for the tribes in Congress. He was already familiar with Indian Territory tribes, having defended many members in the courts of western Arkansas. Most important, he strengthened his associations with these tribes and used those connections in his role as the principal Confederate agent to tribes in Indian Territory.

Out of necessity, the Confederacy looked to the West for expansion and economic needs. Indian Territory was the Confederacy's gateway to the West with its cattle and horses, and as a northern buffer zone between Texas and Union-held Kansas. The

Confederate government in Richmond, Virginia, commissioned Pike to negotiate treaties of alliance between the Confederacy and tribes west of Arkansas, notably the Five Civilized Tribes (Cherokee, Chickasaw, Choctaw, Creek, and Seminole). The design was to make Indian Territory a military district defended by the tribes. Pike first visited each of the Five Civilized Tribes and other tribes in northeastern Indian Territory such as the Quapaw and Osage. He then visited the Caddo, the Wichita, and some Comanche bands in the Leased District to the west. The Cherokee were Pike's first priority, the first tribe he met with on June 1, 1861, and the tribe with whom he eventually leveraged an alliance. He then met with delegates from the Chickasaw, Choctaw, Creek, and Seminole during July and August. The treaties Pike established bound the tribes officially to the Confederate cause, a decision that would be detrimental to the tribes after the war, for the federal government would use them to justify reconstruction treaties that began to chip away at tribal sovereignty and lands.

The Confederate treaties with the Five Civilized Tribes were all similar. Each assured that the Confederacy would assume protection and payments promised in federal treaties. All Indian Territory lands would be annexed to the Confederacy, though each tribe was guaranteed perpetual right to hold tribal lands in common. The Confederacy also offered the tribes greater sovereignty in determining tribal citizenship, controlling trade and tribal finances, and equal standing in surrounding state courts. Reciprocal handling of fugitive slave laws and the legality and perpetuity of slavery were outlined, too. The Confederacy also promised improved roads and mail service. In return, the tribes were to raise troops to defend the region, the troops to be paid and equipped by the Confederacy. Three regiments were formed: a single Cherokee regiment, a combined regiment of Creek and Seminole, and another combined regiment of Choctaw and Chickasaw. In negotiations with other tribes known as the Reserve Indians of the Leased District, Pike offered gifts and rations and pledged arms and ammunition. With the Comanche, he convinced some chiefs to stop stealing horses and making raids into Texas and instead to turn their energies against pro-Union settlements in Kansas.

For his success negotiating the Indian treaties, the Confederate government commissioned Pike a brigadier general and assigned him to Indian Territory to command the Indian regiments there as part of the Confederacy's Army of the West. Pike established his command in the Creek territory near the Verdigris River. Throughout his commission, Pike strived to maintain the tribes' commitments to the Confederacy— especially the Creek and Cherokee, who were divided in their support of the war and plagued by internal strife—while also dealing with racist-minded Confederate commanders. In early March 1862, Pike led eight hundred Cherokee troops at the Battle of Pea Ridge (Elkhorn Tavern) in Arkansas. Though the Confederacy lost the battle, Pike's troops distinguished themselves. Exaggerated Union propaganda about Union soldiers scalped by the Cherokee at Pea Ridge gained Pike an infamous reputation in the North as a "recreant Yankee." Even after his commission ended, Pike remained a dedicated factotum keeping Indian Territory supportive of the Confederacy.

S. Matthew DeSpain

See also Government-to-Government Relationship; Indian Territory; Opothleyahola; Ross, John; Southeast and Florida.

References and Further Reading
Abel, Annie Heloise. 1992. *The American Indian in the Civil War, 1862–1865.* Lincoln: University of Nebraska Press.
Brown, Walter Lee. 1997. *A Life of Albert Pike.* Fayetteville: University of Arkansas Press.
Cottrell, Steve, and Andy Thomas. 1995. *Civil War in Indian Territory.* New York: Pelican.
Fischer, LeRoy. 1974. *Civil War Era in Indian Territory.* Los Angeles: Lorin L. Morrison.
Spencer, John. 2006. *The American Civil War in Indian Territory.* Oxford: Osprey.
Taylor, Ethel Crisp. 2005. *Dust in the Wind: The Civil War in Indian Territory.* Westminister, MD: Heritage Books.

Pitchlynn, Peter
(1806–1881)

A diplomat and Choctaw chief, Peter Pitchlynn successfully fought to preserve tribal sovereignty. After coming to political prominence as the captain of a police force established by the Treaty of Doak's Stand in 1820, Pitchlynn helped negotiate the removal of the Choctaw to Oklahoma in the Treaty of Dancing Rabbit Creek in 1830. He bore primary responsibility for negotiating treaties that enabled the Chickasaws to settle among the Choctaws in 1837 and to have their own domain in 1850. He also served as one of the tribal delegates to the U.S. government to resolve lingering problems related to the Choctaw removal.

Born on January 30, 1806, in Hush-ook-wa, Mississippi, to John Pitchlynn, a wealthy English Indian trader, and Sophia Folsom, a Métis (mixed-blood), Pitchlynn was named Ha-tchoc-tuck-nee (Snapping Turtle) by his Choctaw friends. His education at two mission schools reinforced his white background and separated him from the traditional Native American path. It may also have made it easier for him to negotiate with whites in subsequent years.

Physically impressive at six feet with hazel eyes, brunet hair, and an erect posture, Pitchlynn displayed an early interest in holding a leadership position within the tribe. When the Choctaw established a police force, known as the Lighthorse, according to the provisions of the Treaty of Doak's Stand, Pitchlynn campaigned to lead the unit and won election as colonel in 1824. The Lighthorse closed all the shops in Mississippi that sold liquor to the Native Americans. In recognition of his work, the Choctaws elected Pitchlynn to the national council that adopted the tribe's first written constitution in 1826.

In 1830, the state of Mississippi attempted to gain control over the Choctaws by repealing the laws extending rights and privileges to the tribe. Fearful of the effects of state law upon the tribe, Pitchlynn joined the group that drew up a treaty of emigration and prepared to move west. The terms offered by the U.S. government were unsatisfactory, however, and Pitchlynn helped organize armed resistance to the implementation of the treaty. When the United States agreed to provide additional land reservations, the Choctaws abandoned this small rebellion to sign the Treaty of Dancing Rabbit Creek in 1830 and move to lands that Pitchlynn helped select as the chief of the Northeastern District.

Pitchlynn's position as a district chief was not recognized in Oklahoma, but he still remained a leader. He acted as the principal Choctaw commissioner during negotiations with the Chickasaws in 1837. This neighboring tribe had ceded their Mississippi lands to the United States, and the federal government then attempted to settle the Chickasaws among the Choctaws in Oklahoma. The Chickasaws ultimately bought a district west of the Choctaw settlements.

By the early 1850s, the federal government had still not fulfilled all its removal treaty obligations, and the Choctaws were determined to settle all of their claims. Pitchlynn, who was already familiar with American legal procedure and acquainted with government officials, was chosen in 1853 to resolve all of the remaining issues. The Choctaws admitted that most tribal claims could not be adequately proved. Pitchlynn proposed to give the claimants some justice by combining all the individual complaints into one large demand with any financial settlement to be administered locally by the tribe. A treaty signed on June 22, 1855, gave the Choctaws partial recognition of their claims against the United States, and the Senate approved a monetary settlement in 1859, but the government dawdled on payment.

With the arrival of the Civil War, the slaveholding Pitchlynn wanted the Choctaws to remain loyal to the Union, but Southern influences forced the tribe to sign a treaty of alliance with the Confederacy in 1861. On October 6, 1864, the Choctaws chose Pitchlynn to be their principal chief, although he had not participated in the Southern treaty. Pitchlynn declared that the tribe would continue to support the South, but Union victories forced his hand. On June 19, 1865, he signed a surrender agreement with the United States that granted the Choctaws the protection of the federal government instead of treating them as paroled Confederate supporters. In 1866, while in negotiations with the federal government, he denied that the Choctaw alliance with the Confederacy had revoked all previous treaties with the United States. Later that year, Pitchlynn agreed to a treaty that placed Kansas Indians among the Choctaws and that created a U.S. court in Choctaw territory. The federal government agreed to pay the funds still owed the Choctaws, with all money disbursed by 1889, eight years after Pitchlynn's death on January 17, 1881.

Caryn E. Neumann

See also Aboriginal Title; Indian Removal Act, 1830; Indian Removal and Land Cessions, 1830–1849; Indian Territory; Property: Land and Natural Resources; Pushmataha; Southeast and Florida; Trail of Tears; Treaty with the Choctaw–September 27, 1830.

References and Further Reading

Baird, W. David. 1972. *Peter Pitchlynn: Chief of the Choctaws*. Norman: University of Oklahoma Press.

DeRosier, Arthur H., Jr. 1970. *The Removal of the Choctaw Indians*. Knoxville: University of Tennessee Press.

Kidwell, Clara Sue. 1995. *Choctaws and Missionaries in Mississippi, 1818–1918*. Norman: University of Oklahoma Press.

Pokagun
(c. 1776–1841)

Pokagun was a Potawatomi leader who gained prominence in the early 1830s because of his successful opposition to the removal of his people from the St. Joseph River valley of southern Michigan. Even as other Indian groups in the Great Lakes region signed away their lands and moved west in the years after the Indian Removal Act, Pokagun resisted government efforts and made arrangements to secure lands for his family and his followers. As a result of his labors, the Pokagun community of Potawatomi maintained a presence in Michigan well into the twentieth century.

Although his origins and early years remain somewhat unclear, Pokagun was most likely born in the mid-1770s of either Ottawa or Chippewa parents. He was known among the American and Potawatomi communities in the western Great Lakes region as Pokagun, but his proper name was Sakekwinik, which means Man of the River's Mouth. He did not appear as a headman on any treaties prior to 1826 but affiliated himself with one of the more prominent families among the Potawatomi by marrying a niece of the Potawatomi headman Topenibe. From 1826 to 1833, Pokagun advocated on behalf of his people settled in the St. Joseph River valley of southern Michigan, and he became a known figure among local U.S. officials. At the same time, he also established strong connections with the Jesuits who had recently returned to missionary work in the region, and in July 1830 he was baptized under the name of Leopold Pokagon.

As American settlement increased in the western Great Lakes region, Pokagun encouraged his followers to improve their homes and their lands through an increased reliance on sedentary agricultural practices. Although the Potawatomi already raised crops for subsistence, Pokagun believed that, in moving away from more traditional practices, he and his people had a better chance of avoiding removal. In the fall of 1833, he journeyed with other representatives of the Michigan Potawatomi to the treaty negotiations called for by government-designated commissioners in Chicago. The bulk of the treaty councils focused on land cessions from the United Band of Ottawas, Chippewas, and Potawatomis residing in northeastern Illinois and southeastern Wisconsin Territory. During those negotiations Pokagun served as the spokesmen for those Indian groups that did not want to remove from their lands.

Although the leaders of the United Band agreed to a land cession of approximately five million acres, the Michigan Potawatomi did not. They did not even set up camp with the other Indian delegations but maintained a separate site with the intention of avoiding any undue influence to force their submission to removal. Pokagun particularly stressed the differences in lifestyle and viewpoints between the "Woods" bands of southern Michigan and the "Prairie" bands of Potawatomis, who resided in Illinois and the Wisconsin Territory. His stand and the determination of his band resulted in an addendum to the Treaty of 1833 that allowed them to remain in Michigan while other Potawatomi groups relocated to lands west of the Mississippi River. The specific reason given for this exception in the treaty was the Indians' "religious creed," a reference to their adherence to Catholicism. Pokagun also personally benefited from the treaty, receiving a payment of $2,000 in lieu of an individual land grant.

Although this addendum to the Treaty of Chicago seemingly granted the Michigan Potawatomi a permanent exemption from removal, Pokagun and his people had to fight constantly for their right to remain in the region. In the late 1830s, Pokagun used money he had received from treaties, including the Treaty of 1833, to purchase almost nine hundred acres of land around Silver Creek in southwestern Michigan. Even with this official purchase, Pokagun and his band had to struggle with settlers in the region who desired to lay claim to those very lands. Finally, in 1840, Pokagun traveled to Detroit to secure the legal opinion of an associate justice of the Michigan Supreme Court that established the right of the Potawatomi to remain on these purchased lands. Not long after, on July 8, 1841, Pokagun passed away and left the title to the land as a legacy for his people.

John P. Bowes

See also Indian Removal Act; Treaty with the Chippewa, Etc.–September 26, 1933.

References and Further Reading

Clifton, James A. 1984. *The Pokagons, 1683–1983: Catholic Potawatomi Indians of the St. Joseph River Valley.* New York: University Press of America.

Clifton, James A. 1977. *The Prairie People: Continuity and Change in Potawatomi Indian Culture 1665–1965.* Lawrence, KS: Regents Press.

Edmunds, R. David. 1978. *The Potawatomis: Keepers of the Fire.* Norman: University of Oklahoma Press.

Pontiac
(c. 1720–1769)

Born around 1720 in an Ottawa village near present-day Detroit, Pontiac became one of the most recognizable Native warriors of early American history by organizing and leading what has been called Pontiac's Rebellion against British rule in 1763. During this resistance, Pontiac led the siege of Detroit, one of the last British forts to be assaulted by Native warriors throughout the Great Lakes. Although the siege of Detroit ultimately was broken, Pontiac did wrest concessions from the British, which forced them to revert to many of the earlier trade policies of the French, with whom the indigenous people of the Great Lakes had been allied before the British defeated them in 1760.

Detroit was founded by Antoine Cadillac in 1701, and, in an attempt to establish Detroit as a major fur-trading center, many Native groups were encouraged to relocate to the area. A group of Ottawa was among those who chose to settle in the area, and Pontiac was born in one of these Ottawa villages. His name, Obwandiyag, is said to mean "Stopping It," a reference to his warning of an Iro-

Ottawa chief Pontiac (c. 1720–1769) passes a pipe to Major Robert Rogers in 1760. Pontiac let Rogers and his forces pass safely through Indian territory during the French and Indian War. He led a group of tribes against the British colonists in what became known as Pontiac's War of 1763. (Library of Congress)

quois raid that saved his village. He built on this early experience to become a highly respected war chief, and when the British fought with the French for control of the Great Lakes area, Pontiac led Native people in opposition to British control of the fur trade.

The British, as they took over the trading posts from the French, imposed a trading regime that ignored the long-standing practices established by the French and Native people by mutual agreement and respect. Of course, the British enjoyed none of the respectful family and cultural ties that had been established over the past century of French/Native interaction and marriage; for the British, the fur trade was merely business. Pontiac and many other Native leaders were dismayed by the British defeat of the French in 1760 and led a campaign to convince the British to return to the respectful trade practices of the French. The British were not interested in negotiation, and they refused to accede to Pontiac's demands.

Of course, by this time the Native peoples of the Great Lakes had become dependent on European trade goods, and the new British trade regime threatened that way of life. Pontiac, enlisting the support of Neolin, a Delaware prophet, urged Native people to reject the British disruption of their cultural ways and exhorted them to return to the "old" ways of life before the British.

Pontiac, exasperated by the British refusal to negotiate, laid a clever plan to assault the Detroit fort and expel the British. Yet, when the time for the assault arrived, the commander of the fort, Major Henry Gladwin, appeared to be aware of the ruse, so Pontiac withdrew; on May 9, 1763, he began his siege of the fort. Most of the other British forts throughout the region soon fell to Native warriors; by midsummer only Detroit and Fort Pitt remained in the hands of the British.

Pontiac's biggest problem was that expected support from the French never materialized, and in October he was informed by the French that they had signed a treaty of peace with the British. Facing dissatisfaction from his own warriors and abandonment by the French, Pontiac withdrew his warriors in mid-November, and "Pontiac's Rebellion" was over.

Although the British did ease their trade policies as a result of Pontiac's "uprising," Pontiac himself never regained his war chief stature, and he spent the next few years attempting unsuccessfully to reform the Native confederacy and push the

British out of their homelands. Finally, in 1765, Pontiac made peace with the British and agreed to allow the fort at Detroit to remain but with the understanding that it was on Ottawa land.

After 1765, Pontiac apparently led a rather typical life of trading throughout the region, often spending time in Illinois country, where he had family relations. But his reputation as a war chief did not diminish, and rumors swirled around him and his alleged military intentions. One of these rumors was that he was assembling warriors to lead a raid on Cahokia, a Peoria village on the banks of the Mississippi. The Peoria decided to assassinate him before he could carry out this rumored raid. On April 20, 1769, the assassination was carried out by a Peoria brave as Pontiac walked out of a store in the village. His burial place has never been revealed, although it is assumed to be somewhere near Cahokia, now St. Louis, although no one is willing to venture to guess which side of the river may hold his remains.

Phil Bellfy

See also Fort Pitt, Pennsylvania; Métis.
References and Further Reading
Dowd, Gregory Evans. 2002. *War under Heaven: Pontiac, the Indian Nations, and the British Empire.* Baltimore: Johns Hopkins University Press.
McConnell, Michael N. 1992. *A Country Between: The Upper Ohio Valley and Its Peoples, 1724–1774.* Lincoln and London: University of Nebraska Press.
White, Richard. 1991. *The Middle Ground: Indians, Empires, and Republics in the Great Lakes Region, 1650–1815.* Cambridge: Cambridge University Press.

Powhatan
(c. 1550–1618)
Wahunsonacock, better known to the early Virginia colonists as Powhatan, was the principal chief of what is usually referred to as the Powhatan Confederacy; however, he may be better known as the father of Pocahontas.

The name Powhatan (Falling Waters) was taken from one of his favorite dwelling places, the falls of the James River near present-day Richmond. Powhatan was probably born around 1550. He inherited control over six small tribes in Virginia (most likely from his father) and systematically added other tribes to his dominion through incentives, warfare, and intimidation until he was the

Powhatan (c. 1550–1618) was the principal chief of the so-called Powhatan Confederacy in Virginia during the late sixteenth and early seventeenth centuries. (Library of Congress)

chief of an estimated thirty tribal groups united in what has become known as the Powhatan Confederacy. In total, he was the leader of more than eight or nine thousand people and oversaw an estimated eighty-five hundred square miles of land.

In spite of Powhatan's control over the Tidewater Virginia region, other hostile Native American tribes frequently came into conflict with his people. A series of Indian wars in the sixteenth century compelled Powhatan to maintain a strong warrior class composed of an estimated three thousand men. The Native Americans in Virginia were, therefore, a warring society and constantly fighting to either defend or expand their hunting grounds against other tribes in the area.

By the late sixteenth century, Powhatan had heard about white men who occasionally appeared in North America. In fact, it is possible that a contingent of his warriors killed the last of the Roanoke settlers sometime in the early seventeenth century.

Powhatan was wary of Europeans but viewed them as possible allies in his struggles against other Native American tribes in the region.

About sixty years of age when Jamestown was founded, Powhatan apparently greeted the English colonists with a degree of cordiality at first. Captain John Smith described him as a man of dignified bearing. Powhatan developed a harsher attitude toward the newcomers as relations between the two peoples deteriorated. Nevertheless, for the first few years of the Jamestown settlement, colonists relied heavily on Powhatan and his people for food.

Periodic outbreaks of violence happened between the two groups, making relations difficult; attacks on each other occurred, and both desired mutual trade relations. However, Powhatan managed to maintain peace, and no major wars between the Indians and the settlers erupted during his lifetime. Most devastating to the Powhatans, however, were the diseases the whites had brought with them from Europe, particularly smallpox, which decimated the Indian population. After Powhatan's death from smallpox in 1618, he was succeeded as chief of the Powhatan Confederacy by his half-brother, Opechancanough, who was more aggressive when dealing with the Jamestown colonists.

Edward D. Ragan

See also Jefferson, Thomas; Opechancanough.
References and Further Reading
Hodge, Frederick Webb, ed. 1910. *Handbook of American Indians,* Bureau of American Ethnology Bulletin 30. Washington, DC: Smithsonian Institution.
Rountree, Helen C. 2005. *Pocahontas, Powhatan, Opechancanough: Three Indian Lives Changed by Jamestown.* Charlottesville: University of Virginia Press.
Rountree, Helen C. 1990. *Pocahontas's People: The Powhatan Indians of Virginia through Four Centuries.* Norman: University of Oklahoma Press.

Pratt, Richard Henry
(1840–1924)

Richard Henry Pratt was a leader in American Indian education in the late nineteenth century. Becoming interested in American Indian education in 1875, Pratt founded the noted off-reservation boarding school, the Carlisle Indian School, in Carlisle, Pennsylvania, in 1879. He promoted a combination of academic and industrial training for boys and girls while immersing them in white society. Pratt aggressively promoted his ideas on American Indian education and the need for complete assimilation throughout his twenty-five-year term as headmaster at Carlisle. Carlisle Indian School became the pattern for other off-reservation boarding schools.

Pratt first developed his methods of American Indian education while in charge of Kiowa, Comanche, and Cheyenne prisoners at Fort Marion in St. Augustine, Florida, from 1875 to 1878. He believed that the only way for American Indians to survive was through complete and rapid assimilation into white society. Education was the key. The Fort Marion prisoners were given military uniforms, had their hair cut, and were given lessons in English, Christianity, and adopting white civilization. Pratt tried to instill a work ethic in his prisoners by allowing them to polish sea beans for the tourist trade,

placing the wages they earned into accounts for their benefit.

When the prisoners were released in 1878, Pratt accompanied some to the Hampton Institute, where he helped recruit and oversee American Indian students. In 1879, he was given permission to use the old army barracks in Carlisle, Pennsylvania, to establish a boarding school for American Indian students only.

Pratt believed that people were the product of their environments, and, although American Indian culture was inferior to white culture, American Indians themselves were not. This belief heavily influenced the policies at Carlisle. Most important, the school was located away from the reservations and close to white towns. This allowed the students to be separated from what Pratt saw as the demeaning influence of reservations and tribal status and to be immersed in white society. This important element

Colonel Richard H. Pratt (1840–1924) from New York, sits atop his horse in his military uniform at the Carlisle Indian School, Carlisle, Pennsylvania. Pratt founded the Carlisle school creating the model for off-reservation boarding schools for Native Americans. (Corbis)

of Pratt's education system was not duplicated in other off-reservation boarding schools.

Upon arriving at Carlisle, students were given haircuts and military-style uniforms and were forbidden to speak their Native languages. Harsh discipline was dispensed on those who spoke their Native tongue, misbehaved, or ran away. Courses of instruction included English, religion, reading, writing, basic math, and industrial skills such as farming and harness making for the boys and sewing and cooking for the girls. Through these industrial skills, the students supported the school.

Once students had mastered a certain degree of English and skills, they had the opportunity to enter Pratt's outing program. One of the most significant of Pratt's contributions to American Indian education, the outing system placed students with rural families, where they would gain firsthand knowledge of white society. The student was to live, eat, worship, and work with the family for three months over the summer or for as long as two years. For Pratt, the outing system had a dual purpose: it encouraged students to learn English and allowed them to earn money, and at the same time it broke down prejudice against American Indians in the community.

Pratt traveled widely, recruiting students and promoting Carlisle and a system of off-reservation boarding schools. He also criticized federal policy where he thought it was detrimental to American Indian assimilation. He disliked reservations, the continuation of tribal status, and reservation day schools. Pratt's criticism of federal policy led to his dismissal from Carlisle in 1904 for insubordination.

Pratt was also appointed to lead a commission to submit the Dawes Act to different bands of the Sioux to get their consent in 1888. Pratt's commission had little success in getting the Sioux to agree to the Dawes Act.

The Richard Henry Pratt Papers are housed at the Beinecke Rare Book and Manuscript Library at Yale University.

Tamara Levi

See also American Indian Self-Determination and Education Act of 1975; Assimilation; Leupp, Francis; Treaties and American Indian Schools in the Age of Assimilation, 1794–1930.

References and Further Reading

Adams, David Wallace. 1995. *Education for Extinction: American Indians and the Boarding School Experience, 1875–1928.* Lawrence: University Press of Kansas.

Pratt, Richard Henry. 1987. *Battlefield and Classroom: Four Decades with the American Indian, 1867–1904.* Edited by Robert Utley. Lincoln: University of Nebraska Press.

Reyner, Jon, and Jeanne Eder. 2004. *American Indian Education: A History.* Norman: University of Oklahoma Press.

Pushmataha

(1764–1824)

Pushmataha, Choctaw warrior and statesman, was born about 1764 near the present-day town of Macon, Mississippi, on the Noxubee River. His origins are obscure; he rose to leadership through his outstanding abilities as a warrior and hunter. A natural leader, he was thrust into positions of leadership by his fellow Choctaws, merited by his personal courage and skill in battle and on the hunt. He was also a mesmerizing speaker who succeeded in persuading the young warriors to follow him as he led a path through the difficult times the Choctaw faced in the first quarter of the nineteenth century. On one occasion in 1811, Tecumseh visited the Choctaws in an effort to persuade them to join his pan-Indian movement to stop the American invaders from encroaching further on Indian lands. Pushmataha influenced his warriors to not join the charismatic Tecumseh.

With hundreds of Choctaw warriors in attendance, Tecumseh roused the young men in anger against the Americans, and many of them excitedly agreed to join Tecumseh. After Tecumseh spoke, however, Pushmataha rose. He spoke calmly and eloquently, making the case that the Americans were far too strong and had almost inexhaustible resources and men. He argued that taking up arms against the United States was doomed to failure and that all Indian nations that did so would inevitably lose. He spoke for quite some time; in the end, because of the power of his speech and the force of his personality, most of the young men declined to follow Tecumseh, who departed greatly disappointed. Shortly after Tecumseh's visit to the Choctaws, Pushmataha led a large number of Choctaw warriors as American allies under General Andrew Jackson in the battle against Tecumseh's followers at the Battle of Horseshoe Bend in the Creek (or Muscogee) Nation.

The Choctaws and Cherokees played a decisive role in this battle, which ended in the final defeat of the Muscogee Creek Red Sticks. This battle was a key victory over the Native people who resisted the American invasion of the Southeast, and it signaled the end of the era in which the United States dealt with Indian nations of the Southeast as sovereign nations. From that point on, the United States government knew that it had a military advantage over the Southeastern Native people, and instead of treating these people fairly, the U.S. government inexorably demanded cession after cession of Native lands. Pushmataha's Choctaw warriors also played a key role in the Battle of New Orleans in 1815, where once again they fought as American allies under the command of Andrew Jackson. This battle was the last battle of the War of 1812 and ended in an ignominious defeat for the British. From 1801 to 1824, as the U.S. government demanded land cessions of the Choctaws, Pushmataha cooperated with the Americans in what he saw as the only practical route for them. He signed several cession treaties and continued to aver friendship with the Americans.

In 1820, Andrew Jackson and other treaty commissioners met with the Choctaws to obtain yet another land cession. Despite the resistance of Pushmataha and the other leaders, the Choctaws finally ceded five million acres of their lands to the United States in exchange for thirteen million acres in the West. The U.S. negotiators did not listen when Pushmataha pointed out that there were hundreds of white farmers already living on the lands the United States was giving the Choctaws and that these farmers had built permanent settlements, cleared fields, and would resist in every way possible the emigration of the Choctaws to this area. Jackson scoffed but later found out that Pushmataha spoke the truth. U.S. officials prevaricated and finally asked the Choctaws to exchange this land for an area farther west. In 1824, Pushmataha and the two other main chiefs of the Choctaw Nation went to Washington to negotiate. On December 24, the great chief Pushmataha died in Washington at the age of sixty. He was buried in Arlington National Ceremony with a parade through the streets of Washington and full military honors.

Pushmataha's unfortunate death shattered the Choctaw Nation in its time of great need. The Choctaws became like a ship that had slipped its moorings, and the nation drifted for the next several years, led by men who did not have the prestige or ability of the great Pushmataha.

Donna L. Akers

See also Aboriginal Title; Colonial and Early Treaties 1775–1829; Doak's Stand, Mississippi; Jackson, Andrew; Jefferson, Thomas; LeFlore, Greenwood; Pitchlynn, Peter; Southeast and Florida; Tecumseh; Treaty with the Choctaw–October 18, 1820.

References and Further Reading

Debo, Angie. 1989. *The Rise and Fall of the Choctaw Nation*. Reprint, Norman: University of Oklahoma Press.

DeRosier, Arthur H., Jr. 1970. *The Removal of the Choctaw Indians*. Knoxville: University of Tennessee Press.

White, Richard. 1988. *The Roots of Dependency: Subsistence, Environment, and Social Change among the Choctaws, Pawnees, and Navajos*. Reprint, Lincoln: University of Nebraska Press.

Red Cloud (Makhpiya-Luta)

(c. 1822–1909)

Red Cloud (Makhpiya-Luta) is recognized as one of the most significant Lakota leaders of the nineteenth century. Guiding his nation as a warrior and a statesman from 1841, his determination to maintain the autonomy of the Lakota people continued until his death in 1909. Born about 1822 in present day North Platte, Nebraska, to an Oglala mother and a Brulé father, he was raised by his mother's brother, Chief Smoke. Red Cloud learned warfare as a youth, joining frequent wars against the Pawnee, the Crow, and other Oglala.

While still a teen, he killed a prominent Oglala leader, creating decades of dissension in the Oglala Nation. He continued to distinguish himself as a warrior and leader over the next fifty years in disputes with the Pawnee, Crow, Ute, and Shoshone. The most distinguished recognition Red Cloud would receive in his fight against the U.S. government came in 1868 with the signing of the Fort Laramie treaty, ending two years of warfare along the Bozeman Trail, which ran through the main part of the Lakota lands. Tired of the westward stream of gold hunters and settlers, Red Cloud organized what has been termed the most successful Indian war against the United States.

Lieutenant Colonel William Fetterman and eighty men were killed outside Fort Kearney (in present-day Wyoming) in a battle in December 1866. During the next two years, raiders terrorized travelers and soldiers, which resulted in a treaty that guaranteed the abandonment of forts along the Bozeman

Red Cloud (c. 1822–1909) was an Oglala Lakota leader and warrior who organized what has been termed the most successful Indian war against the United States. (National Archives)

Trail and recognition of Lakota claims to lands in present-day Montana and Wyoming in addition to the western half of South Dakota (including the site of the gold rush in the Black Hills). This treaty continued in force until it was challenged by George Armstrong Custer's Black Hills expedition in 1874.

As a resident of the Pine Ridge Reservation in South Dakota in the 1880s, Red Cloud waged a political war with the federal administration over management, food distribution, and the Indian police force. He rallied sympathizers in the eastern United States and Europe for agency reforms. During the last twenty years of his life, Red Cloud, although no longer officially a leader, continued to lobby to maintain authority over recognized leaders. He issued challenges against the leasing of Lakota lands to whites and disputed the allotment policy of dividing reservation lands into individual parcels.

Pamela Lee Gray

See also Northern Plains; Sitting Bull; Treaty of Fort Laramie with the Sioux, Etc.—September 17, 1851.

References and Further Reading
Hyde, George E. 1937. *Red Cloud's Folk: A History of the Oglala Sioux Indians.* Reprint, Norman, OK: University of Oklahoma Press, 1975.
Larson, Robert W. 1997. *Red Cloud: Warrior-Statesman of the Lakota Sioux.* Oklahoma Western Biographies Series, No. 13. Norman: University of Oklahoma Press.
Olson, James C. 1965. *Red Cloud and the Sioux Problem.* Lincoln: University of Nebraska Press.
Utley, Robert M. 1963. *The Indian Frontier of the American West 1846–1890.* Albuquerque: University of New Mexico Press.

Red Jacket
(c. 1758–1830)

Red Jacket, a Seneca, considered himself an orator first and foremost. An avowed traditionalist, he is most famous for his speeches denouncing the presence of Christian missionaries on the reservations and for opposing the sale of Indian lands. Never actually appointed a sachem, he nonetheless became a very influential Seneca chief. Although he was sometimes accused of cowardice, demagoguery, and alcoholism, his speeches are among the most compelling explanations of aboriginal sovereignty in United States history. In addition to his significance as a political figure in the early national period, Red Jacket became popular because he was an extraordinarily dynamic speaker. His speeches, of which dozens are extant, are notable for their sarcasm and disarming humor.

Red Jacket's birth name was Otetiani (Always Ready). According to anthropologist Arthur C. Parker, he was born to a Seneca mother of the Wolf clan named Ahweyneyonh (Drooping Flower or Blue Flower). His father was Thadahwahnyeh, a Cayuga of the Turtle clan. There are a number of rival stories about the date and location of his birth, but Christopher Densmore argues that he was probably born in 1758 on the west side of Lake Cayuga near either Geneva or Canoga. He was drawn to public speaking at a young age and was rumored to practice the art by himself in the woods, although this story seems fanciful.

Red Jacket served as a message runner for the British during the Revolutionary War. For this work, he was awarded a red jacket, from which his English

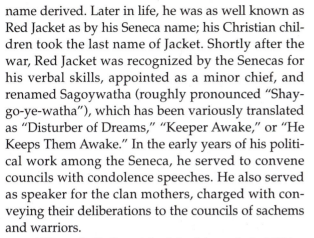

name derived. Later in life, he was as well known as Red Jacket as by his Seneca name; his Christian children took the last name of Jacket. Shortly after the war, Red Jacket was recognized by the Senecas for his verbal skills, appointed as a minor chief, and renamed Sagoywatha (roughly pronounced "Shay-go-ye-watha"), which has been variously translated as "Disturber of Dreams," "Keeper Awake," or "He Keeps Them Awake." In the early years of his political work among the Seneca, he served to convene councils with condolence speeches. He also served as speaker for the clan mothers, charged with conveying their deliberations to the councils of sachems and warriors.

Although distinguished for his verbal abilities during the Revolution, he also earned a reputation for cowardice that followed him for many years afterward. Cornplanter, an influential Seneca warrior, claimed that Red Jacket fled from the Battle of Newtown. Joseph Brant was fond of retelling a story that Red Jacket and a friend smeared themselves with the blood of a slaughtered cow to claim that they had been in battle. As a result, Brant called him Cowkiller, an unflattering name by which he was designated in most British council records of the 1790s and early 1800s. Fighting on the American side during the War of 1812, however, Red Jacket redeemed his martial reputation by fighting with distinction at the Battle of Chippewa.

Several diplomatic triumphs in the 1790s significantly raised Red Jacket's stature. He was an active participant at the U.S.-Haudenosaunee (Six Nations, or Iroquois) councils of Tioga Point and Newtown in 1790 and 1791. He served as a leading spokesman for a Seneca deputation that met George Washington in Philadelphia in 1792. While in Philadelphia, Red Jacket (among other chiefs) was given a large chest medal by the president, which he wore proudly for the rest of his life. Most important, he was a principal negotiator at the 1794 Treaty of Canandaigua, where the Seneca secured nearly four million acres of land in perpetuity. The terms of this treaty have served as the basis for a series of successful Haudenosaunee land claims in New York State since the 1970s.

In 1797, Red Jacket attended the Treaty of Big Tree, where the Seneca sold much of the land guaranteed to them by the Treaty of Canandaigua. At this famous council, Red Jacket spoke on behalf of the sachems to oppose the sale, but, once the warriors and clan mothers overruled the sachems, Red Jacket successfully argued to double the proposed size of the Buffalo Creek Reservation. Because of this apparent change in position, the historian William Leete Stone charged him with duplicitous conduct. The allegation was supported by his Indian political rivals, such as Joseph Brant, but it has little substance.

Red Jacket's most famous speech, a reply to the Reverend Jacob Cram in 1805, was one of several speeches he gave in the early 1800s that explained why the Indians did not want Christian missionaries in their midst. The speech is noteworthy for its condensed history of white-Native relations and its objection to Cram's attempt to "force your religion upon us." Although the level of sarcasm is difficult to gauge, Red Jacket told Cram that the Senecas might ask him back only if they saw that Christianity could soften the habits of the white frontiersmen living on their borders. The speech's authenticity has been a topic of debate, but Red Jacket gave many such speeches on the topic over the decade (Densmore 1999; Robie 1986). Furthermore, Red Jacket had become a minor celebrity on this issue. He often took pride in the publication of his speeches, and he saw to it that they were properly translated.

In addition to his reply to Cram, other famous performances include his May 1811 replies to the Ogden Land Company agent John Richardson and the missionary John Alexander. These speeches contain very clear examples of Red Jacket's acerbic wit. After rejecting Alexander's overtures, Red Jacket concluded with the gentle request that the missionary forbear to extend his generous offers, "lest our heads should be too much loaded, and by and by burst" (Stone 1841, 204).

By the end of the War of 1812, the Senecas lived on ten reservations totaling about two hundred thousand acres. They were beset by land companies externally and Christianity internally.

By 1819, two leading Seneca chiefs, Young King and Captain Pollard, had become Christian. After the conversion of his grandson, Red Jacket allied with the so-called Pagan party, and he began to stridently condemn the encroachment of missionaries and land companies. Every year, he and other traditionalist chiefs lobbied the governor and legislature to support Seneca self-determination. He succeeded in obliging the state to pass a law that prohibited missionaries from living on Native lands from 1821 to 1824.

Red Jacket spent the 1820s denouncing the corrupt practices of the Ogden Land Company agents who succeeded in buying large portions of Seneca lands in August 1826. Red Jacket traveled to Washington to overturn the sale, but he was unable to do so. At the same time, secretary of Indian affairs Thomas McKenney convinced the Christian chiefs to depose Red Jacket as a troublemaker, which they did in 1827. A year later, having proved corruption during the federal inquiry into the sale, Red Jacket was reinstated as a chief in July 1828. Unfortunately, however, even though Red Jacket's protests were successful in preventing federal ratification of the Ogden sale of 1826, the lands were not returned. (Shortly afterward, the land sale of 1838 rendered it a moot issue.) Exhausted by his political efforts, pinched for money, and trying to make peace with his Christian wife, Red Jacket went on a commercial speaking tour the following year, traveling in museum shows from Boston to New York. He died of cholera on January 20, 1830.

There are four principal biographies of Red Jacket. The first, by William Leete Stone, was published in 1841. It contains a wealth of primary and anecdotal information because Stone was able to interview and correspond with many people who knew Red Jacket personally. More important, Stone reprinted as many of Red Jacket's speeches as he could obtain, thinking that future generations of historians would benefit more from the original documents than from historians' glosses of them. Stone's transcripts compare very accurately with extant manuscripts. Stone occasionally changes a preposition or inserts a period for clarity, but he did not dress up the vocabulary. The translations Stone used were principally those of Jasper Parrish, a federal Indian agent who was captured as a child by the Senecas and who spoke both Mohawk and Seneca fluently. The only major weakness of Stone's biography is that he accepted the opinions of Red Jacket's lifelong opponents, namely Thomas Morris, Joseph Brant, and Thomas McKenney, all of whom were invested in protecting their own reputations.

Niles Hubbard's 1886 biography largely reprints Stone's material without Stone's biases. Arthur C. Parker's 1952 biography is important for its sources in Seneca oral tradition, but it seems to have been intended as a children's book, not an academic history. The best recent biography is Christopher Densmore's, which avoids the demonization and hagiography of the earlier works and which puts dates and places to many of the events Stone did not document.

Granville Ganter

See also Agreement with the Seneca–September 15, 1797; Brant, Joseph; Cornplanter; Treaty with the Six Nations–November 11, 1794.

References and Further Reading

Blacksnake, Governor. "Narrative." "Notes of Border History." Lyman C. Draper Collection of Indian Artifacts. [Microfilm.] Reel 47, vol. 4: 13–82. Wisconsin Historical Society.

Densmore, Christopher. 1987. "More on Red Jacket's Reply." *New York Folklore* 13(3–4): 121–122.

Densmore, Christopher. 1999. *Red Jacket: Iroquois Diplomat and Orator.* Syracuse, NY: Syracuse University Press.

Ganter, Granville. 2000. " 'You Are a Cunning People Without Sincerity': Sagoyewatha and the Trials of Community Representation." In *Speakers of the Northeastern Woodlands,* ed. Barbara Mann, 165–195. Westport, CT: Greenwood Press.

Hubbard, Niles J. 1886. *An Account of Sa-Go-Ye-Wat-Ha, or Red Jacket and His People.* Albany, NY: Joel Munsell's Sons.

Parker, Arthur C. 1943. "The Unknown Mother of Red Jacket." *New York History* 24(4): 525–533.

Parker, Arthur C. 1952. *Red Jacket: Last of the Seneca.* Lincoln: University of Nebraska Press. Repr. 1998.

Robie, Harry. 1986. "Red Jacket's Reply: Problems in the Verification of a Native American Speech Text." *New York Folklore* 12(3–4): 99–117.

Stone, William Leete. 1841. *The Life and Times of Sa-Go-Ye-Wat-Ha, or Red-Jacket.* New York: Wiley and Putnam.

Ridge, John Rollin
(1827–1867)

John Rollin Ridge (Cherokee) was also known as Chees-quat-a-law-ny or Yellow Bird. He was born on March 19, 1827, and died on October 5, 1867. John Rollin Ridge—newspaperman, novelist, orator, and poet—was born on a plantation near present-day Rome, Georgia, in an influential Cherokee family before the removals to Indian Territory. He died in Grass Valley, California, in 1867 soon after participating in negotiations with the federal government that reduced Cherokee land holdings by half.

Today, Ridge is distinguished as the first Native American novelist, author of *The Life and Adventures of Joaquin Murieta, the Celebrated California Bandit* (1854); he also wrote more than fifty poems, hundreds of editorials and newspaper articles, and a series of essays about the North American Indian. Though he is remembered as a writer, Ridge was primarily concerned with politics and financial success.

Ridge was the child of a prominent Cherokee, John Ridge, and a white New Englander, Sarah Bird Northrop. Ridge's grandfather, known as Major Ridge, was an accomplished Cherokee warrior, orator, and businessman. The Ridge family defended Cherokee land rights in Georgia for many years but changed their position after the Indian Removal Act passed in 1830. They led the coalition that signed the Treaty of New Echota in 1835, whereby they agreed to give up land holdings in Georgia in exchange for land in Indian Territory. They reasoned that further resistance would lead to further loss, and so they agreed to go. This coalition—known as the Ridge-Boudinot-Watie or Treaty Party—made enemies of John Ross and his allies, who, though they had intended to stay in Georgia and fight a legal battle for their lands, were forced to leave under the Treaty of New Echota. This rift had a long legacy for John Rollin Ridge personally and the Cherokee Nation as a whole. Hostility between the factions reached a high pitch after the Trail of Tears took the lives of between four thousand and eight thousand people in 1838. In 1839, Ridge's father, grandfather, and uncle were murdered by members of the Ross Party.

At age twelve, Ridge witnessed his father's murder; although his family left Indian Territory to live in Arkansas, he swore revenge. Many believe that Ridge modeled his vengeful hero in *The Life and Adventures of Joaquin Murieta* after himself and thereby vicariously satisfied his own desire for revenge. Others have focused more on the way the novel responds to the racist policies of Manifest Destiny, which affected Ridge just as it affected his hero, Joaquin Murieta.

Ridge married Elizabeth Wilson in 1947 and settled down on the family estate in Indian Territory. Soon afterward, he killed a man from the Ross Party in a dispute over a horse and left Indian Territory forever. Ridge joined the gold rush to California, where, after a few months of prospecting, he began his career as a newspaperman. His first job was at *The Sacramento Bee*, but he went on to write for, edit, and publish a number of California papers, including *The California American* and *The Daily Bee* (both in Sacramento), *The California Express* and *The Daily National Democrat* (both in Marysville), *The Herald* (San Francisco), *The Beacon* (Red Bluff), *The Trinity National* (Weaverville), and *The National* (Grass Valley). He also contributed to *The Golden Era, Hesperian, Alta California*, and *Hutchings's California Magazine*. As a newspaperman, Ridge was involved in many public debates, some of which escalated into heated affairs. Most notably, he was at the center of party rivalries before and during the Civil War as an anti-abolitionist Democrat.

Ridge's parents made sure that he received a solid education in boarding schools and from private tutors. Like most Americans of the time, he was taught that social evolution is natural and desirable, that America led the march toward progress, and that Native Americans should assimilate. As a result, he spoke in favor of Native American assimilation throughout his life. Long before the Dawes Act, Ridge wrote that individual land allotment was the best path to assimilation. Ridge also wrote in favor of protecting Native Americans and wanted the importance of Native American cultures to be recognized, though he believed that California Indians were inferior and primitive. Ridge's positions might seem contradictory to twenty-first century sensibilities.

Ridge felt dogged by misfortune; he aimed to take his place as a leader in the Cherokee Nation but never succeeded, in part because his family begged him to stay safely away from Indian Territory. In letters home, he outlined plans to return and establish a newspaper that would preserve Native American history, to publish Native American writers, and to lobby on behalf of the Indian nations. This plan never came to fruition.

In 1866, after eight years of Democratic campaigning, which at times threatened to escalate into armed conflict, Ridge left California for Washington, D.C. to head a Cherokee commission invited to treat with the federal government at the close of the war. The negotiations did not have the results that he had hoped for. He died in Grass Valley the following year.

Deborah Gilbert

See also Assimilation; Boudinot, Elias; Indian Removal; Indian Removal Act, 1830; Indian Territory; Jackson, Andrew; Ridge, Major; Ross, John; Treaty with the Cherokee–December 29, 1835.

References and Further Reading

Conley, Robert J. 2005. *The Cherokee Nation: A History.* Albuquerque: University of New Mexico Press.

Parins, James W. 1991. *John Rollin Ridge: His Life and Works.* Lincoln: University of Nebraska Press.

Ridge, John Rollin. 1991. *A Trumpet of Our Own: Yellow Bird's Essays on the North American Indian.* San Francisco: The Book Club of California.

Woodward, Grace Steele. 1963. *The Cherokees.* Norman: University of Oklahoma Press.

Ridge, Major
(1771–1839)

Kah-nung-da-tla-geh (loosely translated as "The Ridge") was born around 1771 in present-day southeastern Tennessee. By the time he was eighteen, his people were involved in a revolt over conditions and agreements made in the Treaty of Hopewell in 1785. Ridge developed a reputation as a great warrior and mediator, but after ten years of brutal fighting, he tired of the bloodshed on both sides. With his wife, Susanna Wickett (Sehoya), Ridge moved to Pine Log in present-day Barlow County, Georgia.

Ridge joined with Pine Log residents and farmers James Vann and Charles Hicks to forge a new alliance of power in the Cherokee Nation. The old guard and new guard leaders had different plans for the Cherokee government. Susanna and Kah-nung-da-tla-geh started a family that included the future Cherokee leaders, John (Skah-tle-loh-skee) and Walter, also known as Watie. Major Ridge's brother, David Watie (also known as Oowatie), had two sons: Gallegina, popularly known as Buck and later by the Christian name he adopted, Elias Boudinot; and another son named Stand. Ridge's sons and nephews also played pivotal roles in Cherokee history.

Hicks, Vann, and Ridge were disturbed by the actions of the Cherokee Council in 1805. It was determined that the tribe's leaders had sold Cherokee tribal lands for personal profit. The nation lived on land that was important to whites looking for gold and, later, for valuable farmland. Their opposition found Vann and Ridge leaving the tribal government with a small group of followers. This group grew as the two publicized the land fraud charges. The intrigue and plotting on the Cherokee Council rivaled any present-day politics; as a result, Hicks was relieved of his official position, Vann was killed, and Ridge was eventually given the key leadership position in the Cherokee Nation but not without strong and determined enemies. During the Creek War with the Cherokee (1813–1814) and the Seminole War (1818), Ridge led Cherokee volunteer fighters and was given an appointment as major, a title he used for the rest of his life. Based on his bravery in defense of the Cherokee Nation, Major Ridge was elected speaker of the council of the lower house of the Cherokee Nation. (The tribal government was modeled after that of the United States, with an upper and lower house, a judiciary, and an executive.) Ridge's friend John Ross was elected as the tribal leader, and Major Ridge took the key council role until the Cherokee faced removal in the late 1820s.

Major Ridge believed the Cherokee should not be removed from their land, but he was convinced by his son John and his nephew Elias Boudinot (Buck Oowatie) that staying and fighting would not be wise. The Georgia land lottery was a key factor in this decision. The three men followed the Cherokee Nation's challenges to white land acquisition carefully. The U.S. Supreme Court sided with the Cherokee Nation and ruled that the U.S. government could not force removal, but despite the ruling, the federal government continued to take Cherokee land and advocated removal of all Cherokees. It looked as if a treaty offered to the Cherokee Nation would be the most sensible option. The Ross group refused to attend the treaty meeting.

The Ridge group believed that eventual defeat and relocation without any benefits was likely, so they signed the agreement as representatives of the Cherokee Nation in the last days of 1835. This agreement, known as the Treaty of New Echota, was named for the capital of the new Cherokee Nation and the location where it was signed. The four signers of the Ridge Party relocated to new lands in Indian Territory, and when the rest of the Cherokee were removed from their land in Georgia in 1838, a meeting was called to organize the Cherokee Nation in their new home. The Ridge group of treaty-signers attended the meeting, angering a group of Ross Party members, who met in a secret proceeding to declare that the Ridge group had violated a law that prohibited the sale of tribal land to whites. The punishment decreed by this Cherokee tribal law was death, and this sentence was carried out the next day. On June 22, 1839, both of the Ridges and Boudinot were assassinated. Stand Watie had been warned of the plot and managed to escape death.

Pamela Lee Gray

See also Aboriginal Title; Battle of Horseshoe Bend (Tohopeka), 1814; *Cherokee Nation v. Georgia*, 1831; Indian Removal; Indian Removal Act, 1830; Jackson, Andrew; New Echota, Georgia; Ridge, John Rollin; Trail of Tears; Treaty with the Cherokee–December 29, 1835; *Worcester v. Georgia*, 1832.

References and Further Reading
Conley, Robert J. 2005. *The Cherokee Nation: A History.* Albuquerque: University of New Mexico Press.
Wilkins, Thurman. 1986. *Cherokee Tragedy: The Ridge Family and the Decimation of a People.* Norman: University of Oklahoma Press.

Woodward, Grace Steele. 1963. *The Cherokees.* Norman: University of Oklahoma Press.

Riel, Louis
(1844–1885)

More than a century after his execution, Louis Riel (Métis) remains perhaps the most controversial figure in Canadian history. Considered a traitor by some and a hero by others, Riel twice attempted to establish independent provinces in an effort to secure the rights of Native and Métis peoples in the Canadian west. Something of a mystic, Riel led two rebellions against the Canadian government, fifteen years apart, in 1869–1870 and again in 1885.

The son of a Fort Garry (present-day Winnipeg) miller, Riel's father, also named Louis, led the successful Courthouse Rebellion in 1849. The younger Riel attended college in Montreal and returned west in 1869. Canada had become a confederation in 1867, and the newly established federal government wished to establish its control over the western territories as quickly as possible, beginning with present-day Manitoba. In 1869, the government began surveying lands along the Red River and sectioning them into eight-hundred-acre square townships, ignoring Métis land use patterns that were based on the older French system of dividing land into narrow strips, beginning at the waterfront, stretching back through individual fields, and terminating in a common pasture known as the "hay privilege."

Many of the first government allotments were given to the Canada Firsters, Protestant Orangemen from Ontario who detested Catholicism, the French language, and Native peoples. Expecting resistance from the Métis, a party of Canada Firsters seized a small post near Fort Garry but surrendered when Riel arrived with a larger and better armed force. Riel formed a governing body for Manitoba, the Comite National des Métis, and became its president. Unwilling to launch an invasion of the western territories, the Canadian government chose to negotiate with the Métis. At this point, Riel made his first miscalculation.

The Métis released most of their Canadian prisoners, but one of them, Thomas Scott, became embroiled in a confrontation with Riel. Tried by Riel and the Comite National des Métis for bearing arms against the state, Scott was executed in 1870, a move that turned public opinion against the Métis. In response, the Canadian government sent a force to

Louis Riel speaks to supporters in an 1885 depiction published in Harper's Weekly. *He was tried for treason and hanged later that year. (Corbis)*

Manitoba to arrest Riel, who fled for his life. Over the next few years, other members of the jury that had convicted Scott were murdered, while Louis Riel disappeared. However, the Métis elected him to three terms in the Canadian Parliament in absentia.

As Protestant Canadians began moving into Manitoba, Métis peoples moved farther west, settling along the Saskatchewan River. By the 1880s, the Métis, Cree, and other Native peoples recognized that the northern plains were undergoing a dramatic transformation. Violence increased as American whisky traders plied their trade. Bison herds shrank drastically because of overhunting by American and Canadian hide hunters. Canadian government surveyors appeared in Saskatchewan, and, just as they had done fifteen years earlier in Manitoba, they began laying out new square townships.

The most dramatic change, however, was the building of the Canadian Pacific Railroad (CPR), which increased the white presence on the Canadian plains. Worried about retaining their lands and way of life, the Métis decided to organize an opposition to the government under Louis Riel. There was just one problem—no one knew where Riel was. A small party of Métis were assigned the task of finding Louis Riel, and they found him quietly teaching Native children in Montana, where he had married and was raising a family. He agreed to return to Canada to organize a Métis government.

Riel quickly organized the provisional government of Saskatchewan, authored a Métis bill of rights, and put together an army of four hundred men. Riel's initial campaigns against the government attempted to avoid bloodshed. The Métis seized government stores, cut communications, and interfered with the building of the CPR. However, the Métis got into a shooting battle with a force of Mounties at Duck Lake, Saskatchewan. This encounter had two immediate results. First, it persuaded some Crees (but not most) to join Riel. It also prompted the Canadian government to organize a large military expedition to crush the Métis. The troops were shipped west, traveling part of the way on the not-yet-completed CPR. The Métis were defeated at Batoche, and, after hiding in the woods for a few days, Riel surrendered to government troops.

Riel was tried in Regina, charged with the murder of Thomas Scott some fifteen years before. Despite questions concerning his fitness to stand trial and calls for mercy from French Catholics, he was hanged in November 1885.

Roger M. Carpenter

See also Canada; Canadian Bill of Rights, 1960; Canadian Indian Treaties; Métis.

References and Further Reading

Beal, Bob, and Rod MacLeod. 1984. *Prairie Fire: The Northwest Rebellion of 1885*. Edmonton: Hurtig.

Ens, Gerhard J. 1996. *Homeland to Hinterland: The Changing Worlds of the Red River Métis in the Nineteenth Century*. Toronto, ON: University of Toronto Press.

Flanagan, Thomas. 2000. *Riel and the Rebellion: 1885 Reconsidered*. Toronto, ON: University of Toronto Press

Ross, John
(1790–1866)

John Ross was the greatest leader of the Cherokee Nation during the nineteenth century. He led his people through some of the greatest crises they faced yet still managed to preserve them as a nation. He was largely of non-Indian ancestry and had been

John Ross (1790–1866) was the leader of the Cherokee Nation during the early nineteenth century. He led his people during the Trail of Tears to the West and in the Civil War in Indian Territory, yet they still managed to preserve themselves as a nation. (Library of Congress)

trained by his father to live and work in the white man's world. Still, Ross was responsible for preserving the Cherokee, establishing a national press, and instituting a free public school system and a stable, unified political system.

Ross was born on October 3, 1790, at Turkey Town (present-day Center, Georgia) in the Cherokee territory. His father was a Scotsman of loyalist sympathies who had settled as a trader among the Cherokee at the end of the American Revolution. His mother was also Scots but had one quarter Cherokee blood. Ross, whose Indian name was Kooweskowe, was educated at home by a private tutor. He participated in games and rituals as most Cherokee boys did but was more at home in the white world. He probably had only a cursory knowledge of the Cherokee language and apparently never learned its written form.

Around 1805, Ross's father sent him to an academy at Kingston, Tennessee. He learned merchandising and served as a clerk in a trading firm but maintained his connections with the Cherokee. In 1809, a U.S. Indian agent sent him on a mission to the western Cherokee, who had moved from present-day Georgia to Arkansas and Oklahoma. During the War of 1812, Ross served as adjutant of a Cherokee regiment under Andrew Jackson and fought in the Battle of Horseshoe Bend against the Creek. He later established Ross's Landing (now Chattanooga) and ran a ferry and warehouse operation there.

Ross inherited a large home in Rossville from his grandfather and gradually turned from trading between the Indian and white peoples to life as a planter. He moved to a new home at Coosa (later Rome, Georgia) and established a life little different from that of most white, slaveholding plantation owners. As Ross's wealth and influence grew, he became more interested in the political life of the Cherokee. The nation's chiefs selected him as their clerk in 1816. In 1817, he became a member of the National Council of the Cherokee, their legislature. He was elected president of the council in 1819 and held that office until 1826. Ross also was a member of delegations sent to Washington, D.C., to negotiate various issues with the federal government.

During the summer of 1827, Ross was a member of the Cherokee constitutional delegation, and he helped to draft the constitution adopted that year. The constitution was the first among American Indians; it established a republican government and a system of regular elections. Ross served as assistant chief and then was elected principal chief of the eastern Cherokee in 1828. Ross would hold that office through repeated elections until his death.

During the 1830s, the Cherokee Nation faced its greatest crisis as the state of Georgia sought to take over its lands. Ross tried to prevent that by working through the federal courts. In *Cherokee Nation v. Georgia* (1831), the U.S. Supreme Court ruled that the Cherokee were a domestic, dependent nation and that only the federal government could intervene in their affairs. Still, those who favored removing the Cherokee continued to act. Even President Jackson favored removing the Cherokee from Georgia. A minority party of Cherokee who accepted the idea of giving up their land and moving to the Indian Territory signed a fraudulent removal treaty in 1835. Ross, however, resisted peacefully until the very day he was forced to leave his ancestral home.

When the U.S. Army was unable to organize the move, General Winfield Scott turned it over to Ross. He organized the Cherokee Nation into thirteen groups of about a thousand people each. During the winter of 1838–1839, they made the trek to present-day Oklahoma. About a fourth of the tribe died before, during, or after the move. Their route became known as the Trail of Tears because of the many deaths and hardships that the people had to endure. Ross's own wife, Quatie, was a victim of the move; she died in 1839. Quatie was a full-blooded Cherokee; the two had married in 1813, possibly in a marriage of convenience to cement Ross's standing among the Cherokee. He later married Mary Brian Stapler, a Quaker woman many years younger than he.

When the eastern Cherokee settled in Indian Territory, they came into conflict with the "old settlers," western Cherokee who had moved there years before. They joined with signers of the removal treaty against Ross, and a virtual civil war broke out. Peace was restored in 1846, when a new treaty with the federal government settled outstanding disputes and reconciled the factions.

Ross built a fine new home at Rose Cottage, near Tahlequah, the capital of the Cherokee Nation. During the later 1840s and 1850s, the Cherokee prospered under Ross's leadership. They established a national press, a system of free public education, and a stable political system. This golden age came to an end in 1861 with the outbreak of the Civil War. Although Ross was a slaveholder and shared much in common with Southern plantation owners, he favored the Union government. Under pressure from Confederate agents such as Albert Pike from Arkansas, Ross reluctantly agreed to side with the Confederacy and signed a treaty of alliance. He fled north at the first opportunity and pleaded that he had been coerced to sign.

At the end of the Civil War, Ross faced many opponents who accused him of being a rebel at heart. Others attempted to split the Cherokee into different factions. Ross traveled to Washington, D.C., to negotiate a treaty to preserve his people. The treaty, signed in 1866, guaranteed the land rights of the Cherokee and ensured that the Cherokee Nation would remain intact. The treaty was Ross's last accomplishment. He died in Washington on August 1, 1866.

Tim Watts

See also Aboriginal Title; Battle of Horseshoe Bend (Tohopeka), 1814; Cass, Lewis; *Cherokee Nation v. Georgia*, 1831; Indian Removal; Indian Removal Act, 1830; Indian Territory; Jackson, Andrew; New Echota, Georgia; Ridge, John Rollin; Ridge, Major; Trail of Tears; Treaty with the Cherokee–December 29, 1835; *Worcester v. Georgia*, 1832).

References and Further Reading

Harrell, Sara Gordon. 1979. *John Ross*. Minneapolis: Dillon Press.

Lowe, Felix C. 1990. *John Ross*. Orlando, FL: Heinemann Library.

Moulton, Gary E. 1978. *John Ross, Cherokee Chief*. Athens: University of Georgia Press.

Satanta

(1820–1878)

Satanta was a Kiowa war chief who was revered as both a skilled warrior and a persuasive public speaker. Born in 1820, Satanta's real name was Sett'ainte, or White Bear. Eventually, his name was anglicized to Satanta by whites who could not pronounce the difficult Kiowa language. Trained by his medicine-man father, Red Tipi, by his mid-twenties Satanta had grown into a skilled warrior, hunting buffalo and raiding U.S. military camps in the southern plains of New Mexico, Oklahoma, and the Texas panhandle.

During the Civil War, the Kiowa and Comanche began serious raiding on the southern plains while U.S. soldiers at western posts were being sent east. Satanta is credited with several bloody raids in west Texas and Colorado during the war years. By 1867, Satanta was in his mid-forties and an important chief of his band of Kiowa. That year, Satanta represented his band of Kiowa at two peace councils: one at Fort Dodge, Iowa, and the other at Medicine Creek Lodge, Kansas.

At both councils, Satanta showed his oratorial skills by making eloquent speeches on behalf of the Kiowa. His most famous speech, given at Medicine Creek, has been quoted many times over. Lamenting the loss of his native lands, Satanta said, "I love the land and the buffalo and will not part with it . . . I don't want to settle; I love to roam over the prairie; I feel free and happy; but when we settle down we grow pale and die."

Despite Satanta's heartfelt speech, the United States took most of the Kiowa land in exchange for a reservation and promises of goods and supplies. Part of the agreement included the right to hunt buffalo off the reservation, but as whites poured into the southern plains in the post–Civil War years, they took away the hunting lands and killed off the buffalo. In frustration, southern plains Indians began raiding again, and many left the reservation to live with other groups who had not yet surrendered.

In 1871, Satanta organized a raiding party of Kiowa and Comanche and attacked a wagon train

Satanta, or White Bear (1820–1878), was a Kiowa war chief who was revered as both a skilled warrior and a persuasive public speaker. (National Archives)

headed toward Fort Richardson, Texas. They killed seven people, took forty-one mules and other supplies, and burned the wagons. As word spread of what was later referred to as the Warren Wagon Trail Massacre, Satanta and two other chiefs (Satank and Big Tree) were arrested by General William Tecumseh Sherman as he passed through Fort Sill on inspection.

A few months later, Satanta and Big Tree were given a jury trial and convicted of seven counts of murder. Satank had tried to escape before the trial and was killed in the process. Satanta and Big Tree were sentenced to death by hanging, but a local judge and a Quaker Indian agent requested a life sentence instead. Quaker leaders in the southern plains began to work for full pardons for the two chiefs, arguing that reservation conditions had forced such raids. Eventually, the federal government also urged Texas governor Edmund Davis to pardon the men. Finally, in 1873, Satanta and Big Tree were paroled by President Ulysses S. Grant on the condition that they stay permanently on the reservation without hunting rights outside the boundaries.

After his parole, Satanta announced that he would no longer be a warrior or a chief. He gave the symbols of his authority away to his friends and son and presumably began a quiet life on the reservation. In 1874, however, fighting broke out at the Wichita agency, which led to a military campaign to put down the uprising. Satanta and Big Tree happened to be off the reservation hunting at the time of the clash and feared they would be accused of participating because they were in violation of their parole agreement. They finally turned themselves in and were arrested for parole violation. Big Tree was held for only a few months, but Satanta was sent back to prison to finish his life sentence.

Four years later, Satanta became ill, and several officials argued for his release. Sherman opposed his release, however, and Satanta came to believe that he would never see freedom again. On September 11, 1878, ill and discouraged, Satanta reportedly sang his death song and jumped from the second-story window of the hospital where he was being treated. He died within a few hours, at the age of fifty-eight. Although he was buried at the Huntsville prison cemetery, his grandson was finally allowed to move his remains to Fort Sill, Oklahoma, in 1963 so that he could be in his Native lands.

April R. Summitt

See also Indian Territory; Treaty with the Cheyenne and Arapaho–October 28, 1867; Treaty with the Kiowa and Comanche, October 21, 1867.

References and Further Reading

Collins, Michael L., and Everett William Kindig. 2005. *Tales of Texoma: Episodes in the History of the Red River Border*. Wichita Falls, TX: Midwestern State University Press.

Dockstader, Frederick J. 1977. *Great North American Indians*. New York: Van Nostrand Reinhold.

Mayhall, Mildred P. 1962. *The Kiowas*. Norman: University of Oklahoma Press.

Robinson, Charles M. 1997. *The Indian Trial: The Complete Story of the Warren Wagon Train Massacre and the Fall of the Kiowa Nation*. Spokane, WA: A. H. Clark.

Robinson, Charles M. 1998. *Satanta: The Life and Death of a War Chief*. Austin, TX: State House Press.

Wharton, Clarence. 1935. *Satanta: The Great Chief of the Kiowas and His People*. Repr., New York: AMS Press, 1984.

Schoolcraft, Henry Rowe

(1793–1864)

Henry Rowe Schoolcraft was a mineralogist, a geologist, a geographer, and an ethnologist. He was also an author, an Indian agent for the Chippewa (Ojibwa) and Ottawa (Odawa) tribes of northern Michigan and Wisconsin, and a superintendent of Indian affairs for Michigan.

Regarded as a pioneer in Native American studies and criticized for views that support stereotyping, Henry Rowe Schoolcraft was one of the most notable men of the nineteenth century for his interaction with and documented observances of the cultural practices and beliefs of the Eastern Woodland Indians, especially those of the Great Lakes region.

Born in Watervliet, New York, on March 28, 1793, he was formally schooled at Union College (Schenectady, New York) and Middlebury College (Vermont) in mineralogy and chemistry. He was self-taught in geology, Hebrew, German, and French.

His first venture (1817–1818) is reported to have been the first documented exploration of the interior of the Ozark region; upon his return, he published *A View of the Lead Mines of Missouri* (1819). His interest,

An ethnologist who spent much of his life studying Native Americans, Henry Rowe Schoolcraft (1793–1864) from New York, was also an author, explorer, Indian agent, geologist, and, to some extent, the creator of the Smithsonian Institution's Bureau of American Ethnology. (Library of Congress)

however, was not limited to rocks and land formation; his writing indicated the curiosity of a naturalist, including detailed descriptions of plants, animals, and people.

In May 1820, the federal government sponsored the Michigan territorial governor, Lewis Cass, and forty-one other members of a group making an exploratory tour of the region. Schoolcraft, an able geologist and documentarist, was chosen by the U.S. War Department to join Cass.

In addition to his confirmation of the existence of marketable quantities of iron and copper, Schoolcraft developed a keen interest in Indian culture. Upon his return from the expedition, Schoolcraft had published his *Narrative Journal of Travel Through the Northwestern Region of the United States Extending from Detroit Through the Great Chain of American Lakes to the Sources of the Mississippi River in 1820* (1821). Consequently, Governor Cass influenced the decision, made in 1822, to make Schoolcraft Indian agent of the region, with his headquarters located first at Sault Ste. Marie.

Once established, Schoolcraft married Jane Johnston (October 1823), daughter of John Johnston, an influential fur trader of the upper Great Lakes region and a well-respected member of the Ojibwa tribe. She was nicknamed Susan by her Irish husband.

From 1836 to 1841, Schoolcraft served as superintendent of Indian affairs (commissioner) for Michigan. He was originally headquartered at Mackinac but eventually moved to Detroit, with a subagency in Saginaw.

During Schoolcraft's tenure with the Indian agency, millions of acres—all that is now the state of Michigan and some of Wisconsin—were negotiated and acquired for the United States through treaties with the Chippewa, Ottawa, and Potawatomi. The negotiations included Schoolcraft's in-laws (much to their benefit and his). Conflict arose as an increasing number of settlers moved into southern Michigan. Schoolcraft pressed for removal westward rather than assimilation, causing additional apprehension and distrust (Cleland 1992, 225–229). Michigan achieved statehood on January 26, 1837, and Schoolcraft, using interesting and inventive combinations of Chippewa words and non-Indian languages, named many of its counties.

Schoolcraft wrote more than thirty books and published a short-lived, handwritten magazine and many articles. His material on Indian legends was the basis for Henry Wadsworth Longfellow's epic poem, *The Song of Hiawatha*. Schoolcraft is probably best known for his six-volume manuscript, *Historical and Statistical Information Respecting the History, Condition, and Prospects of the Indian Tribes of the United States,* commissioned by Congress and published from 1851 to 1857. "Although Indian culture fascinated Henry, he never empathized with it. He looked upon it as a curiosity, to be studied and to be preserved in books and artifact collections, but not necessarily to be kept alive as a dynamic force" (Brazer 1993, 181). Through this scholarship, even his very early writing foreshadowed the course of events in the nineteenth century trans-Mississippi West.

Schoolcraft remarried in 1847; Jane had died in 1842. His second wife, Mary Howard of Grahamville, South Carolina, also supported him in his literary efforts and on his speaking tours as well as nursing him through a crippling arthritis that would leave him bedridden for the last few years of his life. Henry Rowe Schoolcraft died on December 10, 1864.

Deborah Rubenstein

See also Cass, Lewis; Harrison, William Henry; Michilimackinac, Michigan; Northeast and the Great Lakes; Sault Ste. Marie, Michigan and Ontario; Treaty with the Chippewa–January 14, 1837.

References and Further Reading
Brazer, Marjorie Cahn. 1993. *Harps Upon the Willows: The Johnston Family of the Old Northwest.* Ann Arbor, MI: Historical Society of Michigan.

Caruso, John Anthony. 1961. *The Great Lakes Frontier: An Epic of the Old Northwest.* Indianapolis, IN: Bobbs-Merrill.

Cleland, Charles E. 1992. *Rites of Conquest: The History and Culture of Michigan's Native Americans.* Ann Arbor: University of Michigan Press.

Williams, Mentor L., ed. 1991. *Schoolcraft's Indian Legends.* East Lansing: Michigan State University Press.

Seattle (Seath'tl)
(c. 1788–1866)

Seath'tl was the principal chief of the Duwamish, whose original homeland today comprises an industrial area immediately south of downtown Seattle, a city named with an anglicized version of the chief's name. He was described in 1833 by William Fraser Tolmie, a Hudson's Bay Company surgeon, as "a brawney Suquamish with a Roman countenance and black curley hair, the handsomest Indian I have ever

couver sailed the *Discovery* into Puget Sound and met briefly with the Duwamish and their allies, the Suquamish. Seath'tl later aided his father and other Duwamish in the construction of the Old Man House, a community longhouse one thousand feet long that housed about forty families. The Duwamish and the Suquamish formed an alliance that ringed central Puget Sound. Seath'tl took a wife, La-da-ila, and he became chief of the Duwamish-Suquamish alliance at the age of twenty-two. La-da-ila had died by 1833, when the Hudson's Bay Company established a trading post at Nisqually in southern Puget Sound. In 1841, the first Bostons, as the Duwamish called whites, sailed into central Puget Sound in Seath'tl's territory. Ten years later, the schooner *Exact* delivered the first settlers in what later became the city of Seattle.

From the beginning, Seath'tl resolved to cooperate with the immigrants, but when they proposed naming their city after him, he protested that his spirit would be disturbed if his name was said after he died. The settlers retained the name anyway. Seath'tl had been a Catholic since the 1830s, when he was converted by missionaries. Seath'tl adopted the biblical name Noah at his baptism and began regular morning and evening prayers among his people.

Seath'tl and his band moved westward across Puget Sound after signing the Treaty of Point Elliot with Washington territorial governor Isaac Stevens in 1854. As his people prepared to move, Seath'tl delivered a haunting farewell speech that has come to be recognized as one of history's great pieces of Native American oratory. The speech was given in Salish and translated by Dr. Henry Smith, who published it in 1887. Seath'tl's speech has been published several times after that and sometimes embellished.

Environmental conservation was not a subject of general debate and controversy in the mid-nineteenth century, as European American settlement sped across the land mass of the United States. Yet, from time to time, the records of the immigrants contain warnings by Native leaders whose peoples they were displacing describing how European-bred attitudes toward nature were ruining the land, air, and water.

> Our dead never forget the beautiful world that gave them being. They still love its verdant valleys, its murmuring rivers, its magnificent mountains, sequestered vales and verdant-lined lakes and bays . . . Every part of this soil is sacred in the estimation of my people. Every

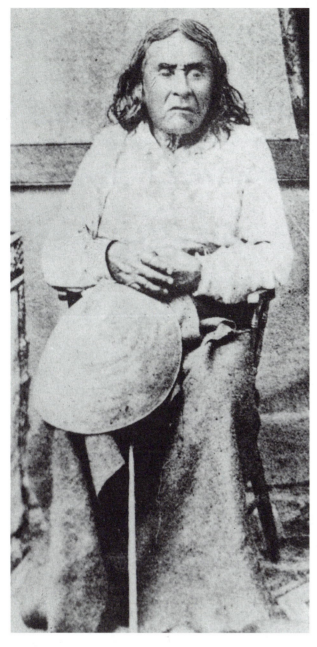

Chief Seath'tl (anglicized as "Seattle") (c. 1788–1866) was a Duwamish and Suquamish leader whose people moved from the present-day site of the city that bears his name. (Library of Congress)

seen" (Johansen and Grinde 1997, 341). David Denny, one of the first white settlers of Seattle, said that Seath'tl's voice could be heard half a mile away when he spoke and that he commanded his people by force of his intellect.

Son of the Duwamish chief Schweabe, Seath'tl probably was born on Blake Island in Puget Sound. He was about seven years of age when George Van-

hillside, every valley, every plain and grove has been hallowed by some sad or happy event in days long vanished. Even the rocks, which seem to be dumb and dead as they swelter in the sun along the silent shore, thrill with memories of stirring events connected with the lives of my people. . . . (Johansen and Grinde 1997, 342–343)

In the development of an environmental philosophy, Chief Seath'tl's words are often cited in the late twentieth century as evidence that many Native Americans practiced a stewardship ethic toward the earth long before such attitudes became popular in non-Indian society. The debate ranges from acceptance of several versions of Seath'tl's speech to a belief that the original translator, Dr. Henry Smith, as well as many people who followed him, put the ecological concepts into the chief's mouth.

In the middle 1850s, when the Yakima War spilled over the Cascades into Seattle under Chief Leschi, Seath'tl and his people looked on from their retreat on the western shores of Puget Sound. He died there in 1866.

Bruce E. Johansen

See also California, Hawaii, and the Pacific Northwest; Treaty with the Dwamish, Suquamish, Etc.–January 22, 1854.

References and Further Reading

Anderson, Eva Greenslit. 1943. *Chief Seattle*. Caldwell, ID: Caxton Press.

Johansen, Bruce E., and Donald A. Grinde, Jr. 1997. *The Encyclopedia of Native American Biography*. New York: Henry Holt.

Vanderwerth, W. C., ed. 1971. *Indian Oratory: Famous Speeches by Noted Indian Chieftains*. Norman: University of Oklahoma Press.

Waters, Frank. 1992. *Brave Are My People*. Santa Fe, NM: Clear Light.

Sitting Bear (Setangya or Satank)

(c. 1800–1871)

Sitting Bear was a noted Kiowa warrior and tribal spokesman whose inability to reconcile himself to reservation life reflected tensions affecting his culture. The particulars of Sitting Bear's life remain largely unknown, but he was probably born in the area encompassed by southern Kansas and northern Oklahoma. His genealogy is poorly understood, though he bore his father's name, and his family

Sitting Bear, or Satank (c. 1800–1871), was a noted Kiowa warrior and tribal spokesman, especially at the Medicine Lodge Council of Southern Plains tribes meeting with U.S. officials in 1867. (National Archives)

enjoyed Sarsi and Kiowa-Apache (now the Apache tribe of Oklahoma) connections. In his youth, he received one of several Bird Shields created as the result of a vision experienced by his cousin Fair Haired Old Man.

Sitting Bear's reputation as a warrior in fights against such traditional Kiowa enemies as the Ute, Pawnee, and Cheyenne, and during raids into Texas and Mexico, led him to a coveted position as leader of the Koitsenko (Real or Principal Dogs, or Sentinel Horses) warrior society, which was composed of the ten bravest men in the tribe.

Kiowa political affairs were dominated by Little Bluff (Dohasan) from around 1833 until his death in 1866, but Sitting Bear's growing influence is indicated by his role as one of six Kiowa signatories of the Fort Atkinson treaty of 1853 (on which "Si-tank-ki" is identified as a "war chief") and as one of the tribe's eleven headmen who put their marks on the Little Arkansas treaty of 1865 (as "Sa-tank"). By 1867, a year after Little Bluff's death, Sitting Bear's name

appeared at the top of the list of the ten Kiowa signatories on the Medicine Lodge Treaty, by which Kiowa, Apache, and Comanche representatives agreed to reside on a reservation in what is now the state of Oklahoma in the vicinity of Fort Sill, established the following year. (Whether they fully understood the provisions and implications of the treaty remains in dispute.)

Sitting Bear had at least six children by four different wives and was adopted father to a captured Mexican boy Kiowas referred to as Short Stay (Aanti). One of Sitting Bear's sons bore his father's name and was killed in 1870 while raiding in Texas. Sitting Bear journeyed to Texas, reclaimed his son's remains, and brought them back to his people. Sitting Bear kept the skeleton inside his tipi, offering it food and referring to his son not as "dead" but merely "sleeping." Sitting Bear's contemporaries regarded this behavior as eccentric, and he acquired a reputation as someone capable of using magic to inflict lethal harm on those who aroused his displeasure.

On May 15, 1871, Sitting Bear joined White Bear (Settainti), Big Tree (Adoetti), Eagle Heart (Tenetendi), Screaming Above (Mamande), and Big Bow (Zebaedal) in leading a raiding party numbering more than a hundred warriors and probably including Apache, Arapaho, Cheyenne, and Comanche. They left the reservation, crossed the Red River, and entered Texas. On May 18, the warriors attacked a freight train of ten wagons on the Butterfield Overland Mail road about twenty miles west of Fort Richardson, killing seven teamsters and capturing forty-one mules.

The day before the attack, General William Tecumseh Sherman, commander of the U.S. Army, traveled the route taken by the ill-fated wagons. Enraged, Sherman adopted a more aggressive Indian policy and ordered the punishment of those responsible for the Warren Wagon Train Raid. Sitting Bear, White Bear, and Big Tree were arrested at Fort Sill. On May 28, soldiers secured them with irons, placed Sitting Bear in one wagon and White Bear and Big Tree in another, and began the journey to a capital offenses trial at Fort Richardson.

About a mile south of Fort Sill, Sitting Bear sang the death song of the Koitsenko warrior society. (One version runs: "O sun, you remain forever, but we Koitsenko must die/ O earth, you remain forever, but we Koitsenko must die.") Somehow, he slipped loose from his chains and produced a knife. (Some Kiowas believed he kept an eagle's wing feather in his stomach and could regurgitate it as a knife when in danger.) After he stabbed a guard and grabbed a rifle, soldiers shot Sitting Bear. Removed from the wagon, Sitting Bear died beside the trail and was buried at the post cemetery. After his death, Sitting Bear came to be known within his tribe as Don't Want To Be Hobbled.

Ron McCoy

See also Lone Wolf (Guipähgo); Satanta; Southern Plains and the Southwest; Treaty with the Kiowa and Apache–October 21, 1867.

References and Further Reading

Mayhall, Mildred P. 1971. *The Kiowas*. Norman: University of Oklahoma Press.

McCoy, Ron. 2003. "'I Have a Mysterious Way': Kiowa Shield Designs and Origin Stories Collected by James Mooney, 1891–1906." *American Indian Art*, 29 (1) (Winter 2003), 64–75.

Mooney, James. 1898. "Calendar History of the Kiowa Indians." In *Seventeenth Annual Report of the Bureau of American Ethnology to the Smithsonian Institution, 1895–96*, 129–445. Washington, DC: Smithsonian Institution.

Mooney, James. 1895–1896. Field Notes. Suitland, MD: Smithsonian Institution, National Anthropological Archives.

Sitting Bull
(1831–1890)

The Siouxan words "Tatanka-Iyotanka" describe a stubborn buffalo seated on his haunches. The name was given to a Hunkpapa Sioux who emerged as a resistance leader against U.S. colonialism in the Northern Plains. He was called Sitting Bull.

Around 1831, Sitting Bull was born along the Grand River at a place known as Many Caches in present-day South Dakota. Originally, he received the name Jumping Badger from his father, who bore the name Sitting Bull. His mother, Her-Holy-Door, created a close bond with him during his formative years. His childhood behavior earned him the alias Slow. He entered combat at age 14, counting his first coup on the Crow and earning the honor of his father's name. With distinction, he entered the Strong Heart, the Kit Fox, and the Silent Eaters societies. He married his first wife in 1851, but she died during childbirth. After his father died in 1859, he married two additional wives. They gave birth to two daughters and a son. In addition, he adopted his nephew, One Bull, as a son.

Sitting Bull became known as a blotaunka, or war chief in the Strong Hearts, a warrior society. Standing five feet ten inches in height, he possessed a muscular frame and dark braided hair. As he matured, Sitting Bull earned acclaim as a singer, an artist, and a dancer. The scars on his chest, back, and arms testified to his repeated sacrifices in Sun Dances. He embodied the cardinal virtues of his people, that is, bravery, fortitude, generosity, and wisdom. He traded furs with the Chouteau company at Fort Pierre and encountered U.S. soldiers at Fort Berthold. In 1864, he fought against blue-clad regulars at the Battle of Killdeer Mountain. Thereafter, he laid siege to the newly established Fort Rice as well as Fort Buford.

By the 1870s, Sitting Bull's reputation as a wichasha wakan, or holy man, elevated his power among the Lakota Sioux. He was anointed wakiconza, a supreme chief, seeking to unite the diverse bands and contentious factions into a spirited resistance movement. In a ceremony, he was borne into a large circle on a buffalo robe and crowned with a magnificent headdress. He denounced the wasichus, or white people, who were invading Sioux country along the Powder and Yellowstone Rivers.

Sitting Bull tried to stop their invasion into the Paha Sapa, or Black Hills, where gold was found by prospectors. Even though the Fort Laramie Treaty guaranteed the "unceded" territory near the Great Sioux reservation as a traditional hunting ground, officials in Washington, D.C., broke their promises. They announced that tribes not settled on the reservation by January 31, 1876, would be considered "hostile." In fact, three columns of soldiers were deployed to drive them into confinement under the surveillance of government agents. One column, led by Brigadier General George Crook, moved north from Fort Fetterman. Under Colonel John Gibbon, another column headed east from western Montana. The third column, commanded by General Alfred Terry, marched westward from Fort Abraham Lincoln. Surrounded on all sides, the Sioux off the reservation had nowhere to escape.

Thus began the Great Sioux war. In the Spring of 1876, Sitting Bull communicated with Wakantanka, or the Great Mystery, at the top of a butte. He received a dream about a dust storm propelled by high winds from the east. He saw uniformed troops advancing, their weapons and horse trimmings glistening in the sunlight. When the approaching fury crashed into a rolling cloud, thunder pealed, lightning cracked, and rains poured. The tempest passed, leaving an open sky.

On June 6, 1876, roughly 3,000 Lakota and Cheyenne joined Sitting Bull for a Sun Dance along the Rosebud Creek in Montana. Following purification in a sweat lodge, he entered the dance circle. After staring into the blazing orb overhead, he offered his flesh and slashed his arms one hundred times. As blood flowed from his body, Sitting Bull received another vision. He foresaw the mounted bluecoats attacking—"as many as grasshoppers." However, they descended upside down toward the ground as they rode. They possessed no ears and therefore could not heed the warnings to turn back.

Inspired by his visions, the Oglala war chief Crazy Horse organized a band of 500 warriors for action. On June 17, he surprised Crook's troops at the Battle of the Rosebud. Then, the Sioux and their allies moved their camps to the valley of the Little Bighorn River at a place the Sioux called Greasy Grass. In search of an elusive enemy, Colonel George Armstrong Custer of the Seventh Cavalry located their camps on June 25 with the help of Crow scouts. Outnumbered more than four-to-one, he ignored the warnings of his scouts and led the troops toward the camps. Along the Little Big Horn, 261 men of the Seventh Cavalry died that day.

After the stunning loss at the Little Big Horn, Lieutenant General Phil Sheridan deployed 2,500 additional troops to avenge the death of Custer. Congress took away the Black Hills in violation of the Fort Laramie Treaty and seized another forty million acres of promised land. Sitting Bull, however, refused to accept defeat. He and his loyalists fled beyond the reach of the armed forces by crossing the border into Canada. General Terry traveled north to offer Sitting Bull a pardon in exchange for settling on the reservation, although he defiantly rejected the offer.

With the buffalo herds dwindling, Sitting Bull finally decided to end his exile. On July 19, 1881, he told his young son, Crow Foot, to hand his rifle to the commanding officer of Fort Buford in Montana. After the gesture, he spoke: "I wish to be remembered as the last man of my tribe to surrender my rifle." He donned a pair of sunglasses to protect his sensitive eyes and boarded a steamer for Bismarck. Dispatched to Fort Randall, he and his followers were prisoners of war for nearly two years.

Assigned to the Standing Rock agency after 1883, Sitting Bull lived in a cabin. Devoted to his family, he retained his two wives. His two adult

daughters were married and presented him with grandchildren. He continued to raise five children in his immediate household, including two pairs of twins and a daughter named Standing Holy. His mother, Her-Holy-Door, lived with the family until her death in 1884. He fathered two more children thereafter. Although he eschewed Christianity, he sent his children to a nearby Christian school to learn to read and to write.

The government agent, James McLaughlin, permitted Sitting Bull to participate in a traveling exhibition in 1884. In 1885, the legendary figure was allowed to join Buffalo Bill's Wild West show, earning $50 a week for appearing on horseback in an arena. On tour, he profited from the sale of his autograph and pictures. He stayed with the show only four months, managing to shake hands with President Grover Cleveland while in Washington, D.C.

After returning home, Sitting Bull spoke against the unjust policies of the agency. He openly defied the land agreements of 1888 and 1889, which threw half the Great Sioux Reservation open to non-Indian settlement and divided the rest into six separate reservations. "I would rather die an Indian," he prophetically stated, "than live a white man." Indeed, he received a vision of a meadowlark telling him that he would die at the hands of the Sioux.

In the fall of 1890, a Miniconjou Sioux named Kicking Bear came to Sitting Bull with news of the Ghost Dance religion, which promised to restore the traditional way of life. Though skeptical of the religion at first, he planted a prayer tree at Standing Rock. He began dancing while wearing a shirt with a painted red cross. When attempting to arrest him at his cabin on December 15, 1890, a Lakota Sioux policeman shot him in the head. Alas, his final vision came to pass. His killing led to the tragic events at Wounded Knee two weeks later.

Sitting Bull died a martyr in the last days of Sioux resistance to U.S. colonialism. He was originally buried at Fort Yates, North Dakota, but in 1953, his remains were relocated to Mobridge, South Dakota. However, researchers continue to disagree about the actual location of his bones.

On March 6, 1996, the Standing Rock Sioux Tribal Council voted to change the name of the tribal community college to Sitting Bull College (SBC). As a tribute to his spirit, the institution adopted its motto from his words: "Let us put our minds together to see what we can build for our children."

Brad D. Lookingbill

See also Northern Plains; Red Cloud (Makhpiya-Luta); Treaty of Fort Laramie with the Sioux, Etc.–September 17, 1851.

References and Further Reading

Anderson, Gary C. *Sitting Bull and the Paradox of Lakota Nationhood*. 1996. New York: Harper Collins.

Ostler, Jeffrey. *The Plains Sioux and U.S. Colonialism from Lewis and Clark to Wounded Knee*. 2004. Cambridge: Cambridge University Press.

Sitting Bull College, http://www.sittingbull.edu (accessed February 14, 2005).

Utley, Robert. *The Lance and the Shield: The Life and Times of Sitting Bull*. 1993. New York: Ballantine Books.

White, Richard. 1978. "The Winning of the West: The Expansion of the Western Sioux in the Eighteenth and Nineteenth Centuries." *Journal of American History* 65 (September): 321–323.

Sohappy, David, Sr.
(c. 1925–1991)

David Sohappy, Sr. was born on April 25, 1925 or 1926, and died on May 6, 1991. He emerged as a symbolic leader of the struggle for Northwest Indian treaty rights in the late twentieth century. His victory in *Sohappy v. Smith* (1969) set the precedent for the Boldt Decision of 1974 and placed off-reservation fishing on firm legal footing. Continued clashes with state, federal, and tribal authorities brought international attention to the cause but ultimately landed him in prison and ruined his health. As one mourner remarked at his funeral, "It's like the government took a knife and turned it in his heart" (Senior 1991, A1).

Sohappy had always followed the subsistence practices and the Washat religion of his Wanapam ancestors. Born and raised on the Yakima reservation in south-central Washington State, he began catching salmon at age five and spent much of each year along the Columbia River. After a brief stint in the army, he farmed his family's allotment and worked various jobs for twenty years before moving to Cook's Landing, an in-lieu fishing site built to replace traditional locations flooded by the Bonneville Dam. There, he became embroiled in the growing controversy between the tribes and the states. In 1968, Sohappy and thirteen other plaintiffs filed a lawsuit to prevent further state interference with off-reservation fishing rights reserved in the Yakama Treaty of 1855. *Sohappy v. Smith* reached federal district court along with *United States v. Oregon*, a supporting action brought by the Justice Department. Judge Robert C. Belloni merged the cases and handed the Indians an important victory, ruling that the states could regulate tribal fishing only when necessary for conservation and that they must guarantee the Indians a "fair and equitable share" of the salmon runs.

Over the next two decades, however, many tribal leaders came to regard Sohappy as a loose cannon. For several years prior to the case, the residents of Cook's Landing had ignored tribal conservation ordinances, which they considered a violation of their spiritual beliefs. The states and the tribes disagreed, and the people at Cook's Landing soon acquired a reputation as poachers. In 1981, a federal-state sting operation netted Sohappy and his son David for selling fish caught with ceremonial use permits. Convinced that Indians had poached forty thousand salmon, agents raided Cook's Landing and apprehended seventy-five Indians. Nineteen faced charges under the Lacey Act, which had recently been amended to make illegal fishing a felony. Although biologists later found the forty thousand "missing" fish, which had been diverted into tributaries by industrial pollution, the Sohappys each received the maximum sentence of five years for selling 345 salmon.

Their conviction placed the Yakama Nation in an awkward position. Anxious to assert its jurisdiction over the Sohappys and three other defendants, the tribe insisted on holding its own trial before handing them over to federal marshals. The jury found all five men innocent, and the tribal council immediately requested presidential pardons, but many Indians objected to the sight of traditionalists being tried by their own government. Some councilmen also supported the ongoing effort of the Bureau of Indian Affairs (BIA) to evict the residents of Cook's Landing. Since the late 1960s, the BIA had insisted that the sites were meant only for temporary access during the fishing season, not as places of permanent residence. In 1984, BIA officials delivered eviction notices to the families at Cook's and four other sites. The Warm Springs and Yakama councils urged them to leave, but the river families insisted that the treaties and their traditional lifestyle gave them the right to stay. In 1986, ten individuals and a group called the Chiefs and Council of the Columbia River Indians initiated a lawsuit to stop the evictions. The U.S. court of appeals upheld their position, but the decision came too late for Sohappy. Although he had received parole in 1988 after suffer-ing a stroke, his health continued to deteriorate. He died just five months before the eviction case closed.

Andrew H. Fisher

See also Boldt Decision (*United States v. Washington*), 1974; Reserved Rights Doctrine; *Sohappy v. Smith* and *United States v. Oregon*, 1969.
References and Further Reading
Dietrich, William. 1995. *Northwest Passage: The Great Columbia River*. New York: Simon & Schuster.
Dills, Barbara, and Paulette D'Auteuil-Robideau. 1987. *In Defense of Che Wana: Fishing Rights on the Columbia River*. Portland, OR: Wheel Press.
Senior, Jeanie. 1991. "Indian Leader Laid To Rest in Tribal Rite." *The Oregonian*, May 10, A1.
Ulrich, Roberta. 1999. *Empty Nets: Indians, Dams, and the Columbia River*. Corvallis: Oregon State University Press.

Spotted Tail
(1823–1881)

Spotted Tail (Sinte Gleska) was a Sicangu (Upper Brûlé Lakota), born in 1823 in the Ring band (*tiyospe*), a community of bilaterally related extended families on the White River in south central South Dakota. He learned to hunt bison, to conduct raiding expeditions against the Pawnee, to protect his community's southern lands that lay beyond the Platte River in western Nebraska, and to take the proper path toward leadership under the guidance of Little Thunder, leader of the Ring band. By midcentury, he had become a Shirt Wearer (Wicasa), the official band executive for the council (Wiscas Itacans), locating good hunting and campgrounds, deciding family disputes, and negotiating with foreign officials.

Traders were part of Spotted Tail's early life, but increased non-Native immigration to Oregon in 1843, to Utah in 1847, and to California in 1849 brought overland travelers through the Brûlés' Platte River territories, and soon the American military followed to protect the immigrants. These events forever changed Spotted Tail's life.

In 1854, a Mormon emigrant abandoned a lame cow and a Minniconju Lakota killed the animal. This "Mormon cow affair" convinced the brash Lieutenant John Lawrence Grattan, a recent West Point graduate, to take a detachment and demand that Little Thunder's Brûlé band pay compensation and release the guilty Lakota to military control. After an unfruitful negotiation, Grattan's

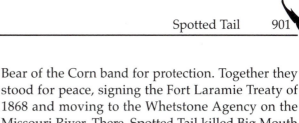

Spotted Tail was a leader of the Brûlé Teton Indians who sought compromise with the invading whites. Spotted Tail disagreed with Oglala Sioux leader Red Cloud, wanting to negotiate to allow whites to pass through Indian lands on their way to the gold mines in Montana. Spotted Tail became the leader of the Oglala Sioux after Red Cloud was deposed in 1881, but he was assassinated shortly thereafter. (Mercaldo Archives)

men fired their heavy artillery, and the Lakota retaliated, killing the entire unit. After learning of Grattan's fate, Secretary of War Jefferson Davis ordered General William S. Harney to prepare a punitive campaign against the guilty tribespeople. The following year, at Ash Hollow in western Nebraska, Harney's expedition attacked Little Thunder's band, killing eighty-six people, taking prisoners. Harney then demanded the surrender and imprisonment of the leading men. Spotted Tail (among others) surrendered at Fort Laramie in the fall of 1855. He was incarcerated at Fort Leavenworth and later at Fort Kearny before returning to his people the following fall. Upon his return, he decided to stand with Little Thunder and avoid war with the whites but to continue to fight the traditional Pawnee foes.

In 1866, Spotted Tail succeeded Little Thunder as headman of the Ring band and joined with Swift Bear of the Corn band for protection. Together they stood for peace, signing the Fort Laramie Treaty of 1868 and moving to the Whetstone Agency on the Missouri River. There, Spotted Tail killed Big Mouth during a leadership dispute in 1869. The agency was moved to northwest Nebraska shortly afterward, and then war began in the north when followers of Sitting Bull and Crazy Horse refused to stay inside the boundaries of the Great Sioux Reservation. At the same time, miners violated Lakota boundaries and invaded the Black Hills. The escalating frustration culminated on the banks of the Greasy Grass Creek when Lakota soldiers and their allies destroyed Brevet General George A. Custer's entire command.

While Crazy Horse and Sitting Bull fought, Spotted Tail's agency was known as a peace camp. As General Nelson Miles pursued the warring chiefs, General George Crook sought Spotted Tail's help and, in the fall of 1876, unilaterally and illegally declared that the United States "recognized Spotted Tail as chief of all the Sioux." Spotted Tail, with U.S. backing, maintained his status by signing the Black Hills Treaty (Agreement) in 1876, which enabled the United States to take control of that region. In early 1877, with Crook's urging, Spotted Tail went north on a peace mission seeking Crazy Horse's surrender. The two men met, and Crazy Horse accepted the terms Spotted Tail presented. The war was nearly over when Crazy Horse surrendered in late spring, and Sitting Bull and his people went to Canada in an effort to retain their independence.

After briefly moving their people to the old Ponca agency on the Missouri River, in the summer of 1878 Spotted Tail and other Upper Brûlé leaders moved to the Rosebud Agency in south central South Dakota. At Rosebud, old tribal conflicts merged into new battles. Spotted Tail tried to follow Lakota tradition but lacked credibility because he owed his position to U.S. intervention. As he attempted to maintain control over all the Brûlé bands, Spotted Tail encountered increasing tension between himself and Two Strike, White Thunder, Crow Dog, and Hollow Horn Bear. Rosebud leaders sent some children to the Carlisle Boarding School in 1879, and Spotted Tail removed the children without Brûlé authority, violating tribal political protocol. These ill feelings erupted following a meeting in early August 1881, when Crow Dog shot Spotted Tail, killing him instantly.

Richmond Clow

See also *Ex Parte Crow Dog,* 1883; Northern Plains; Relevant Court Cases Related to Treaties; Sovereignty.

References and Further Reading

Bray, Kingsley M. 2002. "Spotted Tail and the Treaty of 1868." *Nebraska History* 83(1): 19–35.

Clow, Richmond L. 1998. "The Anatomy of a Lakota Shooting: Crow Dog and Spotted Tail." *South Dakota History* 28(4): 209–227.

Hyde, George E. 1961. *Spotted Tail's Folk: A History of the Brule Sioux.* Norman: University of Oklahoma Press.

Seagle, William. 1970. "The Murder of Spotted Tail." *Indian Historian* 3(4): 10–22.

Worcester, Donald F. 1964. "Spotted Tail: Warrior, Diplomat." *American West* 1(4): 38–46, 87.

Arthur St. Clair (1734–1818), born in Scotland, was appointed territorial governor of the Northwest Territory in 1787. St. Clair's inept diplomacy heightened white-Indian tensions in the Old Northwest Country. (National Archives)

St. Clair, Arthur

(1734–1818)

Arthur St. Clair was a U.S. territorial governor and army commander whose inept diplomacy heightened white-Indian tensions in the Old Northwest. He led the army to one of its most humiliating defeats near the Miami village of Kekionga. A veteran officer and prominent member of the Continental Congress, St. Clair was appointed governor of the newly created Northwest Territory in 1787. Having alienated many moderates among the western tribes with his inflammatory rhetoric, St. Clair concluded the two treaties of Fort Harmar with an unrepresentative gathering of undistinguished chiefs. Rising levels of frontier violence led to a punitive expedition under General Josiah Harmar in 1790. Following Harmar's embarrassing defeat, St. Clair was named major general and commanding officer of a larger expedition, which set out for Kekionga (present-day Fort Wayne) in the fall of 1791. A surprise attack by a numerically inferior force of American Indians led by Little Turtle and Blue Jacket led to the greatest rout of the U.S. Army by Indians in history, with more than nine hundred dead, missing, or wounded. St. Clair was replaced as commanding officer by the more vigorous Anthony Wayne but remained governor of the Northwest and, later, Ohio Territory, until he was fired by President Jefferson in 1802.

Originally from Scotland, St. Clair came to North America during the French and Indian War and served under Lord Jeffrey Amherst and General James Wolfe. He later settled in Pennsylvania and rose to the rank of major general during the Revolu-

tionary War. Immediately prior to his appointment as territorial governor, he served as president of the Continental Congress. As territorial governor of the Northwest Territory, St. Clair was the top U.S. official in the area that is now Ohio, Indiana, Illinois, Michigan, Wisconsin, and eastern Minnesota. Paradoxically, his duties were to placate the Native populations of those lands while clearing the way for possession and development of the lands by whites. Frequently bedridden with gout, largely ignorant of Indian affairs, and at best mediocre as a diplomat, administrator, and military commander, St. Clair soon lost control of the situation.

Implored by his superiors to sign a general peace treaty with the Indians in the region, St. Clair used a minor episode involving a small band of Ojibwas as a pretext to change the council location from the Falls of the Muskingum River to Fort Harmar. This resulted in the alienation of many moderate leaders from the federal government and the rapid rise of more warlike chiefs within the tribal confederacy. Consequently, the treaties negotiated at Fort Harmar had little legitimacy and were, at any rate, primarily a restatement of previous peace treaties. Rather than preventing tension and violence on the frontier, St. Clair's ham-fisted diplomacy convinced many Indians that warfare was the only way to counter American demands for further land cessions.

By 1789, the situation had deteriorated to the point where St. Clair asked that militia be called out to initiate offensive action by the federal government both to punish the Indians and to satisfy the outraged settlers on both sides of the Ohio. The next year, he and General Harmar planned an ambitious expedition against the Shawnee and Miami, manned largely by unfit and unprepared militia troops. When Harmar returned, after great loss of life and without having accomplished the objective of intimidating and pacifying the Indians, St. Clair was named commanding major general and began to plan an even more ambitious campaign for the fall of 1791.

St. Clair's campaign was a fiasco from beginning to end. Incompetence and corruption among the cronies of war secretary Henry Knox resulted in an all but unbearable supply situation. The commander himself emphasized the quantity of troops rather than the quality, hoping to outnumber the enemy. Instead, difficulties in recruitment and logistics, as well as widespread desertion, produced a much smaller force than anticipated. Furthermore, most of the soldiers were inexperienced and undisciplined. At the same time, St. Clair greatly underestimated the skill and experience of the Indian warriors and failed to gather adequate intelligence about enemy movements. Emphatically instructed by President George Washington to "beware of surprise," St. Clair was nonetheless unprepared for the attack by some one thousand Indians from a dozen different tribes shortly before dawn on November 4, 1791. The army was forced into desperate retreat after three hours of lopsided battle, leaving hundreds of dead behind. Shortly thereafter, St. Clair was replaced as commanding officer, but he remained territorial governor until 1802. He suffered numerous reverses in his private life and died in poverty in 1818.

Knut Oyangen

See also Fort Harmar, Ohio; Knox, Henry; Treaty with the Six Nations–January 9, 1789; Treaty with the Wyandot, Etc.–January 9, 1789; Wayne, Anthony.

References and Further Reading
Edel, Wilbur. 1997. *Kekionga! The Worst Defeat in the History of the U.S. Army.* Westport, CT: Praeger.
Smith, William Henry. 1971. *The St. Clair Papers.* 2 vols. New York: Da Capo Press.
Sword, Wiley. 1985. *President Washington's Indian War: The Struggle for the Old Northwest, 1790–1795.* Norman: University of Oklahoma Press.

Standing Bear (Mo-chu-no-zhi)
(c. 1830–1908)

Standing Bear gained national notoriety in the late 1870s during a time of forced removal for the Ponca and other Native peoples on the Great Plains. He led some of the Poncas on a forty-day, five-hundred-mile march from Indian Territory (now Oklahoma) back to Nebraska. In Omaha, Standing Bear became engaged in the first court case to result in a declaration that American Indians are to be treated as human beings under U.S. law. Thus, the army could not legally relocate an Indian by force without cause. The army promptly ignored the court order.

Standing Bear (c. 1830–1908), a Ponca tribal leader, especially known from Standing Bear v. Crook, *1879. (Library of Congress)*

Before they were forcibly removed from their homeland along the Niobrara River in northern Nebraska, the Ponca had gone to great lengths to maintain friendly relationships with the United States. In 1858, they ceded part of their homeland along the Niobrara in exchange for a homeland in the same area that was then said to be theirs in perpetuity. Ten years later, the United States, in a classic example of sloppy bureaucracy, assigned Ponca land to the Sioux, their traditional enemies, in the Laramie treaty of 1868. It took a dozen years for the United States to acknowledge its error, and in the meantime many of the Ponca had died in Oklahoma and on forced marches.

During 1877, federal troops removed 723 Poncas from three villages along the Niobrara River to Indian Territory. The tribe was moved at bayonet point after eight of their leaders had inspected and refused to accept the arid land that the government wanted the Ponca to occupy in Oklahoma. During their march to Indian Territory, several of the Poncas died of starvation and disease.

A year after their removal, a third of the Ponca had died. One of the dead was a son of Standing Bear, who, determined to bury his bones in the lands of his ancestors, escaped northward toward the Niobrara with thirty other Poncas. After two months of walking, including a ten-day stop among the Otoe, the group led by Standing Bear took shelter on land owned by the Omaha, their bloody feet leaving tracks in the snow.

The following spring, army troops arrived at the Omaha camp and began to force the Ponca southward again. They camped for a time outside Omaha, where local citizens obtained a writ of habeas corpus and brought the army into the federal court of Judge Elmer Dundy, who ruled, "An Indian is a person within the meaning of the law, and there is no law giving the Army authority to forcibly remove Indians from their lands" (Johansen and Grinde 1997, 367). Ironically, the case was prepared with the help of the old Indian fighter George Crook, who was swayed by the manifest injustice of the Poncas' case. The harsh treatment of the Ponca also received publicity in Omaha newspaper articles, which were wired to larger newspapers on the East Coast, causing a storm of protest letters to Congress.

Shortly after Omaha federal judge Elmer S. Dundy denied the army's presumed power to forcibly relocate Indians in the case of Standing Bear, his brother Big Snake tested the ruling by moving roughly a hundred miles in Indian Territory from the

Poncas' assigned reservation to one occupied by the Cheyenne. He was arrested by troops and returned in contravention of the judge's ruling. On October 31, 1879, Ponca Indian agent William H. Whiteman called Big Snake a troublemaker and ordered a detail to imprison him. When Big Snake refused to surrender, contending he had committed no crime, he was shot to death. Later, the U.S. Senate called for an investigation of the shooting and other aspects of the Poncas' tragedy.

Following the Senate investigation, Standing Bear's band was allowed to go home. Standing Bear died in his homeland along the Niobrara in 1908.

Bruce E. Johansen

See also *Elk v. Wilkins*, 1884; Indian Removal; Tibbles, Susette LaFlesche (Bright Eyes, Inshta Theamba); Treaty with the Sioux, Etc., and Arapaho–April 29, 1868.

References and Further Reading

Johansen, Bruce E., and Donald A. Grinde, Jr. 1997. *The Encyclopedia of Native American Biography.* New York: Henry Holt.

Massey, Rosemary, et. al. 1979. *Footprints in Blood: Standing Bear's Struggle for Freedom and Human Dignity.* Omaha, NB: American Indian Center of Omaha.

Nabokov, Peter, ed. 1991. *Native American Testimony.* New York: Penguin Books.

Tibbles, Thomas Henry. 1972. *The Ponca Chiefs: An Account of the Trial of Standing Bear.* Lincoln: University of Nebraska Press.

Tecumseh

(c. 1768–1813)

Tecumseh was born about 1768 and died in 1813. He was a Shawnee chief who, along with his brother Tensquatawa (The Prophet), formed an intertribal Indian confederation to oppose land cessions to the United States. While Tecumseh at first tried to maintain peaceful relations with the Americans, he believed that land cessions by treaty brought insufficient monetary compensation to tribes and that bowing to white demands destroyed the Native peoples' dignity and self-sufficiency. He also maintained that cessions could only be made by Native Americans as a group, and not by chiefs of individual tribes.

Tecumseh's father was killed by the Americans in the Battle of Point Pleasant in 1774. From then until the Treaty of Greenville in 1795, there were more than a dozen armed confrontations between the Shawnee and the Americans, including destruction of Tecumseh's village by the Kentucky militia in 1786. These clashes gave Tecumseh the impetus to organize resistance against whites' attempts to expand their settlements on Indian land. Tecumseh participated in the Battle of Fallen Timbers on August 20, 1794, which was a decisive victory for the U.S. over the northwest Indian confederation and ended two decades of border warfare. Tecumseh did not attend the treaty negotiations at Greenville. The result of that treaty was that the southern two-thirds of Ohio was transferred to the United States, and the Shawnee and other tribes were pushed out of where they historically had lived in that region.

Nevertheless, Tecumseh attempted to maintain peace with the United States and concentrated instead on internal reforms such as combating alcoholism, strengthening Native customs and beliefs, and resisting the influences of white culture. Tensquatawa provided the spiritual base for Tecumseh's efforts. Reform was needed because the Indians had been corrupted by sin. If the tribes followed the brothers' teachings, they could recapture their former superiority to whites.

Treaties and supplements to them were often negotiated with separate tribes and tailored to specific groups to make them acceptable. Tecumseh realized that all tribes would have to act as one to halt the shrinkage of landholdings left to them. His idea went beyond previous small-scale alliances between groups with specific affinities of language or custom. His desire for the Indians to act in concert grew out of the belief that no one tribe "owned" any of the lands in question, so no single group had the authority to make land cessions. His particular ire was reserved for those chiefs who negotiated treaties for personal gain. The functional boundary between Indian lands and white settlement had been flexible and constantly moving as white settlement expanded westward, mainly at the behest of whites. Tecumseh wanted to see a permanent boundary established between whites and Native Americans. If Tecumseh's policy of "pan-Indianism" had been accepted by the United States, negotiation of treaties would have become impossible.

Tecumseh's efforts were helped by the fact that, following Greenville, no further treaties were negotiated for several years. This changed when a series of treaties negotiated by William Henry Harrison between 1803 and 1809 resulted in the transfer to the United States of nearly fifty million acres. The treaties of 1809 with the Delaware, Potawatomi, Miami, Wea, Eel River, and Kickapoo, by which

those groups ceded nearly three million acres, marked the end of Tecumseh's willingness to negotiate with the United States. In 1810, he held a council with Harrison at Vincennes and warned the governor that the tribes would oppose the terms of the recently concluded treaty. As Harrison insisted that the treaty would be consummated as written, the council ended disastrously. At a second council the following year, Tecumseh threatened further conflict if white settlers attempted to move onto the ceded land. He then departed for a journey through the South to recruit more tribes for his confederacy. In his absence, Harrison attacked the Indians, who were led by Tensquatawa, along the Wabash near Tippecanoe Creek on November 7, 1811. Harrison's forces were victorious and destroyed the Indians' village.

Tecumseh's further efforts for Indian unity and against the expansion of white settlement were unsuccessful. He cooperated with the British during the War of 1812 and was killed at the Battle of the Thames on October 5, 1813.

Leigh Darbee

See also Battle of Fallen Timbers, 1794; Battle of the Thames, 1813; Battle of Tippecanoe, 1811; Harrison, William Henry; Tippecanoe River, Indiana; Vincennes, Indiana; Wabash River, Indiana.

References and Further Reading
Edmunds, R. David. 1984. *Tecumseh and the Quest for Indian Leadership*. Boston: Little, Brown.
Stefoff, Rebecca. 1998. *Tecumseh and the Shawnee Confederation*. New York: Facts on File.
Sugden, John. 1985. *Tecumseh's Last Stand*. Norman: University of Oklahoma Press.
Sugden, John. 1998. *Tecumseh, a Life*. New York: Henry Holt.

Tibbles, Susette LaFlesche (Bright Eyes, Inshta Theamba)
(1854–1903)

Susette LaFlesche became a major nineteenth-century Native rights advocate through the case of the Ponca Standing Bear, the first legal proceeding (decided in Omaha during 1879) to establish Native American rights as human beings under United States law.

LaFlesche was born near Bellevue, Nebraska, the eldest daughter of Joseph (Iron Eye) LaFlesche and Mary Gale LaFlesche, daughter of an army surgeon. Like her sister Susan, Susette LaFlesche attended the Presbyterian mission school on the Omaha Reservation. Both sisters were among the most brilliant students ever to attend the school. She also studied art at the University of Nebraska.

In the late 1870s, LaFlesche traveled with her father, Joseph LaFlesche, to Indian Territory (later Oklahoma) to render rudimentary medical assistance to the Ponca with Standing Bear, whose people had been forced to move there from their former homeland along the Niobrara in northern Nebraska. When the Ponca attempted to escape their forced exile and return to their homeland, they marched for several weeks in midwinter, finally eating their moccasins to survive and arriving at the Omaha reservation with bleeding feet. The Omaha, particularly the LaFlesche family, granted them sanctuary and sustenance.

Susette accompanied her brother Francis and Standing Bear on a lecture tour of Eastern cities during 1879 and 1880 to support the Poncas' case for a return of their homeland. Newspaper articles about the Poncas' forced exile by Omaha journalist Thomas H. Tibbles helped ignite a furor in Congress and among the public.

Tibbles, an editor at the Omaha *Herald,* was the first journalist to interview Standing Bear as the LaFlesche family sheltered the Poncas. Tibbles's accounts were telegraphed to newspapers on the East Coast. In the meantime, LaFlesche and Tibbles fell in love and married in 1882. Both also toured the East Coast with Standing Bear, "armed with news clippings on the Ponca story and endorsements from General [George] Crook, the mayor of Omaha, and leading Nebraska clergymen," raising support for restoration of Ponca lands (Tibbles 1880, 129).

In Boston, where support for Standing Bear's Poncas was very strong, a citizens' committee formed that included Henry Wadsworth Longfellow. While Susette LaFlesche was visiting Boston with Standing Bear, Longfellow said of her, "*This* is Minnehaha" (Tibbles 1880, 130).

In Boston, Tibbles, LaFlesche, and Standing Bear first met Helen Hunt Jackson. The Poncas' story inflamed Jackson's conscience and changed her life. Heretofore known as a poet (and a friend from childhood of Emily Dickinson), Jackson set out to write *A Century of Dishonor,* a best-selling book that described the angst of an America debating the future of the Native American peoples who had survived the last of the Indian wars. Jackson became a major figure in the European American debate over the future of Native Americans. Standing Bear and his people eventually were allowed to return home to the Niobrara River after Congress investigated the conditions under which they had been evicted. Standing Bear died there in 1908.

LaFlesche also coauthored a memoir with Standing Bear, *Ploughed Under: The Story of an Indian Chief* (1832). During ensuing years, LaFlesche and Tibbles also toured the British Isles. Later, the couple lived in Washington, D.C., but eventually Susette returned to Lincoln, Nebraska, where she died in 1903, and was buried in Bancroft, Nebraska.

In 1994, Susette LaFlesche was inducted into the National Women's Hall of Fame.

Bruce E. Johansen

See also Aboriginal Title; Relevant Court Cases Related to Treaties; Standing Bear (Mo-chu-no-zhi); Treaties and American Indian Schools in the Age of Assimilation, 1794–1930.

References and Further Reading

Jackson, Helen Hunt. 1888. *A Century of Dishonor: A Sketch of the United States Government's Dealings With Some of the Indian Tribes.* Boston: Roberts Bros. Repr., St. Clair Shores, MI: Scholarly Press, 1972.

Massey, Rosemary, et al. 1979. *Footprints in Blood: Standing Bear's Struggle for Freedom and Human Dignity.* Omaha, NB: American Indian Center of Omaha.

Tibbles, Thomas Henry. 1880. *The Ponca Chiefs: An Account of the Trial of Standing Bear.* Repr., Lincoln: University of Nebraska Press, 1972.

Wilson, Dorothy Clarke. 1974. *Bright Eyes: The Story of Suzette LaFlesche.* New York: McGraw-Hill.

Uncas

(1588?–1683)

For most Americans, the name Uncas conjures up the fictional character of James Fenimore Cooper's *The Last of the Mohicans.* The historical Uncas, however, was a Mohegan (not a Mohican) and far from the last of his tribe. Earlier than other Native leaders, Uncas recognized that the arrival of English colonists permanently altered the balance of power in southern New England. He closely allied himself with the newcomers, and for more than four decades he presided over the rise of the Mohegans. Under his leadership, the Mohegans rendered valuable military assistance to both the Plymouth and Massachusetts Bay Colonies during the Pequot War and King Philip's War. Because of Uncas's willingness to enter into alliances with the New England colonies against other Native peoples, as well as his part in slaying the Narragansett sachem Miantonomo, some scholars of Native America have cast him as a historical villain. However, his actions also strengthened the Mohegans, enabling them to retain a measure of independence in colonial New England long after other Native peoples had been displaced or coerced into moving into one of the Praying Towns.

At the time of English and Dutch settlement, the Mohegans were a small southern New England tribe that occupied the lands between the Connecticut and Thames rivers. Dominated by the more numerous and powerful Pequots, the Mohegans paid them tribute in the form of goods and wampum. On at least five occasions, Uncas attempted to undermine the authority—whether by a coup or other means is not documented—of the Pequot sachem, Sassacus. He always failed, and Sassacus forced him into exile among the Narragansetts. Each time, however, Sassacus permitted Uncas to return and retain leadership of the Mohegans, but only after ritually humiliating himself. Sassacus further punished Uncas each time by reducing the amount of Mohegan territory under his control. Uncas and the Mohegans were finally able to throw off Pequot domination by siding with Massachusetts Bay and Plymouth Bay Colonies when the Pequot War erupted in 1637. The colonial military leaders were distrustful of Uncas and the Mohegans at first, but he demonstrated his loyalty by delivering to them four Pequot heads and a captive. He also participated in planning and leading the attack on the Pequot's stronghold at Mystic. As a reward for his services, Uncas received a large share of the Pequot prisoners. Whereas the colonists sold most of their Pequot prisoners as slaves and shipped them to British sugar colonies in the Caribbean, the Mohegans adopted most of their prisoners and incorporated them into the tribe.

Seeking even closer ties to the English, Uncas enhanced his standing with them by occasionally feeding them rumors of Indian plots against their colonies. By presenting himself as an ally, Uncas and his people avoided displacement and received comparably favorable treatment from the English. The Mohegans were able to retain a good deal of autonomy.

Uncas proved useful yet again to the New England colonies when the Narragansett sachem Miantonomo, who had been an English ally during the Pequot War, began to speak out against them.

Miantonomo approached other Native groups and argued that, just as the English thought of themselves as "English," Native people should unite in the face of the European invasion and stop thinking of themselves as Narragansetts, Nipmucks, or Pokonokets. At about this time, Miantonomo signed a treaty with Massachusetts that required him to notify the colony if he went to war against another Native American tribe. Miantonomo sought and was granted permission to attack the Mohegans, who had been waylaying Narragansett hunters. Captured by the Mohegans during the ensuing war, Miantonomo reportedly attempted to purchase his freedom. Despite receiving a ransom from the Narragansetts for Miantonomo's safe return, Uncas turned him over to the colony of Connecticut. Wanting to be rid of a troublesome Native leader but not wanting Miantonomo's blood on their hands, the Connecticut authorities gave him back to Uncas, with the implicit understanding that he would have Miantonomo executed.

Uncas lent further assistance to the New England colonies during King Philip's War in 1675–1676. Although he could no longer lead warriors in the field himself, his son, Oweneco, assisted the English. After the war, Uncas reaffirmed his alliance to the colony and began selling Mohegan lands to them until his death in 1683.

Roger M. Carpenter

See also Metacom; Northeast and the Great Lakes.
References and Further Reading
Jennings, Francis. 1975. *The Invasion of America: Indians, Colonialism, and the Cant of Conquest.* Chapel Hill: University of North Carolina Press.
Oberg, Michael Leroy. 2003. *Uncas: First of the Mohegans.* Ithaca, NY: Cornell University Press.

Washakie
(Pina Quahah, Scar Face)
(c. 1798–1900)

Washakie (Pina Quahah and Scar Face) was born about 1798 and died in 1900. He was the son of a Shoshone mother and Flathead father. Pina Quahah lived with the Shoshone after his father's death and joined the warlike Bannock band of the tribe as a young adult. A large man, standing over six feet tall, he gained a reputation for bravery early in battles against the Blackfeet and Crow, earning the name Scar Face from a scar left by a Blackfoot arrow on his

Washakie (c. 1798–1900) was a Shoshone chief and representative for both the Shoshone and Bannock peoples. He negotiated the surrender of the Green River Valley in eastern Utah and southern Wyoming, which provided for the construction of the Union Pacific Railway. (National Archives and Records Administration)

left cheek. Eventually, Pina Quahah earned his most famous name, Washakie, meaning The Rattle, by adopting the use of a buffalo gourd noisemaker as a weapon to scare opponent's horses in battle.

By 1844, Washakie had established himself as a capable warrior and leader and had attracted to his banner a band of Shoshones that occupied the region from the North Platte and Wind rivers to the Great Salt Lake. Surrounded by hostile Indian tribes, Washakie established friendly relations with the U.S. government and adopted a policy of coexistence to secure his people. In 1847, Brigham Young built settlements around the Great Salt Lake, populated the region with more than fifteen hundred pioneers and opened up trade relations with the Shoshone.

While the Mormons settled the Great Salt Lake region, the Sioux and Cheyenne attempted to check the advance of settlers and gold miners into their region and set the Oregon Trail ablaze, leading the U.S. government to establish military posts along its route. In 1851, the government sought to end its hostilities with the Indians and invited them to a conference at Fort Laramie, Wyoming. Although not invited to the conference, Washakie decided to attend the treaty negotiations to secure his people's lands and interests. But the government ignored Washakie and divided the northern plains into several regions, giving the Crow the Shoshone's northern hunting range between the Powder River and the Wind River Mountains.

Angered at the government, Washakie strengthened his ties with Brigham Young, now the superintendent of Utah's Indian affairs. As a result, Young sent traders and missionaries to the Shoshone. Ignoring the advances of the missionaries, Washakie, impressed with Mormon agricultural techniques and aware of the dwindling buffalo population, urged his people to adopt farming to supplement their diet. However, despite their close relations, Washakie broke his ties with Young in 1857. Though Young petitioned the Shoshone for an alliance, Washakie ignored the plea and met with U.S. officials to claim his neutrality and to request a Shoshone reservation on the traditional Shoshone land the Crow occupied as a result of the Laramie Treaty of 1851. Unable to grant Washakie his request but impressed with his leadership, U.S. officials established an Indian agency intended to deal with the Shoshone and their needs.

Undaunted, Washakie continued to pursue his quest for a Shoshone reservation on their traditional lands. In 1863, Washakie saw an opportunity to fulfill his goal following a failed Indian uprising in 1862. Because he remained neutral during the 1862 uprising, U.S. officials asked Washakie to help them broker a peace settlement with the Shoshone and Ute who had participated in the war. In July 1863, the Indians signed a peace treaty with U.S. officials that allowed the government to construct and maintain telegraph and railroad lines through their territory at the cost of a $20,000 annuity to be paid over a twenty-year period. As a result of this treaty agreement, Washakie's stature grew considerably among both the Shoshone and the Americans.

Over the next few decades, the U.S. government and the Shoshone sought Washakie's counsel and assistance with Indian-white relations during such episodes as the Great Sioux War, in which Washakie and his people assisted U.S. troops with the defeat of the Sioux, Cheyenne, and Arapaho. However, Washakie reached the height of his influence and power in 1868, when he reached a settlement with the government at the Treaty of Fort Bridger that awarded to the Shoshone a reservation of three million acres on their traditional lands in the Wind River drainage. Although the Shoshone eventually ceded much of the land, Washakie succeeded in securing for the Shoshone a reservation on the most desired piece of their traditional lands, a feat many Indian leaders attempted but few, if any, accomplished. As a result of Washakie's great leadership, the government renamed one of its frontier posts Fort Washakie and, when the venerable chief passed on to the next life in 1900, laid him to rest with a full military funeral.

Joseph P. Alessi

See also Treaty with the Eastern Shoshone–July 2, 1863; Treaty with the Eastern Band Shoshone and Bannock–July 3, 1868; Treaty of Fort Laramie with the Sioux, Etc.–September 17, 1851.

References and Further Reading

Hebard, Grace Raymond. 1930. *Washakie: An Account of Indian Resistance of the Covered Wagon and Union Pacific Railroad Invasions of Their Territory.* Cleveland, OH: Alfred H. Clark.

Trenholm, Virginia Cole, and Maurine Carley. 1964. *The Shoshonis: Sentinels of the Rockies.* Norman: University of Oklahoma Press.

Wright, Peter M. 1980. "Washakie." In *American Indian Leaders*, ed. R. David Edmunds. Lincoln: University of Nebraska Press.

Watie, Stand

(1806–1871)

Stand Watie was a leading member of the pro-treaty faction of eastern Cherokees responsible for the Treaty of New Echota. He was also a Confederate brigadier general and principal chief of the Confederate Cherokees. Stand Watie was born at Oothcaloga in the Cherokee Nation, Georgia. He was the younger brother of Elias Boudinot, the nephew of Major Ridge, and the cousin of John Ridge. All four men signed the Cherokee removal treaty, or Treaty of New Echota, in 1835 and immigrated to the Indian Territory in 1837.

Watie was marked for assassination at the same time that anti-treaty Cherokees killed the Ridges and Boudinot in 1839, but he escaped. From that time on, he was regarded as the leader of the Ridge-Watie-Boudinot faction, or Treaty Party of the Cherokee Nation. He became a wealthy planter and slaveowner in the Indian Territory and was strongly in favor of the secession movement. He entered the Confederate army as a colonel in 1861 and was promoted to the rank of brigadier general in 1864, making him the only Native American general on either side in the American Civil War. On June 23, 1865, Watie was the last Confederate general to surrender.

Stand Watie became involved in Cherokee politics at an early age. He was appointed as clerk of the Cherokee Supreme Court in 1828 and later was licensed to practice law within the Cherokee Nation. The Ridge-Watie-Boudinot faction believed that keeping whites out of the Cherokee Nation in the East was hopeless. This was especially true after gold was discovered on Cherokee land in 1828, and President Andrew Jackson refused to enforce the Supreme Court's *Worcester v. Georgia* decision in 1832. Consequently, they became leaders of a Cherokee faction supporting removal to the West. On December 29, 1835, they signed the Treaty of New Echota, giving up all claims to lands in the East in return for compensation and land west of the Mississippi River. A majority of Cherokees (especially the full-blooded element) led by principal chief John Ross bitterly opposed the treaty and fought removal. A previously adopted Cherokee "blood law" called for the death of any Cherokee who surrendered tribal land. Those opposing the treaty marked Watie and the other treaty-signers for death.

In 1837, Watie and the other members of his faction immigrated to the Cherokee Nation West. Watie took up farming and ran a general store at Honey Creek on the east side of the Grand River near the Missouri border in what is now northeastern Oklahoma. The majority of Cherokees continued to resist removal from Georgia. This faction was forcibly removed to the West in 1838 over what became known as the Trail of Tears. On June 22, 1839, anti-removal Cherokees enforced the blood law by killing Major Ridge, John Ridge, and Elias Boudinot. Watie was warned and escaped assassination. He assumed leadership of his faction as civil war broke out between the pro-removal and anti-removal factions. After years of violence, both sides signed the Cherokee Treaty of 1846, and a fragile peace was maintained until the outbreak of the American Civil War.

As a planter and slaveowner, Watie supported secession and joined the Confederate cause when the war began. He was commissioned as a colonel on July 12, 1861, and raised the first regiment of Cherokees for service in the Confederate Army. Principal chief John Ross sided first with the Confederacy and then with the Union, bringing the old split between the Ross and Watie factions into the open once again. Ross eventually fled Indian Territory, and Watie was elected principal chief of the Confederate Cherokees on August 21, 1862. Watie gained renown during the war as a guerrilla fighter and irregular cavalry leader. He was promoted to brigadier general on May 6, 1864, and given command of the first Indian Brigade. His two greatest victories were the capture of the federal steamboat *J.R. Williams* on June 15, 1864, and the capture of a federal wagon train containing supplies valued at $1.5 million at the Second Battle of Cabin Creek on September 19, 1864.

After the war, Watie served as a member of the Southern Cherokee delegation during the negotiation of the Cherokee Reconstruction Treaty of 1866 and was a participant in the *Cherokee Tobacco* case in 1870. In this landmark case, the U.S. Supreme Court ruled that tribes were "independent dependent" nations within the framework of the United States and therefore subject to federal law. Stand Watie died at his longtime home at Honey Creek on September 9, 1871.

Robert D. Bohanan

See also Boudinot, Elias; *Cherokee Nation v. Georgia*, 1831; *Cherokee Tobacco* Case, 1870; Indian Removal; Indian Territory; New Echota, Georgia; Reconstruction Treaties with the Cherokee, Choctaw, Chickasaw, Creek, and Seminole–1866; Ridge, John Rollin; Ridge, Major; Ross, John; Trail of Tears; Treaty with the Cherokee, December 29, 1835.

References and Further Reading

Dale, Edward Everett, and Gaston Litton, eds. 1939. *Cherokee Cavaliers: Forty Years of Cherokee History As Told in the Correspondence of the Ridge-Watie-Boudinot Family.* Norman: University of Oklahoma Press.

Franks, Kenny A. 1979. *Stand Watie and the Agony of the Cherokee Nation.* Memphis, TN: Memphis State University Press.

Knight, Wilfred. 1988. *Red Fox: Stand Watie and the Confederate Indian Nations during the Civil War Years in Indian Territory.* Glendale, CA: Arthur H. Clark.

Watkins, Arthur V.
(1886–1973)

Arthur V. Watkins was the leading congressional proponent of termination, a policy that aimed at ending all federal government relations with American Indian tribes. As Republican senator from Utah from 1946 to 1958 and chair of the Senate Subcommittee on Indian Affairs, Watkins supported a series of bills terminating the federal trust status of more than sixty tribes between 1954 and 1958. Watkins believed that termination would "free" Indians from federal supervision so that they would be able to compete equally within American society.

Watkins was born in Midway, Utah, in 1886 and raised in a devout Mormon family. After completing a mission in New York, he enrolled at the New York University Law School and later at Columbia Law School, graduating in 1912. He returned to Utah and pursued a varied career as a lawyer, ranch-owner, newspaper editor, judge, and manager of water development projects before his election to the Senate in 1946.

Arthur V. Watkins (1886–1973) was a U.S. senator from Utah and author of the termination policy to end the trust relationship between Native Americans and the U.S. Government. (Library of Congress)

Watkins's Mormon religious beliefs and his commitment to free enterprise strongly influenced his approach to Indian affairs. Viewing Indians as a "fallen race," he believed that their interests would be best served by complete assimilation into American society and the termination of federal government support. As he saw it, Indians would be able to better themselves only if they were treated as individuals rather than as members of tribes.

In the cold war era, Watkins's advocacy of termination earned him the support of both conservatives, who opposed John Collier's Indian Reorganization Act as "socialistic," and liberals, who were coming to view reservations as discriminatory institutions. Plans for terminating Indian tribes began to move ahead. In 1947, members of Congress asked acting Indian commissioner William Zimmerman to draw up a list of tribes ranked according to their readiness for the withdrawal of federal supervision. In 1949, Arthur Watkins was appointed chair of the Senate Subcommittee on Indian Affairs; in 1952, with the full support of the new commissioner of Indian affairs, Dillon S. Myer, Watkins sponsored House Concurrent Resolution 108. The resolution declared that it was the intention of Congress to "free" Indian tribes from federal control and subject them to the same laws, privileges, and responsibilities as other citizens of the United States.

After passage of the resolution in 1953, Watkins was eager to make an example. Turning to his home state of Utah, Watkins pushed for the termination of the Southern Paiute and the Northern Ute on the Uintah-Ouray Reservation, even though neither tribe had the economic resources or degree of acculturation that qualified them for immediate termination. Watkins used questionable methods to achieve his goals. After a meeting with the Southern Paiute in December 1953, Watkins claimed that they had accepted termination, despite the fact that the Paiute had been noncommittal. The Paiute then found themselves unable to dispute Watkins's statements at the congressional hearings held in Washington, because they had no money for travel. Consequently, in September 1954, four bands of Southern Paiute were terminated. In the case of the Ute, Watkins used his position as chair of the Senate Subcommittee on Indian Affairs to compel the tribe to use the funds they had been awarded in a federal land claims case to develop programs that included termination provisions. Then, exploiting long-standing divisions on the reservation, Watkins succeeded in getting the Ute to accept a division of assets and termination of federal recognition for the mixed-blood Ute. In addition to these actions in Utah, Watkins played a major role in terminating other tribes, including the Klamath of Oregon and the Menominee of Wisconsin.

The impact of termination on the affected tribes was significant. With the loss of trust status, federal programs to tribes were discontinued, state legislative jurisdiction was imposed, exemption to state taxing power was abolished, and tribal sovereignty was effectively ended. Former tribal members lost lands, federal health service, educational support, and employment assistance.

By the early 1960s, the failure of termination to improve the status of Indians, along with Indian protests, effectively halted implementation of the policy, although termination was not formally repudiated until 1970. Since then, many tribes have successfully campaigned to reverse their termination, including the Menominee, Klamath, and Southern Paiute.

After Watkins was defeated for reelection in 1958, he served briefly as a consultant to interior secretary Fred Seaton. In 1960, President Eisenhower appointed Watkins to the Indian Claims Commission, where he rose to the position of chief commissioner. Ironically, it was during Watkins's tenure that the Indian Claims Commission began negotiations for an $8.25 million settlement of the Southern Paiute land claim suit against the federal government. In 1967, Watkins retired from the commission to write his memoirs. He died in Utah in 1973 at the age of eighty-nine.

Anne Keary

See also Assimilation; House Concurrent Resolution 108, 1953; Indian Claims Commission (ICC); Termination; Trust Responsibility.

References and Further Reading

Burt, Larry W. 1982. *Tribalism in Crisis: Federal Indian Policy, 1953–1961*. Albuquerque: University of New Mexico Press.

Fixico, Donald. 1986. *Termination and Relocation: Federal Indian Policy, 1945–1960*. Albuquerque: University of New Mexico Press.

Metcalf, R. Warren. 2002. *Termination's Legacy: The Discarded Indians of Utah*. Lincoln: University of Nebraska Press.

Wauneka, Annie Dodge
(1910–1997)

Honored by the Navajo Nation and recipient of the U.S. Presidential Medal of Freedom for her effective work as a public health advocate, Annie Dodge Wauneka was one of the most widely respected American Indian women of the twentieth century. The youngest child of prominent Navajo leader Chee Dodge and his reluctant temporary wife, Annie was born in a hogan on the reservation near Sawmill, Arizona, into her mother's Tse níjikíní (Honey-Combed Rock/Cliff Dwelling People) clan. As soon as Annie was weaned, her mother sent her to be raised in her father's household, where she learned to herd sheep before she began boarding school at Fort Defiance. In her first year at school, the 1918 influenza epidemic hit, and eight-year-old Annie was introduced to health work when she helped feed her stricken fellow students after her own recovery. In 1929, in a traditional ceremony, Annie married George Wauneka, a Navajo she had met at Albuquerque Indian School.

The young couple settled in Tanner Springs, Arizona, as managers of her father's large sheep and cattle ranch. Though Chee Dodge stood to lose much through the U.S. government's stock reduction program on the Navajo Reservation in the 1930s, he actively supported it. Annie accompanied her father to meetings all over the reservation to discuss the program, an education in politics that she would put to good use. She was elected to the Grazing Committee of the Klagetoh District chapter house in the 1940s, helping settle range disputes, and later served as chapter secretary.

On his deathbed in 1947, Chee Dodge urged his children to continue his work; four years after that and shortly after the birth of the last of her nine children, Annie followed his advice. Elected as the representative of the Klagetoh and Wide Ruins Chapters in 1951, Annie became only the second woman elected to the Navajo tribal council, a position she held for twenty-seven years. From her first term, she took an active role in the council's debates, expressing herself forcefully and clearly.

Wauneka began her life's work as a health care advocate as chair of the council's health committee in 1953, when she became involved with an experimental public health project aimed at ending the tuberculosis epidemic then rampant on the reservation. Working closely with Cornell Medical School researchers, traditional Navajo healers, and Public Health Service doctors, Wauneka traveled the reservation to patiently explain the disease and its treatment, encouraging Navajo participation. Annie's introduction of such new effective diagnostic and curative procedures as x-rays and antibiotics, in terms the Navajos could understand, made the campaign a great success.

Subsequently, Wauneka focused her prodigious energies on other issues challenging Navajo health: infant mortality, alcoholism, water quality, and sanitation, problems that were more difficult to cure. She never hesitated to try new methods to reach her goals. In the early 1960s, she had a radio show that broadcast her ideas about health in Navajo all over the reservation, emphasizing sanitation and nutrition and urging people to have their children inoculated with the new polio vaccine. She frequently went to Washington, D.C., to lobby for Navajo interests. She also worked on educational issues, helping to establish the federal Head Start program for early childhood education on the reservation and arguing for more Navajo control over BIA schools. In the 1970s, she worked to establish an American Indian medical school that would teach both Native and scientific healing methods; unfortunately, the project faltered. Her career on the tribal council eventually did, too. A controversial dispute with a white lawyer, disagreements with powerful Navajo tribal chairman Peter McDonald, and her outspoken criticism of peyote led to her electoral defeat in 1978.

Tall and imposing, always wearing traditional Navajo dress and turquoise and silver jewelry, Annie Wauneka reaped many honors for her long years of work on behalf of her people. The Presidential Medal of Freedom, which she received in 1964 from Lyndon B. Johnson, was particularly noteworthy. However, Annie valued most of all the Navajo Medal of Honor that was bestowed upon her in 1984 as "Our Legendary Mother" by tribal chairman Peterson Zah on behalf of her grateful Navajo Nation. Honorary doctorates from several universities recognized the importance of her work in building bridges across cultural divides in the interest of health care.

Stricken with Alzheimer's disease, Annie Wauneka died in 1997. Recognized as one of the most important Navajo leaders of the twentieth century, her induction into the National Women's Hall of Fame in 2000 in Seneca Falls, New York, helps ensure that she will also be remembered as a role model for all women seeking to make a difference in the lives of their people.

Helen M. Bannan

See also Canyon de Chelly, Arizona; Long Walk, 1864; Treaty with the Navajo–June 1, 1868.

References and Further Reading

Jones, David S. 2002. "The Health Care Experiments at Many Farms: The Navajo, Tuberculosis, and the Limits of Modern Medicine, 1952–1962." *Bulletin of the History of Medicine.* 76(4), 749–790.

Kasee, Cynthia. 1993. "Annie Dodge Wauneka." In *Native American Women: A Biographical Dictionary*, ed. Gretchen M. Bataille, 274–275. New York: Garland.

Niethammer, Carolyn. 2001. *I'll Go and Do More: Annie Dodge Wauneka, Navajo Leader and Activist.* Lincoln: University of Nebraska Press.

Wayne, Anthony

(1745–1796)

Anthony Wayne was a U.S. military leader who won a decisive victory over the northwestern tribes in the Battle of Fallen Timbers and coerced the Native Americans to significant concessions in the Treaty of Greenville of 1795. Having won a reputation as an audacious yet effective general in the Revolutionary War, Major General Wayne was given command of the new Legion of the United States after the devastating defeats of generals Josiah Harmar and Arthur St. Clair in the Northwest. A staunch Federalist, Wayne believed that a standing army of disciplined regulars was necessary to project the power of the new nation in areas still inhabited primarily by Native Americans and coveted by European powers. After intensive training and planning, Wayne's legion and a substantial number of mounted volunteers headed north from the Cincinnati area in late 1793. His force confronted a smaller army of Native Americans and Canadian militia at Fallen Timbers (near present-day Toledo, Ohio) in August 1794. After an overwhelming victory, Wayne's army burned crops and villages along the Maumee River to starve and demoralize the Native Americans into submission. In the summer of 1795, he negotiated with Native American leaders at Greenville, on August 3 signing a treaty that opened up vast areas to white settlement and decisively ended Native American aspirations to reestablish the Ohio River as a settlement boundary.

Originally a prominent farmer, surveyor, and businessman from Pennsylvania, Wayne became involved in politics in 1774–1775 and later rose to the rank of brigadier general during the Revolutionary War. He proved a brave and successful com-

Anthony Wayne (1745–1796) of Pennsylvania, was one of the best fighters of the American Revolution. He defeated a significant Native American uprising and made possible the settlement of the Old Northwest. (National Archives)

manding officer, but at the same time he gained a reputation for impetuousness, which was reflected in his nickname, Mad Anthony. Wayne was, indeed, a rather vain, pompous man with a penchant for profanity and braggadocio, yet his record shows that he was by no means a reckless military leader. Having been given command of the army in the Northwest in 1792, he spent eighteen months preparing his recruits for battle. Training first at Legionville near Pittsburgh and later at Hobson's Choice near Cincinnati, he emphasized discipline as the key to preventing and withstanding surprise attacks. As peace negotiations broke down in the fall of 1793, Wayne's army marched north with great caution. The constant alertness of the legion and the attached Kentucky Mounted Volunteers prompted the Miami chief Little Turtle to discourage battle with the "chief who never sleeps."

Other chiefs and warriors were more inclined to attack the new enemy leader, especially as Canadian

officials had convinced them that war between Britain and the United States was imminent. Yet the Native American forces (consisting primarily of Delaware, Wyandot, Shawnee, Ottawa, Miami, and Canadian militia) were not allowed to bring British cannon or regular troops against the American army. On August 20, 1794, at the Battle of Fallen Timbers, the Native Americans were swiftly outnumbered and overpowered by Wayne's integrated force of riflemen, musket-armed infantry, cavalry, artillery, and mounted volunteers. The retreating warriors sought shelter in nearby Fort Miami, but the British commander shut the gates and refused to engage the Americans.

Having thus demonstrated the superiority of a disciplined, well-trained army to both the Native Americans and his own government, Wayne ordered the destruction of Miami villages and crops along the Maumee River before returning south to Fort Greenville. The combination of such economic sanctions with military might forced the tribes to seek peace. Assisted by his aide-de-camp, William Henry Harrison, Wayne negotiated a treaty that ensured the cessation of hostilities, an exchange of prisoners, and a system of immediate grants and annual subsidies paid by the U.S. government to the various tribes. More importantly, the Native Americans ceded most of Ohio and a small section of Indiana to white settlement. General Wayne returned to Philadelphia in triumph in 1796 but fell ill and died later that year.

Knut Oyangen

See also Battle of Fallen Timbers, 1794; Greenville, Ohio; Harrison, William Henry; Knox, Henry; St. Clair, Arthur; Treaty with the Wyandot, Etc.–August 3, 1795.

References and Further Reading

Knopf, Richard C., ed. 1960. *Anthony Wayne: A Name in Arms.* Pittsburgh: University of Pittsburgh Press.

Nelson, Paul David. 1985. *Anthony Wayne: Soldier of the Early Republic.* Bloomington: Indiana University Press.

Tucker, Glenn. 1973. *Mad Anthony Wayne and the New Nation: The Story of Washington's Front-Line General.* Harrisburg, PA: Stackpole Books.

Wells, William
(1770–1812)

An interpreter, Indian agent, or warrior, William Wells lived in a divided universe. Although in his youth Native Americans kidnapped and raised him, Wells later returned to the Americans and his socially connected family in Kentucky. While living among the Miami, he married the daughter of Little Turtle, the Miami war chief. Not trusted among whites when he first returned, Wells proved his fidelity to the United States by becoming a spy and, later, an interpreter for General Anthony Wayne at the Treaty of Greenville. Afterward, he was handsomely rewarded with money and land grants.

Due to his firsthand experience of Indian life and decision making, Wells received a government appointment as Indian agent at Fort Wayne, Indiana Territory. In 1803, William Henry Harrison arrived to negotiate a treaty with the neighboring tribes to settle a "dispute" not resolved by the Treaty of Greenville. Most of the Indians present mistrusted Harrison's motives. But Harrison blamed Wells's disloyalty and his connection to Little Turtle as possible reasons the talks had not gone well. The truth was that most of the chiefs present resented the call for more land cessions. The Owl, a leading Miami chief, withheld his presence from the event. Though this treaty was merely the first of many over the next seven years, its rough beginning foreshadowed the difficulties to come.

While treaty negotiations were underway, Harrison received word that his old friend Colonel John F. Hamtramck had died at Detroit. As he was not succeeding in his work, Harrison left the job to Wells, demanding that Wells finish it, and went to Detroit.

In the meantime, the secretary of war ordered Wells to repair to Chicago with a detachment of troops to elicit the support of the local Potawatomi and Winnebago for the construction of a new military post, Fort Dearborn, to commence later that year. Wells was absent for about two weeks; upon his return, he resumed negotiations. By June 7, he had Harrison's treaty.

Over the next nine years, Wells and Harrison continued to work together, although not always peacefully. Harrison continued to doubt Wells's loyalty. Behind Wells's back, he wrote spurious and character-damaging letters to the secretary of war and to Fort Wayne factor John Johnston. On Wells's part, there is some evidence that he was trying to make the best deal for both sides. He had lived among the Indians and knew their ways, shared their belief systems, and intermarried with them. Of course, he would do all he could to be sure they had a fair deal. In the end, war broke out anyway.

When General William Hull ordered the evacuation of Fort Dearborn in early August 1812, Wells was sent with a party of Miami Indians to assist the garrison in making their way through the wilderness to Detroit. Wells had another reason to go there: his niece Rebekah was married to the commanding officer. Despite the ever-increasing gathering of tribes, many of whom did not belong to the district of Fort Dearborn, Wells assisted Captain Nathan Heald with the distribution of supplies the garrison would not need, using them as gifts to ensure protection from the Indians on the overland journey. The promise of safe passage had been secured on August 14.

During the night, however, a wampum belt arrived from Fort Malden calling for the tribes to make war on the Americans. Unaware of the change in attitude, the garrison departed the following morning. A mere mile and a half from the fort, an ambush commenced. During the battle, Wells's horse was shot, and he was pinned under it. He continued to fight until surrounded. Realizing his fate, he allowed himself to be killed, knowing that it was an honor for the warriors to do so.

Sally Colford Bennet

See also Harrison, William Henry; Treaty with the Wyandot, Etc.–August 3, 1795; Wayne, Anthony.

References and Further Reading
Griswold, Bert J., ed. 1927. *Fort Wayne, Gateway of the West, 1802–1813*. Garrison Orderly Books, Indian Agency Account Books. Indianapolis: Historical Bureau of the Indiana Library and Historical Department.
Quaife, Milo M. 1913. *Chicago and the Old Northwest, 1673–1835*. Chicago: University of Chicago Press.
Thornbrough, Gayle, ed. 1961. *Letter Book of the Indian Agency at Fort Wayne, 1809–1815*. Indianapolis: Indiana Historical Society.
Woehrmann, Paul. 1971. *At the Headwaters of the Maumee: A History of the Forts of Fort Wayne*. Indianapolis: Indiana Historical Society.

Williams, Roger

(c. 1603–1683)

One of America's earliest cultural pluralists and advocates of the separation of church and state, Roger Williams founded Providence, Rhode Island, as a safe haven for early European settlers who had suffered religious persecution. He also believed in forging good relations with the Native peoples of New England. Rather than fight for title to the land, Williams argued that colonists should negotiate and pay a fair price for it. His policy proved effective; Rhode Island had the most peaceful Indian relations in all the colonies.

Williams was born in London, England, about 1603. His father was a hardworking shopkeeper who hoped to carve out a better life for his children. Young Roger eventually went off to college at Cambridge University, where he studied to become a minister. He later landed a job as the private chaplain of a nobleman, Sir William Masham. While working for Masham, Williams became increasingly interested in the Massachusetts Bay Colony, of which he had heard rousing stories. In 1631, Williams decided to give up his life in England and set off for America, where he hoped to establish himself in what was already being viewed in some quarters as a land of opportunity.

Once in Massachusetts Bay, Williams found himself at odds with the colony's leadership. He criticized the king and believed that the colony should completely separate itself from the Church of England rather than try to reform or purify it. Williams believed in religious freedom, arguing that governments were not divinely sanctioned and therefore had no right to establish state religions. He also claimed that the colony's royal charter was null and void because the settlers had not purchased the land from the Native people. The colony's leaders considered such talk tantamount to blasphemy, and Williams was eventually banished from Massachusetts Bay in 1636. Rather than head back to England, he decided to move south, and he established the colony of Providence near Narragansett Bay. Williams invited all religious refugees to the new colony and set up a trading post at Cocumscussoc, where he met and befriended the local indigenous people.

Unlike his belligerent neighbors to the north at Massachusetts Bay, Williams made peace and forged positive relations with the Natives. He insisted on adequately compensating the Narragansett Indians for their lands. Only after he fairly purchased the territory around Providence did he apply to London for a colonial charter. But Williams did not stop there. He furthered the Narragansetts' trust by learning their language and familiarizing himself with their culture. He saw in Indian society a degree of harmony, humanity, and hospitality that was decidedly lacking among his own people. Williams docu-

The Narragansett Indians protect British colonist Roger Williams. Williams developed a good relationship with the Narragansetts, a situation that enabled him to negotiate an end to the Pequot War in 1637, thereby helping the Puritans who had exiled him. (Library of Congress)

mented his observations and the Narragansett language in his book, *A Key into the Language of America: Or, An help to the Language of the Natives in that part of America, called New-England* [sic]. Considered the first ethnoanthropological study of American Indians, Williams's account records Narragansett culture, analyzing everything from their religious beliefs to their sleeping habits.

Though Williams was a staunch advocate of Indian land rights, he was also a pragmatist and a realist. Hence, when the Pequots went to war with Massachusetts Bay over that colony's encroachment on Native land, Williams convinced the Narragansetts to remain neutral. He believed that only death and destruction would come to the Indians if they fought the colonists. Williams's peace policy and dealings with the Native peoples were effective; relations between whites and the Narragansetts remained cordial for nearly forty years. But the

burgeoning white population's continual expansion onto Indian lands inevitably led to further conflict.

In 1675, Wampanoag Chief Metacom took on Massachusetts Bay, resulting in what came to be known as King Philip's War—the bloodiest conflict up to that time. Though the Narragansetts had not taken sides in the war, colonists preemptively attacked them, resulting in the Great Swamp Massacre. With five hundred to six hundred dead—most of which were women and children—the Narragansett leadership ignored Williams's pleas and decided to side with Metacom in his fight against the colonists. They launched an assault on Providence, burning the town to the ground. Williams, in turn, accepted a commission as captain in the local militia and fought his former friends. In the end, the Narragansetts and Wampanoags could not match the firepower of the colonists, and they suffered a devastating loss in the war.

After King Philip's War, Williams's vision of a peaceful land where Indians and whites lived side by side, each learning from the other, came crashing down. With all of his former Narragansett friends gone, he lived out his last days a broken man among the rubble and ashes of Providence. Roger Williams died in the winter of 1683.

Bradley Shreve

See also Canonicus; Metacom.

References and Further Reading

Miller, Perry. 1953. *Roger Williams: His Contribution to the American Tradition*. Indianapolis, IN: Bobbs-Merrill.

Rubertone, Patricia E. 2001. *Grave Undertakings: An Archaeology of Roger Williams and the Narragansett Indians*. Washington, DC: Smithsonian Institution.

Williams, Roger. 1643. *A Key into the Language of America*. Repr., Detroit, MI: Wayne State University Press, 1973.

BILL NO. 16.
RESOLUTION.

AUTHORIZING THE PRINCIPAL CHIEF TO TAKE LEGAL STEPS TO RECOVER THE VALUE OF TIMBER UNLAWFULLY CUT FROM PUBLIC DOMAIN OF THE CHOCTAW NATION.

Whereas: Many million feet of pine timber has been cut from the domain of the Choctaw Nation by non-citizens, over the protest of the tribal government; and,

Whereas: The United States Government, through its intercourse laws and treaties solemnly guaranteed protection to our property interests; and,

Whereas: The United States Government, having failed to enforce the laws and treaties, has rendered itself liable to the Choctaw Nation.

THEREFORE

BE IT RESOLVED BY THE GENERAL COUNCIL OF THE CHOCTAW NATION ASSEMBLED.

Sec. 1. That the Principal Chief of the Choctaw Nation is hereby authorized to take the necessary steps to ascertain the amount of timber unlawfully cut from the public domain of the Choctaw Nation, and is hereby further authorized to take such legal action as he may deem necessary to recover the value of said timber from the United States Government.

Sec. 2. That this resolution shall take effect and be in force from and after its passage and approval.

Proposed by DANIEL WEBSTER, Chairman Committee on Chief's Message.

Approved this the 26th day of October, 1905.

GREEN McCURTAIN,
P. C. C. N.

Dis approved February 9" 1906

T. Roosevelt

Treaty Related Issues

Aboriginal Title

Indian tribes in North America first occupied the lands that now make up the United States. They had in place complex systems of government and law, developed over millennia and predicated upon spiritual, political, and social principles, which guided their relationships with each other and the surrounding environment. They consequently also developed culturally distinctive notions of land title. Established land use regimes notwithstanding, increased settler encroachment upon Indian-held territories in the late eighteenth and early nineteenth centuries prompted colonial officials to question the nature of land ownership and title and ask whether Indians in fact could properly govern those lands. There was a perceived need to determine the extent of aboriginal title to the land and how best to affect transfer of said title.

The U.S. government first attempted to address the issue of aboriginal title with the first Indian Nonintercourse Act (1790), which reserved to the United States, as opposed to individuals or states, the right to acquire Indian lands. Under the act, a sale of Indian lands was not valid unless "made and duly executed at some public treaty, held under the authority of the United States." This act created a federal form of land ownership recognized as *aboriginal title*, which was specific to Indian tribes. It assigned to American Indians the right to govern land they occupied at the moment the United States gained its independence from Great Britain. The primary feature of aboriginal title was that the right of possession was superior to that of fee simple title; however, in those cases where Indian title and fee simple title coexisted, aboriginal title prevailed until an act of Congress is passed that extinguishes said title.

The U.S. Supreme Court first addressed the issue of aboriginal title in 1823 in *Johnson v. M'Intosh*, whereby the Court held that the "right to occupancy" indicated aboriginal title; as such, Indian tribes were incapable of conveying their land directly to individuals, but as dependent nations within the United States, extinguishment of aboriginal title was required prior to legal transfer of Indian lands to the U.S. government. Chief Justice

Marshall further concluded that the tribes held their lands by "Indian title." Aboriginal title, in this instance, was not treated as a right of legal propriety and dominion but was more akin to a usufructuary right, or right of occupation to lands that is vested in the sovereign, who, by virtue of the discoveries of European nations, later absorbed by the United States, had "ultimate dominion" over the land.

Aboriginal title also continued to be recognized in the treaty-making process. These treaties between American Indian nations and the United States became the primary instruments employed to extinguish aboriginal title and to open Indian-held territories for settlement. This process ended in 1871. Contemporary American Indian land claims are based on the perspective that the affected tribe occupied the land being claimed at the time of the founding of the United States and that those tribal lands were conveyed to third parties or to state governments without the specific congressional approval required by the Nonintercourse Act. Without congressional approval, the extinguishment of aboriginal title and the transfer of American Indian lands to non-Indian interests were deemed unlawful.

Congressional extinguishment of aboriginal title has been held by the U.S. Supreme Court not to require specific language to that effect in congressional acts; rather, it may be inferred by operation of the act or by congressional extinguishment of aboriginal title in the United States, which is fairly easy to accomplish. Original aboriginal title is extinguished by the federal government with the original issuance of a land patent to an individual. Nearly all the land now set aside for the benefits of American Indians, whether by treaty, statute, or executive order, is held in trust by the United States.

By comparison, in 1973 the Supreme Court of Canada would for the first time formally recognize aboriginal title to land as an aboriginal right. Aboriginal title, in this instance, recognizes an aboriginal interest in the land that is based on the occupancy of the land by contemporary aboriginal peoples as the descendants of Canada's original inhabitants. In *Calder v. Attorney-General of British Columbia*, the Canadian Supreme Court ruled that, if there is a historical aboriginal presence on the land, aboriginal title therefore could be recognized in common law without the need for any action by the provincial or federal governments. Recognizing aboriginal title as a legal right forced the federal government to establish a comprehensive land claims process.

Yale D. Belanger

See also Doctrine of Discovery; Sovereignty; Treaty; Trust Doctrine.

References and Further Reading

Calder v. Attorney-General of British Columbia [1973] S.C.R. 313.

Johnson v. M'Intosh, 21 U.S. (8 Wheat.) 543 (1823).

Prucha, Francis Paul. 1994. *American Indian Treaties: The History of a Political Anomaly*. Berkeley and Los Angeles: University of California Press.

St. Germain, Jill. 2001. *Indian Treaty-Making Policy in the United States and Canada 1868–1877*. Lincoln and London: University of Nebraska Press.

Williams, Robert A., Jr. 1997. *Linking Arms Together: American Indian Treaty Visions of Law and Peace, 16000–1800*. New York and Oxford: Oxford University Press.

Allotments

Parcels of tribal lands were transferred to individual Indians by the federal government as part of the General Allotment Act, also known as the Dawes Act. In an attempt to assimilate Indians and dismantle tribalism, the federal government allotted portions of reservation land to individual Indians between 1887 and 1934. Parcels were held in trust by the U.S. government for a specified period, and at the conclusion of the holding time, each Indian received the land in fee ownership. Once held in fee, individual owners could freely dispose of the land. Through later modifications, the Dawes Act would also authorize the secretary of the interior to negotiate the sale of surplus Indian land for the purpose of non-Indian settlement. Allotment was unsuccessful, and despite its repeal in 1934, its fallout continues to pervade Indian country.

By replacing traditional notions of communal land possession with that of individual ownership, the federal government, through allotment, sought to assimilate Indians into European American culture. Proponents of this policy hoped to transform Indians into "individual American farmers," thereby eliminating governmental dealings with Indians and tribal entities as a whole. Another motivating factor behind this policy was the desire of the federal government to open up fertile Indian land to white settlers.

Under the Indian allotment system, American Indians received individual parcels of former reservation land (allotments) that were held in trust by the United States for a period of twenty-five years. During this trust period, the allotments could not be sold

or mortgaged. After the twenty-five-year trust period, individual allottees received their land in fee, were subject to state laws, became citizens of the United States, and could do with the land as they liked.

The policy of allotment proved to be an utter failure. Using the powers prescribed under the Dawes Act, the federal government sold millions of acres of unallotted Indian land to whites, and the transformation of Indians into farmers as envisioned by the Dawes proponents was unsuccessful. Undersized allotments, and in many cases unfertile ones, coupled with inadequate farming resources, thwarted the policy's success. Additionally, because many allottees died intestate, and their interests in the allotments were divided among their heirs, severe fractionalization occurred. For example, allotments originally held by an individual Indian allottee in time came to be shared by as many as fifty to one hundred people or more. To add to its failure, a large number of American Indians, many of whom were poor, uneducated, and susceptible to fraud, sold their fee simple interests to white settlers shortly after the trust period ended. The cash earned by these sales was often inadequate, and many Native Americans were left with no land and little money.

Allotment resulted in a radical and permanent change in Indian country demographics. Following allotment, many reservations went from having a majority Indian population to a predominantly non-Indian population. A significant number of tribes lost more than 90 percent of their land base to non-Indians, and the total inventory of tribally held land fell by nearly 62 percent because of allotment. Notwithstanding its destructive effects on tribes, the U.S. Supreme Court affirmed general allotment in 1903.

It was not until the passage of the Indian Reorganization Act in 1934 that general allotment came to an end. Despite this, many negative effects continue to plague Indian nations. Tribal land holdings remain low, and excessive numbers of non-Indians continue to reside within tribal territory. This, combined with the probate fractionalization, has created a checkerboard effect on reservations and has fostered tremendously complex problems for tribes.

Ryan L. Church

See also Assimilation; Bureau of Indian Affairs (BIA); Collier, John; Dawes Commission; Dawes, Henry Laurens; General Allotment Act (Dawes Act), 1887; Indian Reorganization Act, 1934; *Lone Wolf v. Hitchcock,* 1903; Meriam Report, 1928; Plenary Power; Sovereignty; Trust Doctrine; Trust Land.

References and Further Reading

Getches, David H. 1993. *Federal Indian Law: Cases and Materials.* 3rd ed. St. Paul: West.

Gould, Scott. 1996. *The Consent Paradigm: Tribal Sovereignty at the Millennium,* 96 Columbia Law Review 809.

Hoxie, Frederick E. 1984. *A Final Promise: The Campaign to Assimilate the Indians.* New York and Cambridge: Cambridge University Press.

Prucha Francis Paul. 1994. *The Great Father: United States Government and the American Indians,* abr. ed. Lincoln: University of Nebraska Press.

Annuities

Annuities were payments of money and/or goods distributed to tribes annually for a specified number of years. Annuities were included in many treaties between tribes and the United States in exchange for land cessions. Many American Indians came to depend on annuity distributions for survival as hunting grounds and other means of support diminished. The government often used the threat of withholding annuity payments to influence tribal behavior. Annuity payments continued after the government stopped negotiating treaties with American Indians.

Annuities were included in many treaties, from the treaty of 1778 with the Delaware through the end of the treaty period in 1871. The government had several reasons for including annuities in treaties. In the *Report of Commissioner of Indian Affairs* for November 1, 1875, Edward P. Smith stated, "The annuity in money or blankets, or bacon and beef, may have a tendency to draw the Indians within the reach of the Government, and prepare them for the beginning of a work of civilization, and also to render them disinclined to take up arms and go upon the war-path. But with any tribe a few years of this treatment is sufficient for the purpose, and after this end has been gained, a continuation of the feeding and clothing, without a reference to further improvement on the part of the Indians, is simply a waste of expenditure" (Washburn 1973, 207).

The distribution of annuities became one of the most important duties of agency personnel and was a complex process. Before distribution each year, the agent took a tribal census to calculate the amount of individual payments. The annuity goods were sent to the superintendent, who was responsible for them until signed payment vouchers were received from the tribe. The distribution was made by the superintendent, agent, and several witnesses to ensure accuracy and legitimacy.

The annuity system was faced with numerous problems, including inferior goods, transportation costs, and corruption. Reformers lobbied for the end of annuity payments, claiming that the annuities increased the dependence of American Indians rather than aided their progress toward self-sufficiency.

Early annuities, in either cash or goods, were paid to the chiefs of a tribe. The chiefs then distributed the payment to the rest of the tribe according to their personal obligations and tribal customs. However, this did not result in the even distribution the government desired. In 1847, the federal government tried to diminish the power and influence of the chiefs by distributing annuity payments directly to heads of families.

Goods distributed in annuity payments included beef, flour, sugar, coffee, corn, pork, shoes, clothing, blankets, beads, mirrors, beds, plows, wagons, and other goods deemed necessary to propel American Indians toward civilization. Individual portions of tribal annuities ranged from a few cents to more than $100. In many instances, cash annuities went directly to traders to pay for goods that had been bought on credit during the year.

The government often threatened to withhold annuity payments to influence the actions of American Indians. The Trade and Intercourse Act of 1834 provided for the payment of depredation claims against a tribe from that tribe's annuity. Tribes could also lose their annuity payments if they returned to ceded land, fought with other tribes or white citizens, resisted allotment, or refused to send their children to school.

Tamara Levi

See also Assimilation, Indian Appropriations Act, 1871; Sovereignty; Treaty; Trust.

References and Further Reading

Priest, Loring Benson. 1975. *Uncle Sam's Stepchildren: The Reformation of United States Indian Policy, 1865–1887.* Lincoln: University of Nebraska Press.

Prucha, Francis Paul. 1984. *The Great Father: The United States Government and the American Indians.* 2 vols. Lincoln: University of Nebraska Press.

Washburn, Wilcomb E. 1973. *The American Indian and the United States: A Documentary History.* New York: Random House.

Assimilation

Assimilation is the process by which members of a minority group become socially, culturally, and institutionally blended into the majority. The U.S. government historically sponsored treaties and policies to encourage or force Indians to exchange tribal institutions, traditional languages and religions, communal property, and the hunting-gathering lifestyle for white officials, English, Christianity, private property, and farming. Assimilation has been saluted by most Americans as a positive process, something that happens naturally and inevitably. This sunny view was popularized in the early twentieth century, when the term *melting pot* illustrated the way individual cultures should disappear into a harmonious whole. In more recent times, the concept of assimilation has been criticized as patronizing and destructive to minority cultures such as those of Native Americans.

Since the seventeenth century, the term *assimilation* denoted the way minorities, particularly immigrants from Europe, acquired American ideas and lost foreign manners. In the late nineteenth century, reformers believed that, if Indians assimilated by becoming farmers, Indians could resist the encroachment of white settlers on their land. In 1887, Senator Henry L. Dawes of Massachusetts sponsored legislation to break the reservations into private, self-sufficient farms. Instead of helping Indians assimilate, however, the Dawes Severalty Act proved disastrous, for it opened the reservations up to unscrupulous government officials and land speculators. Millions of acres were lost from reservations before the reformers understood the worst consequences of the law.

In part because land ownership alone did not seem to bring Indians the benefits of assimilation, white humanitarians turned their zeal toward the foundation of a school system for the children of Native Americans. It was hoped that young Indians, at least, could be taught the values of Christian civilization and independence from tribal institutions. Reformers also realized that, unless Indians learned to understand the ways of whites, became educated in the skills of white society, and knew their new legal rights, the Dawes Act could not achieve the

Native American students in physical education class at the Carlisle Indian School, Carlisle, Pennsylvania, ca. 1902. Richard Henry Pratt, a military officer, founded the school in 1879. (Library of Congress)

goal of assimilating them into American society. Thus, in the name of helping them achieve the full benefits of American citizenship, thousands of Indian children were taken, often by force, to boarding schools, where they were isolated from their families, had their hair shorn, and were given shoes for their feet. There, they were taught to read and write, to tell time, and to master skills considered useful to white society, such as sewing for girls and blacksmithing for boys.

Despite their most dedicated efforts, however, the assimilationists could not get past the basic fact that Indians, no matter how well they mastered literate English, how many skills they possessed, and how ardently they believed in the Judeo-Christian religion, could not blend into white society for being rejected by the mainstream. Worse, once they adopted the ways of whites, many Indians were no longer welcome in their own society and were condemned to lonely and often tragic lives. John Collier, a reformer with experience working with immigrants in New York City, began to speak out against

assimilationist policies in the 1920s. In 1928, the Brookings Institute delivered a devastating indictment of assimilationist policies known as the Meriam Report: "An overwhelming majority of the Indians are poor," the report stated. "They are not adjusted to the economic and social system of the dominant white civilization" (Meriam Report 1928, 1). In other words, despite forty years of active efforts to assimilate the Indians, in fact no assimilation had taken place.

In 1933, President Franklin Roosevelt appointed John Collier commissioner of Indian affairs. Collier proceeded to dismantle the most pernicious allotment policy. The rights of Native Americans to their tribal institutions and reservation lands were confirmed, and the curriculum of Indian schools was changed to celebrate Native cultures and mores. Gradually, the boarding schools were closed and replaced by institutions close to the homes of Indian children. In World War II, Indian men and women helped the United States and served in the armed forces, and the termination and relocation policies

started in the early 1950s tried to assimilate Native peoples.

In the 1960s, the idea of assimilation continued to lose its luster as sociologists and activists spoke against the destruction of Native and immigrant cultures and values. Literature from this period found that full assimilation might not be possible, for even when culturally Americanized, minorities can and do develop their own economic and political institutions and retain many aspects of their own unique cultures. However, recent scholarship suggests that the "melting pot" concept may still be useful if it recognizes that many individual melting pots make up the whole of American society. For Native American tribes, full assimilation into American society need not mean renouncing their own culture but rather being admitted into the full economic and political rights enjoyed by all American citizens. Since the 1960s, American Indians have self-assimilated themselves into a more receptive mainstream America.

Tracey L. Trenam

See also Allotment; General Allotment Act
(Dawes Act), 1887; Meriam Report, 1928.
References and Further Reading
Adams, David Wallace. 1995. *Education for
    Extinction: American Indians and the
    Boarding School Experience 1875–1928.*
    Lawrence: University Press of Kansas.
Kazal, Russell A. 1995. "Revisiting
    Assimilation: The Rise, Fall and
    Reappraisal of a Concept in American
    Ethnic History." *American Historical
    Review* 100 (April): 437–471.
Kelly, Lawrence C. 1983. *The Assault on
    Assimilation: John Collier and the Origins of
    Indian Policy Reform.* Albuquerque:
    University of New Mexico Press.
The Meriam Report. 1928. Baltimore, MD:
    Johns Hopkins University Press.
Prucha, Francis Paul, ed. 1973. *Americanizing
    the American Indians: Writings by the
    "Friends of the Indian" 1880–1900.* Lincoln:
    University of Nebraska Press.

Doctrine of Discovery

The doctrine of discovery was a construct of the Christian European nations devised prior to the onset of treaty making with Native American nations. Two important ideas were contained in the doctrine of discovery. First, Europeans could acquire only land that was *terra nullius* (unoccupied); occupied land could not be sought, for the Native population had held title to the land "since time immemorial." Second, the doctrine of discovery internally regulated European nations upon their discovery of new land.

The first nation to come across land had the immutable right to trade with and acquire title to the land of the Native population. However, during the fifteenth century, the *Bulls of Donation*, issued by the Pope on behalf of Spain, were used in the acquisition of discovered land in the name of Christianity, disregarding the doctrine of discovery and the rights of the Native Americans. The primary factor was that Natives were viewed as religiously inferior—described as "infidels," "heathens," "savages," and "inferior" beings. Native Americans were non-Christians, and the European self-belief of religious superiority dictated that, by imposing Christianity upon the Natives, the Natives would become civilized. This view was the primary one until 1537, when the Pope issued the *Sublimis Deus*, a declaration of human rights, which was the beginning of recognition of the natural rights of the Native peoples.

From the sixteenth century, the doctrine of discovery underwent reform; as international law theorists legitimized and gave credence to Native peoples' right of title and its inherent nature. Such theorists included Francisco de Vitoria, Bartolomé Las Casas, and Hugo Grotius. From this recognition of Native rights, governments began the treaty process, which legitimized Native American nations as sovereign entities.

From the seventeenth century, the emphasis of the doctrine of discovery had been reformed in that it did not divest the Native population of its rights to land title. This was further manifested through the treaty process used by the Dutch, the Swedish, the British, and the United States in acknowledgement of Native American land title to those lands.

Title to land within the United States was settled in the seminal case of *Johnson v. M'Intosh* (1823). European nations were held to be superior, and it was this that entitled the Europeans to exclusive title and possession. The European merchants, agriculturists, and farmers had the superior right to dispose of the Native "savage" and "hunter." Chief Justice John Marshall held that all of Great Britain's land rights transferred to the United States and that the Native peoples were merely occupants. Marshall revised the doctrine of discovery to mean that occupied land could be acquired as a result of the Native peoples being non-Christian savages who practiced hunting and gathering. Implicit in this notion was that the United States would bestow Christianity upon the Native population to civilize them. The United States had the exclusive right to extinguish Native land title, and Native occupancy could be extinguished at any time. Furthermore, Marshall used the doctrine of discovery and converted it into one of conquest, which could not be questioned if it was the law of the land.

However, in *Worcester v. Georgia* (1832), Chief Justice Marshall, *obiter dictum* (a judge's incidental, nonbinding opinion) changed the basis for discovery that he had used in *Johnson v. M'Intosh*, by stating that sovereign Natives could not give up their lands to a country far away. He stated that discovery gave the European powers the sole right to acquire the soil through the right to purchase with the consent of the Native peoples. The doctrine regulated the European nations but did not affect the rights of those already in possession. In *Worcester*, Marshall stated that it was an "extravagant and absurd idea" that small settlements acquired the legitimate right and authority to occupy and claim title to land from coast to coast.

Worcester v. Georgia notwithstanding, Chief Justice John Marshall's earlier definition of the doctrine of discovery as applied in *Johnson v. M'Intosh* is applicable today. It is this doctrine, which was revised in order to promote the development of the United States, that remains the basis of land title and law throughout the current United States of America.

Dewi I. Ball

· *See also* Johnson v. M'Intosh, 1823; Right of
    Conquest; Right of Occupancy/Right of the
    Soil; Sovereignty; *Worcester v. Georgia*, 1832.
References and Further Reading
Deloria, Vine, Jr. 1996. *Behind the Trail of Broken
    Treaties: An Indian Declaration of
    Independence*. Austin: University of Texas
    Press.
Wilkins, David E., and K. Tsianina Lomawaima.
    2001. *Uneven Ground: American Indian
    Sovereignty and Federal Law*. Norman:
    University of Oklahoma Press.
Williams, Robert A., Jr. 1990. *The American Indian
    in Western Legal Thought: The Discourse of
    Conquest*. New York: Oxford University
    Press.

Domestic Dependent Nation

The phrase *domestic dependent nation* refers to the political and legal relationship of Indian tribes to the federal government and state governments (Wilkins 1997, 21–22). Essentially, it means that Indian tribes are governments, separate from local, state, and federal governments, with the power to pass laws, create court and penal systems, levy taxes, and engage in other traditional governmental functions. However, because Indian tribes are within the boundary of the United States and dependent on the United States for protection, they no longer exercise complete sovereignty as they did before their first contact with Europeans. Instead, the United States has limited Indian tribal sovereignty in significant ways, including prohibiting Indian tribes from freely selling the land they occupy on Indian reservations and from entering into treaties with foreign nations (*Johnson v. M'Intosh*, 1823).

Indian tribes were first characterized as domestic dependent nations in 1831 by Chief Justice John

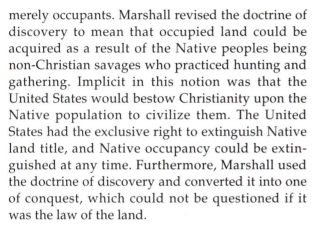

Acts of the Choctaw Nation Bill No. 16 made by the Choctaw tribal government. (Library of Congress)

Marshall in the Supreme Court case *Cherokee Nation v. Georgia* (Deloria and Lytle 1983, 4). In *Cherokee Nation,* Marshall determined that tribal nations were not foreign nations under the U.S. Constitution, because tribes were "completely under the sovereignty and dominion of the United States" (*Cherokee Nation v. Georgia,* 1831). Marshall reasoned that the relationship between Indian tribes and the United States was "unlike that of any other two people in existence," because Indian Territory was geographically located within the boundaries of the United States, the United States had the power to regulate trade between foreign nations and the Indian tribes, and the Indian tribes had conceded in various treaties that they were under the protection and management of the United States (*Cherokee Nation v. Georgia,* 1831). Due to these "peculiar and cardinal distinctions," Marshall declared that Indian tribes were domestic dependent nations and that their legal relationship to the United States was "that of a ward to his guardian" (*Cherokee Nation v. Georgia,* 1831).

Although the Supreme Court has found that Indian tribes are not foreign nations, the Court has held that tribes do constitute "distinct, independent political communities" within the United States, retaining the original right of sovereignty that they possessed prior to the discovery of America by the Europeans (*Worcester v. Georgia,* 1832). Tribes have the inherent power to "make their own laws and be ruled by them" (*Williams v. Lee,* 1959). In order to effectuate their right to self-governance, tribes have adopted criminal and civil laws, exercised their police and taxing power, established courts and regulatory agencies, set rules for determining membership in the tribe, and negotiated state-tribal cooperative agreements (AILTP 1988, 36–39, 47–60).

The status of Indian tribes as domestic dependent nations has two important consequences. First, because Indian tribes are considered wards of the United States, the federal government has a duty to the tribes, called a trust responsibility, to protect and advance tribal interests (AILTP 1988, 23–25). The Bureau of Indian Affairs (BIA), an agency of the Department of Interior, has as its primary purpose the development of federal programs, policies, and regulations that will enable the federal government to fulfill its trust responsibility to Indian tribes (Deloria and Lytle 1983, 37–38).

Second, because Indian tribes possess an inherent, preconstitutional right to self-governance, individual states cannot divest tribes of their sovereignty

(CWAG 2004, 5). Historically, the laws of the various states had no force or effect within the boundaries of an Indian reservation, even if the state law attempted to regulate only the behavior of non-Indians (*Worcester v. Georgia,* 1832). However, in modern-day jurisprudence, many state laws do apply to non-Indians who are physically present within the boundaries of an Indian reservation. These include, among others, state tax laws, state hunting and fishing regulations, and state criminal laws, if the crime is committed by a non-Indian against another non-Indian (CWAG 2004, 126, 165, 312). Nevertheless, state interference in tribal self-governance is still impermissible.

Kimberly Hausbeck

See also *Cherokee Nation v. Georgia,* 1831; Government-to-Government Relationship; Guardianship/Wardship; Indian Territory; *Johnson v. M'Intosh,* 1823; Reserved Rights Doctrine; Sovereignty; Trust Responsibility; *Williams v. Lee,* 1959; *Worcester v. Georgia,* 1832.

References and Further Reading

American Indian Lawyer Training Program, Inc. (AILTP). 1988. *Indian Tribes As Sovereign Governments.* Oakland, CA: American Indian Resources Institute (AIRI).

Conference of Western Attorneys General (CWAG). 2004. *American Indian Law Deskbook.* 3rd ed. Boulder: University Press of Colorado.

Deloria, Vine, Jr., and Clifford M. Lytle. 1983. *American Indians, American Justice.* Austin: University of Texas Press.

Wilkins, David E. 1997. *American Indian Sovereignty and the U.S. Supreme Court.* Austin: University of Texas Press.

Executive Order Reservations

Executive order reservations were formal administrative policy pronouncements by the president of the United States to set aside tracts of land for various tribal nations between the years 1871 and 1919. The president of the United States could create reservations as well as add tracts of land or delete land from existing reservations without congressional input or approval. U.S. presidents used this power for approximately fifty years until Congress formally ended that process in 1919. Many tribal nations gained recognized title to land during this period. For instance, the current Navajo Reservation, the largest reservation in the United States, was created mostly by executive orders in the late nineteenth and early twentieth centuries.

President Franklin Pierce in 1855 became the first president to establish an Indian reservation when he set aside lands for the Ottawa and Chippewa of Michigan. Several subsequent reservations followed. In 1864, President Abraham Lincoln also established a reservation at Bosque Redondo, New Mexico, for the Mescalero Apache and Navajo. Prior to 1871, treaties or statutes ratified by Congress established land boundaries. In 1871, Congress ended treaty making with tribal nations. For the next fifty years, presidents would use executive orders to acknowledge or retract land from tribal nations. No general law existed in the Constitution to allow the president to reserve land from public domain for exclusive Indian occupancy. Congress allowed the president to establish executive order reservations, and the judicial system sustained the action.

An executive order could be changed easily and a new one substituted when the occasion demanded. Many reservation boundaries changed frequently, and some remained in flux. The instability of reservation boundaries through executive orders would lead to future problems. For example, the core of the Navajo Reservation was established in 1868 by treaty. Subsequent additions of land would occur in 1878, 1880, 1884, 1886, 1900, 1901, 1905, 1907, 1917, 1930, 1933, and 1934. Deletions from the Navajo Reservation would also take place in 1908 and 1911. In 1882, an executive order reservation was established for the Hopis and other "Indians." This executive order would lead to boundary disputes between the Hopis and the Navajos for many years. Only recently was the dispute settled, but not before hundreds of Hopi families and thousands of Navajo families were displaced from their ancestral lands.

Executive orders were not uniformed for all tribal nations. The most common form set aside a designated area for a particular tribe for its "use," or "use and occupancy," or as a "reservation" (Prucha 1994, 332). Lands were added to existing reservations such as the Navajo. Some orders restored ancestral lands to tribal nations, whereas other orders substituted land for the reservation. In some cases, the president relied on the secretary of the interior, the superintendent, or the local Indian agent to determine where reservation boundaries would be set. Executive orders designated lands as reservations with no formal input by the Native people.

Presidents used executive orders to establish more than one hundred reservations for nearly fifty years until Congress formally ended the practice in 1919. Congress declared that "hereafter no public lands of the United States shall be withdrawn by Executive Order, proclamation, or otherwise, for or as an Indian reservation except by act of Congress" (Prucha 1994, 332).

For a while, questions existed as to whether executive order reservations were legal and whether Indians had a title to such lands. For instance, there was an attempt in the 1920s to cut tribal nations on executive order reservations out of leasing fees from oil and mineral companies. The Indian Oil Leasing Act in 1927 made sure tribal nations would not be cut out of leasing fees from oil and mineral companies and also that executive order reservation boundaries could not be changed except by an act of Congress. Also, future Supreme Court cases decided that executive order reservations were equated with treaty or statute reservations. Today, there are approximately 151 reservations that were established by executive order.

Lloyd L. Lee

See also Federally Recognized Tribes; Trust Land.
References and Further Reading

Deloria, Vine, Jr., and David E. Wilkins. 1999. *Tribes, Treaties, and Tribulations.* Austin: University of Texas Press.

Prucha, Francis Paul. 1994. *American Indian Treaties: The History of a Political Anomaly.* Berkeley, Los Angeles, and London: University of California Press.

Scholarly Resources, Inc. 1975. *Executive Orders Relating to Indian Reservations from May 14, 1955 to July 1, 1912.* Washington: U.S. Government Printing Office.

Wilkins, David E. 2002. *American Indian Politics and the American Political System.* Lanham, MD: Rowman and Littlefield.

Federal Acknowledgment Process (FAP)

Federal tribal acknowledgment is a formal procedure whereby government officials recognize the legal existence of an Indian tribe. Akin to the recognition of foreign powers, tribal acknowledgment confirms the inherent sovereignty of a tribe and establishes a "government-to-government" relation between an Indian community and Congress. Historically, the federal government recognized tribes by treaty, executive order, legislation, or administrative decisions. In 1978, the Bureau of Indian Affairs (BIA) established an office to handle the growing number of tribal petitions. Federal acknowledgment enables a tribe to secure a reservation, exercise sovereignty, and access federal Indian services. Currently, there are 562 recognized tribal entities in the United States. There are approximately 250 unrecognized Indian communities. Unacknowledged Indian groups exist in thirty-seven of the fifty states.

Traditionally, federal officials conferred tribal status in an inconsistent and arbitrary manner. Many small groups on the East Coast, remnant southeastern tribes, and non-reservation Indian communities on the West Coast failed to secure federal status as a result. With the Indian Reorganization Act of 1934, BIA officials established procedures for acknowledging groups omitted from federal protections. During the 1960s and 1970s, Indian activism and land claims spawned increased attention to the plight and potential rights of unrecognized Indian tribes. In 1978, the BIA established the Federal Acknowledgment Process (FAP) and, later, its Branch of Acknowledgment and Research (BAR) to analyze recognition petitions. To meet the seven FAP criteria, groups must submit written documentation to a team of anthropologists, historians, and genealogists employed by the BIA. Under the rules, unrecognized tribes must provide a governing document, prove they are not forbidden by Congress from securing trust status, and demonstrate that their members are not also members of a previously recognized tribe. More troublesome for most groups, the FAP also requires petitioners to prove that they have been historically identified as Indians, that they have continuously lived in a cohesive community, that they have had a line of political leaders, and that they descend from documented Indian ancestors. After twenty-five years in operation, the FAP has acknowledged fifteen tribes and rejected nineteen others. Since 1978, thirteen tribes have secured acknowledgment through Congress.

Before the creation of the FAP, the three branches of government maintained the right to confer tribal acknowledgment. In certain circumstances, judicial and congressional recognition provided equitable remedies for neglected groups. With the Mashpee Wampanoag case of 1978, however, critics charged that nonexpert juries were incapable of grasping the complexities of race, tribal composi-

tion, and political considerations involved in acknowledgment decisions, and this form of recognition is rarely used today. Similarly, with the congressional recognition of several tribes in the 1970s and 1980s, local interests complained that Congress was too overtly political and inexpert to decide tribal acknowledgment cases. In the 1980s, Indian gaming complicated the picture severely. Federal recognition is a prerequisite for entering into gaming compacts; as a result, public perceptions and attitudes toward unrecognized Indian groups changed markedly. Conservative groups, property owners associations, law enforcement groups, and anti-gambling organizations increasingly turned to litigation to prevent the recognition of Indian communities. On the other hand, gambling interests offered assistance to many groups, bankrolling tribal research in return for casino contracts. In light of the controversies over gaming, Congress and the courts increasingly have delegated tribal acknowledgment decisions to the BIA. More than any other factor, Indian gaming has complicated tribal acknowledgment policy.

The Federal Acknowledgment Process is a controversial Indian identification policy. Given Indian history and government suppression of tribal governments and cultures, many of the criteria for groups have met intense criticism from the Indian and scholarly communities. Critics consistently condemn the FAP for its slow pace, its bias against eastern Indian groups, its claims to scientific objectivity, and its emphasis on written documentation. On the other side, states with an interest in preventing casino development, most notably Connecticut, criticize the FAP for being inconsistent, political, and not rigorous in its scholarship. Leaders of major Indian groups and individual tribal leaders have at various times come out in favor of its strenuous regimen, arguing that it maintains the sanctity of the federal-tribal relationship and screens out dubious claimants. Because of the opposing critiques, since 1994 there have been efforts to ease the FAP's burdens and other attempts to increase its difficulty; however, the essence of the criteria remain.

Mark Edwin Miller

See also Bureau of Indian Affairs (BIA); Indian
    Claims Commission; Indian Gaming Regulatory
    Act, 1988; Statutes as Sources of Modern Indian
    Rights: Child Welfare, Gaming, and
    Repatriation; Treaty.

References and Further Reading
Beinart, Peter. 1999. "Lost Tribes." *Lingua Franca*
    (May/June): 32–41.

Clow, Richard L., and Imre Sutton., eds. 2001. *Trusteeship in Change: Toward Tribal Autonomy in Resource Management.* Boulder: University Press of Colorado.

Miller, Mark Edwin. 2004. *Forgotten Tribes: Unrecognized Indians and the Federal Acknowledgment Process.* Lincoln: University of Nebraska Press.

Wilkinson, Charles. 2005. *Blood Struggle: The Rise of Modern Indian Nations.* New York and London: W.W. Norton.

Federally Recognized Tribes

Federally recognized tribes are those tribes that share a relationship with the U.S. government either through treaty or through congressional legislation. According to international law and treaty, the U.S. government is supposed to protect the tribal lands and tribal resources of federally recognized tribes. Under the same obligation, it is to provide them federal assistance with health care, education, and economic development (O'Brien 1989, 90). These tribes must have officially been recognized by the federal government. The period of self-determination (1968-present) has seen a dramatic shift in legislative policy and attitude toward Indian country evidenced by the passing of acts developed to foster and stimulate economic development in reservation communities. Examples of these acts include the Indian Financing Act and the Native American Programs Act, which establish a revolving line of credit; the Indian Gaming Regulatory Act of 1988, which allows tribes the opportunity to conduct gaming; and the Indian Tribal Government Tax Status Act, which allows tribes to utilize the tax advantages enjoyed by states and to raise money for governmental programs. Unrecognized tribes, frustrated because these benefits are not reaching their communities, petition to become federally recognized. Of the more than 600 tribes to date, 562 tribes are federally recognized. The federal government classifies tribes into four categories: (1) federally recognized tribes, (2) unrecognized tribes, (3) tribes that have been terminated, and (4) tribes recognized by states. More than two hundred tribes are not recognized by the federal government because of termination, have never been formally recognized via treaty or other legislation, or have been decimated by war and disease. Many of these tribes are currently seeking formal recognition in order to receive federal assistance, but tribes that were terminated cannot seek recognition.

The current process, known as the Federal Acknowledgement Process (FAP) was initiated by Congress on October 2, 1978. The secretary of the interior and the Bureau of Indian Affairs (BIA) set forth ethnohistorical, genealogical, anthropological, geographical, and legislative requirements that petitioners must meet to be recognized. A group must be able to prove that it meets these criteria:

(1) The group can be identified by historical evidence, written or oral, as being an American Indian Tribe; (2) its members are descendants of an Indian Tribe that inhabited a specific area, and these members continue to inhabit a specific area in a community viewed as American Indian and distinct from other populations in the area; (3) the Indian group has maintained governmental authority over its members as an autonomous entity throughout history until the present; (4) the membership of the group is composed principally of persons who are not members of any other Indian tribe; and (5) the tribe has not been the subject of congressional legislation expressly terminating their relationship with the federal government. (Pevar 1992, 262)

Many tribes cannot seek recognition because of the fifth clause, termination; but there are other means, beyond the recognition guidelines, that a tribe can pursue, such as Department of the Interior administrative decisions and congressional legislation.

To date, several hundred groups are seeking federal recognition through the Federal Acknowledgement Process by meeting the requirements and submitting to review by the Department of the Interior. The process is costly, more than $250,000 per case. The benefits of reestablishing the relationship between government and tribe are immense. Not only is the tribe eligible for welfare, health care, education, and other federal assistance, but the tribe can enter into and negotiate casino gaming compacts if the state in which it is located allows this form of gaming. Indian gaming is a multibillion-dollar business that has benefited the tribes that operate casinos.

Kurt T. Mantonya

See also Cherokee Nation v. Georgia, 1831; Federal Acknowledgment Process (FAP); Indian Gaming Regulatory Act, 1988; Termination.

References and Further Reading

O'Brien, Sharon. 1989. *American Indian Tribal Governments.* Norman: University of Oklahoma Press.

Prevar, Stephen L. 1992. *An American Civil Liberties Union Handbook: The Rights of Indians and Tribes.* Carbondale: Southern Illinois University Press.

U.S. Senate Committee on Indian Affairs. 2002. *Testimony Before the Committee on Indian Affairs, U.S. Senate. Indian Issues: Basis for BIA's Tribal Recognition Decisions Is Not Always Clear. Statement of Barry T. Hill, Director, Natural Resources and Environment.* Washington, D.C.: General Accounting Office.

Government-to-Government Relationship

The government-to-government relationship between the United States and Native Americans is one based in treaties, statutes, federal and state case law, executive orders, and the U.S. Constitution. Treaties have formed—and continue to form—the strategic link between the federal government and Native American nations. There are nearly four hundred ratified treaties and agreements between the federal government and Native American nations. The relationship is based upon the inherent sovereignty of the Native American nations, and this sovereignty preempts the U.S. Constitution. This preemption is based on the right of Native American nations to self-government, which includes tribal justice systems, protection of their culture, and control of their own resources. The relationship generally bars state interference in tribal affairs without federal and tribal consent. Moreover, the "trust relationship" means that the United States is a protector of the Native Americans and thus does not extinguish the internal sovereignty of Native American nations. The government-to-government relationship has undergone a transformation over the centuries; it is now the United States that is the stronger partner within this relationship, and the Native American nations are quasi-sovereign entities.

The government-to-government relationship between the United States, from its inception and development, and the Native Americans was originally one of sovereign nations capable of interacting in international relations. The federal government used treaties to acquire land, to establish peace, and to provide services and protection for the Native American nations. The government-to-government relationship has undergone transformation, and the United States has gained superiority as a consequence of three seminal U.S. Supreme Court cases. In *Johnson v. M'Intosh* (1823), the Supreme Court revised the relationship by declaring that Native sovereignty and independence were "diminished" and that the land could only be transferred to the United States. In *Cherokee Nation v. Georgia* (1831), Native Americans were deemed wards of the United States and defined as domestic dependent nations, thereby losing their capability to act in international affairs. And in *Worcester v. Georgia* (1832), state intrusiveness into Native American territory was prohibited. Furthermore, Native Americans continued to sign treaties with the U.S. government until 1871, when Congress abrogated that right, although agreements continued to be made until 1914.

The government-to-government relationship was redefined when the plenary power doctrine was adopted in *United States v. Kagama* (1886). This decision established Congress's unfettered right to legislate regarding Native American issues. Additionally, Congress relies on extra-constitutional powers to legislate regarding Native American affairs. Plenary power was affirmed in the Supreme Court ruling in *Oliphant v. Suquamish Indian Tribe* (1978), which denied inherent criminal jurisdiction over non-Native Americans.

The trust relationship between the U.S. government and Native Americans has developed from treaties and case law and is based on the former providing services and protecting Native American lands. Consequently, the trust relationship detracts from the government-to-government relationship. It presupposes a weaker state engaging with a stronger state, and under U.S. domestic law, this means subservience to the federal government.

The government-to-government relationship has depended on many variables, including treaties and federal case law. Politically, the federal government interacts with tribal governments, and the rights of tribes should be taken into account prior to action being taken. The tribes also interact with the states, and this is reflected in tribal-state compacts. Legally, there appears to be a piecemeal approach to Native American law, with many decisions undermining the government-to-government relationship.

Recent case law has also undermined the government-to-government relationship. In *Nevada v.*

Hicks (2001), the U.S. Supreme Court ruled that a tribal court lacks jurisdiction and authority to hear a civil lawsuit against state officials. The government-to-government relationship is further undermined when treaty rights are not protected. In *Brendale v. Confederated Tribes and Bands of the Yakima Indian Nation, et al.* (1989) and *South Dakota v. Yankton Sioux Tribe* (1998), the Supreme Court denied Native American tribes' treaty rights to the exclusive use and occupation of land lost through more recent statutes.

The decisions of the Supreme Court are contradictory. At times, decisions supplement Native American self-government; at other times, the decisions dismiss inherent sovereignty and treaty rights while affirming the destructive plenary power doctrine, which continues to undermine the government-to-government relationship. An enlightening example of the contradictions and the divergent nature of Native American sovereignty appears in *Cherokee Nation v. Georgia* (1831), in which the Cherokee were denied "foreign" status, in contrast to *Idaho v. Coeur d'Alene Tribe* (1997), in which the Supreme Court held that Native Americans should be accorded the status of "foreign sovereigns."

Dewi I. Ball

See also Domestic Dependent Nation; *Johnson v. M'Intosh*, 1823; *Oliphant v. Suquamish Indian Tribe,* 1978; Plenary Power; Sovereignty, Treaty; Trust Doctrine; *United States v. Kagama,* 1886.

References and Further Reading

O'Brien, Sharon. 1989. *American Indian Tribal Governments.* Norman: University of Oklahoma Press.

Wilkins, David E., and K. Tsianina Lomawaima. 2001. *Uneven Ground: American Indian Sovereignty and Federal Law.* Norman: University of Oklahoma Press.

Wilkinson, Charles F. 1987. *American Indians, Time, and the Law: Native Societies in a Modern Constitutional Democracy.* New Haven, CT: Yale University Press.

Guardianship/Wardship

Guardianship/wardship is a theory which holds that tribal nations function under the trust protection of the federal government. The Native nations lack political independence, and state governments cannot intrude on tribal affairs. It is the responsibility of the federal government to ensure that this trust protection is preserved. This theory was pro-posed by Chief Justice John Marshall during two Supreme Court cases, in 1831 and 1832, respectively: *Cherokee Nation v. Georgia* and *Worcester v. Georgia.* The premise of this theory is tribal nations are not sovereign independent entities who can determine their own direction but rather children who must be guided by their parent(s), in this case the federal government. This attitude of ward to a guardian is denoted by the word *paternalism.* The federal government would do what was best for Native people according to white norms, which would lead to the taking of Native peoples' hands and leading them down the path toward white civilization and Christianity.

In the *Cherokee Nation v. Georgia* case in 1831, the Cherokee Nation filed for protection from the state of Georgia. The state of Georgia imposed its own state laws and ruled that Cherokee laws were no longer legal. The Cherokee regarded themselves as an independent nation. Chief Justice John Marshall declared that tribal nations are "domestic dependent nations" and that the federal government has a responsibility to protect Native people. He wrote, "They look to our government for protection; rely upon its kindness and its power; appeal to it for relief to their wants; and address the president as their great father. They and their country are considered by foreign nations, as well as by ourselves, as being so completely under the sovereignty of the United States" (Deloria and Lytle 1983, 30). The Cherokees were declared in a state of pupilage.

The following year, in the *Worcester v. Georgia* case in 1832, the Supreme Court ruled that the state of Georgia did not have the right to interfere with Cherokee affairs. The U.S. government exclusively interacts with tribal nations. Marshall wrote, "The laws and treaties of the United States contemplate the Indian territory as completely separated from that of the states" (Deloria and Lytle 1983, 32). Chief Justice Marshall ruled that the Cherokee people had a right to their own government. Marshall's words became the basis of the guardianship/wardship theory, which guides the relationship between the federal government and tribal nations to this day.

During the rest of the nineteenth century, federal Indian policies illustrated this paradoxical relationship between the federal government and tribal nations. Thousands of Native people were removed from the eastern part of the United States across the Mississippi River into Indian Territory, now known as the state of Oklahoma. Reservation systems were

Native men and boys playing stickball, a game similar to lacrosse. (Library of Congress)

established to remove and restrict Native interaction with non-Native people. Assimilation tactics were imposed to "white out" Native people. The reservations were divided up into individual allotments to destroy the concept of tribal ownership in favor of individual proprietorship.

In the twentieth century, the guardianship/ wardship theory would be demonstrated in various back-and-forth federal Indian policies. Assimilation and allotment dictated the relationship between Native people and the federal government in the early part of the twentieth century. Native people who still needed guiding were looked over, while those people that assimilated to the larger society were forgotten. Under the Dawes Act and its amendments, individuals received land allotments and U.S. citizenship, until the Burke Act of 1906 put these lands into protective trust status for a period of twenty-five years. In the early 1920s, federal courts appointed legal guardians over "incompetent" Indians, who did not understand English and lacked experience in handling business affairs in the white capitalist system.

In 1934, the Indian Reorganization Act was passed and the policy of allotment officially ended. Tribal nations were told to return to practicing tribal ways. A decade later, federal Indian policy shifted back toward assimilating Native people into the larger society of America. Introduced in 1953 with House Concurrent Resolution 108, the new termination policy extinguished tribal nation status by dissolving their trust status. Tribal nations would no longer exist, according to the federal government. The termination policy proved ineffective and costly in the 1960s. A self-determination policy was introduced in the early 1970s to allow tribal nations to direct their own affairs with some federal government guidance. The self-determination policy is still in effect today; yet, the federal government, through different federal organizations such as the Bureau of Indian Affairs and Public Health Service, remains a vital component of Native peoples' lives.

Lloyd L. Lee

See also Allotment; American Indian Self-Determination and Education Act of 1975; Assimilation; Domestic Dependent Nation; Indian Removal; Termination; Trust Doctrine.

References and Further Reading

American Indian Lawyer Training Program, Inc. 1988. *Indian Tribes as Sovereign Governments: A Sourcebook on Federal-Tribal History, Law, and*

Policy. Oakland, CA: American Indian Resources Institute (AIRI).

Deloria, Vine, Jr., and Clifford M. Lytle. 1983. *American Indians, American Justice.* Austin: University of Texas Press.

O'Brien, Sharon. 1989. *American Indian Tribal Governments.* Norman: University of Oklahoma Press.

Indian Country

The legal term *Indian country* is commonly defined as "(a) all land within the limits of any Indian reservation . . . (b) all dependent Indian communities . . . and (c) all Indian allotments" (18 *U.S. Code* § 1151 [2004]). Generally speaking, Indian country is an area that has been set aside for the use and benefit of Indian tribes by the U.S. government (Wilkins 2001, 280). However, Indian country is better understood as a jurisdictional concept rather than a mere geographical concept because it is the "benchmark for approaching the allocation of federal, tribal, and state authority with respect to Indians and Indian lands." (*Indian Country, U.S.A., Inc. v. Oklahoma* ex rel. Okla. Tax Comm'n, 829 F.2d 967 [10th Cir. 1987]). Traditionally, only federal and tribal jurisdiction could be exercised in Indian country; state jurisdiction could not (Pevar 1992, 16). Yet in a series of recent U.S. Supreme Court cases, discussed following, the idea of Indian country has been modified so that state power now extends on to Indian reservations in several situations.

The term *Indian country* was originally a vernacular phrase used by early European colonists to refer loosely to "the lands beyond the frontier," which were occupied by Indians and inaccessible to most settlers (Deloria and Lytle 1983, 58). During this period, tribal sovereignty in Indian country was paramount and largely unchallenged (ibid., 70). After the American Revolution, however, the U.S. Congress began using the term in treaties and statutes such that it developed legal implications (ibid., 60–69). For example, in 1885 Congress passed the Major Crimes Act (23 *Stat.* 362), which gave the federal government exclusive jurisdiction over serious crimes committed by Indians in Indian country. The effect of the act was to eliminate preexisting tribal jurisdiction over this subject matter while, at the same time, precluding state jurisdiction. This act and others like it helped to establish the traditional notion that *Indian country* signified the presence of tribal and federal jurisdiction and the absence of state jurisdiction on Indian reservations (62 *Stat.* 757).

Further development of the term *Indian country* occurred as a result of the passage of the General Allotment Act (Dawes Act) in 1887 (24 *Stat.* 388). The Dawes Act authorized the president to allot to every individual tribal member up to 160 acres of reservation land that had formerly been held in common by tribes (CWAG 2004, 27–31). All surplus land remaining on Indian reservations after the completion of allotment to tribal members was sold by the federal government to non-Indian settlers (ibid.). The sale of large quantities of reservation land to non-Indians produced a checkerboard pattern of landownership on many reservations, with non-Indians owning land right next door to Indians (Deloria and Lytle 1983, 70).

Non-Indians who found themselves situated on Indian reservations eventually challenged tribal and federal efforts to control their activities in Indian country. In 1978, non-Indians met with some success when the U.S. Supreme Court held that only a state court, and not a tribal court, could properly exercise jurisdiction over a non-Indian who committed a crime against another non-Indian while located in Indian country (*Oliphant v. Suquamish Indian Tribe* [1978]). In 1994, state power was extended further regarding Indian reservations when the Supreme Court decided that individual parcels of land, wholly contained within the exterior boundaries of the Uintah Indian Reservation in Utah, had been removed from reservation status when the parcels were sold to non-Indians (*Hagen v. Utah*, 510 U.S. 399 [1994]). This meant that the land owned by non-Indians within the Uintah Reservation had been withdrawn from Indian country, thereby rendering tribal and federal jurisdiction inappropriate but leaving the state free to exercise its power (ibid.)

Thus, Indian country is an evolving concept that not only refers to a geographic place in which an Indian community resides but also defines which government can legitimately exercise power over the Indians and non-Indians on a reservation.

Kimberly Hausbeck

See also Aboriginal Title; Allotments; Assimilation; Dawes Commission; General Allotment Act (Dawes Act), 1887; Indian Territory; *Oliphant v. Suquamish Indian Tribe,* 1978; Trust Land.

References and Further Reading

Conference of Western Attorneys General (CWAG). 2004. *American Indian Law Deskbook.* 3rd ed. Boulder: University Press of Colorado.

Deloria, Vine, Jr., and Clifford M. Lytle. 1983. *American Indians, American Justice.* Austin: University of Texas Press.

Pevar, Stephen L. 1992. *The Rights of Indians and Tribes.* 2nd ed. Carbondale: Southern Illinois University Press.

Wilkins, David E., and K. Tsianina Lomawaima. 2001. *Uneven Ground: American Indian Sovereignty and Federal Law.* Norman: University of Oklahoma Press.

Indian New Deal

The *Indian New Deal* refers to the policies implemented during the administration of Franklin Delano Roosevelt (1933–1945) that are largely the work of John Collier, the commissioner of Indian affairs. The Indian New Deal consisted of many different policies that affected Native Americans across the United States and, historians agree, had mixed results with uneven impact across Native American communities.

The most significant policy of the Indian New Deal was the Indian Reorganization Act (IRA), sometimes called the Wheeler-Howard Act (1934). This act, proposed by Collier but watered down considerably by Congress, ended the allotment period, established a fund to purchase additional land for Native American tribes, and, most important, aimed to write constitutions and set up governments for tribes. It also provided for the creation of tribal corporations to develop tribal economies. Other policies of the Indian New Deal included the Johnson-O'Malley Act (1934), which reversed the assimilationist education policy then in place and provided funds for the development of such things as educational, medical, and welfare services. The Indian Arts and Crafts Board was also formed in 1935 as part of this new government vision for Native Americans. The board aimed to develop the arts and crafts production of reservations as a way of developing tribal economies.

The Indian New Deal sought to overhaul Native American economies and provide a basis for self-sufficiency. John Collier, who had long been involved in "Indian reform," was a strong believer in reviving Native American tribal community. He had long believed that white America could learn from Native American community ways and that this offered a solution to the individualism and selfishness of modern life. He wanted the protection and restoration of Native American cultures. Opposition from many quarters—from those who labeled it "communistic" to the western congressmen who resented any attempt to expand federal control of Native American resources—meant that Collier's vision was never fully realized. The Indian New Deal's major political consequences came about through its goal of setting up tribal governments through the Indian Reorganization Act. Each tribe held a referendum on whether they accepted or rejected such reorganization. Although the figures are approximate, some 181 tribes accepted the act; 77 tribes rejected it. About 93 tribes adopted constitutions as a result. There was some opposition to the IRA from within Native American communities themselves, including those who saw the Indian New Deal policies as a potential hindrance to the process of assimilation, which some believed desirable.

The Indian New Deal did not concern itself much with the issue of Native American treaties, but it did allow the revival and perpetuation of the concept of tribal sovereignty. A sense of tribal consciousness was emphasized by the policies, but the reform showed little concern or awareness of the complexity of tribal relations and tensions. The setting up of tribal governments created tensions and problems that continued well past 1945. Some historians argue that it set in place artificial units of Indian social and political life (that is, the "tribe") and thus prevented political or social organization in any other form (Taylor 1980, 150). As a consequence, local and community organizations and initiatives received little encouragement, and the tribal political structure became inflexible.

The New Deal did initiate Native American political activism, however, and it also began a process of pan-Indian political activism, which would take off in the 1960s. The IRA provided for intertribal contact and conferences and led to the foundation of one of the first intertribal political organizations, the National Congress of American Indians. It also provided for the setting up of the Indian Claims Commission, an important part of the administration of Native American affairs and an important forum for Native American claims. The loss of Native American land was halted, as was the destruction of Native American cultures. Cultural awareness and pride were fostered by the Indian

New Deal, which not only formed an important part of Native American identity and consciousness but played an important role in the Native American political activism that would make treaty rights a key part of its platform.

Amanda Laugesen

See also Collier, John; Indian Claims Commission (ICC); Indian Reorganization Act, 1934.
References and Further Reading
Cornell, Stephen. 1988. *The Return of the Native: American Indian Political Resurgence.* New York: Oxford University Press.
Parman, Donald Lee. 1976. *The Navajos and the New Deal.* New Haven, CT: Yale University Press.
Philp, Kenneth R. 1977. *John Collier's Crusade for Indian Reform, 1920–1954.* Tucson: University of Arizona Press.
Taylor, Graham. 1980. *The New Deal and American Indian Tribalism: the Administration of the Indian Reorganization Act 1934–45.* Lincoln: University of Nebraska Press.

Indian Removal

Indian removal was a concept first envisaged by George Washington in 1783, developed through the early nineteenth century, and legislatively enshrined in the Indian Removal Act of 1830. Removal was for the most part underpinned by the treaty process, in which the federal government acquired Native American land east of the Mississippi River in return for land to the west in what is now the state of Oklahoma. Treaties included the Treaty of Dancing Rabbit Creek (1830) and the Treaty of Payne's Landing (1832). The federal government and its supporters regarded removal as a means of saving the culture and the lives of the Native Americans from white settlers. Conversely, the Native Americans viewed removal as a federal and state land acquisition exercise intent on destroying their existence and detaching them from their ancestral lands. The process of removal involved bribery and intimidation and was devoid of federal government protection of Native Americans in conflict with the states. The process relied on the premise that all tribes were "hunters" and "savages" who did not utilize the land they lived on and who failed to conform to the agrarian ways of the settlers. Indian removal involved many eastern tribes, including the Choctaw, Chickasaw, Creek, Cherokee, and the Seminoles—the "Five Civilized Tribes"—and northern tribes, including the Potawatomi, Shawnee, Seneca, Ottawa, Chippewa,

Miami, Wyandot, Menominee, and Winnebago. Between 1832 and 1842, the federal government removed nineteen tribes and more than fifty thousand Native Americans.

Indian removal, initially developed in the late eighteenth century, permeated the consciousness of many federal administrations. President Thomas Jefferson's Louisiana Purchase in 1803 was land bought for Native Americans west of the Mississippi River, and both Presidents Monroe and John Quincy Adams unsuccessfully sought a congressional removal bill. By 1820, the eastern Native Americans had ceded a land mass equal in size to half the 1812 total.

President Andrew Jackson was elected in 1828, and he used his State of the Union and inaugural addresses to establish the administrative platform of Native American voluntary removal to the west of the Mississippi River. On April 26, 1830, the Senate voted 28 to 19 in favor of the removal bill. The House passed the bill on May 24, 1830, by 102 to 97, and President Jackson signed the bill on May 28, 1830. The Indian Removal Act empowered the president of the United States to convey land west of the Mississippi River to Native American tribes that chose and consented to the exchange of their homeland for land in the West.

Treaties between the tribes and the U.S. government underpinned the sovereign right and authority of Native Americans over their lands and thus excluded state interference. Although removal was voluntary, following the Indian Removal Act of 1830 Jackson stated that the federal government would not protect Native Americans from state law; the tribes would be forced to pay for their own removal, and they would not receive the promised annuities and goods during their first year in the West. Following the attempt of the Five Civilized Tribes to become more "civilized," the process of disenfranchisement began. The Cherokee felt that they had exhausted all avenues and that no redress was available other than to file suit with the U.S. Supreme Court. In *Cherokee Nation v. Georgia* (1831), Chief Justice John Marshall held that the Cherokee were not a foreign state and that they were "domestic dependent nations" under the protection of the U.S. government. This case was followed by *Worcester v. Georgia* (1832), in which Marshall held that Georgia laws that interfered with internal Cherokee affairs were unconstitutional and established the supremacy of federal laws fulfilling Native American treaties. This was a triumph for the Cherokee and the Native American tribes, but removal continued, contrary to the affirmation of Native American sovereignty over state laws by the Supreme Court.

Indian removal resulted in thousands of Native American deaths. One episode that embodies the process was the infamous Trail of Tears, on which thousands of Cherokee died. Removal cost the federal government $68 million to acquire 100 million acres of land in the East and 32 million acres of land in the West. The process of removal was to be voluntary, although it was achieved by coercion, intimidation, and bribery. However, many Native Americans remained on their land in the East and evaded the pressure of the state and the federal government to move west of the Mississippi River.

Dewi I. Ball

See also *Cherokee Nation v. Georgia*, 1831; Indian Removal Act, 1830; Jackson, Andrew; Sovereignty; Trail of Tears; Treaty; Treaty with the Choctaw–September 27, 1830; *Worcester v. Georgia*, 1832.

References and Further Reading

Remini, Robert V. 1990. *The Legacy of Andrew Jackson: Essays on Democracy, Indian Removal and Slavery.* Baton Rouge: Louisiana State University Press.

Satz, Ronald N. 2002. *American Indian Policy in the Jacksonian Era.* Norman: University of Oklahoma Press.

Wallace, Anthony F. C. 1993. *The Long, Bitter Trail: Andrew Jackson and the Indians.* New York: Hill and Wang.

Indian Territory

The term *Indian Territory* refers most commonly to land west of the Mississippi River reserved for the resettlement of Native Americans displaced by expanding European settlement in the eastern United States. Between 1803 and 1907, the West was seen as the logical home for eastern tribes thought to be in the way of American progress. Although passing through many configurations, the land in what was once called the Great American Desert became the new homeland for most of eastern America's Native peoples.

The idea of a western land reserve arose in the early nineteenth century when perceived failed efforts at assimilation prompted the removal of Native Americans from traditional lands. The Louisiana Purchase (1803) made possible such a removal and incredible relocation. The government escalated its military and legal persecution of eastern

Natives during the first two decades of the nineteenth century, and in 1824 President James Monroe proposed to Congress the establishment of a western relocation area. The following year, the first map of the proposed sanctuary was produced; nearly half the lands designated for resettlement were considered uninhabitable.

Although not legally authorized to do so, government agents requested voluntary migrants to the western land. With increasing demand for land by settlers and under pressure from President Andrew Jackson, Congress passed the Indian Removal Act of 1830, which authorized the president to make treaties and offer western land in exchange for eastern tribal lands. The Five Civilized Tribes in the Southeast (the Cherokee, Muscogee Creek, Seminole, Choctaw, and Chickasaw) were critically affected by this act because of their large populations.

Tribal disputes over vague boundaries, competition with already-established tribes, and trespassing white settlers and merchants plagued settlement in Indian Territory. The federal government intervened and in 1832 asked Montfort Stokes to head a commission to identify the problems and make recommendations for improved settlement. The Stokes Commission negotiated new treaties to settle border disputes and to improve relations with displaced Natives. In 1834, the Indian Trade and Intercourse Act further defined the role played by the government in Indian Territory, dictating acceptable relationships between whites and Natives and legally establishing Indian Territory by documenting its geographical boundaries.

The description of Indian Territory in 1834 represented it at its largest size. All lands controlled by the government west of the Mississippi River—excluding Missouri, Louisiana, and the Arkansas Territory—were set aside as Indian land, as were lands east of the Mississippi River still under Native control. Subsequent treaties and laws gradually reduced the size of the territory; by 1854, the Missouri River bordered the territory on the north, the Red River on the south, Missouri and Arkansas on the east, and the 100th meridian on the west.

In 1854, the Kansas-Nebraska Act reduced the territory further. Increased travel across northern Indian Territory by westward-bound settlers and fortune seekers pressured the government to open the land for settlement. Natives who settled on land above 37 degrees north, or the present northern border of Oklahoma, now had to move south. Competition and disputes over land increased as more peo-

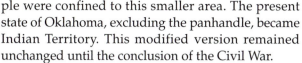

ple were confined to this smaller area. The present state of Oklahoma, excluding the panhandle, became Indian Territory. This modified version remained unchanged until the conclusion of the Civil War.

Questioning Native loyalty, the government concluded that some tribes had supported the Confederacy, whereas others had tried to remain neutral. As a part of Reconstruction in Indian Territory, treaties in 1866 made the western half available for redistribution to other tribes and brought railroads to the area. By 1889, the lands forfeited via treaties became Oklahoma Territory, and it and Indian Territory eventually became better known as the Twin Territories. Eventually applied to Indian Territory in 1891, the Dawes Act (the General Allotment Act of 1887) continued the redistribution and division of tribal lands, diminishing tribal authority. The process was corrupt, and non-Natives reaped the benefits of the land distribution. Eventually, as tribal authority declined and white settlements increased, the Twin Territories merged to become Oklahoma Territory. In 1907, the state of Oklahoma was recognized, and Indian Territory passed into history.

Larry S. Powers

See also Allotments; General Allotment Act (Dawes Act), 1887; Indian Removal; Indian Removal Act, 1830; Jackson, Andrew; Jefferson, Thomas; Reconstruction Treaties with the Cherokee, Choctaw, Chickasaw, Creek, Seminole–1866; Trail of Tears.

References and Further Reading

Baird, W. David, and Danny Goble. 1994. *The Story of Oklahoma.* Norman: University of Oklahoma Press.

Burton, Jeffrey. 1997. *Indian Territory and the United States: 1866–1906, Courts, Government and the Movement for Oklahoma Statehood.* Norman: University of Oklahoma Press.

Hagan, William T. 1976. *United States-Comanche Relations: The Reservation Years.* New Haven, CT: Yale University Press.

Meinig, D. W. 1993. *The Shaping of America: A Geographical Perspective on 500 Years of History,* vol. 2, *Continental America, 1800–1867.* New Haven, CT: Yale University Press.

Inuit

The Inuit are one of the three indigenous peoples of Canada. In 2001, 45,070 people living in Canada self-identified as Inuit. There are eight major groupings of Inuit: Western Arctic, Copper, Netsilik, Caribou, Igloolik, Baffin Island, Ungava and Labrador. They speak dialects of a common language called Inuktitut. Along with similar peoples who live in Alaska and Greenland, the Inuit are often referred to as Eskimos, which means "eaters of raw meat." The Inuit no longer find this description acceptable and prefer the term *Inuit,* which means "the people."

The Inuit traditionally have occupied the northern regions of Canada (Nunavut, the Northwest Territories, the coast of northern Labrador, and about 25 percent of Northern Quebec). The majority live above the tree line in the area bordered by Alaska in the west, the Labrador coast in the east, the southern tip of Hudson Bay in the south, and Ellesmere Island in the north. It is thought that, during the last Ice Age, the ancestors of the Inuit crossed the Bering Strait, a strip of land connecting Siberia and Alaska, and eventually made their home in the eastern Arctic. These ancestors, known as the Pre-Dorset, were inland caribou hunters but adapted to their new conditions by developing skills and technology for catching seals and walruses. The Pre-Dorset matured into the people identified as the Dorset and known as the Tuniit by the Inuit. It is believed that the Dorset, who occupied the eastern Arctic from 800 B.C. to 1000 A.D., were the original architects of snow houses. Sometime after 1000 A.D., the Dorset were replaced or absorbed by the Thule, who had moved into the eastern Arctic from Alaska. The Thule brought with them much of the technology needed to hunt large whales, and this became their economic mainstay. In about 1750 A.D., the Thule evolved into the Inuit, who, like their predecessors, relied on their intimate knowledge of the natural environment around them for survival.

Historically, the Inuit were hunters and gatherers who moved seasonally from one camp to another. Large regional groupings were loosely separated into smaller seasonal groups: winter camps of around a hundred people and summer hunting groups of fewer than a dozen. Until the twentieth century, contact between the Inuit and Europeans was sporadic. The earliest recorded contact is between 1000 and 1200 A.D. with the Norse. The subsequent arrival of explorers, whalers, traders, missionaries, scientists, and others led to many cultural changes.

The Inuit were largely ignored by the Canadian government until after World War II. Although the Canadian Supreme Court ruled in 1939 that the Inuit were a federal responsibility and entitled to receive federal services, it was not until the 1950s that the

Canadian government began providing them with services such as health care, housing, and education. To access these services, the Inuit moved or were relocated to permanent settlements. Although some Inuit maintained their traditional hunting and gathering lifestyle, they also became integrated in all sectors of the economy. The Inuit are known for their creativity; in the 1960s, they began to form marketing cooperatives to help sell local products, including art prints and carvings that have become world famous.

Over the past three decades, the Inuit have struggled to regain much of the autonomy in their day-to-day lives that formerly was lost to the federal government. In this regard, they have created their own political organizations. At present, the two main national organizations are the Inuit Tapiriit Kanatami (ITK), whose mandate is to represent the interests of the Inuit across Canada, and Pauktuutit, which focuses on issues of concern to Inuit women. Through their national and regional organizations, the Inuit have negotiated several land claim agreements that contain self-government components. These include the James Bay and Northern Quebec Agreement, signed in 1975; the Inuvialuit Final Agreement, signed in 1984 with the Inuit located in the western Arctic; the Nunavut Land Claims Agreement, signed in 1993 with the Inuit located in the eastern Arctic; and the Labrador Inuit Land Claims Agreement, signed in 2005.

The Inuit in Canada also work to support Inuit peoples in other countries. In 1977, the Inuit Circumpolar Conference (ICC) was created to represent the interests of Inuit in Canada, Greenland, Chukota (Russia), and Alaska. The ICC, which has enjoyed nongovernmental organization status with the United Nations since 1983, works to strengthen unity between Inuit peoples across borders and promotes sustainable development as well as Inuit interests at the international level.

Ritu Gambhir

See *also* Indian Act of Canada, 1876; Nisga'a Final Agreement–April 27, 1999; Sovereignty; Treaty; Trust; Trust Land.
References and Further Reading
Department of Indian and Northern Affairs Canada. 1990. *The Inuit*. Ottawa: Minister of Supply and Services Canada.
Harring, Sidney L. 1998. *White Man's Law: Native People in Nineteenth Century Canadian Jurisprudence*. Toronto: The Osgoode Society.
McNeil, Kent. 1982. *Native Claims in Rupert's Land and the North-western Territory: Canada's Constitutional Obligations*. Saskatoon: University of Saskatchewan Native Law Centre.
"Nunavut: Special Report on the New Territory." 1999. *Canadian Geographic*, 119(1).
Reiter, Robert. 1994. *The Law of Canadian Indian Treaties*. Edmonton: Juris Analytical Publishing.

Métis

Although it most often refers to people of mixed aboriginal and French ancestry, the term *Métis* (pronounced *may-tee*) can also refer to people with aboriginal and other non-French, European ancestry. During the many centuries of aboriginal and European contact, new cultures arose; the most enduring of these cultures is that of the Métis, which even developed its own "combination" language, called Mischif (mostly a mixture of French and Cree). The Métis, who are concentrated in the Upper Great Lakes and the northern plains, are recognized by the Canadian Constitution of 1982 as aboriginal people (along with First Nations people and the Inuit). The Métis enjoy no recognition, official or cultural, in the United States, as they are not considered an "Indian tribe" under the law.

The French first began to explore the "New World" in the early sixteenth century, sending Jacques Cartier in 1534. Cartier mapped portions of the Maritimes and the St. Lawrence before returning to France. The first settlement of the French in North America was in 1605 in what is now Nova Scotia; Quebec City was founded in 1608. From these ports, the French began building a fur trade empire which, at its height, stretched north throughout the Great Lakes, east to the Appalachians (excepting the Atlantic coastal region), west across the plains as far as Alberta, and south along the Mississippi to New Orleans. The French, unlike the British and Americans who followed them, were not intent on wresting control of the land from the Native people, preferring to foster good relations with them through the process of forming alliances with the indigenous people who lived there. These alliances often were solemnized through marriage with Native women. The Métis culture arose as a result of these marriages and alliances.

Essentially, these Métis families were the backbone of the entire French North American colonial fur trade empire. If not actually trapping (by the

Camp scene of Métis people with carts on the prairie. (National Archives of Canada)

men) and preparing the hides (by the women) for trade, the Métis were the *cour de bois*, transporting the prepared hides to the trading centers for eventual shipment to Europe. Although it is true that the fur trade regime was conducted throughout North America, the prime fur trade areas were those of the Upper Great Lakes, and it is this region in which the Métis thrived and in which their distinct culture arose.

As the Upper Great Lakes fur was being trapped out, the Métis moved west, concentrating themselves in the Red River Valley area of Minnesota and Manitoba. After the confederation of Upper Canada and Lower Canada in 1867, and the Hudson's Bay Company's decision to relinquish control over its land to the new Canadian government effective December 1, 1869, the Métis in Manitoba declared a provisional government under Louis Riel to ensure that the property, language, and religious rights of the Métis would be written into the act that would create the Province of Manitoba. During the life of the provisional government, which lasted from November 1869 to May 1870, the Riel government executed Thomas Scott, who was a

member of an anti-Catholic, anti-Métis militia, for treason. After Manitoba became a province, the Canadian government charged Riel with murder, and he left Canada for exile in the United States.

A similar series of events later played out in Saskatchewan, as the Canadian government moved to incorporate Saskatchewan into its expanding confederation. The Métis were again afraid that their rights were in danger of being trampled by the Canadian government. There, in 1873, they set up another provisional government and elected as governor Gabriel Dumont, who had been Riel's top military commander in the First Riel Rebellion. After a brief time, this government was suppressed by the Royal Canadian Mounted Police (RCMP). By 1884, the Métis were again faced with the prospect of seeing Saskatchewan join the confederation without a guarantee of Métis rights. Dumont, recognizing the need for a charismatic leader to take control of the situation, convinced Riel to return to Canada to declare a second provisional government and lead what has become known as the Second Riel Rebellion. Again, the Métis were successful in establishing their rights as Saskatchewan became a Canadian province, but after the rebellion, Louis Riel was captured and tried for the murder of Thomas Scott. He was found guilty and was hanged on November 16, 1885, in Regina. After the fighting, Gabriel Dumont crossed into Montana, where he lived for the next few years, returning to Saskatchewan in 1893, where he died in 1907.

With the execution of Louis Riel and the death of Gabriel Dumont, the Métis community suffered from a lack of charismatic leadership, and although it was never abandoned, their movement for a national identity and recognition floundered for nearly a century. Their issues and concerns were always a secondary concern, for the Canadian government—if it showed any concern at all—appeared to be interested only in addressing the issues facing First Nations people (those who might be called Indians in the American context).

All of that changed with the repatriation of the Canadian Constitution in 1982, which recognized First Nations, Métis, and Inuit as "Aboriginal People" and enshrined their rights. Consequently, the Métis have been enjoying a cultural renaissance; several national organizations have been formed to promote Métis identity and defend their aboriginal rights. By far the most notable event occurred in 2003, when Métis hunter Steve Powley from Sault Ste. Marie, Ontario, won his case in the Canadian Supreme Court in a decision that recognized an aboriginal hunting right for Métis people.

Another significant event occurred early in 1998, when the government of Canada issued a statement expressing "profound regret" for the mistreatment of aboriginal peoples for most of the country's history, especially for its role in the abuse suffered by aboriginal people in boarding schools. The official statement, although it stopped short of recognizing specific Métis rights, nonetheless did recognize the "contributions of Métis people in Canada" and asked the country to reflect on "Louis Riel's proper place in Canada's history."

Phil Bellfy

See also Constitution Act (Canada), 1982; Riel, Louis; Sahtu Dene and Métis Comprehensive Land Claim Agreement–September 6, 1993; Sault Ste. Marie, Michigan and Ontario.

References and Further Reading
Barkwell, Lawrence J., Leah Dorion, and Darren R. Préfontaine, eds. 2001. *Metis Legacy: A Métis Historiography and Annotated Bibliography*. Winnipeg, MB: Louis Riel Institute and Gabriel Dumont Institute of Métis Studies and Applied Research; Pemmican Publications.
Corrigan, Samuel W., and Lawrence J. Blackwell, eds. 1991. *The Struggle for Recognition, Canadian Justice and the Metis Nation*. Winnipeg, MB: Manitoba Métis Federation; Pemmican Publications.
Peterson, Jacqueline. 1978. "Prelude to Red River: A Social Portrait of the Great Lakes Métis." *Ethnohistory* 25(1): 41–67.
Sawchuk, Joe. 1998. *The Dynamics of Native Politics: The Alberta Metis Experience*. Saskatoon: Purich.
Scofield, Gregory A. 1999. *Thunder Through My Veins: Memories of a Métis Childhood*. Toronto: HarperFlamingoCanada.

Modern Treaties/Comprehensive Land Claim Agreements (Canada)

In 1973, in *Calder v. British Columbia* (1973, 1 S.C.R. 313), the Supreme Court of Canada rendered a decision recognizing the existence of aboriginal land rights in Canada based on aboriginal title. During the same time period, the Cree Nation of James Bay in northern Quebec went to court to stop the development of a massive hydroelectric project that would flood Cree Nation lands. The Quebec superior court ruled in favor of the Cree, leading to the negotiation and signing of what is considered the first modern-day treaty, known as the James Bay and Northern Quebec Agreement.

This series of events during the 1970s led to the announcement of a new policy by the federal government of Canada with regard to First Nations people living in Canada and their rights and title to land. This policy was known as the Comprehensive Land Claim Policy. This policy represented a movement by the government of Canada to settle the longstanding grievances of First Nations with respect to their rights and traditional territories.

A comprehensive claim involves a six-step process through negotiation, which moves from (1) submission of a claim by a First Nation to the Department of Indian Affairs; (2) acceptance (or rejection) of a claim by the department; (3) drafting of a framework agreement if the claim is accepted; (4) an agreement-in-principle; (5) a final agreement; and (6) an implementation plan for the final agreement.

The comprehensive claim process deals with a variety of issues, including creating a certainty of ownership with respect to land and resources, clarifying the rights and duties of the First Nation and the federal and provincial or territorial governments, and providing rules for the establishment and development of self-government for the First Nation. Comprehensive claims also often involve cash settlements paid to the First Nation by the Canadian government for loss of land and/or resources and damages.

When a final agreement is reached between the parties, the agreement must be ratified by members of the First Nation, generally in a referendum vote. Ratification has generally required an absolute majority vote of all members of the First Nation who are eligible to vote. The federal and provincial governments must also ratify the agreement through a vote in the provincial legislature and the federal Parliament.

The whole process of the comprehensive claims policy is very lengthy and costly. Arriving at a final agreement can take anywhere from five to twenty years, and the cost of the whole negotiation process can vary between $15 million and $50 million. The federal government does provide funding for First Nations to cover the legal and historical research costs of presenting such claims. Loans are also available to First Nations for the costs involved with the negotiation process.

The negotiation of these comprehensive claims has often given rise to issues of overlap. The traditional territories of two or more First Nations may overlap because there was a sharing of resources and land in the past between the First Nations, or there may in fact be long-standing disputes between the First Nations over the territory. It is important that these issues of overlap be addressed and resolved before the conclusion of a final agreement. The Department of Indian Affairs is of the opinion that overlap issues ideally should be resolved before an agreement-in-principle is reached.

It is important to note that these final agreements between the parties are constitutionally protected treaties under Section 35 of the Constitution Act (1982). The parties may also reach complimentary or administrative agreements that accompany the treaty, relating to such issues as commercial trapping arrangements, economic development arrangements, or park management arrangements. These complimentary agreements, however, do not have the same constitutional protection.

Lysane Cree

See also Aboriginal Title; *Calder v. Attorney-General of British Columbia* (Canada), 1973; Constitution Act (Canada), 1982; Gwich'in Comprehensive Land Claim Agreement–April 1992; James Bay and Northern Quebec Agreement–November 11, 1975; Nacho Nyak Dun Final Agreement–May 29, 1993; Northeastern Quebec Agreement–January 31, 1978; Self-Government Agreements (Canada); Vuntut Gwitchin Final Agreement–May 29, 1993.

References and Further Reading

Calder v. British Columbia. 1973. 1 S.C.R. 313.

Indian Affairs and Northern Canada. 2003. *Resolving Aboriginal Claims: A Practical Guide to Canadian Experiences*. Ottawa: Department of Indian Affairs.

Royal Commission on Aboriginal Peoples. 1995. *Treaty-Making in the Spirit of Co-Existence: An Alternative to Extinguishment*. Ottawa: Canada Communication Group.

Non-recognized Tribes

Unrecognized Indian tribes are groups that have never been federally acknowledged as Indian nations through treaties, legislation, court decisions, executive orders, or administrative actions. The general public uses the term to differentiate unrecognized groups from federally recognized tribes, although many of these communities possess acknowledgment from the states in which they reside. Because unrecognized groups lack federal status, they are ineligible to exercise full tribal sovereignty and access federal Indian programs of the Bureau of Indian Affairs (BIA) and the Indian Health Service. They are subject to state civil and criminal jurisdiction and, as a result, are unable to enter into gaming compacts. Non-federal Indian communities exist in thirty-seven states, with the majority of groups located in the mid-Atlantic region, the Northeast, the Deep South, California, and Washington State. The communities and racial characteristics of these groups vary considerably, with some resembling stereotypical "tribes" and others appearing fairly assimilated. Most unrecognized Native American communities currently are seeking federal tribal acknowledgment.

Groups lack federal acknowledgment for a variety of reasons. Following the American Revolution, many tribes on the East Coast came under state jurisdiction and never entered into treaties with the central government. In the Deep South, groups of Cherokee, Choctaw, Creek, and Seminole that refused to remove west remained in the region in nonreservation Indian enclaves. In California, dozens of tribes were omitted from federal recognition after the Senate refused to ratify a series of 1850s-era treaties. Other West Coast tribes were so small and peaceful that federal officials overlooked them. In the Pacific Northwest, bands of Snohomish, Samish, and Snoqualmie that refused to remove to Indian reservations became ineligible for federal trust protections. Although many nonfederal tribes possess high degrees of Indian ancestry and have maintained cohesive communities, federal officials traditionally have considered them non-Indians.

The lack of federal reservations and the protection of Indian law had devastating effects on most unrecognized tribes. Most communities lost lands, faced racial discrimination, and were unable to exercise tribal sovereignty. Individuals often intermarried with non-Indians and assimilated the dress, foods, religions, and economic subsistence practices of the surrounding society. The adoption of non-Indian culture did not mean that these tribes ceased to identify as Indian, however, and the civil rights struggles of the 1960s and 1970s inspired unrecognized tribes to organize, reassert their Indian heritage, bring land claims, and demand federal acknowledgment. With the help of attorney Tom Tureen and the Native American Rights Fund, unacknowledged tribes such as the Mashpee Wampanoag of Massachusetts led the 1970s movement to reclaim their rights under federal law. During the 1970s, these neglected tribes prompted the BIA to formulate standardized procedures for tribal recognition; these procedures are called the Federal Acknowledgment Process (FAP). The BIA regimen requires tribes to prove that they have been historically identified as Indians, to have documented indigenous ancestry, to have maintained cohesive communities, and to have a line of political leaders. Currently, many unrecognized tribes put a great deal of time and energy into securing federal tribal status.

Although denied federal Indian programs and status, nonfederal tribes often provide valuable services to their members. State-recognized tribal groups such as the United Houma Nation of Louisiana are eligible for Indian programs sponsored by the Department of Health and Human Services and the Department of Education. As low-income communities, they also can administer programs of the Departments of Labor, Commerce, and Justice. Currently, many unrecognized communities are experiencing a cultural rebirth, serving as the locus of indigenous rebirth in their regions by sponsoring powwows and youth cultural enhancement programs and by fostering pride in their Indian heritage.

The rise of Indian gaming has altered public perceptions of nonfederal tribes. Because federal acknowledgment serves as a gateway to tribal casinos, many local and state officials, conservative groups, and anti-gaming organizations oppose the aspirations of unrecognized tribes in their regions, suing them and lobbying against their acknowledgment petitions. Unrecognized communities counter that they were pursuing federal acknowledgment long before tribal casinos entered the picture. More than other factors, Indian gaming has hindered the aspirations of nonfederal Native groups, aligning powerful forces against their efforts to secure federal recognition of their rights.

Mark Edwin Miller

See also Federal Acknowledgement Process (FAP); Federally Recognized Tribes; State-Recognized Tribes.

References and Further Reading

Campisi, Jack. 1991. *The Mashpee Indians: Tribe on Trial.* Syracuse, NY: Syracuse University Press.

Harmon, Alexandra. 1998. *Indians in the Making: Ethnic Relations and Indian Identities around Puget Sound.* Berkeley: University of California Press.

Miller, Mark Edwin. 2004. *Forgotten Tribes: Unrecognized Indians and the Federal Acknowledgment Process.* Lincoln: University of Nebraska Press.

Plenary Power

The term *plenary power,* when used in reference to Indian affairs, describes the supreme authority exercised by the U.S. Congress over all Indian matters (Pevar 1992, 48–49). Depending on the context in which the term is used, the plenary power of Congress can mean either "exclusive power," "preemptive power," or "absolute and unlimited power" (Wilkins 2001, 13–14). The distinction is important because, although the first two meanings of the term *plenary power* are based clearly on provisions embedded in the U.S. Constitution, the third is not (Pommersheim 1995, 46–48).

When it refers to the ability of Congress to regulate Indians and tribes to the exclusion of the executive and judicial branches of the federal government, the plenary power of Congress is considered "exclusive." However, when Congress exercises its authority to negate or supersede an action by a state government in the field of Indian affairs, the plenary power of Congress is denoted "preemptive." Alternately, when Congress passes legislation that modifies or eliminates tribal sovereignty, its plenary power is deemed "absolute and unlimited" (Wilkins 2001, 98–101). Thus, the precise meaning of the term *plenary power* shifts subtly according to whether congressional power over Indian matters is compared to the power of the other two branches of the federal government, the power of state governments, or the power of tribal governments.

Both the exclusive and the preemptive meanings of congressional plenary power have their origin in constitutional text. The commerce clause—Article I, Section 8, clause 3—of the Constitution confers on Congress "the Power . . . to regulate Commerce with foreign Nations, and among the several States, and with the Indian Tribes." Additionally, the treaty clause—found in Article II, Section 2, clause 2—delegates to Congress the power to approve treaties made with Indian tribes. Finally, the supremacy clause—located in Article VI, clause 2—declares, "This Constitution, and the laws of the United States . . . and all treaties made . . . shall be the supreme law of the land." The U.S. Supreme Court has interpreted these provisions as providing Congress, and only Congress, with complete control over Indian matters (Wilkins and Lomawaima 2001, 102).

In contrast, the "absolute and unlimited" plenary power that Congress exercises in relation to tribal governments does not have a clear constitutional basis (Wilkins and Lomawaima 2001, 106). The Supreme Court first announced this doctrine in 1903 in *Lone Wolf v. Hitchcock*, a case involving tribal opposition to the unilateral modification of an Indian treaty by Congress (Pommersheim 1995, 46). The Supreme Court reasoned that Congress possessed plenary power over tribal governments because such power had been "exercised by Congress from the beginning, and the power has always been deemed a political one, not subject to be controlled by the judicial department of the government" (*Lone Wolf v. Hitchcock*, 1903). Scholars critical of the *Lone Wolf* decision have pointed out that the Supreme Court failed to refer to any constitutional provision supporting this congressional power but instead took what was simply congressional practice and declared it constitutionally permissible (Pommersheim 1995, 46–48).

The plenary power of Congress in this context is so broad that the Supreme Court has stated that tribal self-governance "exists only at the sufferance of Congress and is subject to complete defeasance" (*United States v. Wheeler,* 1978). Under this rubric, Congress not only has continued to abrogate Indian treaties without tribal consent, but it has terminated the sovereignty of numerous tribes (Pommersheim 1995, 47). The only constitutional limitations the Supreme Court has recognized on congressional plenary power over Indian tribes are those contained in the due process clause and the just compensation clause of the Fifth Amendment. The former clause prevents Congress from discriminating against Indians and tribes, whereas the latter clause requires Congress to pay fair compensation for the taking of Indian property (*United States v. Sioux Nation,* 1980).

Kimberly Hausbeck

See also Commerce Clause and Native Americans; *Lone Wolf v. Hitchcock, 1903; McClanahan v. Arizona State Tax Commission, 1973; Morton v. Mancari, 1974;* Supremacy Clause; Termination; *United States v. Kagama, 1886; United States v. Sioux Nation, 1980; United States v. Wheeler, 1978; Worcester v. Georgia, 1832.*

References and Further Reading

Conference of Western Attorneys General (CWAG). 2004. *American Indian Law Deskbook.* 3rd ed. Boulder: University Press of Colorado.

Pevar, Stephen L. 1992. *The Rights of Indians and Tribes.* 2nd ed. Carbondale: Southern Illinois University Press.

Pommersheim, Frank. 1995. *Braid of Feathers.* Berkeley: University of California Press.

Wilkins, David E., and K. Tsianina Lomawaima. 2001. *Uneven Ground.* Norman: University of Oklahoma Press.

Reserved Rights Doctrine

Reserved rights are the "bundle of rights" that is rooted in the inherent or original sovereignty of Indian nations. They are property rights that Indian nations retained and did not give or grant to the United States during the negotiation of a treaty or other formal agreement. When Indian nations negotiated and signed treaties with the U.S. government during the eighteenth and nineteenth centuries, they often retained certain lands as reservations and reserved the right to harvest natural resources on lands they sold or ceded to the United States. In doing so, Native communities reserved property

rights they did not explicitly relinquish to the United States. Such rights are not, as some critics have claimed, "special rights" or rights "granted" to Indian nations by the United States.

The first legal definition of the reserved rights doctrine was articulated by the U.S. Supreme Court in a 1905 decision, *United States v. Winans* (198 U.S. 371 [1905]). The case before the Court was whether or not the Yakama Nation's treaty right to fish in "usual and accustomed places" was being interfered with by fishwheels placed on the Columbia River by non-Indians. In a decision favoring the Yakama, the Court enunciated the reserved rights doctrine. It ruled that non-Indian settlement and landscape change would limit, not eliminate, the Yakama's fishing rights. The Court concluded that the fishing rights could not be taken, because "the treaty was not a grant of rights to the Indians, but a grant of rights from them, a reservation of those not granted. And the form of the instrument and its language was adapted to that purpose." This formulation of the reserved rights doctrine recognizes that Indian nations reserved specific inherent or aboriginal property rights and political powers at the same time they granted specific rights to the United States. The United States was not giving or granting rights or powers to tribes.

Analogies can be drawn between Indian treaty-based reserved rights and power and those of the rights and powers that state governments reserved with the Tenth Amendment to the U.S. Constitution. The Tenth Amendment is a reserved powers clause that protects the sovereignty and powers of state governments. It says that the states reserved all those powers that they did not delegate or give to the federal government by the Constitution. In drawing a direct comparison between Indian and state reserved rights, these scholars demonstrate not only that reserved treaty rights are an inherent aspect of tribal sovereignty—that they have a pre-constitutional basis—but also that, because they are similar to states' reserved rights, there is a legal, if not a moral, basis for the defense of the Indian reserved rights doctrine.

Conflicting interpretations of the reserved rights doctrine have been at the center of legal disputes between state governments and Indian nations over the continuing existence of off-reservation hunting, fishing, and gathering treaty rights. In both the Pacific Northwest and the Great Lakes regions, the reserved rights doctrine has been a key aspect in judicial interpretations of treaty negotiations, the texts of treaties, and historical and contemporary Indian and non-Indian understandings of the meaning of treaties. Anti-Indian treaty rights groups have attacked court decisions employing the reserved rights doctrine as examples of the courts "granting" special rights to Indian tribes.

The reserved rights doctrine has also been important in defining water rights on Indian reservations in the western United States. In *Winters v. United States* (207 U.S. 564 [1908]), the Supreme Court ruled that there was an implicit or "implied" reservation of water rights when Indian reservations were created. According to the Court, even though a treaty or agreement creating a reservation did not explicitly mention or reserve water rights for the tribe, there was an implied reservation of enough water to meet the tribe's needs. Otherwise, the reservation would have little economic (i.e., agricultural) value. As a result of this application of the implied reserved rights doctrine, upstream irrigators and water users cannot legally deprive a downstream tribe of sufficient water to meet their needs.

Steven E. Silvern

See also Aboriginal Rights; Plenary Power; Sovereignty; Treaty; Trust; Trust Lands.

References and Further Reading

Burton, Lloyd. 1991. *American Indian Water Rights and the Limits of the Law.* Lawrence: University Press of Kansas.

Deloria, Vine, Jr. 1996. "Reserving to Themselves: Treaties and the Powers of Indian Tribes." *Arizona Law Review* 38: 963–980.

Wilkins, David E., and K. Tsianina Lomawaima. 2001. *Uneven Ground: American Indian Sovereignty and Federal Law.* Norman: University of Oklahoma Press.

Wilkinson, Charles F. 1987. *American Indians, Time, and the Law.* New Haven, CT: Yale University.

Right of Conquest

The right of conquest is a concept of European civilization. From a non-American view, the concept expressed superiority over the peoples of the Americas, who were perceived as primitive savages. It was used to justify European control of the land if not its immediate possession.

The legal history of the right of conquest is intertwined with the doctrine of discovery. Although the basis for the right of conquest is often cited as William the Conqueror's invasion of England in the twelfth century, the origin of the doctrine of discovery is usually dated to papal bulls in the fifteenth century, which laid the basis for European claims of land in foreign lands.

The two principles—the right of discovery and the right of conquest—were often treated together, as in the eighteenth century when French legal theorist Emer de Vattel, addressing the issues arising from European claims in the "New World," explained that the indigenous peoples' " . . . uncertain occupancy of these vast regions can not be held as a real and lawful taking of possession; and when the Nations of Europe, which are too confined at home, come upon lands which the savages have no special need of and are making no present and continuous use of, they may lawfully take possession of them and establish colonies in them" (Vattel 1758).

English Judge John Blackstone, in his *Laws of Nations*, concluded shortly after Vattel that conquest and treaties were the basis for land acquisition in the United States, stating that "Our American Plantations are principally . . . [ceded or conquered countries], being obtained in the last century either by right of conquest and driving out the . . . or by treaties. And, therefore, the common law of England, as such, has no allowance or authority there; they being no part of the mother country, but distinct, though dependent dominions."

Although these interpretations and a body of treaties with Europeans over the centuries all suggested that Indians retained rights to the soil, legal doctrine in U.S. history was crystallized differently in the watershed case *Johnson v. M'Intosh* in 1823. The U.S. Supreme Court under Chief Justice John Marshall cast the doctrine of discovery in terms of conquest, in effect combining the two distinct historical ideas into a single entity. More important, Marshall's verdict eclipsed earlier rights of occupancy acknowledged by Europeans. This placed the Indians under U.S. jurisdiction and denied them, by right of conquest (due to "discovery"), any rights to dispose of their lands as they desired. Only the U.S. government could do that, Marshall concluded. The Marshall Court maintained that "the title by conquest is acquired and maintained by force. The conqueror prescribes its limits."

The *Johnson* decision effectively annulled Indian rights in favor of a version of the right of conquest by reinterpreting the right of occupation (or right of the soil) such that it was superseded by the doctrine of discovery. By this means, the Indians lost all rights to their land, just as if they had been subject to the right of conquest. Even though Marshall recast this

position yet again in *Worcester v. Georgia* (1832), which finally recognized the right of Indians to make treaties with federal governments, to the present day *Johnson v. M'Intosh* is often cited as the basis for claims at the municipal level. This ruling has been at the core of many legal battles over land rights for American Indians ever since.

Eric R. Smith

See also Doctrine of Discovery; *Johnson v. M'Intosh*, 1823; Right of Occupancy/Right of the Soil; *Worcester v. Georgia*, 1832.

References and Further Reading
Berman, Howard. 1974. "The Concept of Aboriginal Rights in the Early Legal History of the United States." *Buffalo Law Review* 27: 637–668.
Churchill, Ward. 1992. "The Earth Is Our Mother." In *The State of Native America: Genocide, Colonization, and Resistance*, ed. M. Annette Jaimes, 139–188. Boston: South End Press.
Morris, Glen T. 1992. "International Law and Politics: Toward a Right to Self-Determination for Indigenous Peoples." In *The State of Native America: Genocide, Colonization, and Resistance*, ed. M. Annette Jaimes, 55–86. Boston: South End Press.
Story, Joseph. 1873. *Commentaries on the Constitution of the United States*. Boston: Little, Brown.
Vattel, Emer de. 1758. *The Laws of Nations or the Principles of Natural Law*. Trans. Charles G. Fenwick. Repr., Dublin: Luke White, 1762.
Williams, Robert. 1990. *The American Indian in Western Legal Thought*. New York: Oxford University Press.

Right of Occupancy/ Right of the Soil

Europeans who settled the lands occupied by indigenous peoples recognized those peoples' rights to the soil (*jus soli* in the Roman law tradition) through treaties and precedence. Under the doctrine of discovery, however, the need of Europeans to prevent other European powers from claiming these lands often inhibited the full realization of this right of the soil.

Historians and legal scholars generally agree that the existing body of Indian treaties and international legal standards articulated by Europeans even before the American Revolution supported a belief by Europeans and colonists of the Indians' rights to the land. The Europeans, however, were eager to claim land in the new world and did not recognize Indians' rights to dispose of land as they pleased. To protect the land they claimed from being sold to other powers by the indigenous people, Europeans invoked the doctrine of discovery, which subsequently limited the right to the soil in commercial terms.

So, although Indians were entitled to their land, they were not allowed to dispose of it. Only the discovering nation could decide who would be entitled legally to possess it. This principle served the needs of European monarchs, who prevented other imperialist powers from purchasing the land from the Indians who owned it, thereby guaranteeing that only the conquering nation could legally possess the land, although its Native inhabitants could live there.

In the United States, the need for legal cession of Indian land was spelled out in a September 1783 proclamation under the Articles of Confederation and then reiterated on March 1, 1783, by Congress. After the American Revolution, Britain ceded its claims to the United States under the provisions of Vattel's *Laws of Nations*. Writing in 1833, Justice Joseph Story explained that "the Indian tribes . . . maintained a claim to the exclusive possession and occupancy of the territory within the respective limits, as sovereigns and absolute proprietors of the soil." This is the standard understanding of indigenous rights conferred by Europeans.

Still, the U.S. Supreme Court's *Johnson v. M'Intosh* decision in 1823 has been cited as the defining interpretation of the legal principle of the right of the soil, even though the decision was later reinterpreted. Marshall's verdict eclipsed earlier rights of occupancy acknowledged by Europeans. This placed the Indians under U.S. jurisdiction and denied them by right of conquest (due to "discovery") any rights to dispose of their lands as they desired. Only the U.S. government could do that, Marshall concluded. The Marshall Court maintained that "the title by conquest is acquired and maintained by force. The conqueror prescribes its limits." Marshall based the decision on the doctrine of discovery, but many scholars agree that Marshall's interpretation radically departed from earlier understandings of Indian rights, effectively undermining the Native peoples' autonomy. The *Johnson* decision effectively annulled Indian rights in favor of a version of the right of conquest. But Marshall recast this position yet again in *Worcester v. Georgia* (1832), in which opinion the right of Indians to make treaties with federal governments was finally recognized. Unfortunately, even now the *Johnson* case often forms the basis for claims at the municipal level.

Eric R. Smith

See also Doctrine of Discovery; *Johnson v. M'Intosh;* Right of Conquest; *Worcester v. Georgia*, 1832.
References and Further Reading
Berman, Howard. 1974. "The Concept of Aboriginal Rights in the Early Legal History of the United States." *Buffalo Law Review* 27: 637–668.
Morris, Glen T. 1992. "International Law and Politics: Toward a Right to Self-Determination for Indigenous Peoples." In *The State of Native America: Genocide, Colonization, and Resistance,* ed. M. Annette Jaimes. Boston: South End Press.
Story, Joseph. 1873. *Commentaries on the Constitution of the United States.* Boston: Little, Brown.
Vattel, Emer de. 1758. *The Laws of Nations or the Principles of Natural Law.* Trans. Charles G. Fenwick. Repr., Dublin: Luke White, 1762.
Williams, Robert. 1990. *American Indian in Western Legal Thought.* New York: Oxford University Press.

Sacred Sites

Sacred sites are places or landscapes that people identify as different from those of ordinary reality. For many Native Americans, these include natural, historical, and spiritual spaces, such as lakes, springs, mountains, mineral deposits, burial grounds, ancient villages, battle grounds, migration routes, abodes of ancestors, places of divine instruction, and portals between universes. These spaces are often seen not as discrete sites but as broad landscapes that interconnect the sacred and secular, uniting human persistence and natural processes.

Native Americans venerate sacred sites because of the historical events that occurred there or because they are points at which the divine joins with the lives of everyday people. In addition, some sites are revered because they are believed to possess an innate holiness and power that abides outside of human existence. Although many sacred sites have been acknowledged for generations, new locations continue to be revealed through Native American cultural and religious practices.

Sacred sites are experienced and remembered through numerous customs and traditions. Native Americans evoke places through oral histories, stories, myths, dreams, meditation, ceremonial rituals, chants, and songs. When people visit sites during pilgrimages or quests, they regularly leave offerings, make petitions, and give thanks. Because some sacred sites are especially significant or contain an overabundance of power, only a few people may possess knowledge of these specific places and their

associated rites. However, these select individuals by and large take on this responsibility for the well-being of their entire communities and, at times, for all forms of life.

The spiritual and material connections Native Americans make to sacred sites establish their authority as stewards of the land. Through their practices, many Native Americans feel they help maintain the precarious balance among human, natural, and spiritual forces. The landscape is pivotal in helping to record and remember crucial historical moments. Sacred sites also often supply the artifacts, plants, animals, and minerals used in rituals that foster the physical and spiritual health of communities. Sacred places and landscapes preserve and exercise traditional culture, which provides social cohesion and coherence to Native peoples.

Treaties and laws of the United States have long offered only minimal protection for Native American sacred sites. Beginning in the 1800s, several laws directly threatened Native American sovereignty over their sacred lands, including the Indian Removal Act of 1830, the Homestead Act of 1862, the Mining Law of 1872, and the General Allotment Act (Dawes Act) of 1887. The passage of several early cultural resource laws—the Antiquities Act of 1906, the Historic Sites Act of 1935, and the National Historic Preservation Act of 1966—added modest protection of sacred spaces, although the supervision of sites remained firmly outside Native American society. The American Indian Religious Freedom Act (AIRFA) of 1978 was designed to protect Native American religious practices, including activities involving sacred sites. However, AIRFA was found weak when tested in subsequent litigation, most notably the 1988 case *Lyng v. Northwest Indian Cemetery Protective Association*. In the 1990s, Native Americans attained new means of establishing control in the management of sacred sites. The Native American Graves Protection and Repatriation Act (NAGPRA) of 1990 enabled Native American groups to reclaim human remains, funerary items, and sacred objects held in federally funded institutions. NAGPRA also gave Native groups more influence in deciding the ultimate disposition of materials to be recovered from sacred sites in the future. Additionally, an amendment in 1992 to the National Historic Preservation Act furnished greater authority and participatory roles to federally recognized tribes. In 1996, former president Clinton's Executive Order 13007, Indian Sacred Sites, in part directed all federal agencies to accommodate Native American use of

and access to sacred sites and to avoid negatively impacting the physical integrity of these places. Even though the last decade has afforded Native Americans increased control and protection of sanctified lands, they continue to strive for further measures that recognize their sovereignty and responsibilities to the spaces they consider sacred.

Chip Colwell-Chanthaphonh

See also General Allotment Act (Dawes Act), 1887; Indian Removal; Indian Removal Act, 1830; Indian Territory.

References and Further Reading

Deloria, Vine, Jr. 1999. "Sacred Lands and Religious Freedom." In *For This Land: Writings on Religion in America,* eds. Vine Deloria, Jr., and James Treat, 203–213. New York: Routledge.

Gulliford, Andrew. 2000. *Sacred Objects and Sacred Places: Preserving Tribal Traditions.* Boulder: University Press of Colorado.

McPherson, Robert S. 1992. *Sacred Land, Sacred View: Navajo Perceptions of the Four Corners Region.* Salt Lake City, UT: Brigham Young University, Charles Redd Center for Western Studies; distributed by Signature Books.

Mills, Barbara J., and T. J. Ferguson. 1998. "Preservation and Research of Sacred Sites by the Zuni Indian Tribe of New Mexico." *Human Organization* 57(1): 30–42.

Sovereignty

Sovereignty is a concept in which nations are sanctioned to interact in international relations and to make treaties. The origin of nation-state sovereignty was established in Europe following the Treaty of Westphalia in 1648. Sovereignty requires the authority and jurisdiction to act over a defined territory and a specific people, as well as constitutional independence. *Internal sovereignty* is the right of a nation to issue laws independent of another nation and to promote and sustain its culture, heritage, and language. *External sovereignty* defines a nation as part of the international community, which authorizes it to interact in international affairs, symbolized through recognition by other sovereign states and through treaties. Native American nations have nearly four hundred ratified treaties and agreements with the U.S. government. Over the centuries, Native American nations have undergone a transformation from independent sovereign nations to quasi-sovereign nations under the protection of the federal government. The transformation has been developed through federal case law, notably *Johnson v. M'Intosh* (1823), *Cherokee Nation v. Georgia* (1831), *United States v. Kagama* (1886), *Oliphant v. Suquamish Indian Tribe* (1978), and *Nevada v. Hicks* (2001). Additionally, statutes have undermined the sovereignty of Native American nations; such statutes include the Indian Removal Act (1830), the General Allotment Act (Dawes Act) (1887), the Major Crimes Act (1885), House Concurrent Resolution 108 (1953), and Public Law 280 (1953). Moreover, in 1871 Congress unilaterally passed legislation formally ending the treaty-making powers of Native American nations.

Native American sovereignty has changed as a result of U.S. Supreme Court decisions. Chief Justice John Marshall in three seminal decisions laid the foundations for the abrogation of Native American sovereignty. In *Johnson v. M'Intosh* (1823), the sovereignty and independence of Native American nations was "diminished." In *Cherokee Nation v. Georgia* (1831), the Supreme Court described Native Americans as "domestic dependent nations" that were under the protection of the U.S. government. Furthermore, Native Americans lost the right to interact in international relations but kept their internal sovereignty. In *Worcester v. Georgia* (1832), the Supreme Court held that the Cherokee possessed self-government, even though it was dependent on the United States. These three cases have defined the basic construct of Native American sovereignty, and subsequent cases have limited tribal sovereignty.

The cases that have had a direct effect upon Native American sovereignty include *Oliphant v. Suquamish Indian Tribe* (1978), in which the Court denied that a tribal court has criminal jurisdiction over a non-Native American on a reservation. This was one of the most destructive erosions of tribal sovereignty. In *Nevada v. Hicks* (2001), the Supreme Court ruled that a tribal court lacked jurisdiction and authority to hear a civil lawsuit against state officials. Justice Sandra Day O'Connor took the view that the unanimous decision of the Court undermined the right of tribal authority to make and be governed by its own laws.

However, contemporary sovereignty of tribal governments includes the authority to define their own citizenship, and to tax, license, and regulate lands and resources. Criminal and civil laws can be established, to be ruled upon by tribal courts. Tribal government can be developed, structured, and controlled. Additionally, Native American nations have sovereign immunity: inherent sovereignty that predates the U.S. Constitution, general exclusion of state law, and extraconstitutional tribal powers (that is, the U.S. Constitution does not bind or restrict tribes). A "trust relationship" also exists, based on treaties with the federal government, which protects land, assets, and treaty rights. Additionally, tribal governments are responsible for a plethora of governmental activities, which include education, health, housing, social services, court services, and natural resources. Intertwined here is the authority of tribes to protect and preserve their culture, heritage, language, history, and traditions.

To Native Americans, sovereignty is a constantly evolving concept that is defined by the U.S. Supreme Court—the federal government, which continues to have the right to extinguish any aspect of tribal sovereignty—and, more importantly, by Native American nations who can directly influence Congress to protect their sovereignty. Many tribes describe themselves as sovereign nations because they assert that the U.S. government has never conquered them. Native American nations are defending their sovereign right to land, water, and hunting rights through treaties and are advancing their claims through the United Nations and in the international arena.

Dewi I. Ball

See also *Cherokee Nation v. Georgia*, 1831; Government-to-Government Relationship; *Johnson v. M'Intosh*, 1823; *Oliphant v. Suquamish Indian Tribe*, 1978; Plenary Power; Treaty; *Worcester v. Georgia*, 1832.

References and Further Reading

Anderson, Terry L. 1995. *Sovereign Nations or Reservations? An Economic History of American Indians.* San Francisco: Pacific Research Institute for Public Policy.

Pommersheim, Frank. 1995. *Braid of Feathers: American Indian Law and Contemporary Tribal Life.* Berkeley: University of California Press.

Wilkins, David E., and K. Tsianina Lomawaima. 2001. *Uneven Ground: American Indian Sovereignty and Federal Law.* Norman: University of Oklahoma Press.

Specific Claims (Canada)

The relationship between First Nations and the Crown (the British Crown and the Canadian government) has generally been characterized by negotiation and treaty making. However, Canada has not always honored its obligations under treaties or other agreements; the specific claims process was

created in 1973 by the federal government in an attempt to deal with outstanding grievances of First Nations.

Even though the specific claims process became part of public policy in 1973, until 1984 the government of Canada continued to argue before the courts that any federal obligation was of only a political nature. In 1984, however, the Supreme Court of Canada established that the federal government's obligation to protect the reserve lands and other rights of aboriginal peoples constituted a legally enforceable fiduciary obligation (*Guerin v. The Queen*, [1984] 2 S.C.R. 335).

A specific claim can exist in relation to an unfulfilled treaty obligation, an obligation under another agreement or the Indian Act, the mismanagement of funds or other assets (timber, minerals, etc.), or the unlawful surrender or sale of land. From time to time, a specific claim is submitted alleging that an incorrect amount of land was allocated for a reserve; such actions are known as treaty land entitlement (TLE) claims.

Specific claims are subject to a five-step process. First, a First Nation must make a formal submission of its claim(s) to the Specific Claims Branch of the Department of Indian and Northern Affairs. Second, all the evidence presented by the First Nation is reviewed by the government. Third, the Department of Justice produces a legal opinion on the validity of the claim. The federal government then determines whether or not it has an outstanding obligation to the First Nation.

If the claim is accepted, it proceeds to the fourth step, negotiations between the federal government and the First Nation to draft an agreement-in-principle (AIP). Once the AIP is finalized, it becomes the settlement agreement. The fifth and final step is the implementation of the settlement agreement in a formal signing ceremony. If the claim is rejected by the federal government, the First Nation has three possible courses of action. It can submit additional information for further assessment of the claim; it can ask the Indian Claims Commission (ICC), an independent body created in 1991, to intervene and review the claim at issue; or it can undertake litigation.

Over the past twenty-two years, a total of 1,154 specific claims from across Canada have been submitted to the Specific Claims Branch of the Department of Indian and Northern Affairs. Of this total, 528 are currently under review, and 110 are under negotiation. The remaining 516 claims have either been settled (235), have been found not to have a lawful obligation (80), have been resolved under administrative remedy (31), are actively being litigated (61), have been closed (65), or are under review by the Indian Specific Claims Commission (44).

There is no set time period for a specific claim to pass through all of the steps from submission to implementation. In fact, a primary complaint of First Nations has been that the claims process is so arduous that a large number of claims have remained stagnant at the research step for more than a decade. Although it can happen that a claim is settled within a year, some claims have been in the process for as long as eighteen years. The average time to reach settlement is ten years.

Perhaps the most fundamental criticism levied against the Specific Claims process by aboriginal peoples is that, under the process, the government of Canada enjoys the position as final arbitrator of disputes in which it is an interested party. The government has the sole power to decide whether it has violated a lawful obligation and, if so, what damages are appropriate.

A recent federal government initiative was the introduction of Bill C-6, the Specific Claims Resolution Act, into the House of Commons on June 13, 2002. The aim of the bill is to speed up the resolution of specific claims and increase independence in the validation of claims as well as the determination of settlements. Bill C-6 has gone through a first and second reading in the House of Commons and was submitted to the House of Commons Standing Committee on Aboriginal Affairs in the fall of 2002.

This bill would remove the existing Indian Claims Commission (an investigative body) and create the Canadian Centre for the Resolution of First Nations Specific Claims. This centre would encompass both a commission for the review and research of submitted claims and a tribunal to hold hearings and make decisions on compensation.

Many First Nations have rejected Bill C-6, noting that the federal government retains unilateral authority to make appointments to both the commission and the tribunal. First Nations would rather see a joint decision-making power for appointments. The bill also narrows the extent of matters that specific claims can address by excluding from the process unilateral undertakings by the Crown and modern land claims agreements, as well as narrowing the specific treaty obligations that can be addressed only to land (excluding other assets).

In addition, under Bill C-6 a cap of $7 million (CDN) is placed on compensation. This cap can be increased or decreased at the will of the tribunal and can include interest and legal costs as well. The cap will severely limit the number of claims that can be submitted to the tribunal; to date, only three settlements, according to the Indian Claims Commission, have been for less than $7 million. With such limited powers, it is unlikely that the creation of the tribunal for the resolution of First Nations' specific claims will do much to alter current problems with the system.

Anjali Choksi and Lysane Cree

See also Sovereignty; Treaty; Trust Doctrine; Trust Responsibility.
References and Further Reading
Allen, Robert S. 1992. *His Majesty's Indian Allies: British Indian Policy in the Defence of Canada, 1774–1815.* Toronto and Oxford: Dundurn Press.
Dickason, Olive Patricia. 1992. *Canada's First Nations: A History of Founding Peoples from Earliest Times.* Norman: University of Oklahoma Press.
St. Germain, Jill. 2001. *Indian Treaty-Making Policy in the United States and Canada 1867–1877.* Lincoln and London: University of Nebraska Press.

State-Recognized Tribes

State-recognized tribes are Indian communities acknowledged as legal entities by the state governments in which they reside. The term is used generally to set these groups apart from federally recognized tribes, although communities such as the Poarch Creeks of Alabama and the Eastern band of Cherokees of North Carolina are recognized as both state and federal tribes. In the 1990s, thirty-eight states had some form of relationship with the Native communities within their borders. States with historically significant dealings with the tribes in their jurisdictions include Maine, Connecticut, Massachusetts, New York, Virginia, the Carolinas, Georgia, Alabama, Louisiana, and Texas. State-recognized tribes vary considerably in their community composition, political organization, and racial makeup.

Following the Revolutionary War, many states assumed trust responsibility for their Indian populations. Tribes such as the Mashantucket Pequot of Connecticut came to live on state reserves set apart from non-Native inhabitants. Unprotected by federal Indian agents and the full force of Indian law, however, many eastern tribes experienced land loss, assimilation pressures, and economic depravation. During the 1960s and 1970s, the Coalition of Eastern Native Americans (CENA) and the Native American Rights Fund helped state-recognized tribes reinvigorate their communities, pursue land claims, and reassert their Indian identities. In response, states such as North Carolina and Louisiana established Indian commissions to administer state and federal programs for these tribes. Texas, Alabama, Louisiana, and other states also began to recognize actively non-federal groups such as the Tiguas, Poarch Creeks, and Houmas. States faced criticism for lacking standards when acknowledging tribes; as a result, many states, such as Virginia, developed formal recognition criteria modeled directly on the Bureau of Indian Affairs' Federal Acknowledgment Process (FAP).

State recognition provides benefits for groups but is inferior to federal tribal status. After state acknowledgment, groups can qualify for federal Indian programs emanating from the Department of Health and Human Services and the Department of Education, and other general programs of the Departments of Labor, Commerce, and Justice. With a combination of federal grants and aid from the North Carolina Commission of Indian Affairs, the Lumbee Regional Development Association, for example, administers Job Training Partnership Act (JTPA) programs, low-income housing funds, and educational projects for its members. Under the now-defunct Texas Indian Commission, the Alabama Coushatta and Tigua tribes ran successful tourist programs on tax-exempt state reservations, using the proceeds to raise the educational and income levels of their members. Less tangible but also important, Louisiana and other states issue identification cards that tribal members can use to validate their identities. State recognition also confers eligibility for certain affirmative action programs. State tribal status, however, essentially does not alter a tribe's relationship within the federal system. State tribes cannot exercise full tribal sovereignty, pursue Indian gaming, or qualify for federal Indian programs of the Bureau of Indian Affairs and Indian Health Service. Members of state tribes are citizens of the states in which they reside and are subject to local civil and criminal laws; state reservations are not "Indian country" within the meaning of constitutional law.

The genetic and community composition of state tribes varies tremendously. Some, like the Jena Choctaw of Louisiana, have a high degree of Indian ancestry, whereas others have intermarried with non-Indians and possess significant degrees of African and European ancestry. In terms of population, most are small, such as the MOWA (Mobile-Washington) Choctaw of Alabama; however, the Lumbee of North Carolina have more than forty thousand members, and the Houma of Louisiana have more than seventeen thousand, ranking them among the nation's largest Indian groups. In political organization, state tribes also vary markedly. While the once-state-recognized Tigua tribe of Texas maintained a formal tribal structure similar to the Pueblos of New Mexico, most tribes are more loosely organized around family, European-imposed churches, or town governments. Currently, most state tribes are experiencing renewed pride in their Indian heritage. Many are undergoing a significant cultural rebirth, sponsoring cultural programs, powwows, and ethnic exchanges with related Indian peoples. Members of state-recognized tribes are also active in modern indigenous concerns, lobbying for the protection of grave sites, pressing for the repatriation of funeral remains, and protesting negative media portrayals of Native Americans. State-recognized groups have been at the center of federal acknowledgment debates as well; the vast majority are currently seeking federal tribal acknowledgment.

Mark Edwin Miller

See also Bureau of Indian Affairs (BIA); Executive Order Reservations; Federal Acknowledgment Process (FAP); Indian Country; Public Law 280, 1953; Treaty; Trust.

References and Further Reading

Clow, Richmond L., and Imre Sutton., eds. 2001. *Trusteeship in Change: Toward Tribal Autonomy in Resource Management.* Boulder: University Press of Colorado.

Hauptman, Laurence M. 1988. *Formulating American Indian Policy in New York State, 1970–1986.* Albany: State University Press of New York.

Miller, Mark Edwin. 2004. *Forgotten Tribes: Unrecognized Indians and the Federal Acknowledgment Process.* Lincoln: University of Nebraska Press.

Taylor, Theodore W. 1972. *The States and Their Indian Citizens.* Washington, DC: Department of the Interior.

Wilkinson, Charles. 2005. *Blood Struggle: The Rise of Modern Indian Nations.* New York and London: W.W. Norton.

Supremacy Clause

Article VI of the U.S. Constitution accords federal statutes and treaties coequal status as supreme law of the land under the Constitution. Thus, no federal statute or treaty can violate the Constitution, for it has superior status. Similarly, no state law, be it legislation, judicial decision, or executive action, can violate federal law.

Specifically, the supremacy clause of Article VI says:

> This Constitution, and the Laws of the United States which shall be made in Pursuance thereof; and all Treaties made, or which shall be made, under the Authority of the United States, shall be the supreme Law of the Land; and the Judges in every State shall be bound thereby, any Thing in the Constitution or Laws of any State to the Contrary notwithstanding. (U.S. Constitution, Article VI)

The legal doctrine that derives from the supremacy clause is known as the preemption doctrine. Essentially, the preemption doctrine holds that, where state laws and federal laws are at odds on a given subject, the state laws will be preempted and therefore nullified. Federal judges often use this rule to invalidate conflicting state law, and it has been used to make federal agency regulations issued pursuant to statutory authority superior to conflicting state law as well. Preemption can be either express or implied.

When a challenged state law is confronted with express preemption, the only question for the judge is whether Congress intended to do so in the express language of the federal law. However, when implied preemption occurs, the judge must look beyond the statutory language to determine whether Congress has "occupied the field" that the state law attempts to regulate, whether there is a direct conflict in the application of state law with superior federal law, or whether giving effect to state law would frustrate federal purposes.

With regard to Native American tribes and reservations, it is the preemption doctrine that generally keeps at bay state regulation of Indian affairs within Indian country. Because treaties preempt state law, states are prohibited from regulating activities covered by treaty terms, such as those commonly provided for reservation hunting and fishing, even if those treaties are two hundred years old.

Likewise, because federal statutes preempt state law, states are prohibited from regulating activities covered explicitly by statutory provision.

Consequently, the supremacy clause works to help create a sovereignty shield around most tribes and reservations, protecting them from interference by the surrounding state. Without it, Arizona or New Mexico, for example, would be able to freely regulate, tax, or otherwise restrict any activity within the vast Navajo reservation on the same basis as nonreservation areas within the state's borders. Indeed, federal courts now tend to rely more on the preemption doctrine to limit state regulation in Indian country than on the older theory of inherent Indian sovereign status alone.

The Supreme Court explicitly applied the preemption doctrine in the 1973 case *McClanahan v. Arizona State Tax Commission*, wherein Arizona attempted to assert income tax liability against a member of the Navajo tribe for income earned while on the reservation. Writing for the majority, Justice Thurgood Marshall articulated the Court's preference for preemption while not throwing Indian sovereignty theory out completely:

> [T]he trend has been away from the idea of inherent Indian sovereignty as a bar to state jurisdiction and toward reliance on federal pre-emption. The modern cases thus tend to avoid reliance on platonic notions of Indian sovereignty and to look instead to the applicable treaties and statutes which define the limits of state power. The Indian sovereignty doctrine is relevant, then, not because it provides a definitive resolution of the issues in this suit, but because it provides a backdrop against which the applicable treaties and federal statutes must be read. (Marshall *McClanahan*, 164)

Michael J. Kelly

See also Domestic Dependent Nation; Indian Country; Plenary Power; Sovereignty; Treaty; Trust Doctrine.

References and Further Reading

Cipollone v. Liggett Group, Inc., 505 U.S. 504 (1992).
McClanahan v. Arizona State Tax Commission, 411 U.S. 164 (1973).
Pommersheim, Frank. 1997. *Braid of Feathers: American Indian Law and Contemporary Tribal Life.* Berkeley, Los Angeles, and London: University of California Press.
Silkwood v. Kerr-McGee Corp., 464 U.S. 238 (1984).
Wilkins, David E., and K. Tsianina Lomawaima. 2001. *Uneven Ground: American Indian Sovereignty and Federal Law.* Norman and London: University of Oklahoma Press.
Williams, Robert A., Jr. 1990. *The American Indian in Western Legal Thought: The Discourses of Conquest.* New York and Oxford: Oxford University Press.

Termination

Termination emerged as a federal government policy toward Native Americans in 1953. The government wanted to assimilate Native American tribes and tribal members into the broader U.S. population. The Department of the Interior drove this movement to remove Native Americans from their trustee status and to terminate federal responsibility toward Indian people and their tribes.

Although there was not one all-encompassing termination law, House Concurrent Resolution (HCR) 108 provided the foundation for the individual termination bills that appeared before Congress during the 1950s. HCR 108 indicated that all Indians within the United States were to assume all the rights and responsibilities of American citizens. This included being subject to the same U.S. laws that applied to other Americans (*House Report* no. 841). Senator Arthur Watkins of Utah, who also chaired the Senate Subcommittee on Indian Affairs, and Senator Henry M. Jackson of Washington both adamantly believed that termination was the course to equality for Native Americans. Jackson introduced HCR 108 during the 83rd Congress, and on August 1, 1953, Congress adopted it. Congressional recognition did not make it law, but recognition did mean that Congress agreed with the fundamentals of the bill and that it supported a termination policy for Indian tribes (Fixico 1986, 97).

A second force building the momentum to terminate Native American tribes was Public Law (P.L.) 280, which provided for the jurisdictional transfer of criminal and civil matters from Indian tribal control to state control. If the federal government planned to terminate its bureaucratic responsibilities to tribes, the government had to make sure that systems were in place to support an assimilated Indian population.

Following the Korean War, HCR 108 and P.L. 280 both emerged as policies of the U.S. government, not as a result of requests from Native Americans or tribes. Tribes were not consulted regarding

creation of the legislation, nor did anyone ask them whether they desired these changes. After President Dwight Eisenhower approved P.L. 280, he requested Congress to amend it in the following year to include provisions for consultation. Amendments were written, but none were passed. The tribes and tribal members had no voice in the early termination discussions. This was a part of the federal government's effort to withdraw federal responsibilities and for American Indians to apply for state services.

Zealous pursuit of termination as a viable federal policy had begun to wane by the end of the 1950s. Ultimately, 13,263 Indians, or about 3 percent of the total Indian population at that time, would lose their federal trust (Prucha 1995, 1058). Two of the first groups to be terminated, the Menominee of Wisconsin and the Klamath of Oregon, regained federal recognition after decades of battle with the government. Their regaining federal acknowledgement as tribes began a new era of "restoration" in federal-Indian affairs.

Termination was proffered as a simple solution to the complicated relationships between Native American tribes and the federal government. It turned out to be unworkable and costly, and the adversarial atmosphere it created between tribes and the government undoubtedly fueled the Red Power movement of the 1960s.

Laurie Arnold

See also Assimilation; House Concurrent Resolution 108, 1953; *Menominee Tribe of Indians v. United States*, 1968; Public Law 280, 1953; Watkins, Arthur V.

References and Further Reading

Burt, Larry W. 1982. *Tribalism in Crisis: Federal Indian Policy, 1953–1961*. Albuquerque: University of New Mexico Press.

Fixico, Donald L. 1986. *Termination and Relocation: Federal Indian Policy, 1945–1960*. Albuquerque: University of New Mexico Press.

Philp, Kenneth R. 1999. *Termination Revisited: American Indians on the Trail to Self-Determination, 1933–1953*. Lincoln and London: University of Nebraska Press.

Prucha, Francis Paul. 1995. *The Great Father: The United States Government and the American Indians*. Lincoln: University of Nebraska Press.

U.S. Congress. House. HR Con. Res. 108, 83rd Cong., 1st sess. *67 U.S. Statutes at Large* B132; House Report no. 841, 83-I, serial II666.

U. S. Congress. House. Public Law No. 280, § 7, *67 U.S. Statutes at Large* 588–590; House Report no. 848, 83-I, serial II666.

Treaty

A treaty is a binding international agreement made between two or more sovereign nations governed by international law. The European powers that discovered North America used the treaty process as a means of acquiring lands and implicitly acknowledged the bone fide (rightful) sovereignty of the landowners—the Native American nations. Treaties were used for many purposes, and these included land acquisition by the United States, cessation of hostilities, the transference of goods and annuities, trade and commerce, and protection. The treaty process continued with the U.S. government; the first treaty signed between the United States and the Delaware Nation was the Treaty of Fort Pitt, Pennsylvania, on September 17, 1778. This treaty was one of peace, which ceased all hostilities between the two nations; it provided articles of clothing, food, tools of war, and trade. Furthermore, the Delaware allowed the safe passage of U.S. troops through their land. The U.S. government continued to sign treaties with Native Americans until March 3, 1871, when Congress abrogated that right as a rider on an appropriations bill. Agreements continued to be made until 1914—the Ute Mountain Utes engaged in the final agreement with the United States; nearly four hundred ratified treaties and agreements were made between the federal government and Native American nations. Under Article VI, Section 2 of the U.S. Constitution, treaties conducted and made by the United States are the supreme law of the land and are binding thereafter. Treaties have formed and do form the sovereign and governmental link between the United States and the Native American nations. Moreover, treaties underline the inherent sovereignty of the Native American nations as a consequence of their power and authority, deriving from their ownership of the land since "time immemorial."

The relationship between the United States and the Native Americans has undergone transformation; Native Americans, once considered sovereign nations capable of interacting in international relations, are now considered dependent on the federal government. In *Johnson v. M'Intosh* (1823) the Supreme Court ruled that Native American tribes were occupants and thus did not own the lands and could only transfer land to the United States. This was further qualified in *Cherokee Nation v. Georgia* (1831), in which Native American nations were defined not as foreign states but as "domestic dependent nations" under the protection of the United States. Thus, a dichotomy existed between the tribes' ability to conduct treaties with the United States (primarily land cessations and the establishment of reservations) and the incapability of Native American nations to act in international affairs. In *Worcester v. Georgia* (1832), Chief Justice John Marshall ruled that states had no jurisdiction in Native American territory and thus acknowledged that tribal nations had a form of sovereignty. Conversely, Marshall acknowledged that the first treaty between the Delaware and the United States was akin to the model of treaties made between the crowned heads of Europe.

Although the right of Native American tribes to engage in treaty making was annulled, the treaties concluded before 1871 were still binding upon all parties to them; they are still enforced today and are protected under the U.S. Constitution. Conversely, many treaties have been broken and dishonored by the government, many were unilaterally amended by the Senate prior to ratification, and many have been ruled by the Supreme Court to have been annulled by successive acts of Congress, particularly the General Allotment Act of 1887.

In 1871, when Native American treaty-making rights were abrogated, their sovereign status had already began to diminish. It declined further through congressional statutes and Supreme Court decisions. Many cases have declared treaties void; in *Lone Wolf v. Hitchcock* (1903), the Supreme Court declared that Congress had the unilateral authority to abrogate a treaty. Conversely, some cases have ruled in favor of Native American treaty rights. Treaties have been important to Native American nations; in *United States v. Winans* (1905), the Supreme Court referred to treaties as a grant of rights from Native Americans to the United States and not a grant of rights to the Native Americans, thus illustrating that Native Americans had owned the land since "time immemorial." In *Minnesota v. Mille Lacs Band of Chippewa Indians* (1999), the Court ruled that the Chippewa retained the hunting and fishing rights—usufructuary rights—guaranteed to them by the Treaty of 1837. Treaties continue to be the bulwark and the standard bearer of Native American sovereignty. Thus, many centuries later, the treaties remain good law, protected by the Constitution of the United States of America.

Dewi I. Ball

See also Fort Pitt, Pennsylvania; General Allotment Act (Dawes Act), 1887; Government-to-Government Relationship; *Mille Lacs Band v. Minnesota*, 1999; Sovereignty; Trail of Broken Treaties; Treaty with the Delaware–September 17, 1778; *Worcester v. Georgia*, 1832.

References and Further Reading

Prucha, Francis Paul. 1994. *American Indian Treaties: The History of a Political Anomaly*. Berkeley, Los Angeles, and London: University of California Press.

Wilkins, David E., and K. Tsianina Lomawaima. 2001. *Uneven Ground: American Indian Sovereignty and Federal Law*. Norman: University of Oklahoma Press.

Williams, Robert A., Jr. 1990. *The American Indian in Western Legal Thought: The Discourses of Conquest*. New York and Oxford: Oxford University Press.

Trust Doctrine

The evolution of the trust relationship between the United States and American Indian tribes can be traced back to the papal bull *Inter Caetera* (Alexander VI, May 4, 1493), which required training and instruction for the indigenous peoples of the Americas, along with a grant of authority to colonize such lands. An assumption of this responsibility was implicit in the subsequent transfer of claim from one sovereign to another throughout American history. The United States inherited this responsibility from Great Britain in the Treaty of Paris (1783). This marked the first instance of a general trust relationship between the legal and political predecessors of the United States of America and the indigenous peoples of North America as a whole.

The early Plan of Union marked the first instance of official action by the United States to address the trust relationship. In this plan, a grand council and a president general were to share responsibility for Indian affairs and supervision of relationships with Indians. The decision to maintain federal control over Indian affairs after the American Revolution was likely made to avoid conflicts between the states and tribes.

Although the U.S. Constitution contained no wording as to the exact relationship between the United States and American Indian tribes, it provided the federal government with the authority to deal with the tribes and as such has been held to imply a trust relationship. The Indian commerce clause (Article I, Section 8, clause 3) and the treaty-making powers of the president (Article II, Section 2, clause 2) were the most crucial to this interpretation.

The beginnings of the U.S. Supreme Court's perspective on the trust doctrine were found in Chief Justice Marshall's decision in *Cherokee Nation v. Georgia* (30 U.S. [5 Pet.] 1 [1831]). In this case, Marshall characterized American Indian tribes as "domestic dependent nations." He stated that the relationship between the federal government and the tribes "resembles that of a ward to his guardian" (ibid., 17).

During the treaty-making era, the United States signed 374 treaties with American Indian tribes. Many of these treaties contain language that established a protectorate or fiduciary relationship between the United States and American Indian tribes. The Supreme Court recognized the treaty basis of the trust relationship in *United States v. Kagama* (118 U.S. 375, 384–85 [1886]).

It was in *Lone Wolf v. Hitchcock* (187 U.S. 553 [1903]) that the Supreme Court espoused a view of the plenary authority of the U.S. Congress as it derives from the trust relationship. In this case, the Court found that a treaty provision could not limit the ability of Congress to act "in respect to the care and protection of the Indians."

More recently, the cases *United States v. Mitchell* (445 U.S. 535 [1980]), *United States v. Mitchell* (463 U.S. 206 [1983]), *United States v. Navajo Nation* (537 U.S. 488 [2003]), and *United States v. White Mountain Apache Tribe* (537 U.S. 465 [2003]) have further defined the view of the Supreme Court in addressing the trust responsibility. In the Mitchell cases, the Court addressed the multiple doctrines concerning the trust obligations between the United States and American Indian tribes. Especially important in these cases was the distinction between what is known as a *general trust* responsibility (that the United States is obligated to act in the best interest of American Indian tribes—does not indicate a fiduciary duty), a *limited trust* (as in the case of the General Allotment Act [25 U.S.C. § 348], in which the federal government is required to act only in a specific sense short of fiduciary responsibilities), and an *express trust* (as found in the case of the Indian Long-Term Leasing Act [25 U.S.C. § 396], in which the federal government has specific responsibilities, including fiduciary duties). A fiduciary obligation may be found both in an express trust situation and in what may be called an *implicit trust* situation, in which the United States has control or supervision of American Indian resources. In the last instance, such control would need to exceed the level considered to be limited, as in the first *Mitchell* case.

In the later two cases, the Supreme Court distinguished between an enforceable duty and a nonenforceable duty as it relates to the trust doctrine. In *Navajo Nation*, the Supreme Court found that, although the Indian Mineral Leasing Act required the secretary of the interior's approval of any mineral leases negotiated by a tribe, it did not imply an enforceable duty to protect the best interest of tribes in the process. In *White Mountain Apache Tribe*, the Supreme Court found that the United States was responsible for maintaining Fort Apache, which was held in trust for the tribe as expressed in Public Law 86–392 (74 *Stat.* 8, 1960). The statute expressly stated that the secretary has the right to use the fort, which it currently occupies and supervises. These cases are examples of express (*Navajo Nation*) and implicit (*White Mountain Apache Tribe*) trust relationships.

The principles of federal Indian law derive from the unique legal and political relationship between tribes and the federal government. The general trust relationship between the United States and American Indian tribes was not necessarily defined in any particular piece of legislation, treaty, or court case, although it was often referred to in principle for the same. This kind of trust is similar to Executive Order 13175, signed by President Bill Clinton in the year 2000. An example of an implicit trust situation is found in the recent case *Cobell v. Norton* (No. 96–1285), where the Department of the Interior has argued that common-law fiduciary duties do not apply to the Indian trust fund. U.S. District Judge Royce Lamberth suggested otherwise in stating that the range of duties for the department and the nature of such duties "are coextensive with the duties imposed upon trustees at common law."

Martin Reinhardt

See also Bureau of Indian Affairs (BIA); Sovereignty; Treaty; *Worcester v. Georgia*, 1832.

References and Further Reading

Canby, William. 1998. *American Indian Law in a Nutshell.* St. Paul: West.

Deloria, Vine, Jr., and Wilkins, David. 1999. *Tribes, Treaties, and Constitutional Tribulations.* Austin: University of Texas Press.

Native American Law Report, 1(October 2003): 91–92.

Trust Land

Under U.S. law, the Supreme Court, in a series of cases that include *Johnson v. M'Intosh* (1823), and the federal government, in several legislative enactments that include the General Allotment Act and Indian Reorganization Act, recognized that, in accordance with Indian tribal government's "domestic dependent" status, the United States held a trust relationship to Indian tribal governments. As a result of this trust relationship, the United States is the legal title holder of trust assets of Indian tribes and individual Indians, including land. Trust land is real property that may be held in trust for an Indian tribe or an individual. Although the United States holds legal title to the land, an Indian tribe or individual Indian holds beneficial title—the use and benefits that derive from the property.

Historically, Indian tribal government ownership of lands set aside as reservations gradually eroded as a result of the federal government's allotment policies of the late nineteenth and early twentieth centuries. An Indian affairs social reform movement, arising first outside and then within the federal government, called for the legislative measures to be implemented to restore and protect Indian lands. Reformers noted that tribal governments' loss of a geographic base resulted in crippling Indian poverty throughout the United States. Consequently, in 1934 the U.S. Congress authorized the secretary of the interior to take land in trust for the benefit of Indians under the Indian Reorganization Act. Today that section is codified as 25 U.S.C. §465.

By 1999, there were roughly fifty-five million acres of tribal lands held in trust by the federal government and nearly eleven million acres held in trust for individuals Indians. As a general rule, state and local laws regarding matters such as taxation, zoning, and land use have no application on Indian trust lands. Although this is the general rule, P.L. 280 enables certain states to exercise criminal and civil jurisdiction over tribal lands within their borders. An Indian tribe and a state might enter into a compact or cooperative agreement to clarify the role of courts or law enforcement on trust lands when the relationship is legally uncertain or when authorized or mandated by Congress. For instance, public roads crossing trust lands may legally be considered Indian country, but the practical implications for law enforcement may be unclear.

Because the United States is legal title holder, the federal government is a necessary part in all leases and dispositions of resources including trust land. For example, the secretary of the interior must approve any contract for payment or grant by an Indian tribe for services for the tribe "relative to their lands" (25 U.S.C. §81).

Today, Indian tribes may request the federal government to acquire additional land in trust by purchase or acquisition from surplus federal lands, including former military bases. Indian tribal governments may acquire land through the approval of the Department of the Interior application and regulatory process pursuant to 25 U.S.C. §465 and 25 C.F.R. §151 or legislatively conferred trust status. The applicable federal regulations were subsequently modified and now require the BIA to notify "the state and local governments having regulatory jurisdiction over the land to be acquired" and to provide those governments with a thirty-day time period "in which to provide written comment as to the acquisition's potential impacts on regulatory jurisdiction" (25 C.F.R. § 151.11[d] 2004). Placement of newly acquired tribal land into trust has impacts on tribes as well as state and local governments. The land-into-trust process under the regulations is rigorous, requiring the secretary to review several criteria, including Indian tribes' need for the land, the purpose for which the land will be used, the impact on the state and local political subdivisions (especially concerning taxation and any jurisdictional considerations), and compliance with National Environmental Protection Act of 1969.

The status of trust lands has seen the most profound criticism in the context of Indian gaming. All gaming and gaming-related acquisitions must be approved by the assistant secretary, pursuant to the Indian Gaming Regulatory Act. The practice of placing land into trust for proposed gaming facilities is especially contentious for land outside an Indian tribe's aboriginal homeland. Such off-reservation trust acquisitions must still be formally approved by the Bureau of Indian Affairs. The tribe must also submit an application and supporting documents to the BIA requesting such approval under 25 U.S.C. §465 and pursuant to 25 C.F.R. Part 151.

Litigation challenging the Department of the Interior's trust acquisition authority—on the grounds that 25 U.S.C. § 465 is an unconstitutional delegation of legislative power to the Department of Interior because the statute contains no express limits on the secretary's discretion and no judicial review standards—has met with little success. Courts have found that 25 U.S.C. § 465 does in fact place limits on the secretary's discretion, and the legislative history identifies goals by which a court may examine the secretary's discretion, including "rehabilitating the Indian's economic life" and "developing the initiative destroyed by . . . oppression and paternalism," and must assure continued "beneficial use by the Indian occupant and his heirs."

Peter D. Lepsch

See also Bureau of Indian Affairs (BIA); *Cherokee Nation v. Georgia,* 1831; Sovereignty; Treaty; Trust.

References and Further Reading

Clow, Richmond, and Imre Sutton, eds. 2001. *Trusteeship in Change: Toward Tribal Autonomy in Resource Management.* Boulder: University Press of Colorado.

Deloria, Vine, Jr., and David E. Wilkins. 1999. *Tribes, Treaties, and Constitutional Tribulations.* Austin: University of Texas Press.

Pommersheim, Frank. 1995. *Braid of Feathers: American Indian Law and Contemporary Tribal Life.* Berkeley, Los Angeles, and London: University of California Press.

Prucha, Francis Paul. 1994. *American Indian Treaties: The History of a Political Anomaly.* Berkeley: University of California Press.

Wilkins, David E., and K. Tsianina Lomawaima. 2001. *Uneven Ground: American Indian Sovereignty and Federal Law.* Norman: University of Oklahoma Press.

Williams, C. Herb, and Walt Neubrech. 1976. *Indian Treaties: American Nightmare.* Seattle, WA: Outdoor Empire.

Williams, Robert A. 1997. *Linking Arms Together: American Indian Treaty Visions of Law and Peace, 1600–1800.* New York: Oxford University Press.

Trust Responsibility

The definition of the relationship between the U.S. government and the Indian nations of the land evolved over the first century of American history from one of theoretical equals to one of subservience and dependency. The trust responsibility of the federal government is the result of that transition.

The U.S. Constitution recognized that Indian tribes had sovereignty just as other European nations did. Of course, the Constitution was written at a time when most tribes existed outside the borders of the United States on land that was often in dispute with European colonial powers. Because of these disputes, tribes were able to exert influence on the balance of power on the continent, as the con-

stantly shifting alliances were pertinent to all conflicts from the colonial wars of the early eighteenth century through the War of 1812. Often militarily and politically powerful at a time when the United States was not, groups such as the Iroquois Confederacy were able to retain their sovereignty.

As the United States grew in population, territory, and military power, however, the balance of power on the continent shifted away from the Indian nations. Although the Constitution still held that a nation-to-nation relationship existed, many politicians and frontier settlers believed that the United States could claim Indian land by right of conquest.

The conflict between theory and reality was put to the test during the 1830s, when the Supreme Court ruled on a number of cases that, along with President Andrew Jackson's actions, would have long-lasting repercussions for Indian nations. The case of *Cherokee Nation v. Georgia* in 1831 stated that the tribes were not nations in the European sense but rather "domestic dependent nations," to be regulated by the federal government. In the decision of 1832 in *Worcester v. Georgia,* the Supreme Court ruled that, because the Cherokee tribe was thusly sovereign, it was therefore exempt from the laws of the state of Georgia.

This seeming diminution and, at the same time, reinforcement of tribal sovereignty forms the rationale and the basis for the trust relationship. As domestic dependent nations under the protection of the federal government, the United States assumed a responsibility to enforce treaty agreements and protect Indian interests. This responsibility has played out in numerous areas, ranging from land, water, and natural resource rights to health care, among others.

The power inherent in this relationship was designed to protect tribes from state abuse, but, ironically, it was used during the late nineteenth and early twentieth centuries to diminish tribal sovereignty. The Supreme Court decisions in *United States v. Kagama* (1886) and *Lone Wolf v. Hitchcock* (1903) gave Congress, as guardian of the tribes, "plenary powers" to make whatever use of tribal resources and whatever decisions in tribal affairs they saw fit, without the courts to serve as arbiter.

In essence, the trust relationship gives all of the branches of the federal government both heightened responsibilities and increased powers over the tribes. The trust relationship has existed to protect Indians and Indian groups, but it has done neither. The history of enforcement—or the lack thereof—of treaties

between the federal government and Indian nations is evidence enough of federal neglect of the government's responsibilities in the relationship.

Although federal courts have been reluctant to recognize a breach of trust by Congress, during the 1990s President Clinton announced a renewed government-to-government relationship between all parts of the federal government and Indian tribal governments. However, by 1999 it had become clear to the National Congress of American Indians (NCAI) that, once again, the federal government had not met its lofty ideals. In resolution # PSC-99–000, NCAI leaders called attention to the continuing neglect of treaty rights despite the Clinton administration's rhetoric. Even the Bureau of Indian Affairs, the primary federal guardian of Indian rights, is a part of the federal Department of the Interior, the same department that oversees the Bureau of Reclamation and the Bureau of Land Management, two bureaus whose goals have often conflicted and usually superseded those of the Indian tribes (Clarke and McCool 1995).

Over the years, as the tribes have sought to increase sovereignty and self-determination, they have, at times, both relied on the protections and chafed under the paternalistic implications of the trust relationship. The fact that the federal government has been and continues to be uneven in its application of the responsibility and in its protection of Indian treaty rights only serves to increase the apprehension of Indian peoples toward the BIA and the federal government as a whole.

Steven L. Danver

See also *Cherokee Nation v. Georgia*, 1831; *Federal Power Commission v. Tuscarora Indian Nation*, 1960; Indian Civil Rights Act, 1968; *Lone Wolf v. Hitchcock*, 1903; *Menominee Tribe of Indians v. United States*, 1968; Nixon's Message to Congress, July 8, 1970; *Tee-Hit-Ton Indians v. United States*, 1955; Trust Doctrine, Trust Land; *United States v. Kagama*, 1886; *Worcester v. Georgia*, 1832.

References and Further Reading

Clarke, Jeanne Nienaber, and Daniel C. McCool. 1995. *Staking Out the Terrain: Power and Performance of Natural Resource Agencies*. 2nd ed. Albany: State University of New York Press.

Clow, Richmond L., and Imre Sutton. 2001. *Trusteeship in Change: Toward Tribal Autonomy in Resource Management*. Boulder: University Press of Colorado.

Getches, David H. 1998. *Cases and Materials on Federal Indian Law*. 4th ed. Eagan, MN: West.

Prucha, Francis Paul. 1995. *The Great Father: United States Government and the American Indians*. Lincoln: University of Nebraska Press.

Resources

Alternate Tribal Names and Spellings

Tribal Name	Alternate Tribal Name(s)
Abenaki (western)	Alnonba, Abnaki
Absaroke	Crow
Adai	Nateo
Adamstown	Upper Mattaponi
Alabama	Alibamu
Aleut	Alutiiq, Unangan
Anadarko	Nadaco
Anishinabe	Chippewa, Ojibwa
Apache	N de,Tinneh, Dine, Tinde, Unde, Shis Inde, Aravaipa, Bedonkohe, Chihene, Chiricahua, Chokonen, Cibecue, Jicarilla, Kiowa, Lipan, Mescalero, Mimbres, Nednhi, Tonto, Yuma
Apache Mohave	Yavapai
Appomattoc	Apamatuks
Arapahoe	Inunaina, Atsina
Arikara	Northern Pawnee, Ricara, Ree
Assiniboine	Hohe
Athapaskan	Dene
Atsina	Haaninin
Aztec	Nahua, Nahuatl
Bannock	Panaiti
Bear River Indians	Niekeni
Bellabella	Heiltsuqu, Heiltsuk
Bellacoola	Nuxalk
Beothuk	Beathunk, Betoukuag, Macquajeet, Red Indians, Skraelling, Ulno
Blackfeet/Blackfoot	Niitsitapi, Nitsi-tapi, Piegan, Ahpikuni, Pikuni (northern); Siksika, Sisaka (southern), Sihasapa, Ahkainah
Blood	Kainai, Ahkainah
Boothroyd	Chomok
Brule Sioux	Si can gu
Caddo	Adai, Eyeish, Hasinai, Hainai, Kadohodacho, Kadohadacho Confederacy, Natchitoches
Cahuilla	Agua Caliente, Cabazon, Kawasic, Morongo, Los Coyotes, Painakic, Wanikik
Calusa	Caloosa, Calos, Calosa, Carlos, Muspa
Campo	Kumeyaay
Carrier	Dakelh, Wet'suwet'en
Catawba	Esaw, Iswa, Iyeye, Nieye, Ushery
Cayuga	Kweniogwen, Iroquois
Cayuse	Wailetpu, Te-taw-ken
Chakchiuma	Shaktci Homma
Chehalis	Copalis, Humptulips, Qwaya, Satsop, Sts'Ailes, Wynoochee
Chemainus	Tsa-mee-nis

Alternate Tribal Names and Spellings (cont.)

Tribal Name	Alternate Tribal Name(s)
Chemehuevi	Nuwu, Tantawats
Chetco	Tolowa
Cherokee	Tsa-la-gi, Ani-yun-wiya, Anikituhwagi, Keetowah
Cheyenne	Dzi tsi stas, Sowonia (southern), O mi sis (northern), Tse-tsehese-staestse
Chilcotin	Esdilagh, Tl'esqox, Tl'etinqox, Xeni Gwet'in
Chimakum	Aqokdlo
Chippewa	Anishinabe, Ojibwa
Chitimacha	Chawasha, Pantch-pinunkansh, Washa, Yagenechito
Choctaw	Chakchiuma, Chatot, Cha'ta
Chumash	Santa Barbara Indians
Clackamas	Guithlakimas
Clallam	S'klallam, Nusklaim, Tlalem
Cocopah	Xawitt Kunyavaei
Coeur d'Alene	Skitswish, Schee chu'umsch, Schitsu'umsh
Comanche	Detsanayuka, Kotsoteka, Nermernuh, Noconi, Nokoni, Numunuu, Padouca (Sioux word), Penateka, Pennande, Quahadi, Yamparika
Comox	Catloltx
Copane	Kopano, Quevenes
Cora	Nayarit
Coree	Coranine
Coushatta	Koasati, Acoste
Cree	Kenistenoag, Iyiniwok, Nehiawak or Nay-hee-uh-wuk (Plains Cree), Sah-cow-ee-noo-wuk (bush Cree)
Creek	Muscogee, Abihika, Abeika, Hitchiti, Homashko
Crow	Absaroke, Apsaalooke
Cupenos	Kuupangaxwichem
Cuthead	Pabaksa
Dakelh	Carrier
Delaware	Lenni Lenape, Lenape, Abnaki, Alnanbai, Wampanoag, Munsee, Unami, Unalachitgo, Powhatan-Renápe
Dieguenos	Comeya, Tipai, Ipai, Kumeyaay
Ditidaht	Nitinaht
Eskimo	Inuit, Inupiat, Inuvialuit, Yupik, Alutiiq
Equimalt	Is-Whoy-Malth
Fox	Mesquaki, Meskwaki, Mshkwa'kiitha
Gabrieleno	Tongva
Ganawese	Conoys, Piscataways
Gitanyow	Kitwancool
Gitxsan	Tsimshian
Goshute	Kusiutta
Gros Ventre	Atsina (prairie), Hidatsa (Missouri), A'ani', Ah-ah-nee-nin, Minnetaree
Gwich'in	Loucheux
Hainai	Ioni
Havasupai	Suppai
Heiltsuk	Hailhazakv
Hidatsa	Gros Venture
Hohokam	Hoo-hoogam
Hopi	Hopitu, Hopitu Shinumu, Moqui, Hapeka
Hualapai	Hwal'bay, Walapai
Huichol	Wirrarika, Wixalika

Alternate Tribal Names and Spellings (cont.)

Tribal Name	Alternate Tribal Name(s)
Hupa	Natinnohhoi
Huron	Wendat, Wyandot
Ingalik Athapaskans	Deg Het'an
Iowa	Pahodja
Iroquois	Haudenosaunee, Hodenosaunee, Ongwanosionni, Hotinonshonni
Jemez	Tuwa
Jicarilla Apache	Tinde
Kalispel	Pend d'Oreilles
Kamia	Tipai
Kansa	Hutanga, Kansas, Kanza, Kaw,
Kato	Tlokeang
Keres	Pueblo, Acoma, Cochiti, Isleta, Laguna, San Felipe, Santa Ana, Santo Domingo, Zia
Kickapoo	Kiwigapawa
Kiowa	Kwuda, Tepda, Tepkinago, Gaigwu, Kompabianta, Kauigu
Kiowa Apache	Nadiisha Dena
Klamath	Eukshikni Maklaks, Auksni
Klickitat	Qwulhhwaipum
Kootenai	Kuronoqa, Kutenai, Kootenay, Yaqan nukiy, Akun'kunik', Ktunaxa
Koso	Panamint
Karok	Karuk, Arra-arra
Ktunaxa	Kootenay
Kumeyaay	Diegueño, Barona, Sycuan, Viejas, Campo, Cuyapaipe, Ewiiaapaayp
Kutchin	Gwich'in
Kutenai	Asanka
Lancandon	Maya, Hach Winik
Lemhi Shoshone	Agaidika, Salmon Eaters, Tukudika, Sheep Eater
Loucheux	Gwich'in
Lillooet	Lil'wat, St'át'imc, T'it'kit
Lipan	Naizhan
Lower Sioux	Mdewakanton, Wahpekute
Luiseño	Ataxum, La Jolla, Pechanga, Soboba, Quechnajuichom
Lumbee	Cheraw
Maicopa	Xalychidom Piipaash, Pipatsji
Makah	Kwenetchechat, Kwi-dai-da'ch
Mandan	Metutahanke or Mawatani (after 1837), Numakaki (before 1837)
Manhattan	Rechgawawank
Manso	Maise, Mansa, Manse, Manxo, Gorreta, Gorrite, Tanpachoa
Maricopa	Xalychidom Piipaash, Xalchidom Pii-pash, Pipatsje, Pee-posh
Miami	Twightwis, Twa-h-twa-h, Oumameg, Pkiiwileni
Micmac	Mi'kmaq
Miniconjou	Mnikawozu, Mnikowoju, Minnicoujou
Mi'kmaq	Lnu'k, L'nu'k
Missouri	Niutachi
Mixtec	Ñusabi, Nusabi
Moapa	Moapariats
Modoc	Moatokni, Okkowish
Mohave	Mojave, Tzinamaa, Ahamakav, Hamakhava
Mohawk	Kanienkahaka, Kaniengehage, Abenaki, Iroquois, Akwesasne
Mohican	Muh-he-con-neok, Mahikan, Mahican
Molala	Latiwe

Alternate Tribal Names and Spellings (cont.)

Tribal Name	Alternate Tribal Name(s)
Mono	Monache
Moratoc	Nottoway
Mosopelea	Ofom
Munsee	Minasinink, Homenethiki
Muscogee	Creek, Homashko
Nanticoke	Unalachtgo, Onehtikoki
Navajo	Diné, Dineh, Tenuai, Navaho
Nez Perce	Nee-me-poo, Nimipu, Kamuinu, Tsutpeli, Sahaptin, Chopunnish
Nisga'a	Tsimshian
Nootka	Nuu-chah-nulth
Northern Ojibwa	Saulteaux, Sauteux
Nuu-chah-nulth	Nootka
Nuxalk	Kimsquit, Kwalhnmc, South Bentick Sutslmc, Taliyumc
Ogallala	Okandanda
Ojibwa	Chippewa, Anishinabe, Missisauga, Odjbway, Saginaw
Okanagon	Isonkuaili
Omaha	UmonHon
Oneida	Iroquois
Onondaga	Iroquois
Oohenupa	Two Kettle, Oohenonpa
Osage	Wa-Shah-She, Wakon, Wazhazhe
Ottawa	Adawe, Otawaki
Otto	Chewaerae
Oulaouaes	Necariages
Oweekeno	Kwakiutl, Oweehena
Pacheenaht	Nootka
Paiute	Numa, Nuwuvi, Kuyuiticutta
Papagos	Tohono O'odham, Ak-chin, Yohono Au'autam
Parianuc	White River Utes
Passamaquoddy	Peskedemakddi
Patchogue	Unkechaug
Pawnee	Pariki, Panyi, Chahiksichahiks, Ckirihki Kuruuriki
Pechanga	Luiseño
Pecos	Pueblos from Jemez
Pend d'Oreilles	Kalispel
Penobscot	Pannawanbskek, Penaubsket
Petun	Khionontateronon, Tionontati
Piegan	Blood, Kainai, Pikuni, Pigunni, Ahpikuni
Pima	Onk Akimel Au-authm, Akimel O'odham, A-atam, Akimul Au'autam, Tohono O'odham (incorrectly)
Piro	Tortuga
Pit River	Achomawi, Atsugewi
Poosepatuck	Unkechaug
Popolucas	Chochos
Pyramid Lake Paiute	Kuyuidokado
Quapaw	Quapah, Akansea, Ouaguapas, Ugakhpa
Quechan	Yuma
Quileute	Quil-leh-ute
Quinault	Qui-nai-elts
Sac and Fox	Sauk, Asakiwaki, Meshkwakihug, Fox
Sahwnee	Shawadasay

Alternate Tribal Names and Spellings (cont.)

Tribal Name	Alternate Tribal Name(s)
Salish	Okinagan, Slathead
Saanich	Pauquachin, Tsawout, Tsartlip, Tseycum, Malahat
Sans Arc	Itazipco
Santee	Sisseton
Saponi	Monasukapanough
Sauk	Hothaaki, Sac, Sack, Sock, Thakiki
Scioto	(Five Nations of the Scioto Plains) Shawnee, Wyandot, Delaware, Munsee, Seneca
Seminole	Ikaniuksalgi, Alachua, Mikasuki
Seneca	Iroquois
Serrano	Cowangachem, Mohineyam, Qawishwallanavetum, Yuhavitam
Shawnee	Savannah, Chillicothe, Hathawekela, Mequachake, Piqua
Shoshone	Shoshoni, Snake, Nimi, Tukudeka, Agaidika
Sioux	Brule, Dakota, Hunkpapa, Isanyati, Itazipco, Lakota, Mnikawozu, Mnikowoju, Nakota, Ocheti Shakowin, Oglala, Oohenunpa, Sicangu, Sihasapa, Sisseton, Sisitonwan, Teton, Titunwan
Sissipahaw	Haw
Skagit	Humaluh
Skoskomish	Twana
Squinamish	Swinomish
Slotas	Red River Metis
Songish	Lkungen
Southern Paiute	Numa
St. Francis	Abenaki
St. Mary's Indian Band	A'qam, Ktunaxa
St. Regis Mohawk	Akwesasne, Kaniengehage
Stockbridge	Mahican
Snuneymuxw	Nanaimo
Susquehanna	Susquehannock, Conestoga, Minqua, Andaste
Taidnapam	Upper Cowlitz
Tarahumara	Raramuri
Taviwac	Uncompahgre Ute
Tejas	Hasinai, Cenis
Tenino	Melilema
Tequistlatecos	Chontales of Oaxaca
Teton	Brule, Hunkpapa, Itazipco, Mnikowoju, Oglala, Oohenunpa, Sicangu, Sihasapa, Titunwan
Tewa	Pueblo, Nambe, Pojoaque, San Ildefonso, San Juan, Santa Clara, Tesuque
Thompson	Nlaka'pamux
Tigua	Pueblo, Tiwa, Tortuga
Tillamook	Killamuck
Timucua	Utina, Acuera
T'it'kit	Lillooet
Tiwa	Pueblo, Tortuga
Tlaoquiaht	Clayoquot
Tlatlasikwala	Nuwitti
Tobacco	Khionontateronon, Tionontati
Toltec	Chiaimeca Mochanecatoca
Tonkawa	Titskan Watitch, Titskanwatitch, Tonkaweya
Tubatulabal	Bahkanapul, Kern River

Alternate Tribal Names and Spellings (cont.)

Tribal Name	Alternate Tribal Name(s)
Tunica	Yoron
Tuscarora	Skarure, Iroquois, Coree
Tututni	Tolowa
Twana	Tuadhu
Two Kettle	Oohenonpa, Oohenupa
Umpqua	Etnemitane
Uncompahgre Ute	Taviwac
Upper Chehalis	Kwaiailk
Upper Sioux	Sisseton, Wahpeton
Ute	Noochi, Notch, Nuciu, Yamparka, Parianuc, Taviwac, Wiminuc, Kapota, Muwac, Cumumba, Tumpanuwac, Uinta-ats, Pahvant, San Pitch, and Sheberetch
Viejas	Quimi
Wampanoag	Pokanoket
Wappo	Ashochimi
Warm Springs	Tilkuni
Wasco	Galasquo
Watlala	Katlagakya
Wea	Eel River, Gros, Kilataks, Mangakekis, Pepicokia, Peticotias, Piankeshaw, Wawiyatanwa
Whilkut	Redwood Indians
Winnebago	Winipig
Wichita	Kitikiti'sh, Wia Chitch (Choctaw word)
Winik	Maya
Wishram	Ilaxluit, Tlakluit
Wyandot	Huron, Talamatans
Yakama	Waptailmin, Pakiutlema, Yakima
Yaqui	Yoeme, Surem, Hiakim
Yazoo	Chakchiuma
Yoncalla	Tchayankeld
Yuchi	Chisa
Yuma	Quechan, Euqchan
Zapotec	Binigulaza
Zuni	Ashiwi, Taa Ashiwani

Source: Phil Konstantin

Tribal Name Meanings

Tribal Name	Meaning
A'ani'	white clay people
Abnaki	those living at the sunrise (easterners)
Achomawi	river, people that live at the river
Acolapissa	those who listen and see
Agaidika	salmon eaters
Ahousaht	facing opposite from the ocean, people living with their backs to the land and mountains
Ahtena	ice people
Aitchelitz	bottom
Akun'kunik'	people of the place of the flying head
Akwesasne	land where the partridge drums
Alabama	I clear the thicket
Apache	enemy (Zuni word)
Apalachicola	people of the other side
Apalachee	people of the other side
A'qam	people of the dense forest or brush
Arikara	horns or elk people, or corn eaters
Assiniboine	ones who cook using stones (Ojibwa word)
Atakapa	man eater
Atsina	white clay people
Atsugewi	hat creek indians
Avoyel	people of the rocks
Bayogoula	people of the bayou
Bedonkohe (Apache)	in front at the end people
Bidai	brushwood (Caddo word)
Binigulaza	people of the clouds
Brule	burned thighs
Caddo	true chiefs
Cahuilla	leader, master, powerful nation (all questionable)
Calusa	fierce people
Canim	canoe, broken rock
Catawba	river people
Cayuga	place where boats were taken out, place locusts were taken out, people at the mucky land
Cayuse	people of the stones or rocks (French-Canadian word)
Chakchiuma	red crawfish people
Cheam	wild strawberry place, the place to always get strawberries
Chehalis	sand, beating heart
Chemehuevi	those that play with fish (Mojave word)
Cherokee	cave people (Choctaw word), people of different speech (Creek word)
Cheslatta	top of a small mountain, small rock mountain at the east side
Chetco	close to the mouth of the stream
Cheyenne	red talkers (Dakota word), little Cree (Lakota word)
Chickahominy	hominy people
Chihene (Apache)	red paint people
Chilcotin	young man river
Chipewyan	pointed skins (Cree word)
Chitimacha	men altogether red, they have cooking vessels
Chokonen (Apache)	rising sun people
Chontal	stranger (Nahuatl word)
Choula	fox

Tribal Name Meanings (cont.)

Tribal Name	Meaning
Chowanoc	people at the south
Chumash	people who make the shell bead money
Clallam	strong people
Clatsop	dried salmon
Clayoquot	people of other tribes
Cocopah	river people
Coeur d'Alene	those who are found here or heart of an awl (French words)
Comanche	anyone who wants to fight me all the time (Ute word)
Comox	place of abundance
Cowichan	warm country, land warmed by the sun
Crow	crow, sparrowhawk, bird people, people of the large-beaked bird
Dakelh	people who travel by water
Dakota	allie
Ehdiitat Gwich'in	people who live among timber or spruce
Erie	long tail or cat people (Iroquois word)
Eskimo	eaters of raw meat (Algonquin or Cree word)
Esquimalt	the place of gradually shoaling water
Fox	red earth people
Gingolx	the place of the skulls
Gitanmaax	people who fish with burning torches
Gitwangak	place of rabbits
Gwich'in	people who live at a certain place
Gros Ventre	big bellies, one who cooks with a stone, he cooks by roasting (see Atsina)
Hach winik	true people
Hagwilget	gentle or quiet people
Han	those who live along the river
Haudenosaunee	people of the long house, people of the extended lodge
Havasupai	people of the blue green water
Heiltsuk	to speak or act correctly
Hesquiaht	people of the sound made by eating herring eggs off eel grass
Hidatsa	willow (speculation)
Hiute	bowmen
Hohokam	those who have gone
Honniasont	wearing something around the neck
Hopi	peaceful ones, people who live in a peaceful way
Houma	red
Hualapai	people of the tall pines
Huchnom	mountain people
Huichol	healers
Hul'qumi'num	those who speak the same language
Hunkpapa	campers at the opening of the circle
Hupa	trinity river
Huron	ruffian (French word)
Hwal'bay (Hualapai)	people of the tall pines
Ihanktonwan	dwellers at the end
Ihanktonwana	little dwellers at the end
Iowa	sleepy ones (Dakota word)
Iroquois	real adders (Algonquian word) or we of the extended lodge
Jatibonicu	people of the great sacred high waters
Jatibonuco	great people of the sacred high waters

Tribal Name Meanings (cont.)

Tribal Name	Meaning
Jicaque	ancient person (Nahuatl word)
Jicarilla	little basket weaver (Spanish word)
Kainai	many chiefs
Kamloops	the meeting of the waters
Kan-hatki	white earth
Kanienkahaka	people of the place of flint
Kanza	people of the south wind
Karok	upstream
Kaskaskia	he scrapes it off by means of a tool
Kato	lake
Kawchottine	people of the great hares
Ketsei	going in wet sand
Kickapoo	he stands about
Kiowa	principal people, pulling out, coming out, people of the large tent flaps
Kispiox	people of the hiding place
Kitamaat	people of the falling snow
Kitkatla	people of the salt, village by the sea
Kitselas	people of the canyon
Kitsumkalum	people of the plateau
Klallam	strong people
Klamath	people of the lake
Klickitat	beyond (Chinook word)
Kluskus	place of small whitefish
Kotsoteka	buffalo eaters
Kutcha-kutchin	those who live on the flats
Kuupangaxwichem	people who slept here
Kuyuidokado	cui-ui eaters
Kwalhioqua	lonely place in the woods (Chinook word)
Kwayhquitlum	stinking fish slime
Kwuda	people coming out
Lakota	friend or ally (same with Dakota and Nakota)
Latgawa	those living in the uplands
Lenni Lenape	genuine men
Lheidli T'enneh	people of the confluence of the two rivers
Lillooet	wild onion
Loucheux	people with slanted or crossed eyes
Machapunga	bad dust
Mahican	wolf (incorrect translation per the Mohican Nation, Stockbridge-Munsee Band)
Makah	cape people
Malahat	infested with caterpillars, place where one gets bait
Maliseet	broken talkers
Maricopa	people who live toward the water
Massachuset	at the hills
Matsqui	easy portage, easy travelling
Mdewankantonwan	dwellers of the spirit lake
Menominee	wild rice men
Metlakatla	a passage connecting two bodies of salt water
Miami	people on the peninsula, cry of the crane
Michigamea	great water
Mimbres (Apache)	willow (Spanish word)

Tribal Name Meanings (cont.)

Tribal Name	Meaning
Miniconjou	planters by water
Minnetaree	they crossed the water
Minqua	stealthy
Missouri	great muddy, people with wooden canoes
Moapa	mosquito creek people
Moatokni	southerners
Modoc	southerners
Mohave	three mountains, people of the water/river
Mohawk	the possessors of the flint, coward or man eater (Abenaki words)
Mohegan	wolf
Mohican	the people of the waters that are never still
Moneton	big water people
Munsee	at the place where the stones are gathered together
Musqueam	place always to get iris plant root
Nahane	people of the west
Nak'azdli	when arrows were flying
Narragansett	people of the small point
Nanticoke	people of the tidewaters
Nanoose	to push forward
Natsit-kutchin	those who live off the flats
Navajo	cultivated field in an arroyo (Tewa word)
Nehalem	where the people live
Nicomen	level part
Nihtat Gwich'in	people living together as a mixture
Nipmuck	freshwater fishing place
Nokoni	those who turn back
Nooksack	mountain men
Nootka	along the coast
Nusabi	people of the clouds
Oglala	scatters their own
Ojibwa	to roast till puckered up
Okanagan	head, top of head
Okelousa	blackwater
Okmulgee	where water boils up
Omaha	upstream people or people going against the current
Oneida	a boulder standing up, people of the standing stone
Onondaga	people on top of the hills
Opata	hostile people (Pima word)
Ottawa	to trade
Otto	lechers
Oweekeno	those who carry on the back, people talking right
Pahodja	dusty nones
Pakiutlema	people of the gap
Pamunkey	rising upland
Pantch-pinunkansh	men altogether red
Papagos	desert people, bean people
Pascagoula	bread people
Passamaquoddy	plenty of pollock
Paugusset	where the narrows open out
Pawnee	horn people, men of men, look like wolves
Pechanga	place where the water drips

Tribal Name Meanings (cont.)

Tribal Name	Meaning
Penateka	honey eaters
Penelakut	something buried
Pennacook	down hill
Penobscot	it forks on the white rocks or the descending ledge place, at the stone place
Pensacola	hair people
Penticton	permanent place, always place
People of the lakes	tribes near the great lakes
Peoria	carrying a pack on his back
Pequot	fox people or destroyers
Piegan	scabby robes
Piikani	poor robe
Pilthlako	big swamp
Pima	river people
Pojoaque	drinking place
Potawatomi	people of the place of the fire, keepers of the fire (fire nation, fire people)
Powhatan	falls in a current of water
Pshwanwapam	stony ground
Puyallup	shadow
Qawishwallanavetum	people that live among the rocks
Quahadi	antelope
Qualicum	where the dog salmon run
Quapaw	downstream people
Quatsino	downstream people
Qwulhhwaipum	prairie people
Raramuri	foot runner
Sac (Sauk)	people of the yellow earth or people of the outlet
Salish	flatheads
Sans Arc	without bows
Schaghticoke	at the river forks
Schitsu'umsh	the ones that were found here
Sekani	dwellers on the rocks
Semiahmoo	half moon
Seminole	separatist or breakaway, peninsula people
Seneca	place of stone, people of the standing rock, great hill people
Shawnee	south or southerners
Sicangu	burned thighs
Sihasapa Sioux	blackfeet
Siksika	blackfeet
Sioux	snake (French version of other tribe's name)
Sisitonwan	dwellers of the fish ground
Siska	uncle, lots of cracks in the rocks
Skidegate	red paint stone
Skokomish	river people
Skookumchuck	strong water
Snuneymuxw	people of many names
Spallumcheen	flat along edge
Spokane	sun people or children of the sun (generally accepted)
Spuzzum	little flat
Sts'Ailes	the beating heart

Tribal Name Meanings (cont.)

Tribal Name	Meaning
Sumas	big flat opening
Tahltan	something heavy in the water
Taino	we the good people
Takelma	those living along the river
Tamarois	out tail
Tanima	liver eaters
Tangipahoa	corn gatherers
Tantawats	southern men
Tarahumara	foot runner
Tatsanottine	people of the copper water
Tawakoni	river bend among red hills
Teetl'it Gwich'in	people who live at the head of the waters
Tejas	friendly
Tenawa	down stream
Tennuth-ketchin	middle people
Teton	dwellers of the prairie
Tewa	moccasins
Thlingchadinne	dog-flank people
Titonwan	dwellers of the plains
Tl'azt'en	people by the edge of the bay
Toltec	master builders (Nahuatl word)
Tonawanda	confluent stream
Tonkawa	they all stay together or most human of people
Toquaht	people of the narrow place in front, people of the narrow channel
Tsa-mee-nis	bitten breast
Tsattine	lives among the beavers
Tsawout	houses raised up
Tsawwassen	beach at the mouth, facing the sea
Tsay Keh Dene	people of the mountains
Tsetsaut	people of the interior (Niska word)
Tseycum	clay people
Tsleil-Waututh	people of the inlet
Tubatulabal	pinenut eaters (Shoshone word)
Tukudika	sheep eater
Tuscarora	hemp gatherers, the shirt wearing people
Two Kettle	two boilings
Uchuckledaht	there inside the bay
Ulkatcho	good feeding place where animals get fat
Unalachtgo	tidewater people
Viniintaii Gwich'in	people who live on or by the caribou trail
Vuntut Gwitch'in	dwellers among the lakes
Vvunta-ketchin	those who live among the lakes
Wahpekute	shooters among the leaves
Wahpetonwan	dwellers amoung the leaves
Wailaki	north language (Wintun word)
Wakokai	blue heron breeding place
Walapai	pine tree people
Wallawalla	little river
Wampanoag	eastern people
Wappo	brave
Waptailmin	people of the narrow river

Tribal Name Meanings (cont.)

Tribal Name	Meaning
Wasco	cup, those who have the cup
Wea	the forest people, light-skinned ones, people who live near the river eddy
Whel mux	people of spirit, people of breath
Wichita	big arbor (Choctaw word)
Winnebago	filthy water people
Wiwohka	roaring water
Wyandot	people of the peninsula, islanders
Yakama	runaway
Yamparika	rooteaters or yapeaters
Yaqan nukiy	the people where the rock is standing
Yavapai	people of the sun, crooked mouth people
Yoncalla	those living at ayankeld
Yuchi	situated yonder
Yuhavitam	people of the pines
Yuki	stranger (Wintun word)
Yurok	downstream (Karok word)

Source: Phil Konstantin

Treaties by Tribe

Tribe	Treaty Name
Aionai	Treaty with the Comanche, Aionai, Anadarko, Caddo, Etc., 1846
Anadarko	Treaty with the Comanche, Aionai, Anadarko, Caddo, Etc., 1846
Apache	Treaty with the Apache, 1852
	Treaty with the Apache, Cheyenne, and Arapaho, 1865
	Treaty with the Cheyenne and Arapaho, 1865
	Treaty with the Comanche, Kiowa, and Apache, 1853
	Treaty with the Kiowa, Comanche, and Apache, 1867
Appalachicola	Treaty with the Appalachicola Band, 1832
	Treaty with the Appalachicola Band, 1833
Arapaho	Treaty with the Apache, Cheyenne, and Arapaho, 1865
	Treaty with the Arapaho and Cheyenne, 1861
	Treaty with the Cheyenne and Arapaho, 1865
	Treaty with the Cheyenne and Arapaho, 1867
	Treaty with the Northern Cheyenne and Northern Arapaho, 1868
	Treaty of Fort Laramie with Sioux, Etc., 1851
	Treaty with the Sioux—Brulé, Oglala, Miniconjou, Yanktonai, Hunkpapa, Blackfeet, Cuthead, Two Kettle, Sans Arcs, and Santee—and Arapaho
Arikara	Treaty with the Arikara Tribe, 1825
	Agreement at Fort Berthold, 1866
	Treaty of Fort Laramie with Sioux, Etc., 1851
Assinaboine	Treaty of Fort Laramie with Sioux, Etc., 1851
Bannock	Treaty with the Eastern Band Shoshoni and Bannock, 1868
Belantse-Etoa or Minitaree	Treaty with the Belantse-Etoa or Minitaree Tribe, 1825
Blackfeet	Treaty with the Blackfeet, 1855
	Treaty with the Blackfeet Sioux, 1865
Blood	Treaty with the Blackfeet, 1855
Brothertown	Treaty with the New York Indians, 1838
Caddo	Treaty with the Caddo, 1835
	Treaty with the Comanche, Aionai, Anadarko, Caddo, Etc., 1846
Cahokia	Treaty with the Peoria, Etc., 1818

Treaties by Tribe (cont.)

Tribe	Treaty Name
Cayuga	Agreement with the Five Nations of Indians, 1792
	Treaty with the Six Nations, 1784
	Treaty with the New York Indians, 1838
	Treaty with the Six Nations, 1789
	Treaty with the Six Nations, 1794
Cayuse	Treaty with the Walla-Walla, Cayuse, Etc., 1855
Chasta	Treaty with the Chasta, Etc., 1854
Cherokee	Treaty with the Cherokee, 1785
	Treaty with the Cherokee, 1791
	Treaty with the Cherokee, 1794
	Treaty with the Cherokee, 1798
	Treaty with the Cherokee, 1804
	Treaty with the Cherokee, 1805
	Treaty with the Cherokee, 1805
	Treaty with the Cherokee, 1806
	Treaty with the Cherokee, 1816
	Treaty with the Cherokee, 1816
	Treaty with the Cherokee, 1816
	Treaty with the Cherokee, 1817
	Treaty with the Cherokee, 1819
	Treaty with the Western Cherokee, 1828
	Treaty with the Western Cherokee, 1833
	Treaty with the Cherokee, 1835
	Treaty with the Cherokee, 1846 [Western Cherokee]
	Treaty with the Cherokee, 1866
	Treaty with the Cherokee, 1868
	Agreement with the Cherokee, 1835 (Unratified)
	Agreement with the Cherokee and Other Tribes in the Indian Territory, 1865
	Treaty with the Comanche, Etc., 1835
Cheyenne	Treaty with the Apache, Cheyenne, and Arapaho, 1865
	Treaty with the Arapaho and Cheyenne, 1861
	Treaty with the Cheyenne Tribe, 1825
	Treaty with the Cheyenne and Arapaho, 1865
	Treaty with the Cheyenne and Arapaho, 1867
	Treaty with the Northern Cheyenne and Northern Arapaho, 1868
	Treaty of Fort Laramie with Sioux, Etc., 1851
Chickasaw	Agreement with the Cherokee and Other Tribes in the Indian Territory, 1865
	Treaty with the Chickasaw, 1786
	Treaty with the Chickasaw, 1801
	Treaty with the Chickasaw, 1805
	Treaty with the Chickasaw, 1816
	Treaty with the Chickasaw, 1818

Treaties by Tribe (cont.)

Tribe	Treaty Name
Chickasaw (cont.)	Treaty with the Chickasaw, 1832
	Treaty with the Chickasaw, 1832
	Treaty with the Chickasaw, 1834
	Treaty with the Chickasaw, 1830
	Treaty with the Choctaw and Chickasaw, 1837
	Treaty with the Chickasaw, 1852
	Treaty with the Choctaw and Chickasaw, 1854
	Treaty with the Choctaw and Chickasaw, 1855
	Treaty with the Choctaw and Chickasaw, 1866
Chippewa	Treaty with the Chippewa, Etc., 1808
	Treaty with the Chippewa, 1819
	Treaty with the Chippewa, 1820
	Treaty with the Ottawa and Chippewa, 1820
	Treaty with the Chippewa, 1826
	Treaty with the Chippewa, Etc., 1827
	Treaty with the Chippewa, Etc., 1829
	Treaty with the Chippewa, Etc., 1833
	Treaty with the Chippewa, 1836
	Treaty with the Chippewa, 1837
	Treaty with the Chippewa, 1837
	Treaty with the Chippewa, 1837
	Treaty with the Chippewa, 1838
	Treaty with the Chippewa, 1839
	Treaty with the Chippewa, 1842
	Treaty with the Chippewa of the Mississippi and Lake Superior, 1847
	Treaty with the Chippewa, 1854
	Treaty with the Chippewa, 1855
	Treaty with the Chippewa of Saginaw, Etc., 1855
	Treaty with the Chippewa, Etc., 1859
	Treaty with the Chippewa of the Mississippi and the Pillager and Lake Winnibigoshish Bands, 1863
	Treaty with the Chippewa—Red Lake and Pembina Bands, 1863
	Treaty with the Chippewa—Red Lake and Pembina Bands, 1864
	Treaty with the Chippewa, Mississippi, and Pillager and Lake Winnibigoshish Bands, 1864
	Treaty with the Chippewa of Saginaw, Swan Creek, and Black River, 1864
	Treaty with the Chippewa—Bois Forte Band, 1866
	Treaty with the Chippewa of the Mississippi, 1867
	Treaty with the Ottawa, Etc., 1807
	Treaty with the Ottawa, Etc., 1816
	Treaty with the Ottawa, Etc., 1821
	Treaty with the Ottawa, Etc., 1836
	Treaty with the Ottawa and Chippewa, 1855
	Treaty with the Pillager Band of Chippewa Indians, 1847
	Treaty with the Potawatomi Nation, 1846
	Treaty with the Chippewa of Sault Ste. Marie, 1855
	Treaty with the Sioux, Etc., 1825
	Treaty with the Winnebago, Etc., 1828

Treaties by Tribe (cont.)

Tribe	Treaty Name
Chippewa (cont.)	Treaty with the Wyandot, Etc., 1785
	Treaty with the Wyandot, Etc., 1789
	Treaty with the Wyandot, Etc., 1795
	Treaty with the Wyandot, Etc., 1805
	Treaty with the Wyandot, Etc., 1815
	Treaty with the Wyandot, Etc., 1817
	Treaty with the Wyandot, Etc., 1818
Choctaw	Agreement with the Cherokee and Other Tribes in the Indian Territory, 1865
	Treaty with the Choctaw and Chickasaw, 1837
	Treaty with the Choctaw, 1786
	Treaty with the Choctaw, 1801
	Treaty with the Choctaw, 1802
	Treaty with the Choctaw, 1803
	Treaty with the Choctaw, 1805
	Treaty with the Choctaw, 1816
	Treaty with the Choctaw, 1820
	Treaty with the Choctaw, 1825
	Treaty with the Choctaw, 1830
	Treaty with the Choctaw and Chickasaw, 1854
	Treaty with the Choctaw and Chickasaw, 1855
	Treaty with the Choctaw and Chickasaw, 1866
	Treaty with the Comanche, Etc., 1835
	Treaty with the Comanche and Kiowa, 1865
Clack-A-Mas	Treaty with the Kalapuya, Etc., 1855
Columbia	Agreement with the Columbia and Colville, 1883
Colville	Agreement with the Columbia and Colville, 1883
Comanche	Treaty with the Comanche, Etc., 1835
	Treaty with the Comanche, Aionai, Anadarko, Caddo, Etc., 1846
	Treaty with the Comanche, Kiowa, and Apache, 1853
	Treaty with the Kiowa and Comanche, 1867
	Treaty with the Kiowa, Comanche, and Apache, 1867
Creeks	Agreement with the Cherokee and Other Tribes in the Indian Territory, 1865
	Treaty with the Comanche, Etc., 1835
	Treaty with the Creeks, 1790
	Treaty with the Creeks, 1796
	Treaty with the Creeks, 1802
	Treaty with the Creeks, 1805
	Treaty with the Creeks, 1814
	Treaty with the Creeks, 1818
	Treaty with the Creeks, 1821
	Treaty with the Creeks, 1821
	Treaty with the Creeks, 1825
	Treaty with the Creeks, 1826

Treaties by Tribe (cont.)

Tribe	Treaty Name
Creeks (cont.)	Treaty with the Creeks, 1827
	Treaty with the Creeks, 1832
	Treaty with the Creeks, 1833
	Treaty with the Creeks, 1838
	Treaty with the Creeks and Seminole, 1845
	Treaty with the Creeks, 1854
	Treaty with the Creeks, Etc., 1856
	Treaty with the Creeks, 1866
	Agreement with the Creeks, 1825 (Unratified)
Crow	Treaty with the Crow Tribe, 1825
	Treaty with the Crows, 1868
	Agreement with the Crows, 1880 (Unratified)
	Treaty of Fort Laramie with Sioux, Etc., 1851
Dakota	Treaty with the Blackfeet Sioux, 1865
	Treaty of Fort Laramie with Sioux, Etc., 1851
De Chutes	Treaty with the Middle Oregon Tribes, 1865
	Treaty with the Tribes of Middle Oregon, 1855
Delaware	Treaty with the Delawares, 1778
	Treaty with the Delawares, Etc., 1803
	Treaty with the Delawares, 1804
	Treaty with the Delawares, Etc., 1805
	Treaty with the Delawares, Etc., 1809
	Treaty with the Delawares, 1818
	Treaty with the Delawares, 1829
	Treaty with the Delawares, 1829
	Treaty with the Delawares, 1854
	Treaty with the Delawares, 1860
	Treaty with the Delawares, 1861
	Treaty with the Delawares, 1866
	Agreement with the Delawares and Wyandot, 1843
	Supplementary Treaty with the Miami, Etc., 1809
	Treaty with the Shawnee, Etc., 1832
	Treaty with the Wyandot, Etc., 1785
	Treaty with the Wyandot, Etc., 1789
	Treaty with the Wyandot, Etc., 1795
	Treaty with the Wyandot, Etc., 1805
	Treaty with the Wyandot, Etc., 1814
	Treaty with the Wyandot, Etc., 1815
	Treaty with the Wyandot, Etc., 1817
	Treaty with the Wyandot, Etc., 1818
Dwamish	Treaty with the Dwamish, Suquamish, Etc., 1855
Eel River	Treaty with the Delawares, Etc., 1803
	Treaty with the Delawares, Etc., 1805
	Treaty with the Delawares, Etc., 1809
	Treaty with the Eel River, Etc., 1803

Treaties by Tribe (cont.)

Tribe	Treaty Name
Eel River (cont.)	Supplementary Treaty with the Miami, Etc., 1809
	Treaty with the Miami, 1828
	Treaty with the Wyandot, Etc., 1795
Five Nations	Agreement with the Five Nations of Indians, 1792
Flathead	Treaty with the Blackfeet, 1855
	Treaty with the Flatheads, Etc., 1855
Fox	Treaty with the Foxes, 1815
Gros Ventres	Treaty with the Blackfeet, 1855
	Agreement at Fort Berthold, 1866
	Treaty of Fort Laramie with Sioux, Etc., 1851
Illinois	Treaty with the Kaskaskia, Etc., 1832
	Treaty with the Peoria, Etc., 1818
Iowa	Treaty with the Iowa, 1815
	Treaty with the Iowa, 1824.
	Treaty with the Iowa, Etc., 1836.
	Treaty with the Iowa, 1837
	Treaty with the Iowa, 1838
	Treaty with the Iowa, 1854
	Treaty with the Sauk and Fox, Etc., 1830
	Treaty with the Sauk and Fox, Etc., 1861
	Treaty with the Sioux, Etc., 1825
Kalapuya	Treaty with the Kalapuya, Etc., 1855
	Treaty with the Umpqua and Kalapuya, 1854
Kansa	Treaty with the Kansa, 1815
	Treaty with the Kansa, 1825
	Treaty with the Kansa, 1825
	Treaty with Kansa Tribe, 1846
	Treaty with the Kansa Tribe, 1859
	Treaty with the Kansa Indians, 1862
Kaskaskia	Treaty with the Delawares, Etc., 1803
	Treaty with the Eel River, Etc., 1803
	Treaty with the Kaskaskia, 1803
	Treaty with the Kaskaskia, Etc., 1832
	Treaty with the Kaskaskia, Peoria, Etc., 1854
	Treaty with the Peoria, Etc., 1818
	Treaty with the Seneca, Mixed Seneca and Shawnee, Quapaw, Etc., 1867
	Treaty with the Wyandot, Etc., 1795
Ka-Ta-Ka	Treaty with the Kiowa, Etc., 1837
Keechy	Treaty with the Comanche, Aionai, Anadarko, Caddo, Etc., 1846

Treaties by Tribe (cont.)

Tribe	Treaty Name
Kickapoo	Treaty with the Delawares, Etc., 1803
	Treaty with the Eel River, Etc., 1803
	Treaty with the Kickapoo, 1809
	Treaty with the Kickapoo, 1815
	Treaty with the Wea and Kickapoo, 1816
	Treaty with the Kickapoo, 1819
	Treaty with the Kickapoo, 1819
	Treaty with the Kickapoo, 1820
	Treaty with the Kickapoo of the Vermilion 1820
	Treaty with the Kickapoo, 1832
	Treaty with the Kickapoo, 1854
	Treaty with the Kickapoo, 1862
	Treaty with the Wyandot, Etc., 1795
Kik-Ial-Lus	Treaty with the Dwamish, Suquamish, Etc., 1855
Kiowa	Treaty with the Comanche, Kiowa, and Apache, 1853
	Treaty with the Comanche and Kiowa, 1865
	Treaty with the Kiowa, Etc., 1837
	Treaty with the Kiowa and Comanche, 1867
	Treaty with the Kiowa, Comanche, and Apache, 1867
Klamath	Treaty with the Klamath, Etc., 1864
Kootenay	Treaty with the Blackfeet, 1855
	Treaty with the Flatheads, Etc., 1855
Lepan	Treaty with the Comanche, Aionai, Anadarko, Caddo, Etc., 1846
Long-Wha	Treaty with the Comanche, Aionai, Anadarko, Caddo, Etc., 1846
Lummi	Treaty with the Dwamish, Suquamish, Etc., 1855
Makah	Treaty with the Makah, 1815
	Treaty with the Makah Tribe, 1825
	Treaty with the Makah, 1855
Mandan	Agreement at Fort Berthold, 1866
	Treaty with the Mandan Tribe, 1825
	Treaty of Fort Laramie with Sioux, Etc., 1851
Me-Sek-Wi-Guilse	Treaty with the Dwamish, Suquamish, Etc., 1855
Menominee	Treaty with the Chippewa, Etc., 1827
	Treaty with the Menominee, 1817
	Treaty with the Menominee, 1831
	Treaty with the Menominee, 1831
	Treaty with the Menominee, 1832
	Treaty with the Menominee, 1836
	Treaty with the Menominee, 1848
	Treaty with the Menominee, 1854

Treaties by Tribe (cont.)

Tribe	Treaty Name
Menominee (cont.)	Treaty with the Menominee, 1856
	Treaty with the Sioux, Etc., 1825
Miami	Treaty with the Delawares, Etc., 1803
	Treaty with the Delawares, Etc., 1805
	Treaty with the Delawares, Etc., 1809
	Supplementary Treaty with the Miami, Etc., 1809
	Treaty with the Miami, 1818
	Treaty with the Miami, 1826
	Treaty with the Miami, 1828
	Treaty with the Miami, 1834
	Treaty with the Miami, 1838
	Treaty with the Miami, 1840
	Treaty with the Miami, 1854
	Treaty with the Seneca, Mixed Seneca and Shawnee, Quapaw, Etc., 1867
	Treaty with the Wyandot, Etc., 1795
	Treaty with the Wyandot, Etc., 1814
	Treaty with the Wyandot, Etc., 1815
Middle Oregon Tribes	Treaty with the Middle Oregon Tribes, 1865
	Treaty with the Tribes of Middle Oregon, 1855
Minitaree or Belantse-Etoa	Treaty with the Belantse-Etoa or Minitaree Tribe, 1825
Mitchigamia	Treaty with the Peoria, Etc., 1818
Modoc	Treaty with the Klamath, Etc., 1864
Mohawk	Treaty with the Mohawk, 1797
	Treaty with the Six Nations, 1784
	Treaty with the Six Nations, 1789
	Treaty with the Six Nations, 1794
Molala	Treaty with the Kalapuya, Etc., 1855
	Treaty with the Molala, 1855
Muscogee	Treaty with the Comanche, Etc., 1835
Munsee	Treaty with the Chippewa, Etc., 1859
	Treaty with the New York Indians, 1838
	Treaty with the Stockbridge and Munsee, 1839
	Treaty with the Stockbridge and Munsee, 1856
	Treaty with the Wyandot, Etc., 1805
Navajo	Treaty with the Navaho, 1849
	Treaty with the Navaho, 1868
New York Indians	Treaty with the New York Indians, 1838
Nez Percé	Treaty with the Blackfeet, 1855

Treaties by Tribe (cont.)

Tribe	Treaty Name
Nex Percé (cont.)	Treaty with the Nez Percé, 1855
	Treaty with the Nez Percé, 1863
	Treaty with the Nez Percé, 1868
Nisqually	Treaty with the Nisqualli, Puyallup, Etc., 1854
Noo-Wha-Ha	Treaty with the Dwamish, Suquamish, Etc., 1855
Omaha	Treaty with the Omaha, 1854
	Treaty with the Omaha, 1865
	Treaty with the Oto, Etc., 1836
	Treaty with the Sauk and Fox, Etc., 1830
Oneida	Agreement with the Five Nations of Indians, 1792
	Treaty with the Six Nations, 1784
	Treaty with the New York Indians, 1838
	Treaty with the Oneida, Etc., 1794
	Treaty with the Oneida, 1838
	Treaty with the Six Nations, 1789
	Treaty with the Six Nations, 1794
Onondaga	Agreement with the Five Nations of Indians, 1792
	Treaty with the Six Nations, 1784
	Treaty with the New York Indians, 1838
	Treaty with the Six Nations, 1789
	Treaty with the Six Nations, 1794
Osage	Agreement with the Cherokee and Other Tribes in the Indian Territory, 1865
	Treaty with the Comanche, Etc., 1835
	Treaty with the Osage, 1808
	Treaty with the Osage, 1815
	Treaty with the Osage, 1818
	Treaty with the Osage, 1822
	Treaty with the Osage, 1825
	Treaty with the Great and Little Osage, 1825
	Treaty with the Osage, 1839
	Treaty with the Osage, 1865
Oto	Treaty with the Oto, 1817
Oto & Missouri	Treaty with the Confederated Oto and Missouri, 1854
	Treaty with the Oto and Missouri Tribe, 1825
	Treaty with the Oto and Missouri, 1833
	Treaty with the Oto, Etc., 1836
	Treaty with the Oto and Missouri, 1854
	Treaty with the Sauk and Fox, Etc., 1830
Ottawa	Treaty with the Chippewa, Etc., 1808
	Treaty with the Ottawa and Chippewa, 1820
	Treaty with the Chippewa, Etc., 1829

Treaties by Tribe (cont.)

Tribe	Treaty Name
Ottawa (cont.)	Treaty with the Chippewa, Etc., 1833
	Treaty with the Ottawa, Etc., 1807
	Treaty with the Ottawa, Etc., 1816
	Treaty with the Ottawa, Etc., 1821
	Treaty with the Ottawa, 1831
	Treaty with the Ottawa, 1833
	Treaty with the Ottawa, Etc., 1836
	Treaty with the Ottawa and Chippewa, 1855
	Treaty with the Ottawa of Blanchard's Fork and Roche De Bœuf, 1862
	Treaty with the Potawatomi Nation, 1846
	Treaty with the Seneca, Mixed Seneca and Shawnee, Quapaw, Etc., 1867
	Treaty with the Sioux, Etc., 1825
	Treaty with the Winnebago, Etc, 1828
	Treaty with the Wyandot, Etc., 1785
	Treaty with the Wyandot, Etc., 1789
	Treaty with the Wyandot, Etc., 1795
	Treaty with the Wyandot, Etc., 1805
	Treaty with the Wyandot, Etc., 1815
	Treaty with the Wyandot, Etc., 1817
	Treaty with the Wyandot, Etc., 1818
Pawnee	Treaty with the Grand Pawnee, 1818
	Treaty with the Noisy Pawnee, 1818
	Treaty with the Pawnee Republic, 1818
	Treaty with the Pawnee Marhar, 1818
	Treaty with the Pawnee Tribe, 1825
	Treaty with the Pawnee, 1833
	Treaty with the Pawnee—Grand, Loups, Republicans, Etc., 1848
	Treaty with the Pawnee, 1857
Peoria	Treaty with the Kaskaskia, Etc., 1832
	Treaty with the Kaskaskia, Peoria, Etc., 1854
	Treaty with the Peoria, Etc., 1818
	Treaty with the Seneca, Mixed Seneca and Shawnee, Quapaw, Etc., 1867
Piankeshaw	Treaty with the Delawares, Etc., 1803
	Treaty with the Eel River, Etc., 1803
	Treaty with the Kaskaskia, Peoria, Etc., 1854
	Treaty with the Piankeshaw, 1804
	Treaty with the Piankashaw, 1805
	Treaty with the Piankashaw, 1815
	Treaty with the Piankashaw and Wea, 1832
	Agreement with the Piankeshaw, 1818 (Unratified)
	Treaty with the Seneca, Mixed Seneca and Shawnee, Quapaw, Etc., 1867
	Treaty with the Wyandot, Etc., 1795
Piegan	Treaty with the Blackfeet, 1855

Treaties by Tribe (cont.)

Tribe	Treaty Name
Ponca	Treaty with the Ponca, 1817
	Treaty with the Ponca, 1825
	Treaty with the Ponca, 1858
	Treaty with the Ponca, 1865
Potawatomi	Treaty with the Chippewa, Etc., 1808
	Treaty with the Chippewa, Etc., 1829
	Treaty with the Chippewa, Etc., 1833
	Treaty with the Delawares, Etc., 1803
	Treaty with the Delawares, Etc., 1805
	Treaty with the Delawares, Etc., 1809
	Supplementary Treaty with the Miami, Etc., 1809
	Treaty with the Ottawa, Etc., 1807
	Treaty with the Ottawa, Etc., 1816
	Treaty with the Ottawa, Etc., 1821
	Treaty with the Potawatomi, 1815
	Treaty with the Potawatomi, 1818
	Treaty with the Potawatomi, 1826
	Treaty with the Potawatomi, 1827
	Treaty with the Potawatomi, 1828
	Treaty with the Potawatomi, 1832
	Treaty with the Potawatomi, 1832
	Treaty with the Potawatomi, 1832
	Treaty with the Potawatomi, 1834
	Treaty with the Potawatomi, 1834
	Treaty with the Potawatomi, 1834
	Treaty with the Potawatomi, 1834
	Treaty with the Potawatomi, 1836
	Treaty with the Potawatomi, 1836
	Treaty with the Potawatomi, 1836
	Treaty with the Potawatomi, 1836
	Treaty with the Potawatomi, 1836
	Treaty with the Potawatomi, 1836
	Treaty with the Potawatomi, 1836
	Treaty with the Potawatomi, 1836
	Treaty with the Potawatomi, 1836
	Treaty with the Potawatomi, 1837
	Treaty with the Potawatomi Nation, 1846
	Treaty with the Potawatomi, 1861
	Treaty with the Potawatomi, 1866
	Treaty with the Potawatomi, 1867
	Treaty with the Sioux, Etc., 1825
	Treaty with the Winnebago, Etc, 1828
	Treaty with the Wyandot, Etc., 1789
	Treaty with the Wyandot, Etc., 1795
	Treaty with the Wyandot, Etc., 1805
	Treaty with the Wyandot, Etc., 1815
	Treaty with the Wyandot, Etc., 1817
	Treaty with the Wyandot, Etc., 1818

Treaties by Tribe (cont.)

Tribe	Treaty Name
Puyallup	Treaty with the Nisqualli, Puyallup, Etc., 1854
Quapaw	Agreement with the Cherokee and Other Tribes in the Indian Territory, 1865
	Treaty with the Comanche, Etc., 1835
	Treaty with the Quapaw,1818
	Treaty with the Quapaw, 1824
	Treaty with the Quapaw, 1833
	Treaty with the Seneca, Mixed Seneca and Shawnee, Quapaw, Etc., 1867
Qui-Nai-Elt	Treaty with the Quinaielt, Etc., 1855
Quil-Leh-Ute	Treaty with the Quinaielt, Etc., 1855
Ricara	Treaty with the Arikara Tribe, 1825
	Agreement at Fort Berthold, 1866
	Treaty of Fort Laramie with Sioux, Etc., 1851
Rogue River	Treaty with the Rogue River, 1853
	Treaty with the Rogue River, 1854
	Agreement with the Rogue River, 1853 (Unratified)
Sac & Fox	Treaty with the Fox, 1815
	Treaty with the Iowa, Etc., 1836.
	Treaty with the Sauk and Fox, 1804
	Treaty with the Sauk, 1815
	Treaty with the Sauk, 1816
	Treaty with the Sauk and Fox, 1822
	Treaty with the Sauk and Fox, 1824
	Treaty with the Sauk and Fox, Etc., 1830
	Treaty with the Sauk and Fox, 1832
	Treaty with the Sauk and Fox Tribe, 1836
	Treaty with the Sauk and Fox, 1836
	Treaty with the Sauk and Fox, 1836
	Treaty with the Sauk and Fox, 1837
	Treaty with the Sauk and Fox, 1837
	Treaty with the Sauk and Fox, 1842
	Treaty with the Sauk and Fox of Missouri, 1854
	Treaty with the Sauk and Fox, 1859
	Treaty with the Sauk and Fox, Etc., 1861
	Treaty with the Sauk and Fox, 1867
	Treaty with the Sioux, Etc., 1825
	Treaty with the Wyandot, Etc., 1789
Sa-Heh-Wamish	Treaty with the Nisqualli, Puyallup, Etc., 1854
Sah-Ku-Meh-Hu	Treaty with the Dwamish, Suquamish, Etc., 1855
Scotons	Treaty with the Chasta, Etc., 1854

Treaties by Tribe (cont.)

Tribe	Treaty Name
Seminole	Agreement with the Cherokee and Other Tribes in the Indian Territory, 1865
	Treaty with the Creeks and Seminole, 1845
	Treaty with the Creeks, Etc., 1856
	Treaty with the Florida Tribes of Indians, 1823
	Treaty with the Seminole, 1832
	Treaty with the Seminole, 1833
	Treaty with the Seminole, 1866
Seneca	Agreement with the Cherokee and Other Tribes in the Indian Territory, 1865
	Treaty with the Comanche, Etc., 1835
	Agreement with the Five Nations of Indians, 1792
	Treaty with the Six Nations, 1784
	Treaty with the New York Indians, 1838
	Treaty with the Seneca, 1802
	Treaty with the Seneca, 1802
	Treaty with the Seneca, 1831
	Treaty with the Seneca, Etc., 1831
	Treaty with the Seneca and Shawnee, 1832
	Treaty with the Seneca, 1842
	Treaty with the Seneca, Tonawanda Band, 1857.
	Treaty with the Seneca, Mixed Seneca and Shawnee, Quapaw, Etc., 1867
	Agreement with the Seneca, 1797
	Agreement with the Seneca, 1823 (Unratified)
	Treaty with the Six Nations, 1789
	Treaty with the Six Nations, 1794
	Treaty with the Wyandot, Etc., 1814
	Treaty with the Wyandot, Etc., 1815
	Treaty with the Wyandot, Etc., 1817
	Treaty with the Wyandot, Etc., 1818
Seven Nations of Canada	Treaty with the Seven Nations of Canada, 1796
Shawnee	Agreement with the Cherokee and Other Tribes in the Indian Territory, 1865
	Treaty with the Chippewa, Etc., 1808
	Treaty with the Delawares, Etc., 1803
	Treaty with the Seneca, Etc., 1831
	Treaty with the Seneca and Shawnee, 1832
	Treaty with the Seneca, Mixed Seneca and Shawnee, Quapaw, Etc., 1867
	Treaty with the Shawnee, 1786
	Treaty with the Shawnee, 1825
	Treaty with the Shawnee, 1831
	Treaty with the Shawnee, Etc., 1832
	Treaty with the Shawnee, 1854
	Treaty with the Wyandot, Etc., 1795
	Treaty with the Wyandot, Etc., 1805
	Treaty with the Wyandot, Etc., 1814

Treaties by Tribe (cont.)

Tribe	Treaty Name
Shawnee (cont.)	Treaty with the Wyandot, Etc., 1815
	Treaty with the Wyandot, Etc., 1817
	Treaty with the Wyandot, Etc., 1818
S'homamish	Treaty with the Nisqualli, Puyallup, Etc., 1854
Shoshoni	Treaty with the Eastern Shoshoni, 1863
	Treaty with the Shoshoni—Northwestern Bands, 1863
	Treaty with the Western Shoshoni, 1863
	Treaty with the Eastern Band Shoshoni and Bannock, 1868
Shoshoni-Goship	Treaty with the Shoshoni-Goship, 1863
Sioux	Treaty with the Blackfeet Sioux, 1865
	Treaty with the Hunkpapa Band of the Sioux Tribe, 1825
	Treaty with the Sioune and Oglala Tribes, 1825 (Also Ogallala)
	Treaty with the Oto, Etc., 1836 — Yankton and Santee Bands
	Treaty with the Sauk and Fox, Etc., 1830 — Medawah-Kanton, Wahpacoota, Wahpeton, Sissetong [Sisseton], Yanckton [Yancton] and Santie Bands
	Treaty with the Sioux of the Lakes, 1815
	Treaty with the Sioux of St. Peter's River, 1815
	Treaty with the Sioux, 1816
	Treaty with the Teton, Etc., Sioux, 1825 — Teton, Yancton and Yanctonies Bands
	Treaty with the Sioux, Etc., 1825
	Treaty with the Sioux, 1836
	Treaty with the Sioux, 1836
	Treaty with the Sioux, 1837
	Treaty with the Sioux—Sisseton and Wahpeton Bands, 1851
	Treaty with the Sioux—Mdewakanton and Wahpakoota Bands, 1851 (Also Med-ay-wa-kan-toan and Wah-pay-koo-tay)
	Treaty of Fort Laramie with Sioux, Etc., 1851
	Treaty with the Sioux, 1858 — Mendawakanton and Wahpahoota Bands
	Treaty with the Sioux, 1858 — Sisseeton and Wahpaton Bands
	Treaty with the Sioux—Miniconjou Band, 1865 (Also Minneconjon)
	Treaty with the Sioux—Lower Brulé Band, 1865
	Treaty with the Sioux—Two-Kettle Band, 1865
	Treaty with the Sioux—Sans Arcs Band, 1865
	Treaty with the Sioux—Hunkpapa Band, 1865 (Also Onkpahpah)
	Treaty with the Sioux—Yanktonai Band, 1865
	Treaty with the Sioux—Upper Yanktonai Band, 1865
	Treaty with the Sioux—Oglala Band, 1865 (Also Ogallala; O'Galla)
	Treaty with the Sioux—Sisseton and Wahpeton Bands, 1867 (Also Sissiton)
	Treaty with the Sioux—Brulé, Oglala, Miniconjou, Yanktonai, Hunkpapa, Blackfeet, Cuthead, Two Kettle, Sans Arcs, and Santee—and Arapaho,
	Treaty with the Sioux, 1805

Treaties by Tribe (cont.)

Tribe	Treaty Name
Sioux (cont.)	Agreement with the Sisseton and Wahpeton Bands of Sioux Indians, 1872 (Unratified)
	Amended Agreement with Certain Sioux Indians, 1873 — Sisseton and Wahpeton Bands
	Agreement with the Sioux of Various Tribes, 1882–83 (Unratified) — Pine Ridge, Rosebud, Standing Rock, Cheyenne River, and Lower Brulé Agencies
	Treaty with the Yankton Sioux, 1815
	Treaty with the Yankton Sioux, 1837
	Treaty with the Yankton Sioux, 1858
Six Nations	Treaty with the Six Nations, 1784
	Treaty with the Six Nations, 1789
	Treaty with the Six Nations, 1794
Skai-Wha-Mish	Treaty with the Dwamish, Suquamish, Etc., 1855
Skagit	Treaty with the Dwamish, Suquamish, Etc., 1855
S'klallam	Treaty with the S'Klallam, 1855
Sk-Tah-Le-Jum	Treaty with the Dwamish, Suquamish, Etc., 1855
Snake	Treaty with the Klamath, Etc., 1864
	Treaty with the Snake, 1865
Snohomish	Treaty with the Dwamish, Suquamish, Etc., 1855
Snoqualmoo	Treaty with the Dwamish, Suquamish, Etc., 1855
Squawskin	Treaty with the Nisqualli, Puyallup, Etc., 1854
Squi-Aitl	Treaty with the Nisqualli, Puyallup, Etc., 1854
Squin-Ah-Nush	Treaty with the Dwamish, Suquamish, Etc., 1855
St. Regis	Treaty with the New York Indians, 1838
	Treaty with the Seven Nations of Canada, 1796
Stehchass	Treaty with the Nisqualli, Puyallup, Etc., 1854
Steilacoom	Treaty with the Nisqualli, Puyallup, Etc., 1854
Stockbridge	Agreement with the Five Nations of Indians, 1792
	Treaty with the New York Indians, 1838
	Treaty with the Oneida, Etc., 1794
	Treaty with the Stockbridge and Munsee, 1839
	Treaty with the Stockbridge Tribe, 1848
	Treaty with the Stockbridge and Munsee, 1856
Suquamish	Treaty with the Dwamish, Suquamish, Etc., 1855

Treaties by Tribe (cont.)

Tribe	Treaty Name
Swinamish	Treaty with the Dwamish, Suquamish, Etc., 1855
Tah-Wa-Carro	Treaty with the Comanche, Aionai, Anadarko, Caddo, Etc., 1846 Treaty with the Kiowa, Etc., 1837
Tamarois	Treaty with the Peoria, Etc., 1818
Tenino	Treaty with the Middle Oregon Tribes, 1865 Treaty with the Tribes of Middle Oregon, 1855
Teton	Treaty with the Teton, 1815
Tonkawa	Treaty with the Comanche, Aionai, Anadarko, Caddo, Etc., 1846
T'peek-Sin	Treaty with the Nisqualli, Puyallup, Etc., 1854
Tum-Waters	Treaty with the Kalapuya, Etc., 1855
Tuscarora	Agreement with the Five Nations of Indians, 1792 Treaty with the Six Nations, 1784 Treaty with the New York Indians, 1838 Treaty with the Oneida, Etc., 1794 Treaty with the Six Nations, 1789 Treaty with the Six Nations, 1794
Umatilla	Treaty with the Walla-Walla, Cayuse, Etc., 1855
Umpqua	Treaty with the Chasta, Etc., 1854 Treaty with the Umpqua—Cow Creek Band, 1853 Treaty with the Umpqua and Kalapuya, 1854
Upper Pend D'oreille	Treaty with the Blackfeet, 1855 Treaty with the Flatheads, Etc., 1855
Utah	Treaty with the Utah, 1849 Treaty with the Utah—Tabeguache Band, 1863
Ute	Treaty with the Ute, 1868
Waco	Treaty with the Comanche, Aionai, Anadarko, Caddo, Etc., 1846
Walla-Walla	Treaty with the Middle Oregon Tribes, 1865 Treaty with the Tribes of Middle Oregon, 1855 Treaty with the Walla-Walla, Cayuse, Etc., 1855
Wasco	Treaty with the Middle Oregon Tribes, 1865 Treaty with the Tribes of Middle Oregon, 1855
Wea	Treaty with the Delawares, Etc., 1803 Treaty with the Delawares, Etc., 1805 Treaty with the Kaskaskia, Peoria, Etc., 1854

Treaties by Tribe (cont.)

Tribe	Treaty Name
Wea (cont.)	Treaty with the Wea and Kickapoo, 1816
	Supplementary Treaty with the Miami, Etc., 1809
	Treaty with the Piankashaw and Wea, 1832
	Treaty with the Seneca, Mixed Seneca and Shawnee, Quapaw, Etc., 1867
	Treaty with the Wea, 1809
	Treaty with the Wea, 1818
	Treaty with the Wea, 1820
	Treaty with the Wyandot, Etc., 1795
Winnebago	Treaty with the Chippewa, Etc., 1827
	Treaty with the Sioux, Etc., 1825
	Treaty with the Winnebago, 1816
	Treaty with the Winnebago, Etc, 1828
	Treaty with the Winnebago, 1829
	Treaty with the Winnebago, 1832
	Treaty with the Winnebago, 1837
	Treaty with the Winnebago, 1846
	Treaty with the Winnebago, 1855
	Treaty with the Winnebago, 1859
	Treaty with the Winnebago, 1865
Witchetaw	Treaty with the Comanche, Etc., 1835
	Treaty with the Comanche, Aionai, Anadarko, Caddo, Etc., 1846
Wyandot	Treaty with the Chippewa, Etc., 1808
	Agreement with the Delawares and Wyandot, 1843
	Treaty with the Eel River, Etc., 1803
	Treaty with the Ottawa, Etc., 1807
	Treaty with the Seneca, Mixed Seneca and Shawnee, Quapaw, Etc., 1867
	Treaty with the Wyandot, Etc., 1785
	Treaty with the Wyandot, Etc., 1789
	Treaty with the Wyandot, Etc., 1795
	Treaty with the Wyandot, Etc., 1805
	Treaty with the Wyandot, Etc., 1814
	Treaty with the Wyandot, Etc., 1815
	Treaty with the Wyandot, Etc., 1817
	Treaty with the Wyandot, Etc., 1818
	Treaty with the Wyandot, 1818
	Treaty with the Wyandot, 1832
	Treaty with the Wyandot, 1836
	Treaty with the Wyandot, 1842
	Treaty with the Wyandot, 1850
	Treaty with the Wyandot, 1855
Yakima	Treaty with the Yakima, 1855

Source: Charles J. Kappler, Indian Affairs: Laws and Treaties (Washington DC: Government Printing Office, 1904). Digital copy courtesy of the Oklahoma State University Library Electronic Publishing Center

Common Treaty Names

Common Name	Full Treaty Name
Albany, Treaty of	Treaty of Albany with the Five Nations–July 31, 1684
Canandaigua Treaty	Treaty with the Six Nations–November 11, 1794
Chicago, Treaty of	Treaty with the Chippewa, Etc.–September 26, 1833
Dancing Rabbit Creek, Treaty of	Treaty with the Choctaw–September 27, 1830
Doak's Stand, Treaty of	Treaty with the Choctaw–October 18, 1820
Doaksville, Treaty of	Treaty with the Choctaw and Chickasaw–January 17, 1837
Fort Bridger, Treaty of	Treaty with the Eastern Band Shoshone and Bannock–July 3, 1868
Fort Harmar, Treaty of	Treaty with the Wyandot, Etc.–January 9, 1789
	Treaty with the Six Nations–January 9, 1789
	(Addendum) Treaty with the Cherokee–June 26, 1794
Fort Laramie, Treaty of	Treaty of Fort Laramie with the Sioux, Etc.–September 17, 1851
Fort McIntosh, Treaty of	Treaty with the Wyandot, Etc.–January 21, 1785
Fort Stanwix, Treaty of	Treaty Conference with the Six Nations at Fort Stanwix–November 5, 1768
	Treaty with the Six Nations–October 22, 1784
Greenville, Treaty of	Treaty with the Wyandot, Etc.–August 3, 1795
Holston, Treaty of	Treaty with the Cherokee–July 2, 1791
Hopewell, Treaty of	Treaty with the Cherokee–November 28, 1785
Medicine Creek, Treaty of	Treaty with the Nisqually, Puyallup, Etc.–December 26, 1854
Medicine Lodge Creek, Treaty of	Treaty with the Cheyenne and Arapaho–-October 28, 1867
New Echota, Treaty of	Treaty with the Cherokee–December 29, 1835
Northwest Angle Treaty	Canadian Indian Treaty 3–October 3, 1873
Prairie du Chien, Treaty of	Treaty with the Sioux, Etc.–August 19, 1825
Qu'Appelle Treaty	Canadian Indian Treaty 4–September 15, 1874
St. Louis, Treaty of	Treaty with the Sauk and Fox–November 3, 1804

Selected Bibliography

Abele, Charles A. 1969. "The Grand Indian Council and Treaty of Prairie du Chien, 1825," Ph.D. dissertation, Loyola University of Chicago.

Anderson, George E., W. H. Ellison, and Robert F. Heizer. 1978. *Treaty Making and Treaty Rejection by the Federal Government in California, 1850–1852.* Socorro, NM: Ballena Press.

Anderson, George E., and Robert F. Heizer. 1978. "Treaty-making by the Federal Government in California 1851–1852." In *Treaty Making and Treaty Rejection by the Federal Government in California, 1850–1852,* eds. George E. Anderson, W. H. Ellison, and Robert F. Heizer, 1–36. Socorro, NM: Ballena Press.

Anderson, Harry. 1956. "The Controversial Sioux Amendment to the Fort Laramie Treaty of 1851." *Nebraska History* 37 (September): 201–220.

Asch, Michael, ed. 1998. *Aboriginal and Treaty Rights in Canada.* Vancouver: University of British Columbia Press.

Balman, Gail. 1970. "The Creek Treaty of 1866." *Chronicles of Oklahoma* 48 (Summer): 184–196.

Barce, Elmore. 1915. "Governor Harrison and the Treaty of Fort Wayne, 1809." *Indiana Magazine of History* 11 (December): 352–367.

Barnes, Lela. 1936. "Isaac McCoy and the Treaty of 1821." *Kansas Historical Quarterly* 5 (May): 122–142.

Bell, Catherine, and Karin Buss. 2000. "The Promise of Marshall on the Prairies: A Framework for Analyzing Unfulfilled Treaty Promises." *Saskatchewan Law Review* 63(2): 667.

Bigart, Robert, and Clarence Woodcock, eds. 1996. *In the Name of the Salish and Kootenai Nation: The 1885 Hell Gate Treaty and the Origin of the Flathead Indian Reservation.* Pablo, MT: Salish Kootenai College Press/University of Washington Press.

Bird, John, Lorraine Land, and Murray MacAdam, eds. 2002. *Nation to Nation: Aboriginal Sovereignty and the Future of Canada,* 2nd ed. Toronto: Irwin.

Bischoff, William N., and Charles M. Gates, eds. 1943. "The Jesuits and the Coeur D'Alene Treaty of 1858." *Pacific Northwest Quarterly* 34 (April): 169–181.

Borrows, John. 1992. "Negotiating Treaties and Land Claims: The Impact of Diversity within First Nations Property Interests." *Windsor Yearbook of Access to Justice* 12: 179.

Borrows, John. 2005. "Creating an Indigenous Legal Community." *McGill Law Journal* 50: 153.

Boxberger, Daniel L. 1979. *Handbook of Western Washington Indian Treaties.* Lummi Island, WA: Lummi Indian School of Aquaculture and Fisheries.

Boxberger, Daniel L., and Herbert C. Taylor. 1991. "Treaty or Non-Treaty Status." *Columbia,* 5(3): 40–45.

Boyd, Mark F. 1958. "Horatio S. Dexter and Events Leading to the Treaty of Moultrie Creek with the Seminole Indians." *Florida Anthropologist,* 11 (September): 65–95.

Brooks, Drex, and Patricia Nelson Limerick. 1995. *Sweet Medicine: Sites of Indian Massacres, Battlefields, and Treaties.* Albuquerque: University of New Mexico Press.

Brown, George, and Ron Maguire. 1979. *Indian Treaties in Historical Perspective.* Ottawa: Research Branch, Indian and Northern Affairs Canada.

Bugge, David, and J. Lee Corell. 1971. *The Story of the Navajo Treaties.* Window Rock, AZ: Research Section, Navajo Parks and Recreation Department, Navajo Tribe.

Burns, Robert Ignatius, ed. 1952. "A Jesuit at the Hell Gate Treaty of 1855." *Mid-American* 34 (April): 87–114. Report of Adrian Hoechen.

Bushnell, David I., Jr. 1916. "The Virginia Frontier in History–1778." Part 5, "The Treaty of Fort Pitt." *Virginia Magazine of History and Biography* 24 (April): 168–179.

Campisi, Jack. 1988. "From Stanwix to Canandaigua: National Policy, States' Rights, and Indian Land." In *Iroquois Land Claims,* eds. Christopher Vecsey and William A. Starna, 49–65. Syracuse, NY: Syracuse University Press.

Campisi, Jack. 1988. "The Oneida Treaty Period, 1783–1838." In *The Oneida Indian Experience: Two Perspectives*, eds. Jack Campisi and Laurence M. Hauptman, 48–64. Syracuse, NY: Syracuse University Press.

Canada. 1905. *Indian Treaties and Surrenders from 1680–1890*. Ottawa: S. E. Dawson. Repr., Saskatoon: Fifth House, 1992.

Canada. 1971. *Indian Treaties and Surrenders from 1680 to 1890*. 3 vols. Ottawa: Queen's Printer.

Clark, Blue. 1994. *Lone Wolf v. Hitchcock: Treaty Rights and Indian Law at the End of the Nineteenth Century*. Lincoln: University of Nebraska Press.

Clifton, James A. 1980. "Chicago, September 14, 1833: The Last Great Indian Treaty in the Old Northwest." *Chicago History* 9 (Summer): 86–97.

Cohen, Fay G. 1986. *Treaties on Trial: The Continuing Controversy over Northwest Indian Fishing Rights*. With contributions by Joan La France and Vivian L. Bowden. Seattle: University of Washington Press.

Cohen, Felix S. 1942. "Indian Treaties." In Cohen, *Handbook of Federal-Indian Law*, ed. Felix Cohen. Washington, DC: U.S. Government Printing Office.

Cohen, Felix S. 2005. *Handbook of Federal Indian Law*. Newark, NJ: LexisNexis.

Colby, Bonnie G., John E. Thorson, and Sarah Britton. 2005. *Negotiating Tribal Water Rights: Fulfilling Promises in the Arid West*. Tucson: University of Arizona Press.

Commissioner of Indian Affairs. 1975. *Article Six, Treaties between the United States and the Several Indian Tribes from 1778 to 1837*. Millwood, NY: Kraus Reprint.

Costo, Rupert, and Jeannette Henry. 1977. *Indian Treaties: Two Centuries of Dishonor*. San Francisco: Indian Historian Press.

Danziger, Edmund J., Jr. 1973. "They Would Not Be Moved: The Chippewa Treaty of 1854." *Minnesota History* 43 (Spring): 174–185.

Daugherty, W. E. 1981. *Maritime Indian Treaties in Historical Perspective*. Ottawa: Indian and Northern Affairs Canada.

Decker, Craig A. 1977. "The Construction of Indian Treaties, Agreements, and Statutes." *American Indian Law Review* 5(2): 299–311.

Deloria, Vine, Jr. 1974. *Behind the Trail of Broken Treaties: An Indian Declaration of Independence*. New York: Delacorte Press.

Deloria, Vine, Jr. 1996. "Reserving to Themselves: Treaties and the Powers of Indian Tribes." *Arizona Law Review* 38(3): 963–980.

Deloria, Vine, Jr., and David E. Wilkins. 1999. *Tribes, Treaties, and Constitutional Tribulations*. Austin: University of Texas Press.

DeMallie, Raymond J. 1977. "American Indian Treaty Making: Motives and Meanings." *American Indian Journal* 3 (January): 2–10.

DeMallie, Raymond J. 1980. "Touching the Pen: Plains Indian Treaty Councils in Ethnohistorical Perspective." In *Ethnicity in the Great Plains*, ed. Frederick C. Luebke, 38–51. Lincoln: University of Nebraska Press.

DePuy, H. 1917. *A Bibliography of the English Colonial Treaties with the American Indians: Including a Synopsis of Each Treaty*. New York: Lennox Club.

Downes, Randolph C. 1977. *Council Fires on the Upper Ohio: A Narrative of Indian Affairs in the Upper Ohio Valley until 1795*. Pittsburgh, PA: University of Pittsburgh Press.

Duff, Wilson. 1969. "The Fort Victoria Treaties." *BC Studies* 3 (Fall), 3–57.

Dustin, Fred. 1920. "The Treaty of Saginaw, 1819." *Michigan History Magazine* 4 (January): 243–278.

Edmunds, R. David. 1978. "'Nothing Has Been Effected': The Vincennes Treaty of 1792." *Indiana Magazine of History* 74 (March): 23–35.

Ellison, William H. 1978. "Rejection of California Indian Treaties: A Study in Local Influence on National Policy." In *Treaty Making and Treaty Rejection by the Federal Government in California, 1850–1852*, eds. George E. Anderson, W. H. Ellison, and Robert F. Heizer, 50–70. Socorro, NM: Ballena Press.

Fay, George Emory. 1971. *Treaties Between the Potawatomi Tribe of Indians and the United States of America, 1789–1867*. Greeley, CO: Museum of Anthropology: University of Northern Colorado.

Fay, George Emory. 1972. *Treaties and Land Cessions Between the Bands of the Sioux and the United States of America, 1805–1906*. Greeley, CO: Museum of Anthropology: University of Northern Colorado.

Fay, George Emory. 1977. *Treaties Between the Tribes of the Great Plains and the United States of America: Cheyenne and Arapaho, 1825–1900 Etc.* Greeley, CO: Museum of Anthropology: University of Northern Colorado.

Fay, George Emory. 1982. *Treaties Between the Tribes of the Great Plains and the United States of America: Comanche and Kiowa, Arikara, Gros Ventre, and Mandan, 1835–1891*. Greeley, CO: Museum of Anthropology, University of Northern Colorado.

Ferguson, Clyde R. 1979. "Confrontation at Coleraine: Creeks, Georgians and Federalist Indian Policy." *South Atlantic Quarterly* 78 (Spring): 224–243.

Ferguson, Robert B. 1985. "Treaties between the United States and the Choctaw Nation." In *The Choctaw before Removal*, ed. Carolyn Keller Reeves, 214–230. Jackson: University Press of Mississippi.

Fielder, Betty. 1955. "The Black Hawk Treaty." *Annals of Iowa* 32 (January): 535–540.

Fisher, Andrew H. 1999. "This I Know from the Old People: Yakama Indian Treaty Rights as Oral Tradition." *Montana, The Magazine of Western History* 49 (Spring): 2–17.

Fisher, Andrew H. 2004. "Tangled Nets: Treaty Rights and Tribal Identities at Celilo Falls." *Oregon Historical Quarterly* 105 (Summer): 178–211.

Fisher, Robert L. 1933. "The Treaties of Portage des Sioux." *Mississippi Valley Historical Review* 19 (March): 495–508.

Fixico, Donald L. 1984. "As Long as the Grass Grows . . . The Cultural Conflicts and Political Strategies of United States-Indian Treaties." In *Ethnicity and War*, ed. Winston A. Van Horne, 128–149. Milwaukee: University of Wisconsin System, American Ethnic Studies Committee/Urban Corridor Consortium.

Foreman, Carolyn Thomas. 1955. "The Lost Cherokee Treaty." *Chronicles of Oklahoma* 33 (Summer): 238–245.

Foreman, Grant, ed. 1936. "The Journal of the Proceedings of Our First Treaty with the Wild Indians, 1835." *Chronicles of Oklahoma* 14 (December): 394–418.

Foreman, Grant. 1948. "The Texas Comanche Treaty of 1846." *Southwestern Historical Quarterly* 51 (April): 313–332.

Franks, Kenny A. 1972–1973. "An Analysis of the Confederate Treaties with the Five Civilized Tribes." *Chronicles of Oklahoma* 50 (Winter): 458–473.

Franks, Kenny A. 1973. "The Impeachment of the Confederate Treaties with the Five Civilized Tribes." *Chronicles of Oklahoma* 51 (Spring): 21–33.

Gates, Charles M., ed. 1955. "The Indian Treaty of Point No Point." *Pacific Northwest Quarterly* 46 (April): 52–58.

Gerwing, Anselm J. 1964. "The Chicago Indian Treaty of 1838." *Journal of the Illinois State Historical Society* 57 (Summer): 117–142.

Getches, David H., and Charles F. Wilkinson. 1998. *Federal Indian Law: Cases and Materials*, 4th ed. St. Paul: West.

Gibson, Ronald V. 1977. *Jefferson Davis and the Confederacy and Treaties Concluded by the Confederate States with Indian Tribes*. Dobbs Ferry, NY: Oceana Publications.

Gold, Susan Dudley. 1997. *Indian Treaties*. New York: Twenty-First Century Books.

Goodman, Edmund Clay. 2002. "Indian Reserved Rights." In *Nontimber Forest Products in the United States*, eds. Eric T. Jones, Rebecca J. McLain, and James Weigand, 273–281. Lawrence: University Press of Kansas.

Hagan, William T. 1956. "The Sauk and Fox Treaty of 1804." *Missouri Historical Review* 51 (October): 1–7.

Haines, Francis. 1964. "The Nez Perce Tribe versus the United States." *Idaho Yesterdays* 8 (Spring): 18–25.

Halbert, Henry S. 1902. "The Story of the Treaty of Dancing Rabbit Creek." *Publications of the Mississippi Historical Society* 6: 373–402.

Harmon, George D. 1929. "The North Carolina Cherokees and the New Echota Treaty of 1835." *North Carolina Historical Review* 6 (July): 237–253.

Harring, Sidney L. 1994. *Crow Dog's Case: American Indian Sovereignty, Tribal Law, and United States Law in the Nineteenth Century*. New York: Cambridge University Press.

Hawkinson, Ella. 1934. "The Old Crossing Chippewa Treaty and Its Sequel." *Minnesota History* 15 (September): 282–300.

Hawley, Donna Lea. 1990. *The Annotated 1990 Indian Act: Including Related Treaties, Statutes, and Regulations*. Toronto: Carswell.

Hayden, Ralston. 1920. *The Senate and Treaties, 1789–1817: The Development of the Treaty-Making Functions of the United States Senate during Their Formative Period*. New York: Macmillan.

Heilbron, Bertha L. 1941. "Frank B. Mayer and the Treaties of 1851." *Minnesota History* 22 (June): 133–156.

Heizer, Robert F. 1978. "Treaties." In *Handbook of North American Indians*, vol. 8, *California*, ed. Robert F. Heizer, 701–704. Washington, DC: Smithsonian Institution.

Henderson, Archibald. 1931. "The Treaty of Long Island of Holston, July, 1777." *North Carolina Historical Review* 8 (January): 55–116.

Henderson, James [Sakej] Youngblood. 1997. "Interpreting Sui Generis Treaties." *Alberta Law Review* 36(1): 46.

Henderson, James [Sakej] Youngblood. 2000. "Constitutional Powers and Treaty Rights." *Saskatchewan Law Review* 63(2): 719.

Henslick, Harry. 1970. "The Seminole Treaty of 1866." *Chronicles of Oklahoma* 48 (Autumn): 280–294.

Hill, Burton S. 1966. "The Great Indian Treaty Council of 1851." *Nebraska History* 47 (March): 85–110.

Holmes, Jack. 1969. "Spanish Treaties with West Florida Indians, 1784–1802." *Florida Historical Society,* 48 (140–154).

Hoover, Herbert T. 1989. "The Sioux Agreement of 1889 and Its Aftermath." *South Dakota History* 19 (Spring): 56–94.

Horsman, Reginald. 1961. "The British Indian Department and the Abortive Treaty of Lower Sandusky, 1793." *Ohio Historical Quarterly* 70 (July): 189–213.

Hosen, Fredrick E. 1985. *Rifle, Blanket, and Kettle: Selected Indian Treaties and Laws.* Jefferson, NC: McFarland.

Hough, Franklin B., ed. 1861. *Proceedings of the Commissioners of Indian Affairs, Appointed by Law for the Extinguishment of Indian Titles in the State of New York.* 2 vols. Albany, NY: Joel Munsell.

Hryniewicki, Richard J. 1964. "The Creek Treaty of Washington, 1826." *Georgia Historical Quarterly* 48 (December): 425–441.

Hryniewicki, Richard J. 1968. "The Creek Treaty of November 15, 1827." *Georgia Historical Quarterly* 52 (March): 1–15.

Humphreys, A. Glen. 1971. "The Crow Indian Treaties of 1868: An Example of Power Struggle and Confusion in United States Indian Policy." *Annals of Wyoming* 43 (Spring): 73–90.

Ibbotson, Joseph D. 1938. "Samuel Kirkland, the Treaty of 1792, and the Indian Barrier State." *New York History* 19 (October): 374–391.

Imai, Shin. 1999. *Aboriginal Law Handbook.* 2nd ed. Scarborough, ON: Carswell.

Isaac, Thomas. 2001. *Aboriginal and Treaty Rights in the Maritimes: The Marshall Decision and Beyond.* Saskatoon: Purich.

Jaenen, Cornelius J. 2001. "Aboriginal Rights and Treaties in Canada." In *The Native North American Almanac,* ed. Duane Champagne, 1–6. Los Angeles: University of California Press.

Jennings, Francis, ed. 1985. *The History and Culture of Iroquois Diplomacy: An Interdisciplinary Guide to the Treaties of the Six Nations and Their League.* Syracuse, NY: Syracuse University Press.

Jones, Dorothy V. 1982. *License for Empire: By Treaty in Early America.* Chicago: University of Chicago Press.

Jones, Douglas C. 1966. *The Treaty of Medicine Lodge: The Story of the Great Treaty Council as Told by Eyewitnesses.* Norman: University of Oklahoma Press.

Jones, Douglas C. 1969. "Medicine Lodge Revisited." *Kansas Historical Quarterly* 35 (Summer): 130–142.

Josephy, Alvin M., Jr. 1965. "A Most Satisfactory Council." *American Heritage* 16 (October): 26–31, 70–76.

Kane, Lucile M. 1951. "The Sioux Treaties and the Traders." *Minnesota History* 32 (June): 65–80.

Keller, Robert H. 1971. "On Teaching Indian History: Legal Jurisdiction in Chippewa Treaties." *Ethnohistory* 19 (Summer): 209–218.

Keller, Robert H. 1978. "An Economic History of Indian Treaties in the Great Lakes Region." *American Indian Journal* 4 (February): 2–20.

Keller, Robert H. 1989. "America's Native Sweet: Chippewa Treaties and the Right to Harvest Maple Sugar." *American Indian Quarterly* 13 (Spring): 117–135.

Kellogg, Louise Phelps. 1931. "The Menominee Treaty at the Cedars, 1836." *Transactions of the Wisconsin Academy of Sciences, Arts and Letters* 26: 127–135.

Kelsey, Harry. 1973. "The California Indian Treaty Myth." *Southern California Quarterly* 55 (Fall): 225–238.

Kessell, John L. 1981. "General Sherman and the Navajo Treaty of 1868: A Basic and Expedient Misunderstanding." *Western Historical Quarterly* 12 (July): 251–272.

Kickingbird, Kirke, Lynn Kickingbird, Alexander Tallchief Skibine, and Charles Chibitty. 1980. *Indian Treaties*. Washington, DC: Institute for the Development of Indian Law.

Kickingbird, Lynn, and Curtis Berkey. 1975. "American Indian Treaties—Their Importance Today." *American Indian Journal* 1 (October): 3–7.

Kinnaird, Lucia Burk. 1932. "The Rock Landing Conference of 1789." *North Carolina Historical Review* 9 (October): 349–365.

Kvasnicka, Robert M. 1988. "United States Indian Treaties and Agreements." In *Handbook of North American Indians*, vol. 4, *History of Indian–White Relations*, ed. Wilcomb E. Washburn, 195–201. Washington, DC: Smithsonian Institution.

Lambert, Paul F. 1973. "The Cherokee Reconstruction Treaty of 1866." *Journal of the West* 12 (July): 471–489.

Lanchart, David. 1985. "Regaining Dinetah: The Navajo and the Indian Peace Commission at Fort Sumner." In *Working in the Range: Essays on the History of Western Land Management and the Environment*, ed. John R. Wunder, 25–38. Westport, CT: Greenwood Press.

Landau, Jack L. 1980. "Empty Victories: Indian Treaty Fishing Rights in the Pacific Northwest." *Environmental Law* 10: 413–456.

Lane, Barbara. 1977. "Background of Treaty Making in Western Washington." *American Indian Journal* 3 (April): 2–11.

Larson, Gustive O. 1974. "Uintah Dream: The Ute Treaty—Spanish Fork, 1865." *Brigham Young University Studies* 14 (Spring): 361–381.

Laurence, Robert. 1991. "The Abrogation of Indian Treaties by Federal Statutes Protective of the Environment." *Natural Resources Journal*, 31 (Fall): 859–886.

Lehman, J. David. 1990. "The End of the Iroquois Mystique: The Oneida Land Cession Treaties of the 1790s." *William and Mary Quarterly*, 47(4): 523–547.

Leonard, Stephen J. 1990. "John Nicolay in Colorado: A Summer Sojourn and the 1863 Ute Treaty." *Essays and Monographs in Colorado History* 11, 25–54.

Lindquist, G. E. E. 1948–1949. "Indian Treaty Making." *Chronicles of Oklahoma* 26 (Winter): 416–448.

Litton, Gaston L., ed. 1939. "The Negotiations Leading to the Chickasaw-Choctaw Agreement, January 17, 1837." *Chronicles of Oklahoma* 17 (December): 417–427.

Madill, Dennis. 1981. *British Columbia Indian Treaties in Historical Perspective*. Ottawa: Indian and Northern Affairs Canada.

Mahan, Bruce E. 1925. "The Great Council of 1825." *Palimpsest* 6 (September): 305–318.

Mahan, Bruce E. 1929. "Making the Treaty of 1842." *Palimpsest* 10 (May): 174–180.

Mahon, John K. 1962. "The Treaty of Moultrie Creek, 1823." *Florida Historical Quarterly* 40 (April): 350–372.

Mahon, John K. 1962. "Two Seminole Treaties: Payne's Landing, 1882, and Ft. Gibson, 1833." *Florida Historical Quarterly* 41 (July): 1–21.

Mainville, Robert. 2001. *An Overview of Aboriginal and Treaty Rights and Compensation for Their Breach*. Saskatoon: Purich.

Manley, Henry S. 1838. "Buying Buffalo from the Indians." *New York History* 28 (July 1947): 313–329, Buffalo Creek Treaty.

Manley, Henry S. 1932. *The Treaty of Fort Stanwix, 1784*. Rome, NY: Rome Sentinel.

Martin, John Henry. 1975. *List of Documents Concerning the Negotiation of Ratified Indian Treaties, 1801–1869*. Millwood, NY: Kraus Reprint.

McCool, Daniel. 2002. *Native Waters: Contemporary Indian Water Settlements and the Second Treaty Era*. Tucson: University of Arizona Press.

McCullar, Marion Ray. 1973. "The Choctaw-Chickasaw Reconstruction Treaty of 1866." *Journal of the West* 12 (July): 462–470.

McKenney, Thomas L. 1827. *Sketches of a Tour to the Lakes, of the Character and Customs of the Chippeway Indians, and of Incidents Connected with the Treaty of Fond du Lac*. Baltimore: Fielding Lucas, Jr.

McNeil, Kinneth. 1964–65. "Confederate Treaties with the Tribes of Indian Territory." *Chronicles of Oklahoma* 42 (Winter): 408–420.

Morris, Alexander. 1880. *The Treaties of Canada with the Indians of Manitoba and the North-West Territories*. Repr., Toronto: Coles, 1971.

Morse, Bradford. 2004. "Aboriginal and Treaty Rights in Canada." In *Canadian Charter of Rights and Freedoms/Charte Canadienne des droits et Libertés*, 4th ed., eds. Gérald-A. Beaudoin and Errol Mendes, 1171–1257. Markham, ON: LexisNexis Butterworths.

Nesper, Larry. 2002. *The Walleye War: The Struggle for Ojibwe Treaty and Spearfishing Rights*. Lincoln: University of Nebraska Press.

Parker, Arthur C. 1924. "The Pickering Treaty." *Rochester Historical Society Publication Fund Series* 3: 79–91.

Partoll, Albert J., ed. 1937. "The Blackfoot Indian Peace Council." *Frontier and Midland: A Magazine of the West* 17 (Spring): 199–207.

Partoll, Albert J. 1938. "The Flathead Indian Treaty Council of 1855." *Pacific Northwest Quarterly* 29 (July): 283–314.

Perdue, Theda, and Michael D. Green, eds. 1995. *The Cherokee Removal: A Brief History with Documents.* Boston: Bedford Books of St. Martin's Press.

Phillips, Charles, and Alan Axelrod. 2000. *Encyclopedia of Historical Treaties and Alliances.* New York: Facts on File.

Phillips, Edward Hake. 1966. "Timothy Pickering at His Best: Indian Commissioner, 1790–1794." *Essex Institute Historical Collections* 102 (July): 185–192.

Pittman, Philip M., and George M. Covington. 1992. *Don't Blame the Treaties: Native American Rights and the Michigan Indian Treaties.* West Bloomfield, MI: Altwerger and Mandel.

Powless, Irving, and G. Peter Jemison. 2000. *Treaty of Canandaigua 1794: 200 Years of Treaty Relations Between the Iroquois Confederacy and the United States.* Santa Fe, NM: Clear Light.

Price, Monroe E., and Robert N. Clinton. 1983. *Law and the American Indian: Readings, Notes and Cases.* Charlottesville, VA: Michie.

Price, Richard, ed. 1979. *The Spirit of the Alberta Indian Treaties.* Montreal: Institute for Research on Public Policy. Repr., Edmonton: University of Alberta Press, 1999.

Prucha, Francis Paul, ed. 1975. *Documents of United States Indian Policy.* Lincoln and London: University of Nebraska Press.

Prucha, Francis Paul. 1994. *American Indian Treaties: The History of a Political Anomaly.* Berkeley, Los Angeles, and London: University of California Press.

Quaife, Milo M., ed. 1918. "The Chicago Treaty of 1833." *Wisconsin Magazine of History* 1 (March): 287–303.

Quinn, William W., Jr. 1990. "Federal Acknowledgment of American Indian Tribes: The Historical Development of a Legal Concept," *American Journal of Legal History* 34 (October): 331–364.

Rakove, Jack N. 1984. "Solving a Constitutional Puzzle: The Treatymaking Clause as a Case Study." *Perspectives in American History*, s.n., 1: 233–281.

Roberts, Gary L. 1975. "The Chief of State and the Chief." *American Heritage* 26 (October): 28–33, 86–89. Creek Treaty of New York, 1790.

Royal Commission on Aboriginal Peoples. 1995. *Treaty Making in the Spirit of Co-Existence: An Alternative to Extinguishment.* Ottawa: Canada Communication Group.

Royal Commission on Aboriginal Peoples. 1996. *Report of the Royal Commission on Aboriginal Peoples.* Ottawa: Canada Communication Group.

Royce, Charles C. 1899. *Indian Land Cessions in the United States.* Washington, DC: U.S. Government Printing Office.

Rutland, Robert A. 1949–1950. "Political Background of the Cherokee Treaty of New Echota." *Chronicles of Oklahoma* 27 (Winter): 389–406.

Satz, Ronald N. 1991. "Chippewa Treaty Rights: The Reserve Rights of Wisconsin's Chippewa Indians in Historical Perspective." *Transactions of the Wisconsin Academy of Sciences, Arts and Letters*, 79(1). Madison: Wisconsin Academy of Sciences, Arts and Letters.

Schwartzman, Grace M., and Susan K. Barnard. 1991. "A Trail of Broken Promises: Georgians and the Muscogee/Creek Treaties, 1796–1826." *Georgia Historical Quarterly* 75 (Winter): 697–718.

Silliman, Sue I. 1922. "The Chicago Indian Treaty of 1821." *Michigan History Magazine* 6(1): 194–197.

Slattery, Brian. 2000. "Making Sense of Aboriginal and Treaty Rights." *Canadian Bar Review* 79: 196.

Smith, Dwight L. 1954. "Wayne and the Treaty of Greene Ville." *Ohio State Archaeological and Historical Quarterly* 63 (January): 1–7.

Smith, Dwight L. 1978. "The Land Cession Theory: A Valid Instrument of Transfer of Indian Title." In *This Land Is Ours: The Acquisition of the Public Domain*, 87–102. Indianapolis: Indiana Historical Society.

St. Germain, Jill. 2001. *Indian Treaty-Making Policy in the United States and Canada, 1867–1877.* Lincoln and London: University of Nebraska Press.

Stanley, Henry M. 1967. "A British Journalist Reports the Medicine Lodge Peace Council of 1867." *Kansas Historical Quarterly* 33 (Autumn): 249–320.

Stern, Theodore. 1956. "The Klamath Indians and the Treaty of 1864." *Oregon Historical Quarterly* 57 (September): 229–273.

Sullivan, Julie E. 2004. "Legal Analysis of the Treaty Violations That Resulted in the Nez Perce War of 1877," 40 *Idaho Law Review* 657.

Surtees, Robert J. 1988. "Canadian Indian Treaties." In *History of Indian White Relations,* ed. Wilcomb E. Washburn, 202–210. Washington, DC: Smithsonian Institution.

Taylor, Alfred A. 1924. "Medicine Lodge Peace Council." *Chronicles of Oklahoma* 2 (June): 98–117.

Townsend, Michael. 1989. "Congressional Abrogation of Indian Treaties: Reevaluation and Reform." *Yale Law Journal*, 98 (February): 793–812.

Trafzer, Clifford E., ed. 1986. *Indians, Superintendents, and Councils: Northwestern Indian Policy, 1850–1855.* Lanham, MD: University Press of America.

Treaty 7 Elders and Tribal Council with Walter Hildebrandt, Sarah Carter, and Dorothy First Rider. 1996. *The True Spirit and Original Intent of Treaty 7.* Montreal: McGill-Queen's University Press.

Van Doren, Carl, and Julian P. Boyd. 1938. *Indian Treaties Printed by Benjamin Franklin, 1736–1762.* Philadelphia: Historical Society of Pennsylvania.

Vaugeois, Denis. 2002. *The Last French and Indian War: An Inquiry into a Safe-Conduct Issued in 1760 That Acquired the Value of a Treaty in 1990.* Montreal: McGill-Queens University Press/Septentrion.

Vaughan, Alden T. 1979. *Early American Indian Documents: Treaties and Laws, 1607–1789.* Washington, DC: University Publications of America.

Vipperman, Carl J. 1989. "The Bungled Treaty of New Echota: The Failure of Cherokee Removal, 1836–38." *Georgia Historical Quarterly* 73 (Fall): 540–558.

Watts, Charles W. 1959. "Colbert's Reserve and the Chickasaw Treaty of 1818." *Alabama Review* 12 (October): 272–280.

Watts, Tim J. 1991. *American Indian Treaty Rights: A Bibliography.* Monticello, IL: Vance Bibliographies.

Wells, Samuel J. 1983–1984. "Rum, Skins, and Powder: A Choctaw Interpreter and the Treaty of Mount Dexter." *Chronicles of Oklahoma* 61 (Winter): 422–428.

Wells, Samuel J. 1986. "International Causes of the Treaty of Mount Dexter, 1805." *Journal of Mississippi History* 48 (August): 177–185.

Wicken, William C. 2002. *Mi'kmaq Treaties on Trial: History, Land and Donald Marshall Junior.* Toronto: University of Toronto Press.

Wilkins, David E. 1996. "Indian Treaty Rights: Sacred Entitlements or 'Temporary Privileges?'" *American Indian Culture and Research Journal* 20(1): 87–129.

Wilkins, David E., and K. Tsianina Lomawaima. 2001. *Indian Sovereignty and Federal Law.* Norman: University of Oklahoma Press.

Wilkinson, Charles F. 1991. "To Feel the Summer in the Spring: The Treaty Fishing Rights of the Wisconsin Chippewa." *Wisconsin Law Review* (May–June): 375– 414.

Wilkinson, Charles F. 2000. *Messages from Frank's Landing: A Story of Salmon, Treaties, and the Indian Way.* Seattle: University of Washington Press.

Wilkinson, Charles F., and John M. Volkman. 1975. "Judicial Review of Indian Treaty Abrogation: 'As Long as Water Flows, or Grass Grows upon the Earth'—How Long a Time Is That?" *California Law Review* 63 (May): 601–661.

Williams, C. Herb, and Walt Neubrech. 1976. *Indian Treaties: American Nightmare.* Seattle: Outdoor Empire.

Wright, J. Leitch, Jr. 1967. "Creek-American Treaty of 1790: Alexander McGillivray and the Diplomacy of the Old Southwest." *Georgia Historical Quarterly* 51 (December): 379–400.

Wrone, David R. 1986–1987. "Indian Treaties and the Democratic Idea." *Wisconsin Magazine of History* 70 (Winter): 83–106.

Wunder, John R. 1985. "No More Treaties: The Resolution of 1871 and the Alteration of Indian Rights to Their Homelands." In *Working the Range: Essays on the History of Western Land Management and the Environment,* ed. John R. Wunder, 39–56. Westport, CT: Greenwood Press.

Index

Note: Page locators in **boldface** type indicate the location of a main encyclopedia entry.